BEYOND
THE DESKTOP

Tools and Technology
for Computer Publishing

BARRIE SOSINSKY

BANTAM BOOKS
NEW YORK • TORONTO • LONDON • SYDNEY • AUCKLAND

A Bantam Book/September 1991

Interior Design by Nancy Sugihara
This book was produced by DMC & Company, Acton, MA.

ISBN 0-553-35244-X

Published simultaneously in the United States and Canada

Bantam Books are published by Bantam Books, a division of Bantam Doubleday Dell Publishing Group, Inc. Its trademark, consisting of the words "Bantam Books" and the portrayal of a rooster, is Registered in U.S. Patent and Trademark Office and in other countries. Marca Registrada, Bantam Books, 666 Fifth Avenue, New York, New York 10103

PRINTED IN THE UNITED STATES OF AMERICA

0 9 8 7 6 5 4 3 2 1

If you are thinking about purchasing a computer system or expanding your current system to do desktop publishing, graphic, or design work, then *Beyond the Desktop* is written specifically for you. This is the fourth book in the ITC-Bantam series of books that focuses on computer design and production. The goal of this series is to provide intermediate and advanced computer users with information about how to get the most out of today's technology.

Beyond the Desktop surveys personal computer technology, both the hardware and software, and provides working concepts that will enable you to make informed decisions and selections of hardware and software to accomplish a wide range of DTP-related projects. The concepts discussed contain detailed information on each topic, supported by a wealth of practical detail on how to best use the technology. For example, how various software combinations will save you time when you are working in a group environment, and help you to avoid common and technological pitfalls.

Beyond the Desktop is not a style book. It is about understanding and properly utilizing the available technology. This book's aim is to show how the technology works best, in a manner that allows you to do your job more successfully, armed with tools that you more fully understand.

Beyond the Desktop is not filled with technical jargon. It is written in language easily understood by the everyday user. It is also a very effective reference work. You can dig in at any point, or use the cross-reference material to discover specific areas of related interest or problem solving. Since *Beyond the Desktop* addresses technological concepts and not specific hardware or software issues, it will still be useful as new and improved technologies appear on the market.

International Typeface Corporation, as a leading purveyor of high-quality typeface designs, has a personal objective to support the many people who use typeface designs by providing them with the quality tools and educational products which enable them to more professionally achieve their communication objectives.

This joint venture with Bantam is one more step in ITC's commitment to help all communicators create highly effective pieces most efficiently. We believe that the intelligent use of technology, allied to necessary traditional skills, and with the best of tools, such as high quality typefaces, will produced effective and efficient high-standard results.

In short, ITC's goal is to help you achieve higher, better standards in less time for less money.

Mark J. Batty
President and CEO, ITC.

Why This Book Was Written

The personal computer is an engine of technology in the 1990s. New personal computers have put the power of what was, not too long ago, a mainframe on the desks of the general public. Thus empowered, average computer users now find themselves compelled to accomplish projects once restricted to highly trained technical specialists and forced to grapple with issues from a broad spectrum of disciplines. Suddenly typewriting becomes typesetting, drawing becomes computer-aided design, handouts turn into presentations, photographs are replaced by digital imaging, and printing evolves into desktop publishing. Yet most publishing that starts on the desktop now extends electronically far beyond those confines to high-end color workstations, phototypesetting machines, and super-fast short-run printers.

Beyond the Desktop surveys personal computer technology and its impact on publishing and design. Its goal is to provide you with working concepts that will allow you to make informed selections of hardware and software to accomplish the projects of your choice. In the quicksilver world of computers, companies and products come and go. This book attempts to examine the underlying similarities and differences separating one computer or operating system from another, and one class of program from

v

Figure P-1
Calculated shapes (called rendering), and light sources (called ray tracing) can re-create lifelike scenes, such as this chessboard. In the '70s, these techniques were refined on $100,000 graphic work-stations using packages that cost $10,000 or more. They are now found on powerful microcomputers. The $495 StrataVision 3D on a $5,000 Macintosh II was used. *Courtesy of Strata (St. George, UT).*

another. It is hoped that this approach will give the book a more lasting value.

I am a computer enthusiast, and *Beyond the Desktop* represents an outgrowth of my own thoughts, questions, and experiences doing short-run prototype work on computers. My original use of computers to design products for a small business has led me to undertake projects in desktop publishing and graphics. It has also led to a career as a writer and computer consultant. Many of the issues and concerns I address here come from my own experience, or represent experiences of friends and colleagues; I've also included some of the more interesting stories I have heard in the past two or three years. Much of the material arises from discussions with friends. Tips and hints are responses to their problems.

Who Is This Book For?

If you are thinking about purchasing a computer system to do desktop publishing, graphics, or design work, then this book is for you. It should help you get a handle on what type of hardware you

Figure P-2
Many programs ship
with sample layouts or
designs called templates
(see Chapter 12) that
you can use and modify
for your work. This is a
template from Aldus
PageMaker. Many pro-
grams also ship with
libraries of artwork,
called clip art (see Chapter 9). Additional pieces
are in the public
domain; many portfolios
are also commercially
available.

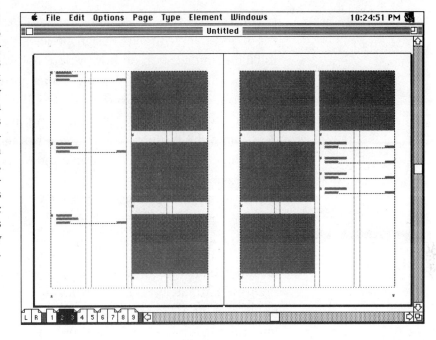

need and perhaps give you a feeling for the relative importance of various devices you might want to buy. If you haven't had much experience in computers (and are therefore unprejudiced), I present the advantages and disadvantages of some of the more common operating systems. Is the Mac better than MS-DOS, or vice versa? What about Windows, GeoWorks, or OS/2? All experienced computer users develop their own prejudices, and you can adopt some of mine, if you like.

I try to explain in a straightforward manner some of the basic concepts that you need to know in order to understand how a computer creates images, works with type, draws, paints, creates pages, and outputs the data to printers and other devices. You'll get an overall picture, and enough specific information on each topic to help you buy relevant software in an informed manner. This book also serves as reference to more advanced and specialized treatises. So if any of the individual chapter topics that will be described later interest you, this book will be worth your time. It is not my goal to overwhelm you with technology, just to provide you with enough to help you accomplish the tasks described.

This book is also about doing projects in groups. How do you· assign and track complex design projects? Who .should do what? You'll find information on how various software combinations will save you time when you're working in a group, and perhaps help you avoid some of the pitfalls others have encountered. Networked workgroups of personal computers have penetrated deeply into the business world, and a workgroup project enables closely interacting groups of people with multiple talents to create complex projects.

This is Not a Style Book

Most books that deal with design, graphics, and desktop publishing topics are style books. *Beyond the Desktop* is a technology book. Style issues are introduced only when the concepts are important to understanding technology. For example, it is important to understand the vocabulary of typography in order to know how a computer displays, outputs, or modifies characters. Then you can build a type library or use a printer correctly. Therefore, there is some discussion of typography in this book, but you won't find information about what font looks best where; that is a design issue and not a technology problem. Unfortunately the issue is not always that cut and dried, and it is becoming more and more difficult in the world of small computers to separate the two. Communities of both designers and computer users will, I hope, find this information of value.

You can find the subjects addressed in *Beyond the Desktop* scattered about in the trade press for small computers, PC and Macintosh, and in publications on graphics and desktop publishing. Reference is made to these sources, as appropriate. Perhaps, if you had the time, you could extract this information yourself. You would probably find that many of the conclusions drawn are both contradictory and inconclusive. That is a consequence of multiple authorship; it has both advantages and disadvantages. The advice in this book is filtered through just one person. The questions are those that I hear asked daily; the solutions are the most common-sensical ones I have found.

The best computer books are imprinted with their author's opinions. To be valuable a book must name names and take no prisoners. *Beyond the Desktop* names names: They are listed in the product index at the back of this book. If you see "black-and-white stripes" on a product, (both "pro" and "con" judgments), you'll be told why. There are few zebras floating around on the pages to follow; bad products are rarely mentioned. Space dictates that only the market leaders and significant new products can be discussed. These are products that have already impacted the marketplace, and some whose impact is just beginning to be felt. Products generally reach a prominent position for some positive reason(s). You can bet that any product in its third version has had plenty of user input in its redesign.

This is the fourth book in the Bantam-ITC Series, books that focus on computer design and production. The first book was *The Ventura Publisher Solutions Book* by Michael Utvich; the second was *Real World PageMaker 4, Macintosh Edition,* by Olav Martin Kvern and Stephen Roth; the third, *Roger Black's Desktop Design Power*. The goal of this series is to provide intermediate or advanced computer users with information about how to get the most out of technology. The previous books were hands-on, solution-oriented books. Their focus was, as business folk are wont to say, on benefits rather than on features. And so it is with *Beyond the Desktop*.

This Is Not a User's Guide

You won't find many discussions of specific keystrokes in *Beyond the Desktop*; this is not a user's guide. If this book turns you on to a great piece of software, or turns you away from a bad purchase, then it has served its purpose. And if *Beyond the Desktop* starts you down the road toward creating something that makes the world (or maybe just *your* world) a more interesting place, so much the better.

What You Should Know

This book assumes some previous computer experience. To get the maximum benefit from the text, you should be comfortable working with a modern word processor, and it would be helpful if you have used a paint or draw program as well. You should be familiar with files, menus, commands, dialog boxes, and other similar concepts.

Hardware

Most of the examples used in this book are drawn from the Apple Macintosh and the IBM PC families of computers. At the moment, these are what most people work with. The Apple and IBM companies represent more that 85 percent of the personal computer market, with about 50 to 60 million machines installed. These companies are also where most computer users start. By virtue of being the market leaders, their computers illustrate best the trends you will encounter in the future. But don't be afraid if you know only one of these computer systems. As the computer industry matures, concepts born on one machine are refined on another.

Many other fine computers are mentioned in this book, and some have devoted followings. Amigas, NeXTs, SPARCStations, and so on are mentioned when they introduce a new concept. They certainly fit the definition of a desktop computer, and each has much to recommend it. But as they currently lack consumer market penetration, a detailed discussion of each is beyond the scope of this book. To their fans I offer an apology, with the hope that future versions of this book will report on their success.

Software

The same may be said for software discussed in this book. According to current estimates, there are around 50,000 commercial software packages available for the IBM PC; perhaps 6,000 offerings for the Macintosh. Both computer systems—or platforms as they are called—support a vigorous programming community producing shareware (try-it-before-you-buy-it-software) and freeware (no money asked). So obviously I couldn't discuss all the marvelous software. I've tried to include some of the best to amplify on the concepts discussed.

How to Use This Book

As the range of subjects discussed in *Beyond the Desktop* is broad, I couldn't cover each topic on a first-principles basis. As space permits and it is relevant to the discussion, this book delves into how things work; otherwise you'll find general references to articles in the Bibliography at the end of the book.

This book can be read cover to cover. But if you have specific needs, by all means dig in at any point. Each chapter, which can be read as a unit, cross-references related sections of interest.

Part I: The Big Picture introduces how computers can help you do design and publishing work. It describes some of the important general concepts you need to be aware of right from the start.

Chapter 1: Why Extend Your Reach? describes the history of publishing technology, the rise of desktop publishing, and the basic considerations involved with DTP purchasing decisions. As manufacturing and information management becomes more central in our lives, computers take over more of the tasks we do. Futurists call this the information age. Clearly our society is changing greatly because of it. This chapter is about leveraging technology for publishing.

Chapter 2: Issues and Standards discusses some necessary general computer issues, including exactly what you should have sitting on your desktop and what you should access. Those of us buying the equipment are not joking when we refer to the "leading edge" as the "bleeding edge." That PostScript printer you bought for $6,000 two years ago costs $1,500 today. Memory chips that cost $1,000 today are as cheap as postage stamps tomorrow. Have you ever felt that software developers are trying to turn you into a beta tester for their product? I have! So this chapter attempts to present a coherent philosophy on how to get the maximum mileage out your computer system.

Chapter 3: The Electronic Production Cycle introduces the impact that computers are having on the print industry. The chapter describes and contrasts the steps required in going from concept to press using the traditional methods of just a few years ago versus some of the methods in practice today. Where does a computer save you time and money, and where is its use still just a fad?

Part II: The Tools describes some of the major personal computer systems currently available for use in design work.

Chapter 4: Publishing Hardware details microcomputer hardware and related operating systems. The computer system you buy will affect the choices you can make in hardware and software for years to come, so it's the first, most important decision you will make. In this chapter you will find the major options available, plus a discussion of which features are particularly useful. There's also a strategy presented for building a system over time.

Chapter 5: Displays considers the factors important in selecting and using a computer monitor. Do you need color, or will black and white do? You'll learn about display standards, black and white versus grayscale monitors, color standards, computer graphics cards, and graphics accelerators. Large-size monitors can substantially boost your productivity; you'll see when they are most useful.

Chapter 6: Input and Storage Tools describes equipment that you can use to create, store, and transport computer data. We discuss various types of disk drives; size, speed, price, and accessibility are the factors that differentiate them. You can transfer data electronically as disk files using modems and fax modems, the tools that enable your computer to interact with the outside world. The emphasis is on how they work and what their advantages and disadvantages are.

Chapter 7: Output Tools is a primer on printers. In it you will find information on how a computer prepares and sends a file to a printer, page description languages, and how a printer processes the data. Dot matrix, ink-jet, and laser printers are described, and their cost and quality is compared. Related technologies of plotters, film recorders, and other output methods are also introduced.

Part III: The Systems introduces the software needed to work with text, graphics, images, and type; and how to combine all these elements into a page layout. You'll learn what a file format is, how to work with these files, and how to convert them when needed. There's also an introduction to using a computer for color work. The emphasis is on getting your work into a form that can be reproduced, so you'll also learn about prepress and how to work with a printer. Last, Part III offers some principles on working in a group and on buying outside services.

Chapter 8: Preparing Text describes the important features of a word processor. What's essential, and what's fluff. What are some of the better programs and add-ons you can buy, and how do you save and move text data? Modern word processors offer sophisticated formatting and layout capabilities that can save you time, and their relationship to page composition is considered.

Chapter 9: Working With Graphics introduces graphics programs for illustration and design. Each program offers specialized tools for creating images, and the aim here is to show which are essential. The chapter discusses some examples of the applications of computer graphics to publishing, art, engineering, and business. You'll see how paint programs can create modern art, and how draw programs such as computer-aided design (CAD) can design an object, a complex office form, or presentation graphics and slides.

Chapter 10: Digital Imaging shows how a computer creates a digital image using scanners and cameras. Important principles of hardware and software are introduced, and some of the interesting applications are proposed. While you can certainly use digital images in your publishing applications and the quality of the technology is rapidly improving, there are also other applications. You'll see how images are processed, retouched, or altered and where this can be applied. The chapter also addresses the related technology of optical character recognition (OCR), where scanned text is converted to a disk file. It's an example of where the field of artificial intelligence is having impact on computer technology. If you handle large amounts of text, as many law firms do, then OCR can be a great time saver.

Chapter 11: Typography offers a primer on fonts or type families, and how computers display and output them. You'll see what the industry standards are, and how to build and work with a font library. Large computers have long been used for high-quality type work, but now personal computers offer the same capabilities. We also discuss some programs that are able to transform type into high art.

Chapter 12: Page Composition describes page layout programs used in desktop publishing. The aim is to show what features are important and how to best merge illustrations and text. Page layout marries text, graphics, images, and type into a single file. By understanding the overall process, you can learn how to make each of the steps involved complement each other, where to take shortcuts, and how to manage the process.

Chapter 13: Transferring Data details the mechanics of moving files between programs, discusses file formats, and describes how to convert between formats. Formats are the manner in which a program stores and displays data, and they are particularly important when integrating data from various sources into a page. This chapter also introduces you to telecommunications programs and how to use them to transmit your data to output devices.

Chapter 14: Working With Color describes how a computer displays and prints color. Using color on computers is a rapidly changing subject; tremendously satisfying and exciting, but filled with many pitfalls. In this chapter you'll learn the basic principles, including: color models, how color is prepared for output (separated), issues and difficulties, how to output files for prepress, how to get color fidelity, and traps to beware of.

Chapter 15: From Prepress to Print offers a look at the final part of the process in publishing. Your role in the print process doesn't end with the creation of a master copy. How you intend your printer to "manufacture" your work will impact on what you provide, how long it takes, what you're charged, and the overall quality of the piece. It's infinitely better to involve a printer from the start, and this chapter discusses what you need to ask and what some of the options are. In it you'll find a basic discussion of some of the different print options. Probably no single area of computer technology will change faster than the link between very high quality typesetting equipment and the microcomputer. Soon you will be able create a piece on your desktop, send it by modem to a service bureau, and have it print out at a quality level used by the best magazines.

Chapter 16: Network/Workgroup Publishing describes the mechanics of setting up a multiperson publishing project. Issues include what sort of hardware/software you'll need to connect the group and how to best handle file transfers. Options discussed include networks, electronic-mail, and bulletin board systems. Group publishing requires planning and coordination, so this chapter describes some of the software tools you can use to assign the work and track it. Production concerns include who does what part best, and how to create project specifications.

Chapter 17: Using Service Bureaus returns to the concept of leveraging technology. This chapter describes exactly what services are commonly offered at a service bureau, what they cost, and what you need to know to use them. There's a discussion on how to tell the difference between a good service bureau and a mediocre one. You can rent time, equipment, and help, if you need it, from service bureaus. This chapter describes the process of equipment rental and some of the considerations involved.

Part IV: Emerging Technologies explores developments of the near future that will change the manner in which you interact with your personal computer and the kinds of projects you may be able to accomplish with it as a result.

Chapter 18: Multimedia examines the fusion of sight and sound that turns a computer into a stage. It's possible to author scenes, even to animate them to a degree, using your personal computer. In this chapter you'll learn about the hardware you need to do this sort of work and about the software currently on the market. Hypertextual, hypermedia authoring programs can integrate digitized sound with pictures and drawing; they can even create animation by inserting intermediate states between frames, all with a mouse click or a menu command. More powerful computers can modify your output, shading and rendering, or solidifying the objects you created on a PC into more lifelike ones, and sequencing and extending the animation. Hollywood uses these tools, and so can you.

Chapter 19: A Look Ahead offers a view of upcoming publishing technologies, including hardware and software, page description standards, full digital press and electronic publishing. We'll even take a look at virtual reality as a form of publishing.

Appendix A discusses how this book was produced. **Appendix B** contains magazine references, organized by chapter, for nearly all the book's topics. **Appendix C** is the bibliography. **Appendix D** is an index of publishing products.

Book Conventions

I've tried to keep the number of conventions down to the absolute minimum. Any words you see on your computer monitor are set in Chicago font (Macintosh), such as:

System Error 13. Your Computer is Smoking!

In the very rare instances that you are meant to type something, you will see that entry in Courier (typewriter) font, as in:

```
COPY A:VENTURA/DISK FILE C:BTD/CH2 \v
```

Products mentioned in this book are listed in Appendix A, product index. Program versions discussed are always the one listed unless otherwise stated. *Beyond the Desktop* discusses many programs that have versions on multiple computer systems. To differentiate which version is being discussed, the platform is appended to the name. Thus you'll often see PageMaker (Mac), PageMaker (PC), or PageMaker (OS/2). If a section discusses Macintosh software only, you may see a program listed by itself. When discussing a specific computer its name will be mentioned, but only very rarely will the term PC be applied to all personal computers. The term IBM PC refers to all IBM-compatible PCs, including clones.

There just isn't enough space in *Beyond the Desktop* to discuss many subjects in the detail they deserve. Therefore, subject references are listed at the end of the book. Most often subject references are articles, but sometimes they're chapters in a larger work. A great deal of information is available in the references, much more than is possible to include in these pages.

So much for the trivial pursuits!

And just one more thing... If you don't see your favorite program here, or want to share the experiences you've had, both good and bad, with the technologies described in this book, let

Figure P-3
MacDining Room, a digital window on the world.

me hear from you. We may include them when we do the next edition. Your opinions are welcome. No one, after all, can have a perfect perspective. You can contact me on CompuServe at 72020,2311 or through America OnLine, where my screen name is "BASman." Or you can write me care of Bantam Computer Books, 666 Fifth Avenue, New York, NY 10103.

Think of your personal computer as a window, and now let's go beyond the desktop.

Barrie Sosinsky
Newton, Massachusetts, USA
May, 1991

A C K N O W L E D G M E N T S

This book was originally conceived at a lunch during the Boston 1989 SIGGRAPH conference with Josef Woodman, publisher of Ventana Press. It began as a book on how to use service bureaus and the equipment in them to create project prototypes. Josef suggested I place the book through Bill Gladstone's literary agency, Waterside Productions (Cardiff-by-the-Sea, CA). Bill contributed to the project by helping me to broaden its scope and improve the proposal, by negotiating a good contract, and by finding an appropriate publisher. This book found life through Kenzi Sugihara's group at Bantam Electronic Publishing, and through the support of Mark Batty and Skip Wilhelm at International Typeface Corporation (ITC).

It's rare that an author gets to write a book with an editor who is an expert on its subject area. Michael Roney's expertise in electronic publishing is reflected throughout this book in its breadth and scope, and in its attention to detail. Many of his contributions to the field may be found in *Publish* magazine, where he is a contributing editor. Working with Mike has been a pleasure. Even when the scope of this project grew well beyond our initial expectations, and slipped beyond our intended time frame, he retained his overall perspective and his consummate professionalism. He kept the focus of this book straight and true.

I would like to thank my readers for the project: Terry Moore of MicroPrint, independent consultant David Drucker, Greg Wallace of SIS, Inc., Bob Janukowitz of Optronics, and Bob Weibel of *Publish* magazine. They all took time from their very busy schedules to lend their special expertise to the project. Terry Moore gave me invaluable insight into the workings of a service bureau; her contributions added greatly to Chapter 17. David Drucker gave focus to Chapter 18. Bob Weibel provided valuable technical input throughout the book.

Bob Janukowitz was a special friend to me and helped me in many ways. In addition to coordinating the production of the color pages at Optronics, he lent me his LaserWriter IINTX for many months while I ground out the pages that became this book. His perspective is one born out of years of experience in the electronic publishing industry, and he freely shared it with me. I hope I got it right.

Many thanks are also due to the management and staff at Optronics (Chelmsford, MA) for their help throughout the project.

Another very important contributor to this book was Donna Chernin, who co-designed and executed the color pages. Donna also went on to compose the text pages. You can find details of the process in Appendix A. I look forward to our next project(s) together.

Overall production was handled by Bantam Electronic Publishing's Managing Editor, Maureen Drexel, who made things run smoothly. Thanks are also due to the many behind-the-scenes people at Bantam who helped produce this work and share in its success.

Brian Wallace, the collections manager at The Computer Museum, very generously allowed me to use elements of the museum's collection in this book. If you visit Boston, you should plan to spend some time visiting the museum and its world-class exhibition. The museum has a continuing interest in documenting the history of computing, and it actively seeks participation of the public in building its collection.

I appreciate the loan of an H-P ScanJet Plus scanner from Lois Clifton's group at the Greeley Hardcopy facility, and of a Toshiba 3100SX laptop from Toshiba, Inc. Both were put to good use. Paul Parisi helped with some of the IBM PC screenshots found in this book. As always, I acknowledge the contribution of the Boston Computer Society (world's greatest user group) to my interest and education in computers.

You will find the contributions of many vendors in this book. Apple Computer, particularly, supplied a library of photos, so too did Hewlett Packard. Microsoft, Freda Cooke at Aldus and Katerina Krebs at Micrografx were especially helpful. Catherine Hartley and Stefan Winnek at Bitstream provided insight by allowing me to visit with them and discuss digital type. Bob Wagner at Xerox provided me with the opportunity to visit the introduction of the DocuTech Production Publisher in New York, and to see a bit of the future. Many vendors provided software, information, or figures that enriched this book. To them all I say thanks.

Much of this book was written late at night when the phone stops ringing. To Larry King, whose talk show was my late night writing companion, I can only say this: Now that this book is done I will surely "rest well."

This book is dedicated to Carol Westheimer, my best friend.

Contents

CHAPTER 9

Working with Graphics 233

C H A P T E R   1 2

Page Composition 357

CHAPTER 19

A Look Ahead 599

The Third Wave Starts Here

We have intelligence and imagination that we have not yet begun to use.
Alvin Toffler, THE THIRD WAVE

This is a book about state-of-the-art publishing technology, which happens to be based upon microcomputers. The capabilities of our powerful, low-cost publishing tools far exceed those of the room-sized computers and million-dollar dedicated systems of years past. In order to fully appreciate where we are now, and where publishing technology is headed, we need to first take a short journey down memory lane.

In the Beginning

The first widely recognized personal computer appeared on the January 1975 cover of *Popular Electronics*. It was a hobbyist's kit from a small company called MITS in Albuquerque, New Mexico. Dubbed the "Altair 88" after a star that was the destination of starship *Enterprise* in the television series *Star Trek*, and the Intel 8088 microprocessor that powered it, the Altair 8800 was in reality nothing more than a box of parts, wires, and lights. The first prototype was lost in shipment. So with deadline time approaching, Ed Roberts, the president of MITS, and Les Solomon, the technical editor assigned to the *Popular Electronics* article, shot the cover

1

Figure I-1
The January 1975 cover
of *Popular Electronics.*
Courtesy of the Ziff-
Davis Company.

photo from an empty casing. It's ironic then, that the original PC
was an illusion.

MITS, which was near bankruptcy at the time, was struggling to
fill a backlog of 4,000 orders for the Altair 8800 three months later.
David Bunnell, a MITS vice president, wrote the first company
newsletter, called *Computer Notes*. Mainly for MITS employees, it
also circulated to 12,000 others. Bunnell went on to publish a
string of other computer magazines including *PC World* and *Mac-
World*, and is now working on one of the first integrated maga-
zine/electronic news services for the biotechnology community
called *BioWorld* (described in Chapter 19).

The Altair 8800 didn't do much at first. A year later Paul Allen and Bill Gates wrote a version of BASIC for the Altair that allowed users the chance at least to create their own programs. Finally there was something you could do with the Altair—run a program and receive an answer as a pattern of lights. From that start Allen and Gates went on to found and build Microsoft Corporation.

Computers were hobbyists' dreams in 1975. Heathkit introduced a computer kit that went nowhere. In the towns surrounding Stanford University where an electronics industry had grown up around such companies as Hewlett-Packard, Varian, and Intel, people began to build their own computers. The microprocessor made that possible. Two young men, Steven Wozniak and Steven Jobs, whose first product was a freak phone tone dialer, went on to build computer motherboards in their garage. The Apple I shipped out to electronics stores, no assembly required. If you wanted a case, you could have one made of wood.

Three personal computers appeared in 1977, jump-starting the industry: the Apple II, the Radio Shack TRS-80, and the Commodore PET computers. Four years later, in 1981, IBM introduced

Figure I-2
Steven Jobs's garage where the original Apple I motherboard prototypes were constructed. *Courtesy of Apple Computer, Inc.*

the original IBM PC, designed from vendor parts in its Boca Raton labs. It was an astounding success. Four years after that came the Apple Macintosh. In eight short years the personal computer advanced from a curiosity to a fixture and affected the lives of hundreds of millions of ordinary people. *Byte Magazine's* fifteenth anniversary issue (September 1990) has an article on the history of personal computers done in capsule format with pictures that show the rush of technology measured against world events.

Figure I-3
Steve Wozniak (left) and Steve Jobs holding up an Apple I board.
Courtesy of Apple Computer, Inc.

Computers Today

If you consider that each generation of computer may be delineated by the sophistication of the microprocessor that runs it, then we are coming to the end of the third generation of the PC—roughly. There is enough processing power in an Intel 80386 or Motorola 68030 chip to run a workstation. A workstation is a single-user computer that is used for powerful processing projects, such as graphics or as a server in a network system. Workstations are smaller than minicomputers and generally more powerful than personal computers. Recently some of the more powerful PCs have nearly achieved workstation status, blurring the division between these categories. Creative tasks that once were limited to very few are now in the hands of many. It's not that creating art on a computer is new, or that publishing with a computer is new, or even that animation with a computer is new. What is new is that individuals can now do these things on equipment they can afford.

Today's personal computer bears little relationship to the Altair 8800. What you're likely to buy for home or office use today has as its true ancestor the minicomputer of the late '60s and early '70s—equipment similar to Digital Equipment's VAX series, or the Xerox Alto computer (see Chapter 4) with the graphical user interface that inspired the Apple Macintosh. The benefit of real-time

Figure I-4 The Apple Macintosh IIfx motherboard (1990). *Courtesy of Apple Computer, Inc.*

user/computer interaction has led to the introduction of true graphics-oriented computer systems. Even character- or text-based operating systems such as MS-DOS have adopted graphically based user interfaces (GUIs) in order to simplify their command structure and to attain a higher level of user interaction.

The proliferation of the microcomputer has also meant that the best new programs are now appearing on personal computers. This book describes the best word processors, paint programs, desktop publishing packages, and so on. Most have appeared as new products meant for a mass audience. A much smaller number have migrated downward from the world of larger computers with their power intact (often increased) and with their prices slashed. Programs that started their lives as version 1.0 on your personal computer are now potent competitors for programs that run on the big iron (mainframes). This trend of bottom-up development is likely to escalate with time.

Once looked upon as so-called smart terminals capable of off-loading some of the simpler functions of a host computer, personal computers are now viewed as the central players in a distributed information network. Each user has undergone brain enhancement. Now the main purpose of a larger computer is to serve as a repository of data or to perform the execution of a task requiring raw speed. Apple Computer buys a Cray supercomputer to design the next Macintosh. Cray buys Macintosh computers to build the next Cray. And so the circle is closed.

What of the trends for the future that Alvin Toffler wrote of in *The Third Wave*? The electronic cottage is a reality for many professionals who rely on the personal computer and related devices to run their businesses and interact with the outside world. A phone, computer, copier, modem, fax, digital scanner, and printer comprise the office of the present. Separate now, but in the years to come how many of these functions will be integrated into the next generation of personal computer? Stereo sound, massive information storage and retrieval capabilities, and new types of information exchange are already appearing. Will the next computers be the brain of the home of tomorrow? Probably. If it all sounds too futuristic, it shouldn't. The technology exists today and only awaits competitive pricing in the marketplace and public acceptance.

Every day or two I log onto CompuServe to "talk" with my editors at *MacUser* in England, to a coauthor in New York, or a friend in Saskatoon. CompuServe is a networked database, an information giant with over 600,000 users. At the prompt you can go to any of hundreds of forums and libraries. Even better is the point-and-click approach of America OnLine. I've uploaded articles to an editor in San Francisco using America OnLine. There I can find reviews of products I've done for *MacWorld* Magazine in the months past, as well as many others. Telecommuting? Yes. Most professional writers and journalists I know operate this way, and so do many other people operating as independents or running businesses small and large.

The personal computer is also the single best prototyping tool yet devised by man. Newspapers and magazines are full of stories of individuals and businesses using personal computers to create pilot products. Ad agencies use them for designs or for advertisement, architects construct buildings using computer-aided design (CAD) programs or create visualizations of designs that you can actually walk through. Desktop publishing has revolutionized how newsletters and magazines are created. Today many major newspapers are using page layout programs and networked personal computers to create your morning newspaper; many more are experimenting with their use.

It is in this spirit that this book is offered. Vignettes of the modern age, the new tools to aid you in your publishing work, the current standards, and the standards to be. Hardware, and software, systems are discussed, as is a philosophy to guide you in choosing between them. The 1990s is an era of consolidation in the personal computer industry as the industry matures and the choices become blurred. Old architecture is swept aside to make room for advancing technology. Let's pick a place to start.

Figure 1-5 *The National,* a sports daily, was one of the first newspapers to adopt a cradle-to-grave desktop publishing approach. *Courtesy of* The National.

PART I

The Big Picture

Why Extend Your Reach?

Invention breeds invention.
Ralph Waldo Emerson

The technology of publishing has changed tremendously over the centuries, and has evolved at an even greater pace since the advent of personal computers. Today's publishing tools are less expensive, more portable, more controllable, and easier to use than ever before. These factors have popularized publishing, extending the reach of millions of people who would never have participated in the process otherwise. They have also precipitated a rush to the new technology from within the professional publishing community.

Whether you're a publishing newcomer or a professional, your decision to embrace this powerful and rapidly changing technology must result from careful consideration of trade-offs in costs, control, changing job descriptions, training, and the ultimate quality of your publication. This chapter presents a capsulated summary of publishing's evolution, and lays the groundwork for the issues that affect computer-based publishing today.

The Printed Word

Publishing in the form of clay tablets may have appeared in Crete as early as 1500 B.C. and in China and Korea in the eleventh century, but it was the introduction of movable type by Johann Gutenberg in Germany in 1440 that impacted most significantly on Western

11

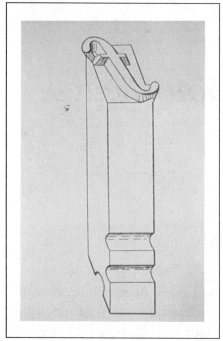

Figure 1-1 A piece of lead type.

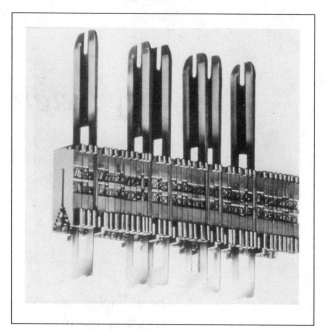

Figure 1-2 A line of handset type.

Figure 1-3 Two manual letterpress printing presses in the Athenaeum, Cambridge, Massachusetts.

civilization. Historians mark that date as the end of the Middle Ages and the beginning of the Renaissance. Gutenberg introduced poured lead type (see Figure 1-1) created from carved letter-molds. Coupled with block letterpress, introduced early in Europe, the movable-type machine was a revolutionary invention. Individual "slugs" of type were hand-set into lines (see Figure 1-2), and bound into pages called proofs. As recently as the early 1900s, hand-composed pages were the predominant method for printing. You still can find letterpress type in specialty print shops catering to artistic page print, but they are an anachronism.

Automation of type casting began with the invention of a typesetting machine by the American Dr. William Church in 1822. Ottmar Mergenthaler's invention of the linotype machine (literally "line o' type") in 1886 was the first practical commercial typesetting machine that could automatically cast lines of type with appropriate spacing; a process called justification. Other significant typesetting machines included the Monotype, invented in 1887 by Tolbert Lanston; the Ludlow Typograph, invented in 1906 by Washington I. Ludlow, and the Intertype (based on the linotype) invented in 1911.

In 1950 you could still "pull" a proof from a type tray in a printing plant. You could choose letters from the upper and lower parts of the case (hence upper and lower case), you would insert size spaces to justify lines and lead strips for line spaces (leading) just as early printers had done five hundred years ago. But no more. The computer has changed all that.

Electronic Typesetting and Printing

Typesetting is now done on computers of all sizes. Software controls type size, shape, and placement. Whereas typesetters place type on a page, more modern devices called imagesetters compose an entire page, with both text and graphics (see Chapter 7). Photographic elements traditionally created by cameras and film are now often converted into digital files by electronic scanners for direct incorporation into an electronic page. Color art can be digitized by color scanners and separated digitally by computer software, which can then produce the film needed to prepare each printed process color. Color proofs can be made directly from digital computer files. On the horizon is full digital press, bypassing film entirely.

In the past, craftsmen called layout artists worked with pasteboards, tape, glue, scissors, and the like to assemble the elements of the printed page onto a master page. Setting a page could take hours. Complex designs such as newsprint pages could take a day. Once a design had been decided upon, there wasn't time to experiment with alternatives. Today all of the elements of a page are integrated in a special type of software package called a page layout program, composed, and sent to an output device. Now, design experimentation is the name of the game.

Magazines and catalogs are often produced on large offset presses, some of which are capable of printing at 2,500 feet per minute. That's nearly half a mile each minute! As impressive as that is, to futurists it is technology of the industrial age. The technology of the information age to come is based on high-quality, short-run production. Computer-controlled, laser-driven imagesetters can create the master copy you take to a printer, and a desk-

Figure 1-4
The Linotype Co. of Hauppage, Long Island evolved from mechanical typesetting to electronic typesetting in the 1950s. Their Linotronic line of imagesetters are the most popular page composition devices on the market today and are widely found in service bureaus. Shown here is the 2,540 dots-per-inch Linotronic 530 offering image sizes of up to 18 by 120 inches. *Courtesy of Linotype Hell Co.*

top laser printer can do short-run prototype printing. You can have a printing press on your desktop. Better yet, you can now send desktop-produced files directly to digital printers such as the Xerox Docutech Production Publisher for high-speed short runs.

The introduction of the computer has led to all these changes in the printing industry. We are entering an age of entirely filmless print composition and of new print technologies. Low-priced laser and ink-jet printers are being built that approach imagesetter quality, and other electronic methods are replacing printing presses for short-run work. Links are being established from desktop computers to the high-end equipment used in design for mass production. Individuals do the time and intellectually intensive prototyping work; automation does the labor-intensive work.

The Birth of Desktop Publishing

The phrase "desktop publishing" or DTP, was coined on January 28, 1985, by Paul Brainard, president of Aldus Corporation, at an Apple Computer annual stockholder meeting. Aldus was the developer of the PageMaker page layout program which, combined with a Macintosh computer, Aldus PageMaker, Adobe's PostScript page description language, digital type licensed from the International Typeface Corporation, and an Apple LaserWriter, created a new medium-resolution publishing system. The original Apple LaserWriter was a printer that created images at a resolution of 300 dots per inch (DPI). It used the Canon LCB-CX print engine, and was built around the technology used for photocopiers, in particular, the Canon Personal Copier cartridge line. (See Chapter 7.)

Linotype, also at that Apple meeting, had a high-quality imagesetter driven by a PostScript (Adobe's page description programming language) interpreter that provided high-quality output. The Linotronic could output at 1,270 dots per inch, and later models at 2,540 dpi. "Going to lino" has become synonymous with creating the master copy for a printer. These developments meant that for the first time a microcomputer could be used as a typesetter and proofing system, and the results could then be high-quality output. This was a price/performance breakthrough in the market-

Figure 1-5 Aldus PageMaker and the Apple Macintosh popularized the concept of desktop publishing. This is the original version (1.0) and the Mac Plus from 1985. *Courtesy of Aldus Corporation.*

place. Sales for the Macintosh, which had been only crawling along, became respectable, and many industry analysts today claim that these watershed announcements may have saved Apple's bacon.

In concept the heavily hyped so-called Macintosh Office did at least provide a ready solution to medium-quality printing needs. If you were willing to create black and white pages, using scanned photos of modest quality, this solution provided complete electronic page construction. For a small tradeoff of flexibility you could specify where your photos should be placed (the so-called FPO, or "for position only") using the scanned image. You could then turn around and have your printer use photographic prints for photos, and an imagesetter to create type, rules, and other design elements for a high-quality printed piece. Spot color also was easily incorporated. So, for millions of people with Macintoshes, creating a newsletter, brochure, or advertisement electronically was (and is) viable. Although they have lagged somewhat behind in the range and quality of graphics tools available, the IBM PC and clones have undergone, and continue to undergo, rapid product growth in the desktop publishing arena.

New Frontiers and Integrated Solutions

Currently the new developments in personal computers are in color processing—not just spot color, but full four-color work. This is as much a migration of technology down from more powerful computer systems as it is a bottom-up development of advancing technology in general. *USA Today* is among the major publications who desktop publish (its weather charts and illustrations are produced entirely electronically on Macintoshes). These other publications include *The New York Times*, *Arizona Republican*, *Newsweek*. Some newspapers and magazines are adopting a cradle-to-grave approach using desktop publishing with every element of their newspaper produced by a microcomputer. Most

Figure 1-6
The weather page from *USA Today* was among the first to use Macintosh graphics integrated with page layout programs. Today microcomputers are almost universally used in magazines and newspapers with tight production schedules. © *1991,* USA Today, *reprinted with permission. All rights reserved.*

(especially those for whom color reproduction is important) are experimenting, trying to decide when the new technologies are mature enough to provide the required quality of output.

Not all publications have been able to adopt a complete DTP approach, even when they're committed to the process. *Mac-World Magazine* and *Publish* currently are completely desktop published, except for full-color pictures. It is still more cost effective to send color pictures out to be stripped photographically rather than electronically. Color matching, as it turns out, has proven to be a difficult computer problem to solve for reasons that we discuss in Chapter 14. Advanced computer preprint systems are nearly good enough to replace traditional methods, but the price/performance ratio is not compelling enough yet nor is the technology stable enough (it is changing rapidly) to impell smaller operations to make a major investment in it.

Going Desktop: The Initial Decisions

Because nearly every design project requires the use of a mixture of technology, it's important to think strategically right from the outset. You need to ask yourself a number of pointed questions about the work you're about to undertake in order to determine what you should do yourself and what you should have others do for you, or do yourself on the outside. Let's look at some of the important factors in your decision.

Crunching Numbers: Financial Considerations

Financial considerations are straightforward. If the design you're attempting costs more to do on the outside than in-house over a reasonable period, then buy the equipment and do it yourself. Consider how much the equipment costs, how much materials and services to run the equipment costs, and how much manpower is going to cost you. For example, an imagesetter costs $50,000, materials and services cost $5 for every piece of printed output, an operator costs $25 an hour, and throughput is five images an hour, then you need to calculate a break-even point for the number of images you would have to run in order to justify a purchase. If you normally pay out $15 per image, then you would need to run roughly 2,000 hours of time on the imagesetter, or 10,000 prints, to break even. In real life, you would probably be able to depreciate the equipment and expenses over a three-year period, so that might bring the numbers down to 1,400 hours and 7,000 prints. These are just ballpark figures, but this is the type of analysis you need to do.

Most people find that 7,000 prints from an imagesetter costs quite a lot, even spread over three years. It is out of reach for most individuals and small companies, and impractical for large companies as well. If you put out a glossy monthly magazine of 200 pages, and output at 2 pages to a proof sheet, that means you have a yearly consumption of 3,600 pages over a three year-period. When most glossy magazines went to desktop publishing, they sent much of their work out to service bureaus.

The Division of Labor

Even when you can make the financial numbers work out, if the work is technically difficult, and/or you don't perform the task frequently enough to produce acceptable results, it still may make more sense to have it done on the outside. Imagesetters, for example, are known to be ornery critters. The counterargument is that, if you require special services, or unusual technical specifications, you might be better off to do the work yourself. Technical issues can't always be quantified financially, so figuring this out will definitely make your creative juices flow.

In the last few years, a large number of graphic arts service bureaus have been established. In Chapter 17 we'll have a closer look at the range of services they provide, and how you go about using them properly. The range of services offered can include print (black and white or color), duplication, computer rental, slide making, file translation services, and so on.

One typical service bureau is MicroPrint in Waltham, Massachusetts. Established three years ago, now with a staff of twelve, it includes the services of artists, designers, and page layout specialists. MicroPrint offers Linotronic output (based on PostScript) using (mostly) Macintoshes and some IBM PCs in a local area network (LAN). Its clients include large Boston area corporations, small companies, and individuals. You can rent equipment time and do the work on premises, or have MicroPrint do the work for you. Projects range in complexity from laser prints and photcopies, to books and annual reports. Often volume printing is subcontracted out to a specialist.

Buying Your System

If you are trying to buy software and hardware for your computer, perhaps you are suffering from future shock. There's no better definition of future shock than that feeling you get when you see the next version of your computer in a magazine the day *after* you get yours home. It is even more critically applied when you're involved with buying an imagesetter or a prepress system that's been superseded in the marketplace. Since this is a common problem, let's look at how one rationally decides what to buy.

In Search of the Killer Apps

Whenever you can find one, buy a killer app. A killer app is any application that is so irresistible that you must purchase the computer or system needed to run it. Dan Bricklin and Robert Frankston's VisiCalc program released in 1979 for the Apple II was a killer app; so was Mitch Kapor's Lotus 1-2-3 released in 1982 for the IBM PC; and the 1985 release of PageMaker for the Apple Macintosh. A killer app defines a new category of task that you can accomplish with a computer, and is the dream of every software and hardware vendor in the industry. Normally you don't have to search for killer apps; the skills they empower you with force themselves upon you.

As the personal computer industry is maturing, each of the killer apps from successful companies is written to run on several different computers. This negates the necessity of a particular computer system, and changes your decision to that of deciding between several systems. PageMaker, Ventura Publisher, and Auto-CAD run on the Apple Macintosh, Windows (PC), and on the Presentation Manager for OS/2 (PC). Which version of a program you use is now more dependent on hardware considerations and on secondary pieces of sofware. Being able to run a file created by a program on one computer using the same program on another computer is referred to as *interoperability*.

It's not that killer apps are not still appearing as singularities on the event horizon of software. They are, but they often don't have the broad universal appeal of earlier killer apps. Spreadsheets such as Lotus 1-2-3 or Excel can be used by accountants, scientists, banks, businesses, and anyone with a need for enhanced calculation capabilities. But 1-2-3 and Excel now run on several platforms and have noteworthy competitors such as Borland's Quattro Pro (PC) and Informix's Wingz (Mac, PC), so they're no longer as compelling as that they used to be. Most often killer apps are written by small companies. Now that the microcomputer marketplace has grown explosively, competitive products appear quickly. Killer apps are also now more likely to appear as specialized products in niche markets. If you are running a newspaper that does color print work, then Scitex Visionary running on an Apple Macintosh (just as an example) might be your killer app. Or, if you're an ad agency specializing in advertising commercials, then MacroMind Director (Mac) for desktop animation might be your killer app.

The Latest and Greatest

One of the major problems you face as a graphic artist or designer is the increasing complexity of software that are called upon to learn. This trend has been exacerbated by increasingly sophisticated hardware available to the average user, and a competitive marketplace. If twenty key features are selling points, then how about one hundred? Constant upgrades are the rule in the software game as vendors strive to differentiate their products in some way from others and to add value. Upgrades are incentive to users to own a product, and they fund the research and development necessary to create new products, not just the upgrade.

You can learn a lot about a company by studying the upgrade history of its products. Microsoft, for example, regularly upgrades every two years, just like clockwork. It's almost as if Bill Gates has the future of the personal computer planned in a

Microsoft Project file on his desktop. Then there's WordPerfect: The word processing giant ambles along, quietly improving its product. A major change to its best-selling DOS word processor came with just a minor version number change, 5.0 to 5.1, right out of the blue. What sense can be made of life on the upgrade path in that instance?

Often it's wise to wait a while before you upgrade software. This is particularly true of system software. Be cautious when upgrading system software to a new major version number. First releases of Apple system software (versions 4.0, 5.0, 6.0, etc.) have been notoriously buggy; secondary "mid version" releases (4.2, 6.0.7, etc.) have been stable. Microsoft Word 3.0 was a legend in the Macintosh community for documented bugs. Microsoft upgraded users to 3.01 for free (many users wanted to be paid for their upgrade), and the company never forgot the experience. In 1989 Microsoft delayed the introduction of Works and Word several months in order to produce stable releases, even at the expense of short-term profit. Similarly, many in the DOS community today steadfastly refuse to upgrade from MS-DOS 3.3 to version 4.0 or 4.01.

Users therefore face a dilemma when deciding just what features they really need versus what is just a convenience. As you read about software in this book, please keep in mind that the number of features offered is not necessarily a benefit. If a complex product is not well designed, or if it is weighed down by features you don't need, its value to you will be greatly diminished. If you choose the simpler pachage, you will be rewarded by a reduced learning curve and substantially reduced training headaches.

Learning the Software

When you set about to do a design project, you need to allow enough time to learn a program well. A full-featured drawing program, such as Micrografx Designer (Win), or Adobe Illustrator (PC or Mac), can take a full day of work (or play, depending how you feel about it) to feel comfortable with, perhaps a week really to master. I use Adobe Illustrator, but not frequently enough to have a good feel for the product. In the two years I've used the product, I always have to go back and review its features before each project. Illustrator is not unusual in that regard; I find Bezier curves (see Chapter 9) to be nonintuitive. Designer and artist friends of mine using Adobe Illustrator or Aldus FreeHand for their living do not have these problems. It can take a person several days to a week of constant work in order to come up to speed, a month to fully master a CAD package such as AutoCAD, or a desktop publishing package such as QuarkXPress (Mac). There just aren't any shortcuts, and you have to make provisions for this.

Frankly, most of the documentation that software vendors provide is poor. There are noteworthy exceptions, and good technical documentation should be a major consideration when deciding on a software purchase. Yet it's usually the last thing you get to look at. When evaluating documentation, consider whether it is benefits-oriented rather than features-oriented. The key is whether it is easy to figure out how to do a particular task. Are commands listed in a logical way? Is there a good mixture of tutorials and project ideas built in? Microsoft's MS-DOS manuals read like the Manhattan phone book; Apple's system software manuals are generally highly regarded, being task-oriented with very good technical illustrations. So by all means read the documentation that comes with the product, or at least scan it so that you know what information it contains. Many of the questions that are asked could easily have been answered by looking at a program's docs. Any "expert" who claims to have gotten that way by just hacking his or her way to knowledge is either pulling your leg or is no expert. Modern software is too complex to guess at. You will enjoy your work more and be more efficient by using applied study, so factor that time into your purchase.

An outstanding software package with poor documentation is not necessarily a write-off, however. Numerous publishers have produced a library of fine computer books that you can use to supplement a product's original documentation. Ask experienced members at a users' group what they would recommend, or find a technical bookstore in your town and ask the staff. That's how major publishers figure out what's good. Different users have different approaches to learning; there is no "right" way. If you learn best from hands-on tutorials, then take a class, buy a tape, or use training disks to get up to speed. There are many good training aids on the market today.

Expertise at the Bleeding Edge

So what are you as a computer user to do when working with systems that are leading edge? You will often face the dilemma of equipment and software obsolescence coupled with less expensive impending technology. That's the bleeding edge. There isn't any easy answer to this problem. If you can use the technology to increase your skills, a purchase might translate into increased revenue that you might not anticipate. It's always a gamble, but more often than not these decisions work out.

Test Drive Hardware and Software

Your enterprise might force you to be a pioneer, but consider each acquisition for all of its risks and rewards. If it's possible, try to spend some time with a piece of software or hardware before you've committed to buy it. Go into a store that sells the software, and sit down with a computer and play with it. Ask for a return period in case you're not happy with it. These are good reasons to buy from a retail outlet. If you buy from a mail order firm, try to do it from one with a generous return policy, such as PCConnection or MacConnection.

Consider renting the equipment for a trial run. Maybe you don't really need to own the equipment in the first place, for all the reasons we've discussed. Service bureaus often have had the leading-edge experiences you need to make informed selections, so do users' groups.

You can also find specialized help on various bulletin boards and information services. You can find a desktop publishing forum on CompuServe (type GO DTPFORUM at the ! prompt), for example; nearly every other big service offers one.

Often you can get technical support from the companies themselves. Some companies, such as WordPerfect, are renowned for their phone support. WordPerfect spends $1 million *per month* on technical support; lines are open nearly twenty-four hours a day, and they will answer questions from all users (not just registered ones).

Read Magazines

The computer industry moves quickly, and many seek advice from magazines, believing that they are the most current source. Most publishers shy away from survey-type books believing that technology is moving too quickly to be contained in a book with any long-term shelf life. Conventional wisdom says that you can get up-to-date, unbiased opinions from the computer trade press, the magazines you see on your bookstore rack. But that's rarely the case. Most of the magazines you pick up on the newstands have a strong bias toward the type of reader they serve. Although you would expect that a magazine that serves a specific machine's readership to show bias, often you'll also find that general-purpose magazines aimed at new users are highly prejudiced too.

The best way to gain a perspective when you are interested in a particular discipline is to to seek out specialty magazines with that focus. *Publish* magazine has a useful general focus for a DTP audience, and it tries to discuss both major DTP platforms (Mac and PC) along with their products. If you are primarily interested in choosing a platform for CAD work, then you should seek out a specialty CAD magazine. It might be prejudiced toward one system or another, but at least that prejudice should coincide with your own purpose.

Talk to Other Users

The best place to find out about the joys or trials you're likely to encounter when trying to use a particular piece of hardware or software for a certain purpose is to ask users actively involved in that pursuit. Chances are, if they're having a tough time, then you will as well. You can trade notes with other users in one of the hundreds of on-line bulletin boards found around the country, or in user groups that meet regularly in cities and towns everywhere.

Keep in mind that computer equipment has a very narrow product window, maybe two to three years on average, five years maximum—if you buy a watershed product at the beginning of its product cycle. Try to think strategically, and invest in watershed technology whenever you recognize it.

Summary

Let's summarize the discussion in this chapter regarding the use of computers in graphic design work and briefly look at the advantages and disadvantages of doing a project by computer. Benefits are:

- Retaining Artistic Control: Using a computer often allows you to do more parts of the production in-house. For a desktop publishing project you could complete nearly all aspects of a project, including short-run production work, on a micro-computer system.

- Rapid Turnaround: Doing a design project on a computer often results in substantially reduced completion times. This is particularly true when the designers or operators have done similar projects on the system before.

- Customization: Computer technology offers unparalleled opportunities to experiment with design parameters. You can make rapid changes to designs and create individual solutions for clients.

- Cost Savings: After the cost of a computer system is amortized, you can often achieve substantial cost reduction in many segments of the production process.

- Competitiveness. All of these factors may make your enterprise more competitive than your counterparts who do design work traditionally.

- Quality of Work: Retaining artistic control, customizing a project for an individual need, and shortening design time can greatly enhance the quality of the work done. As a side benefit, computers also improve the quality of the life of the individual workers by eliminating repetitive tasks.

- Increased Opportunities: The expansion of your skills set with computer tools often allows you to compete in areas you hadn't previously anticipated, thereby leading to further gains.

Balanced against all of the preceding benefits are the costs involved with computerizing your design projects. They include:

- High Initial Cost: Computer systems and software are expensive and depreciate rapidly. The useful lifetime of a computer system may be three to five years.

- Steep Learning Curve: Learning to operate a computer system for specialized design work can take a long time. Training tends to be expensive. These hidden costs often are overlooked, but they must be factored into any decisions or purchases.

- Quality of Work: Computers tend to be faddish tools. Often the traditional methods are superior to computer tools, but novices opt to bypass them and use the new "toys." For example, photographic techniques are still generally superior to digital imaging for quality, but if you have a scanner available you might take a shortcut and use a digital image.

- Distractions: Knowledge workers rely heavily on computer tools, but computers can distract them from their primary job. Many companies require reports from skilled workers (such as engineers), but they often find these workers will spend considerable time doing design or DTP projects, not at all what their companies desired.

Issues and Standards

The computer is no better than its program.
Elting Elmore Morison, MEN,
MACHINES, AND MODERN TIMES

No matter what brand of personal computer you consider, basic microcomputer design is fairly standardized. There is a central microprocessor with some volatile memory (RAM), connected by a sort of data highway, called a *bus,* to various input and output peripheral devices. Input can be from keyboard, mouse, scanner, or storage devices (disk drives). Output can be to monitors or other display mechanisms and also to storage devices, printers, or the other recording media. This chapter elaborates on some of the basic principles separating one computer system from another and how these variables may affect your publishing tasks. A general discussion of hardware and operating systems is included.

The CPU

The central logic unit, or *central processing unit* (cpu), in any microcomputer you might consider is most likely based on one of these two types of microprocessorchips: an Intel 80x86 (x = omitted, 2, 3, or 4) or a Motorola 680 x 0 (x = 0, 2, 3, or 4). Higher numbers of x denote more advanced chips with higher speeds and advanced capabilities. The Intel 8088 chip powered the original IBM PC computers. The Intel 80286 chip powers the IBM PS/2 models 25, 30, 50, and 60 as well as the IBM PC AT; the 80386 and 80486 are in the new, more advanced IBM PCs and clones, including the IBM PS/2 models 70 and 80. The original Macintosh used the 68000 series (roughly equivalent in features to the 80286), as does the Mac Plus, Mac SE, and Macintosh Portable. The original Mac II and the new Mac LC use the 68020 chip, while the 68030 chip is included in the Mac SE/30, Mac IIcx, Mac IIci, Mac IIsi, and Mac IIfx machines. (A table of features for the Macintosh and IBM PS/2 line of computers can be found in Chapter 4.)

When purchasing a computer to do design or graphics work, buy an Intel 80386 S/X or Motorola 68030-based machine, or better. You will need a machine of this class to run many of the graphics programs described in this book well.

▼ *Tip: It may be tempting to save money by buying a less powerful microprocessor. Don't do it!*

The cpu will define your system capabilities for many years to come. Whenever possible, make the better cpu a priority; it will extend the useful life of your entire computer system. Others may argue that you can always insert an upgraded board into your computer later on, but this is rarely done and is a wasteful practice. Remember, for graphics you always have "the need for speed."

Speed: Clock Speed and Throughput

One of the important characteristics of a microprocessor is its speed. Speed is measured by the frequency with which the cpu fetches new instructions. This is referred to as the *clock rate* and is measured in megahertz (MHz). A computer processes instructions in cycles of three operations: fetch, decode, and execute. The entire cycle is called the *instruction cycle*. As megahertz is a frequency measurement, you can convert clock rates to system cycles by taking their reciprocal: A 10 MHz machine cycles every 100 billionth of a second or every 100 nanoseconds; a 50 MHz machine is five times faster.

Often the microprocessor is faster than the electronic channel, called the *bus,* that carries the instructions from input/output

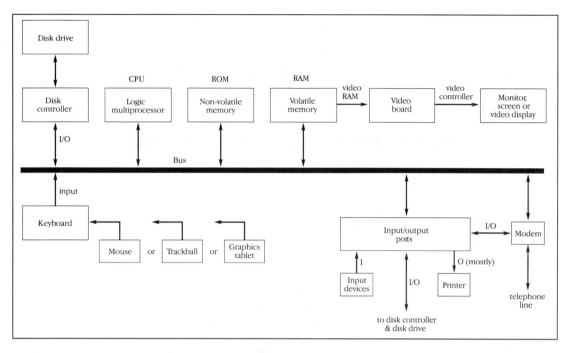

Figure 2-1 A conceptual figure of a microcomputer.

(I/O) devices. Manufacturers can build time delays in the cycle called *wait states* to compensate for this imbalance or design in system *caches* to hold needed instructions. A cache is high-speed RAM reserved for required or recently used instructions. Whenever possible, buy a computer with a zero wait state specification. The highest performance chips sold by Intel and Motorola for the personal computer market range from 33 to 50 MHz.

Another measure of computer speed, the *throughput*, represents the number of instructions that pass through a microprocessor (or more generally through the entire computer) per unit time, and is commonly quoted in *million instructions per second* or MIPS. The Mac SE runs at about 1 MIPS, the Mac II at 4 MIPS, and the Mac IIfx at about 16 MIPS. Mainframe or supercomputers can run at 100 MIPS or more.

While clock rates or throughput may seem somewhat esoteric, graphics applications are computationally very intensive, and the level of performance is a major consideration in determining what

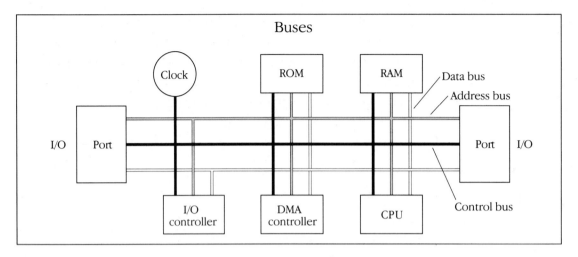

Figure 2-2 A computer's bus is the wiring that connects all the devices in a computer and serves as the data's pathway.

software you can run effectively. You will need an IBM PC AT class or better (or a clone of similar specifications) running at 16 MHz or more to effectively run Windows (see Chapter 4). Windows 3.0 is one of the best graphical user interfaces currently on the market for IBM PCs. Many of the important graphics applications on the PC use this environment.

Clock speed and throughput numbers as an absolute indicator of computer performance can be deceiving, however. The Apple Macintosh was originally *designed* as a graphics computer, and graphics routines are directly encoded into the read-only memory (ROM) chip in the computer. Because of this, graphics drawn to the display or sent out to a printer are executed faster than in a system where interpretation is required. One of the faster IBM PCs operating Windows 3.0 at 33 MHz may be no faster than a Macintosh II running the Finder at 12 MHz. Similarly, Microsoft Excel running on a Mac IIcx at 16 MHz is faster than the same program running on a Compaq Systempro 386/33.

The Bus

Of less importance at the moment, but worth mentioning, is the width of the bus structure in a computer. The computer bus is the system of "wires" that electrically connect all of the computer parts. All input/output occurs through the bus. A bus can physically be a set of wires, but it also includes the integral connections inside the various microchips in your computer. The width of the computer bus is a measure of the size of data chunks that may move through it, which can be thought of as computer "words." Since 8 bits of information equal 1 byte, a 16-bit bus moves data along in 2-byte packets. Similarly, a 32-bit bus moves data in 4-byte packets. Just as a wider pipe can transfer more fluid per unit time, bus width has a direct effect on data flow.

Figure 2-3
Bytes are "computer words," and they are determined by both hardware (chips and wires) and software considerations.

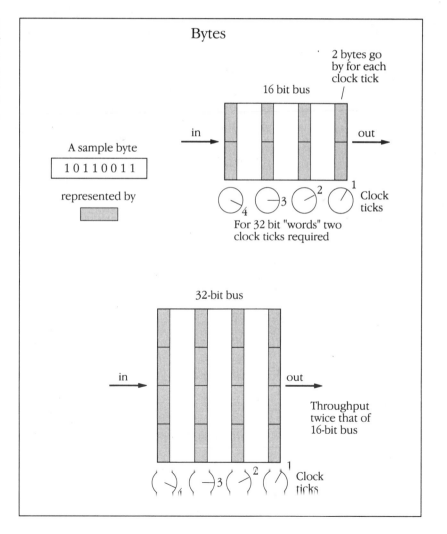

Originally, early microcomputers used 8-bit buses (such as that used on original IBM PC), and each word was 8-bits (or electrical on/off signals). More modern buses tend to use 32-bit structures. In order to fully utilize a bus size, you need a microprocessor to match. The 8086 and 80286 chips were 16-bit cpus, 80386 and 80486 chips are 32-bit microprocessors.

IBM PCs use the standard AT bus architecture (16-bit bus) commonly referred to as the *industry standard architecture*, or ISA. The more recent standards of *microchannel architecture* (MCA) promulgated by IBM in its Personal System 2 (PS/2) line of personal computers (and also found licensed in NCR PCs), or the competing *extended industry standard architecture* (EISA) promoted by Compaq and others are also 32-bit bus structures. MCA offers complete compatibility to IBM mainframes, which may be important to you if you work in a large business; EISA offers backward compatibility to the previous ISA standard and has not been demonstrated to be incompatible with mainframes. Right now, the consensus is that EISA has a very slight advantage.

In principle, a 32-bit bus structure in both the bus and the microprocessor should have faster throughput than a 16-bit bus structure, but in practice this speed advantage rarely seems to be realized. Some of the new 80486 machines using the AT bus (such as the Northgate or Gateway systems) turn in average or better-than-average performance when compared to other machines in this class using the MCA or EISA standard bus. The bus width does not limit you in any way to particular applications. If you are using an application that includes full color and describes each pixel with 32 bits of information, then a 16-bit bus structure moves this data as two consecutive words.

All Macintosh computers are 32-bit machines. The Mac II series uses the NuBus architecture (a 32-bit bus) which provides for self-configuring add-in boards. (NuBus is a high-speed expansion bus that uses special 96-pin boards.) The Macintosh IIfx, exhibits a trend that probably will be seen on many of the more powerful personal computers to come: It incorporates split bus structures and separate microprocessors for off-loading I/O functions from the main cpu. The MCA bus also supports split bus architecture. I/O is seen as a major bottleneck in the current computer design, and both of these solutions help speed up a system's performance.

Competing Operating Systems

Every computer system requires a program to control, assist, or supervise all the other programs that run on it. That program is called the *operating system*. Like the conductor of an orchestra, it dictates the order in which events occur. The operating system normally controls input and output, plus disk operations or printing commands. Operating systems can be stored in read-only memory, as a program loaded from disk at startup, or as any combination of these two possibilities. The more instructions stored on ROM, the less memory is required to load the operating system at startup, and the more room you have to run applications.

DOS

The best-known operating system is the one that runs on the IBM PC and compatibles, the Microsoft Disk Operating System, or MS-DOS for short. Using commands typed at the prompt, users can do file management, control display characteristics, or output to peripheral devices. DOS commands are *procedural*—nothing happens unless you specifically command DOS to act; but you can create sets of commands in a *batch* file (indicated by filename.bat) and have the entire set executed automatically. Programs that run on DOS are *executable* files (indicated by filename.exe or filename.copy). MS-DOS is described in more detail in Chapter 4.

Macintosh System

The Macintosh has its own operating system, built mostly into ROM. It includes a set of graphics instructions, or routines, based on its proprietary graphics language called QuickDraw, and a collection of command routines called *managers*. The entire set of commands are grouped into the Macintosh Toolbox. The Macintosh operating system does not currently offer a procedural command language, although one may be included in its System Software version 8. Most people mistakenly believe that the Macintosh Finder is its operating system, because that is how they interact with their Macintosh. The Finder is an *interface*(defined below), and you use the menu commands or their keyboard equivalents in the Finder or mouse input to access the underlying operating system commands. This type of interaction is termed *event driven*. The Macintosh monitors its condition and doesn't act until it senses an event as detected by the Event manager.

The Interface

An interface is a program that runs on top of an operating system and interacts with the user. It can be as simple as the command-line prompt in DOS, or as complicated as the menu system for the Macintosh Finder. Very little processing is needed to draw a prompt on the screen, but quite a lot of processing is required to draw all the menus, graphics, and icons for the Finder. The purpose of an interface is to provide a standard set of commands that all programs use. A user then needs only to learn that single command set to be competent on all applications that run on the interface.

The Macintosh Finder is an example of a *graphical user interface* (GUI) for the Macintosh. Windows, GeoWorks, GEM, and the OS/2 Presentation Manager are PC GUIs. Much of Chapter 4 is devoted to a discussion of various GUIs and the advantages one has over another. GUIs are intrinsically slower than command-line interfaces, but they offer graphical icons and simulated "buttons," instead of commands and substantially reduced training times and cost. Nearly all of the graphics and DTP programs discussed in this book are run on GUIs. Many DOS users appreciate its power and prefer it for file management, but graphics programs require an extensive command set and options settings, and the GUI offers significant advantages. All GUIs and the graphics programs that run on them are event-driven systems; that is, the computer monitors its current state for events (such as mouse clicks, keyboard entries, network signals, or disk insertions) and takes appropriate actions when it detects them.

Long-time DOS users may bemoan the fact that GUIs are the coming thing for the PCs, but new users benefit greatly from GUI use. The Macintosh Finder or Windows will mediate among a user, a program, and the operating system of the Mac and PC respectively. Things such as printer drivers and font (type) management are already "built into" the interface.

Some people refer to interfaces as *shells*, and the core operating system is considered a computer's *kernel*; both of these terms arise from the UNIX operating system.

Platforms

A *platform* is defined as the marriage of a computer, operating system, and interface that defines a unique working environment. The Apple Macintosh is one platform, the IBM PC with its DOS operating system is another. It's possible to have several platforms on the same hardware, especially if the installed user base is large enough. For example, both DOS and OS/2 could run on the same PS/2 computer, so each configuration could be considered a separate platform. Chapter 4 discusses platforms in depth.

The 1990s will see tremendous new capabilities built into operating system/interface combinations. Features will include automatic data linking, data flow control, enhanced intercomputer communication, sophisticated typography, and so on. Pay particular attention to the platform you choose—especially the first one—because you might not buy or want to use another. Your platform will define your ultimate capabilities, which is far more important than to realize an initial advantage by saving $1,000 or $2,000 on cheaper hardware just to get started with computer technology.

Memory Access

Memory is the Achilles' heel of the personal computer. How much memory you have and how your computer uses that memory speaks volumes about the quality of an operating system's design. It limits your system capability, and it can directly affect program operation and speed. With enough memory you can load programs into separate sections of memory so they're all ready to go. All Macintosh computers and IBM PCs with 80286 chips or better allow you to do this—as long as you have *enough* memory and the right interface (MultiFinder or System 7 on the Mac; Windows 3.0, OS/2, or DESQview on the PC). Having several programs in memory allows you to move quickly between them, called *context switching*. This is a particularly valuable feature for graphics because you are often called upon to do several related tasks requiring different programs at the same time.

Multitasking

If an operating system permits it, you can have more than one program running at once, a process called *multitasking*. Multitasking doesn't actually run multiple programs at the same time, but through a process called *time slicing*, two or more programs may appear to be executing simultaneously. Multitasking allows you to work on one program, such as a word processor, in the foreground, while you're downloading a file in a telecommunications package in the background. Many operating systems allow limited *background processing* even when they don't fully permit generalized multitasking. Multitasking is an advanced feature built into the chips, and it is often touted as a reason for upgrading to a more powerful operating system.

OS/2 has full multitasking and displays a property called *multithreading*, which allows near-simultaneous processing of multiple applications. In practice, the appeal of multitasking is somewhat limited. Even current high-end microcomputers don't have the speed to run two or more programs well at the same time. For example, running PageMaker in OS/2 while printing in the background will slow the execution of both tasks. Future generations of microcomputers with clock speeds of 50 MHz and above will likely have enough horsepower to make multitasking practical.

Protected Memory

Much more important is the notion of *protected memory*, the capability to insulate one program in memory from another. The Macintosh operating system has limited multitasking abilities under MultiFinder (see Chapter 4), but most of its capabilities really might be termed context switching. When a program running under MultiFinder intrudes on another's memory, an error message is posted, and the assigned memory is released. That is what happens when you see a message on a Macintosh that states:

Application XYZ unexpectedly quit.

You then go on to remedy the problem. But anyone who has worked with a Macintosh recently has noticed that system errors and application bugs shut down a Mac more frequently than one might care to admit. So a Macintosh has limited protected memory, an outgrowth of the way the computer builds its memory stack (described below). *Multitasking* may then be seen as the unique opportunity to crash two or more programs at the same time. *Protected memory* is therefore a valuable feature of any multitasking operating system.

The DOS 640 K Limit

MS-DOS imposes a 640 kilobyte (KByte) limit on the memory available for applications (programs) to run in, even though most basic IBM PC systems have a full 1 megabyte (MByte:1024 KB) of RAM as "address space." The remaining 340 KBytes at higher memory addresses are used to control system functions such as display and input/output functions. This is a serious limitation because full-featured programs, including nearly all of the graphics programs discussed in this book, typically require from 500 KBytes to 2 to 3 MBytes on the high end. It is a major failing of the DOS operating system, and it really shows how old DOS has become.

Figure 2-4
The DOS 640 KByte application memory partition.

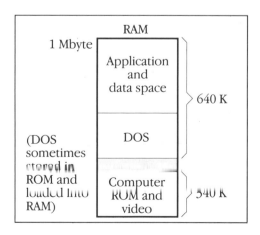

There are numerous schemes around, however, for extending DOS. Breaking the 640 KByte DOS limit is a major goal of software vendors. Most use a technique called *page swapping* where instructions, code, and data are swapped in and out of a narrow window—usually 64 KBytes in size—from main RAM borrowed from unused space normally reserved for ROM. Called *expanded memory* (for EMS, or Expanded Memory Specifications 4.0), it can address 8 MBytes of RAM. Quarterdeck's DESQview and QEMM-386 programs offers a multitasking environment or interface based on this page swapping technique, allowing you to run several DOS programs at once.

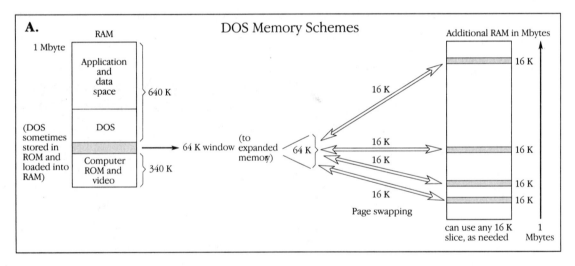

A.   DOS Memory Schemes

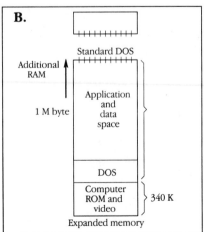

Figure 2-5
Two schemes for extending MS-DOS memory. **(A)** Expanded memory page swaps RAM, instructions out to (and back from) additional installed RAM, making it appear as if more (and much slower!) RAM is installed. **(B)** Extended memory refers to a situation where the application assesses all available RAM directly.

B.

Expanded memory is less desirable than the scheme called *extended memory*, which uses all the installed memory in a PC as a single unit addressing it directly. IBM PC AT class and other 80286 machines can address 15 MBytes of memory if the operating system can run programs in the protected mode. The 80386 machines can address nearly 4 gigabytes (4,000 MBytes) of memory directly. Windows 3.0 allows programs to run in protected mode, and will access the entire memory, as will OS/2. Unfortunately, expanded and extended memory are not interchangeable, but you can buy Above Disk from Above Software to transform extended memory or disk memory into expanded memory. You will need 2 to 3 MBytes of RAM to run Windows, over 4 MBytes to run OS/2. Expanded memory is really a relic of the past; extended memory is a feature of the future.

Figure 2-6
The Windows memory partition chart from the Memory Viewer, part of the hDC First Apps package. Also shown is the hDC animation editor. *Courtesy of hDC.*

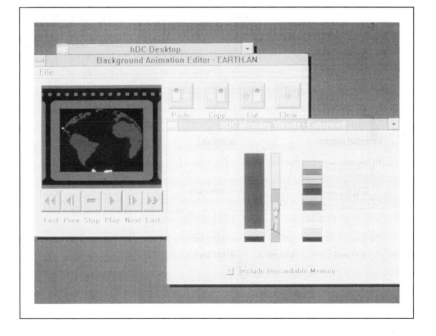

Memory Management on the Mac

Memory management is much simpler on the Apple Macintosh where all memory is available for programs. The system loads into the bottom addresses in memory, and applications load into the top addresses. The system grows (uses up memory addresses) upward, and the applications grow downward until there are no more addresses to be assigned. An application can have its memory allocation adjusted in MultiFinder through the Get Info dialog box. When an application is closed, its addresses are released, but you need to have enough free contiguous space in memory to load an application. Often you reach a point where memory frag-

Figure 2-7
Memory allocation in Macintosh MutiFinder. Choose the About the Finder command from the Apple menu.

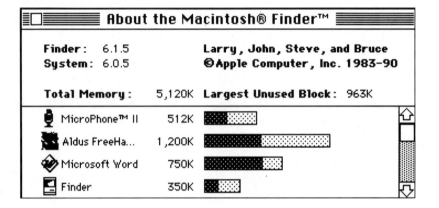

Figure 2-8
Setting an application memory partition from the Get Info box on a Macintosh. Click on the application icon, then select the Get Info command from the File menu to view.

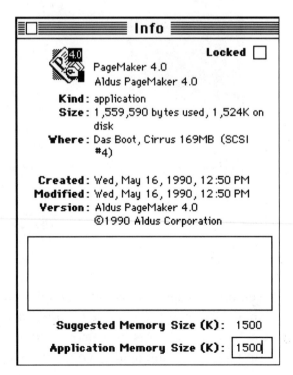

mentation is so great in the memory stack that you must reboot. This is a defect in the system software.

The Apple Plus, SE, SE/30, and LC can carry up to 4 MBytes of additional RAM in the form of single in-line memory modules, or SIMMs installed into the available eight banks. The Mac II series can hold up to eight SIMMs using 1-MByte SIMMs, for a total of 8 MBytes. When 4-MByte SIMMs become available, that number will jump to 32 MBytes. It is possible to install considerably more RAM in the form of NuBus cards, but the current operating system will access only 8 MBytes. Apple's A/UX UNIX operating system allows considerably more memory access, and future versions of the Macintosh system software also will expand memory access.

Figure 2-9
The memory scheme for the Apple Macintosh.

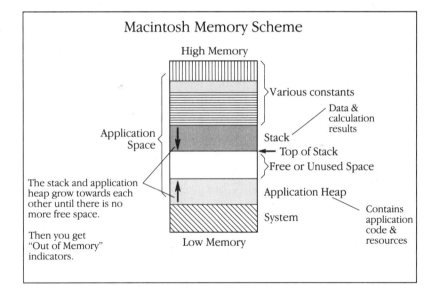

If you are low on installed RAM, you can use a software program to allow a portion of your hard disk to be used as RAM. This is called *virtual memory*. Connectix's Virtual is a program that allows up to 15 MBytes of virtual memory for a Mac II with five out of six empty NuBus slots. System 7 (see Chapter 4) will offer a virtual memory module, but in order to use this feature you must have a 68030-based Macintosh or a 68020 with a paged memory management unit (PMMU) chip installed. Virtual memory programs, also exist on the IBM PC.

When you have additional free RAM, you can set aside a portion of it as a cache where recently and often-used RAM instructions can reside dynamically. These instructions are updated as needed and page-swapped in and out of RAM, offering a system performance increase. There are RAM disks on the market made from a collection of SIMMs. RAM disk access times are around 0.1 millisecond, 200 times faster than a fast hard drive. These disks are valuable for manipulating large graphics files, and their use will increase as the price of memory chips continues to decline.

Memory is a complex and developing topic in the microcomputer field. Space limits this discussion to a simple introduction, but we will return time and again to the limits that memory imposes on your computer's working environment.

File Formats and Graphics Standards

There are three classes of data used by computers: characters, objects, and bit maps.

Characters

Characters are letters, numbers, symbols, control codes, and a number of special symbols that can be accessed by holding down modifier keys (Alternate, Option, Shift, Control, and Command keys) as part of keystrokes. The computer industry has standardized characters into a coding scheme called the *American Standard Code for Information Interchange*, or ASCII for short. Using the ASCII code, one computer can read another computer's files, and one user can transmit data to another without the need for much interpretation. Data created in ASCII is called text, and any file consisting of ASCII characters is called a text file.

The 256 characters and symbols that make up the ASCII code can be expressed in binary, decimal, or hexadecimal form. The letter Z is character 90, and that codes as 101101 in the binary language that computers understand. An 8-bit byte, such as the code just given, allows 256 combinations, hence a byte is sufficient to specify the entire ASCII character set. Only ASCII 32 through 127 are used for letters and numerals; the additional are codes and symbols that are generally customized to a specific platform. You can generally find a copy of the ASCII code that applies to your computer in the back of the operator's manual. Many books on specific programs, such as databases or telecommunications, also specify the ASCII code as an appendix.

You may use ASCII code-based text in telecommunications sessions or in other situations when you want to communicate with another computer. Because ASCII characters 32 through 127 are standard, they can be used to communicate with other computers, and any computer can understand and interpret (see Chapter 13). You can also save a word processor file as ASCII or "text only."

Most applications work with additional characters which are outside the basic ASCII set. These characters define unique appearances and styles for text and graphics and create what is known as *formatting*.

Formats are the special features that make one program more powerful or easier to use than another, and if a file is saved in a standard, specified manner, it is referred to as a file format. A Word 4.0 (file type MSWD) or MacWrite II file (file type MACA) on the Mac is a special format, so is the file you create with WordPerfect (*filename.wp*), WordStar (*filename.WS*), or Word (*filename.DOC*) on the PC. When you save a formatted file as "text only" you lose all information except the ASCII characters themselves.

Understanding file formats is a necessary requirement for working with complex multiprogram projects, and most of Chapter 13 is devoted to this subject. Always keep in the back of your mind how to convert one file format to another and which file formats are standards. The inability of a program to save a file in a standard file format is a good reason for not purchasing it. Your data are useful only if you can move it around, and fortunately most major programs have this capability.

Objects

Computers can describe shapes as well as characters. One type of graphic format is that described by a mathematical expression, called *object-oriented* graphics or *drawings*. A line is described by its end points and width. A circle can be described by its origin, radius, line width, line fill, and fill of the circle. This form of graphics allows the description of such complex objects as Bézier curves, outlined type (characters), halftones (simulated grays), and other features. You can also scale or resize an object perfectly, without distortion or loss of resolution. Draw programs, CAD, and even some word processors make use of this kind of graphics, including: Claris MacDraw, Adobe Illustrator, Aldus FreeHand, Claris CAD on the Macintosh; CorelDRAW!, Micrografx Designer, GEM Draw, Lotus 1-2-3, and AutoCAD on the PC.

Bit Maps

Graphics also can be described by *bit-mapped* or *paint* graphics. A file stores a picture of the image on your screen literally as a map with each *pixel* (the smallest point that can be described on the screen) turned on or off, shaded, or colored in some specific way. Shapes, type (characters), and any image can be bit-mapped. The resolution that you achieve is dependent , however, on the resolution of your input or output device. A 13-inch monitor, for example, contains about 371,200 pixels (640 x 580). Saving an image on screen requires 46.4 KBytes of memory in black and white (using two bits to describe the appearance of each pixel), eight times as much using an 8-bit per-pixel color board. In contrast, only about 3 or 4 KBytes are required to save a page of text using a word processor. Paint programs include: Claris MacPaint, Adobe Photo-Shop, Letraset ColorStudio, and SuperMac PixelPaint on the Mac, and Publisher's Paintbrush IV and GEM Paint on the PC. We discuss paint graphics in more detail in Chapter 9.

While early computer printers, so-called line printers, could output only ASCII text, today most printers can print both ASCII characters and graphics, although you can specify that a printer return to just character-based printing. In order to determine how graphics will be printed your computer must "create" an image of a page in memory. This can be done either by your computer's memory or in a printer's cpu and memory, and this is where page description languages come in.

Page Description Languages

We describe page description languages (PDLs) in detail in Chapter 7, but a brief definition is necessary for our purposes here. A PDL is a graphics programming language that allows you to place text, objects, and images on a page, and modify them through the use of various commands. There are several PDLs in use today, of which PostScript is perhaps the best known. The Macintosh QuickDraw routines are a PDL, as is the language of the Hewlett-Packard Laserjet III, which is called PCL.

What's not widely appreciated is that PostScript actually describes graphics on a page using a text-based file. If you use a program such as Illustrator or FreeHand to create a drawing with text (see Figure 2.10), the software application will actually describe your drawing with a text file that can be opened, read, and modified with any word processor (see Figure 2.11).

Working with the commands in this text file, you can alter any graphic element ultimately printed on the page. Working this way with the text file is useful for creating special effects or for optimizing your printer in ways not possible by simply using the drawing tools of the application.

▼ *Tip: You can import PostScript code directly into your word processor and edit it to achieve many different effects.*

Consult the books on PostScript referenced in Appendix B and your word processor's manual for details.

Using a Text file you can specify all the objects and settings to be displayed in any program that can read PostScript, or printed to any device that can read PostScript, by simply coding them in the PostScript language. If you know how to program in PostScript, you can create many useful effects. Some applications allow you to "program" in PostScript with a click and a drag on a mouse, select-

Figure 2-10
A simple Adobe Illustrator draw file with a square and some sample text.

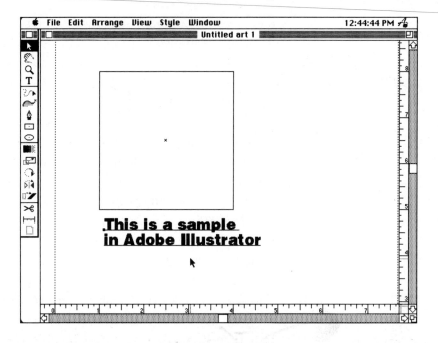

Figure 2-11
The associated PostScript file for Figure 2.10 opened in Microsoft Word.

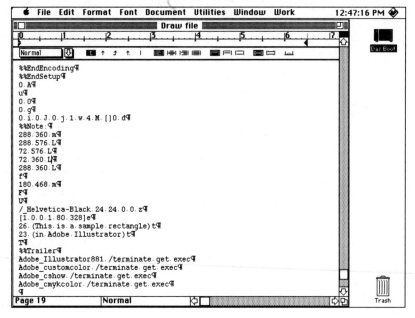

ing from icons or menu commands. They shield you from the complexities of the language. So, when you fire up Adobe Illustrator, Aldus FreeHand, or Aldus PageMaker, you are turning yourself into a PostScript programmer.

You can also embed a PostScript text file in any word processing document to achieve special effects when printing out to a PostScript printer. This allows you to supplement the graphics capabilities of a word processor with the entire range of fills, rotations, halftones, and so on, few of which are contained even in today's industrial-strength word processors. The procedure involves inserting some code in front of the paragraph to be affected. Note that normally you can't view the effect on-screen unless you have a computer with display PostScript (as in the NeXT computer), but when the print file is executed on a PostScript printer the effect is applied.

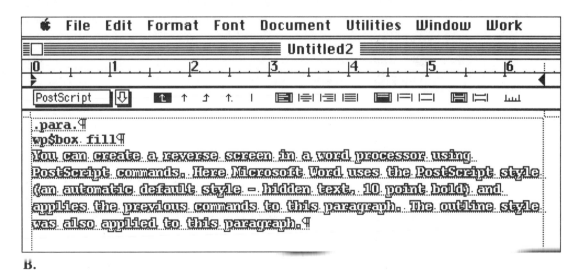

A.

B.

Figure 2-12 **(A)** Reverse screen and **(B)** PostScript code needed to implement it.

A PostScript language file can be sent to a printer, an imagesetter, a slide recorder, or any device that supports PostScript. The PostScript interpreter that resides in the printer will then *interpret* the PostScript code in order to create a bit map of the image in the printer's particular resolution. This interpreter is called a raster image processor (RIP). A RIP in the printer turns it into a computer in its own right. This off-loads processing from the computer driving the printer to the printer itself, thereby freeing the computer for further work.

Device Independence

The purpose of a page description language is to create a file that can be used to output to a range of output devices. A PostScript file is *device independent;* it will output to the maximum resolution of any device that can read a file in that format. Having device independence means that you can view a file on your screen at 72 dots per inch, print to a laser writer at 300 dpi, and create output on an imagesetter at 2,450 dpi, all with the same code in the same file that you created in your application. You no longer have to worry about respecifying a page when the resolution of the output device changes—the page description language takes care of that. Line breaks, page breaks, graphics, and other formatting occurs in exactly the same relative locations on a page as you see on your computer monitor. Format your file once, and then forget it.

Having device independence also means that you have a simple way of transporting and storing computer graphics output. Think of it as a way of storing a print file without having to worry about what printer or device is being specified. A file can be sent down a phone line to a remote location where the printing is to be done. Device independence also means that you get the best-quality output possible. It's a revolutionary improvement over the photographic method of creating and resizing printing masters. Compare that to the process and quality of a modern fax transmission.

Prepress Links

The use of imagesetters (printers that can place both text and graphics) to compose a page has changed how printing is done. Whereas prepress work (preparing text and images for the press) used to be done by hand, it can now take place entirely on a computer system. Because of device independence, standard file format input into a high-end device can output as camera-ready copy right from your desktop.

You might not choose to implement the entire prepress process electronically, for reasons explained in Chapter 1, but the point is that you could if you wished to do so. That is a powerful concept, because with some planning you can now create publications of the finest quality right from your own computer. The links between your computer and the desktop applications that you use to do this kind of work and high-end prepress systems such as the ones supplied by Scitex, Optronics, Hell Graphics, and so on are being established now. These systems, which just a few years ago ran on workstations costing $200,000 to $500,000, now operate from desktop computers. The imagesetters, allowing for full color separations and color proofs, now cost between $50,000 and $100,000, with costs dropping steadily.

Although large printing operations can afford such prepress installations today, they will be much more readily available in the near future as prices drop and quality improves. Your service bureaus should begin installing them in the next couple of years; in five years they may be common. In Chapter 15 we look more closely at some of these prepress systems and what they offer. But first let's take a general look at how the electronic publishing process works, how it's different from traditional methods, and how you can make use of it in your own work.

The Electronic Production Cycle

You see him laboring to produce bon mots.
Molière, LE MISANTHROPE

Every step in the design and production of graphic arts, from conception to master copy, to short-run production, can be accomplished from your desktop. Many graphics professionals would take exception to this bold statement because they've defined their desktop as their own personal computer, scanner, and printer. If you are similarly limited, then you are certainly better off striking a balance between the new and the traditional when attempting DTP projects. In this chapter we look at the various steps in a DTP production scheme and attempt to decide where and when electronic tools are best adopted.

Sewing Electronic Threads

Taken individually, each step in the electronic production cycle is direct and well defined. Text can be electronically formatted in typographic detail; graphics created, or scanned; and all these pieces can be assembled in page composition or layout software in the form of disk files. This compares to the process of creating copy by a linotype or other manual typesetting machine, art drawn by pen, and photographs or camera-ready artwork all hand "pasted-up" on a board. However, when you try to integrate both electronic and conventional processes to create a whole smooth production flow, you must define exactly what you are trying to achieve, how much you are willing (or able) to spend, and what compromises you are willing to make to strike a balance between them. Let's take a close look at the process.

Traditional Versus Desktop Methods

Preparing Text

Traditional Method Creating hand-written copy or composing copy on a typewriter requires very little training or specialized computer knowledge, but there is little flexibility or editing capability, and it's difficult to incorporate into a design process. The typewriters of today come with microprocessors, create disk files, and include such automatic editing or authoring tools as spell checkers. They just don't require the user to be computer literate.

Desktop Method Text prepared as disk files in a word processor on a computer is easy to edit, makes use of automated text tools, and incorporates a compact disk file into a page composition scheme. Specialized computer knowledge of operating systems and file structures is required, however.

Conclusion The strong advantages word processors offer compels their use. See Chapter 8 for discussion.

Paint or Draw Graphics

Traditional Method Paper and pen or pencil are the traditional media of artists. Advantages include low cost, ease of use, and many special effects such as variable line width that are difficult to achieve on a computer. Contrarily, artwork isn't easily altered, isn't very precise, and is hard to adapt to a production process.

Desktop Method Computer paint and draw programs with digital file output are easy to alter, include many special effects, are precise, and adapt easily to an electronic production cycle. Disadvantages include high cost of equipment, and lengthy rendering times of complex art at final output stage.

Conclusion Electronic art is more frequently becoming the choice for a production process, but the advantages are not always overwhelming, depending on the art form. See Chapter 9 for a discussion of computer graphics.

Photographic Elements

Traditional Method Camera-generated artwork is low cost, high quality, easy to generate, and can incorporate many special effects. But it is difficult to alter and include into an electronic production process.

Desktop Method Using scanned artwork you can alter an image and create certain special effects not offered by film. Disadvantages are cost of equipment and storage, training, and highly varying quality, depending on equipment.

Conclusion Traditional photography is preferred in all situations except where moderate quality is acceptable or where there is access to very high quality computer equipment. See Chapter 10 for a discussion of digital imaging.

Page Layout, Typesetting, and Composition

Traditional Method Paste-up boards result in a high-resolution master. However, they are time-consuming and expensive to produce.

Desktop Method Page layout programs have the support of automation tools, offer device independence, and are low cost and of good quality. Disadvantages include complex design strategy, lengthy setup times for initial run, and immature color and digital image technologies.

Conclusion Desktop page layout is a better choice for composing a page, particularly for repetitive situations. See Chapter 12 for a discussion of page composition.

Printing

Traditional Method Letterpress, offset, gravure, screen printing, and heat-transfer printing offer high quality and low cost per unit, give better color reproduction, and offer large page sizes.

Disadvantages include high setup costs and time and low adaptability for mixed print runs.

Desktop Method Personal laser printers and imagesetters are adaptable and have short setup times. Quality is variable but can be from good (laser printers or copiers) to excellent (for imagesetters, but with high costs).

Conclusion Use desktop methods to do mixed or short-run print jobs of moderate quality or to produce a high-quality printing master. See Chapter 7 for a discussion of print and output technologies.

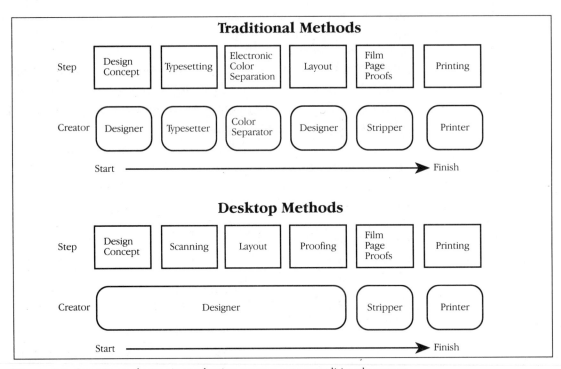

Figure 3-1 Steps in an electronic production process versus traditional process.

Desktop Publishing Quality Considerations

DTP cradle-to-grave gets a bad rap from many professionals who are attempting to bring a project to completion with only modest computer tools. But with proper resources, it is possible to achieve results today at any quality level. If you are one of the lucky people who has access to some of the newer tools mentioned in this book, you may already share this viewpoint. If not, rest assured that time will bring these new technologies to you in a form that you can use. The high-end commercial system of today is the microcomputer of 1995 and the technology available on those platforms will be available to you by then.

Page Layout and Publication Design

Almost any layout design can be implemented electronically, but rarely do you realize any cost or time savings until you automate the process. If you are laying out a newsletter or a newspaper, your initial design costs are normally the same for both traditional and desktop methods. It isn't until you create a standard design format or layout that desktop publishing starts to save you money. Saved standard formats are called *templates*. Normally they incorporate specified type styles called *style sheets*, along with pictures and other graphic elements of various sizes placed in designated places. If you can buy a template designed for commercial use, then you can realize savings using DTP methods right from the start.

The switch to computer layout from hand pasteup actually started many years ago, appearing first on minicomputers and later on workstations. Early layout systems contained text and graphics embedded with typesetter's codes that placed objects precisely on a page. These types of layout programs are briefly discussed in Chapter 12. They are best exemplified by such programs as TeX, which runs on a variety of UNIX platforms, and have microcomputer analogs such as TeXtures and LaTeX on the Macintosh. You won't see much discussion of coded systems in the microcomputer trade press, but it continues to be used in the UNIX world.

Coded systems can produce very good results, but they require lengthy training times and a dedicated operator for production work. Coded systems are particularly useful with mathematical and engineering formulas—in fact, Microsoft Word 4.0 on the Macintosh incorporates them into text commands. Recent coded programs like MagnaType have incorporated preview screens that give a WYSIWYG display (what you see is what you get, pronounced wizzy wig). However, true WYSIWYG layout programs, such as Aldus PageMaker, Ventura Publisher, QuarkXPress, Letraset DesignStudio, and others, are easier to learn, understand, and work with and currently seem to have enough typographical control to recommend their use.

Typesetting and Composition

Typesetting is an artform, almost a lost artform. Using traditional typesetting equipment, trained typographers could look at a line of type (a *slug*) and adjust letterspacing, kerning (subtracting the space between two characters) and line spacing (*leading*) to a pleasing compromise. Typographers might have a table of set spacing parameters, but they would often use their judgment and finesse to make the small adjustments that make a page of type really work. Traditional typography makes use of special letter pairs that run together, called *ligatures* (eg., œ, æ, fi, fl, Æ, etc.). A typographer has a choice of hundreds of character sets built up over the centuries to choose from. But today such typography is available only in small shops devoted to carrying on the traditions of the past.

Manual typesetting and composition is just too expensive and time-consuming to be practical in today's world. So computers have replaced humans, and certain compromises have been made. Today you can compose a page proof electronically but you would choose from perhaps only 1,000 typefaces, although the number is growing rapidly. Page layout programs allow fine spacing control, but require advanced desktop publishing sophistication and practice to implement. A human typographer can kern letters with any spacing. Most electronic programs let you manually kern, but also use automatic pair kerning. Adobe's character sets come with about 100 kerned pairs; Bitstream fonts contain about 300 pairs.

Electronic type just doesn't have the sophistication of the trained human eye, although more sophisticated computers and artificial intelligence are being applied to typography even as you read this. (Macintosh System 7 is shipping with a Layout Manager that could create new ligatures and type sets, and Apple's demonstration of the technology was impressive.) Even experienced typographers acknowledge that the best tools for creating new type are those that exist today on computers. We look more closely at typography in Chapter 11.

What you get electronically in page layout packages is great speed, automated spell checking, spacing, hyphenation, justification (H & J) control, and the ability to compose text and graphics. In theory, composing a page by DTP methods offers speed and quality. But in order to get those advantages you have to make use of style sheets, tags, and other formatting codes in your word processor that automate the process of incorporating text into a layout (see Chapter 7). If you don't, you can lose that cost and speed advantage. Such use requires both knowledge and planning, and it separates a polished computer user from a novice.

Electronic printing is not quite device independent. Page description languages such as PostScript are a great boon, because a page printed on a laser printer looks similar to one created on an imagesetter. However, higher-resolution devices do present problems; sometimes it's hard to spot small features on the copy. For example, hairline rules are often hard to match; and if you have different colors that abut and you don't know how to build traps, you are going to end up with poor color quality (see Chapter 14). Often you can't tell at lower resolution. Only on a high-resolution proof do many complex issues, such as poor registration or improperly formed halftones, show up. Manually, when you typeset, you do so at high resolution only. Your graphics are photographic or art originals, so quality issues aren't hidden.

Creating Master Copies or Mechanicals

A master is the original piece of art used by a printer to make a printing plate; it is often referred to as *camera-ready copy*. Sometimes the terms *mechanicals* or *boards* are also used to describe masters. The quality of your master is dictated by the printing process and paper you want to use for the final product. It makes little sense to print fine small serifs on highly textured paper stock, where you might lose that detail. Master copy should contain all page elements. If it doesn't and it specifies that the printer add some elements, it is probably better referred to as a mechanical or, as a printer would say *artwork*.

Mechanicals often have tissue or acetate overlays with instructions to the printer written in red ink or grease pencil. When precise registration is required, written instructions leave the work to the printer. A mechanical with written instructions is called a *keyline*. But when you submit a master copy, you are responsible for any error it contains (such as misregistrations). Therefore, be very careful to proof a master copy completely.

Halftones and Line Screens

The printer converts every element of camera-ready copy into line art. Even photographs are screened to produce intersecting lines that appear as halftone dots (see Chapter 10 for a fuller discussion of halftones). Photographically, a fine screen is placed in front of the original master. The resulting photograph produces a dot pattern. If fine enough, that dot pattern simulates shades of gray or grayscale. The reason for using halftones is that the modern printing process uses opaque inks. Tonality and color can be achieved only by converting continuous tones into a fine pattern of dots that the human brain blends together.

The size of the dots and their spacing are dependent on the printing process used. For newspapers printed on a web press on absorbent rough paper with watery inks, line screens of 85 lines per inch (lpi) giving 85 halftone dots per inch (dpi) provide the best compromise. A finer screen (such as the 133 to 150 lpi used in magazines) would result, on newsprint, in the dots running together and would degrade image quality.

Most scanners can digitally create line screens, and many digital image processing programs offer special effects or filters that imitate the special filters you can place on a camera to create photographic effects. Often your printer can tell you about the necessary settings for a particular printing process. Color Figure C-5, in this book's color pages shows how a color halftone is built from a set of screens.

Figure 3-2
The halftone process and its relation to printing.

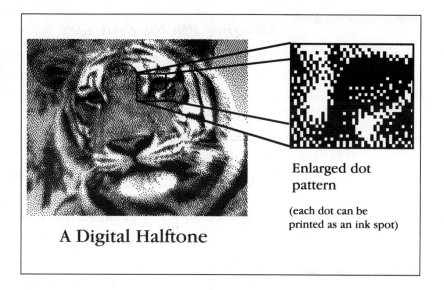

Enlarged dot pattern

(each dot can be printed as an ink spot)

A Digital Halftone

Spot Color

When the print job you're creating has color elements in it, you will require two (or more) color layers or separations. Most page layout programs support spot color to accentuate areas of a page. Each color is normally separated into a single master copy and used for each run of ink on a press. For one or two spot colors it is sufficient to show position and specify a color match using the Pantone ink matching scheme, or something similar. You can either create multiple masters for each process color or create one mechanical with the appropriate number of overlays.

Process Color

A full-color print job, on the other hand, where color photographs are reproduced, requires a four-color printing process. Most of the more powerful page layout programs, such as QuarkXPress and Aldus PageMaker, now have links to programs that support process color separation. Each process ink color—cyan, yellow, magenta, and black, or CYMK—requires its own master copy to specify where each colored halftone dot must be placed. As dots to create various colors must be placed next to each other and not on top of one another, the screens for each of the four process colors are rotated with respect to the original perpendicular screens. Chapter 14 describes this technology more fully.

Merging Photos and Text

Traditionally, text mechanicals were pasted up and keylined, with spot colors, process color, and all photos or line art shot separately and physically "stripped in" to the final press film by the printer. Now, using desktop tools for layout, scanning, and image manipulation, almost all artwork can be merged with text electronically, and an imagesetter can then print out composite film with all art in place. This has truly revolutionized the production process and has shifted and compressed job rules. We discuss these processes and issues in detail in Chapter 15.

Comparing Printing Costs and Results

Computer technology has not yet advanced enough in some areas of printing to be cost effective (or quality effective) for an individual user. Some electronic methods approach the quality attained traditionally only when produced on the most advanced systems (color photography, for example). As with prior steps in the production process, it may make sense to use a mixture of electronic technology and traditional methods to yield the best results. Let's look at examples of work in ascending order of quality.

Quick Printing

Until very recently, this method has been typical of a quick-copy shop, low-quality printing, or photocopying. It has been appropriate for fliers, forms, newsletters, and some newspapers. Quick printing has normally produced black-and-white photographs that are recognizable but not crisp, limited color, and modest registration (precise placement of details). A good strategy at this level has been to use laser printing combined with scanned artwork to create a master copy of modest quality.

However, things are changing. Now the Canon Color Laser Copier (CLC) 500, available at many quick-print shops, can be outfitted to accept PostScript files and print them at 600 dpi. Digital QuickColor, Inc. (DQI), or Sir Speedy, will soon be offering quick color printing service for printshops.

Good Printing

Good printing can be obtained as low-end work from a commercial printer, coupled with high-speed printing. It might be used for direct mail catalogs, most color books, retail packaging, and most magazines, such as *Time* or *Newsweek*. This category has strong black-and-white photos with good gray levels (see Chapter 10), good but not exact color reproduction, and close registration. At this level, a good idea is to use an imagesetter for master copy and incorporate artwork. If you have access to one, use a good black-and-white scanner for photos. If not, use the original black-and-white photos and put your scanned images into the artwork to show them for position only. Use a commercial stripper for color pictures, incorporating color photos only when you have access to high end prepress systems.

Quality Printing

Quality printing is available as high-end work from a commercial printer, coupled with high-speed printing. This is the level of printing required by the better mail-order catalogs that need to portray colors accurately and such magazines as *National Geographic*. It is characterized by sharp black-and-white/grayscale photos, very good color work that accurately matches the original photograph, and tight registration. Printing at this level requires imageset type and artwork. Photographs are normally handled traditionally (photographically), although many of the larger organizations are installing and experimenting with digital photo manipulation.

Museum Printing

Museum printing is available from a limited number of printers with the best equipment. This level of work is found in museum reproductions, some brochures, and some annual reports. Materials and execution are nearly flawless, registration is perfect to the naked eye, and colors are well matched to the original. At this level, it is necessary to create a master with the best typesetting equipment you can find, probably either a minicomputer-based Atex type system or by traditional handset type. Masters should be created photographically, and pictures should be handled photographically. Museum-quality imagesetters and scanners are only just starting to come to market and aren't widely available.

Composition and Printing Costs

To compare relative costs between DTP and traditional methods, keep in mind that you must amortize the cost of your equipment. Until you do a fair amount of DTP work, you can't really disregard those costs. In the discussion that follows, the costs of equipment are not factored into DTP costs, although they are part of the cost borne from outside services.

Typesetting is normally at least one half to one third as expensive on a DTP system compared to traditional means. A page of type costs roughly $12 to set by DTP, versus $30 traditionally. A scanned black-and-white image might cost $20 to prepare; photographic methods would have a similar cost. Spot color work costs about $50 to separate, $10 to create a color key proof. Done traditionally, spot color costs about the same.

Color photos cost approximately $30 to scan on a prepress system (assuming an hour for the process and a three-by-three inch image); separated color film and a color proof costs around $80. Done traditionally, a similar color separation costs about $100.

Layout and production costs around $25 per hour for the labor in either case, but it normally takes up to twice as long to do traditional paste-up than to do electronic page layout. Any special effects or requirements could, of course, change these prices significantly.

Going to Print

The goal of any publication process is to produce a printed final product. But surprisingly, talking to the printer is the last thing most desktop publishers think of. In fact, it should be one of your first steps. Your printer can help you define what your master must contain or what guidelines it must conform to. In this section you'll find some general considerations about printing. Chapter 15 discusses this topic in more detail.

Obviously, the printing press you decide on will limit you to a particular size, but there are many other subtle, less-obvious specifications that your printer can spell out for you. In any print process there are restrictions on total ink coverage that you might need to know about when separating color elements. Each printing process also has quantity/quality/price formulas that you might not be familiar with. Why bother to go to the trouble of creating imageset pages if your budget and size of your print run only allows you to photocopy a master copy? In that case laser printing will do. Folding and binding imposes a page order called an *imposition* that few page layout programs currently address. A printer's master copy might position your pages together correctly as a *signature* for folding and binding after printing. Your printer can help you order your master pages into a set of signatures that will save you money and time.

Find a good printer who is familiar with the type of work you do and visit him or her early in your electronic production cycle. Bear in mind that each print shop varies in quality and cost. Send the job out for bids to several printers who do the kind of work you want. Give the job to the printer who bid somewhere in the middle, and whom you think you can work with. Don't select on price alone; if you do, chances are you won't see your job on time or that the printer will cut corners with quality.

A good printer normally recommends printing a page proof before the final job is run and will ask you to sign that proof to ensure that it has been reviewed. This is the time to review each page carefully for errors. Many experienced desktop publishers create page proofs themselves. For quick printing, photocopies are often used as prepress proofs. Photostats (or stats, for short) are camera-generated prints used for black-and-white work. Color printers and color imagesetters print output; Chromalin, Matchprint, Gevaproof, or Transfer Key print proofs are used for four-color processes. Color overlays (called Color Keys for the 3M brand name) are used for color proofs of spot color work.

Although exact color matching isn't provided at the proof stage, many problems, such as registration or moiré patterns (misregistration of halftone dots), will show up. New-generation color printers such as DuPont's dye sublimation 4CAST printer are ideal for this purpose. Chapter 7 includes a discussion of new proofing technologies. The ideal proof is a *press proof* (or press sheet), one of the first setup pages that comes out of a press run, but it is very expensive to catch errors at that late stage. For expensive, long-run print jobs you should be at your printer's when the print job is on-press to check a press proof.

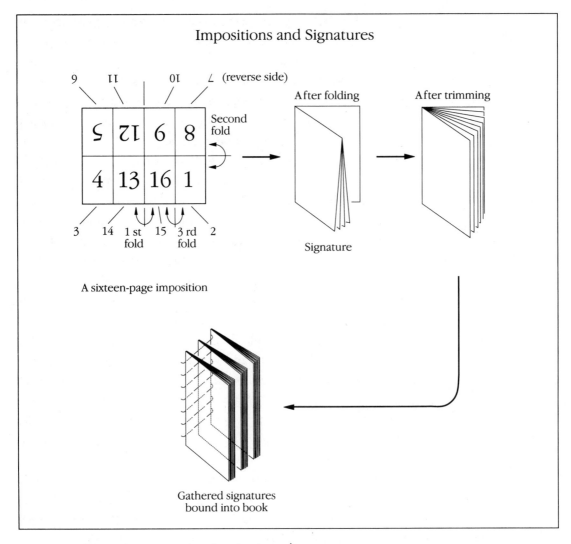

Figure 3-3 The imposition process and a related signature.

Always allow extra time for printing, as there are often unforeseen delays. It may be expensive to make changes when the job is being run, but doing so will prevent you from being stuck with a ruined job. Chapter 15 has a section entitled "Working with Your Printer." For more discussion of printing etiquette, picking a printer, and getting the print quality you require, see *Getting It Printed* by Beach, Shapiro, and Russon.

If you need under 500 pieces, then printing is not particularly cost effective, and you should consider photocopying, or using a laser printer or other short-run device. Printing becomes cost effective at quantities of 1,000. Generally, runs of 5,000 and more amortize the setup cost and result in no further quantity discounts. While costs of two-color printing are significantly higher, they are not twice as high as a single print color. Three-color printing is usually not cost effective, and you might as well consider a full four-color print job; it's normally no more expensive and allows color photography to be used. Five- and six-color print jobs also exist and are supported by printing presses that allow that many process colors. When using five and six process colors, obviously some, if not all, of the ink colors are not the primary CYMK inks, those extra inks can be used to match a particular color.

PART II

The Tools

Publishing Hardware

One user, one CPU.
Silicon is cheaper than iron.
Two of Jerry Pounelle's laws,
BYTE MAGAZINE

Because you interact with both hardware and system software as a unit, any evaluation of a particular computer system requires that you consider both. This is often hard to do. If you are a novice, you don't normally have the experience to weigh one choice against another; and if you are an experienced user, you probably have some strong built-in biases toward the computer and operating system you are using at the moment. Using a particular computer system has almost religious overtones for some users, so remember that advice is likely to be biased.

Few people want to bother learning to work on more than one computer. Using any of the computer systems described in this chapter it should be possible to do an acceptable level of desktop publishing, drawing, painting, CAD, and other graphics tasks. When I say a computer is more advanced than another computer in a particular area, I mean that it offers a better set of additional tools. Advanced should also mean that it's easier to perform a certain task. In this chapter we explore the advantages of one computer over another.

71

Graphic User Interfaces (GUIs)

Nearly all of the programs discussed in this book are based on a *graphical user interface*, or GUI, as we described in Chapter 2. GUIs use menus, dialog boxes, icons, and other elements that allow a user to work with a program in a standardized manner. GUIs either can be built into the system software at the operating system level or can be programmed to run on top of the operating system. GUIs are *event-driven* environments where the computer reacts to user-generated actions. A program written to run on a GUI is structured to cycle through an event loop reacting only to user-generated or system events.

GUIs put all of the commands and operations on the screen so that they don't have to be remembered. They have the advantage of being highly visual, action oriented, and intuitive. GUI users tend to learn their systems and software faster, require less training, and use more software packages in their work than those who use command-line (also called command prompt) interfaces.

A GUI may be contrasted to MS-DOS, which is a procedural operating system. In DOS the user issues commands at a command prompt. For example:

```
C:\> COPY A:\*.* C:\LETTERS
```

This command copies all of the files (*.*) from drive A (normally the first floppy disk drive) to a subdirectory (the equivalent of a folder on the Macintosh) called LETTERS or drive C (normally your hard drive). To complete this process on a Macintosh, you would double click on the A disk icon, select all of the file icons, and then drag them into the folder called LETTERS on your hard disk. The result is the same, but the process is very different.

Other interfaces offer a menu system with a set of choices activated by different keystrokes. For example, you might see the following hypothetical screen:

Press a key to initiate these actions:

Open another file.

Copy file(s) to another destination.

Save current file's contents.

Print current file.

Help.

Quit the Program.

A menu system is more flexible because more choices are shown, but there is no real uniformity between menus. Each one is different, and what you learn by using one menu doesn't carry over to any other menu.

Longtime DOS users prefer the control that their operating system gives them from the command prompt. The MS-DOS command-line interface is hard to learn, and often confusing to use. If you could collect a dollar for every DOS shell (GUI or menuing system running on top of DOS) ever written, you could retire comfortably to a nice tropical island.

Not one major graphics-oriented program runs strictly on DOS. The reason is simple; DTP packages, graphics programs, and other sophisticated applications require the use of many more commands and settings than DOS offers. In DOS you can include options with the twenty or so commands. For example, the command **DIR/W** will list your current directory in the wide format. However, any action that requires more than, say, two or three different settings necessitates a different approach; GUIs use special options selection screens, called dialog boxes, in those instances.

WordPerfect (DOS) is the leading word processor for the PC, with about 60 percent of the market, and it's a good example of an application with a nongraphical user interface. The WordPerfect opening screen displays only an insertion prompt and a position indicator. A very complete writing environment underlies this apparent simplicity, however. Conceptually, WordPerfect looks like a typewriter, clean and highly functional. Simple command keys bring up a full range of word processor utilities.

Figure 4-1
(A) WordPerfect
opening screen.
(B) WordPerfect
command template
or help screen.

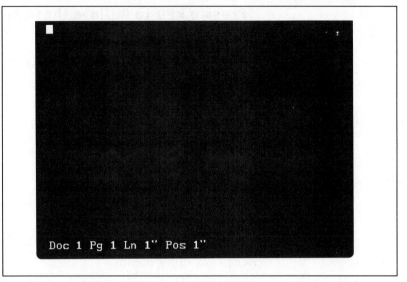

A.

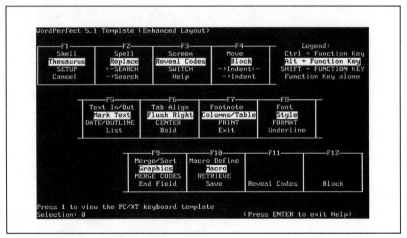

B.

W. E. "Pete" Peterson, executive vice president of WordPerfect, has described WordPerfect (DOS) this way: "What makes WordPerfect attractive is that it gets out of your way. It's like a well-mannered house guest who is kind enough not to disrupt your life or the way you do things."

However, most new users require a keyboard template to help them remember WordPerfect's many, many commands. Now, there's nothing wrong with this approach; you can learn any program well if you're willing to spend the time. The problem is that the knowledge of WordPerfect is isolated in its utility—it doesn't carry over to other programs. Fortunately, other versions of Word-Perfect for Windows and the Macintosh take the GUI approach. WordPerfect seems to run on every platform; I expect to see a toaster version one day.

Looking for Integration

Bill Joy (a founder of Sun Microsystems) has said that a standard GUI doesn't offer the best interface for every type of application; that DTP might benefit from a stand-alone environment, different from, say, a CAD application. But that's a contrarian viewpoint at the moment.

GUIs are generally your best bet when melding several disparate applications into a working environment. They allow you to accomplish complex tasks using different applications without having to remember more unique commands than necessary. Anyone who has ever tried to use a word processor's formatting features (such as WordPerfect's) structure recognizes how much easier it is to lay out a book in Ventura Publisher or in Aldus Page-Maker. It may well be that the future will offer newer and better computer interfaces with much more sophisticated use of sound, such as voice input and speech recognition, or maybe even direct brain input. But for now, a GUI is the current state of the art.

▼ *Tip: If this book has one strong prejudice, it is this one: Adopt a GUI, learn it well, and use applications that exploit it as much as you possibly can.*

This will enable you to be much farther along the road to power user status. You'll spend less time learning and more time producing.

The best advice concerning equipment selection has always been to let the choice of software guide your equipment purchase. If there isn't a compelling reason for choosing one operating system over another, or one particular application over another, then you should attempt to focus on the computer system that offers the best integration. Unfortunately, most people buy for price first and ultimately end up spending more than if they had bought their computer for functionality. And actually, when you sit down and price a particular computer function, you'll find that most computers are similarly priced.

Macintosh

In the mid-1970s Steve Jobs visited Xerox's Palo Alto Research Center (PARC) as part of the payoff for a million-dollar Xerox purchase of Apple stock. There he saw Xerox's highly graphic Alto computer, which featured a GUI. It served as a model for many of the features of the Apple Lisa released in 1983. (See Figure 4.2) The Lisa wowed the critics, but its nearly $10,000 price tag kept it from becoming a commercial success or attaining small-office penetration. Originally scheduled for release at the same time as the Lisa, the Apple Macintosh borrowed heavily from the Lisa development project, but it ran twice as fast and cost a quarter of the price.

Figure 4-2
The Apple Lisa was the predecessor of the Macintosh and was used in developing the Mac. It was Apple's first graphically oriented computer.

The Apple Macintosh was introduced in January 1984. Conceived as an "appliance computer," simple to use, with a plug-and-play design, this was a computer for computer phobics. The original Macintosh used a Motorola 68000 cpu, ran at 8 MHz clock speed, had 128 KBytes of memory, a floppy disk drive, and shipped bundled with three applications: MacWrite, MacDraw, and MacPaint. It was meant to be used "as is," and had no expansion slots or capabilities. Even opening the case, which required a special hex wrench, could void the warranty.

Figure 4-3
The introductory ad for the Macintosh appeared during the 1984 Superbowl and featured an athletic young woman with a sledgehammer breaking down the walls of conformity represented by the IBM PC. *Courtesy of Apple Computer, Inc.*

This kind of closed architecture made it less versatile, and that, along with very limited memory space, drove the Macintosh through several product upgrades very quickly. The 512 (512 Kbytes of RAM) was introduced in 1985, the 512KE in 1986, and the Mac Plus (1 Mbyte RAM, expandable to 4 MBytes) in 1986. The Mac SE (for system enhancement), introduced in 1987, added the Apple Desktop Bus (ADB), a small network for daisy-chaining input devices, and the SCSI (small computer standard interface) bus for I/O ports for connecting disk drives and other peripheral devices, such as scanners. The Macintosh II series shipped in 1987, with a 68020 cpu and six expansion NuBus slots. Later Mac

Figure 4-4 Steve Jobs with three original Macintoshes (from r to l): Apple's MacWrite word processor, MacPaint paint program, and Microsoft's Multiplan spreadsheet. *Courtesy of* MacWorld Magazine.

II's shipped with 68030 cpus and either three (IIcx and IIci: the c or compact series) or six (IIx, IIfx: the x or expansion series) NuBus expansion slots. Now Apple has released a 68000-based classic model, a 68020-based LC, and a 68030-based IIsi. All Macintosh models come "network ready," with Apple's network communication protocol, AppleTalk, built in. The Macintosh models are described in more detail in the section "Models—Descriptions, Pros and Cons" later in this chapter.

The Macintosh was conceived with graphics at its core, the first commercially successful personal microcomputer with a graphical user interface. Its operating system includes a complete set of graphical routines for screen display and printing called Quick-Draw that makes Macintosh significantly different from the IBM PC computer where all screen display in DOS is character based. The advantage of building graphics routines into system software is that fewer machine processing steps or interpretations are required. It's possible to build a graphics platform as a shell to a character-based computer (Windows running on DOS, described subsequently, is an example), but graphics shells require extra command interpretation that exacts a performance penalty.

On average, a 68000-based Macintosh performs like an 80286 PC. Put in terms of clock speed, a 68030 Macintosh IIcx running at about 16 MHz runs Microsoft Excel (a GUI spreadsheet) at roughly the same speed as a Compaq 38633 MHz SystemPro. These two machines are similar in price/performance ratio, thus adhering to the axiom that you get what you pay for. Nowhere is that more true than in personal computers. The industry has made the personal computer a viable commodity product, feature for feature, dollar for dollar.

The operating system of a Macintosh is updated in software and uses the instruction set encoded in ROM. Thus, when you *boot up*, or start a Macintosh, you load a file called the System from either a floppy disk or your hard drive that makes the appropriate calls to ROM to create your operating system.

The Finder is the part of the Macintosh operating system that functions as a desktop metaphor for the file structure. It is a shell in the classic definition, since it shields the user from operating system commands, such as those required for disk input and output. Unlike most classic shells, the Finder makes direct operating system calls and is integrated into the operating system. The Finder is an application program/shell hybrid. The current version of the Finder provides for limited multitasking and context switching in MultiFinder, where each application runs in a layer or partition of memory. Finder runs in its layer, as does each application, along with a set of small programs called desk accessories, which are available within any application.

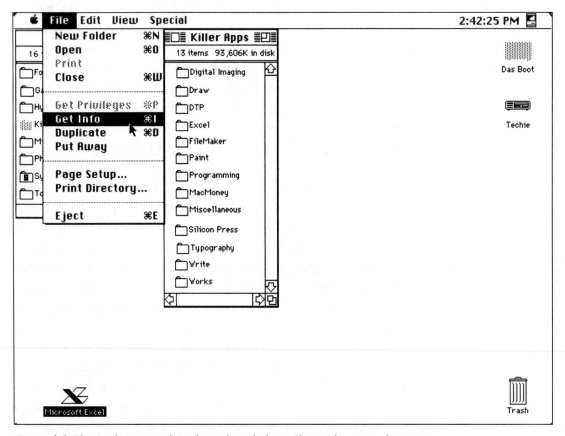

Figure 4-5 The Apple Macintosh Finder with its desktop. Shown also are its distinctive pop-down menus designed by MacPaint author Bill Atkinson. Files have associated icons; directories are represented by file folders.

As in any computer operating system, Macintosh programs and data documents are saved as files. Macintosh files have a binary structure to them and are separated into *forks*, a data fork and a resource fork. Characters saved as Text can be opened and read with any word processor or Text editor; programs saved as code appear as ASCII characters and control codes (those other odd symbols in the ASCII code). Macintosh uses the resource fork to store letterforms (fonts), sounds, pictures, and other objects that might be used by a program for manipulation. If the System file is opened using a resource editor (Apple Computer supplies one called ResEdit, but there are others), the System file is seen to be largely composed of resources. Applications can have attached resources also.

Macintosh volumes (any storage device, such as a hard drive or floppy disk) each have a hidden Desktop file in the top folder that serves as a table of contents for all files stored on that volume. Information saved includes the physical location of each file (which sector), which icon to display on the desktop, the size and format of each window, and creator or file types. Other file attributes stored include creation date, last modification date, whether the file is locked and can't be modified, if the file should be run (initiated) at startup, if it's an application or document, which application to use to open a document, and several other file attributes. All this information facilitates many of the niceties of the Macintosh operating system, such as opening the creator application by double clicking on a document's icon, arranging files by various views, or doing incremental backups.

We discussed Macintosh memory access in Chapter 2. RAM can be used for video memory, parts of the operating system, utility programs, desk accessories, current font data, icon images, the Finder, disk directories, and application programs. RAM also contains data you create or use in an application or data held in the Clipboard, which is a portion of RAM used for cutting and pasting data between or within documents and applications.

The Clipboard offers "cut and paste," a very powerful means for data transfer that is proprietary to the Macintosh system and all of

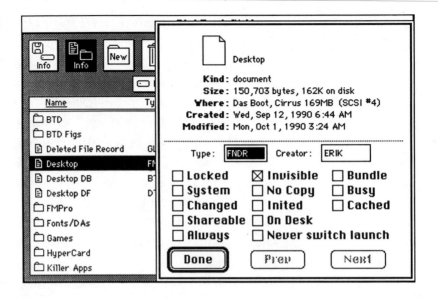

its applications. It is a noteworthy data storage device, and it is a memory buffer that can be used to hold temporary data. Apple specifies the file formats that can be transferred in and out of the Clipboard; these include: Text; pictures in the file formats of PICT, PICT2, or TIFF; sound; and anything that can be stored as a resource in a file. Full 32-bit color images are supported. The Clipboard can even support special proprietary program file formats for internal application use. We discuss file formats more fully in Chapter 13.

The commands on Macintosh's Edit menu are used for Clipboard manipulation. They are:

- Cut command: removes a selection and places a copy on the Clipboard.

- Copy command: leaves the selection intact and places a copy on the Clipboard.

- Paste command: copies the contents of the Clipboard to your current location.

- Clear command: flushes the Clipboard, removing all data.

- Undo command: not specifically part of the Clipboard, the Macintosh stores the last action in buffered memory. This command restores your previous state.

▼ *Tip: To measure how well a Macintosh program is constructed, see if all the actions you try can be reversed with the Undo command.*

Different programs implement undo actions at different levels. The word processor Nisus, for example, allows user access to virtually unlimited numbers of undos; in it you can backward reconstruct an entire document's evolution, if you wish.

These commands are found in every Macintosh application running under the Finder, as are some of the commands in the File menu. The main benefit of this consistency is the resultant superior data handling compared to other operating systems. Microsoft Windows Version 3.0 on the PC has a Clipboard, but the range of data that may be transferred is not as wide as in the current version of Macintosh System 6. In desktop publishing, where data transfer is critical, a Macintosh's well-implemented Clipboard offers a major advantage.

Today the Macintosh is the premier microcomputer for desktop publishing. Its advantages include good system integration, excellent data handling, full color support, and an excellent portfolio of application software. In the last two years more innovative software has been written for the Macintosh than for any other personal computer, especially in graphics and media applications.

System 6

Introduced in 1988, System 6 has been the recommended version for all production Macintoshes from the Plus on up. Its most recent release at press time is Finder version 6.1.7 and System version 6.0.7. Most of the System 6 enhancements were minor improvements to the Finder, memory handling, control panel devices, printing, and color.

System 6 furthers the development of MultiFinder, which was included first in System 5. MultiFinder is a system for partitioning available RAM between several applications, and is capable of some limited multitasking, where two or more applications run concurrently, but its greatest use is in background processing, (such as printing or telecommunicating) while a second applica-

Figure 4-7
The Macintosh Control Panel allows configuration of many system variables through the use of control panel devices.

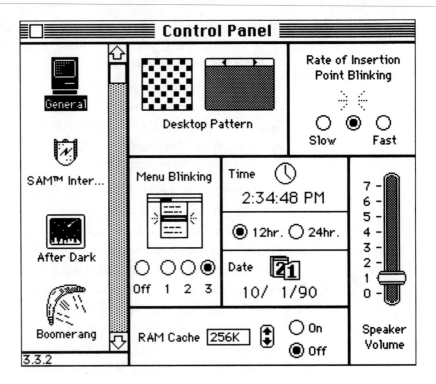

tion operates in the foreground. You can switch between Multi-Finder, or the Finder, which runs one application at a time. The current minimum requirement for RAM is 1 megabyte.

Also new in System 6 is the Apple File Exchange utility, a software package that lends support to Apple's 1.44 Mbyte, high-density floppy disk drive called SuperDrive. Using Apple File Exchange, a utility that comes with each Mac system, you can translate a file created on MS-DOS or on Apple's ProDOS (used in the Apple II series) to Macintosh format. File conversion using Apple File Exchange is described more fully in Chapter 13.

System 7

Apple has introduced a major system software upgrade about every two years, and System 7 was released in May, 1991. System 7 requires 2 MBytes of RAM to run and runs on all Macintosh computers. Enhancements in System 7 include:

- Virtual Memory: expands RAM using a disk swapping technique (see Chapter 2). The full 32-bit memory space now addresses up to 1 *gigabyte* of virtual memory.

- Enhanced Finder: will run only as MultiFinder.

- Outline Fonts: technology called TrueType (see Chapter 11) allows scalable fonts on-screen. An imaging technology called TrueImage emulates PostScript, but will have other Mac and Windows-specific functions. TrueType and TrueImage are cross-licensed and scheduled to appear in Microsoft's Windows 3.1 and O/S 2 Presentation Manager.

- Interapplication Communications: a system of linking data created with one application to a document created by another application allows for instant update of data appearing in multiple locations (see Chapter 16).

- 32-Bit QuickDraw: already released, this technology allows for photographically realistic color and better grayscale.

Two delayed modules of System 7 of particular interest to publishers are:

- Layout Manager: allows fine typographical controls with new intelligence. Particularly useful for foreign letterforms and writing styles.

- Print Architecture: better background printing, mixed print jobs, and so on.

System 7 appears to be the most significant Macintosh system software upgrade in four years, as much of an advance as System 5 was. Just how significant for desktop publishers System 7 is remains to be seen. Full color support, already introduced, has opened up the Macintosh to high-end prepress systems. File and program sizes previously limited by available RAM finally will become less of an obstacle for publishers as virtual memory allows users to set memory requirements by their available storage. Adobe's PostScript has established outline fonts, and it is not yet known whether System 7's TrueType and TrueImage can compete with an already fine and steadily advancing Adobe technology. A probable effect of this emerging standard is an increase in competitiveness, and lower font and printer prices.

The results of many of the improvements System 7 offers are difficult to gauge. Interface niceties and enhancements undoubtedly will be welcome—they've been on user wish lists for quite some time—but features such as aliasing, which allows for multiple icons for the same file, while useful for the advanced user, are confusing for novices. Clearly, there need to be new means for controlling documents that pass through several versions and contributors. Will interapplications communications provide the right set of tools? It's hard to tell. Overall it appears that System 7 will please longtime users and make Macintosh MIS managers' jobs more difficult as they attempt to support less experienced users.

Models— Descriptions, Pros and Cons

In summary, the current Macintosh product line consists of three machine types: the "classic" Macintosh, the Macintosh Portable, and the modular Macintosh II series. Table 4.1 summarizes the current models. With the release of System 7, it is recommended that you purchase a Macintosh with 2 MBytes RAM minimum and a 68030 cpu or 68020 with a Paged Memory Management Unit (PMMU) chip if you want to have virtual memory available.

Table 4.1 Macintosh Computer Models

Model	CPU	Speed (MHz)	RAM (MBytes)	Screen (pixels inches)	Storage (floppy hard drive)	Ports
Plus (N/A)	68000	8	1, up to 4	512 by 342 9"	800 K	EDD, SCSI, Snd, SP(2)
SE (N/A)	68000	8	1, up to 4	512 by 342 9"	1.44 M	Exp, EDD, SCSI, ADB(2), SP(2)
Classic	68000	8	1 or 2, up to 4	512 by 342 9"	1.44 M	Exp, MP, ADB(2), SCSI SP(2), SSD
SE/30	68030	16	1, up to 8	512 by 342 9"	1.44 M	Exp, EDD, SCSI, SSnd, ADB(2), SP(2)
Portable	68000	16	1 or 4	640 by 480 AM display	1.44 M	Exp, VP, EDD, SCSI, SSnd, ADB, SP(2)
LC	68020	16	2, up to 8	12" or 13" color RGB	1.44 M	Exp, MP, OBV, PDS, ADB, SP(2), SCSI, EDD, VP, SSnd

Table 4.1 (*continued*)

Model	CPU	Speed (MHz)	RAM (MBytes)	Screen (pixels inches)	Storage (floppy hard drive)	Ports
II (N/A)	68020 68882 cp	16	1, up to 8	640 by 580 13": MOD,	800 K 1.4 M (option)	NB(6), EDD, SCSO, SSnd ADB(2), SP(2)
IIsi	68030	20	2 or 5, up to 17	12" or 13" color RGB	1.44 M	SCSI, MP, OBV, ADB, SP(2) VP, Exp
IIx	68030	16	1, up to 8	MOD	1.44 M	NB(6), SCSI, SSnd, ADB(2) SP(2)
IIcx (N/A)	68030	16	1, up to 8	MOD	1.44 M	NB(6), EDD, SCSI, SSnd, ADB(2), SP(2)
IIci	68030	25	1, up to 8	MOD	1.44 M	NB(3), SCSI, SSnd, ADB(2), SP(2), VP, CC
IIfx	68030	40	4, up to 8	MOD	1.44 M	NB(6), SCSI, SSnd, ADB(2), SP(2), PDS, OBV

Key: ADB=Apple Desktop Bus; SP=Serial port; AM display= Transistor active matrix display; CC=Cache connector for memory cache; EDD=External floppy disk drive port; Exp=Expansion slot (unique ones for SE, SE/30, and Portable each); MOD=Modular, you can select any external monitor; MP=Microphone input; N/A=Not available; NB=NuBus slot; OBV=On-board video; PDS=Processor direct slot; Snd=Sound port; SSnd=Stereo sound; VP=Video port; 68882cp=Paged memory management chip can be added (all 68030 chips include this feature); 800 K=800 KByte floppy disk drive; 1.44 M=SuperDrive 1.44 Mbyte floppy disk drive; (2)=Number of ports, here 2.

Source: Macintosh Products Brochure, Spring 1990, Apple Computer.*

The "classic" Macintosh series includes the Mac Classic, Mac Plus, Mac SE, and Mac SE/30. These models are characterized by 9-inch diameter screens and roughly 9-inch square footprints. Their usefulness for publishing is severely limited, however, because they don't offer color and because of the small screen sizes. The Mac Plus and Mac SE can be upgraded to a 68030 machine through add-on boards, and all of the classic Macs can have large screens attached as add-ons, but it's more cost efficient to buy a Mac II series machine. In late 1990 Apple replaced the Plus and SE

*See also: *MacUser Magazine*, December, 1990. 110–11, for a more recent listing.

Figure 4-8
The classic Macs
were exemplified by
(A) the Mac Plus and
(B) the Mac SE/30. The
Mac Classic is now the
only "traditional" Macin-
tosh manufactured by
Apple. *Courtesy of Apple
Computer, Inc.*

A.

B.

with the Mac Classic, an entry-level machine that is similar to the SE and shares the same limitations. A more interesting machine is the Mac LC (for low-cost color), which serves the need for a lower-cost work and design terminal. The LC has a pizza box configuration, it lacks NuBus slots, and has only one direct processor slot. The LC would be a good choice for text and low-end design work.

Radio ads say that a Mac Classic will get you get started in DTP, but because of its slower speed and small black-and-white screen, you wouldn't want to do graphics and layout work on it for long. It is primarily useful for word processing, data handling, and telecommunications because it runs all Macintosh applications. You can try to work around the small screen size, but when you go to print your file you will find that there's almost always some small detail wrong. It's impossible to get a sense of the overall scale of things. We talk more in Chapter 5 about how important screen size is for graphics both in terms of getting an overall view of a layout and making sure that fine details are correct, but suffice it to say that a small screen exacts a severe penalty when doing DTP.

The Macintosh II series offers good computers for graphics or DTP. The Macintosh II, now discontinued, was a 68020 machine with six NuBus slots. This series of computers has separated into a compact series with three NuBus slots, the Mac IIcx and the IIci, and the full-size models with six expansion slots, the Mac IIx and the new IIfx. Within each type the models are differentiated largely by cpu clock speed. Most users can get by just fine with three expansion slots; in fact, the vast majority of people use only one slot for their video cards. A compact model is often the best choice. The people who require six NuBus slots are those with special needs for data acquisition or analysis, such as laboratory workers, for example; multimedia applications also often require several NuBus boards. Apple introduced the Mac IIsi compact 68020 computer as a lower-cost solution for design work. It features a 68030 processor and a single direct (non-NuBus) slot.

The current top of the line is the IIfx, which uses a fast, 40 MHz-68030 cpu. (Apple will release a 68040-based model in the fall of 1991.) It runs roughly four times faster than the original Mac II, seven times faster than a Mac Plus. It would be a good choice as a

Figure 4-9
The Mac II line is exemplified by **(A)** a three-slot compact or c-series and **(B)** a six-slot or x-series. Shown here are the Mac IIci and the Mac IIfx (with PixelPaint and PageMaker on the screen). *Courtesy of Apple Computer, Inc.*

A.

B.

CAD station, or for desktop publishing when full-color processing work is required. The IIfx has video built into the motherboard and a separate I/O bus and coprocessor, which eliminates a Mac input/output bottleneck. To make good use of an fx, you should purchase a graphics accelerator board or even a separate video adapter. An fx is overkill for most DTP applications, as that kind of speed has very limited critical application.

The SCSI port on the Macintosh allows for the connection of up to seven daisy-chained devices: hard disk drives, scanners, and so on. The ADB ports are for daisy-chaining input devices: mice, keyboards, graphics tablets, and the like. All Macintosh computers include AppleTalk wiring, a proprietary networking system. AppleTalk allows for printers (such as a LaserWriter) to be connected in a local area network (LAN). Even just one Macintosh connected to a single laser printer is by definition an LAN.

The new Mac LC (for lowest cost, color capable) has some DTP applications. It can be configured with up to three monitors directly without an additional video card. Up to 16 colors can be displayed on the AppleColor High Resolution RGB monitor ($1,000), or 16 grays appear on the 12-inch Monochrome Display ($300). Although these screens are large, they have poor color and resolution and are not suitable for quality DTP work. The standard 12-inch Apple RGB Display ($600) can display up to 256 colors on screen. An additional SIMM module can be added that brings the high-resolution and monochrome monitors up to 256 colors or greys, and allows 32,000 colors for the RGB display.

The most important feature of the Mac LC is the optional card that allows it to run all of the Apple II software. If you add SoftPC, then the Mac LC can probably run more software than any other personal computer. Another great feature of the LC is that if you add a flat panel LCD projection display, its low weight and flat profile makes it a nearly ideal machine for a presentation or road show. Apple has positioned the LC as the entry level machine to the Macintosh line for Apple II owners, and is expected to promote the machine heavily in the education market.

The Mac IIsi uses a 68030 20 MHz cpu, and is meant to be a low-cost alternative to the Mac II line; it is positioned to replace the Mac II. The IIsi has only one expansion slot, a direct slot. Apple sells an adapter card ($250) that fits in the slot and allows it to take either a NuBus card or one of the Direct Slot cards used in the SE/30. The adapter card comes with a 68882 floating point coprocessor chip useful for spreadsheet, CAD, and graphics programs. The IIsi should not be purchased without the adapter card. The Mac IIsi should appeal to many users as a good machine for design work, and it is priced at a very attractive level.

The Mac IILC and IIsi are in what commonly is referred to as a pizza box configuration. The Sun SPARCStations were the first PCs to come in this configuration: the compact design is achieved by eliminating NuBus slots, the rationale being that most users only include a video board in their computers and don't require the expendability. Once the video board is integrated into a motherboard, most uses don't require that one additional slot. Your ultimate needs should determine whether this configuration is suitable for your work; it's fine for word processing or page layout, but it wouldn't be suitable for multimedia applications.

IBM and Compatibles

The mid-1970s saw one large company after another flounder in the attempt to create successful personal computers. Then, in 1979, IBM gave twelve engineers in the Entry Level Systems Unit at the Boca Raton Lab in Florida the mandate to produce a small computer within a year. Project Chess yielded the IBM PC (code-named the Acorn) on August 12, 1981. Based on the Intel 8086 chip, the PC was an open architecture machine that set a new standard for its time. It was expandable, with 48 KByte RAM, two floppy disk drives and a monochrome monitor. An additional 256 KByte RAM cost $2,000. The system was greeted with enthusiasm: with a predicted 250,000-unit lifetime product run, it shipped 500,000 in 1983 alone.

So great was the demand that IBM couldn't keep up, and other manufacturers rushed in with less expensive IBM-compatible computers called *clones*. By the end of 1983 there were over 150 manufacturers all claiming compatibility, but the first to truly achieve it was Compaq Computers. Many others followed, and today there are scores of "IBM-compatible" computer models from which to choose. Many "clones," such as those produced by Leading Edge or Dell, are very reliable and can be purchased for a fraction of what you'd pay for a "true blue" IBM machine.

DOS and DOS Shells

Of course, a computer needs operating system software in order to function, and the new IBM PC was no exception. IBM first approached Digital Research's Gary Kildall, the author of an older operating system called CP/M to have his company write the operating system. Kildall declined, but his company went on to develop several successful products for the IBM PC, including the GEM graphics environment (described subsequently).

IBM eventually signed an agreement with Microsoft, and MS-DOS was born. Version 1.0 of MS-DOS, called PC DOS, shipped with the original IBM PC1 in 1981. Version 2.0 offered three times the commands of version 1.0 and shipped with the IBM PC2 and XT, the 8088 sequels to the original PC. Version 2 accommodated the introduction of the hard drive with a hierarchical file system (treelike structure) borrowed from the UNIX world, with a directory structure and a file allocation table (FAT) for tracking the use of disk space.

Versions 3.0 and 4.0 of MS-DOS are those currently in use; 4.01 is the latest version, with version 5 slated for a June 1991 introduction. MS-DOS 4.0 introduced the DOSShell, a menu interface allowing mouse support, which longtime DOS users seem to hate. Many PC power users believe that DOS has reached the end of its useful life, and the cognoscenti at *PC Magazine* are pushing their readership to upgrade to PCs capable of running GUIs, such as Windows or the OS/2 operating system.

Literally hundreds of DOS shells have been written to shield PC users from DOS procedural commands. Some, such as Tandy's DeskMate, come bundled with their computers. The new IBM

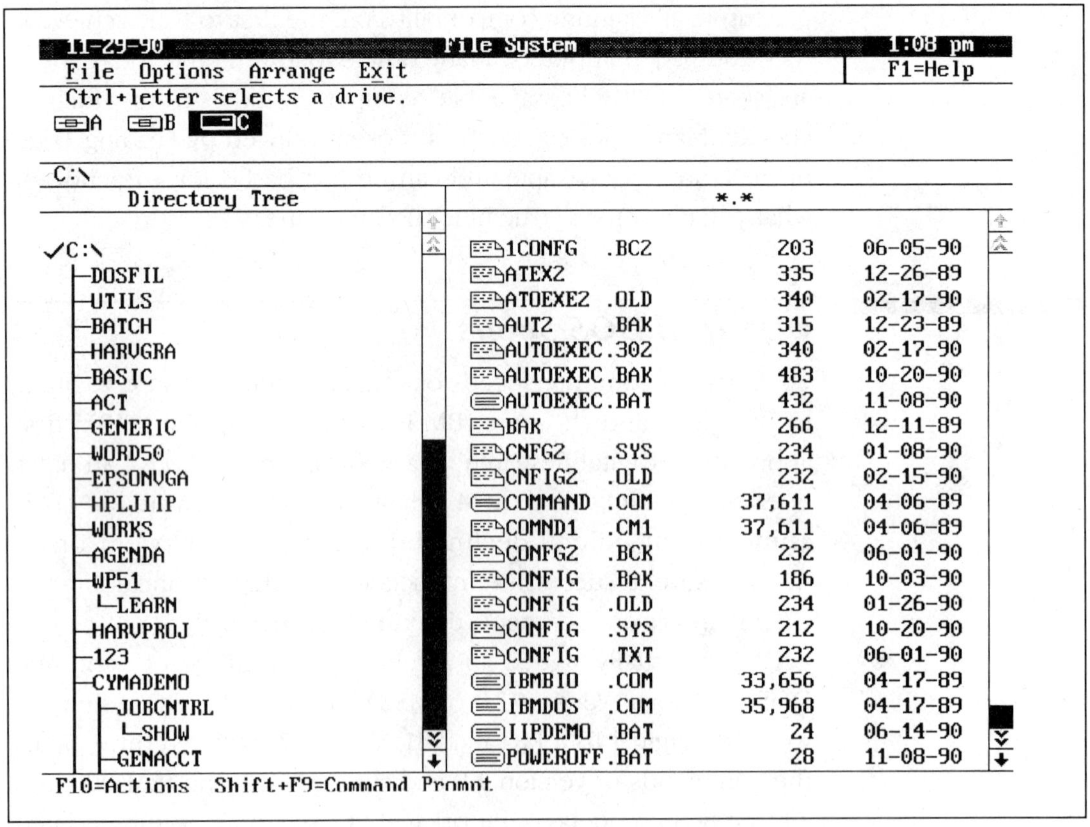

```
11-29-90                      File System                    1:08 pm
 File   Options   Arrange   Exit                          F1=Help
Ctrl+letter selects a drive.
  ▭A    ▭B   ▭C


C:\
        Directory Tree                              *.*

 ✓C:\                            ▤1CONFG   .BC2         203      06-05-90
    ├─DOSFIL                     ▤ATEX2                 335      12-26-89
    ├─UTILS                      ▤ATOEXE2  .OLD         340      02-17-90
    ├─BATCH                      ▤AUT2     .BAK         315      12-23-89
    ├─HARVGRA                    ▤AUTOEXEC .302         340      02-17-90
    ├─BASIC                      ▤AUTOEXEC .BAK         483      10-20-90
    ├─ACT                        ▤AUTOEXEC .BAT         432      11-08-90
    ├─GENERIC                    ▤BAK                   266      12-11-89
    ├─WORD50                     ▤CNFG2    .SYS         234      01-08-90
    ├─EPSONVGA                   ▤CNFIG2   .OLD         232      02-15-90
    ├─HPLJIIP                    ▤COMMAND  .COM      37,611      04-06-89
    ├─WORKS                      ▤COMND1   .CM1      37,611      04-06-89
    ├─AGENDA                     ▤CONFG2   .BCK         232      06-01-90
    ├─WP51                       ▤CONFIG   .BAK         186      10-03-90
    │  └─LEARN                   ▤CONFIG   .OLD         234      01-26-90
    ├─HARVPROJ                   ▤CONFIG   .SYS         212      10-20-90
    ├─123                        ▤CONFIG   .TXT         232      06-01-90
    ├─CYMADEMO                   ▤IBMBIO   .COM      33,656      04-17-89
    │  ├─JOBCNTRL                ▤IBMDOS   .COM      35,968      04-17-89
    │  │  └─SHOW                 ▤IIPDEMO  .BAT          24      06-14-90
    │  └─GENACCT                 ▤POWEROFF .BAT          28      11-08-90
 F10=Actions  Shift+F9=Command Prompt
```

Figure 4-10 The DOS shell was introduced in version 4.0 of MS-DOS.

PS/1 computer has DOS on a chip and boots up with a DOS shell. Nearly all PC users end up working with shells to aid in their file management, but most of those shells offer a menuing system and not a full graphical user interface. The best of these packages is PC Tools Deluxe version 6.0; other highly rated ones are XTree Gold 4.1, the Norton Commander 3.0, and Magellen 2.0. DESQView from QuarterDeck Systems is a shell that offers extended memory management (access to additional memory through four 16-KByte page swaps in a narrow DOS partition) and a windowing system (discussed in Chapter 2). None of these programs is used as a working environment for graphics programs because their screens are character based rather than bit mapped, but all can be useful for managing a portfolio of programs—particularly on slower PCs.

Figure 4-11
PC Tools Deluxe
offers a sophisticated
menu-driven/interface
shell for DOS that allows
for many functions
necessary to file
management and main-
tenance. It is a favored
MS-DOS shell. *Courtesy
of Central Point Soft-
ware, Inc.*

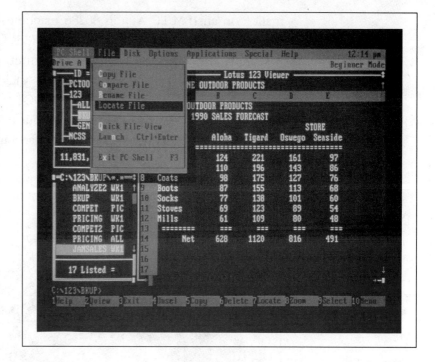

The two major GUIs for DOS, Digital Research's GEM environment and Microsoft Windows, are described below. A third one,
GEOS (Graphical Environmental Operating System), from
GeoWorks is also covered. It runs well on 8088 and 80286 PCs, but
it doesn't have many applications yet, in spite of its favorable
advance press. Many graphics programs that run on these GUIs
use *run time versions* of the interface: When you startup Page-
Maker from its executable file in DOS, you see the Windows interface. You can open and close files from within PageMaker, but
when you quit the program you are back at the DOS prompt. Similarly, Ventura Publisher started out its life on the GEM environment as a run-time product.

GEM

GEM is Digital Research's Graphical Environment Manager, a bit-
mapped, windowed DOS-shell GUI. GEM's main advantage is
speed. It was written to execute quickly, much more so than
Microsoft Windows. For PC users looking for acceptable perfor-

mance on an IBM PC AT (an 80286 machine), the GEM environment offers a workable DTP solution. GEM is fast because it is limited in its functions, and provides no multitasking capabilities. One of its main disadvantages is that it's stuck with the 640 KByte application memory allocation of MS-DOS. Generally speaking, the GEM interface can be installed without the manual, and most of the applications that run on this interface are intuitive and easy to learn.

Figure 4-12
Artline is an excellent draw program from Digital Research that runs on the GEM interface. *Courtesy of Digital Research, Inc.*

A few miniapplications are built into GEM: a calculator, clock, and a print spooler. Some IBM PC XT and AT–class computers come bundled with the GEM environment and the GEM Collection; they're what you see when you go into a department store to buy a low-cost, no-name clone. The GEM Collection includes a word processor, paint, and draw package. Digital Research and third-party vendors sell a range of DTP and graphics programs; perhaps 500 commercial graphics products run on GEM. These include publishing software (GEM Desktop Publisher, Publish-IT, and Ventura Publisher), presentation software (Presentation Team), object-oriented drawing (Artline), and several other product categories.

▼ *Tip: GeoWorks and the GEM interface and all of its applications are the best choices for low-end systems, IBM PC AT or XT.*

If you are interested in doing DTP on an old PC or XT, then these are probably your only choices for a GUI. They're also particularly good choices for novices, as the products are simple and easy to learn.

The GEM interface is aging technology, as are the machines it's optimized to run on. It has a niche market, at this point most PCs, but that will change rapidly in the next year or two. Windows 3.0 appears to have generated enough customer and developer interest to suggest that few new significant applications will be written for the GEM environment in the future.

Windows

Windows is the DOS shell that provides MS-DOS-based computers with a GUI that looks and operates somewhat like the Macintosh interface. It runs on a minimum configuration of 2 MByte AT class 80286 machine or better (12 MHz), but it really requires a 2 MByte 16 MHz 80386 S/X machine for acceptable performance. On the PC, Windows seems to be the emerging standard for switching from DOS to a GUI.

The latest version, Windows 3.0, is most significant for a number of reasons. Although still a DOS shell, Windows 3.0 breaks the DOS 640 KByte application memory allocation, allowing memory-hungry applications, such as many graphics programs, access to 16 MBytes of RAM. If there's insufficient RAM installed, Windows can page swap RAM instructions out to disk (virtual memory). By having access to all installed RAM, Windows 3.0 runs significantly faster than version 2.0.

Windows can provide a fair amount of multitasking. Programs that run on Windows can run in protected memory on an 80286 or 80386—also calledprotected mode—thus making the system fairly stable. On 80286 machines (with 640K) Windows can operate in what's called real mode, where the environment goes back to single tasking, as if you started up the application from DOS. It can return to the DOS prompt, run a program, and when the program is quit, return to Windows. It also has good network support built in.

Version 3.0 of Windows is a handsomely designed product that contains many useful interface features. The Program Manager, the iconic interface is shown in Figure 4.13 (A) File Manager, shown in Figure 4.13 (B), replaces the awkward MS-DOS Executive file manager from version 2.0 for users who prefer a more traditional file menuing system. Fonts are installed with the interface (as they are on all GUIs), and Windows manages them for all installed applications as it does printer drivers and other system-wide utilities. Version 3.1 of Windows will include the TrueType outline font technology and TrueImage page description language. One notable feature of Windows is its ability to reduce applications to an icon (called minimizing) and reactivate them (maximize) by double clicking. There is also a Task Manager (the task list) for grouping applications so that you can switch quickly between them.

Windows ships with several applications already built in: Write, a text editor and basic word processor; Draw, an object-oriented drawing program; Paintbrush, a color paint program; and Terminal, a communications application. You'll find fuller discussion of each of these Windows applications later in the book. None of these is a power application, and alone each would not be sufficient for any but the most basic publishing tasks. Windows also includes several accessories: a Calculator, Calendar, Cardfile, Clock, Notepad, a macro Recorder, a Print Spooler, and PIF editor (program information file) used for storing information needed to run applications. One of the nicest features is good, context-sensitive help in a hypertextural, or nonsequential retrieval, application

Figure 4-13
(A) The Windows Program Manager presents an iconic graphical user interface for point and shoot computing. **(B)** Users who prefer a more menulike interface can switch from Windows into the File Manager program.

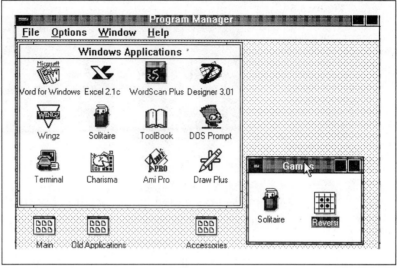

A.

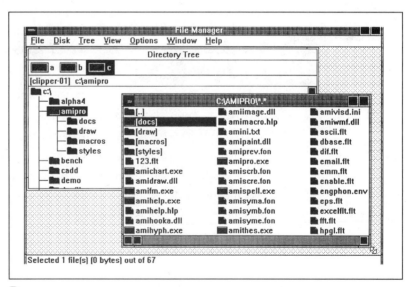

B.

setting. Just click on a key word to go to more information. Windows has a Clipboard and a Notepad, and many of the utilities are installed within a Control Panel.

Windows has lacked the Mac's color capability, but Windows 3.0 now has good color support. It can support 256 colors on screen (8-bit color) and offers choices from a full 24-bit palette of 16.8

Figure 4.14
The Windows
Control Panel allows
many system variables
to be changed.

million colors, which means it supports the emerging Super VGA standard. Windows may emerge as a very important multimedia platform in the years to come, as hypertext and animation tools continue to appear and as PC hardware continues to improve.

Windows Versus the Macintosh

How does Windows stack up against the Macintosh? It is about 75 percent as functional as a Macintosh, and has some features that have yet to be incorporated into a Mac. Overall, though, the Macintosh has better color support, much better sound, and smoother system functions that make it a better graphics platform. Apple's Macintosh *Human Interface Guidelines*, a set of specifications designed to promote common interfaces and functionality among Mac software programs, have resulted in applications that work better together, fewer file formats, and easier data transfer. Though surface differences seem subtle, they are numerous. A Macintosh is more expensive than a similar PC running Windows, but it does more things well. Windows 4, when it comes, may change all this.

Windows offers the most handsome collection of IBM PC applications of any environment—some 500 major applications by early 1990. It is the product of choice for PC graphics. Most of the important DTP programs already have versions running on Windows, and there is so much pent-up demand for PC graphics that development in the next two years will substantially narrow the gap between the Macintosh and Windows environments. This goes for software and hardware alike. We discuss Windows throughout this book.

GeoWorks

Unlike all of the promotional hoopla that surrounded Microsoft's $10 million PR campaign in 1990 for Windows, one of the most significant products introduced that year was from a small company. GeoWorks (Berkeley, CA), formally Berkeley Softworks, shipped a DOS shell (GUI) written in object assembly that is one of the handsomest, most functional GUIs yet seen. Based on the GEOS operating system (graphical environment operating system) that GeoWorks has previously worked on Apple IIs and Commodores. GeoWorks/PC is a fully multitasking, multithreaded GUI that runs well on a 640 KByte XT class machine. It contains a good file management system, virtual memory, scalable fonts (Nimbus Q engine), wide and capable peripheral device control, an excellent menuing system, and a user interface based on the OSF Motif standard developed by the Open Systems Foundation of Cambridge, Massachusetts.

▼ *Tip: If you own an IBM PC XT or AT computer, or an 8088 or 80286 laptop, consider adopting GeoWorks Ensemble as a work environment; it is an exceptional GUI.*

The product is sold as a $195 package of software applications called GeoWorks Ensemble. Included in the package are: GeoWrite (a medium-level word processor); GeoDraw (a vector draw package); GeoDEX (a card file and phone dialer); GeoPlanner (a diary); GeoComm (a simple communications program); the NotePad (an ASCII text processor); and a bundled version of America Online software. Vendors are aware that GeoWorks could run on 20 million PCs that will never run Windows, and the ultimate sucess of the product is dependent on the release of major independent software packages. The next version of GeoWorks is due out in fall 1991.

OS/2 and Presentation Manager

OS/2 is IBM's next operating system, and the Presentation Manager is Microsoft's graphical user interface that runs on OS/2. The Presentation Manager interface looks remarkably similar to that of Windows 3.0. OS/2 has many features to recommend it, most notably full multitasking, multithreading, and sophisticated memory management. Running OS/2 requires a 80386 machine with at least 4 MBytes of RAM, although 6 MBytes or more is better. Version 1.2 is current; 2.0 is slated for 1991 release and will include TrueType outline fonts and TrueImage PDL.

Programmers generally seem to like the power in OS/2 but have found it difficult for developing applications. Very few significant programs that desktop users want are currently offered on OS/2. This is a major obstacle for publishers or designers who like to work with a range of applications to accomplish complex tasks. Early adopters of OS/2 have discovered numerous problems, the most onerous of which are poor printing and unstable device drivers, and OS/2 development has been very slow.

The introduction of Windows 3.0 has probably set back the future of OS/2 by two or three years, perhaps permanently. The cognoscenti, of course, say that OS/2 is better, more solidly programmed, and that users will naturally migrate to it for all of its benefits. But the cognoscenti don't buy many computers. For the next couple of years most of the best software will be written for Windows. A fine version of Aldus PageMaker runs better on OS/2, but not significantly better than the version on Windows. Recently a highly praised version of Lotus 1-2-3 called 1-2-3/G (for graphics) has appeared on OS/2, as has a version of Ventura Publisher, and eventually buyers may shift into OS/2, but the incentives to do so are still too subtle to drive the conversion en masse anytime soon. Windows client workstations may end up communicating with servers running OS/2 as a standard in large installations, but for the average PC user wanting to do DTP or graphics, Windows is it for now.

Hardware

When purchasing a computer, one of your choices is whether to buy a signature PC from someone like IBM, Compaq, and the six or seven other major vendors, or to buy a clone mail order from someone like Dell, Zeus, Northgate, Gateway, or many others. Buying an IBM computer means that you will always have compatibility and that you can expect good service from a company that will be around for a while.

A signature brand will cost you anywhere from 35 to 100 percent more than a clone. Frankly, unless you are in a large organization that will foot the bill, I think it makes sense to look at the clones. As all of the pieces of a PC are standardized (IBM hasn't demonstrated that Microchannel Architecture is essential to efficient computing), you might find that Beacon Street Computers (my favorite brand), manufactured from a garage, produces every bit as good a machine as Big Blue. You certainly can't go wrong buying mail order from one of the more established clone vendors, because most offer on-site repair contracts and rapid turnaround. Then buy a laser printer and go on vacation with the money you save.

The current line of IBM Personal System 2 computers (PS/2) serves as the models for clone makers in terms of power, speed, accessories, ports, and features. Table 4.2 lists the specifications for the IBM PS/2 line. In 1990 IBM launched the PS/1 line of computers for the home market. Based on the 80286 cpu, and with limited expandability, this series was not the great leap forward and will probably suffer the same sad fate as previous "home computers," such as the PCjr. But the PS/2 line models remain reliable and expandable. Although it's been a while since IBM has led the PC marketplace, it's likely to do so again one day—not with the PS/2 line but with some future models.

Table 4.2 IBM PS/2 Computer Models

Model	CPU	Speed (MHz)	RAM (MBytes)	Screen (pixels inches)	Storage (floppy hard drive)	Ports
Model 25	8086 8-bit PCB	8	640 K	640 by 400 12" MCGA	720 K 3.5"	SP, PP, MP, KP, 2XS, (8-bit)
Model 30	8086 8-bit PCB	8	640 K to 2.6	640 by 400, 12" MCGA or VGA	720 K 3.5"	SP, PP, MP, KP, DP, 3XS (8-bit)
Model 30 286	80286 16-bit AT	10	1, up to 16	640 by 400, 12" VGA	1.44 M 3.5"	SP, PP, MP, KP, DP, 3XS (16-bit)
Model 50 Z	80286 16-bit MCA	10	1, up to 16	640 by 400 VGA	1.44 M 3.5"	SP, PP, MP, KP, DP, 3XS (16-bit)
Model 55 SX	80386SX 16-bit MCA	16	2, up to 16	640 by 480, 13":VGA	1.44 M 3.5"	SP, PP, MP, KP, DP, 3XS (16-bit)
Model 60	80286 16-bit MCA	10	1, up to 16	640 by 480, 13":VGAor 1,024 by 768	1.44 M (3.5") 1.2 (5.25")	SP, PP, MP, KP, DP, 7XS (16-bit), SCSI
Model 65 SX	80386SX 16-bit MCA	16	2, up to 16	640 by 480, 13":VGA or 1,024 by 768	1.44 M (3.5") 1.2 (5.25")	SP, PP, MP, KP, DP, 7XS (16-bit), SCSI
Model P70 386 (Port)	80286 16-bit MCA	16, 20	2, up to 16	640 by 480, GP, VGA	1.44 M (3.5") 1.2 (5.25")	SP, PP, MP, KP, DP, 1XS (16, 32-bit)
Model 70 386	80386 32-bit MCA	16, 20, 25	2, up to 16	640 by 480, 13":VGA or 1,024 by 768	1.44 M (3.5") 1.2 (5.25")	SP, PP, MP, KP, DP, 3XS (2 16-bit, 1 32-bit)
Model 70 486	80486 32-bit MCA	25	2, up to 16	640 by 480, 13":VGA or 1,024 by 768	1.44 M (3.5") 1.2 (5.25")	SP, PP, MP, KP, DP, 3XS (2 16-bit, 1 32-bit)
Model 80 386	80386 32-bit MCA	16, 20, 25	2, up to 16	640 by 480, 13":VGA or 1,024 by 768	1.44 M (3.5") 1.2 (5.25")	SP, PP, MP, KP, DP, 3XS (2 16-bit, 1 32-bit), EDSI, SCSI option

Table 4.2 IBM PS/2 Computer Models *(continued)*

Model	CPU	Speed (MHz)	RAM (MBytes)	Screen (pixels inches)	Storage (floppy hard drive)	Ports
Model P75	80486 32-bit MCA	33	8 to 16	1,024 by 768 10" XGA	1.44 M (3.5")	SP, PP, MP, SCSI
Model 90	80486 32-bit MCA	25 or 33	4 to 64	1,024 by 768 12" XGA	1.2 (5.25") 1.44 (3.5")	2 SP, PP, MP, KP, DP, 4XS (32-bit)
Model 95	80486 32-bit MCA	33	4 to 64	640 by 400, 12" 12" XGA	1.2 (5.25") 1.44 (3.5")	SP, PP, MP, KP, DP, 8XS (32-bit)

Key: AT=AT bus; DP=Display port; EDSI=Enhanced small device interface bus; GP=Gas plasma; KP=Keyboard port; MCA=Microchannel architecture bus; MP=Mouse port; PCB=PC bus; (Port)=Portable; PP=Parallel port; SCSI=Small computer system interface bus; SP=Serial port; #XS=Expansion slots (#=number of slots).

Source: *IBM Personal System/2 Reference Guide,* IBM, July 1990.

It just doesn't make sense to buy a PC that can't run Windows well, which means, at *minimum,* a 16 MHz 80386 S/X (an 80386 is better) computer, with 2 MBytes RAM (4 is better). A 3 1/2-inch floppy drive is preferred, but buy a 5 1/4-inch drive as a second floppy drive. A monochrome VGA machine for grayscale with a hard drive should cost around $2,000 from a respected clone manufacturer; color VGA adds another $300. (VGA should be your minimum graphics requirement.) Most important, don't purchase a PC with a hard drive smaller than 80 MBytes; the larger, the better. You will be amazed at how much disk space Windows applications take up. Pass up the 80386 machines in favor of 80486 machine if you have the money to go big time; it won't cost you all that much more if you shop around.

Other Platforms

NeXT Introduced in October 1988, the matte black, square-foot NeXTcube is a noteworthy publishing and media system for many reasons. It was the first desktop computer to offer both Display PostScript (on screen) and PostScript output, a megapixel display

(1 million pixels at 92 dpi), a 256 MByte erasable optical drive, an object-oriented interface builder or development environment called NeXTStep (licensed by IBM to run on its RISC workstation), and a digital signal processing (dsp) chip that can record and play CD-quality stereo sound and aid in voice recognition.

Included on the motherboard is a 68030 cpu, four NuBus slots for expansion, and an Ethernet port for networking applications. A 400 dpi laser printer shipped with the original system, although there is now a 400 dpi scanner as well. The NeXT computer is a design achievement that may someday sit in a museum of technology. A system including the optical drive, monitor, and laser printer costs about $10,000 at Businessland, its primary dis-

Figure 4-15 The NeXTcube is an innovative computer with a distinctive interface and with many features that make it an impressive development environment and desktop publishing platform. Shown here are the NeXTcube and NeXTstation computers. *Courtesy of NeXT Computer, Inc.*

tributor. A 25 MHz 68040 cpu NeXTcube is now available, and a lower-cost pizza box computer called the NeXTstation is also on the market.

The NeXTcube is a UNIX workstation built by Steve Jobs's company NeXT Computer. It runs a variant of the Mach UNIX kernel developed by Carnegie Mellon University, which is a superset of the Berkeley UNIX V. 4.3. UNIX is the operating system developed by AT&T in 1969 at Bell Labs by Kenneth Ritchie and Kenneth Thompson on a DEC minicomputer. It provides a set of system standards that can be set up on any computer. UNIX offers full multitasking, background processing, a hierarchical file system, many utilities, and is a mature operating system that runs on hundreds of computers, from mainframes to micros. UNIX has long been known for being "user-hostile," but the NeXT interface, called NeXTStep, goes a long way toward making UNIX "smile."

It is strange that a computer with as much to offer as the NeXT hasn't been more successful, unit sales-wise. Part of the problem is that version 1.0 of the system software didn't ship until September 1989 (version 2.0 is now current). In the interim, new versions of IBM PC 80386 and 80486 machines and Macintosh computers closed the performance gap. Recent reviewers have felt that the machine based on Motorola's 68030 chip (roughly equivalent to an 80386 in the PC world) is too slow to multitask effectively. It's effective as a single-user machine, but sluggish as a multi-user system, and color was slow in coming. Other problems include slow application development, although a very respectable application set now can be obtained. The NeXTcube sells for $7,995, with the NeXTstation selling for $4,995. The color NeXTstation is priced at $7,995. NeXT is a well-funded, innovative company and is likely to have a hit version of a low-cost workstation/PC in the near future.

Amiga/Atari

Commodore makes a series of desktop computers called the Amiga that have gained a cult following similar to the one the Macintosh had in the old days; particularly in Europe. Approximately 1.5 million Amigas have shipped. The Commodore Amiga 500, 2000, 2500, and 3000 computers offer true multitasking, good color support (4,096 colors in the palette), stereo sound (two-channel, four-voice), NTSC video (TV or VCR input), and some very innovative programming techniques made possible by a proprietary chip set. The 500, 2000, and 2500 are 68000-based, with the 2500 capable of supporting a 68030 coprocessor that allows alternate operation. The Amiga 500 is primarily a game machine. The newly introduced 3000 is 68030-based, and there aren't many applications shipping for it at the moment. A 3000 with the 25 MHz cpu and a 40 MHz hard drive lists for $3,999. The Amigas ship with between five and seven AT-styled expansion slots; boards are also available that allow an Amiga to run PC software, plus one that runs Macintosh software (apparently quite well). The Amiga has a proprietary GUI called the Workbench that is well developed; version 2.0 is scheduled for release soon.

The Amiga offers many fine games, some of the important larger applications, such as WordPerfect, an excellent set of applications for multimedia manipulating sight and sound, and MIDI (musical instrument digital interface). But the Amiga has only a couple of moderately powered page layout programs and is therefore not on the cutting edge of desktop publishing. Leading packages on the Amiga include the WordPerfect 5 word processor, Deluxe Photo Lab paint program from Electronic Arts, and Professional Page and Publishing Partner Professional page layout programs.

The Amiga does have the advantage of being fairly inexpensive, so if you are interested only in doing intermediate-quality DTP, the Amiga 2000 or 3000 series may provide an interesting solution. Although offering only 8-bit color at the moment, the Amigas are first-class graphics machines for design, visualization, and multimedia work. Many design studios producing television ads use Amigas, and there are excellent special tools available at low cost on this platform. The Amiga is a serious desktop computer that might have been significantly more successful if it had been developed by a company that had been a little more skillful at selling it. Its success is one of those rare instances where technology triumphs over marketing.

Products and specifications subject to change.

Figure 4-16
The Commodore Amiga is a favored, low-cost machine for graphics and animation work. It has a devoted European following. *Courtesy of Commodore, Inc.*

Atari

Several of Atari's computers, aimed primarily at the home market, offer low-priced DTP solutions. The Atari 1040ST^E, a replacement for the Atari 1040ST computer, is based on an 8 MHz 68000 cpu. It runs a variant of DOS and comes bundled with Digital Research's GEM environment, described earlier in this chapter. Originally growing out of Nolan Bushnell's start-up company for Atari games, after sale to Warner Communications and subsequent spin-off, the

Atari computers have evolved into solid home microcomputers. There are serial and parallel ports, stereo ports, built-in MIDI ports, and NTSC direct video input support. Ataris can read MS-DOS formatted disketts and through a cartridge port can be set up to read Macintosh files as well.

The 1040ST^E has a good library of software and is a very inexpensive solution to DTP if you are willing to live within its limitations. Atari is touting a more upscale Atari called the Mega (model 2 and 4, for 2 and 4 MBytes RAM) as a DTP solution. For about $3,000 you can obtain a Mega, an Atari laser printer, and a layout program and do DTP work of reasonable quality, comparable to a PC but not a Macintosh. Page printing on an Atari laser printer is very quick.

Figure 4-17
The Atari Mega and its low-cost fast Atari SLM804 provide a low-cost DTP solution. *Courtesy of Atari, Inc.*

The main problem with the Amiga and Atari computers has less to do with their feature set and more to do with the size of their installed base here in the United States. You are unlikely to find these computers supported at a service bureau, and many of the traditional DTP tools, such as font libraries and application support, are limited. However, they can output your documents as PostScript files, which can be printed on imagesetters from Macs or PCs. They are good, low-cost home solutions.

High-End Systems

Those of us who have grown up on microcomputers may be surprised to learn how important desktop publishing has been on minicomputers and workstations. Complex publishing applications, such as Interleaf Publisher and FrameMaker, are just now making their way onto microcomputers. They started life on UNIX machines, a product category that includes $20,000 to $50,000 packages. Others, such as Intergraph's Distributed Publishing System, XYVision's Parlance, ArborText's The Publisher and their coded TEX system, still run exclusively on these more powerful computers.

These are really full documentation publishing systems including integrated text, drawing, painting, image processing, and page layout tools. As such, they are better referred to as *electronic technical publishing* systems (ETP). These systems are usually sold as a set that can be installed on several computers (nodes) in a network, often attached to a server minicomputer on a LAN. Two types of ETP may be found: interactive or WYSIWYG systems, and coded or batch systems; both seem popular. Only WYSIWYG DTP packages have been commercially successful on micros, however. Chapter 12 discusses the difference between these two approaches.

Documentation has been a major concern of the military and of commercial firms developing sophisticated equipment, such as aircraft. A Boeing 747 has a maintenance and repair manual set roughly the size of the *Encyclopaedia Britannica*. Not surprisingly, Boeing was one of the first companies to reduce its manuals to a compact disk. Current microcomputers are not capable of DTP projects on that scale.

With its concern for documenting widgets, do-hickeys, and thingamabobs, coupled with its interest in getting competitive bids on all systems, radar, nuts, bolts, and toilet seats, the military has established a set of publishing guidelines for vendors to follow as part of a DOD Computer-Aided Acquisition and Logistic Support (CALS) initiative. CALS specifies what's called the Standard

Generalized Markup Language (SGML) format for text, the IGES format for vector (object-oriented or draw) graphics, Consultative Committee International Telegraph and Telephone (CCITT) Group 4 format for bit-mapped graphics, and the MIL (military) STANDARD 1840A tape format for document file organization. All ETP packages currently support the CAL standard.

Figure 4-18
An Intergraph workstation running the Distributed Publishing System.

To learn the future of high-end DTP on microcomputers, you have only to look at these systems to see what they're capable of. A simple edit on a page can cause your entire manual to repaginate, the placement of all graphics to alter, including how text wraps around them, and the placement of footnotes to adjust. On an ETP system you can edit to your heart's delight in the foreground while your computer repaginates quietly in the background. Hundreds of pages can be reformatted in seconds. Many packages contain very sophisticated indexing systems, and the best spell checkers and hyphenation and justifications (h & j) routines available. While indexing and cross-referencing can take hours or days on a micro, these systems can do them in minutes. Some systems contain sophisticated equation builders that will actually solve the equations you specify. And, because these are UNIX computers, you have full multitasking and some of the best computer print utilities at your disposal.

Sun Microsystems is one of the leaders in the workstation market (a very hot market at that), and in 1989 it successfully downsized its product line into the under-$10,000 category. The SPARCStation 1 and the Sun-3/80 computers set new performance/price point standards for the workstation category at that time, with the former machine rated at over 12 MIPS. Sun has not yet positioned itself in the personal computer market, preferring to sell through dealers and VARs (value added resellers), but it may become a name to be reckoned with in years to come. The SPARC chip set, upon which the SPARC series computers are based, has been licensed for cloning, and there is now a $10,000 SPARC laptop on the market in Japan. Stephen Roth, a DTP industry analyst, has suggested that powerful SPARC-based clones from Taiwan may become available in 1993 for under $2,000; this development could change the face of desktop publishing.

What's Important in a Computer Graphics Setup?

You have to buy hardware that lets you run the software necessary to do your work. Always try to buy equipment that will allow you to expand your system over time. This means buying a computer with the most advanced cpu you can afford in order to give your system the longest useful life. Your system should include the following:

- Personal computer: with enough RAM to use your most complex program.

  Low End: Computer—Mac Plus or SE, IBM PC AT, Atari 1024ST^E; RAM—1 MByte.

  Mid Level: Computer—Mac IILX or si, IBM compatible 80386 S/X, Commodore Amiga 2500 or 3000; RAM—2 MByte.

  High Level: Computer—Mac IIci or IIfx, IBM compatible 80386 or 80486, Sun SPARCStation 1, or NeXT; RAM—4 to 8 MBytes.

- Display monitor and high-resolution graphics board: read Chapter 5 for information on displays.

  Low End: Monochrome or grayscale monitor with an 8-bit video board (Mac) or a VGA board (PC).

  Mid Level: Small color monitor, large portrait, or two-page grayscale monitor with 8-bit video board (Mac) or VGA board (PC).

  High Level: Portrait or two-page color monitor with 24-bit video board (Mac), or with SuperVGA board (PC). Most high-end systems have video boards built into the motherboard.

- Graphical User Interface:

  Low End: Macintosh (Mac OS), GEM (for IBM PC AT and Atari), Tandy's DeskMate, or GeoWorks (PC).

  Mid Level: Windows 3 (PC), Mac OS, and Amiga OS.

  High Level: Mac OS, Windows 3, NeXTStep, and other dedicated UNIX boxes.

- Hard Drive: storage device options are discussed in Chapter 6.

  Low End: 40 MByte fixed hard drive or 45 MByte removables (preferred).

  Mid Level: 80 MByte fixed hard drive and/or 45 MByte removables.

  High Level: 170 to 330 MByte hard drive, erasable optical drive, and 45 MByte removables. The large drives and removables are particularly necessary for color files.

- Mouse or other pointing device: a mouse, a trackball, or a graphics tablet is the usual choice. See Chapter 6 for details.

- Printer: see Chapter 7 for more details.

  Low End: dot matrix printers or other impact printer.

  Mid Level: Ink-jet Printer, or color ink jet for proofing, or low-cost personal laser printer.

  High Level: Networkable PostScript Printer, imagesetters, and thermal transfer color printers.

You will also need writing, painting, drawing, and page layout software that works with the choices you've just made. A scanner is a very useful device for illustration, particularly at the midlevel DTP quality. Black-and-white scanners and digital image processing software are well developed; together a good set would cost about $1,500. Full-color desktop scanners have recently dropped considerably in price, and low-cost color retouching software has also been introduced. A color setup might cost $2,200. For more information on scanners, see Chapter 10.

Displays

But the bravest are surely those who have the clearest vision of what is before them, glory and danger alike, and yet notwithstanding go out to meet it.

Thucydides, c. 460–400 B.C.

A good display improves your performance and the quality of your work. Computer video systems have three main components: a monitor, a video interface, and a software driver. These components affect the color content, resolution, and other important factors that you work with in publishing projects. Other technologies are being introduced to make smaller, larger, and better displays. In the sections that follow we examine how a computer display system works, some related display equipment, important considerations in their purchase and use, and the current and emerging video technologies.

Display Technology

Cathode ray tubes (CRTs), or what we now call monitors, were invented in the 1930s and appeared on military equipment in World War II, but it wasn't until the summer of 1961 that they were attached to computers. At that time, the American Research Project Agency (ARPA), which was responsible for funding large-scale computer research, had projects in interactive computing in progress at its Interactive Processing Techniques Division, headed by J. C. R. Licklider. ARPA also had program running at MIT, and there a video

117

monitor was hooked to a DEC PDP-1. By 1962 Slug Russell had pro-grammed the world's first video game called Spacewars where an enemy blip was blasted by torpedoes on a display.

The CRT monitor is the display of choice today for most com-puter users because of its low cost, high resolution, fast imaging speed, and shading/color capabilities. And although CRT monitors are also bulky and emit low-energy radiation, they are likely to remain the display of choice for some time to come. No other competitive technology, and there are several—(liquid crystal, gas plasma, active light-emitting transistors, and projection displays), has yet demonstrated the capacity to display as much information at as low a cost as the venerable CRT.

How Computer Video Works

A computer creates an image on a CRT monitor by moving an electron beam over the inner surface of the picture tube. The movement of the beam is called *raster scanning*. Chemical phos-phors painted on the inner CRT screen in a dot pattern are excited by the electrons and glow with a measurable lifetime. The smallest resolving unit imaged on the screen is called a picture element, pel, or pixel, and there can be several phosphor dots to a pixel.

Monochrome monitors are coated with a single glowing phosphor. Colors for these monitors include white on black, amber on black, green on black, and some others. The reverse, achieved by creating a negative image, are monitors that are black on white, black on amber, and so on. Shadings are possible when a monitor has phosphors that can be excited to lesser or greater degree. The range of shadings highlight detail, and because most monitors of this type are the white-on-black variety, they have been dubbed *grayscale* monitors. Grayscale imitates black-and-white photography, but at a lower resolution. Black-and-white photography offers an almost infinite range of grays because the silver particles in the developed emulsion can be of any size and reflect light of any wavelength. But, depending on your computer's video setup, most grayscale monitors only offer up to 256 shades of gray. The human eye cannot distinguish more than that.

As color TV sets, a computer monitor can have a surface coated with three different phosphors that glow red, green, or blue when struck. These monitors are therefore called *RGB* monitors. RGB monitors use three electron beams to excite the RGB phosphors, which are arranged as triads of dots or vertical stripes. Each electron beam has a different energy so that it excites only its assigned color. As in most monochrome monitors, a metallic screen isolates each pixel so that a beam can excite only one at a time.

When you mix the three primary colors in equal amounts, you get a shade of gray or, to put it another way, a white of a certain brightness. What that means is that you can write the same data to each primary color in a pixel and re-create a monochrome monitor using a color monitor. When you go into the Control Panel of a Macintosh or Windows and set the colors to black and white, that is what you are doing. You can set it further so that only so many shades of gray or colors can be displayed.

Each RGB signal travels down its own separate wire, as does a mixing signal for synchronization, or "sync" signals. Monitors that can have their frequency changed so that they can work with multiple computer systems are called *multisync* monitors. The NEC multisync series is highly regarded. By contrast, a TV screen uses

Figure 5-2
Phosphors, pixels,
and pitch on a
CRT monitor.

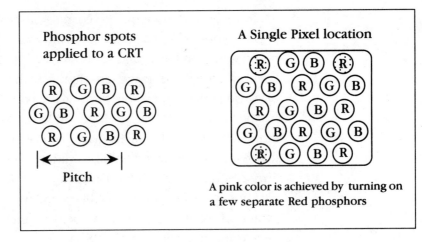

Phosphor spots applied to a CRT

A Single Pixel location

Pitch

A pink color is achieved by turning on a few separate Red phosphors

one cable that merges RGB and sync and is referred to as a *composite signal* (for which the NTSC, also called the RS170, standard is used). Composite video technology is simpler, but images are less detailed and clear than on RGB video.

An image of the screen is created in a section of your computer's memory (video RAM) and then transferred to the screen. The more advanced a display is, the greater the size of the video RAM it requires. Video RAM is more often part of an add-in board called a video card, but it can be built right onto the motherboard of your computer itself (a future trend). The advantage of add-in cards is that they give you the option to buy as much video as you require and no more. When you buy a monitor you must buy a video card to match. While you don't have to buy the two from the same vendor, you must always check for compatibility. Many vendors sell monitors and video cards as a matched set.

Drivers

Software is required to control the video process; any peripheral device on a computer requires a device driver, termed *video driver;* the Macintosh Monitor CDEV in the system folder is an example (see Figure 5-3). On an IBM PC, under DOS, each application provides a choice of PC monitor standards. GUIs simplify the situation by supporting all the major video standards as part of the Setup program for all the applications that run on it. (Printers require printer drivers, covered in Chapter 7.)

More advanced computers store more video frames and write new video data onto monitors faster. Video requires a lot of work by the computer's microprocessor, and many advanced models have accelerators built into their video boards in the form of an extra cpu; they can also contain instructions hardwired into a video ROM. Because a graphics coprocessor has a specialized narrow function, generally a RISC (reduced instruction set chip) is used; fewer instructions run faster. Acceleration is particularly important where many objects must be manipulated on screen and their colors mapped. CAD users in particular benefit from graphics acceleration, but if you do color graphics for desktop publishing on a large screen you will also benefit from an accelerator board. Look for the next generation of high-end personal computers to come with built-in video acceleration.

Figure 5-3
The Macintosh Monitor CDEV from the Control Panel menu, allows you to pick a monitor if you have additional video cards, turn color on and off, and set the bit density.

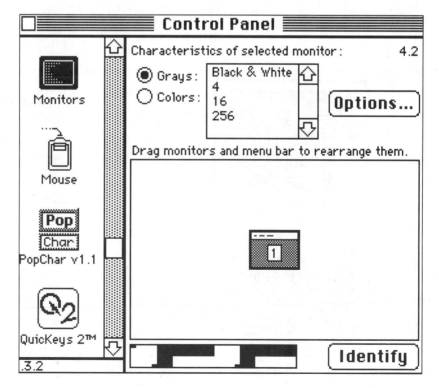

Computer Writing

A computer forms a bit map of your screen in video RAM; that is, it stores display information in the form of bits that it maps for each pixel on your monitor. Normally a computer writes (raster scans) to the screen starting in the top left corner and sweeping right to complete a line. The electron beam then shuts off, returns to the left side one line down, and continues to write the next line. Macintosh programs also number pixels in this manner: left to right, top to bottom.

A Macintosh writes every line one after the other (the scan line) and writes the entire screen 60 or more times a second (the frame rate, or refresh rate). This kind of display is called a *noninterlaced* display. The IBM EGA and VGA graphics standards are also noninterlaced; U.S. television, which conforms to standards developed by the National Television Standards Committee (NTSC), *is* interlaced. It sends only half the screen information (every other line) at a time, fooling the eye. It has the advantage of needing a smaller video frame (or narrower bandwidth), but it is more likely to suffer from display flicker. At 60 times per second on a nonin-

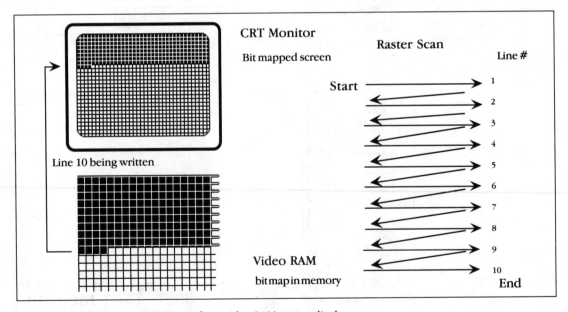

Figure 5-4 How a computer writes from video RAM onto a display screen.

terlaced display, your brain averages the signal, and you can detect the writing process only when the monitor is out of balance and needs adjustment.

In the early days of microcomputers, manufacturers hooked computers to TV screens, but TV screens lack sufficient resolution and informational capacity to display information accurately. Text looked very poor. The RGB monitors in use on computers today are of much higher resolution. HDTV (high density television) has the potential to merge computers with televisions (see Chapter 19); even today add-in boards can put a TV inside your computer. Radius makes one for the Macintosh (see Chapter 18). Computers write to screen 50 to 100 percent faster than a TV does, but most computers require special conversion boxes to be transformed to the TV NTSC standard . An exception is the Commodore Amiga, which has built-in NTSC.

Display Standards

Monitors and display standards are classified in part by the number of pixels they show. A 13-inch Macintosh monitor is 640 by 480 pixels (wide by high) and contains 371,200 pixels; this is the same resolution that a VGA graphics board supports on an IBM PS/2 computer. Resolution and the information density displayed at each pixel are both important elements.

To display black and white on a monitor requires that one data bit, on or off, 1 or 0, be stored for each pixel. These are called 1-bit displays although they are sometimes less correctly referred to as 2-bit. The Macintosh Plus and SE have 1-bit monitors, but appear to show grays, achieved by grouping a set of pixels into a "super-pixel". This process, called *dithering*, results in a substantial loss of resolution. The gray-looking scroll bars of a Macintosh window results from dithering; the process is also used for scanning and printing technologies.

Eight bits of data can describe 256 shades of gray (2^8), or 256 colors if you have a color monitor. For the standard Macintosh II 13-inch display, you can buy either an 8-bit or a 24-bit color video

Figure 5-5
How screen size,
pixel number, and
resolution relate to
one another.

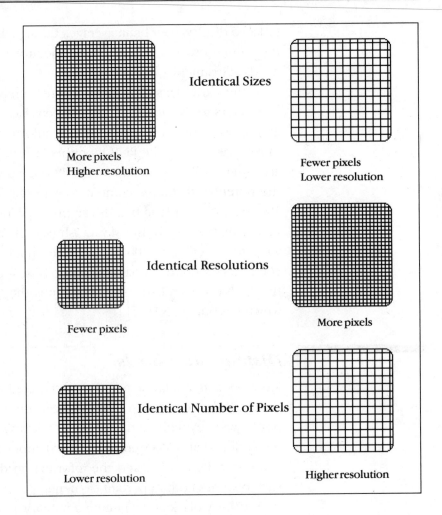

Identical Sizes

More pixels
Higher resolution

Fewer pixels
Lower resolution

Identical Resolutions

Fewer pixels

More pixels

Identical Number of Pixels

Lower resolution

Higher resolution

card. Different bit densities are illustrated in Figure C-4 in the color section of this book.

It's confusing, but "32-bit" graphics computers use only up to 24 bits to describe color inside a computer. That's a 16.8 million color palette (2^{24}). Psychologists have found that 16.8 million is considerably more colors than a human being can recognize. The remaining 8-bit part (the so-called alpha channel) of the 32 bits available to describe a colored pixel is used for special effects such as describing an object's transparency (see Chapter 14). So if you have a video display that can show only 256 colors on screen, as an 8-bit card does, where do all the other colors go? Your computer contains a color look-up table that translates a color value to the one closest to that which can be displayed. So, if your monitor is grayscale, then that color value is translated into the appropriate value of gray. The information is still there internally, you just can't see it. Switch over to a 24-bit card and each pixel can have a unique color up to the limit of the number of pixels on the screen.

▼ *Tip: All the extra processing required for color slows your computer down. If you have a color monitor and need faster computer performance, turn off the color to increase its speed. The speed enhancement is quite considerable.*

Some monitors offer several resolutions, and you can switch among them. This is particularly useful in the IBM world where different programs support different video standards, but it can also be useful on the Macintosh where you might want a crisper display for a large spreadsheet and a lower resolution for larger graphics. In general you'll want to use the highest resolution a display offers, and one way to do this is to adopt a GUI.

Macintosh

Early computers could draw only characters on a screen and then print characters to a printer. This made for very fast screen display and fast printing because very little information (only the ASCII code value) had to be stored for each position. The pixels were turned on and off based on where they fell in a character's cell. That's what MS-DOS is all about; it's a character-based operating system. Character-based systems have tremendous performance advantages, especially for intensive number crunching like database work on a mainframe. They're not as useful as the front-end systems for users accessing that database; GUIs are better solutions for that.

The Macintosh is a graphics computer. It uses an imaging scheme called QuickDraw to create what you see on its screen. (However, some applications, such as Adobe Illustrator, render their own graphcs, and largely bypass QuickDraw.) PostScript can also be used as a screen-imaging model. The best-known desktop computer currently using Display PostScript is the NeXT computer, but you can license PostScript for your Mac (or the subset

Figure 5-6
The Sigma Designs
L*View monitor offers
six different resolutions
(adjusted in software)
for the Apple Macintosh.
This is a solution to the
problem of monitor ori-
entation. You can also
use software indepen-
dently to address this
problem, but without
the increase in apparent
screen resolution.
*Courtesy of Sigma
Designs, Inc.*

of it that creates screen type) by buying the Adobe Type Manager (discussed in Chapter 11). QuickDraw also can be used to print; it drives an ImageWriter printer, for example, or can be interpreted into PostScript by the LaserWriter printer driver. Having a graphics language imaging your monitor is a distinct advantage when draw-ing complex graphics to the screen. Character-based models limit a monitor's capabilities.

The resolution of the "classic" Macintosh screen is 74 dots per inch, very close to a typographer's *point* size of 72 dpi. A point was specified as the smallest dimension a typographer could make on a letterform by the point of an engraving tool. In this day and age of 300-dpi laser printers, 2,450-dpi imagesetters, and 800-dpi handscanners, a 74-dpi screen may seem awfully coarse, but it was, and is, considered to be a fairly crisp display compared to the character-based display standards running on IBM PC and clones. Apple monitors have the following display characteristics:

- Classic Compact Macs: 512 by 342 pixels, 74 dpi, and 9-inch landscape.

- Apple monochrome monitor: 640 by 480 pixels, 80 dpi, 12-inch landscape.

- Apple color RGB monitor: 640 by 480 pixels, 80 dpi, 13-inch landscape.

- Two-page monochrome monitor: 1,152 by 870 pixels, 77 dpi, and 21-inch landscape.

- Macintosh portrait display: 640 by 870 pixels, 80 dpi, and 15-inch portrait.

▼ *Tip: Use a screen saver to protect your monitor. Clean your monitor with a soft, dry tissue and elbow grease. Cleaners leave a residue on the monitor.*

Turn your monitor off if you are leaving your computer for several hours to allow the display to degauss, and to cut down on wear. Only turn your monitor when it is off to prevent distortions. These precautions are particularly important for large color monitors. A monitor should be set up by turning the brightness completely up and lowering it until the edge band appears black. Then the contrast should be adjusted to your preference.

Video cards for the Macintosh II are available as NuBus boards; the current standards are 8-bit boards (256 colors or gray levels on screen) and 32-bit boards (16.8 million colors or gray levels available on screen). Keep in mind that a 13-inch Apple monitor has

Figure 5-7
The three different sizes of Apple modular monitors are shown here. Top left: the 13-inch Apple RGB monitor; bottom left: the Apple Full-Page display (9 by 12 inches, about 15 inches corner to corner); right: the Apple Two-Page display (18 by 12 inches, about 21 inches corner to corner). *Courtesy of Apple Computer, Inc.*

307,200 pixels, so you can have only that many unique colors on screen regardless of the palette size. The new Apple video cards are called the Display Card 4•8 (a 24-bit board), and the Display Card 8•24 (a 32-bit board). The Display Card 8•24 GC offers an accelerator option using an Advanced Micro Devices (AMD) RISC. Currently about 150 dpi is the high end for resolution on a computer monitor.

IBM PC

Display video is a major weakness among IBM-style personal computers. The proliferation of standards and its overall lower quality of screens compared to the Macintosh have impeded growth of the PC as a graphics platform. That is likely to change considerably over the next couple of years. The PC video standards that exist, and continue to evolve, are:

- Monochrome Display Adapter (MDA): The original IBM character display for monochrome monitors; good, text display with just one color (often green with a black background). Unsuitable for graphics and not sold on modern PCs. 720 by 350 pixels.

- Hercules Graphics Card (HGC): For use on a monochrome display. Has a resolution of 720 by 348 pixels, about 72 dpi horizontally. A non-IBM standard, but has been adopted and cloned by many manufacturers. A low-cost solution to DTP; cards in this class can be obtained for around $80, and monitors can be had for a similar amount.

- Color Graphics Adaptor (CGA): The original IBM PC standard for RGB monitors with multiresolution capabilities. Low resolution is 320 by 200 pixels; switching into monochrome display allows a 640 by 200 pixel display; which represents a 64 by 27 dpi resolution, and is unacceptable for graphics or DTP applications. Up to 16 colors or grays can be displayed. CGA costs about $150 for a video card, around $350 for a monitor, and is not recommended for modern applications.

- Enhanced Graphics Adaptor (EGA): The IBM color standard that was competitive with the Hercules graphics card. Text and graphics can be displayed in up to 64 colors or shades of gray. It has 640 by 350 pixel resolution (about 64 by 47 dpi), judged to be medium resolution. With VGA adapters selling for $99, EGA is effectively obsolete.

- Multicolor Graphics Array (MCGA): An IBM PS/2 standard for text and graphics at low to medium resolution. Can display up to 256 colors.

- Video Graphics Array (VGA): The current standard for the IBM PS/2 line of computers. VGA displays up to 16 colors at a resolution of 640 by 480 pixels and up to 256 colors at a resolution of 320 by 200. However, only 6 bits can be assigned to each primary color, so VGA is limited to showing only 2^6 or 64, grayscale (R + G + B). VGA is the current recommended minimum display standard for use in IBM PC graphics applications.

- SuperVGA: An emerging standard that displays 256 colors at 1024 by 768 pixels. Recommended.

- IBM 8514/A: Designed specifically for OS/2 and the PS/2 computers and clones, this high-end 1024 by 768 interlaced pixel display is most often used for CAD or for more precise color graphics work. Alternate 1024 by 768 monitors and standards may emerge as the future standard. In 1991 IBM introduced a standard called XGA similar to 8514/A with 256 colors out of a 16.7 million color palette, interlaced or noninterlaced, with a new associated display architecture.

- TARGA: Originally developed by AT&T, this 24-bit technology allows you to view up to 16.7 million colors at a resolution of 1024 by 768 pixels. TrueVision markets today's TARGA boards, and RasterOps and Hercules both have their own 24-bit display adapters with roughly the same capability. This is what you want if you're doing color prepress and/or working seriously with photographic color images.

VGA is the standard for PCs, but it's unclear what the future standards may be. Edsun Laboratories (Waltham, MA) and Analog Devices (Norwood, MA) have developed a chip for digital-to-analog (DAC) conversion called Continuous Edge Graphics (CEG). It takes VGA and uses interpolation techniques to antialias (smooth and blend) jagged lines and colors on a monitor, and allows a much larger palette of apparent colors to be displayed (some claim up to 800,000). The result is crisper screen display and more photorealistic images. If this technology is adopted, it has the potential to extend the VGA standard's lifetime significantly, and would be available at a much lower cost than other standards. This chip will be built into VGA boards and be transparent to the user.

PC applications give video instructions by sending a call (programming instruction) to DOS or by sending calls directly to the video card's memory. Writing video directly to video RAM is more efficient and faster. Microsoft Word (DOS version) actually writes directly to video RAM. Another advantage of direct video write is that hot keys are supported, so all of those useful memory resident programs can run. All this means is that if your applications bypass DOS, you must be particularly careful that any high-resolution monitor you purchase faithfully emulates one of the display standards. Of the monitor types, choose among secondary displays, primary DOS displays, and primary display with hardware emulation; avoid a primary display *without* hardware emulation.

As mentioned previously, Windows and GEM have display managers (a set of routines) that write directly to your video card. So a Windows application such as Arts & Letters Graphic Editor writes to Windows video driver, bypassing DOS entirely. In the OS/2 Presentation Manager, the video driver of the GUI is part of the operating system itself.

Types of Displays

Most displays are rectangular. When a display is wider than it is tall, it is called a *landscape* display; one taller than it is wide is called a *portrait* display. Each has its use and application. A landscape monitor works nicely to show a wide spreadsheet, or a horizontal graphic, while a portrait display serves well as a one-page display monitor for page layout. Radius makes a new monitor called the Pivot that turns on its axis, switching from landscape to portrait; a color version is also available.

Figure 5-8
The new Radius Pivot monitor changes from landscape to portrait configuration by rotation. A mercury sensing switch evaluates position and software reconfigures the display characteristics. This 15-inch monitor solves the problem of whether you should buy a landscape or a portrait monitor. *Courtesy of Radius, Inc.*

Monitors can be divided into three groups. Low-resolution monitors have fewer than 640 by 350 pixels and cost less than $500. They are the least legible and require the most screen movement to view information. Medium-resolution monitors are less than 1024 by 768 pixels and cost between $500 and $1,000. Most good DTP monitors fall into this intermediate range. High-resolution monitors display about 1024 by 768 pixels and can cost from $1,500 to $40,000. This class of monitor is more likely to be used for engineering, but can be useful in high-end color prepress work.

Buying a Monitor

Buying a computer monitor, particularly a color one, can be a highly subjective purchase; some users prefer one color cast over another. You could take sophisticated equipment with you and evaluate a monitor's characteristics, but better yet, read the information here and some of the reviews cited at the end of this chapter. Remember, the light in which you view a monitor shouldn't be important; you are dealing with emitted and not reflected light. Assuming you don't need color calibration, there are several details that separate good monitors from bad.

- Fine character display. Don't be bashful, take a magnifying glass to the monitor to see how fine features, such as serifs (those little letter endings), are displayed. As long as the same imaging language is used on a set of monitors, they may be compared.

- Flatter edges. A curved monitor means that the manufacturer didn't take the time or trouble to incorporate recently developed dynamic beam shaping circuitry. Check the resolution at the edges of the screen. This is always a good criterion.

- Good glare protection. This requires special coatings, and careful manufacturing includes this feature. Check how a flashlight shines off the monitor face. Poor glare protection can lead to image degradation (some monitors use silica-coated or etched glass that absorbs light); the best monitors use true antireflective coatings.

- Multiple resolutions. This is particularly important for the PC and for DOS, and it is also useful for different graphics views on the Macintosh. GUIs are likely to reduce the future need for multiple resolution standards.

If you have to do color matching for prepress, then your best bet is to buy a color-matching and self-adjusting monitor. Barco (the Calibrator) and Radius (Color Display System), among others, sell them. Color-calibrating monitors contain compensating circuitry to adjust beam intensity as your monitor ages (as they all surely do). You can also buy a color calibration device (Radius, SuperMac, and others sell them) and do manual calibration for your monitor, or you can buy a monitor with automatic adjustment circuitry built in. These monitors tend to be expensive (around $5,000), but they are invaluable for work requiring exact color matching, such as prepress.

Remember to protect your monitor from image burn-in by installing a screen saver. A screen saver is a program that blanks the monitor when it detects a certain period of inactivity. This protects the monitor from having an image permanently burn into the phosphors on the screen. It isn't necessary that the screen go black, only that the image change with time. Some of these screen savers are "way cool": After Dark (Mac, Win) puts flying toasters on your screen, with flapping-wings sounds. It has thirty other modules with an infinite number of settings. Pyro! has color fireworks, a superb aquarium where big fish eat little fish, and many other animations.

Figure 5-9
After Dark has animated screen savers that have to be seen to be believed. These are flying and flapping toasters (!) Is this the killer app you've been waiting for?

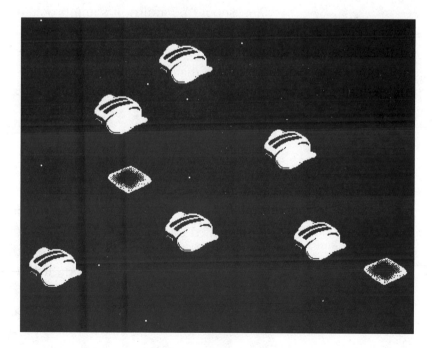

Your Monitor and Your Work

For DTP applications, the ideal monitor size is a two-page display. Doing layout work on facing pages is generally acknowledged as the most effective way to work. But two-page displays can be expensive; some color monitors of this size (minimum 18-inches wide by 12-inches tall) can cost many thousands of dollars, more than the computer they sit next to. You can write text on a 9-inch Macintosh screen—it ain't that pleasant, but you can get used to it. Basically, laying out pages on anything other than a full-page size screen is a major chore. You are forever fiddling with getting things aligned, or trying to locate a small detail on a page. Once you work on a large monitor, you'll never go back to a small one.

▼ *Tip: Size is so important to layout work that it generally makes sense to buy a two-page grayscale monitor if you can't afford a color one.*

Ask yourself—do you really need color for your work? You may want to spend some time on a large-size display or a color monitor at your friendly service bureau.

You should be aware of some problems that arise from large monitors. Their size often requires that you use your mouse a lot more, moving your cursor from one end of the screen to another. Applications that offer keyboard shortcuts and tear-off menus are a distinct advantage, for "tear-off" menus can be moved anywhere on the screen. They're found on the NeXT machines interface (NeXTStep), Apple's System 7 software, and sometimes come bundled with the software that large-screen vendors offer with their monitors (such as RadiusWare from Radius monitors, Figure 5.10). Utilities that allow you to modify menu sizes or change type sizes are also helpful. Personality, Click Change, and the shareware product called Layout are three examples for the Macintosh.

Many desktop publishers pooh-pooh the need for color displays in their black-and-white work. If you don't need color, why buy it? One reason for choosing a color monitor is that modern interfaces use color to detail interface features. Color gives you

Figure 5-10
You can see the importance of size in layout work by comparing a Macintosh SE/30 with its 9-inch classic screen with a Radius Two-Page Display (19 inches). You can barely fit the menus on the smaller screen. Here the Radius Tear-off Menus feature of the RadiusWare package is shown. *Courtesy of Radius, Inc.*

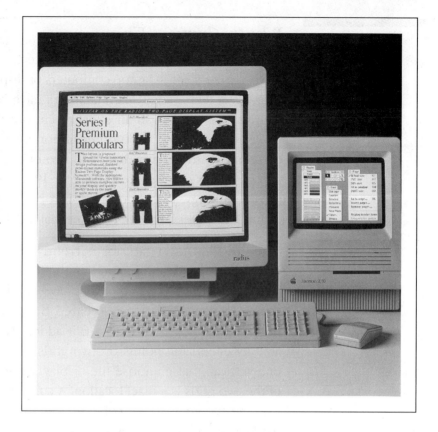

clues as to what's going on and where to find things. You can get that from grayscale monitors, but the effect isn't as dramatic. Studies also find that workers who use color monitors don't get tired as quickly. So don't be suckered into what passes for common wisdom these days—that color monitors don't matter. They do.

You can never have enough resolution or speed on your monitor. A fast, colored, highly detailed display is a thing of beauty. You may have to settle for less than you might want, but if you make your living with your computer, the right monitor can make your life much nicer. A CAD user on a large display without an accelerator might wait 15 seconds for a screen redraw compared to 1 second with acceleration; and that could be the difference between a computer tool being used or not.

What's Coming Up

Most of the action in innovative display technology is not in desktop computers, it's in laptop computers or display systems used for projection technology. Manufacturers have been experimenting with various displays in an effort to cut down on their bulk and power consumption. The other important hurdle laptops must overcome, is the power drain and size of the mechanical components, such as disk drives. In Chapter 19, we talk more about laptop technology. Here, however, is a brief look at some of the technologies that have been commercialized for flat panel displays.

Gas Plasma

Some of the better laptops currently use gas plasma display screens for VGA display, such as the Toshiba 3100 S/X or 5200 series computers. They typically have an orange or red cast to them. Plasma displays are created by turning on an array of neon/argon bulbs, each individually addressable. The image is created by energizing points on two grids of wires, one horizontal, one vertical, that comprise the display surface. Each intersection of the two grids is a pixel location. A current is sent through each row line and kept low on column locations, thus creating an electric field where a discharge is to be created. While the image has good contrast and is flicker free, I personally find it difficult to see graphics applications on plasma displays. They consume 15 to 20 watts of power and are expensive compared to CRTs.

Electroluminescent Displays

Electroluminescent (EL) displays are similar to gas plasma displays. The main difference is that the neon/argon gas is replaced by a phosphorescent thin film such as zinc sulfide and sometimes manganese that is thin enough to be transparent. Again, a set of column and row electrodes light up the phosphor layer at points where electricity passes between a vertical and horizontal electrode. A black background absorbs light and gives the image a dark background. EL displays have a characteristic green-yellow color that some users find attractive, draw as much power as plasma displays, and cost about 20 percent more than plasma displays. They are not in widespread use.

Figure 5-11
In an early experiment, IBM installed a plasma display on an IBM PC. Never commercialized, this working model sits at the Boston Computer Museum. *Courtesy of the Boston Computer Museum.*

LCDs

Liquid crystal displays (LCDs) are found on most of the lower-cost laptop computers and also on projection panels for presentations. Display quality ranges up to VGA, but most are EGA graphics, which makes them lower-end graphics displays. LCDs have a thin layer of organic crystals called biphenyls (used also in digital watches) that can be polarized by an electric current. Two types of LCDs are in use: nematic liquid crystals with a 90-degree polarization angle and supertwist liquid crystals with a 270-degree polarization angle. A mirror reflects light through this film and a polarizing filter blocks out all light from locations where the liquid crystals have been electrically aligned.

Commonly, LCDs have a blue surface with black lettering; examples are the Toshiba 1000, 1200, or 1600 laptops; the NEC Superlite; and the Compaq LTE laptops. GRID, which makes higher-end laptops, has a Windows-specific model with a VGA screen and ISO-Point cylinder pointing device (found also on the Macintosh compatible portable from Outbound) that replaces a mouse. LCDs generally use less power than gas plasmas, but they have the dis-

Figure 5-12
(A) The Toshiba
3100 S/X laptop
utilizes a gas plasma
VGA screen.
*Courtesy of
Toshiba, Inc.*

A.

advantage of utilizing transmitted light. They tend to have poor contrast, can have a dead angle when tilting the screen, and have restricted viewing angles. In order to improve contrast, many LCD screens use extra lighting behind their polarization filter, referred to as backlit displays.

In a gutsy move, Apple Computer chose yet another technology for the Apple Macintosh Portable (see Figure 5-12) introduced in 1989, the active matrix display. An active matrix display consists of a panel of light-emitting transistors that can be turned on and off. This display is a 1 bit, but it has remarkable resolution and, as a

Figure 5-12
(continued)
(B) The GRID GRID-
CASE 1550sx has a
VGA LCD screen.
*Courtesy of GRID
Systems, Corp.*

B.

(C) The Apple
Portable uses an active
matrix (transistor dis-
play) and has a trackball
pointing device.
*Courtesy of Apple
Computer, Inc.*

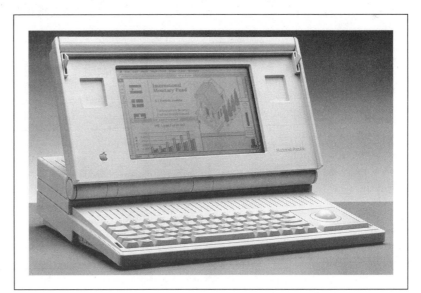

C.

light emitter, has excellent contrast. Active matrix displays tend to be expensive but have very low power requirements.

New projection displays and virtual displays are on the horizon for later in this decade, and new technology continues to be developed. CRTs are still the undisputed king of graphics displays and the monitors of choice, but future advances in this area are exciting to contemplate. While photorealistic color is available, future advances continue to create greater and greater resolutions, propelling computer graphics technology into many new applications.

Input and Storage Tools

Give us the tools, and we will finish the job.
Winston Churchill

A computer would be worthless without the ability to move information in and out of it. In this chapter we'll look at the various components used to transmit and store your documents and graphics. These include keyboards, mice, trackballs, and graphics tablets, as well as modems and disk drives of various capacities and descriptions. We'll also take a look at input connections and various schemes for compressing files.

Input Devices

Graphical user interfaces were created so that complicated commands could be displayed and organized in a standardized, logical manner, across multiple applications. Yet, no set configuration of input devices will work well for every user. Different people have different adaptive skills and require complementary methods of interacting with the computer.

There are two main catagories of input devices: absolute and relative. A graphics tablet is an absolute input device because the driver for the tablet maps the position on the table to the position on your computer monitor. The top left corner of the tablet corresponds to the top left corner of your screen, and when you move to the bottom right corner the cursor, pointing arrow, or position indicator on your monitor moves to the bottom right of the screen. Part of the initialization procedure for a tablet is to indicate manually where these two corners are. Graphics tablets can have over ten times the resolution of your monitor (1000 dpi versus 50 to 100 dpi), and can be much larger or smaller than your monitor, but the tablet driver automatically scales the movement you make.

By contrast, a mouse is a relative device. A computer boots up and places the cursor on your screen in a default position. When you move your mouse some direction or distance, the cursor moves similarly. Pick up your mouse and put it down on the other side of your desk, and your screen cursor remains fixed in position. It isn't until you move the mouse on a flat surface that your cursor moves. The motion relative to where you start rolling the mouse is what counts. You can adjust the sensitivity of a mouse through the Control Panel in Windows or the Macintosh, and that will change the scaling factor of the movement, but screen movement still depends on a vector of motion: starting and ending points, and direction. Macs ship with a mouse; other popular mice for the PC include the Microsoft Mouse and the Logitech Mouse.

All of this discussion about absolute versus relative input devices has important real-world implications. Certain applications lend themselves to one or the other type of input. For example, when tracing an outline of a figure from a template what you need is absolute motion. The template is fixed and you have to traverse along its boundary. Drawing, on the other hand, requires only relative motion because your screen movement is independent of any other coordinate system. Users know this intuitively, and that knowledge is the basis of choice for one input device over another.

Unfortunately, many motions are a combination of both absolute and relative motions. Menu commands are an example. Obviously it is much faster to hit a keystroke (a single key, or a combination of keys struck simultaneously) than it is to mouse up to the menu, pull it down, find the command, and then activate it. But you have to remember what keystroke goes with what command, and that takes some training. So it's been found that a mouse helps users get started, and a keyboard helps them become more efficient in GUI applications. Some users are so visual that they never make the transition to many keyboard shortcuts.

The keyboard is both an absolute and relative input device. When you type the letter "Q" on your keyboard, its ASCII code is inserted into your file and that letter appears on your screen. Or type the Command-Q keystroke on a Macintosh, or the "Alt-F-X" keystroke in Windows (for activating the File menu), then giving the Exit command) to quit an application. These are absolute motions. But if you press an arrow key, you move your pointer or cursor one position over in the direction indicated. That's relative motion.

Many programs allow you to assign keystrokes to actions you define. These small programs are called macros, or less commonly, scripts. Then there are utilities that allow you totally to remap your keyboard in many different ways. A few examples are SuperKey (PC), Tempo II (Mac/Win3), and QuicKeys (Mac). QuicKeys is particularly slick because it uses a graphical approach to defining keystrokes. You can define keystrokes to produce character strings, launch applications and documents, clicks, time/date, and many others. You can also define keystroke macros for sequences of actions. Utilities like these are great productivity enhancers because they let you create an environment that works for you in your own special way. Macros are so useful that Apple now bundles a macro recorder called MacroMaker as part of its system software (version 6.0). Macros are also showing up in most modern major applications.

The 1990s will be an era of great change in input devices, and some are discussed in Chapter 19. Today these devices are appearing on computers for the handicapped, and are pushing the boundaries of interactive computing. Refer to the article by Joseph J. Lazzaro in the Bibliography for more information. Use input devices to personalize your computer and have it your way!

Figure 6-1
QuicKeys 2 from CE Software is a world-class utility that allows you to remap your keyboard and create complex macros, thereby greatly enhancing your productivity. Shown here is the control panel device (CDEV) for creating the macros.

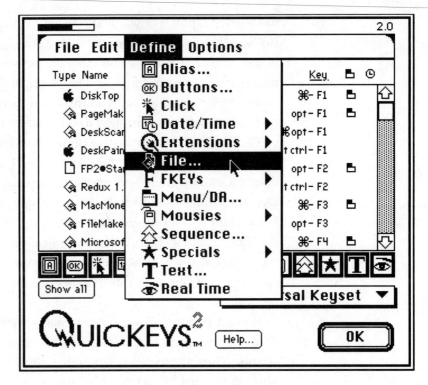

Input Connections for Macs

Input devices can be classified as slow or fast, input only, or input with feedback. In this chapter we have been surveying slow input devices without any feedback. (An example of a fast input device requiring feedback is a digital scanner.) Different devices require different ports or I/O connections. The slow I/O port for an Apple Macintosh is the Apple Desktop Bus (ADB) which has two connections. The fast I/O port is the single SCSI port (see "Hard Drives" later in this chapter). Additionally, Macintosh computers have two serial ports that serve interchangeably for the modem and printer and are AppleTalk networkable. Slow data transfer normally occurs over the serial ports as a single stream asynchronous of data; data from the host is returned to the input device synchronously using handshaking. Asynchronous communication is data sent that is not synchronized with a clock signal but is sent as a package (or set of packages) with start and stop markers called start bits and stop bits to mark the data unit(s). Handshaking is a method for controlling serial communications where transmission signals are exchanged to make sure all settings and protocols are correct. Fast data transfer uses parallel ports where several data streams are transferred in both directions at the same time with synchronization.

The ADB allows for a maximum data transfer rate of 4.5 KByte per second. A maximum of 16 ADB devices including keyboard(s), mice, trackball(s), graphics tablet(s), bar code readers, some simple OCR devices, and others can be connected in a daisy chain. The ADB is much too slow to support MIDI (musical instrument digital interface) devices like musical keyboards that can generate and modify sound. An ADB is similar to a local area network in the sense that each input device must have its own simple ADB microprocessor and requires its own device driver software, which is stored as INIT files in the System folder. Information can be transferred in either direction, but as drivers are part of the system heap in RAM, you should always shut down your computer to reconfigure your ADB. Stray charges can also damage a Mac's ADB chip if shorted while power is on, leading to an expensive repair (possibly a motherboard replacement). ADB devices are self-configuring.

Input Connections for PCs

The situation for IBM PCs is quite similar. PS/2 computers contain both serial and parallel ports. The COM ports (for communications) are serial ports that can be used for modem or serial mice such as the Microsoft Mouse, Logitech Mouse, or PS/2 Mouse. Bus mice also exist and they are connected by an adaptor to an add-in expansion board. MS-DOS allows sophisticated control over COM ports by setting lines for COM1: in the CONFIG.SYS file, and through use of the MODE command. Parallel ports are normally used for printers and are configured with the device names LP1, LP2, and LP3 (for line printer). Alternately, a device named PRN is specified; it's the same as LPT1.

All peripheral devices require device drivers, small programs that boot up to extend the operating system's capability to recognize and work with the specific hardware device. In MS-DOS and OS/2, device drivers normally carry the .SYS suffix. A user writes the command to auto-load that driver by placing a line such as DEVICE = MOUSE.SYS in the CONFIG.SYS file. Many installation programs for peripheral devices shield you from this level of complexity by writing the command line in the CONFIG.SYS file automatically. MS-DOS doesn't require DEVICE commands to work with keyboards (called, together with the display, the console or CON), monitors, and printers; that support is built into the operating system. However, you do need a driver for a mouse, and if you erase your CONFIG.SYS file, the mouse will not operate. Windows 3.0 installs any of several different mice, keyboard types, and other peripheral devices through its SETUP program.

Keyboards

It's amazing, but people pay $2,000 and up for a computer, worry about the clock speed of their cpu or the access time of their hard drive, then skimp on the one input device that they spend their time actually touching—the keyboard. A bad keyboard causes many missed keystrokes and bad typing angles. Coupled with a poor chair and bad body position, it's actually possible to develop carpal tunnel syndrome, a condition similar to arthritis where calcium deposits build up on the wrist and cause painful hand motion.

IBM spent hundreds of thousands of dollars sitting people down and testing keyboards. The result of this effort was the IBM PC AT keyboard, reputed by some to be the finest keyboard ever made for layout and tactile feel. It has served as the model for a whole generation of keyboards that other manufacturers call "extended keyboards," or "101 keyboards." The combination of typing angle, click sound and feel, and general layout is what makes it a standout. I know people who own ATs and won't upgrade their computers because they love their keyboard so much.

Keyboards are so ingrained in our culture from their introduction in the teletype and typewriter that the reasons for their design have been clouded in the mystique of the past. But they are not optimized input devices. Most Americans type on a keyboard called the QWERTY keyboard, so called for the first letters on the top left row. This keyboard was laid out to prevent the most commonly used keys from jamming together when they struck the typewriter ribbon. Unfortunately, this design also slows down the user. Nonetheless, when IBM converted to computers, it modeled them after its typewriters. An Wang's company in Boston actually bought and stripped IBM Selectrics for their keyboards, then connected them to microprocessors and monitors to create the Wang WPS (word processing system). At one time Wang was the biggest purchaser of Selectrics and owned 30 percent of the world's word processing market, more than IBM itself. QWERTY keyboards again.

Studies now show there are better configurations of letter placement than QWERTY. One keyboard, designed by August Dvorak in 1932, placed the letters struck most often on the home row. Speed tests have proved that trained DVORAK keyboard typists can achieve 200 words per minute versus 80 wpm for QWERTY typists. Other designs, such as the one called the Maltron introduced by Lilian Malt and Stephen Hobday in the late 1970s, have split keyboards contoured to fit each hand, and with keys raised to different heights. New keyboards appear all the time. Two years ago Tony Hodges developed a prototype keyboard that actually bent in two in the middle; another inventor, Dr. Johan Ullman, built one with palm rests and sloping sides.

Handedness is also important. DataDesk has just introduced a keyboard called the Switchboard that offers DVORAK and QWERTY keypads, trackball, LCD Calculator, vertical function keys, numeric keypad, arrow cursor, graphics tablet, and 3270 mainframe emulation keypad modules. You can mix and match modules and set up the keyboard for right- or left-handed users. The Switchboard can be configured to attach to an IBM PC as a PS/2 keyboard, to an Apple Macintosh as an ADB Apple Extended Keyboard or as a Mac Plus non-ADB keyboard. The feel of this keyboard is excellent.

Mice

Mice are palm-sized input devices that control cursor position and initiate actions. A distance measurement mechanism (either mechanical or optical) and switch button is built in. The most common mouse in use today is an optical mechanical mouse: the

Figure 6-2
The Switchboard from DataDesk International is the first truly customizable keyboard introduced with interchangeable parts. It is really an input device development platform.

Macintosh mouse and the Microsoft mouse. A roller ball on the bottom of the mouse is coupled to two rotating vanes with slits in them, one for the horizontal and one for the vertical directions. As the ball is rotated, slits in the vane interrupt beams from light-emitting diodes that illuminate phototransistors. Each interruption event marks a movement.

Doug Englebart is generally credited with inventing the mouse at the Augmentation Research Center (ARC) at the Stanford Research Institute (SRI) in the early 1960s. Introduced widely at the 1968 Fall Joint Computer Conference in San Francisco by Englebart in a bravura performance, his vision of interactive computing and multimedia shown that day is regarded as one of the high points of early personal computer history.

Most buttons have a mouse-up and mouse-down (pressed) position, and the computer monitors for these conditions. Remember, a GUI is an event-driven program (see Chapter 4). The Macintosh mouse is a single-button animal, but many mice in the DOS world contain two or three buttons. The mouse on the Calcomp Wiz graphics tablet has three buttons, but each position has an up and a down position yielding six specific actions.

In GUIs, the most common mouse action for a button is the click. A click can initiate an object selection or associated action like a pull-down (actually a pop-down) menu activation. Combining a click and a drag (click-drag) is another action that will move an object or select a command on a menu. When the mouse button is released, that command is activated.

Mice are very valuable input devices for graphical user interfaces. They take up some space on your desk, but they are relative devices, an advantage, as noted earlier. Keep in mind that the direction of mouse movement depends on the absolute orientation of the mouse; if you move a mouse vertically, pick it up and rotate it 90 degrees, and then move it, the movement of the cursor on the screen is in the same direction. There are three types of mice: bus, serial, and regular. Bus and serial mice have already been described; regular mice connect to a special mouse port on the computer (IBM PC). There are also wireless mice on the market.

Trackballs

Trackballs are esentially mice turned upside down. Instead of moving the trackball about a surface, your hand rotates a ball inside the assembly. The mechanism is the same. It's generally believed that trackballs should have two buttons, one for clicking and the second for click-locking or latching. Latching allows you to activate a menu command and release it by clicking the latch button once more. This is easier for some people to use because without the latch you need good coordination to do the equivalent action of dragging with a mouse.

Trackballs require only their own footprint on your desk, which is a major advantage in tight space situations. However, most users find them harder to use for drawing or graphics applications, but comparable to the mouse for navigating an application's menu, selecting and manipulating objects, and doing general work with a GUI. Trackballs have perhaps a 10 percent penetration in the third-party replacement market for mice. Many users have both a mouse and trackball. I have used a Kensington TurboMouse trackball for the past two years exclusively, ever since the day I cut through my mouse cord and fried my ADB chip, and thus was given yet another opportunity to replace my motherboard.

New versions of trackballs and mice are at the forefront of development for three-dimensional input devices; this is particularly important for visualization and three-dimensional modeling. Graphic workstations often come with these devices, which combine movement in three dimensions. Before the 1990s end, microcomputers will ship with three-dimensional input devices standard.

Graphics Tablets

Graphics tablets, sometimes called digitizing tablets, are absolute input devices that allow a user to translate a mouse, puck, or pen movement to the screen. They come in many sizes and shapes, from a 12-inch square up to 3-foot square, and generally attach through a serial bus for a PC or the ADB on a Macintosh. Because a tablet takes up desk space, it's generally best to buy the smallest one that suits your needs. Obviously, if you are an architect tracing blueline drawings, you need a large tablet.

If you are working on a tablet, it doesn't make sense to try to use a keyboard at the same time. Most graphics tablets, therefore, support the use of templates that have most application commands defined. Different areas of the tablet are reserved for special actions. For example, it is possible to buy a template for AutoCAD with its menu commands defined. Click in a specific area, and that command is executed. The user can also define areas for complex macros. Certain graphics tablets are being specially built to recognize handwriting through artificial intelligence programs, a variant of OCR where the user must train the program to recognize character styles.

It takes some training to get used to tablets, but they reward you with extremely fine resolution and the ability to create special effects. Good tablets are made by Kurta, SummaGraphics, and Calcomp, along with many others. One notable set of tablets from Wacom offers a pressure-sensitive electronic pen. Coupled with a color paint application, such as Time Art's Oasis (Mac) or its PC version called Lumena, it's possible to create in 24-bit color a piece of art that a French impressionist master would be proud of.

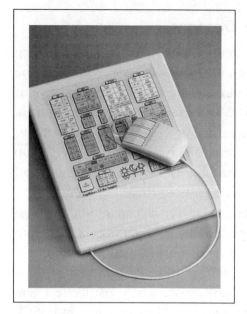

A.

B.

Figure 6-3 **(A)** The Wiz from Calcomp is a small, 1000 dpi resolution graphics tablet for either the PC (serial or mouse port) or Mac (ADB device) with dedicated application templates. It comes with either a multiple button (and function) mouse, or an electronic pen or stylus. *Courtesy of Calcomp.* **(B)** The graphics tablet from Kurta features large sizes, templates, and good ergonomics. *Courtesy of Kurta.*

Tablets are most useful for paint programs and as freehand tools for draw programs (including CAD).

Most first-time users of graphics tablets dislike them, but that is true of most new input devices. It takes time to learn a new input device, and some patience. CAD users know and use graphics tablets, and many artists and graphic designers have learned to use them as well. Artists find that graphics tablets have a natural drawing motion, but tablets probably aren't for the average computer user. Tracing can be very time consuming, and most casual users find that their tracing needs are better served by a digital scanner where autotracing functions built into graphics programs can convert a bit map to an outline (called raster-to-vector conversion; see Chapter 9).

Disk Drives/Storage Devices

If you are gearing up to do a desktop publishing project or getting involved with computer graphics, you will soon recognize the necessity of large storage devices. Aside from the rather obvious need to have a place to put WordPerfect or PageMaker, both of which use about 5 MBytes of storage in their current incarnations, files created on graphics programs can be enormous. A good setup for DTP and graphics uses at least four or five major programs and several minor utilities. You need a hard drive large enough to accommodate your complete working environment and any files you create. You also need some method of getting the data into your computer. In this chapter we consider various equipment options for working with your files and creating data input.

Text files created on a word processor such as WordPerfect generally are small because they require only a position and ASCII character description. A two- to three-page letter to a friend takes up about 4 KBytes. An average chapter in this book, which consists of 40,000 to 70,000 character, ranges from 40 to 80 KBytes in size in Microsoft Word 4.0 (Mac). Do the appropriate arithmetic and you'll find that about 10 percent of a word processor file is used for extra formatting marks. (Check this out by saving a file as "Text only" and comparing file sizes.) The text for an entire 500-page book can fit onto a single 1.44 MByte floppy disk with a little space left over.

You can also get a few pages of layout text from a DTP layout program onto a 1.44 MByte floppy, provided it doesn't contain many graphics. Lines, boxes, and text—anything that your computer can store as an object—are stored compactly. Patterns or fills also are described compactly using a unit cell description (like building a crystal). Any feature requiring a bit map, however, such as a scanned image that has nonregular features, can quickly eat your supply of floppies. Combine color and bit maps and you are into the multimegabyte range. Mix in animation and some sound, and you are in the hundreds of megabyte to gigabyte range. So it's easy to see why having the right storage is so important.

A single scanned 8½- by 11-inch page containing 24-bit color pictures might run from 5 to 10 MBytes or more. That one image requires 30 to 40 MBytes (without file compression) to create the four digital separations that will become the masters for the process colors you turn over to your printer. A typical page of advertising laid out in QuarkXPress (a leading Macintosh DTP layout programs and a leader in prepress color) might average 1 or 2 MBytes in size because it creates links to the graphics files that are to be embedded in it. That Quark file is still attached by the links to the four process color files, 30 to 40 MBytes in size.

The page layout file for a book that includes all of the graphics and page elements can be enormous; its size depends almost entirely on how many graphics there are. With only simple line art as graphics, a 500-page book still can easily fill up a medium-size hard drive. This book, if it had been done entirely digitally, would have taken maybe 1 gigabyte (1,000 MBytes) of storage and maybe twice that amount to prepare master copy for printing. An optical disk (see "Optical Drives") can be a valuable, cost-effective solution for storage at this level.

Anyone who has ever backed up a 40 MByte hard drive with floppies will probably understand the strange looks and spirited conversation you get from digital separation people (who feed the high-end imagesetters) when you hand them a few boxes of floppies for color seps. Who wants to spend an hour copying a file? Having a portable hard drive helps, but you're unlikely to want to mail it back and forth for jobs. The answer to this kind of problem is to invest in megafloppies, SyQuest or Bernoulli cartridges, or other removable hard drive disks.

There are answers to file size dilemmas. The most promising one for the near future is file compression. Using software, you can squeeze files, although it's too slow for problems in animation or sound. But for files of static images used in DTP or graphics software, software compression works fine with floppies when your files are under 5 MByte. Software compression applications are described at the end of this chapter. Motion and sound require hardware solutions, and these are discussed in Chapter 18. The threshold will be raised enormously when compression is combined with optical storage, such as CDs.

Floppy Drives

Every microcomputer user works with floppy disk drives; currently they are the means of distribution of most of the software bought and sold in the world today. The invention of the floppy disk arose out of research work done at the IBM San Jose Laboratory for the System/370 mainframe in 1967. A team of researchers, led by Alan Shugart, enclosed a disk made out of the same material used for magnetic tape inside a nonwoven fabric envelope. So named to differentiate it from the hard platter disks in use (Winchester drives), the floppy disk contributed mightily to the explosion in the personal computer industry by providing a low-cost storage solution. Prior to the introduction of the floppy disk, microcomputers used audio-type tape storage. Audio tape was low-density storage allowing only serial access whereas floppies greatly increased storage capacity and provided random disk access.

Floppy disks come in two basic sizes: the 5 ¼-inch flexible floppy disk used in the IBM PC, PC compatibles, and the Apple II series of computers; and the rigid 3 ½-inch plastic-case–enclosed floppy disk developed by Sony Corporation and used on the Apple Macintosh and also on many IBM PCs and compatibles. Over the years the floppy disk has increased in data density and storage capability by lowering the required magnetic field strength of the read/write heads and using denser media. Thus it is possible to format a 1.44 MByte microfloppy (1.6 MByte unformatted) for a Macintosh at either the full 1.44 MByte density using a Macintosh floppy disk high density (FDHD) drive (also known as the SuperDrive), or to format that disk using an 800 KByte drive. There are 2.88 MByte floppies on the market now; one is used with the NeXT computers.

The Macintosh SuperDrive reads 800 KByte disks and formats them. You can tell the difference between a 800 KByte disk, which Sony calls double density (DD), and a 1.44 MByte disk called high density (HD) by the addition of a second locking window on the upper left-hand corner of the disk. On the Macintosh, an 800

KByte drive will not recognize a 1.44 MByte formatted disk, and will request that you reformat it. Note: Doing so erases your data. You can use an 800 KByte disk drive to format a 1.44 MByte disk in the 800 format, but it is not recommended. The increased strength of the magnetic field in the 800 KByte disk drive can damage the HD disk and will eventually lead to disk errors and lost data.

Keep in mind that although a disk has a capacity of 800 KBytes, some space is used up when you initialize the disk to write the circular lines that mark the *track* and the straight radial lines that separate each track into a *sector*. Additionally, floppies maintain a directory file called the Desktop file on a Macintosh and a File Allocation Table (FAT) on an IBM PC. On a Macintosh, 779 KBytes is available; 7 KBytes are used for the Desktop, and the remainder are used for marking the disk. Hard drives operate in a similar manner.

Similarly, you can buy flexible floppy disks that can be formatted as 1.2 MByte, 800 KByte, 720 KByte, or 400 KByte disks, depending on the specifications of the drive in your computer or the settings you use with DOS's Format command. MS-DOS allows you automatically to format a disk at a certain density, but you can change this to a lower density if desired. However, an 800 KByte drive can only format a disk to 800 KBytes. The IBM PC world is in the process of converting from flexible floppies to rigid ones, and if you are purchasing an IBM PC or clone it makes sense to get both a 5 ¼-inch and a 3 ½-inch drive at the highest density ratings. Whatever disk you buy or use, try to be cognizant of the format when using it or sending it to someone else to use.

You can buy external floppy disk drives for both Macintosh and PCs that allow you to format and read the various size disks, and to convert from one machine's format to another. One example of a Macintosh diskette drive with IBM compatibility is the DynaFile. Certain utilities allow you to mount PC files on the Macintosh desktop, others such as the Apple File Exchange (supplied as part of the Macintosh system software) allow for file conversion. The better networks, like TOPS, that connect Macs and IBM PCs together also offer some file translation, which changes a file's internal formatting. Chapter 13 examines this aspect of intermachine communication; "File and Disk Conversion" looks specifically at some of the products on the market.

Megafloppy Drives

Floppies are nearing the end of their useful life as the standard for low-end storage . If you don't believe that, trying loading some of the current generation of sophisticated applications into your computer. Windows 3.0 takes seven 720 KByte disks. Some of the recent games from Sierra On-Line shipped as *boxes* of disks. Sierra is now introducing two games on CD ROM and is also planning to sell a CD ROM drive. CD ROM technology is fertile ground for interactive games, new methods of paperless publishing, and dense storage of read-only data. It is discussed in Chapter 19.

It's been estimated that the current type of floppy can be made with as much as 5 MByte storage capacity. Several companies are working with prototypes at this level. However, by the time 5 MByte floppies are introduced in 1992, they will have been eclipsed by a megafloppy format in the tens or hundred-mega-byte range. Several are on the market today, and their wide acceptance as a primary storage device awaits only mass production and downpricing. The drives are about twice as expensive as floppy drives; the disks are about 1.5 times the cost on a per-megabyte basis.

Medium-size magnetic removable storage devices, which many people refer to as "megafloppies," or removable media drives, have been on the market for about three or four years and are reliable. Many companies offer this technology, but there are only a small number of primary manufacturers or original equipment manufacturers (OEMs) of these mechanisms and the matching disks. Three OEMs are Iomega, SyQuest, and Kodak/Verbatim. They license the technology to other companies that serve as value added resellers (VARs) for packaging and sale. These VARs include companies such as Microtech, PLI, MassMicrosystems, MicroNet, LaCie, and many others. The situation is similar for hard drives. Companies such as Seagate, Quantum, Imprimis-Wren, Conner, and Rodime sell to dozens of other companies. Right now there are only three or four optical drive mechanism manufacturers, including Sony, Ricoh, and Maxtor.

Iomega pioneered the removable drive with its Bernoulli box. Its bulky 10 MByte cartridges have since been replaced by slim 44 MByte, 5 ¼-inch cartridges. Inside a Bernoulli box is a flexible disk that spins on a cushion of filtered air. A change in air pressure brings the media within the appropriate distance of the read/write head. If a dust particle is on the media, the disk flexes to accommodate it. Bernoulli boxes have excellent reliability and are not subject to disk crashes. They are sold for both the IBM PC and Macintosh.

Kodak/Verbatim disks are ultra-hard floppy disks that can store up to 20 MBytes of data. While they are faster than floppy disks, they are slower than other removable technology and have not had major impact in the marketplace.

The 45 MByte removable drives have become popular as backup units for large hard drives, as replacements for hard

Figure 6-5
A 44 MByte Bernoulli
drive, mechanism,
and cartridge.

drives, and as work disks for special projects. (Quoted drive capacity depends on the formatting software used and the company's veracity. The one I use has a 42.5 MByte capacity, but it's billed as a 44 MByte drive.) They are great media for doing desktop publishing work, are very portable, and are handy for transporting large graphics or publication files to service bureaus. They have flexible disks or hard drive platters that spin at hard drive speeds, and their access times have dropped to 20 milliseconds, only slightly slower than some of the best hard drives on the market today. Fast hard drives have access times that range from 12 to 16 milliseconds. After several years of backing up onto floppies, few things are more satisfying than using Redux software to back up my Quantum 170 (from APS) to my Microtech SyQuest drive. SyQuest cartridges range from $70 to $130; drives cost between $650 and $1,300, depending on where and how you purchase them. SyQuest has introduced an 88 MByte cartridge drive (in a format incompatible with its 45 MByte drives).

Removable-media megafloppies will serve you well. They offer unlimited capacity, flexibility, convenience, security, and moderate media cost. In all of the modern applications described in this book where hard drives are used, megafloppies are a useful alternative. Keep in mind that if you have a removable drive and you intend to use the cartridge elsewhere (say at your friendly service bureau), each drive requires its own specific device driver. It is an INIT file on a Macintosh or a device driver loaded by your CONFIG.SYS file on the PC.

Hard Drives

Hard drives developed as a result of research at IBM in the mid-1950s, and rate as one of the most significant early achievements in computer technology. The first data written from card to disk is purported to have taken place in 1954. The first mass storage file server was shipped with the IBM 305 RAMAC computer in 1956. That file server had two read/write heads for 50 double-sided disks; the IBM 1301, introduced in 1961, had 100 heads, one for each disk in the drive. By the late 1960s the IBM 3040 disk unit had two 14-inch platters with 1.7 million bits per square inch that stored 30 MBytes of data each. The 3040 was dubbed the "Winchester" by Ken Haughton at IBM after the 30-30 caliber and powder weight configuration of the Winchester rifle he kept at home. Even today many people refer to hard drives as Winchesters. Alan Shugart and Finis Conner formed Seagate Technology in 1979 and shipped the first 5 ¼-inch Winchester drives for personal computers six months later. This was a year after the first trio of modern microcomputers appeared on the scene.

The basic concept of the hard drive is very similar to that of the floppy, except that it uses one or more rigid disks, called platters, spinning at high speed. Platters store data at several times the density of floppy disks, spin constantly (floppies spin only when being accessed) in an order of magnitude faster speeds, and have very exacting tolerances. A particle of dust can cause the read/write head to impact the platter instead of riding on a thin cushion of air. This is called a *head crash* (or disk crash), and in these days of hardened coating, crashes generally lead to soft errors requiring reformatting rather than permanently damaged sectors or clusters. To protect the platter, hard drives are enclosed in air-filtered boxes and contain fans to throw off the heat they generate.

Connecting Hard Drives and Megafloppies

Hard drives or megafloppies connect to your computer through a parallel port where data moves in and out in several concurrent data streams. For the Macintosh, that interface conforms to the small computer system interface (SCSI) standard. Other I/O bus standards exist for the IBM PC, but IBM seems to be endorsing SCSI for its PS/2 line of computers, and it is a recommended standard for that platform as well. Peripheral devices such as hard drives, scanners, and so on that conform to this standard are called *SCSI devices,* and connecting them together is done in a daisy-chain fashion referred to as a *SCSI chain.* In a daisy chain, devices are connected in a linear fashion via cables. The devices are assigned unique addresses between 0 and 7 (7 represents the highest priority). Eight devices may be connected in a chain; the Macintosh itself counts as one device.

In theory, it's easy to take your Macintosh hard drive (provided it's an external drive), carry it down to your local service bureau, or across the country, connect it to a Mac and be up and running in seconds for a whiz-bang product demo. Practice works as theory so long as you do not have multiple devices on the SCSI chain. You must be particularly careful when configuring SCSI chains with multiple devices because the current SCSI implementation is one ornery beast. Problems include nonfunctioning devices, data transfer errors, and damaged disk structures. Plug a SCSI device into a computer that is on and you may cause damage to your computer's circuits.

Hard drives are a highly recommended element of a fully configured microcomputer. In fact, it's just not practical to try to do most of the work described in this book with only one or two floppy disk drives. External drives offer portability and do not tax your computer's power supply, but they do take up extra space. After endless debate over the merits of internal versus external drives, I decided to go with external drives not only because of the reasons just mentioned, but because they are more straightforward to configure in an SCSI chain. The speed of your disk drive will make a noticeable difference in the overall speed of your computer. You can get a significant performance boost by buying a faster drive.

Future developments of virtual memory, special disk caching schemes, and new disk controllers will continue to make hard drives important in microcomputers for several years to come. Also, as hard drives become larger, and backup becomes more important, many vendors will build mirroring and duplexing into their hard drives. Mirroring is a software technique for writing the data from one hard disk to another, and it takes twice the time of a single-write system. Duplexing is a hardware technique in which a disk controller (normally an add-in bus card) writes data to two hard drives at the same time.

How much disk drive capacity is enough? That depends on what your applications are. Minimum configurations have 40 MBytes of storage, enough for five major applications in a working environment. You can do page layout and word processing, along with some graphics, but not scanned art, color, sound, or animation. A much more reasonable minimum is an 80 or 100 MByte drive, which gives the additional space to work with scanned art and color separate one complex page. If you are doing prepress, animation, or sound, then your need for disk storage is exceptional, probably in the hundreds of megabytes. Popular large hard drives are now sold in the 300, 600, and even a gigabyte range, and they are also used as servers on networks. Prices for hard drives have dropped dramatically in the recent past; 80 MByte drives sell for $600, 170 MByte drives for under $1,000. Optical storage devices, described next, begin to be practical at the 600 MByte range.

▼ *Tip: Working with large hard drives or megafloppies increases your need for regular backup and disk maintenance. Try to purchase disk storage and your backup device at the same time. Whereas a corrupted floppy disk can ruin a project, a corrupted hard drive has the potential of destroying everything you've painstakingly created. File recovery utilities installed on your hard drive are useful but not totally reliable; the best insurance is a mirror-image backup to another media. Make triple copies of important projects. Then if your drive is damaged you still have a chance of recovery on another computer or storage device.*

Optical Drives

Optical storage technology comes in three varieties: CD ROM (see Chapter 19), WORM (write once, read many), and erasable optical drives. Optical disks store information as microscopic pits on the disk surface. (Erasable optical uses magnetic polarization of the media as well.) Laser reflections from the surface of pits and flat surfaces are read as binary ones and zeros. These technologies are amazingly reliable because they read and write with light and there is no mechanical contact, but the formats are not compatible. Jukebox optical drives on the market offer truly astronomical storage capabilities; they are useful for government archival storage and other large database users.

WORM drives have been on the market for nearly three years now, and their primary use is in archival or backup applications. Their estimated life span for data integrity is 100 years. Platters store 650 MBytes per side on double-side cartridges, with gigabyte sizes becoming common. WORM drives are compatible with Macs and PCs, requiring only connectors and a new software driver. WORM technology began on mainframes and has migrated down to microcomputers. A major disadvantage of WORM technology is that there are several incompatible standards; disks are even incompatible between drives. It is widely believed that erasable optical technology will lead to the demise of WORM drives, but given a 100-year storage lifetime, WORM continues to appeal in niche markets such as data archives for government and libraries.

Erasable magneto-optical drives appeared on the market for small computers in 1989. They combine the great storage capacity of optical drives (300 MBytes per side, 600 MBytes per disk on average) with the read/write capability and portability of removable media. Optical floppies, which some wags call "flopticals," are being developed in labs today and are starting to appear as commercial products. The typical size is 150 MBytes for 3 ½-inch platters. Optical storage is nearly ideal for applications such as full-color publishing, digital sound, and animation projects attempted from the desktop.

The first computer to ship with an erasable optical drive was the NeXTcube. Initially 5 ¼-inch erasable optical drives cost between $3,500 and $6,000, with cartridges costing around $150 each. Optical technology is still rather expensive, but competitive with other technologies on a per-megabyte basis, and it will get cheaper. It is estimated that within the next three or four years optical drives will be preferred over magnetic hard drives as standard deep storage on personal computers.

So-called flopticals and other erasable optical drives are not yet standardized and are still too slow to serve as primary drives, but they are improving. Their current access times range from about 35 to 90 milliseconds, about two to five times as fast as modern magnetic floppies, but three to four times slower than fast hard drives and two to three times slower than digital audio tape. Sony estimates media life and data integrity from ten to twenty-five years for its new glass substrate disks. It also believes its optical devices will approach hard drive speeds within five years.

Digital Tape

Magnetic tape drives have never really disappeared from the scene, and although they are no longer used as primary storage devices, they are excellent for data backup. There are many units on the market today, the most popular based on cassette tape cartridges in the 40 to 80 MByte size manufactured by 3M Corporation. Pricing is from $650 to $1,500 for cassette units, with $25 to $50 for the cassettes. Open reel nine-track units run from $4,000 to $8,000 and store 150 MBytes of data. Cassette tapes hold 250 MBytes and more; times have changed.

The problem with tape storage is that you must access data serially, and that limits its potential to serial applications. Also, standards are not formalized between vendors. You can restore a drive, or use tape to access and play a large file, but it's impractical to use this technology to achieve multiple access to files; it is simply too slow. Tape does have the potential to work with very large single files, but it is too slow a medium to work in real-time applications.

However, the introduction of digital audio tape (DAT) for computer applications will greatly enhance the storage capacity of tape drive technology. DAT, the same technology that allows nearly flawless copies of audio to be made, can be applied to tape storage using almost the same equipment as its audio counterpart. DAT offers storage in the 1 to 2 gigabyte range for a cassette no bigger than a standard audio cassette. It's the perfect complement to optical storage devices. Early DAT units have been introduced as network backup units and have been fairly pricey, in the $4,000 to $5,000 range, but by 1992 units in the $800 range will be on the market.

Modems

Modems are devices for converting electronic signals into audio signals so that text and files, including DTP documents, can be transmitted over phone lines. The name comes from the contraction of the terms for modulation of the digital signals into audio signals and demodulation of the audio signal into digital data. Modem transfers are rated by their speed in bits per second (bps) or, less precisely, in a related unit of their baud rate, where baud refers to the number of transfer "events" per second. At high speeds modems can transmit multiples of two, four, or more event codes per bit. A 1200 baud modem can transmit 600 events per second. Most modems are quoted in baud speed, and you can get modem rated at 300, 1200, 2400, 4800, 9600, and soon at 19,200 baud top speed. The faster a modem is, the more expensive it is. Prices for 2400 baud (the current standard) range from $120 to $350. When a modem connects with a slower modem, both communicate at the slower speed. A noisy telephone line will also reduce the transfer rate. Using modems, direct file transfer between computers is fairly easy to achieve by phone, even between dissimilar computers.

Faster transfer rates reduce connect charges and phone tolls. Although a 9600 baud modem can cost $1,000 to $1,500, and on-line services charge more for higher transfer rates, heavy users of telecommunication services can generally recover the cost of the modem over time. Modems are especially practical when shared by multiple users on a network. Although 9600 baud protocols are not yet standardized, several on-line services support them. High-speed (and higher priced) modems often come with such niceties as communications software, error correction, data compression, and long warranties. Most 300 and 1200 baud modems use Bell protocols. Higher 2400 and 9600 baud modems use CCITT standards. Hayes-compatible modems and their instruction set have become a de facto industry standard. The Hayes command set is a desirable feature, although few modems emulate them exactly.

Telecommunications sessions have a bewildering array of settings and agreed conventions (called *protocols*) that must be set before data transfer can take place. These include: speed rates, character width, stop bit (end mark for a character), parity (error detection), handshake (a pause message), and file transfer protocols such as XModem, Binary, YModem, and ZModem, among others. Good telecommunications packages such as Microphone II (Mac, Win, NeXT), White Knight (Mac), and DynaComm (Win), offer canned settings for services and special built-in scripts or macros to guide you through an on-line session. On-line services also have caught on and now offer their own proprietary software to guide the user through the maze of services, forums, and databases. Telecommunications is discussed in more detail in Chapter 13.

Modems and DTP

Modems and telecommunications have a definite place in desktop publishing, although they are not as pervasive today as they will be in the future. The data transfer rate in use today limits the applications to which you can apply telecommunications. At 2400 baud, it takes an hour to transfer about an 800 KByte floppy disk's worth of data. That's fine for communicating notes (equal to about 400 pages of text per hour) but it limits you severely in terms of transferring graphics. Even with the fastest modems in use today, we will need a new communications architecture to allow rates fast enough to transfer large files.

Fax Modems

A fax (from the word facsimile) is the process by which a document may be imaged and transferred to another user. Stand-alone fax machines have become business standards. They scan a page, code it into a bit-mapped image using a transmission protocol standard (the Group 3 CCITT standard), and transmit by phone a 9600 (4800 or 2400 for a noisy line) baud signal. A second fax receives the transmission, rasterizes the page, and then prints it out. Standard fax machines offer 200 by 100 dpi resolution, or 200 dpi in both directions if the "fine" mode is used; only 2-bit black and white is supported. That's pretty crude by computer graphic standards. A Group 4 standard that's in the works will improve greatly on current resolution, making graphics transmission more acceptable. Information International Inc. (Triple-I) already markets a product dubbed the 3750 Facsimile Film Scanner, which allows the transmission of page film at over 1,000 dpi resolution.

Still, high-resolution fax film scanners are very expensive, costing thousands of dollars. There's a cheaper solution: a modem to communicate, a scanner as an input device, and a printer as an output device. The machine or board used to create the file transfers is referred to as a fax modem. These modems, which can be purchased as external units or add-in boards, have the CCITT standard with its associated compression and error correction built in. They can send whole data files and graphics to a fax machine or another computer without loss of quality, and give you the best level of resolution available.

Fax modems offer many benefits over dedicated fax machines. If you already own a computer, then they offer economy of integration and are less expensive than dedicated faxes. Other advantages include: superior printing, sophisticated queueing, no scanning noise or crooked alignment problems, and no loss of quality for transferred documents. Since fax modems also double as regular modems, there is some savings in having a combined unit. On the other hand, fax machines are cheaper as stand-alone units, don't require a scanner if you want to transmit a document that wasn't created on a computer, don't tie up your computer while images are created, don't tie up your printer or modem ports, and don't necessitate leaving your computer on to receive messages. Other problems experienced in current fax modem technology include difficulty in attaching signatures (see MyScript listing, Appendix A), PDL coding inclusion, and mismatched type resolution that requires the use of an outline font renderer, such as the Adobe Type Manager.

Early adopters of fax modems have generally liked the overall idea of the technology while being somewhat dissatisfied with its implementation. Poor hardware and software have plagued early units, but the technology is improving over time. Software in particular has been a major problem and should be important in guiding your purchase in this technology. Solutions, Inc., sells a set of fax software products for the Macintosh (BackFAX, FAXGate, and CommGATE) that have been well received. Fax modems are now available as send-only 4800-baud units for as low as $250. Send-and-receive units at the standard 9600 baud cost between $700 and $1,000.

Even if you don't own a fax modem you can participate in fax madness. Commercial on-line services, such as CompuServe, MCI Mail, AT&T Mail, and Connect allow you to upload text files and send them to fax machines. Some can also send graphics files. They charge extra for the service, but not as much as you would pay if you went down the street to your friendly copy center to send a fax. Western Union's EasyLink accepts ASCII files up to 300,000 characters, or graphics files up to 2 MBytes in PostScript, TIFF, or .PCX formats. (See Chapter 10 for a discussion of these formats.) Current charges are 55 cents for the first 1,250 characters, 35 cents for each additional 1,250 characters. Sending PostScript allows you to embed formatting, select fonts and point sizes, and customize your document. EasyLink and MCI Mail will store your letterhead, and add text as you wish. The AT&T Mail service is called MailFax, and it transmits graphics files. Cost is 55 cents for the first half page, 40 cents for each additional half page. MCI Mail calls their service Fax Dispatch. MCI Mail allows only ASCII Text for its fax dispatch service.

Be aware, however, that fax technology is an inefficient way of sending ASCII text because it takes character-based data and translates it into bit maps. This turns a 3 KByte text file into a 50 KByte file (120 KByte for fine mode). It is, on the other hand, a useful way of transferring graphics files where images are bit mapped initially. Once better standards are implemented for faster transmission and higher resolutions, and the optical character recognition (OCR) standard for reconversion back to ASCII is added, this technology will become more practical. Intercomputer communications are almost always more efficient sent as computer files, but for dissimilar computers and in desktop publishing applications for graphics transfers, fax is useful technology.

Level 2 PostScript will give rise to PostScript fax devices in 1991. A PostScript fax printer allows a person to send a full-resolution document to another person with a PostScript Fax printer as easily as printing on a network printer. If the fax is sent to an ordinary fax machine, a PostScript fax printer converts the file to the standard CCITT format.

File Compression

Formatted text, and particularly graphics files, contain considerable redundant information. When you draw a square in a paint program, your computer stores a representation of it as a bit map when all that really needs to be stored is its boundaries, fill pattern (maybe represented by a primitive cell or smallest representative unit), line weight, and fill. Scanned and color images, in particular, are unnecessarily large. Describing them in this alternative way, similar to the way draw programs operate, would save a lot of storage space. Certain computer routines or algorithms (equations) allow you to compress files into special storage formats called *archives*. When you need to use the compressed files again, you run the complementary algorithm to decompress the files. Many computer programs, including database managers, graphics and digital image programs, among others, employ compression utilities internally as part of their programming in a manner that is transparent to the user to prevent unwieldy operation.

How much compression you can achieve is dependent on the file and the particular algorithm you use. There are two main types of compression: *lossless* and *lossy*. Lossless compression preserves all the original file data, but can achieve only a 2:1 compression ratio. Lossless is used for compressing files like binary programs, where every bit is important. Lossy compression, on the other hand, allows some data loss (fine for graphics) and can achieve ratios of up to 200:1.

You can achieve 35-percent to 50-percent reduction for formatted word processor files, 50 percent for draw files, 65 percent for database files, 85 percent for paint files, and over 95 percent for scanned and full-color images. These are ballpark figures and can vary depending on the programs used.

File compression routines have long been used for telecommunication purposes to save on transfer and connect charges, and they're built into many telecommunication protocols. Nearly all on-line services and bulletin boards store their files as archives and require users to decompress them. In the IBM PC world the

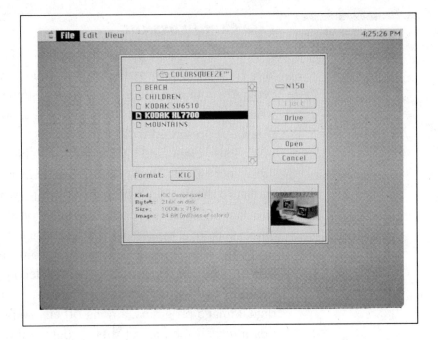

Figure 6-7
The Kodak Color-
squeeze Open File dia-
log box shows in the
lower right corner a
thumbnail image of a
highlighted file in Kodak
Image Compression
(KIC) format. Users can
view the reduced image
to decide if they want to
decompress the image.
Pixel measurements are
also shown. An 800
KByte file can be com-
pressed to 40 KBytes
within 40 seconds using
this program. *Courtesy
of Kodak, Inc.*

original standard for telecommunication compression was ARC
from System Enhancement Associates. The program is a "shareware" and may be found on many bulletin boards such as ARC.xxx,
where xxx is the version number; 500 and above is current. Perhaps the most popular compression utility today on the PC for
telecommunication applications is the PKZIP utility. Compressed
files generally bear the .ARC or .ZIP suffix to indicate that they are
archives. One program on the PC for graphics file compression is
ImagePrep (Win).

StuffIt is the compression standard for the Apple Macintosh.
Written by Raymond Lau when he was fifteen years old, StuffIt
started life as a shareware program and evolved into StuffIt
Deluxe, with a reputation for being nearly bulletproof. (A shareware version called StuffIt Classic with a reduced feature set of
StuffIt Deluxe is still offered.) StuffIt allows folders and file hierarchy to be maintained in an archive and supports several compression schemes. Archives stored in this format are given the .SIT
suffix. StuffIt Deluxe can UNZIP ZIP files and allows for the cre-

ation of self-decompressing archives, as do other compression utilities. Two other highly regarded Macintosh file compression utilities are DiskDoubler and Compactor Pro. This class of utility is worth its weight in gold.

Figure 6-8
StuffIt Deluxe from Aladdin Systems supports various compression schemes, file structure maintenance, viewing inside an archive, and many useful utilities.

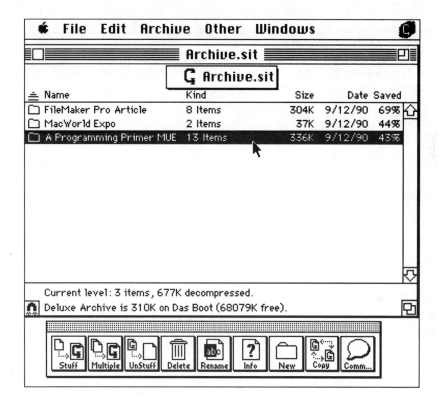

There are many proprietary programs for compressing files that haven't been mentioned here due to space considerations, but be assured, the next generation of personal computers all will have compression routines heavily embedded into various parts of their operation systems. Color, sound, animation—all of the leading edge technologies demand it. While compression can be achieved in software, it operates much faster when the program is encoded in a silicon microchip. See Chapters 10 and 18 for further discussions of file compression for graphics.

Output Tools

Nor ever once ashamed
So we be named
Pressmen; Slaves of the Lamp; Servants of the Light.
                                                    Sir Edward Arnold

Professional publishing from microcomputers would never have come to be if it were not for revolutionary advances in page description and printer technology. Whereas all desktop printers were once character based, they now have the ability to output almost any typeface or graphic element. What's more, device-independent page description languages (PDLs) like PostScript have made it possible to create a document, proof it on one type of output device (such as a desktop printer), then output it on a separate, high-resolution typesetter or imagesetter.

In this chapter we'll take a brief look at the evolution of micro-computer output, then survey the current field of PDLs, printers, imagesetters, plotters, film recorders, and other output technology.

Graphics Imaging

Once, all computer printers were character based. Characters were sent to a line printer in an ASCII stream, and if graphics were required they were composed of characters. ASCII includes some special codes for such things as carriage return, end of page, tabs, and so on, but no formatting. You can see an example of character-based graphics when you log onto a text-based on-line service.

173

Users often type the symbols :) to show that they are happy, or the symbol :(to show that they are angry or sad. You can compose elaborate graphics using characters, but the resolution of images is quite poor, limited by the smallest character and the size of the grid that you place them on.

MS-DOS is a character-based operating system, and you can print to a line printer with an ASCII stream through Edlin, DOS's built-in text editor; as you can any program that saves a file as "Text only." Graphics programs that run on top of MS-DOS use internal programs (routines) to create files that have graphics programs embedded in them. When printing graphics files, the printer driver executes the internal programs in that file to create graphic output that a particular printer can understand. You choose a printer driver from the Chooser desk accessory for the Macintosh, the Setup program for Windows or as part of the installation procedure for individual programs that run on MS-DOS. (You saw an example of an embedded PostScript program in a Microsoft Word file in Chapter 2.) The Apple Macintosh uses a

Figure 7-1
Printing a document requires a fusion of text and graphics by both software and hardware. Depending on your operating system and your printer, the final page is described either in your computer's or your printer's CPU. RAM in either device stores the page description until it can be printed by your printer's marking engine.

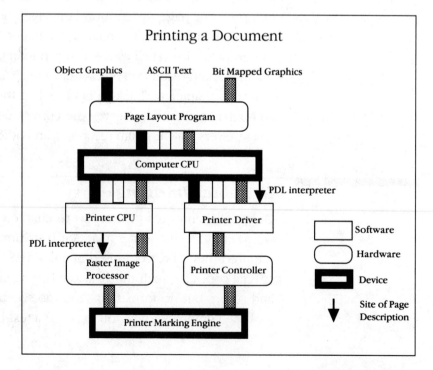

graphics-based operating system and manipulates objects with the QuickDraw. It doesn't require further interpretation if it outputs to a QuickDraw device, and thus has a speed advantage.

Today's printers can be switched from a character mode to a graphics mode by the print file they are executing at the moment. In a graphics mode the computer attempts to control the smallest feature that the printer can output. For a 9-pin dot matrix printer, the smallest resolvable feature is the spot that forms when each pin impacts the ribbon. For a laser printer or imagesetter, the smallest feature is the minimum spot size of the laser beam that is turned on and off to create the latent image on the photosensitive drum to which the toner sticks (or doesn't stick).

▼ *Tip: Always choose the printer driver before beginning a work session with a program. Your choice will affect all aspects of page definition, including margins, tab settings, character sizes, and so on.*

There is a limit to what computers can achieve. On certain output devices, images can be resolved at a level that is too dense to be fully exploited. Film has the capacity to record up to 12,000 lines per inch (lpi). In film recorders your computer is limited by the size of the pixels that it can create on the miniature CRT monitor inside the recorder; for a 7-inch screen, a spot 0.04 mm can yield 4,000 lines per inch on a 35 mm slide. This is at the high end of what can be achieved by computer imaging at this time.

Screen Description Versus Page Description

GUIs have Print Managers, a set of routines that serve as a referee between an application and needed device drivers. They assure that all applications that run on them print similarly. For a GUI, the process by which output is imaged is very similar to the process by which a screen frame is created. In the NeXT computer, the same imaging model, PostScript, describes both the screen and printer output. With Adobe Type Manager, fonts are described for both screen and printer using the same imaging model. What you see on the screen is therefore a close approximation to what you see in your output: WYSIWYG graphics. The output must be described as a file that can be executed by the device driver to write the image, just as electron beams write the image of a frame from the frame buffer in video RAM to your monitor.

Whatever the output media, whether ink on a page or silver crystals in film emulsion, the goal of your computer system is always to achieve the best resolution of which the output device is capable. This is called device independence, and we discussed its importance to graphics work in Chapter 2. Increases in microcomputer CPU speed and complexity and in memory size continue to motivate the development of new, more sophisticated imaging models for output. Whatever imaging model your computer uses will ultimately determine how successful it will be in trying to output a page at the highest resolution the output device allows, the kinds of equipment it can drive, and of what manipulations it's capable.

Page Description Languages

A page description language is a programming language that is used to describe printer output in a device-independent set of commands. A PDL tells the output device everything that will appear on the page. It describes:

- Type description and modification. Most PDLs create character outlines and a set of rules based on artificial intelligence to convert those characters to a bit map. This process is described in more detail in Chapter 11.

- Object definition. Graphics primitives, such as an object's fill, its line width (stroke) and fill, and its position can be described.

- Object groupings. PDLs allow objects to be grouped so that they can be manipulated in logical layers.

- Colors sets and/or grayscale values. Additional code describes how to create the patterns of ink a printer will use to create the finished piece (see Chapter 10).

- Special operators. Lines, arcs, dashes, miter joints, transformations, and so on may be part of a PDL description.

A PDL has a decisive influence in the quality of output. A program that outputs a file in a PDL can be output on any device that can interpret the commands contained in that file; your computer doesn't have to issue the standard printer control codes of a character-based printer. It uses the PDL codes instead. A PDL interpreter, which holds the page description code, can be implemented in software running on top of the operating system, or it can be hardwired into a ROM chip inside the output device. This is the case in printers called "PostScript," "TrueImage," or "PCL." Interpreters not built into printers and other output devices can be included as add-on boards or plug-in cartridges; these implementations are faster than incorporating the interpreter in software.

Because the file is interpreted, the output is dependent only on the resolution of the output device. PDLs are object-oriented programming languages. They describe a circle as a mathematical equation or a set of lines that can be scaled to any size and retain the resolution of the device interpreting the program. By contrast, a circle described as a bit map (as in a paint program) scales each bit by the resolution ratio of the output device, thus distorting the circle.

PDLs offer another technological advantage over controlling software that just passes ASCII characters to a printer. Using PDLs, it is possible to transfer the print file to the printer's memory (called downloading), and use the printer's microprocessor, thus alleviating some of the processing burden on your computer and freeing it up for other work.

PDLs and Graphics Printers

A graphics printer is composed of three elements: a page description language, a PDL interpreter, and a raster image processor (RIP).

Graphics printers, such as laser printers or imagesetters, are computers in their own right, as they have both memory and CPUs. Some, such as the impressive Optronics ColorSetter that was used to print the color plates in this book, are full-fledged, networked UNIX workstations. All this extra hardware is part of what makes them more expensive than simple line printers; the other added expense is in the license of the proprietary PDL that they might contain. Printers on the Macintosh that are called QuickDraw actually use the Macintosh CPU as a controller to drive the laser engine. TrueImage, the new PDL from Apple and Microsoft, will be first implemented in software.

The final element in a graphics printer is the controlling software that drives the marking engine. The interpreted graphics page is converted to a bit-mapped image of the page at the appropriate device resolution. This is very similar to the rasterizing process in a CRT monitor. It is referred to in output imaging as raster image processing, or RIP. A laser beam sweeps the drum in a laser printer; the controlling software turns the beam on and off, sweeps a line, and then sweeps the next line (see Figure 5.4). For a 300 dpi laser printer, this means 7 million dots on a letter-size page, a considerable amount of computation. RIP is a CPU-intensive process, and many graphics printers (especially higher-end devices such as imagesetters) contain specialized RIP boards built especially for this purpose.

Figure 7-2
The desk accessory Laser Queue is part of the SuperLaserSpool package. Print order is controlled by simply dragging the filenames. A good spooler offers the ability to change printers, change setup, pause or resume, and turn it off.

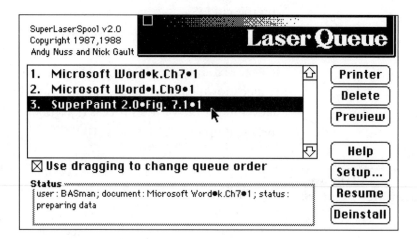

Print spoolers such as those built into Macintosh system Software or Windows, or commercial programs such as SuperLaserSpool (Mac) or SuperPrint (Windows 3.0), can free up your computer, as can print buffers. SuperLaserSpool (5th Generation

Software) offers print queueing for the Macintosh. It actually writes a file to your hard drive, thus freeing up your computer's CPU. A print buffer is a piece of hardware that contains RAM specifically for containing print files. It can be built into a printer or purchased separately. When a printer uses bit-mapped type built into the ROM, printing can be "rippingly" fast; but when fonts have to be "built" (constructed from outlines in software) and each dot's color or grayscale value must be calculated, printing can be agonizingly slow.

PostScript

PostScript is an advanced device-independent page description language developed by Adobe Systems (Mountain View, CA). Its introduction in 1985 was a key component in the desktop publishing revolution, and over the last five years it has become a de facto industry standard. It is licensed to several mainstream personal computer vendors, in over fifty printers, and in many other output devices. Many printers that do not come with built-in PostScript, such as the popular Hewlett-Packard LaserJet II and III, offer plug-in PostScript cartridges; Adobe sells the PostScript Cartridge and Pacific Data sells the PacificPage for the LaserJet II and III. The Adobe cartridge is somewhat cheaper and gives better results than the PacificPage. If you need to print PostScript files to non-PostScript printers on the IBM PC, you can use utilities such as the Printer Control Panel from LaserTools.

PostScript clones (emulation software) are also on the market today, including Freedom of the Press from CAI (Billerica, Massachusetts) (see Chapter 11). This device driver software (an emulator or interpreter) can turn a non-PostScript printer into a PostScript one. A professional version of Freedom of the Press supports varying levels of color. PostScript clone printers, such as the Qume CrystalPrint Publisher (an LCD-based printer), are also available.

PostScript has nearly 250 commands, far more than most other high-level programming languages. All of them are devoted to graphics and object manipulation. Its syntax is similar to FORTH, another high-level programming language. This example of a PostScript program would draw a simple box.

```
1.  gsave
2.  newpath
3.        270 72 moveto
4.        0 72 rlineto
5.        72 0 rlineto
6.        0 -72 rlineto
7.        -72 0 rlineto
8.  4 setlinewidth
9.  stroke
10. grestore
11. showpage
12. end
```

Figure 7-3
The square produced by the PostScript code just given in text. Note the notch in the lower left corner. PostScript lines are set from the center of the lines; therefore, a unit square does not get filled in. Using the endcap line feature, it is possible to complete the square.

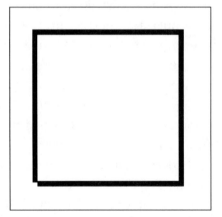

This example, taken from Michael Waite's chapter "Introduction to PostScript" in *Desktop Publishing Bible*, draws a box 72 pixels (6 inches) on each side with a 4-pixel line width (or stroke). You might ask, "Why bother learning PostScript? After all, it's built into the command structure of many graphics programs." The simple answer is that you can create many special effects with the language that are not available any other way. You can go into the text file that describes a page layout file and tweak a figure, create a starburst with any number of rays, or modify the screening pattern, fill pattern, or some portion of the page to your liking.

PostScript is a very rich graphics programming language, and like all PDLs, it includes tools for describing fonts as a set of outlines and then converting those fonts to bit maps. We discuss the process for this conversion, how subtle features in fonts are hinted in software using artificial intelligence routines, how they're encrypted, and the various font standards in Chapter 11. Font standards are intimately related to the imaging PDL that creates them, and font libraries and type manipulations are a prominent feature of PDLs. Adobe's fonts are built from Bézier curves, which you work with in PostScript drawing programs. Adobe has one of the largest font (type) libraries on the market; nearly 500 Adobe fonts have been licensed from several of the type houses.

The inside word on PostScript is that it has been deficient in creating complex halftone and color images. Adobe has worked hard over the last couple of years and released a new set of specifications for its second-generation PDL standard called PostScript Level 2. PostScript Level 2 products are currently available. This technology is an expanded superset of the original PostScript with significant speed enhancement for digital imaging, improved halftone screening algorithms, new data compression, composite fonts, device-independent color spaces, and support for printer-specific features. It should continue to maintain PostScript's dominant position in the electronic imaging market through 1993.

▼ Tip: At the moment, PostScript printers still offer some compelling technological advantages.

They are: compatibility with the higher-end imagesetters that you find at service bureaus; support for draw programs such as Adobe Illustrator, Aldus FreeHand, CorelDraw, Arts & Letters, and Micrografx Designer that use Bézier curves; encapsulated PostScript support (EPS, see Chapter 13); a larger typeface library; and standardization across a wide range of computer platforms including Mac, PC, UNIX, DEC, and others. See Appendix B for more references.

PCL

PCL is the page description language from Hewlett-Packard, and it comes built into Hewlett-Packard's LaserJet series of laser printers. These printers currently have 60 percent of the laser printer market outselling PostScript printers nearly five to one, and they are the standard for IBM PC users. The current version of this language is PCL5; it has the Agfa Compugraphic Intellifont scalable font technology and comes with several Intellifonts built into it. H-P offers many other typefaces based on Agfa's library, which is one of the largest in the industry. Only Bitstream's and Adobe's font libraries are larger.

Figure 7-4
The Hewlett-Packard LaserJet Series III is a 300-dpi, eight-page-per-minute laser printer with a feature called Resolution Enhancement. This is the LaserJet IIID printer. The D stands for duplex; each printer ships with two 200-sheet letter-size paper trays and allows for two-sided (duplex) printing. The top tray is an automatic 50 envelope feeder. *Courtesy of Hewlett-Packard.*

PCL is a less powerful PDL than PostScript but yields very good results for type. For applications that don't require sophisticated graphics manipulation, such as business correspondence, PCL5 is a good choice. Hewlett-Packard LaserJet series printers consistently earn very high marks from reviewers for the excellent features/cost ratios and their unusually high reliability.

Figure 7-5
Hewlett-Packard's
resolution enhancement
is an example of
advanced printing tech-
nology based on variable
dot size and artificial
intelligence techniques
for curve fitting.

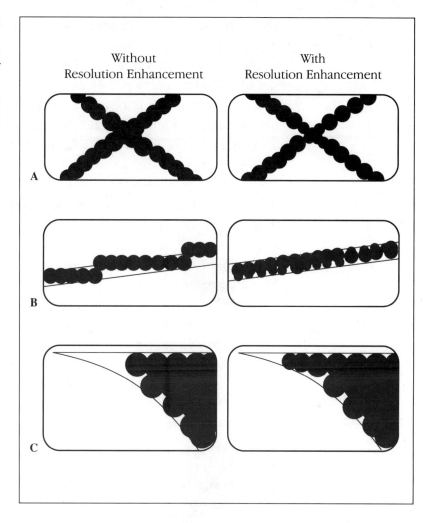

Without
Resolution Enhancement

With
Resolution Enhancement

A

B

C

**TrueType/
TrueImage**

Apple announced a new scalable outline font technology called
Royal in 1988–89. In it, fonts are stored and rendered using
quadratic equations, and the outlines for fonts are stored and rendered as part of the operating system software. This is an extension of Apple's proprietary Macintosh graphics routines called
QuickDraw, which images a screen and can output to a printer.

Microsoft purchased a company that created a PostScript clone
PDL, and in 1989 Apple and Microsoft cross-licensed each other's
technology to create what has come to be called the TrueType
fonts and the TrueImage PDL. TrueType/TrueImage is built into the
Macintosh system software (System 7), and into Microsoft's

Windows and the OS/2 Presentation Manager. As such, it will run on all of the most important GUIs for microcomputers in the next couple of years, with a basic set of fonts shipping with each.

Early demonstrations of TrueType/TrueImage have been impressive, and early adopters of the technology (especially Bitstream) have touted its technological advantages over PostScript. The announcements of TrueType/TrueImage lit up the computer industry's trade press in 1989. The battle of Adobe's PostScript versus Apple's Royal technology was dubbed the "Font Wars" (see Chapter 11). TrueType products were scheduled for mid-1991. The main benefit that TrueType currently offers is that it is keeping legions of computer writers employed. It's primary disadvantage is that whole forests have died describing it, thus adding to the greenhouse effect.

Service bureaus (and many users) at first disliked TrueType because it looked like it would muddy the waters and force them to support a second standard. However, it now appears that TrueType/TrueImage will download its rasterizing technology to non-TrueImage printers, and TrueImage printers will faithfully output PostScript files. Also, TrueType/TrueImage has broken Adobe's stranglehold on microcomputer PDLs and fonts (which can cost $300 a typeface), leading it to publish the specifications for its Type 1 font technology (which included much-coveted "hinting" instructions for high-resolution display of fonts at small point sizes). This opened up the PostScript font market to many more vendors, resulting in more and cheaper high-quality fonts.

Most likely, all computer users will benefit from these developments. The struggle to control the PDL technology is basically the struggle to control low-cost, high-quality print technology. A substantial amount of the price of a true PostScript printer was the cost of licensing PostScript inside the printer, so TrueImage printers will probably cost less. Microtek (Torrence, CA) introduced the first TrueImage printer, called TrueLaser, with thirty-five resident TrueType fonts built in; it also interprets PCL5 and PostScript. TrueImage will be built into the operating systems, and promises to be a faster technology than PostScript. As the basic set of TrueType fonts will be free, it will no doubt be used by average computer users and widely supported, but TrueType/TrueImage products will not be competitive with PostScript until 1993 at the earliest.

Printers and Imagesetters

Printer Architecture

Printers consist of a paper transport system, a marking engine, and a controller. Paper transport is normally belt or roller driven. The marking engine is driven by a print controller; it creates the marks on the page. In previous sections we addressed the software/hardware controller of a graphics printer. In this section we examine the important features of the marking engine.

Marking engines can be either positive- or negative-image print devices, more commonly referred to as write-black or write-white. An impact printer, such as a dot matrix or daisy wheel printer, is a write-black mechanism; pins or characters are impacted onto a ribbon, and the image is transferred directly to paper. For a laser printer or imagesetter, write-black places markings onto a latent imaging mechanism (normally a drum) that toner is attracted to; that toner is then transferred to paper. By comparison, a laser printer write-white mechanism creates the negative of the image to be transferred. Toner is *not* attracted to the latent image of a write-white printer, only the unwritten portion, and the transfer creates the desired positive image. Write-black results in better type quality at small point sizes because positive dots give fuller characters (as shown in Figure 7.6), for finer line strokes.

Print Resolution Versus Quality

The main difference between a graphics printer and an imagesetter is one of image resolution. Low-quality dot matrix printers can create a dot size of around 7 mm, or up to 150 dpi, referred to as letter- or near-letter quality printing. Laser printers commonly have medium dot resolutions of 3.3 mm or 300 dpi, moderate quality that permits for sharp type down to around 6 point, and mediocre digital images. Imagesetters have dot resolutions of 0.4 mm or 2,450 dpi; this is high quality that results in sharp type

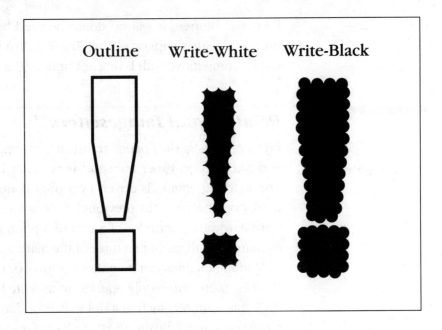

down to around 3 point and medium-quality digital images. Put another way, desktop printers produce ragged dots, imagesetters produce clean dots. Table 7.1 summarizes how resolution affects the results you can achieve.

Table 7.1 Printing Resolution Versus Application

Resolution	*Output Device*	*Application*
Low, less than 125 dpi	Dot matrix impact printer	Letters, short reading session material; poor type, very poor images
Low to moderate, 125 to 250 dpi	Near letter-quality impact printer, thermal transfer printers	Business correspondence; newspapers; moderate sans serif type, poor serif type quality, poor images

Table 7.1 Printing Resolution Versus Application *(continued)*

Resolution	*Output Device*	*Application*
Moderate, 300 to 500 dpi	Ink jet, thermal transfer, or laser printers, some daisy wheel printers	Brochures, books (mass market), magazines, and journals; good sans serif type, some serif type, modest image quality
High quality, 1000 to 2500 dpi	Imagesetters (and high-end microcomputer laser printers)	Books and other prolonged reading material; color work, advertising, annual reports; good type reproduction, good image quality
Very high quality, 2500 up	Film recorders	Photographic material; suitable for all materials, can be enlarged

As technology advances, low-cost laser printers are being built with advanced print engines, new marking engines are being introduced, and more sophisticated printing is appearing on the desktop. Enhancements such as variable dot sizes and AI routines for curve-fitting different size dots are being built into desktop printers to improve their overall image quality. Different dot shapes are being experimented with, but so far only round dots are used in print technology. LaserMax sells 1,000 dpi and 1,200 dpi laser printers, and the Mx6 $2,795 printer controller board for upgrading Apple LaserWriters to either 400 by 400 or 800 by 800 dpi. Clearly the differences between printers and imagesetters are blurring with time. In the sections that follow we examine the underlying technologies for output.

Dot Matrix Printers

The dot matrix printer has been the primary output device of the desktop computer industry. It is a low-speed impact printer that gives modest business-quality correspondence but is unsuitable for desktop publishing applications. Dot matrix printers are normally connected to serial ports (LPN for the PC, or the Printer or Modem port for the Macintosh). They are normally rated in characters per second. Printers of this type are the best solution available for applications requiring impact printing, such as business forms. For low-cost printing with extremely high reliability, this is proven technology.

The only other solution for impact printing is the daisy wheel printer. These printers have higher quality (up to 700 dpi), but don't offer graphics printing. Each font or character set for a daisy wheel is a separate type or font wheel and must be loaded onto the print mechanism, whereas dot matrix printers can create any pattern of dots.

Dot matrix printers have engine lifetimes (provided they receive regular yearly cleaning and maintenance) rated in the many hundreds of thousands of pages, which translates into ten years use in a busy office. The cost of printing can be a tenth of a cent, about the cost of the ribbon. A host of ribbon colors are available, and four-color ribbons can be used on many printers. Colored ribbons are usually blue, red, yellow, and black. Although four-color printing with ribbons is fairly ugly, spot colors and color type effects can be effective. Many applications support four-color dot matrix printing, particularly labeling programs. Check your application's documentation for specific instructions.

▼ *Tip: Printer ribbons often benefit from re-inking prior to use; even brand new ribbons perform better when ink is added.*

Once a ribbon is spent, you can re-ink it again for reuse. With care, a ribbon may be re-inked up to 50 times, but it should be discarded at the first sign of fraying. Computer Friends (Portland, OR) sells a series of re-inking machines called the MacInker and a PC equivalent for between $25 and $60, special inks, and even four-color ribbon ($15) re-inkers that quickly pay for themselves.

The printing mechanism in a dot matrix printer is a set of pins or tiny wires driven by solenoids (electronically switchable magnets) to impact on an inked ribbon. The most common dot matrix printer has nine pins, although some of the near letter-quality printers have as many as 24 to 30 pins. You should expect to pay anywhere from $300 for the former, up to $1,400 for the latter. The number of pins a printer has, and the number of passes the pin set makes for each line of type, directly affects the print quality you receive.

Certain printers, such as the Apple ImageWriter II (an Epson clone printer manufactured by Toshiba), offer three print qualities: best (144 vertical by 160 horizontal dpi), faster (72 by 80 dpi), and draft. The ImageWriter is a 9-pin printer with a pin size of 0.4 mm (16/1000 inches), dot size is 7 mm in diameter. In draft mode, the Macintosh reverts to character printing and sends the ASCII code to the ImageWriter. The ImageWriter then prints one of its built-in fonts encoded in printer ROM. When faster mode is selected, the Macintosh creates a bit map that prints a pixel for representation of your Macintosh screen display, along with an 11-percent horizontal distortion that can be removed by choosing the Tall Adjusted printing option. The best mode prints at twice the resolution of the Macintosh screen by passing over each line twice. For the second pass the page is advanced half a dot height so that the dots overlap by 50 percent.

▼ *Tip: When printing pages containing significant amounts of black ink, it's important to allow the printer to cool off between pages. The pins and solenoids of impact printers can heat up to such an extent that the print heads can bend and be destroyed, requiring expensive replacement. Use caution.*

Ink Jet Printers

Ink jet printers are low-cost, moderate-quality printers that can generate either black-and-white or color output at 225 to 300 dpi, for modest cost per page. They operate by squirting ink under pressure through small holes in the print head and are proven mature, reliable technology with high engine lifetimes. (A related technology called bubble jet printing uses heated bubbles to force ink through the nozzles. Ink dries somewhat faster, but otherwise output is similar.) Black-and-white output is competitive with laser printer output in resolution. Costs are about 1 cent to 2 cents per page. The print engine for an ink jet printer is generally slower than a laser printer with a typical rating of a page per minute. A good ink jet printer, such as the DeskJet 500 (PC), also called the DeskWriter (Mac), from Hewlett-Packard is much cheaper to purchase than a laser printer; it costs about $700 discounted. The major consumable for ink jet printers is the ink well (about $25), which can be difficult to refill and reuse. The DeskJet uses the PCL page description language; the DeskWriter uses QuickDraw.

This technology is delightfully quiet, very reliable, and a great, low-cost solution for desktop publishing and graphics applications where impact printing is not required. By adding the Adobe Type Manager (Mac or Win), it's possible to add scalable font technology to the DeskWriter or DeskJet, making its print quality nearly indistinguishable from a laser printer. Ink used on ink jet printers dries fast but not instantly, and care should be taken in handling fresh copy to avoid smudges. Graphic Utilities sells a line of waterfast inks for the H-P DeskJet.

Apple released an ink jet printer called the StyleWriter ($599) in spring 1991 based on the Canon BubbleJet engine. The StyleWriter is positioned to compete with the very successful H-P DeskJet and DeskWriter printers. The StyleWriter is a ½-page-per-minute printer with very high print resolution (360 dpi, as compared to the H-P printer's 300 dpi) but with smaller footprint and lighter weight (< 5 lbs). Early adopters have found that the StyleWriter gives better output, although Apple uses inks that tend to smudge somewhat more than H-P printers. The StyleWriter's and the BubbleJet's portability makes them good choices for laptop companions. If you can live with the slow printing speeds (they are really only personal printers), then these printers are superb solutions for small business and personal appplications. The introduction of TrueType fonts in Macintosh System 7 and Windows 3.1 will increase the value of these printers in DTP applications, and the Adobe Type Manager provides access to PostScript Type 1 fonts. Full PostScript compatibility can be achieved through the use of a PostScript emulation program such as Freedom of the Press.

Laser Printers

Laser printers are based on the xerographic process developed for copier machines. Canon developed their basic marking engines for personal copier machines with the original Canon CX engine, and then adapted them for computer printers. The printer gets its name from the computer-guided laser that writes the latent image on a photosensitive drum. Electrostatic toner is then attracted to the drum, and the latent image is transferred onto the paper by an electrostatic attraction developed by a transfer corona, an electric field created by a very hot wire.

Figure 7-7
The Hewlett-Packard LaserJet series (from front to back): The LaserJet IIP personal laser printer, the Laser-Jet III, and the LaserJet IIID (shown without the envelope feeder). *Courtesy of Hewlett-Packard.*

▼ *Tip: To print double-sided documents without the use of a duplex printer, print the pages first by putting even-numbered pages before odd-numbered pages that precede them (e.g., 2, 1, 4, 3, 6, 5, and so on). Then reverse the order of the pages (5, 6, 3, 4, 1, 2), put the printed pages in the paper tray face down, and print again on the blank sides. You will end up with two copies of double-sided documents.*

PostScript laser printers follow this printing sequence:

1. The user gives the Print command, and the application creates an executable file. This file is translated to PostScript.

2. The printing resource or driver transmits PostScript commands to the printer, often through a network.

3. A PostScript interpreter converts the vector-oriented page description into a bit-map image at the correct resolution.

4. The charging corona, a wire at high voltage, ionizes the photoconductive drum and attracts air molecules to the drum surface.

5. The laser beam is reflected from the rotating mirror onto the drum surface, and the beam is turned on and off at the correct locations (modulated). Wherever the laser beam strikes the surface of the drum, the photoconductive surface conducts electricity; negative charges are drained off, and these areas have a positive potential that attracts toner.

6. Toner, a low-temperature plastic resin containing carbon black and magnetic particles, adheres to the photoconductive drum in the areas of the latent image.

7. The drum turns, and paper is fed within close proximity to where a transfer corona charges the paper positively, attracting the negative toner to the paper.

8. Heat and pressure fuse the plastic toner to the paper.

9. A blade scrapes the drum, and a lamp illuminates the surface, neutralizing all remaining charges and preconditioning the drum for additional copies.

▼ *Tip: Toner cartridges can be refilled several times, but be careful who recharges them for you because eventually they have to be reworked.*

You should always insist on getting your own cartridge back so that you can monitor the number of recharges. If you weigh the cartridge when it is first empty, later you can tell from its weight how close to empty it is. When you get near empty and the print quality fades, you can often get a few more days of use out of a cartridge by shaking it vigorously and turning up the darkness setting.

Laser printers are graphics page printers. Whole pages are composed in RAM either in the printer itself or in the computer, and then printed. Most laser printers are built with CPU to offload the processing, and come with 1 to 2 MBytes of RAM standard, often upgradable to 8 MBytes or more. As driving the laser requires considerable data, the instructions must be stored in the laser printer prior to the actual printing. At 300 dpi, the 8 million bits of data occupies about 1 Mbyte RAM. Most laser printers are built to be network compatible so that the printer's high cost can be amortized over several users. Although they are a complex technology, laser printers have excellent reliability and are rated with MTBF (*mean time before failure*, also called *duty cycle*) rates of several hundred thousand pages or more. Laser printers are among the most reliable pieces of computer equipment that you can purchase.

A fully configured Apple LaserWriter II NTX (PostScript) costs over $6,000. It is an eight-page-per-minute printer, with a Motorola 68020 microprocessor and 2 MBytes RAM. Like all LaserWriters, it runs on the AppleTalk network built into every Macintosh. The NTX allows for a SCSI hard drive to be attached to serve as a font library. Apple has just introduced a Personal LaserWriter (both a QuickDraw and PostScript model) series to compete with the Hewlett-Packard LaserJet III series in the $2,500 price range. Highly rated laser printers for the Macintosh are the DataProducts LZR1260i and the Varityper VT600P. If you don't require PostScript graphics, several lower-cost laser printers, such as the GCC PLP (Personal Laser Printer) for $1,700, are available that use a Macintosh CPU to create QuickDraw page descriptions, or the H-P Laser-Jet III. For the IBM PC market, the HP LaserJet series is often highly rated; the Texas Instruments microLaser PS17 (the PS35 for the Mac) was recently rated as best buy in the under-$3,000 category. Refer to reviews in the Appendix for specific information.

Figure 7-8
(A) The Apple Personal LaserWriter was introduced in 1990. It has a fine marking engine, prints four pages per minute, and can be configured as a QuickDraw or PostScript printer, networked or direct.
(B) The Apple Laser-Writer II NTX is an eight-page-per-minute networked PostScript printer that was both a *Byte* and *PC Magazine* product of the year a couple of years ago. Still considered a fine printer, it has lost some of its competitive advantage. *Courtesy of Apple Computer, Inc.*

A.

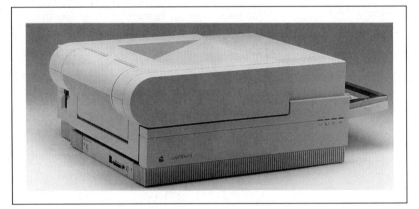

B.

Apple began to introduce low-cost laser printers in 1990 and 1991 to compete with the very successful H-P LaserJet series printers and other lower-cost printers, and to supplement their Laser-Writer IINT ($3,999) and IINTX ($4,999) network printers. Initial offerings included the Personal LaserWriter II series and models LC ($1,299), SC ($1,299), and NT ($2,599) printers. The PLP LC and SC models are meant for users not requiring network operation, PostScript output, or fast printing (PLPs are 4 ppm printers). The PLP NT is a PostScript, networkable printer. The print quality of the Apple PLPs are actually better than the LaserWriters, but the duty life is half as long. The Personal Laser Printer LC's and SC's attractiveness will increase when TrueType becomes more prominent. But users who need to preview or print PostScript graphics are better off buying the PLP NT or higher-priced LaserWriter series, or looking into a PostScript emulation program.

The most important marking engines for laser printers are:

- Canon CX. The original laser printer engine included in the LaserWriter, LaserWriter Plus, H-P LaserJet, LaserJet Plus, QMS PS-800, and PS-800 Plus. This write-black engine uses a disposable imaging drum and toner supply.

- Canon SX. This engine replaced the CX, and is used in the LaserWriter II series, the LaserJet Series II, and the QMS PS-810. The SX uses a disposable drum and toner supply, and is not interchangeable with the CX.

- Casio LCS-130. A light-duty, 300,000-page duty cycle, (non-laser) write-black, liquid crystal shutter (LCS) imaging engine that uses a halogen lamp light source shining through an array of over 2,000 liquid-crystal shutters (each shutter is 1/300 inch in diameter). Shutters are turned on and off electrically and serve to either block or transmit the light falling on the drum. This technology doesn't require a rotating mirror to focus a laser beam, so it claims to be sharper at the edges of the page and to provide more precise image control. It's found in the Qume CrystalPrint and several other manufacturer's laser printers.

- NEC 890. Found in the NEC SilentWriter 890 PostScript printer, this engine uses an array of 2,400 light-emitting diodes (LEDs) that flash on and off to expose the latent image on the drum. Like the LCS-130 engine, it has the advantage of fewer moving parts than a traditional laser engine.

- Ricoh 4081. The 4081 is the most common write-white engine, with a 600,000-page duty cycle. It's found in the AST TurboLaser/PS and the TI OmniLaser 2108. This engine uses an organic photoconductor belt, with toner stored in a separate hopper.

- Ricoh 1060. A compact write-black engine with a 180,000-page duty cycle. It is found in the GCC PLP and Business Laser-Printer, IBM Personal Page Printer II, and TI OmniLaser 2106. It has a disposable drum with toner held in a separate hopper.

- Other recent entries. Minolta (the SP 140 laser), Toshiba (the A-739 laser), Fujitsu (LED), Canon (the LX and UX lasers), Kyocera (laser), Printware (laser diode), Sharp (Ipia laser), TEC (laser), Okidata (LED), and more.

Some fonts are built into the ROM of a laser printer; the Apple LaserWriter comes with thirty-five typefaces standard. Other laser printers, such as the LaserJet series, allow for the use of plug-in ROM cartridges containing other font families. If a font is not contained in the ROM of the laser printer, a screen bit-mapped version of the font is created, then printed. Fonts and their handling are described more fully in Chapter 11.

Opaque Ink Color Printers

There are two basic methods for color printing. One method uses opaque inks. The second blends colorants together and is far superior for continous tone images. Opaque ink printers place dots next to each other in clusters called halftone cells. The eye dithers, or blends, the colors together. Opaque inks compromise the range of colors available on the page (called the *printer color gamut*) by lowering the resolution (see Color Figure C6). This is a property of all opaque color print technologies, and requires extremely high resolution to address the full color palette suitably. Graininess in the print is a giveaway of this kind of technology. Many folks find this type of printing to be artistic and attractive, but it does not lend itself to color photograph reproduction. Currently all professional printing is done this way.

Color ink jet technology represents a good, low-cost solution for moderate-quality color printing using opaque inks. It uses the same technology as black-and-white ink jets, but with four process ink colors. It is useful for color comp work to serve as a proofing aid before final printing, or acceptable for work such as high detail maps where dot structure is not a problem. The Hewlett-Packard PaintJet is the best-selling printer in this category, costing about $1,500. Other printers in this category retail up to $4,000.

Figure 7-9
The Hewlett-Packard
PaintJet and PaintJet XL
with a Macintosh IIx
computer. *Courtesy of
Hewlett-Packard.*

Thermal Transfer Printers

The most common opaque ink color print technology may be loosely termed *thermal transfer* printing. Most of the high-priced color printers in the $5,000 to $12,000 range are based on this technology, which uses dye, dyed ribbons, colored plastic or wax, or some other material that can be heat-flowed from a reservoir or a set of process color sheets onto the page. Often the transfer mechanism in the print head is a set of heated elements, wires, or pins (similar to the arrangement on impact printers). The paper makes three or four passes through the printer to transfer the process colors, a registration disadvantage, although better printers in this category can lay down the colors in a single pass. QMS,

Shinko, Cal Comp, and Tektronix make good printers in this category. One printer, called the PixelMaster ($7,500), from Howtek uses funky colored crayons and coats the page with a raised texture that looks almost impressionistic. The PixelMaster was recently adapted to print in Braille for the blind. It uses opaque colorant technology, and output costs about $1 per page. Data Products sells an upscaled version of the PixelMaster called Jolt. The Jolt printer has the advantage of printing on plain paper.

Continuous Tone Color Printers

The second kind of color printing is called continuous tone (contone). It has a photographic quality because the colorants can be blended together on a single pixel without requiring a superpixel mechanism. One class of thermal transfer printers, now called dye sublimation printers, uses nearly the same mechanism as thermal transfer printers to achieve contone printing. The colorant is a set of sublimable dyes that interact with the printing paper and allow the light of other process colors through. Layers of dye can create

Figure 7-10
The DuPont 4CAST printer delivers near-photographic PostScript color output, 300 dpi, and continuous tone. This printer debuted in 1989 for $75,000; today it costs about $45,000.
Courtesy of DuPont, Inc.

the whole palette of colors with up to 300 dpi. The Mitsubishi S340 ($14,000) delivers 150 dpi, the Kodak XL7700 ($25,000) 200 dpi, and the DuPont 4CAST printer ($49,000) gives 300 dpi. The output from the 4CAST is remarkable, just like fine photographic prints; many slide services offer them for comp generation.

Imagesetters

For finished typographical copy or separation masters used for printing, only typeset quality is acceptable. Such copy can be obtained by traditional typesetting or through electronic printing from imagesetters. Imagesetters are high-quality laser printers, sometimes referred to as typesetters or linos (although the term typesetters is more appropriately used for type-only equipment, and not printers that print pages with both type and graphics).

"Linos" is derived from the Linotype Company (Hauppauge, NY) series of imagesetters found in most service bureaus (see Figure 1.4). The three Linotronic printers in use today are the 200P, 300, and 500 series printers (from $25,000 to $125,000). The original model was the L100. Linos are black and white, paper, or film devices that can print at either 600, 1,270 or 2,540 dpi. Recent models go as high as 3,386 dpi. They are all PostScript printers with internal hard drives and external SCSI drive connections for large font library collections (up to 500 fonts for 80 MBytes). Figure 7.11 shows one of the more popular imagesetters found in service bureaus today, the Linotronic 330.

Imagesetters all contain built-in RIPs, and their writing engines are helium-neon lasers that write *directly* onto photosensitive paper or film without the need for forming a latent image on a drum. Direct write is a feature of all high-quality imagesetters. As such, their cassettes are light-tight and require photographic processing. Having an on-board RIP and a very high quality drive mechanism allows imagesetters to pause midpage to receive more data; an 8 ½-by 11-inch page at 2,540 dpi contains 600 million pixels or 75 MBytes of data, and takes about ten minutes to print (that's really ripping!) A very clean type is obtained, with no excess toner marring the white areas, as is found in laser printer

Figure 7-11
The Linotronic 330.
*Courtesy of Linotronic
Corporation
(Hauppauge, NY).*

output due to the smearing effect of the xerographic process. Dot size can be smaller than 1 mil or 2.5 mm. Expect to pay about $10 to $25 for imageset pages at a service bureau; if done in-house, output costs about $2 to $5.

The imagesetters market is very competitive, with many new models being introduced every year. Agfa Compugraphic (Wilmington, MA); Crossfield, Linotronic-Hell; Optronics (Chelmsford, MA); and Varityper (Hanover, NJ), to name but a few, are imagesetter manufacturers. Color imagesetters based on proprietary screening and halftoning algorithms capable of museum-quality printing, are coming to market. One such imagesetter is the Optronics ColorSetter 2000 ($60,000), a high-end UNIX workstation that is finding favor with many magazines and prestige catalog publishers.

Figure 7-12
The Optronics ColorSetter 2000, a color imagesetter that delivers museum-quality color printing, is based on a UNIX workstation with proprietary color print technology. It was used to print the color plates in this book. It is shown here with the three platforms it supports: Mac, PC, and Intergraph workstation. *Courtesy of Optronics.*

Plotters and CAD/CAM Devices

A plotter is a device that creates images by mechanically moving pens across paper. This process is nearly ideal for creating object graphics, such as lines or curves, but it creates bit-mapped graphics at the lower resolution of the pen tip. In publishing, plotters are very useful for large size artwork and color output. They also offer high resolution, particularly for line art. Plotters can create printouts of enormous size and are especially good at drawing graphics used in CAD/CAM applications. Architects or engineers make frequent use of plotters; they are used to create wall-size schematics of microchips.

Plotters prices begin at about $1,500 and rise to $8,000 for industrial-strength behemoths. Output can cost from 5 cents to 10 cents a copy based on size. Plotters use opaque inks, and their color output has the same qualities as color dot matrix printers, but at higher resolutions. The Hewlett-Packard plotters are industry standards, and their .HPGL format is also an engineering standard. Plotters come in all shapes and sizes, with output quality from good to excellent, as seen in Figure 7-13.

Figure 7-13
Hewlett-Packard makes a series of highly regarded moderate-cost plotters. *Courtesy of the Boston Computer Museum.*

Electrostatic plotters are a cross between laser printers and plotters. They achieve near-contone printing at high speed. In an electrostatic plotter, a set of writing heads (one for each process color) images the paper just before it passes over each toner station. The ColorWriter 400 ($120,000) from Synergy achieves 400 dpi output in a single-pass system. These plotters are often networked printers used for high-quality mapping, technical blueprints, or engineering applications.

Film Recorders

Film recorders are output devices used to print images (including page layouts) to film. They are not to be confused with slide scanners or slide recorders, which are devices used to scan and digitally record images on slides, respectively. Because film is a continuous tone medium, film recorders offer some of the best-resolution output you can achieve from computers. (Continuous tone changes color smoothly and gradually, like a photograph.) There are several different competing technologies for film recording, depending on the quality you are trying to achieve.

Low-cost film recorders in the $2,000 to $7,000 range employ miniature monochrome CRTs inside a sealed light box; less expensive analog recorders use color CRTs but have the limitation of poor resolution. Good film recorders in this price range are the Mirrus FilmPrinter (Santa Cruz, CA), American Liquid Light Imprint for the Amiga (Torrence, CA), Still Light Polaroid for the Mac II (Cambridge, MA), Turbo Palette (PC), Polaroid Bravo Comp, Slide Maker for the Mac and PC and Matrix Instruments SlideWriter (Orangeburg, NY). The image is captured by a commercial 35 mm camera that is placed inside the box and exposed for long periods of time—many seconds to minutes—depending on film speed and type. Such lengthy exposure leads to the best results. Film recorders of this type produce slide film with resolutions of up to 2,000 lines per image and have excellent color gamuts. This is as high a resolution as the human eye can see. Compare this output with high-quality color printers yielding 400 lpi. A couple of film recorders on the market use character wheels for type output; they give sharp output but slow recordings.

At the high end, film recorders range up to $150,000. The recording can be done on large film format directly written by raster beams into the film. This kind of equipment can achieve a dot placement accuracy of 0.02 percent of a CRT-based film recorder; it is ten times as accurate as CRT film recorders. The quality of this output is astonishing and lends itself to the most demanding of applications, including electronic prepress, satellite photo interpretation, science and engineering applications, and output that requires large enlargements without image loss.

Genigraphics (Syracuse, NY) manufactures high-end film recorders. One is called the Masterpiece 8700 ($40,000 to $70,000). Along with Autographix (Waltham, MA) and Magicorp, Genigraphics also offers state-of-the art slide-making services on a nationwide basis. Other slide-imaging services include Management Graphics (Minneapolis, MN), Dicomed (Burnsville, MN), and Visual Business Systems (Atlanta, GA). Many of the better presentation programs, such as Aldus Persuasion, Microsoft Powerpoint, and Harvard Graphics, actually write PostScript files in the correct format. You can mail in a disk or, if you prefer, use the device drivers the aforementioned programs ship with so you can modem the files to these companies. Slides are typically $10 to $20 each with a $50 minimum, plus courier or transmission charges. Making about 500 slides would justify purchasing your own $6,000 recorder, but these services offer high quality and are convenient.

PART III

The Systems

Preparing Text

Writing is turning one's worst moments into money.
J. P. Donleavy

Preparing text is an important part of the desktop publishing process. Depending on the programs you choose, they can speed your work, allow documents to be formatted for later inclusion into a page layout package, or even take the place of a page layout program itself. In this chapter we discuss the important text preparation software: word processors and utilities. We also discuss their usefulness in the DTP process and some of the factors you need to be concerned about in handling text.

Textverabetung

After many false starts beginning nearly three centuries ago, the "Type-Writer" was introduced by a Wisconsin newspaper editor and printer named Christopher Latham Sholes in 1867. Refined by Sholes and Gibbons in 1875, it was sold by E. Remington & Sons. Remington was a noted firearms manufacturer, and later as Remington Rand the company would go on to produce the UNIVAC computer in 1951, the first commercial computer in the United States. Writers have always loved writing devices, and one Samuel

Clemens (otherwise known as Mark Twain) pecked away at the "Type-Writer." He reputedly was the first author to submit a typed manuscript to his publisher (by his recollection, *Tom Sawyer*, but his biographers claim it was *Life on the Mississippi*). Clemens was enamored of writing machines. He later sunk his entire life fortune of $300,000 into a New York company trying to perfect an automatic typesetting machine, but the company never commercialized the product. Shortly thereafter, the Linotype machine was introduced, and the author went bankrupt.

Early computers were large, beastly things, and the coven that tended them believed that typewriter emulation was a trivial thing to do. Still, it was useful to enter programming code, and word processing programs, like one called the "Expensive Typewriter," were written early on. The IBM Selectric, an electric typewriter with a golf ball print head, was introduced in 1961 and quickly added to the IBM 7030 "Stretch" computer. By 1965 a German IBM employee named Ulrich Steinhilpher renamed what IBM called power-typing as "textverabetung," or word processing, a term that stuck. By 1972 An Wang's company was buying 65 percent of the production of Selectric typewriters produced to create its word processing system. By 1980, word processors were being written for microcomputers. The first was called the Electric Pencil, followed by Screenwriter, and the smash hit of yesteryear, WordStar.

It seems amusing in retrospect that there could have been any resistance at all to word processing. The word processor is the single most important application ever written for a computer, and it certainly is the most ubiquitous. Most people spend the majority of their time on a computer working in their word processor, and most people develop strong preferences based on their personal experience with one program or another. In the sections that follow we discuss what makes one word processor better than another, different utilities for aiding your writing, and how you can use your word processor to speed your publishing efforts.

Overall Considerations

Perhaps it is trite to say so, but a word processor frees you from the demands for perfection imposed by a typewriter. No more whiting out mistakes or retyping a page. Make a mistake, and just use the Delete or Backspace key to correct it. Cut, Copy, Clear, and Paste selections let you play a what-if game with your work until it's the way you want it. A word processor is the single best reason to buy a computer, and nobody goes back to a typewriter once he or she uses one.

Everyone you talk to will give you different opinions on what makes a good word processor. Many people, particularly those who have grown up on MS-DOS–based computers, believe that response or speed is an important factor in choosing a word processor. Still others starting on GUI-based computers feel that ease of remembering and accessing powerful features are the most important considerations. Manufacturers would have you believe that a comparison of the number of features should be the deciding factor, and they price (or overprice) their programs accordingly.

In reality, you can use very simple word processors called text editors to do your work. An example of a text editor would be the NotePad utility that ships with Windows. You can use NotePad to examine and modify the various Windows preference files such as WIN.INI. A similar utility called Note Pad (a desk accessory) ships with Macintosh system software. But whatever you use, the most important feature in a computer is its ability to get your data out of a word processor and into your other programs, with as much of your formatted text intact as possible. This minimizes the work that must be repeated. Most of today's word processors are capable of exporting and importing files, but they all support a varying range of formats, and their ability to support the more widely used formats must be considered.

This is a graphics book, the applications described in this book are graphics applications, and the goal is to create an environment to do graphics. It makes sense to buy a word processor that behaves like other applications on the GUI that you choose to work with. That's my prejudice. It saves time because you don't have to learn and remember a unique command set. When you buy a non-GUI word processor, you have to be concerned with such features as printer or other device support, file formats supported, type handling, and other factors that a standardized interface would provide.

Choices

Certainly there are some fine word processors that run in their own environments. A market leader such as WordPerfect 5.1 (DOS) allows you to save your formatting in an accessible file format that can be read by most programs that use text on the PC. It's a complete 5 MByte writing environment that comes with every accoutrement you can think of. There's extensive device and printer support, and a wide range of file formats are supported. If you work in an office environment where IBM PCs and ATs are used, it makes sense to run WordPerfect. With 60 percent of the PC market, it's the word processor users are most familiar with and is also the most widely supported at the moment.

Other popular non-GUI choices on the PC are Microsoft Word 5.5, WordStar 6, XyWrite III, and Q&A Write. For GUI PC programs, Ami Professional 1.2 and Word for Windows 1.0 are the popular choices running on Windows 3.0; also Legacy has recently been released, while WordPerfect for Windows is in the last phase of development. Windows 3.0 comes with its own modest word processor, called Write, built in.

All Macintosh programs are, by definition, GUI programs. Microsoft Word 4.0 (Mac) has about 70 percent of the Macintosh word processing market, making it something of a standard on that machine. Other highly rated and popular Mac programs are MacWrite II, WriteNow 2.2, WordPerfect 2.O, Nisus 2.11, and Full-Write Professional 1.1. Microsoft Works, with its midlevel capabilities based on Word 1.0 has a large installed base.

Layout in Word Processors

A WYSIWYG word processor is particularly valuable for doing simple page layout and formatting. Elements such as multiple columns, side-by-side paragraphs, lines (or rules), boxes, justification, line spacing, tab settings, and so on are all layout features that most word processors support. If your formatting needs are simple, with graphics that don't need precise placement or extensive flexibility, you should consider the capabilities of a word processor to serve as a substitute for a page layout program.

Figure 8-1
Mishu, the Macintosh desk accessory/word processor that creates some 6,763 Chinese characters and allows users to do desktop publishing in Chinese. Characters can be pasted into other Macintosh programs. Various fonts and configurations are offered.

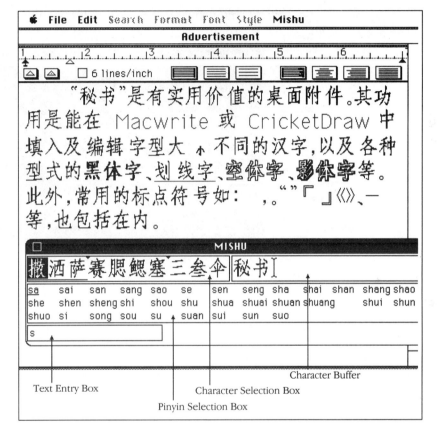

You don't need PageMaker, Ventura Publisher, QuarkXPress, FrameMaker, or any other $800, 5 MByte, fire-breathing monster layout program to do a letter with two columns or to incorporate simple graphics. You can avoid those programs, and even the $295, lean and mean, personal publisher, garden-variety layout programs by getting to know your word processor well enough to make full use of its layout potential. Some word processors are even capable of indexing, generating table of contents, automatic footnotes and references, creating complex tables, equation notation, sorting, and other advanced features you wouldn't normally expect. This is not to say that doing layout in a word processor is easier than in a layout program; complex layouts in a word processor can get Byzantine, and then you need a page layout program.

```
 File Edit Search Layout Mark Tools Font Graphics Help

0,76 L
0,77 M
0,78 N
0,79 O
0,80 P
0,81 Q

0,82 R
0,83 S
C:\WP51\CHARACTR.DOC                          Doc 1 Pg 2 Ln 1.17" Pos 1.6"
[                                             ]
0,80 P[HRt]
0,81 Q[HRt-SPg]
0,82 R[HRt]
0,83 S[HRt]
0,84 T[HRt]
0,85 U[HRt]
0,86 V[HRt]
0,87 W[HRt]
0,88 X[HRt]
0,89 Y[HRt]

Press Reveal Codes to restore screen
```

Modes

Word processors have become almost universally modal—that is, only one aspect of the program can be worked with at a time—and they offer several different modes of operation to support the type of work in progress. In one mode, all page formatting is turned off and the word processor emulates a simple text editor with the expected increase in speed. Many programs call this *draft* or *galley mode*. Another mode can show page formatting applied at actual size in what is called *page mode*. Still a third mode shows how pages look in reduced form, side by side in the so-called *page preview mode*. Other programs offer more specialized views of your writing. An important one offers an outline view that collapses each of your paragraphs down to the first line in each paragraph. *Outlining* means you can do global organizational changes by moving around a single line that represents a paragraph. Figure 8.3 illustrates two of the modes. As even non-GUI word processors, such as WordPerfect 5.1 and WordStar 6.0, now have page preview, in a sense all word processors are now WYSIWYG. A word

Figure 8-3
Two different views
of Microsoft Word.
(A) Draft or
galley mode.
(B) Page preview
mode.

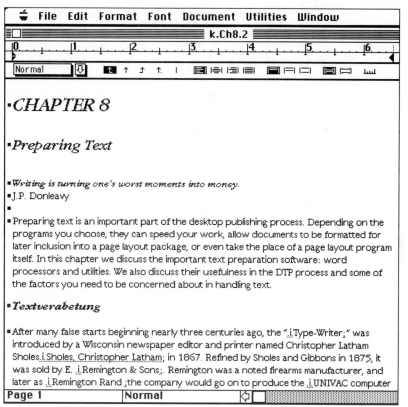

A.

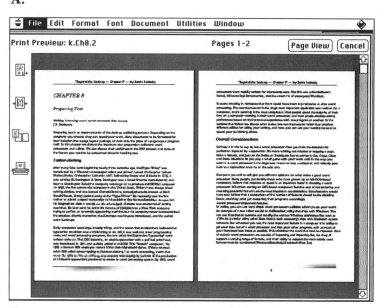

B.

of warning: Stay away from programs like XyWrite III and Q&A Write that either don't have preview modes or have poorly implemented ones.

Let's consider what the views in these modes help you accomplish. The outline helps you organize your thoughts and then do major adjustments in your flow of logic. This is possible even when your document runs to tens of pages, because reducing each paragraph to its first sentence makes it easier to see your logic and the order of presentation. An outline view also allows you to collect headings as entries in a table of contents. Expand the outline to galley view and you have a text editor for speed. Page view gives you WYSIWYG editing, and page preview lets you see your margins and how pages relate to one another. You could buy utilities to do these extra features, but it's nice to have them all there in a unified package. My best writing has been done with outlining, and I wish I could say that I use it all the time, but I don't as much as I should.

Codes and Style

One important feature of a word processor that is most often overlooked by new computer users are the embedded *formatting codes*. With the "show codes" or "show formatting" feature turned on (normally by a menu command or a preference setting), each move you make is highlighted. When you type the Tab key, for example, a tab mark is shown. Similarly, each tap of the Spacebar key shows a space mark code, and pressing on the Return or Enter key shows a return mark. It's a little distracting to see all of these markers, so many programs either hide them or allow you to turn them on and off. You can't know why a space is a certain size without seeing its mark, or why the format or style you are trying to apply only works for a certain range or selection. You can format text as hidden that will not print; some programs use this kind of formatting to create indexes. That's what these codes tell you.

▼ *Tip: Formatting codes allow you to figure out what the program is doing, and understanding them is the most important thing you can learn about your word processor to aid your work. It separates the novices from experienced users.*

Figure 8-4
Embedded word
processor codes help
you understand why
things happen.

> selection. You can format text as ;i.hidden text ;that will not print, some programs use that
> kind of formatting to create indicies. That's what these codes tell you. ;i.word
> processors:formatting codes; i.indexing;¶
> ¶
> ■ **Tip**¶
> ■ Understanding formatting codes allows you to figure out what the program is doing, and it's the single best thing you
> can learn about your word processor to aid your work. It separates novices from experienced users.¶
> ■ **End of Tip**¶
> ¶
> ■ *** **Figure 8.4.** — Embedded word processor codes help you understand why things happen. ***¶
> ¶
> ■ All word processors ;i.*wordwrap* ;text, going to the end of a line and then starting on the
> next line automatically. This is very different from a typewriter where a carriage return is

All word processors *wordwrap* text, that is, go to the end of a line and then start on the next line automatically. This is very different from a typewriter where a carriage return is used, and this difference is fundamental to understanding how data is handled in a word processor. When you press the Return key (Enter on some keyboards), you are making an end-of-paragraph marking. A word processor actually writes all of the formatting for a paragraph, including that of the preceding characters back to the previous paragraph mark, *within* that carriage return symbol in the data file. And while you can format any range of characters in a file, the overall global formatting that you can apply relates only to particular paragraphs. These global formats are called a *style* or a *tag*, and they provide a powerful means for altering your document quickly. By defining and using styles for each element in a document—headings, footnotes, body text, and so on—you can quickly change each element at will for an entire document, or apply a format with a click of a mouse or a keystroke. It's a great time saver. Always let your word processor wordwrap unless you really mean to end a paragraph at that line.

▼ *Tip: Assign macros to each style or tag in your word processor; they are great time savers. If your word processor doesn't offer a macro recorder or assignment utility, purchase a program such as QuicKeys (Mac) or Tempo II (Mac or Win3) that does. Both the Macintosh and Windows ship with basic macro recorders.*

Styles or tags can be overridden for any part of a paragraph, but when a style is chosen it returns you to that style definition. Some word processors will maintain italic or bold text and change only font, size, and other style attributes when you apply a style. What a style or tag can support depends on the program. Some can embed tab settings, nonbreaking paragraphs, grouped paragraphs, and so on, while others incorporate dependent style families, which means that changing the base or normal style also changes all related ones. Being able to determine styles is the single most important difference between word processors and text editors. Most important is that many page layout programs allow for the importation of collections of tags or styles, called style sheets. In PageMaker, you can import Word styles; in Ventura, you can import WordPerfect tags.

Figure 8-5
An established style sheet for a project. Shown here is the style sheet in Word (Mac) for this book.

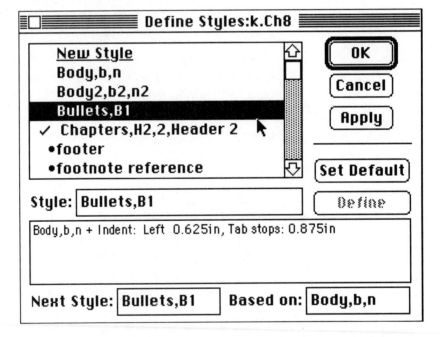

▼ *Tip: Code text styles or tags in your word processor. Whenever possible, use a combination that allows you to import styles from your word processor into your page layout program.*

You can save as much as 20 percent of the cost of a page layout operation by using style sheets, and more important, if you do your own layout work it's faster to format in your word processor.

Also, do your editing in your word processor. Keep in mind that the best combination of page layout program and word processor imports and exports, intact, as much of your formatting work as possible, not just tags and styles, but tab settings, dashes, quotes, and so on. This minimizes your text cleanup work.

It's been a trend to try to get users to do as much formatting in their word processor as possible because page layout programs support a large interface overhead and are slow. Faster microcomputers and more powerful page layout programs are dissipating this trend somewhat as newer layout programs incorporate word processor features in them. PageMaker 4.0 (Mac) now ships with a story editor; it is a program mode that emulates a simple word processor or text editor. Spell checkers are now common to both types of programs, and some even check for style attributes.

Many books tell you that it doesn't matter what word processor you use, only that you feel comfortable with it. You know, don't worry, be happy. I don't ascribe to that philosophy because a full-featured modern word processor changes the way you write. Speed generally is an insignificant factor though, because most people don't input on a keyboard fast enough to challenge even the slowest word processors. (If you do have such a slow computer, however, then you probably won't be able to use it for many of the graphics programs described in this book.) Stylish, easy-to-understand features, especially ones that organize your thoughts, guide your structure, and aid your writing flow are the important factors. You don't need a full-featured word processor to be a good writer, but it certainly helps.

Text Applications

There are many word processors, and there's not enough space in this book to cover them all. Some of the best-known and most widely selling commercial programs are the ones mentioned in this section and chapter, but new programs appearing on the market all the time offer improved features over the market leaders.

While it's important to know how to use the market leaders on the computer of choice in order to work at service bureaus, to enable other people to work on your equipment, or to share files with friends, always be on the lookout for a new product that may have a special feature that is just right for you. For example, Word 4.0 (Mac) is a market leader, but the more recently introduced Nisus has some unique features. It offers an essentially unlimited number of undos (300 is the initial default) through its GREP feature, which ports over from the UNIX world. Many programmers like Nisus because they can work backward through their coding if they are creating that code as text in a word processor. You may want to check the references at the end of this chapter for more detailed product reviews, but here are several of the most well-known word processors.

- Ami Professional 1.2 (Win3): One of the most satisfying power word processors running on the Windows environment. It has full editing features, great file handling, and uses the Windows interface well. Consider either Ami or Word for Windows as first choices.

- FullWrite Professional 1.1 (Mac): A powerful but slow word processor with strong layout features. It requires a Mac II or SE/30 with 4 MBytes RAM for acceptable performance. A full utility set is missing only a macro feature.

- Legacy (Win3): A full-featured word processor with strong formatting and layout capabilities. Its initial version was thought to be slow and wasteful of disk space; writes large files.

- MacWrite II 1.1 (Mac): A major upgrade of the first Macintosh word processor. Unlike the original, MacWrite version II is a powerful midlevel word processor with a full range of utilities. This product is noted for its ability to translate many different formats of text with its XTND technology, proprietary to Claris. It will even import graphics files directly.

- Nisus 2.11 (Mac): A high-end product with many unique features. It has sophisticated graphics built in, an enhanced Clipboard, unlimited undos, strong macro capability, and a powerful search utility. Nisus is more suitable to advanced users and to technical documents.

- Signature (Win3): Developed by Xyquest and now owned by IBM, this high-end word processor features powerful formatting tools (just like its predecessor, XyWrite) and a friendly Windows interface.

- Word for Windows 1.0 (Win3): One of the two best Windows word processors. It is powerful, fast, and uses the Windows interface well. This program ships with a full range of utilities. It has file compatibility with other versions of Word.

- Word 4.0 (Mac): The best-selling Macintosh program. It is very powerful and has some unique command assignments that some reviewers dislike. It's hard to think of a feature it doesn't have, but it is weak on long document handling and there's no searching for formatting. It has the most easily modified menu structure of a Mac word processor; novice users can even go to a short menu option. All major Macintosh programs support the Word format and you can use the Microsoft rich text format (rtf) to exchange files with the PC versions.

- Word 5 (DOS): The non-GUI version of Word. It has strong page layout features and is a powerful word processor. If you have an XT or AT you might consider this program; for a 386 S/X and better, consider Word for Windows in its place. Word 5.5 (the upgrade) is now available for the PC; MacWrite II and WriteNow are my alternate choices.

- WordPerfect 5.1 (DOS): The best-selling IBM PC program, driven through the use of ten function keys and four modifier keys. It's difficult to learn and powerful to use. It's a complete writing environment that takes up over 5 MBytes on your hard drive. Be ready to glue the accompanying templates to your keyboard, or reach for the F3 or Help key. WordPerfect uses embedded codes that you can view in a split screen and supports style sheets or tags for entry into Ventura Publisher. You add a draw module by buying the companion program from WordPerfect called DrawPerfect, and a calendar by using WordPerfect Office. All versions of WordPerfect can interchange files. Longtime WordPerfect users seem to like it.

- WordPerfect 2.0 (Mac): One of the nicest word processors on the Macintosh market. It follows the interface guidelines faithfully and has good response. It has excellent layout capabilities and is easy to understand and use. It is a new product, and a great improvement over the first Mac version.

- WordPerfect 1.0 (Win3): Scheduled for release in the fall of 1991.

- WordStar 6.0 (DOS): The first of the power word processors, a version of the program shipped with the 8-bit CP/M machines. Allows you to turn off automatic text formatting, so you can format paragraphs manually. Version 6.0 has windows, a great page preview, H-P LaserJet printer and font support, plus a full utility set. It has an unfriendly command set, but longtime users seem to like the program, reviewers don't. It still can run on a floppy-based system.

- WriteNow 2.2 (Mac): A midlevel writing package that is easy to learn and very fast. It runs well on older Macs and fits a floppy disk. Users like WriteNow for its logical structure, complete feature set, and well thought out use of the Macintosh interface. A version of WriteNow runs on the NeXT computer.

File Formats

All word processors save files in one or more different forms. The simplest format is the "Text only," TEXT, *filename*.TXT, and so on that saves text characters only. This format ignores all of the extra formatting you add, such as italic or bold designations, font information, and layout instructions like tab settings. Only keyboard entries that are ASCII characters are saved, and this can cause problems. For example, using the Option key on a Macintosh produces non-ASCII characters that are interpreted as spurious ASCII symbols. Smart quotes in Microsoft Word (Mac) show up as U in a text file. In addition, Text only is the lowest level of information that you can transfer, and nearly every word processor supports it; but if you have to transfer as Text only, you will spend considerable time reformatting your document. So this is the worst type of file transfer. Text only is used primarily for communications transfers or in electronic mail systems.

You might wonder how you can locate all of the characters that your computer is capable of producing. Many programs create a virtual keyboard to show you the symbols that keystrokes produce. Key Caps is one desk accessory that ships with the Macintosh systems software (see Figure 8.6A); a shareware version, called PopChar (see Figure 8.6B), is an INIT that creates a pull-down menu. These are very useful utilities.

Figure 8-6 Virtual keyboards show you what characters you can type. **(A)** Key Caps. **(B)** PopChar. Both are for the Apple Macintosh.

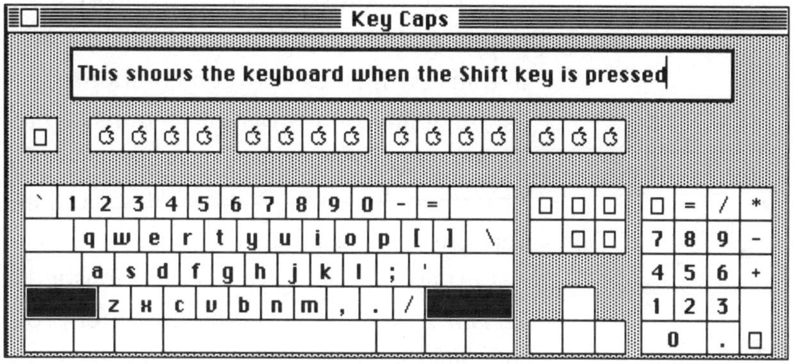

A.

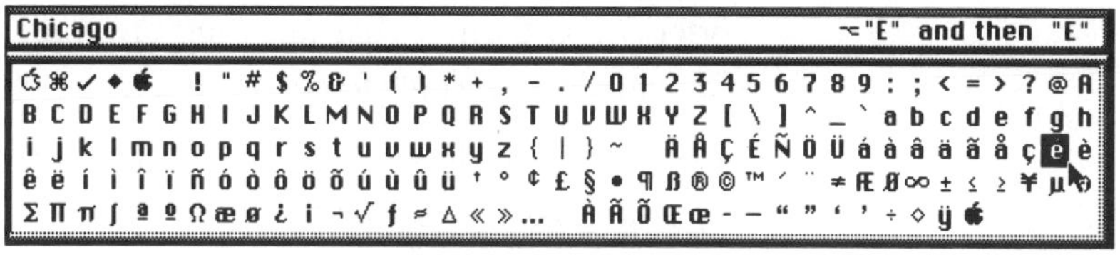

B.

In general, you'll want to save your files in a more complex format that saves all of the information you enter. Every program saves files in a proprietary format known as a *native* document in order to maximize its own feature set. Formatting commands and codes are interspersed with text, and there is no standard format. Many programs also can save files in other program formats as well, but it's far more common for a program to be able to interpret (read) another proprietary format than to write it. If you can transfer a native format you can effect a complete file transfer, and this is the best type of file transfer.

It's a good idea to name your files with extensions that describe what they are. This is particularly true for PC files to be used by a layout operator who will need to be able to identify them. Use suffixes like .TXT for ASCII, .DCA for DCA, .DOC for MS Word files, .WP for WordPerfect, .WS for WordStar, and so on. File extensions also can serve as a way of organizing a DTP project. Note: These extensions are less necessary on the Macintosh.

Interchanges

There are two types of file interchanges: interapplication transfers on the same computer and transfers between applications on different computers. Most word processors support a reasonable number of interapplication transfers and are much less forgiving in transferring files between computers. Interoperability is defined as the ability of a program to transfer files across computer platforms with formatting intact. WordPerfect and Microsoft Word save their files in an accessible format that enables all their various versions to read a file.

Certain formats have been established as *interchange files*, are *revisable,* and can be edited by other programs. Not all formatting information is saved and transferred, but much is, including margins, tabs, columns, and line spacing. A *revisable document* is coded in a format that another program can read. Some of the more important ones for text are:

- Distributed Office Support System (**DISOSS**): A standard interchange format for the IBM office computer products that are part of the SNA (System Network Architecture). DIOSS has two key format designs or architecture, DCA and DIA.

- Document Content Architecture (**DCA**): Defines layout attributes such as page sizes, tab settings, and so on. There are two forms of DCA, Final-Form-Text DCA (DCA-FFT) and Revisable-Form-Text DCA (DCA-RFT). DCA is finding wide support as an interchange format between word processors.

- Document Interchange Architecture (**DIA**): Specifies the communication protocols for transmission of DCA files.

- Rich Text Format (**RTF**): A word processing exchange format developed by Microsoft that improves on DCA by managing more text attributes and features. RTF is saved as pure ASCII characters and can be sent over electronic mail services.

Other kinds of interchange formats are the SYLK (Symbolic Link—Microsoft Excel) and WKS (Lotus 1-2-3) formats for spreadsheets, and DIF (Data Interchange Format). DIF was created by Software Arts for VisiCalc and is supported by some spreadsheets and databases.

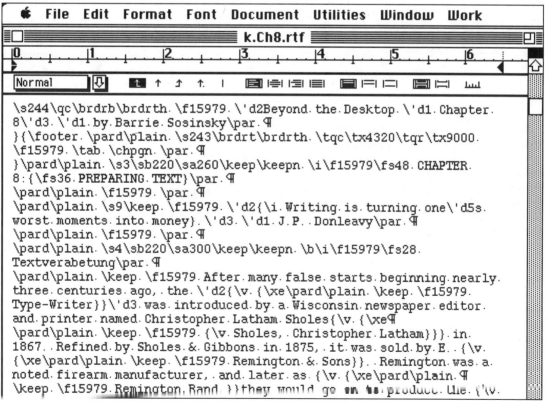

Figure 8-7 Microsoft's RTF format is reminiscent of typesetting codes in coded page layout programs. It lets you exchange file formatting with other programs on other platforms that support RTF.

Filters/Conversions

Some word processors do not save files as Text only, while others insert symbols derived from formatting information that need to be removed. You sometimes can get around this problem by using a Print to disk option. Print to disk is the ASCII character stream sent out to a printer and saved as a disk file, and is more common for PC programs than Mac programs. Once a file is saved as Print to disk, you can go through and do a search and replace for unwanted characters.

WordStar saves text using 8 bits for each character, instead of the more common 7 bits. The extra bit must be removed by special programs, some of which are in the public domain. Such programs are called *filters*, and they literally remove unwanted characters or replace them with more appropriate ones. File conversion uses filters to convert and read native formats. The telecommunication program White Knight actually allows you to define a filter that translates each ASCII symbol to the symbol of your choice.

Figure 8-8
Claris has developed a proprietary conversion utility (external commands) called the XTND technology for doing automatic file translation. Third-party developers can write new file filters for Claris applications.

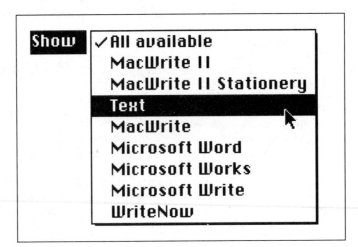

Actually, formatted text translation between word processors is normally not a major problem, especially if you work with market leaders such as the ones mentioned previously. They all read several other word processor formats for their own platform and can convert between them. While Word 4.0 (Mac) converts MacWrite II documents automatically, it can open any file by holding the Shift key while giving the Open command. Similarly, most page layout programs read the major text formats, but if you are using a less common product you should inquire what formats are supported for that translation. All text conversion utilities are either shareware or freeware, demonstrating their limited market. This isn't the case for graphics; there are many different formats and commercial products available for this purpose. Also, commercial products are available to help you convert files from one computer format to another. We discuss graphics file translations and intercomputer file conversions more fully in Chapter 13.

Built-in Utilities

What are some utilities to look for in a word processor? Utilities can be grouped into six categories: editing tools, long document checkers, customization tools, workgroup editing, formatting, and graphics. Some will be important to you, and some won't be.

Editing Tools

Editing tools include glossaries, mail merge, outliner, spell checker, styles or tags, thesaurus, undo, math functions, equation editor, automatic timed saves, context-sensitive help, draft mode, maximum number of windows, number and types of import/export formats. *Glossaries* are collections of character strings that you can save and assign a keystroke to. Entries might include mailing addresses or any other commonly used text. They are useful but not essential. *Mail merge* is a utility that allows a word processing program to import data from a data file to create individualized documents.

Outliners are utilities that allow you to view a document as headings. They can also be invoked as a mode of a word processor. *Spell checkers* are a blessing, and no document should ever be sent out without being first run through a spell checker. Use it in your word processor because most page layout programs don't have good ones, although this is changing. When you work with a page layout program that does have a spell checker, do a second spell check. You are likely to find one or two extra text strings you might want to correct. A good spell checker not only searches for misspelled words, it can also locate formatting problems, double words (the the), and double spaces. Finding words that sound alike but are improperly used (homonyms such as to and two) is another useful feature. The 1990s will see spell checkers evolve into syntax and lexicon evaluators.

Styles or tags are the formats or codes applied to stylize a range of characters, generally a paragraph. The *thesaurus* offers you alternative words with similar meanings as the word or expression you want to replace.

Long Document Tools

These tools include indexing, table of contents, cross-referencing, character/word/ line/paragraph counter, and page marks. *Indexing* marks words or phrases with hidden codes for collection into an index. *Table of contents* generators collect outline headings and the page numbers that they appear on to create the contents page once a document is complete. *Counters* are particularly valuable for those writers who, like Charles Dickens, get paid by the word.

Customization

Customization tools include the all-important macros, menu editing, data links, and updating.

Workgroup

Document notes, strike-through, and document summaries comprise this group of utilities.

Formatting

Style sheets, conditional page breaks, orphan/widow control, automatic hyphenation, justification, snaking columns, kerning and tracking control, document queues, and background printing are all part of formatting. An *orphan* is a flaw created when the first line of a paragraph is separated from the rest of the paragraph it belongs to by a page break or column break. A *widow* is a formatting flaw in which the last line of a paragraph appears at the top of a new column or page. Both orphans and widows can be controlled through automatic settings of word processors.

Hyphenation is the automatic process that breaks up words syllabically so that line spacing is improved, especially when text is fully justified. *Justification* is the alignment of multiple lines of text. Options are: along the left margin (left justified, flush left, ragged right) or the right margin (right justified, flush right, or ragged left), center justified (about the center), or fully justified (flush with both sides).

Graphics

Graphics tools import file formats, size, crop, and rotate graphics; they move graphics frames, flow text around graphics, preview pages, draw lines/boxes/borders, and can include a drawing program and a table editor.

Figure 8-9 (A) The Word spell checker. **(B)** The Find/Change dialog box from QuarkXPress allows formatting searches.

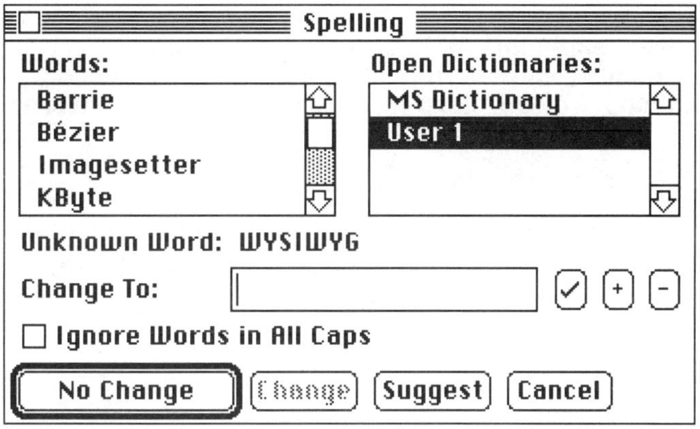

A.

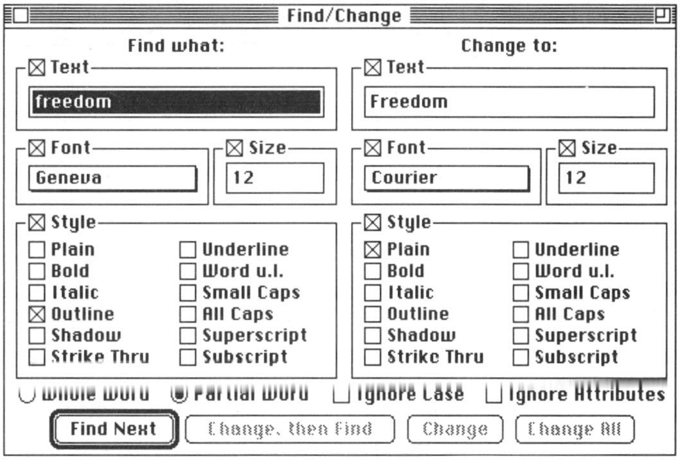

B.

Add-on Utilities

While industrial-strength word processors may have many, or even most, of the utilities listed, you can always supplement your word processor through the purchase of add-on utilities. Many commercial, shareware, and even freeware utilities on the market work as well as or better than the utilities that ship with most word processors.

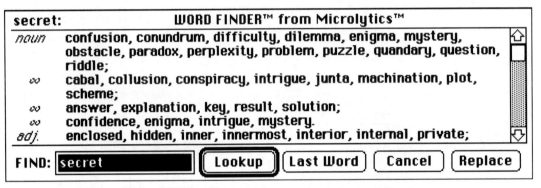

Figure 8-10 A thesaurus is a valuable utility for finding just that right word. Word Finder from Microlytics is available on many computers, even hand-held calculators.

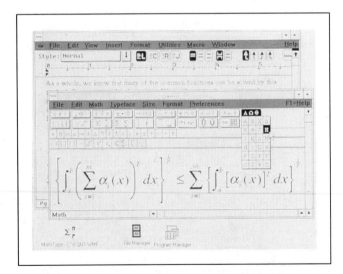

Figure 8-11 Math Type is an equation editor for Windows. Few word processors and page layout programs offer this kind of formatting device, although they are a particular strength of TeX-based (coded) page layout systems (see Chapter 12). Milo and Expressionist are two Macintosh-based equation editors.

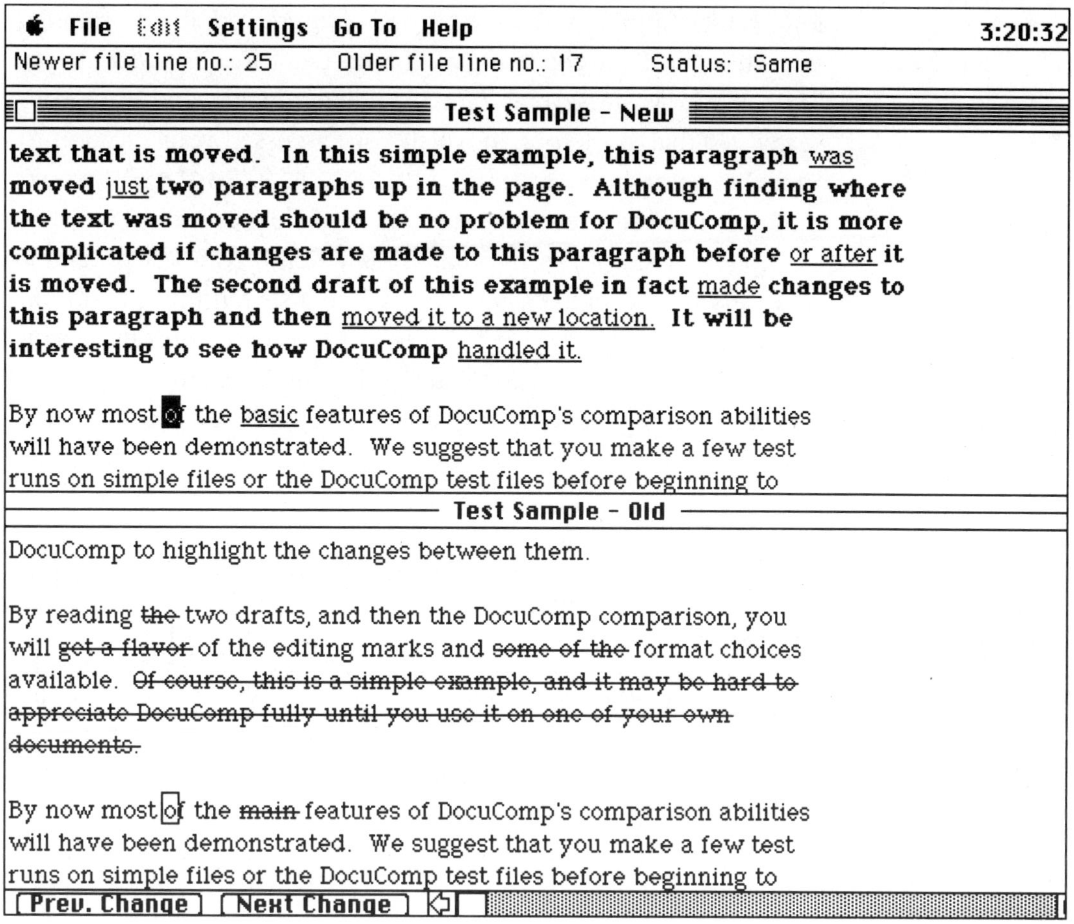

File Edit **Settings** **Go To** **Help**   3:20:32
Newer file line no.: 25   Older file line no.: 17   Status: Same

▣▤▤▤▤▤▤▤▤▤▤▤▤▤▤▤▤▤▤▤ **Test Sample - New** ▤▤▤▤▤▤▤▤▤▤▤▤

text that is moved. In this simple example, this paragraph <u>was</u>
moved <u>just</u> **two paragraphs up in the page. Although finding where
the text was moved should be no problem for DocuComp, it is more
complicated if changes are made to this paragraph before** <u>or after</u> **it
is moved. The second draft of this example in fact** <u>made</u> **changes to
this paragraph and then** <u>moved it to a new location.</u> **It will be
interesting to see how DocuComp** <u>handled it.</u>

By now most█ the <u>basic</u> features of DocuComp's comparison abilities
will have been demonstrated. We suggest that you make a few test
<u>runs on simple files or the DocuComp test files before beginning to</u>

──────────────── **Test Sample - Old** ────────────────

DocuComp to highlight the changes between them.

By reading ~~the~~ two drafts, and then the DocuComp comparison, you
will ~~get a flavor~~ of the editing marks and ~~some of the~~ format choices
available. ~~Of course, this is a simple example, and it may be hard to~~
~~appreciate DocuComp fully until you use it on one of your own~~
~~documents.~~

By now most│of│ the ~~main~~ features of DocuComp's comparison abilities
will have been demonstrated. We suggest that you make a few test
runs on simple files or the DocuComp test files before beginning to

[**Preu. Change**] [**Next Change**] ◁▷

Figure 8-12 DocuComp compares two versions of a text file and highlights the
changes made. It allows you to follow the history of a document and is a first step
to coordinate versions in workgroup utilities.

▼ *Tip: Do not use your word processor's hyphenation and
justification feature. Generally the h&j feature in page
layout programs are more powerful. Also, when you
hyphenate words you may leave hyphens embedded in
the text.*

Text Search   Text search utilities can be very valuable additions to a working
environment. These programs will search a hard drive for a text
string that you specify, in a location you designate, or through
your entire hard drive, or through a specific type of file. Search

logic can be applied so that the search is narrowed, if, for example, you know your target string occurred near another text string. Thus, if you wrote several letters to Elysian Fields, and wanted to search for that single one in which you discussed your vacation to Santa Fe, a search for "**Elysian Fields**" NEAR "**Santa Fe**" would bring up the required document. GOfer 2.0 (Mac and PC) is an example of a simple search utility; higher-end, complex programs have very exotic search algorithms. When a search utility builds an index file (normally about 1 to 2 percent the size of all your files on a volume), its search can be blindingly fast. OnLocation (Mac) works this way and can search 100 MBytes of data in 20 seconds. Text search will become very important as large volume applications such as CD ROM become more popular (see Chapter 19).

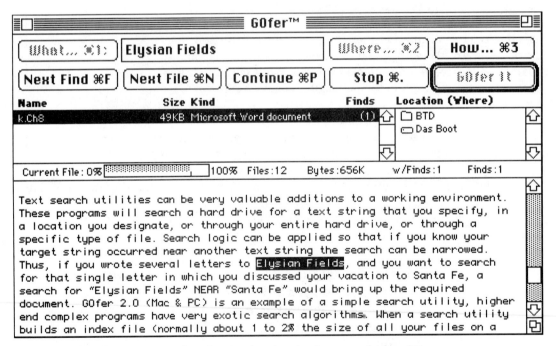

Figure 8-13 GOfer is a text search and retrieval system that is very useful for editing long documents stored as sections or for finding data from anywhere on a hard drive.

Grammar Checkers

One class of utilities beginning to find favor are called grammar checkers or proofreaders. These utilities use a set of logic-based rules and artificial intelligence routines to suggest editing changes. Writers are fascinated by proofreaders, and they get considerable trade press. Good products in this category are Grammatik (Mac and Win), RightWriter, Sensible Grammar, Correct Grammar, and MacProof. Proofreaders flag run-on sentences, improper writing sophistication (grade level), improper punctuation, typos, inappropriate phrases, double words, poor capitalization, bad phrase selection, and other problems that a spell checker can't correct.

The general impression seems to be that grammar checkers are useful, but not essential; not quite ready for prime time. Reviewers and authors who use them say that they're not ready to replace their editors just yet. They delight in running classics, such as Lincoln's Gettysburg Address, through grammar checker just for grins or in checking their grade levels using the Flesch or Gunning Fog indexes. Ernest Hemingway writes at a suprisingly low grade level that is deemed very appropriate for the general readership. Nonetheless, intelligent style and grammar checkers are likely to become increasingly important over the next few years.

Figure 8-14
Most reference works, such as dictionaries and encyclopedias, are CD-ROM based (see Chapter 19). One that is disk based is the Random House Electronic Encyclopedia.

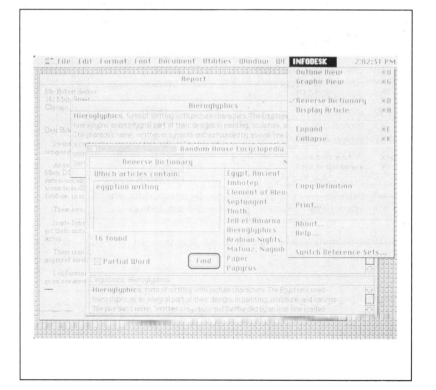

**On-line Style
Guide**

One computer writing aid that is quite valuable is an on-line style guide. For years writers have reached for copies of such books as *The Chicago Manual of Style* or Strunk and White's *The Elements of Style*. In Hypertext format this type of tool becomes even more powerful, allowing the writer to jump from subject to subject by simply clicking on an icon, subject, or key word of interest. Petroglyph's Editorial Advisor is a set of expert stacks running on HyperCard 2.0 that achieves this kind of integration, making it a valuable weapon in a writer's arsenal.

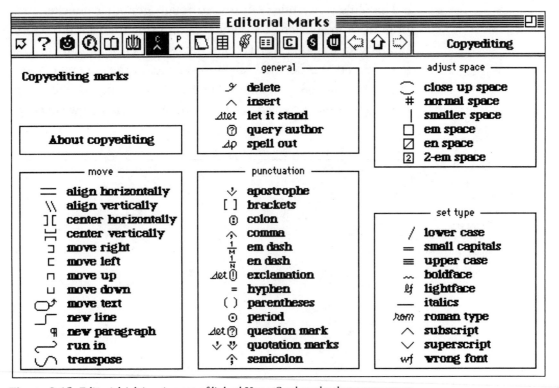

Figure 8-15 Editorial Advisor is a set of linked HyperCard stacks that serves as an on-line style guide.

Working with Graphics

These is not art to me, all these squares and things.
Real art has, you know, like a Madonna in it.
Copied from a guest book at an exhibition of modern art

In December 1951 renowned CBS reporter Edward R. Murrow "interviewed" a computer called the Whirlwind on national television. The computer flashed the greeting "HELLO MR. MURROW" on a monitor screen, then displayed a graph depicting values for a rocket's trajectory, speed, and fuel consumption.

One decade later, MIT doctoral candidate Ivan Sutherland programmed Sketchpad, the first draw program, on the TX-Z computer. By 1963 an operator pressing a light pen onto the screen could direct Sketchpad to create lines, do rotations, join line segments, and perform a number of other manipulations that were extraordinary then, although they seem commonplace now. Interest in computer graphics has always been high, and the technology early on found its way into design labs in many industries and onto the silver screen.

Now, because of the miniaturization of microchips and other electronic components, PCs have more graphic processing power than ever before. Sketchpad's descendants, MacDraw (Mac), Adobe Illustrator (PC and Mac), Arts & Letters (PC), CorelDraw (PC), AutoCAD (PC and Mac), and many others now do magic— creating rich electronic paintings, complex technical drawings, and crisp page geometries that we take for granted. In this chap-

Figure 9-1
Sketchpad, running
on the TX-O, was the
ancestor of a generation
of drawing programs.
*Courtesy of the Boston
Computer Museum.*

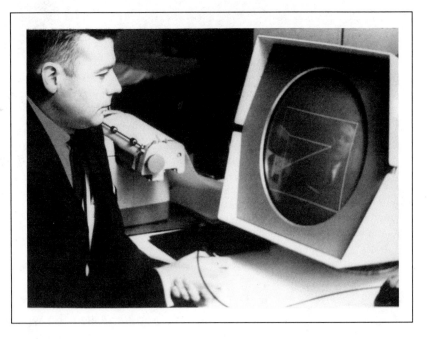

ter, we take a look at the state of desktop-based graphic technology, and explore its tools, standards and uses.

Resolution Versus Quality

As mentioned earlier, the 72 dpi resolution of a medium-quality CRT allows the display of a graphic element roughly the size of the typographer's unit called a point. A *point* was considered the smallest size that a craftsman could make with his tools in creating a letterform in poured lead type. Certainly 72 dpi looks crisp on a screen, but as we saw in Chapter 7, it's a very crude resolution for the printed page, about the quality of a poor dot matrix printer. The reason for this disparity in quality is that a monitor has pixels that perfectly abut one another, whereas the dots created by the pins in the printer require more dpi to create a perfect replica.

The original MacPaint program that once came bundled with every Macintosh saves files in a 72 dpi format called the PAINT or, more commonly, the MacPaint format. It looks fairly crude when printed. Save a bit-mapped picture in a program that supports 300 dpi bit maps, such as SuperPaint II's LaserBits mode, and that 300 dpi will look much finer when printed on a laser printer than a 72 dpi bit map would. However, both the 72 dpi and the 300 dpi bit maps, when printed on a 2,540 dpi imagesetter look the same as they each did on a 300 dpi laser printer. How can one take advantage of an output device capable of higher resolution? It's done by describing images as mathematical formulas rather than as bit maps. Both methods have their pros and cons.

▼ *Tip: If you use traditional methods and photographically reduce the size of a bit-mapped image, you can achieve considerable resolution enhancement.*

A 72 dpi bit-mapped image reduced by a factor of four will have a resolution enhancement and appear as if it is a 288 dpi figure, near laser printer quality. At 300 dpi, that reduction gives the typeset quality of 1,200 dpi.

Objects Versus Bit Maps

Computer graphics come in two different forms: *object-oriented* (also called vector) graphics and *bit-mapped* graphics. Not only do these two classes of software and images look and behave differently, but the concepts used to define them are different. Object-oriented graphics—those described by formulas—normally look smooth on a display and are rendered evenly at any size or orientation. Bit maps are a mosaic of individual pixels. When enlarged, they reveal exaggerated jaggedness.

Object-Oriented Graphics

Object-oriented graphics are computer constructs that can be defined mathematically by equations or through the use of formulas or mathematical specifications that have both dimension and direction associated with them. As such, objects always display at the maximum resolution that your hardware allows, and they scale or resize without distorting the object. Other properties can also be associated with objects besides their mathematical shape, including line width (or stroke), fill pattern, line fill, colors, and so on. Fills are created by a mathematical algorithm for dot placement and they are a built-in feature of page description languages. For an object, all of these must be specified, and each can be manipulated individually.

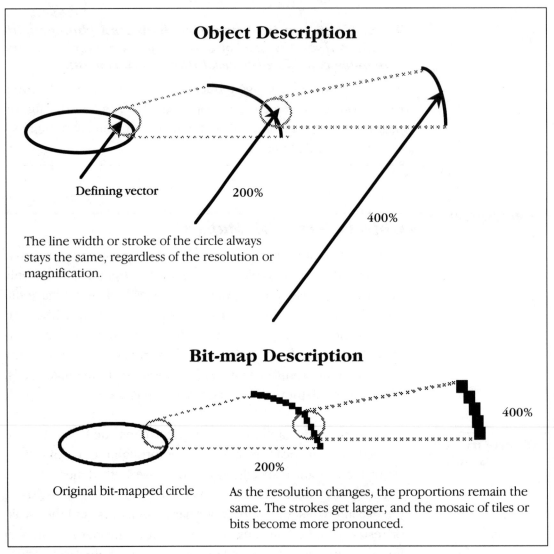

Figure content:

Object Description

Defining vector

200%

400%

The line width or stroke of the circle always stays the same, regardless of the resolution or magnification.

Bit-map Description

400%

200%

Original bit-mapped circle

As the resolution changes, the proportions remain the same. The strokes get larger, and the mosaic of tiles or bits become more pronounced.

Figure 9-2 Objects versus bit maps.

When you draw, move, or change an object's appearance, an internal database that keeps track of each object is updated. You can place objects in different layers, order layers back to front, and specify object groups, unlike bit maps, which have only one layer. Even objects hidden by other objects are described and can be fully manipulated. Object graphics can be compactly described and are relatively quick to calculate and display, real advantages that make them ideal for work that requires precision and rapid manipulation. One disadvantage to representing complex images with objects, however, is that many objects must be specified. A smooth sphere would require several triangulated or pentagonal faces to give the appearance of an even surface. Objects don't have to appear sharp or hard, however. Graceful curves, subtle shadings, and gradient screens are possible with tools provided by many of the better programs coupled with correct technique. Object description does lose its file size advantage when the image being drawn has many small features that need to be represented (such as a photograph or halftone); then bit-mapped graphics have a smaller file size and are more appropriate.

Object graphics software programs are called *draw* programs. Special-purpose draw programs are used for architecture, engineering, and design applications that require drafting tools. Examples include technical illustrations, floor plans, maps, diagrams, and charts.

Bit-mapped Graphics

Bit-mapped graphics store images as a set of binary digits (bits) mapped to a specific display location called a picture element (pixel or pel). With black-and-white graphics, each pixel is either on or off (1 or 0), but for grayscale or color graphics a computer actually calculates some binary value for each pixel that is referenced to a color table stored internally in the system software. Bit-mapped graphics scale poorly except at special whole integer multiples or fractions that are defined by the display system's attributes. Bit maps also rotate properly only at specified angles. For rectangular pixels that angle is 90 degrees; hexagonal pixels rotate properly at 60-degree angles.

Figure 9-3
Moving objects versus moving bit maps. An object can be selected and moved only in its entirety; it shows handles when selected. A bit map can be partially selected and manipulated.

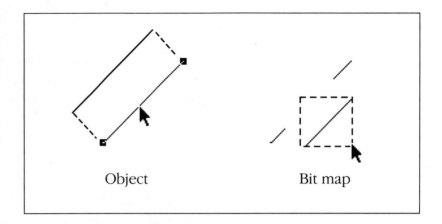

Object   Bit map

The advantage of bit maps is that individual elements can be manipulated and controlled; their disadvantage is that any changes to be made to a group of pixels of bits must be individually calculated for each bit independently. That requires considerable processing power. A 13-inch CRT monitor with 371,200 pixels (640 by 480) must store and manipulate 371 K bits every sixtieth of a second to refresh the screen. For 256 grayscale colors, eight bits of data are needed to describe each pixel. (Color plate Figure C4 shows different values of color and grayscale.) Bit-mapped files are large (five to ten times the size of an object description), and thus bit-mapped graphics production is slow. Even though computers use special techniques to minimize RAM requirements, such as saving and displaying only pixels that change, or breaking down bit maps to a set of regions (sometimes called graphics ports), bit-mapped graphics files and descriptions are always considerably larger than object graphics.

A real-world analogy of bit-mapped graphics would be a mosaic of tiles. To describe a color or gray value that isn't available, you can group tiles together to blend them into that color. That process is called *dithering*. Also, a bit map has only one layer. When you move pixels you are leaving a hole behind, and the pixels cover over the area into which they are moved .

Software programs that manipulate bit maps are called *paint* programs, and they find applications in the arts, imaging, mapping, and other scientific areas. Although bit-map graphics have

Figure 9-4
Whether graphics are created in "paint" or "draw" formats greatly affects the manner in which they can be manipulated. **(A)** We start with two sets of three overlapping objects. **(B)** In a bit-mapped paint format, these elements cannot be separated into individual objects: one can only select and move a field of contiguous bits.

(C) However, in an object-oriented draw format, the elements can be selected and moved as individual objects. Here, we've used a "Move to back" command to juggle their locations in multiple drawing layers.

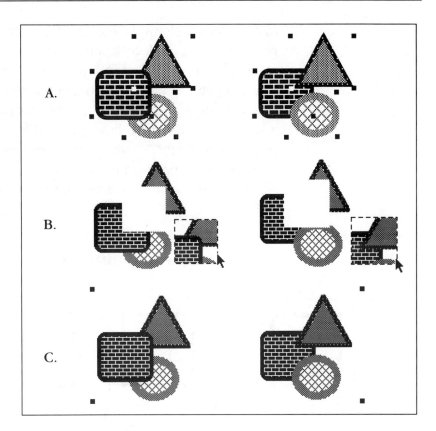

many limitations, many artists are uncomfortable with object graphics. With bit-map graphics, you can achieve effects similar to traditional painting with extraordinary control. Photo retouching or digital image processing programs are special types of bit-mapped paint programs that are the default graphics for scanned images. Chapter 10 discusses digital imaging in detail.

Paint Versus Draw Programs

It's fairly easy to tell what kind of graphics description you are working with. If you can select any part of an object and manipulate it, you are working with bit-mapped graphics in a paint program. If you can only manipulate an object as a whole, then you are working with object graphics in a draw program. Consider the same rectangle drawn in Figure 9.5 by both a draw and a paint program. Using a selection arrow, you can move any part of the rectangle that you select in a paint program, while in the draw program you can only select the entire rectangle for translation. Think of a draw program for object graphics as being composed of a set of tools similar to those you find in a drafting kit: pencils, pens, rulers, French curves, compasses, and the like. Paint programs for bit-mapped graphics, on the other hand, have tools that you might find in an artist's kit: pencils, pens, charcoals, crayons,

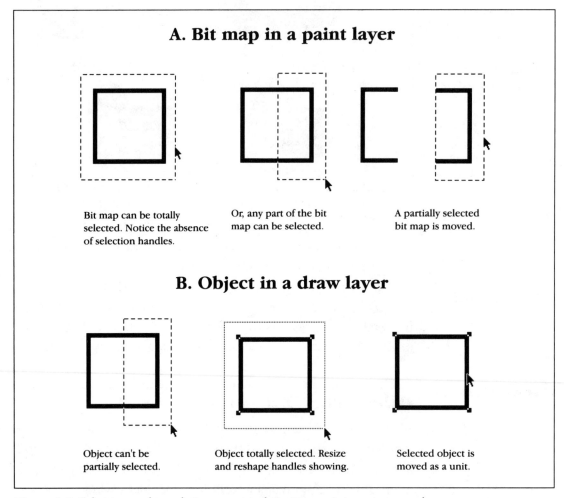

Figure 9-5 Selecting and translating a rectangle in **(A)** a paint program, and **(B)** a draw program.

paintbrushes, and paint. A paint program is more effective for problems dealing with imagery; draw programs are better suited to technical drawing and illustration.

Although objects can be altered in many ways, you can't manipulate parts of an object; only global changes are allowed. If a command acts on part of an object, it acts by changing the underlying mathematical description of the object as a whole. When selected, a unique drawing tool such as a freehand Bézier that you might find in Adobe Illustrator (PC and Mac), Aldus FreeHand (Mac), Micrografx Designer (PC), or CorelDraw (PC) allows curves to be edited by dragging the handles about a control point. When you drag a control point handle, you are actually changing the mathematical description of the curve defined. Bézier curves are hard to master but allow for infinite modification without image degradation.

Figure 9-6
Editing a Bézier curve changes the underlying mathematical description. **(A)** A single segment curve is created and selected. **(B)** When endpoints are selected, the reshape handles are shown. **(C)** Moving a reshape handle changes the shape of the curve. Both endpoints have two reshape handles. **(D)** When you use a freehand draw tool, your drawing is unconstrained. The program assigns Bézier curves based on a set of rules. From Adobe Illustrator.

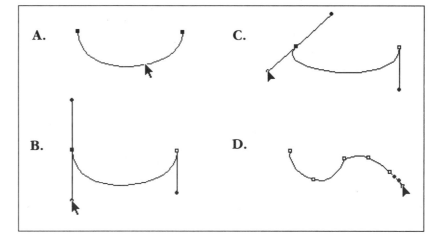

But, no matter how a computer calculates an object image, when it displays, outputs, or prints that image, it must translate it into the technology of the system's output device. That's what device drivers do. For a standard CRT monitor the display technology is a bit-mapped model at the somewhat crude resolution of 72 to 75 dpi on a Macintosh monitor (depending on the model), or as high as 150 dpi on high-resolution screens from third-party vendors. Computers allow you to store characters or lines either as an object or a bit map. No matter how precisely described an object is internally (very precisely, actually!), it can be displayed only as a translated bit-mapped representation. So on your screen a smooth object diagonal line appears staircased to the eye even though the underlying description is considerably smoother. (This particular problem in regard to type is discussed in Chapter 11.) Take that same precisely described object and output it as a bit map to a Linotronic printer at 2,450 dpi, and you now have a line that looks more perfect. The bits have become smaller, and it takes a magnifying glass to spot the imperfections.

These same limitations apply to bit-mapped graphics. You can create a high-resolution bit map, say a letterform described by many thousands of bits, but you can display only what the technology allows you to; the bit maps are reduced to the resolution allowed. At small point size, that might be only a few pixels. When a bit-mapped image is compressed, you usually observe an image quality *enhancement*. There is more information than is needed to describe the bits that are being created. When you must scale a bit map up, you have fewer pieces of information available than necessary and you see an image quality *degradation*. The software doesn't know how to represent precisely those additional pixel values it must create for the scale-up. This is a problem for complex graphics, such as photographs, that are digitally imaged (see Chapter 10).

The principle of resolution enhancement is apparent in the process by which computers handle type. If a computer has an object representation of a letterform, it computes the mathematical translation of that letter to a bit map. Considerable processing is involved in tweaking the letter so that it looks right, especially at small sizes. Yet this is more efficient than having to store bit maps for that character at all of the different sizes and styles; it takes up less storage space. But suppose an object character is not available. Then the computer looks for a bit-map font to work with, ideally one at two to three times the size to reduce, thus obtaining a resolution enhancement for the output bit map.

Thus a graphic is represented by the translation of its underlying image to a device. This phenomenon has important ramifications on how an object looks on screen versus how it prints. Consider Figure 9.7 where the same rectangle is created as both an object and a bit map. Rotate both images by a non-ideal angle and both look distorted on screen. However, when the object is printed, it prints fine because the underlying description is that of the whole entity. A PostScript file can take a long time to manipulate certain features on screen, including graduated screens. Therefore, some programs use a file format called Encapsulated PostScript (EPS) that allows for both an object description and a reduced-resolution bit map. The latter is used with on-screen work. Often EPS figures look awful because you are seeing the bit-map representation, but they print fine because the object representation is output. You have to understand what the file format represents to make sense of its behavior.

Figure 9-7
Rotating a bit map versus an object image. A rectangle looks the same, but when rotated at a nonideal angle, only the drawn object prints properly. The bit map is distorted.

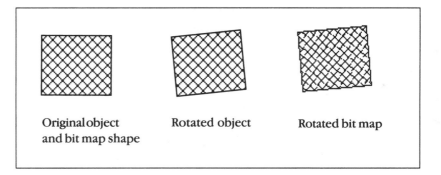

Original object   Rotated object   Rotated bit map
and bit map shape

Paint Programs

Bill Atkinson's MacPaint program was a wonder when it appeared in 1984 bundled with the first Macintosh. Tightly coded so that it would run on a 128 KByte machine, this black-and-white (1-bit) program had excellent performance and many well thought out tools. It has served as the model for a whole generation of paint software that has appeared since on many different computers. As explained earlier, paint programs have a single layer of pixels and require special tools to select and manipulate individual pixels and regions of pixels, and there are pattern tools and shape tools. One of MacPaint's most unique features was its *fat bits* mode, a zoom-in view where the entire bit map was substantially enlarged on screen for modification.

Paint programs vary widely in their power and purpose. Windows 3.0 ships with a simple black-and-white application called Paintbrush that is based on ZSoft's PC Paintbrush, a more fully developed product. Similarly, the Microsoft Mouse comes with Microsoft Paintbrush based on the same product. ZSoft also sells Publisher's Paintbrush for DTP applications. The GEM interface ships with GEM Paint as part of its basic package. Claris has developed MacPaint into MacPaint II, which is considerably faster, more powerful, and easier to use than the original program.

A host of powerful paint software exists on the Macintosh. Zedcor's desk accessory called DeskPaint packs enormously powerful paint power into a very small program. It handles higher-resolution paint-type images that are created by digital scanners (TIFF format, see Chapter 13). The Hewlett-Packard DeskJet Plus scanner comes bundled with a version of DeskPaint for use as an image editing program. Similarly, PC Paintbrush IV Plus, a full-featured PC paint program, can drive a scanner and create and edit images in both color and black and white.

When a program has both draw and paint tools, it can create special effects. Silicon Beach's SuperPaint program combines a paint layer and a draw layer in the same program. You can switch from layer (or mode) to layer creating appropriate graphics. When the image is printed, both layers are output in place. SuperPaint II is a best-selling product with many advanced tools, including 300 dpi bit maps. One very special black-and-white paint program from Electronic Arts, called Studio/1, contains many special tools to provide animation. Adobe Illustrator, a draw program, can import a bit map in a noneditable grayed-out layer that's used as a template, and an artist draws over it (see "The Draw Toolbox"). This process is akin to copying a drawing with tracing paper (see Chapter 10). A combination draw/paint package allows one layer to be converted to another. By selecting an object and then using the Cut to Paint layer, you can turn an object into a bit map, a process called vector-to-raster conversion.

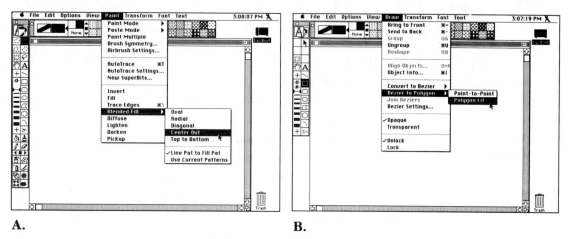

A.   **B.**

Figure 9-8 SuperPaint has both **(A)** a paint and **(B)** a draw layer.

▼ *Tip: When working in a program that allows both bit maps and objects, use object type to lower file size, speed printing, and improve print quality.*

Color Paint Programs

In the last couple of years, a new generation of color paint programs have been introduced, especially on the Macintosh. Color paint programs are slowly but steadily replacing their black-and-white cousins with low-cost, 32-bit programs, such as Color Mac-Cheese (Mac). The first of these full-featured programs was SuperMac's PixelPaint (Mac), an 8-bit color program (see color Figure C8). Electronic Arts introduced a highly rated 8-bit program called Studio 8 (Mac), and both of these products have received excellent reviews. The 8-bit color video technology shows 256 colors from a palette of 16.8 million colors, and 8-bit color is an adaptation on IBM PC compatible computers.

Macintosh computers have begun to ship with 24-bit color, also called 32-bit color because 8 bits are used for other information and special effects. PixelPaint Professional (Mac) and Studio/32 (Mac) have begun to take advantage of this new photorealistic standard. If you work with 32-bit color paint programs, you should consider purchasing a graphics accelerator board to improve screen display response. Both raster and vector accelerator boards are available. The 32-bit color paint programs are being used in a number of areas, including fine art, design, and animation.

Note: Here we are defining paint programs as bit-mapped-based graphics software used to create art by hand. These differ from photo retouching and color prepress applications, such as Adobe Photoshop (Mac) or U-Lead's PhotoStyler (Win3), which are covered in Chapter 10.

Paint Palette Tools

Because a paint program must manipulate pixels both individually and in groups, a good toolbox offers a number of specialized tools for selecting, creating, and manipulating pixels. All tools, even ones that create shapes, do so with pixels in mind. With a good paint program, generally you can constrain shapes to perfect shapes, constrain motion to restrict angles, and change the way tools operate in many other ways by holding down *modifier keys*. Modifier keys are usually the Shift, Control, Option, Command (Mac), Alternate or Alt (PC) keys.

Figure 9-9
Elements of a paint program toolbox. From SuperPaint II.

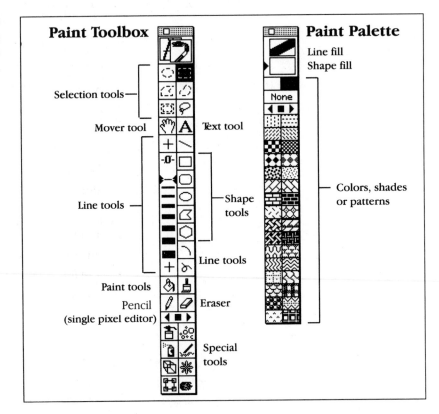

It's impossible to describe all the tools included in paint programs, but this list of tools can serve as a guide for your selection.

- Selection tools. Various tools are generally offered. A selection rectangle and oval select a regular-shaped area by dragging the cursor. A polygon is sometimes added. Often there is a free tool to select irregular areas. Most useful is a lasso for selecting all pixels within the traced area. Sometimes a tool is supplied to move the whole painting.

- Shape tools. Text, rectangles, ovals, polygons (irregular straight-edged shapes), multigons (regular straight edged shapes), and line tools are usually supplied. Remember, these are *bit maps*, but you can normally assign line weight and fill, and shape fill (color, shade, pattern, etc.) to these shapes.

- Paint tools. These include a paintbrush for painting a color, shade, or pattern; a pencil tool for freehand drawing of a single-pixel line; or a freehand tool. They also include a paint bucket for pouring a color, shade, or pattern into an enclosed area; an airbrush for spray-painting a fill pattern with an adjustable rate of flow, spray area, and dot size; and a freeform paint tool. A color and/or pattern palette is typical, with assignments for both fills and strokes (lines); blend and smear tools are also common. The ability to create custom palettes and assign special colors and patterns is very useful. A paint mode can be assigned, allowing for opaque or transparent paint, paint on black areas, and inverted pixel color painting.

- Viewing modes. Zoom-in and zoom-out tools are often supplied for close-in editing or global changes. In Macintosh paint program, such as MacPaint, clicking Command when the Pencil tool is active zooms into the fat bits mode so that you can do single-pixel editing.

- Editing tools. An eraser tool is used to white-out black or colored areas. Cut, copy, paste, clear, and delete are standard Duplicate and replicate, or step and repeat tools are also common. Good programs allow you to create your own color or pattern palette assignments. Most tools can be edited to change their size, shape, lines, and so on. Masking, which is the ability to edit an image either inside or outside of a defined boundary, is very useful. Smears, blends, pattern mapping (duplicating a pattern elsewhere), image merging, and masking are advanced features.

- Position tools. Rulers, grids, constrained motion, rotation, reflection, and shearing, shaping, and position indicators are common, although they are more often associated with draw programs.

Part of what makes one paint program better than another is how easily the tools can be selected and modified. How easy is it to select a color or a pattern? Does the program appear logically designed? Paint programs are among the most feature-laden programs on the market, and it can take several days of work to fully appreciate the power of some of the better ones. Color Figure C8 shows the color palette and screen for PixelPaint. Expect to pay from $75 to $150 for a black-and-white paint program, and $100 to $700 for a color paint program for professional uses.

Paint Software Gallery

The best paint software currently is found on the Macintosh. This is particularly true of color paint software, where the Macintosh II series has about an eighteen-month lead over the IBM PC compatibles. In microcomputer workstations, the Mac IIfx, IBM RISC machines, Sun SPARCStation 1, and others are roughly comparable, but the more innovative paint software is still to be found on the Macintosh, with some good software appearing on the Amigas. The introduction of successful GUIs such as Windows and OS/2 Presentation Manager for the PC will narrow the difference, and throughout 1991 a number of successful PC paint programs should be introduced and refined.

Among the more successful paint programs available commercially today are:

- Color MacCheese (Mac): A low cost, 24-bit color paint program with a good feature set.

- DeskPaint 3.0 (Mac): The paint twin of DeskDraw DA. Very powerful, a perfect DTP companion. File formats supported include Paint/PICT, PICT, PICT2, TIFF, and EPS.

- GEM Paint (PC): A modest paint program that is bundled with the GEM GUI (as is GEM Draw Plus). Comes with standard tools and doesn't recognize objects. It has a fat bit mode called Microscope, and comes with a screen shot utility called Snapshot. This program uses the .IMG format.

- LaserPaint Color II (Mac): A complete color graphics environment with paint/PostScript draw tools, text and image editing, color scanning, and four-color separations. A version called LaserPaint is a smaller set of these features.

- MacPaint II (Mac): A middle-of-the-road paint program with a clean interface and standard Macintosh tool set with limited color support. It is starting to show its age. Only MacPaint/PICT is supported.

- Paintbrush (Win3): Supplied with the Microsoft Windows package, and based on ZSoft's PC Paintbrush. It's a much-improved version of the program called Windows Paint that shipped with Windows 2.0 and was based on a program supplied from Micrografx. Windows has a metafile format called .MSP.

- PC Paintbrush IV Plus (Win3): An 8-bit color package with a scanner driver and image editing tools built in. With a good tools set, this program is a high-end standard. A version for MS-DOS comes with a virtual memory manager to deal with large images and uses a mouse-driven, pull-down menu interface (not Windows or GEM), with good device support.

- Publisher Paintbrush 2.0 (Win3) A similar program without virtual memory and with enhanced device support for DTP work. File formats supported include the .PCX (ZSoft's own standard) and TIFF.

- PixelPaint 2.0 (Mac): The first full featured color paint package. It is highly rated, very successful, and competes directly with Studio/8. Has the widest choice of color selection methods and supports several different color matching methods. File formats supported include MacPaint/PICT, PICT2, TIFF (black and white and grayscale), and EPS.

- PixelPaint Professional (Mac): The 24-bit version of PixelPaint. Has a unique color mixing scheme. Supports same file formats as PixelPaint 2.0 plus TIFF (color), and now does image editing.

- Studio/1 (Mac): A full-feature black-and-white paint program, most notable for its animation features. Does figure tweening, creating snapshots of figures between two specified positions and states. File formats supported include MacPaint/PICT, PICT2, TIFF, and EPS.

- Studio/8 (Mac): One of the two favored color paint packages. It has a well thought out tool set with many special tools and effects. Texture patterns are included. File formats supported are similar to Studio/1, except for EPS.

- Studio/32 (Mac): A professional paint program modeled on the popular Studio/8. Same file formats supported as in Studio/1.

- SuperPaint II (Mac): A combination paint/draw package that is the best-selling black-and-white graphics package on the Macintosh. Exceptionally good interface with a full set of tools and wide file format support. Limited color support, mostly in the object layer. Many special effects and tools, autotracing, Bézier curves, rotation, and 300 dpi precision bit maps. File formats supported are: MacPaint/PICT, PICT2 (except for 24-bit bit maps) and TIFF (monochrome only).

- Ultrapaint (Mac): A paint/draw package with color and some grayscale support for image processing, autotracting, Bézier curves, rotation, and 600 dpi precision bit maps. Very large feature set. File formats accepted are MacPaint/PICT, PICT2, and TIFF (monochrome and grayscale).

Several paint packages meant specifically for digital image processing and discussed in Chapter 10 include Digital Darkroom, Enhance, ImageStudio, ColorStudio, Photoshop for the Macintosh, Aldus Snapshot, Grey F/X, Image-In, ImageEdit, Picture Publisher, PC Paintbrush IV, and Windows ColorLab for the PC. These packages differ from the paint programs discussed here only in that they contain fuller sets of tools for photographic-type manipulations, plus device drivers for various scanners. They have enhanced sets of filters, and color or grayscale value calibration and measurement tools, but fewer shape tools, and few or no patterns or color palettes, and fewer masks.

Draw Programs

Graphics that are used to evaluate or model, rather than image, are usually draw programs. Business, presentation, and design software such as CAD and graphing or statistical software are typical examples. Draw programs lend themselves to integrated applications and programs that run in a limited operating system environment. Microsoft Works, the low-end integrated package that comes bundled with the IBM PS/1, many laptops, and many personal computers, has a draw module. The important benefit for limited RAM or storage size situations is that a large video frame is not necessary for bit maps and compact file storage. At the high end, draw software in the form of computer aided design (CAD) has specialized tools that require sophisticated intensive processing techniques, specialized numerical coprocessors, video graphics (vector) accelerators, and the power of workstations in order to run. Draw software is used in a broad spectrum of applications. Draw programs are ideal for PDL support.

**The Draw
Toolbox**

The fact that draw programs are different from paint programs can be somewhat confusing to new computer users. Many of the tools are identical for both paint and draw tools, but when a draw program defines a square, it does so by defining positions and line segments. When a paint program defines a square, it does so by defining the pixels that compose the square. The square looks the same, but what you can do with it is unique to each. Selecting an object square normally shows resize or reshape handles. Selecting a bit-map square actively selects the constituent pixels without providing manipulation devices, such as handles.

Figure 9-10
Two technical
PostScript draw
programs for the
Macintosh.
(A) Aldus FreeHand
(B) Adobe Illustrator
uses a tracing paper
metaphor to import
grayed-out bit maps as
templates for drawing.

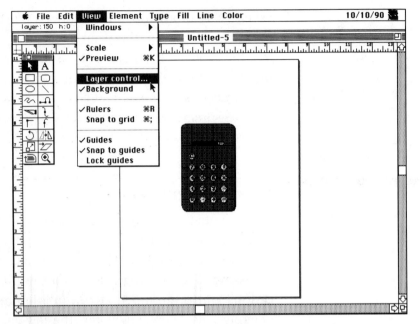

A.

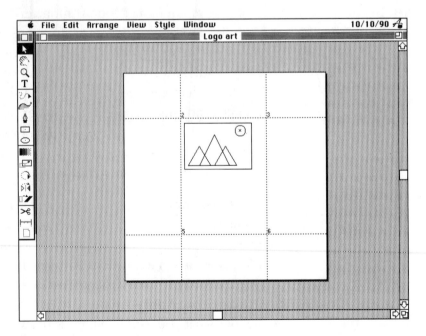

B.

Because draw programs allow many layers of objects, commands are necessary to manipulate these layers so that you can access the objects that may be hidden. Such commands as *Send to back* or *Bring to front* are common. And, as most objects are made from a collection of other objects, the only reasonable way of manipulating a compound object is by object grouping; therefore, *Group* and *Ungroup* are typical commands. *Join*, *Average*, and *Blend* are also sometimes found. Layering and grouping commands have no paint counterparts.

A good draw program allows you to create shapes. Refining shapes, constraining motion to restricted angles, and changing the way tools operate are accomplished using the modifier keys described in "The Paint Toolbox," but generally the smoothness and fineness of the control is greatly enhanced. If a paint program constrains perfect line angles to 45-degree line angles, a draw program might allow 5-degree line angles.

A draw program lacks certain tools and commands that are prominent in a paint program. Selection tools are obviously more modest for a draw program because only an entire object can be selected. Also, there are generally fewer freehand tools in draw programs because they require a mathematical object description. Pencils and paintbrushes aren't required, nor is the eraser tool that acts on pixels, not objects. Draw software uses deletion instead.

A good draw toolbox includes:

- Selection tools: A single arrow selection tool is common. Only whole objects are selected.

- Shape tools: Text (or type), rectangles, ovals, polygons, multigons, and line tools, are the norm. Although these are objects, most draw programs allow you to assign line weight and fill, and shape fill (color, shade, pattern, etc.) to these shapes. Fills can be bit maps that draw programs support. Because shapes are not as editable as objects, often there is support for such properties as line end curves (called miters) and line connections (called joins).

Figure 9-11
Elements of a draw
program toolbox. From
SuperPaint II.

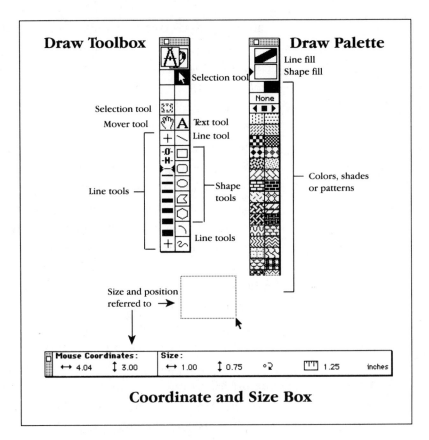

- Draw tools: Bézier curves are the single most important tool unique to draw programs. Also, freehand Bézier tools are common. Both types give editable curves. Autotrace tools that convert bit-mapped shapes into editable object shapes are common.

- Viewing modes: Zoom-in and zoom-out tools are often supplied for close-in editing or global changes. Some programs allow bit maps to be imported for use as templates.

- Editing tools: Cut, copy, paste, clear, and delete are standard commands. Duplicate and replicate (clone), or step and repeat tools, are common, and their precision is much higher than in paint programs. Most tools can be edited to change their size, shape, lines, and so on. Layer commands such as Bring to Front or Send to Back are common. Group, Ungroup, Join, Segment, and Average commands are found.

- Position tools: Rulers, grids (with snap-on and snap-off), constrained motion, rotation, reflection, and shearing, shaping, and position indicators are very important. Various types of alignments are supported.

Tools for converting bit maps to objects, called autotrace tools, are particularly impressive and satisfying. Raster-to-vector conversion can lop literally hours off of a drawing project by creating an editable figure to work with. Most high-level draw programs have autotrace modules built in, but this is such a valuable feature that Adobe Streamline is marketed as a stand-alone application. Autotrace works best with high-contrast line art. It is an algorithm that searches for adjoining pixels that have a certain adjustable color or grayscale value difference or similarity. For that reason, however, images with subtle variations of shades are difficult candidates for autotracing. Micrografx Designer has a unique color autotrace module.

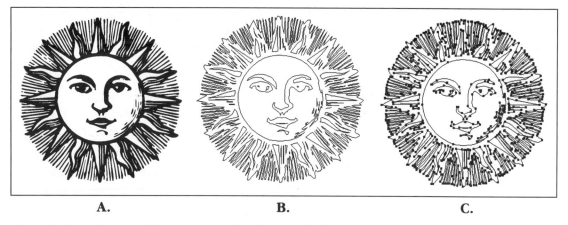

A.   **B.**   **C.**

Figure 9-12 Adobe Streamline is a high-end product specifically sold for converting bit maps to objects—raster-to-vector conversion. **(A)** The symbol for Streamline is first scanned as a bit map. **(B)** The conversions to bit map yields an editable outline. **(C)** In this figure, all of the figure is selected and the individual control points are shown. *Courtesy of Adobe Systems, Inc.*

Expect to pay from $75 to $150 for a basic draw program. Technical illustration packages that output PostScript and have a full toolbox can cost from $250 to $700. CAD programs range from $150 to $300 for enhanced drawing programs, $500 to $800 for midlevel drafting programs, to $800 to $3,000 for professional CAD packages. Special-purpose drawing programs for use in visualization or in special market niches can cost thousands of dollars, sometimes much more than the computers they run on. Draw programs can be simple and take no more than a few hours to learn, while technical drawing packages require several days of work for familiarization.

**Draw Software
Gallery**

Very good draw software is found on both IBM PC compatibles and the Macintosh. The most important CAD packages, such as AutoCAD, started life on the PC and have migrated to the Macintosh, but the product category is crowded for both. AutoCAD on OS/2 (PC) may be one of the most important and strongest products yet released for that platform. Low-end draw software for the Macintosh tends to perform better than similar products on the PC. High-end draw packages and CAD are normally the first applications written for microcomputer workstations such as the Mac IIfx, IBM RISC machines, or Sun SPARCStation 1. The arguments made about a consistent interface easing training time apply strongly to complex draw software.

Among the more successful draw programs available commercially today are:

- Adobe Illustrator 3.0 (Mac): One of the two favored (with Aldus FreeHand) technical illustration drawing programs for the Mac; based on PostScript. Illustrator uses a tracing paper metaphor, importing bit maps into a separate grayed-out layer that you draw over. Illustrator is faithful to the Mac interface and has logical menu commands. Type handling is much improved from version 2.0, with outline font editing possible. Color is available in a preview window, with color separation output accomplished using Adobe Separator. Modest autotrace; Adobe Streamline is recommended for that purpose. File formats supported are MacPaint/PICT (import and display only), PICT (object), PICT2 (object), and EPS.

- Adobe Illustrator 1.1 (Win3): An easy-to-use program with a strong interface. Color is available only in preview mode, and typographical controls are modest. Uses a template metaphor to import TIFF, .PCX, and .PNT (MacPaint) bit maps for tracing. Saves EPS files as artwork and exports them to page layout programs. Supports CYMK color RGB and requires the Adobe Separator utility (available on Macintosh only) for color output. Autotrace is modest; Adobe Stream-line (PC) is recommended for this purpose, an additional expense. Has many nice features, but not as well reviewed as either CorelDraw or Micrografx Designer.

- Adobe Streamline (Mac and Win): A good stand-alone auto-trace application, but not significantly better than many included in high-end packages such as CorelDraw or Micro-grafx Designer.

- Aldus FreeHand 3.0 (Mac): A highly rated technical drawing package (my favorite) with a good toolbox. Strong color sup-port and an editable preview mode. Supports up to 100 undo/redo's and 200 design layers. Formats supported include MacPaint/PICT (import and print only), PICT (object), PICT2, TIFF, and EPS (import and print only).

- Artline 2.0 (PC): Runs on the Digital Research GEM interface and is an excellent choice for low-end computers such as PC ATs. Good toolbox, excellent blend tool, and good pattern control. Has good text handling and ships with thirty-five fonts. Three color models supported.

- Arts & Letters Graphic Editor 3.1 (Win3): A high-powered drawing program from Computer Support Corp., which allows artists and non-artists alike to easily produce profess-sional illustrations. Version 3.1, released in mid-1991, ships with 5,000 pieces of editable clip art.

- CA-Cricket Draw (Mac): A good middle-of-the-road draw pro-gram that is now somewhat out of date.

- Canvas 2.1 (Mac): A precision drawing program with many features making it a good value for the money. Formats sup-ported include MacPaint/PICT, PICT, PICT2, and TIFF (1-bit).

- CorelDraw (Win3). One of the highest-rated PC draw pro-grams, it started life as an outline text editor and has excep-tional typographical tools. A deceptively simple toolbox has several modes per tool and is powerful. The autotrace tool is excellent, importing either .PCX or TIFF. Patterns are limited. Objects are drawn as wireframes and can be difficult to manipulate. The program ships with 6 MBytes of clip art and seventy-five typefaces.

- DeskDraw 3.0 (Mac): The surprisingly powerful desk accessory draw package twin of DeskPaint DA. Excellent tools for a low-priced package, the twins are wonderful DTP companions. File formats supported include Paint (import/view), PICT (object), PICT2, and TIFF.

- GEM Draw Plus (PC): A simple, easy-to-use draw program for the GEM GUI. Runs well on PC XT and AT class computers, but Artline is the recommended product for that class. Saves files in the .GEM format.

- MacDraw II (Mac): The updated version of the program that originally came bundled with the Macintosh. Excellent interface and logical toolbox make this a very accessible middle-of-the-road application.

- Mass-11 Draw 6.0 (PC): A low-end package that runs well on PC ATs and XTs. Its CAD-like features and color support make it a good choice for those machines. Type handling is poor.

- Micrografx Designer 3.0 (Win3): A powerful drawing package with strong drafting tools. Has good text editing, impressive autotracing, and good color support (32 bit). Color autotrace is notable. Has a strong CAD-like design feel, but with many artistic enhancements. Includes a slide show feature. Designer has the widest file format support on the IBM PC, including .PIC, .DRW, .EPS, and .DFX. Its large toolbox makes it difficult to learn but powerful to use. Ships with a large library of clip art.

- Micrografx Draw (Win): A low-end product for Windows that is somewhat outdated.

Many computer users find that the tools contained in these drawing packages are sufficient for very technical design work, and it's not unusual to find CAD work being done in a package such as MacDraw or Micrografx Designer.

Figure 9-13
Two of the best high-end IBM PC draw programs. For Windows **(A)** CorelDraw started life as a type manipulation program and is a complete drawing environment with strong tracing (CorelTrace) capabilities. **(B)** Micrografx Designer is an excellent draw program with many utilities. It ships with several megabytes of clip art and has fine color tools. *Courtesy of Corel Systems. Courtesy of Micrografx, Inc.*

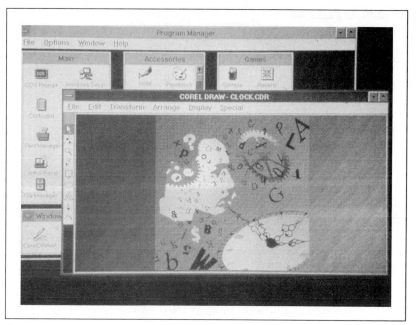

A.

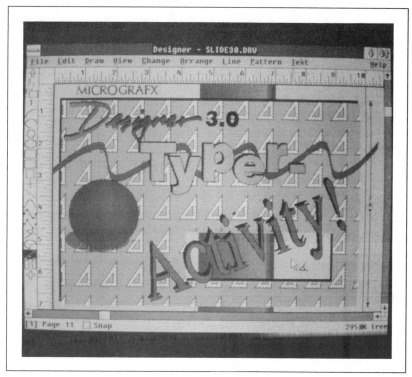

B.

Beyond Drawing

Draw graphics comprise a large product category and new products appear every month. In the following sections are brief discussions of three unique draw product categories: forms software, CAD, and presentation graphics. Each category could be the subject of an entire book on its own. For more information on each refer to the articles referenced in Appendix B.

CAD: Enhanced Draw

Computer aided design (CAD) software is a multibillion-dollar product category. Although often associated with workstation computers, most of the units shipped are for powerful personal computers, such as the Mac IIs and 80368 and 80486 computers. CAD is an extended drawing package with specialized tools that comes in two basic flavors: 2D and 3D. Marked with somewhat different tool sets, and modeling capabilities, they address different market segments with 2D the larger of the two categories. It finds favor in drafting applications, such as blueprints, printed circuit board, or microchip design. 3D CAD is used for general-purpose and architectural drafting, animation, surface modeling, and solid modeling applications. 2D CAD is a planning aid, 3D CAD addresses visualization applications. Because of the complexity of the command and tool structure, the precision necessary for tracing graphics, and other input issues, digitizing tablets using a puck or pen stylus are the favored input devices for CAD applications (see Chapter 6).

Drawing programs are vector applications and programmed databases, and CAD builds on this concept to support the use of *object libraries*. When drawing an aircraft turbine you have to create only a single blade in the library. By repeating, rotating, and positioning that blade, you can build the turbine. The underlining library stores just the single blade description, thus saving file storage and increasing processing speed. If a bolt hole is required, you can use the description for the hole size stored in the library, and not have to create one.

Furthermore, because an object library can store attributes of an object, it's possible to attach properties such as cost to an object. An architect creating an apartment building can draft the floor plan of a single apartment configuration, including doors, fixtures, piping, and so on, and then have the CAD program calculate and list all the costs and bill the client. All of the materials used to create all the apartments can be output directly to a database. CAD supports a vigorous third-party add-on market, and although these applications don't come cheap, they can be the engine of your businesses.

A number of innovations are in development to make CAD a more friendly beast. Programmers are adding artificial intelligence properties into their interfaces to anticipate the desired action. Ashlar Vellum is notable in this regard: for example, if you place your cursor near a line midpoint, the program asks if you want to select that midpoint; if you are near a tangent to a curve, it will ask you if you wish to create a tangent. *Parametric drawing* can also resolve a drawing by resizing and positioning objects to fit a set of constraints that you define. If an object must have a certain surface area, once you specify a shape, Vellum returns the appropriate dimensions for that surface area.

CAD is an interesting product category to watch because many of the most innovative new trends in software are being pioneered there. They include interapplication communications (linking data between programs), groupware, specialty tools, shading and rendering, and virtual reality applications. CAD applications are among the most sophisticated available for computers. This very complexity can mean from a week to a month of work before a user becomes fully competent in all of a program's nuances. Simple packages are similar to technical drawing programs and can be learned in a few days. Prices vary with a product's capabilities,

Figure 9-14
DynaPerspective offers
3D CAD with visualiza-
tion tools. Shown here
is a city plan by ELS/
Elbanasani & Logan
Architects, Berkeley, CA.
(A) Cityscape shown in
wireframe view.
(B) A fully rendered
3D cityscape. Produced
on a Macintosh.
*Courtesy of
Dynaware, Inc.*

A.

B.

The CAD market leaders for the Mac and PC market are:

- Ashlar Vellum 1.0 (Mac and Win): A 2D CAD program that pioneered many AI techniques for intelligent drafting with built-in parametrics. A 3D product is due out soon. Symbol libraries are available.

- AutoCAD (Mac, PC, Win, OS/2): A powerful 3D (only) CAD package that has a huge market following. The overall product category leader in the CAD market. The Mac version was not well received, but the OS/2 version is considered excellent. AutoCAD's .DFX file format is an industry standard.

- Claris CAD (Mac): The best-selling CAD package on the Macintosh. A professional 2D package with a good interface that's easy to learn. Feels like a very upscale version of Mac-Draw II. Supports the .DFX (AutoCAD) and industrywide IGES file standards.

- Dreams 1.1 (Mac): A strong midlevel 2D CAD package that competes with Claris CAD. Strong visualization features.

- Generic CAD (Mac, PC): A midlevel 2D package for the Mac and PC. The PC version has three levels that can be upgraded in functionality. Level 3 (PC) is equivalent to the Mac version.

- MacBravo (Mac): A high-end, complex package from Schlumberger for CAD/CAM work. Has excellent tools aimed at the professional market. Has a Detailer package for 2D drafting, a Facilities package for facility design and management, and a Modeler for 3D mechanical designwork.

- MacDraft 2.0 (Mac): A low-end 2D CAD package that initiated the category of extended drawing. A recent version has substantially updated this best seller. A very easy package to learn and use.

- MicroStation 3.5.1 (Mac, PC): A powerful 3D CAD program for professional workstation-type applications.

- VersaCAD (Mac, PC): The favored high-end Macintosh package with a good feature set and a logical interface. The PC version is popular, but not as popular as AutoCAD.

There are so many other fine programs in this category that it doesn't seem fair to stop with this list. For more information, see the references at the end of this chapter. Solid and surface modeling, rendering, and other visualization CAD packages are discussed more fully in Chapter 18.

Desktop Presentation Graphics

Depending on how you define this product line, presentation graphics can be a huge category. Such products as Lotus 1-2-3, Excel, and WingZ are charting applications that let you build object-oriented graphs of many kinds. DeltaPoint's DeltaGraph (Mac) adds even more tools for color charting imported spreadsheet data and will output to high-resolution PostScript devices. Draw programs are used more often than paint programs to create presentation graphics because of the device-independent nature of the object description. Many programs, such as Micrografx Designer, have built-in slide show capabilities. The user specifies an image order and a timing sequence—and it's show time, folks. It is also possible, using a picture database or a hypertextural application such as HyperCard, SuperCard, Toolbox, and Plus, to create very effective multimedia-styled presentations (see Chapter 18).

Many products designed specifically for the corporate presentation market offer specialized tools for organizing, presenting, and outputting work. Presentation products share elements of several product categories, including text outliners, draw graphics, paint graphics (less frequently), page layout tools, templates (35 mm slide, overheads, etc.), and slide sorters. They also have a notes page, automatic numbering, hot or warm linking of data to the application that created it, wide file format support for importing data, support for many output devices, and drivers for sending slides to a service bureau or an overnight slide service (see Chapter 7).

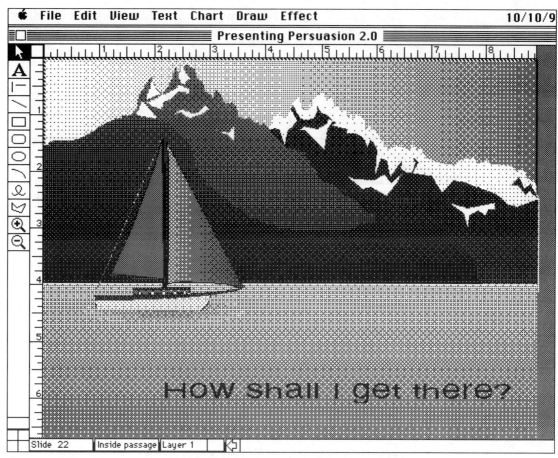

A.

Figure 9-15
(A) Aldus Persuasion 2.0 is one of the top Macintosh presentation packages with a wide range of attractive design features. **(B)** Micrografx Charisma is a fine new package just released for Windows. *Courtesy of Micrografx, Inc.*

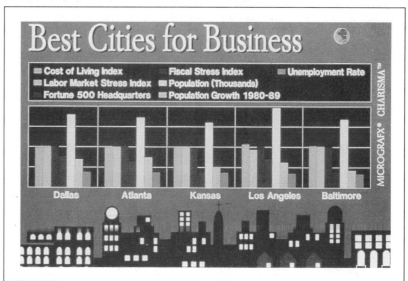

B.

In a typical desktop presentation sequence you would follow these steps:

1. Launch the program and create a master layout(s) or use a template(s) for a slide or overhead. A choice of attractive color and type combinations, blends, shadings, and other eye-catching backgrounds are offered.

2. Open the outliner and create a slide order with slide headings and subheadings.

3. Close the outliner, go from slide to slide adding charts and graphics. Headings are already in place. Many programs offer full word processors and spreadsheet modes.

4. View your slide order and change if necessary. These programs will renumber your slides and if you are collecting them as hard copy for session notes, they are automatically rearranged.

5. Print your notes and output your slides to either a laser printer (laser printers accept transparent foils, 8 ½- by 11-inch sheets from Avery are good enough to cut up into 35 mm holders), color printer, film recorder, or by modem to an overnight slide service.

6. Give your performance.

7. Collect your raise!

However, you don't need these specialized programs to give presentations. You can output files from Adobe Illustrator, Mac-Draw, or Aldus FreeHand, CorelDraw, or Micrografx Designer as color PostScript files. But if you do a lot of presentation work, then dedicated presentation packages will dramatically increase your efficiency and the quality of your sessions. Some have simply amazing effects, such as transitions between slides, dissolves and wipes, superb color graphics that draw an audience's attention, plus commonsense style features built in to prevent over-styling of your slides. All of the following products come with device drivers for commercial slide-making services. As an alternative to creating slides and overhead transparencies, you can hook up an LCD Panel to your computer. By placing the LCD Panel on an overhead projector, you can use your presentation package to display onto a screen.

The best packages in desktop presentation graphics are:

- Aldus Persuasion 2.0 (Mac and Win): The market leader (on the Mac side) that has won admiration for its intelligent style tools. Graphic artists seem to feel very comfortable with its design feel. Has a wide range of import file formats and supports PostScript output. Aldus Persuasion 2.04 (Win3) is scheduled for a late 1991 release.

- CA-Cricket Presents (Mac)/Xerox Presents (PC): A strong package with many special tools for charting and graphing. Not considered as strong a design tool as Persuasion, or as logically presented as Powerpoint.

- Charisma (Win): A graphing and charting package specifically aimed for business presentation users. It accepts input from Lotus 1-2-3, Excel, and Harvard Graphics. Comes with drawing and freehand tools, a large clip art collection, and can create a computer-based slide show.

- DeltaGraph (Mac): A graphing and charting package that can import spreadsheet data to create very attractive slide materials. Good for Excel owners, with even better graphing than found in Wingz. For Macintosh scientific and engineering applications, see KaleidaGraph from Synergy Software.

- Harvard Graphics 2.3 (PC): The market leader on the PC, it runs in its own menu-driven interface, which, although a little outdated, has many loyal users. Excellent range of features.

- Lotus Freelance Plus (PC): A graphing and charting package that accepts spreadsheet data in Lotus 1-2-3 format to create slides and other output.

- Microsoft Powerpoint 2.0 (Mac and Win): A solid product with excellent organizational tools, plus a good, easy-to-learn interface. Has an excellent built-in color scheme. Highly recommended.

- More II (Mac): Began life as the favored outliner and grew into a full-featured desktop presentation package. Still strong in its organizational ability but somewhat unfocused.

- Pixie (PC): Business graphics presentation package noted for its direct manipulation of graph elements. Zenographics' Pixie has built-in color schemes, a standard 98-color palette and can support up to 16 million user-definable colors. The Import and Export formats are extensive, as are its editing and enhancement tools.

- Standout! (Mac): The presentation companion to Letraset's ReadySetGo! page layout program with modest features.

Forms Generation Software

Computer programs for generating complex business forms have appeared on the market and are a significant niche product. Two different product types are available: form design tools and linked automatic entry systems that are basically databases. Professional forms designers often use PostScript draw programs with strong drafting features or page layout programs for form design. Page-Maker, Illustrator, Designer, and FreeHand also are used. However, dedicated form design software has many features that make form design easier and more professional. Features found in good form design software include combs (those tiny lines used to separate letters in a field), multipage or multipart designs, special field tools for split fields, and so on.

Many of the better high-end packages, such as SmartForms (Mac), InFormed Designer, and perForm (PC), not only offer design but also allow you to build intelligence into your forms. When coupled with their associated data entry modules, you can use database concepts to do automatic data entry, validation, and calculations for your forms. This combination isn't as powerful or flexible as a dedicated database, but the forms are simpler to construct and can be valuable to organizations that have considerable form-based data entry requirements. FormBase (PC) is a forms-oriented program with an underlying relational database; File-Maker (Mac) is a database with strong graphical and forms capabilities that are useful for automated forms management.

Figure 9-16
Shana Corporation's
InFormed Designer is a
powerful, specialized
object draw package
that integrates with
their miniManager to
create data entry sta-
tions based on intelli-
gent forms. *Courtesy of
Shana Corp.*

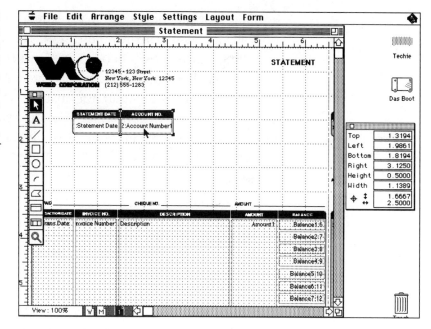

TrueForm (Mac) takes another approach eschewing design, and using instead a scanned form as a template for placing fields and building automation.

Miscellaneous

**Screen-Capture
Utilities**

Screen capture (sometimes called a *screen dump*) is a graphics program or routine that allows you to take a snapshot of your computer screen and send it out to a printer, print it to disk as a file (in one of several formats), or place it into RAM (memory). Capture utilities are often built directly into system software, or they are terminate-and-stay-resident (TSR, or memory-resident) programs on the PC (called INITs and CDEVs on the Macintosh). Simple screen-capture utilities often show up in the public domain, but the best and most stable programs are those sold commercially.

Pressing Command-Shift-3 on a Macintosh creates a MacPaint file in your root directory; Command-Shift-4 sends the file out to your printer. The Command-Shift-Number combination is called an FKey (for function key); many simple utilities in the public domain can be assigned to these keys. This is different from the Shift-PrtSc function built into MS-DOS that is used for ASCII character output; here graphic file formats are created. Screen capture can save the video frame in a format like MacPaint at the same screen resolution (72 dpi), which is crude. Alternatively, many capture utilities save a file in the internal file format before it is converted to a bit map. This format is PICT for the Macintosh.

Use screen capture for:

- Computer documentation: About 75 percent of captured screens end up in technical documentation, such as books or magazine articles.

- Slide shows or demos: Create slide shows from many different programs.

- File format conversion: Many screen-capture utilities offer several save formats, some do image editing (paint tools), and many are significant products for file conversion (see Chapter 13).

- Color printing: When a program has better color on screen than it can print, you can sometimes work around the problem by using the capture utility's print enhancement routines.

- Image editing: Using a capture program with editing capabilities you can resize, annotate, manipulate, and modify an image. Some programs allow you to do translations of color to grayscale or black and white.

PC Paintbrush IV (PC) ships with its own built-in screen capture called FRIEZE, which has editing and format conversion capabilities. DoDot is recommended for Windows, and PMCAP.ARC (available on CompuServe's PC MagNet) is good for OS/2's Presentation Manager. Advanced color standards on the PC, such as SuperVGA, can often lead to problems, but the more standard VGA (and below) generally present no problem. MicroPro's WordStar, Microsoft Word, WordPerfect, and Lotus PC word processors ship with screen-capture utilities. The best screen-capture programs

Figure 9-17
(A) Capture from Mainstay is a simple Macintosh screen-capture utility (a CDEV-control panel device) that's easy to use.
(B) HotShot Graphics is a favored PC screen-capture utility with full-menued graphics editing capability.

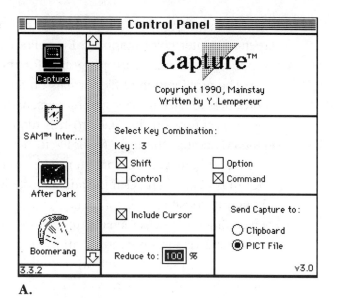

A.

B.

for the PC are the higher-end products HotShot Graphics and Pizazz Plus. They provide broad file format capability and excellent editing capabilities. HotShot Graphics has excellent editing, and has a Windows and Presentation Manager screen-capture capability. HotShot saves files in its .HSG format and converts them to more standard file formats with a batch process. Pizazz Plus is noted for strong printer support and the most sophisticated screen-to-printer color mapping. ImagePrep, and Tiffany Plus, are also strong screen-capture programs for the Windows environment. The proliferation of file formats on the PC makes these useful products to have in your graphics arsenal.

Screen capture on the Macintosh is more straightforward than on the PC because there are fewer file formats that need to be supported, and better, more consistent color standards. The favored program is Capture. It is simple and almost always works properly, although it doesn't work for arcade games (no utility seems to). For a graphics editing screen capture, Exposure is recommended.

One class of screen-capture utility goes a screen dump one better; they've been dubbed print-to-disk utilities. SuperGlue II (Mac) is the best example. When activated it captures an entire document in a proprietary file format, in TEXT, or in the Scrapbook format. Graphics, text, data in tables—anything can be saved. Using an application or desk accessory that you can distribute freely from the package called SuperViewer, people can open, view, and modify a document even if they don't have the applications that the document was created in. This is superior to a screen capture because there isn't any size restriction, the process saves data—not a bit-map rendition—thus allowing you to edit it, and PICT is a higher-resolution file format than MacPaint/Paint. A bit map prints poorly to a PostScript printer; a PICT file prints better. SuperGlue's ability to save in TEXT format means you can create ASCII text files from applications that can't create them directly themselves.

Clip Art

A vast library of computer art exists. Much of it is in the public domain and can be downloaded from on-line services and bulletin boards. Some of the best clip art is in commercially available collections; some may come bundled with your favorite graphics package. Clip art is a boon to desktop publishers and to computer users in general. Named when people took scissors and clipped pictures out of magazines or newspapers to paste into their work, today's canned artwork incorporates computer power.

Depending on the source, either you have an unlimited license to use and alter the art, or you must seek permission for use from the copyright holder. In this era of high-quality desktop scanners, it's wise to be careful. To use copyrighted artwork, you must obtain permission from the publisher to reprint it. Depending on subject matter, most will grant that permission with the addition of a source reference. Some require a small fee to license the rights.

The quality of the clip artwork can vary widely, and not just because of the artist's contribution. Bit-mapped art will not print well on a PostScript printer. On the other hand, art saved as drawn objects can be printed at the output device's best resolution. High-resolution artwork tends to be more precise and expensive because publishers perceive their product as applying to a more professional market. Collections are nearly always thematic—a disk might have computer images, borders, maps, or food as its subject. Collections range from $20 per set up to several hundred dollars; some are sold on a subscription basis with new images mailed every month. Collections of clip art are becoming available on CD ROM, an excellent distribution medium. A CD ROM can hold 600 MBytes of images—hundreds to thousands depending on the file format—and the relatively slow access speed of the disk is not a disadvantage for this application. While computer clip art can be expensive, traditional clip art is not. If you have access to a scanner, you may want to consider looking into the collection from Dover Publications whose books cost between $5 and $10. Fenton and Morrissett's book *Canned Art* is a good place to start.

The commercial clip art library is much larger for the Macintosh than for the PC, a result of the Macintosh's more graphic orientation. To take advantage of that fact, many PC graphics programs read and write MacPaint/PICT images and allow for cross-platform transfer of graphics files in general. The most common file formats for clip art are MacPaint/PICT (bit-mapped for the Mac), .PIC (bit-mapped for the PC), PICT (object), .CGM (object, computer graphic, metafile-PC), EPS (object-Mac or PC), and very rarely TIFF (bit-mapped but high-resolution, Tagged Image File Format-Mac or PC). TIFF files are generally too large to be distributed economically (except when compressed), but they look nice when printed.

If you download artwork from an on-line service, you are likely to encounter the graphics interchange format (.GIF) developed by CompuServe for the PC, or the run length encoded (.RLE) format; both are PC standards. Viewer and conversion utilities for .GIF, like GIFDESK are available in the public domain. Graphics files on-line are often compressed by StuffIt (Mac) and ZIP or ARC (PC). Refer to Chapter 6 for more information about the aforementioned utilities. Whew! Alphabet soup. For more information about graphics file formats and converting them into something your particular program can open, see Chapter 13.

Organizing Picture Books

Eventually, DTPers and other electronic Gutenburgs can end up with large collections of artwork. Short of printing out images and collecting them in looseleaf binders, there are several different approaches to organizing images. If you own a Macintosh, then you can create multiple Scrapbooks in which to store your images. SmartScrap and The Clipper are two desk accessories that allow you to switch between Scrapbooks, name each book and each image, and search for names. The Clipper part of the package allows you to resize and manipulate images on the Clipboard, that area of RAM reserved for cut-and-paste operations. SmartScrap and the Clipper are invaluable. MultiClip is another program that gives you multiple scrapbooks.

The Curator offers an even more powerful approach. It builds an index of thumbnail sketches so that you can visually scan several pictures at one time. The Curator accepts most Mac file formats (not simple PostScript, however), and allows you to catalog images with keywords or names. It accepts graphics saved in SuperGlue format and Solutions International's print-to-disk utility (see "Screen-Capture Utilities" above), and can do some file format conversion. The utility Scrapbook Plus serves the same functions as a Clipboard, file conversion program, and picture library builder for Windows.

Digital Imaging

You can't depend on your eyes when your imagination is out of focus.

Mark Twain

In 1989, just after TV talk show host Oprah Winfrey completed her diet, a full-length picture of her appeared on the cover of *TV Guide*. Readers were astonished at her svelte appearance. In reality, Oprah Winfrey's head had been pasted onto the body of actress Ann Margret using a computer.

How a Computer Forms a Digital Image

Digital imaging can make old photographs new, new photographs blue, and turn you into a magician. It's about as much fun as you can legally have with a computer. You can use the same technology that is used to enhance satellite photos from space to create art, remove wrinkles, or add hair (would that it were so!) to roll away the years, enhance your publishing projects, and synthesize new images quickly. Digital imaging opens up a world of new possibilities that are also great fun. It is much easier than going on a diet or finding new genes. In this chapter, we'll look at the way digital imaging works, consider its power and pitfalls, and survey the range of tools for creating, modifying, and publishing digital images.

275

Your computer is digital; it stores information in binary code: on or off, 1 or 0, logical yes or no. Often the images you want to work with are analog, continuous images containing an infinite range of shades, tones, and colors. To convert an analog image to a digital image, a sampling process occurs that creates discrete finite picture elements and assigns to them both a location and a color or gray value. This is the process called *digital imaging* or digitizing. Although it degrades a continuous image somewhat, at sufficient quality digitizing is nearly an ideal medium for composing images to be used in a DTP project. *Video capture* is the process of taking and displaying the images rapidly in real time; this naturally has application in the animation and film industries (see

Figure 10-1
Using image processing those old family photos can be resurrected and retouched without any loss of image quality. **(A)** The before photo of three children. **(B)** After image processing the restored picture. *Photo courtesy of Shirley J. O'Lear and Silicon Beach Software.*

A.

B.

Chapter 18). In the 1990s electronic imaging will replace film as the major technology in many industries (see Chapter 19).

We perceive images by the light that reflects off an object; this light has both color and intensity. Digital imaging uses an electronic photoreceptor to create an electrical signal (voltage) that is proportional to the amount of light it receives (black objects absorb light, white ones reflect light). An analog-to-digital converter converts the electrical signal from the photoreceptor to digital form, and timing circuitry that measures the value of light

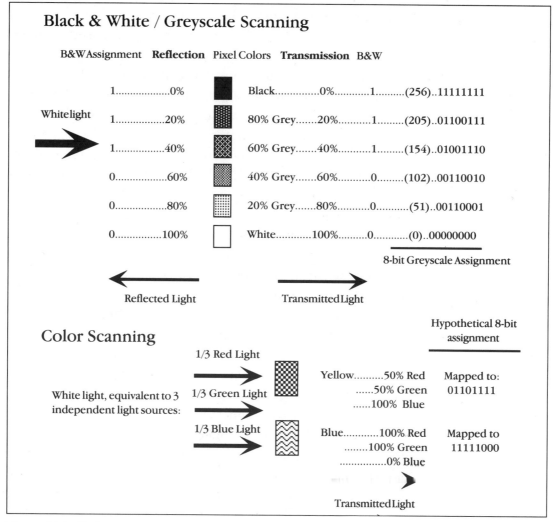

Figure 10-2 The scanning process.

received at each specific sampled time interval maps those data to a specific location or pixel. The size of the photoreceptor, its sensitivity, and the sampling rate are of primary importance in determining the resolution and quality of the scanning process.

The most commonly used photoreceptor is the *charge-coupled device* (CCD), formed from an array of transistors (typically 4,096) made from a variety of light-sensitive semiconductor materials. Changes in light intensity entering the transistor cause corresponding changes in electrical current. CCDs can be very small, but they are not small enough yet to produce the extremely fine definition needed to mimic fine photography.

An alternative photoreceptor technology is based on liquid crystal displays. In displays, LCDs work by forming aligned crystals where electric potential occurs. Light shining through the display appears dark where these aligned "domains" are formed. For photoreceptor applications, certain crystals can be light-stimulated to form domains. If electric potential is applied, the variable resistance can be measured. This may be interpreted in terms of light intensity. However, just as with CCDs, LCDs form domains that are too large for very fine resolutions.

Various methods are used to improve the data density of digitizing processes. In *scanning*, an array of photoreceptors are used and the picture to be digitized is swept by this array, or vice versa. Scanners minimize the number of CCDs or LCDs needed to digitize an image. The highest-priced scanners, called transmissive scanners, use rotating drums, light transmitted through film (transmitted light has a wider dynamic range), and two-dimensional photo arrays. The quality of drum scanners is so fine that they can be used in mapping applications. High-resolution scanners are just starting to show up in the publishing industry. More common are reflective scanners with a linear array of CCDs. A flat image is moved past the scanning head, and the line of CCDs is translated into a line of pixels. Desktop scanners are a staple of the DTP industry, and they are rapidly improving in both quality and price. They are similar in design to photocopy machines, but print to disk instead of to paper.

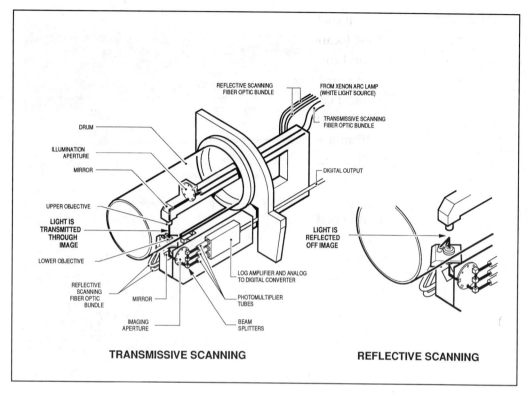

Figure 10-3
Transmissive versus reflective scanning. *Courtesy of Optronics, Inc.*

The data obtained from the scanning process are handled similarly, in many respects, to the process used to create screen display. If you recall from Chapter 5, computers require a considerable amount of RAM to store a bit-mapped video frame. That video buffer is sent to your monitor thirty times a second, and for each display a new frame is composed. The size of the buffer required depends on the pixel density necessary to describe the color value of each pixel. An 8-bit description (grayscale or color) requires eight times the RAM of a 1-bit description. For 8 bits,

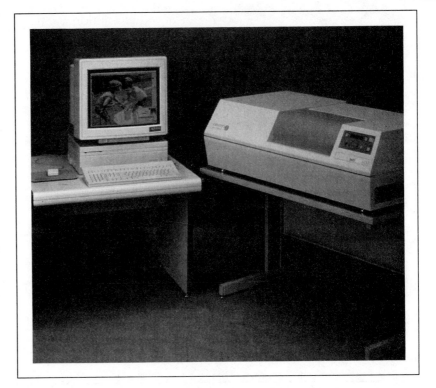

00000000 is black and 11111111 is white; software sets the threshold for each color value. The color value of a pixel is compared to
a table of values called a color lookup table, or simply a lookup
table, and then assigned to the display or output device utilizing
the scanned information. Scanning also requires large bit-mapped
image frames be composed in RAM. To increase the amount of
memory available, some software spools the image from RAM to
disk; this reduces the RAM requirement but has a concomitant
storage and speed penalty.

Resolution Versus Quality

The size of the digitizing element affects the quality of a scan. The
physical size of the photoreceptor is a major factor in determining
the maximum resolution of a picture element. While you can compress the sampling rate to improve quality, you can't compress the
minimum size of your digitizing element. An 8 ½-inch linear array
(thin strip) of 2,450 CCDs moved over an 11-inch page in 3,300
steps (the sampling rate) produces an image with close to 300 dpi

by 300 dpi resolution. Resolution in one dimension is fixed, while the other dimension trades off resolution for scanning speed.

Rendering a scanned image cleanly is a software, not a hardware chore, so software is an important element of a scanning package and should play a major role in your selection process. Appropriate algorithms must be applied to clean up the image, remove smudges and smears, and fill in any gaps. Lines can be recognized and completed, and using pattern recognition, arcs, curves, type, and other objects can be rendered more cleanly. Some scanning software attempts to increase resolution through a process called *interpolation,* where pixel density is doubled by averaging adjacent pixels to fill in a new intermediate pixel. This process works well for continuous images but is less useful for digitizing line art.

Line Art

There are three types of images that you might choose to reproduce with scanning: line art, continuous tones, and halftones. Line art is the type of illustration generated by a 1-bit image, the kind you get from a program like MacPaint, and almost any scanner adequate for line art. Your main concern for line art reproduction is the resolution of the scanner (dpi)—the quality of the lines and whether they reproduce properly depends entirely on this factor. With insufficient resolution, all curved or diagonal lines will appear jagged or staircased; even straight lines will exhibit this defect.

Figure 10-5 illustrates different types of scanned art. The picture of Jimmy's Chowder King in Boston, Massachusetts, was taken from black-and-white Kodalux processed film. Scanned on an H-P ScanJet Plus desktop scanner at 300 dpi, all files were saved in TIFF format. These images were printed with Digital Darkroom (Silicon Beach) and opened with gray levels derived from pixel cells 4 by 4 in size, using Digital Darkroom's normal halftone print algorithm.

Staircasing, technically called *aliasing*, is an artifact of any bit-mapped representation (refer back to Figure 9.2), whether it is a display or a digital scan. Depending on the resolution of the scan and the output medium used, aliasing may or may not be noticeable. It is most apparent at the boundary of two areas of very different color values. Adding a set of pixels with intermediate color

Figure 10-5
Different types of
scanned art .**(A)** A 256
grayscale results in the
largest files, but also the
best contrast and detail .
(B) A diffusion algo-
rithm is applied (like a
frosted diffusion filter
on a camera), washing
out some of the contrast
but maintaining detail.
This effect helps print
dark images on a
printer .**(C)** A normal
halftone of an image
creates good quality at
moderate file size by
patterning pixels into
groups. **(D)** Line art is
black and white only. It
results in small files, and
poor image quality on
continuous tone images,
but gives excellent
results for text and
drawn line with
high contrast.

A.

B.

C.

D.

Figure 10-6
In this figure the bottom line of text "the Desktop" is antialiased to smooth its bit-mapped font. The word "Beyond" is not. Note how much smoother the second line looks, especially in the reduced figure. The algorithm used here surrounded the letters with two successively lighter frames of gray. Any graphic with sharp distinct edges can be improved with this approach.

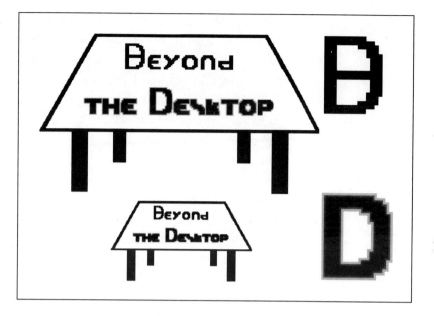

values at the boundary causes a blurring effect called *antialiasing,* which reduces contrast and produces a sharper contour. Antialiasing can be used to great effect for smoothing jagged type, especially on displays.

Grayscales

If you viewed a digitized black-and-white photograph made up of sufficiently small pixels, the result would appear to be a continuous spectrum of shades. Your mind's eye would blend together (dither) patterns of black and white into the various shades of gray, resulting in a photographic effect. A better scheme for creating realistic photographic images varies the intensity of light at each individual pixel element between black and white, producing a *grayscale* image. Here the color (or hue) remains constant, while the intensity (or lightness) is varied. Just as a monochrome grayscale monitor has pixels that can be individually excited and phosphors whose glow intensity can be variably adjusted, grayscale scanners have photoreceptors whose output voltage can be resolved into a number of intensity levels defined by your computer.

The number of shades of gray is determined by the formula GS $= 2^n$, where n is the number of bits resolved. One, 4, 8, and 16 bits have zero, 16, 64, and 256 shades of gray, respectively. As black isn't a gray, one shade of gray should be subtracted from these numbers. You don't usually find a system with more than 256 shades of gray because the human eye can't distinguish more than that. The VGA standard (PC) can theoretically display up to 256 grays but has an actual limit of 64 (see Chapter 5). The 8-bit Apple video board can display all 256 grays. Color Figure C4 shows the effect of grayscale on image quality.

Digital Halftones

As the number of gray shades increases, one level of gray becomes indistinguishable from its nearest neighbors, forming a continuum of tones called a continuous tone image. The most common example of a continuous tone grayscale image is a black-and-white photograph, where particles of silver form any size in the specified range, and allow an infinite level of grays.

Printing presses use opaque inks, and therefore cannot reproduce images with true continuous tones. The continuous tone effect has to be simulated by reducing a photograph to patterns of small dots of varying size. This results in a *halftone.* Conventional halftones created from photographs are made by placing a glass screen (or a film-based screen) with fine-line mesh between the camera and the image. Dots in light areas of the image are small, while the dots in the dark area of the image are large. Dots can be of any shape, but are always spaced evenly at the screen mesh spacing, also called a *pitch* or *screen ruling*. Varying the wire mesh alters the shape of the dots and, depending on the output process, can produce effective results.

The resolution of a halftone depends on the spacing of the dots in the halftone screen. The traditional measure is based on the line frequency from one line of dots to the next. This is normally measured in lines per inch, or lpi. As a rule of thumb, for newspapers or simple desktop publishing projects, a relatively coarse 65 to 85 lpi is sufficient. Absorbent paper, rapid web presses, and thick ink cannot support a finer dot size. Magazine work generally requires 120 to 150 lpi; fine art requires 200 lpi or above.

Computers create halftones by grouping pixels together into a *superpixel* or *halftone cell*. The electronic algorithms that create a digital halftone screen representation are proprietary features of both hardware and software vendors, and they greatly affect the quality of a digital image. Most scanner software saves files either as halftones or grayscales. Halftones take 12 to 25 percent of the file size of the grayscale, but will not scale well because the image quality is lower. A halftone of a scanned halftone gives poor results.

Dithering, the process by which the human mind recognizes levels of gray, creates a halftone image with a much lower resolution than the original photograph. If you create halftone cells of 16 pixels each, you reduce the apparent resolution to 75 dpi for a 300 dpi laser printer. At 16 pixels per cell you have created sixteen levels of gray. Raising the levels of gray to sixty-four (a much more acceptable output) lowers the resolution to 50 dpi. Scanned images output on an imagesetter at 2,450 dpi with halftone cells of eight pixels per side yield 256 levels of gray at 150 dpi resolution.

Figure 10-7
Photographic output from a 300 dpi laser compared to a 2,450 dpi Varityper 4300P.

Halftone resolution, expressed as lines per inch (lpi), relates to the maximum resolution of the output device (RES, in dpi) and the number of gray levels (GL) by the following formula: $lpi^2 = RES^2/GL$.

For example, a halftone of 75 lpi on a 300 dpi laser printer will have $(300/75)^2$, or 16 gray levels, with one additional level (a seventeenth) for a white pixel. What this means is that with any given output resolution, an increase in lpi will result in a decrease in grayscale range. You'll generally get a better quality halftone if you reduce lpi in favor of more gray tones.

Halftone output calculation also depends on the *screen angle* at which the halftone dots are aligned. The preceding formula assumes an angle of 0 degrees or 90 degrees. Altering the screen angle changes the dot shape. Experiments show that the best results are obtained at angles closer to 45 degrees, where grays are more easily perceived. This screen angle more successfully retains the overall balance of the halftone resolution versus the gray levels, and alters the equation. For 300 dpi output (a laser printer), the 50 lpi result with 36 shades of gray at 90 degrees changes to 53 lpi and 32 shades of gray at 45 degrees. Table 10.1 details a more realistic assessment of the relationship of grayscale to halftone at various printer resolutions for the 45-degree screen angle.

Table 10.1 Number of Gray Levels for Halftones

for 0° or 90° screen angle	*Halftone Resolution (lpi)*					
Printer Resolution (dpi)	*50*	*75*	*90*	*100*	*120*	*150*
300	36	16	11	9	6	4
600	144	64	44	36	25	16
1000	256	178	123	100	69	44
1270	256	256	199	161	112	72
1693	256	256	256	256	199	127
2540	256	256	256	256	256	256

Note that a laser printer substantially limits your options for balancing grayscale and resolution. Both are effectively lowered to below acceptable levels. Many scanners will not allow you to reduce your scan below 150 dpi to make the tradeoff.

▼ *Tip: For commercial printing with anything above 85 lpi, use film as your output medium. It costs more to print film, but eventually you would have to spend more on camerawork and stripping for hard copy.*

At too high a line screen you may experience dot gain, plugging, and loss of detail. Find out from your printer what dot gain is allowed; a range of 4 percent to 93 percent is common. If you use a complete range of dot sizes, certain areas will have black blobs (called plugging), and others will have white spots. Use the new range to alter the contrast curve in your image editing program for best results.

Color Scans

As discussed earlier, any color can be broken down into percentages of the three primary colors, red, green, and blue (RGB). A scanner digitizes a color image by measuring its reflected or (in the case of film) transmitted red, green, and blue light. It then assigns a value to each, and combines the results to color each digital pixel.

Reflected light has a lower contrast or a greater dynamic range than transmitted light, so you can obtain higher quality from transmission scans. A scanner that uses transmitted light from 35 mm slides is called a *slide scanner*; the Nikon LS-3500 and the Barneyscan are two good examples. Slide scanners normally give excellent results, but they are fairly slow (20 minutes to an hour, or more), yield huge file sizes (45 to 70 MBytes is common), and are fairly expensive.

Impart Research offers a product called KaleidoSCAN that consists of a set of filters and instructions specific to several scanners and programs enabling you to turn your grayscale scanner into a color scanner. The new color scanners from Epson and LaCie actually use three different color light sources to achieve their imaging, and don't require the use of filters.

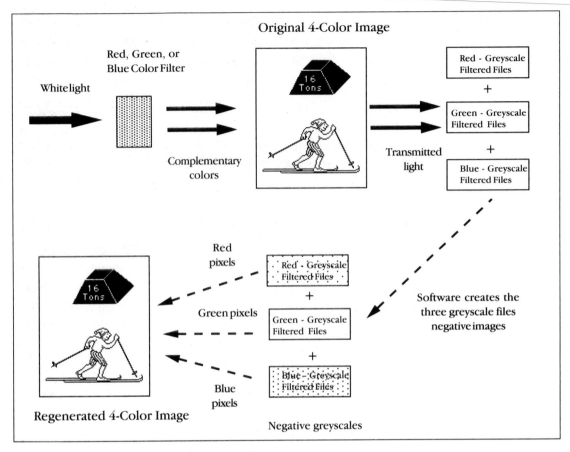

Figure 10-8 How a grayscale scanner inputs color images.

▼ *Tip: If you are preparing a manuscript and want to create For Position Only (FPO) comps from slides, you can save a great deal of time by using your desktop scanner in place of a slide scanner.*

Place your slide on a flatbed scanner and shine a strong light through it using an overhead lamp (not too strong or you will melt a slide). When you scan the slide at 300 dpi or better you will obtain an acceptable low-resolution image that you can give to reviewers or resize, crop, and alter to put in place on your page layout package. Use TIFF first, PICT, or .PCX as a second choice. A 35 mm slide scanned in this manner will be about 100 KBytes in size and can be scaled acceptably up to 400 percent. Some brightness, contrast, and sharpening is helpful to improve the image quality.

Image File Formats

Once again we return to the issue of graphics file formats, those routines that programs use to store and manipulate files. Digital imaging is a bit-mapped representation, and the most important file formats are the ones that offer strong bit-mapped support. File formats abound, but choosing one for a particular image is important because the quality of the data determines what you can eventually do with it. Clearly, images saved in 72 dpi black-and-white (1-bit) MacPaint format cannot match 300 dpi-256 grayscale scans saved in TIFF. So the general rule of thumb is to get the best-quality scan possible right from the start. File formats are a software issue, and most scanner driver software can save images at several resolutions and in several formats. Scanner drivers are almost always bundled with scanners; it's part of the OEM's added value. Some are small programs, such as the Macintosh desk accessory DeskScan bundled with the H-P ScanJet Plus. Some drivers are built into major image processing applications, such as PC Paintbrush IV (PC), Digital Darkroom (Mac), Adobe Photoshop (Mac), Image-In-Color (PC), PhotoStyler (PC), and Picture Publisher Plus (PC). These programs can actually control the scanner's hardware. The full-featured image editing and processing programs described here all accept several formats and can convert them to other formats. That's one of the strengths of image editing programs, and it separates them from other paint and graphics programs.

Chapter 13 defines file formats in more depth. Here the focus is on formats used in imaging. There are many specialized programs for converting files from one format to another. Some, such as Micrografx's XPort(PC), are stand-alone applications; others, such as HiJaak (PC) and HotShot Graphics (PC), are part of screen-capture facilities. Some cross-platform support, Mac to PC and vice versa, is built into many of these programs. There are more graphics standards on the PC than on the Macintosh, but file translation is not the major issue it once was if you understand what file formats do.

It's almost impossible to list programs versus supported file formats because these features change constantly. In Chapter 13 you will find one such chart. Programs can either open or read formats, or save or write them. A program may be able to open a file but not save it. In certain instances, a format may be incompletely read or written, so your best bet is always to experiment before beginning critical work; some programs print better than others and you can find that out only by attempting to print some images. There aren't many universal standards, but TIFF and .PCX are the most common for the PC, and TIFF and MacPaint for the Macintosh.

The most important scanning file formats are:

- **TIFF** (Mac and PC): The most universal file format for scanning, developed by Aldus (the creators of PageMaker) with Microsoft's participation. The latest version of the TIFF specification (5.0) supports grayscale up to 8 bits per pixel or 256 levels of gray, color images, and black and white. When possible, work in TIFF. Be aware, however, that TIFF creates very large graphics files. Conversion of TIFF between Mac and PC is best done by a program that reads compatible files, such as PageMaker.

- **.PCX** (PC): A format used by ZSoft's PC Paintbrush and Publisher's Paintbrush. Most PC scanners can create .PCX formatted files, and most DOS DTP programs can read them. Originally .PCX was a 1-bit black-and-white format, useful for line art. It dithered images to create an imitation grayscale. .PCX released in 1987 now works with 256 grayscale and color. Creates compact files.

- **RIFF** (Mac): A proprietary file format developed by Letraset for ImageStudio and its DTP package Ready, Set, Go! RIFF allows substantial compression of file space, but is useful only when working with these specified programs. When transferring data to another program, you will probably want to create a TIFF file.

- **MacPaint** (Mac): A 1-bit graphics file format, a Macintosh standard. Images are 72 dpi. Most useful for scanning images to display on a monitor only. Useful for some special effects but with no real image editing capability because grayscale information is missing.

- **Encapsulated PostScript (EPS)** (Mac and PC): A standard file format developed by Altsys. Sometimes abbreviated as EPSF; EPS encapsulates a bit-map representation of a vector or object description composed of Bézier curves. Creates large file sizes. Cross-platform programs such as Illustrator allow for easy conversion between Mac and PC.

- **.IMG** (PC): Used by GemPaint, GemScan, and other programs running under the GEM windowing environment. Can be read by the page layout package from Xerox, and Ventura Publisher (Gold Series—GEM, Win3, Mac, OS/2).

- **PICT** (Mac): A universal Macintosh object-oriented drawing format. All Macintosh graphics programs save and read PICT files. A newer version, called PICT2, saves bit-mapped images with grayscale information. As PICT2 is the endorsed Apple file format, it is a platform standard and widely supported.

- **Computer Graphics Metafile (CGM)** (PC): This is a device-independent, object-oriented format supported by Harvard Graphics, Lotus Freelance Plus, CorelDraw, Arts & Letters, MicroGraphx Designer, Ventura Publisher, Page-Maker, WordPerfect, Word, and many other applications. Files in the format have the extension .CGM.

- **FAX** (Mac and PC): The Group III facsimile standard, .FAX files on the PC. FAX machines are scanners with 216 dpi resolution and no grayscale (see Chapter 6). Some scanners support it so that they can be used to transmit faxes. Considered a poor standard, it is scheduled for upgrade in 1992 to include higher-quality graphics.

- **Miscellaneous Formats** (PC): Examples include the Halo DPE format (1-bit), which has its own file format called CUT, .PIC (from Dr. Halo), .PFF (Epson printers), and .CAT (Computer Aided Technologies—a scanner manufacturer). Use these formats only when you intend to work within these programs.

▼ *Tip: Not all versions of TIFF are entirely compatible.*

TIFF was designed to be modular and flexible for both software and hardware developers. TIFF files can be compressed through the use of proprietary algorithms that are generally incompatible with one another. Xerox/Datacopy's MacImage driver saves files in three types of TIFF formats: compressed TIFF, uncompressed TIFF, and TIFF PackBits. PackBits can be read by LaserPaint and Image-In-Color (PC).

File Sizes

Digital imaging makes extreme demands on RAM and disk storage space. It's not uncommon to use an entire removable 44 MByte cartridge for a 24-bit color scan and four-color separation files. An IBM PC XT using DOS has only 640 KBytes of RAM; you need at least a 286 (AT) chip to extend this limit. Several companies offer an expanded memory specification, or EMS board (added RAM), with a scanner driver built in. Intel 80286, 80386, and 80486 PCs have memory management, and can also use extended memory as an image buffer. Macintosh computers can utilize total installed RAM without a special memory manager. Table 10.2 illustrates file size versus image depth (pixel density).

One advantage of using a GUI such as Windows, or an operating system such as the Macintosh, is that it can provide a disk-swapping scheme from RAM to disk, appropriating a portion of disk space as overflow RAM. Image processing programs on these platforms often use this scheme, called *virtual memory*, effectively. It provides a work-around for RAM memory limitations but requires disk space and exacts a speed penalty. Many programs also do file compression, generally to proprietary file formats, as part of their disk swapping.

File sizes depend on the following factors:

- Scanned Area: File size is linearly dependent on the area to be scanned.
- Pixel Density: The bits saved are linearly dependent and have a direct effect on file sizes. For an 8 ½- by 11-inch 300 dpi scanned image, line art would require 1,085 KBytes; 16 grayscale (a 4-bit image) needs 4,332; and 256 grayscale (8-bit

image) requires 8,661 KBytes. Color scans show similar relationships. If a 1-bit black-and-white image needs 1 MByte of storage, a 24-bit color image needs at least 24 MBytes! So plan accordingly.

- Scan Resolution: An 8,661 KByte scan at 300 dpi is reduced to 4,492 KBytes at 216 dpi, 1,997 KBytes at 144 dpi, and 449 KBytes at 72 dpi. While this relationship is direct, it is not linear—the number of pixels saved goes up as a squared function of the resolution.

- File Format: Some file formats are compact, especially line art scans. Others, such as EPS and TIFF, which are bit-mapped grayscale, can be quite large. A file format may be compressed and then uncompressed by the program that opens it in order to be manipulated. RIFF from Letraset is one example; it offers about 4:1 compression.

Table 10.2 Image File Sizes (KBytes)

Square Inches	Resolution (dpi)			
	75	*150*	*200*	*300*
6	33	132	234	527
9	49	198	352	791
12	66	264	469	1055
15	82	330	586	1318
20	110	439	781	1758
24	132	527	938	2109
30	165	659	1172	2637
36	198	791	1406	3164
40	220	879	1563	3516

Table 10.2 Image File Sizes (KBytes) *(continued)*

Square Inches	Resolution (dpi)			
	75	150	200	300
48	264	1055	1875	4219
56	308	1230	2188	4922
64	352	1406	2500	5625
72	396	1582	2813	6328
80	439	1758	3125	7031

At times you may not want the highest resolution available. When scanning line art for a 300 dpi resolution scanner, you can reduce the resolution to 150 dpi, thus halving the file size. This is valuable when you are planning to reproduce the figure at a smaller size. It works well with thick lines, but fine line detail will be lost. You also can save file space by scanning only the image portion that you need. Most scanning software provides the necessary controls to portion the image scanned. Many preview the image in a first pass at low-resolution, and scan at high resolution only after you have selected the desired area.

▼ *Tip: Use a grayscale image of a resolution of no more than twice the line screen rating that you will print at.*

For a known output size you can use the following formula for optimum screen resolution: (Line Screen (in lpi) X 1.25 X final width)/original width = scanning resolution (in dpi).

Graphics File Compression

If digital image file sizes have you gasping, you're not alone. Bulky 24-bit color files 8 ½ by 11 inches can chew up 25 MBytes, fill hard drives and removable cartridges, and make floppy disks or telecommunications impractical. However, emerging standards for file compression can shrink digital files down to practical levels (see Chapter 6). File compression works well for storage, but it does not solve the problem of working with the file in memory unless the application you use supports it; few do at present. There are two kinds of compression: *lossless* and *lossy*; the former preserves all data and gives compression of up to 4:1, the latter degrades the data set at progressively higher compressions. Practical limits, depending on the application, are 25:1 to 100:1. Traditional algorithms used in telecommunications, such as Huffman, Run-length encoded (RLE), and so on, are lossless; the JPEG and DVI standards are lossy.

Utilities based on the Joint Photographic Experts Group (JPEG) standard can reduce files with compressions of 25:1 or more. Intel's Digital Video Interactive (DVI) technology is an alternative

Figure 10-9
With Kodak's ColorSqueeze JPEG file compression utility, you can view a thumbnail of your compressed image prior to decompression. *Courtesy of Kodak, Inc.*

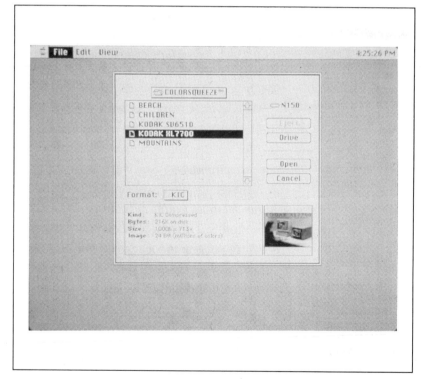

standard. Currently, compressions of 100:1 and above are attainable, but some image degradation occurs. Compression can be accomplished in software, or can be hardwired into a microchip for faster performance. The former is fine for static images, the latter is necessary for processing animation sequences (see Chapter 18). Kodak ColorSqueeze (Mac) is a JPEG software package that can compress a 20 MByte image file in under a minute to less than 800 KBytes, less than a floppy disk worth. C-Cube's CL550 Processor may find its way into color printers, video boards, digital cameras, and color copiers, considerably reducing image buffer requirements and greatly speeding up performance. This technology will begin to show up on more equipment over the next couple of years, and should become standard fare on computer motherboards in the next year or two. The Color NeXT Station ships with a CL550 Processor.

Scanners

Scanners are hot, with the market growing at about 250 percent each year. The hardware offered for the IBM PC and the Macintosh is competitive. As with laser printers, there are only a few manufacturers of scanner mechanisms, but many assemblers. (Refer to the references at the end of this chapter for more in-depth coverage.) Software is another matter. There is a clear advantage in Macintosh image processing software at the present time. As in all graphics matters, the PC market is playing catch-up, but rapidly. The first full-color scanners and best digital image processing programs for microcomputers have appeared on the Macintosh. Two popular types of scanners are on the market today: hand-held and flatbed or desktop units.

Hand-held Scanners

Hand-held scanners cost from $250 to $400 and can deliver up to 256 grayscale tones with images at an effective resolution of 400 dpi, and scan widths of from 4 to 5 inches. Hand-held scanners are very convenient for imaging small areas, but they can be hard to master because they don't always roll perfectly straight when you

Figure 10-10
(A) The Logitech's ScanMan features good grayscale editing and stitching. *Courtesy of Logitech, Inc.*
(B) The Typist is the first hand-held scanner to offer higher-end OCR scanning based on Caere's OmniPage package. *Courtesy of Caere Corporation.*

A.

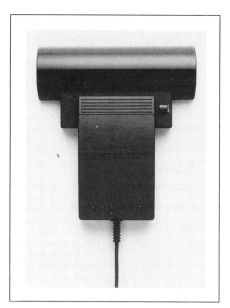

B.

push them. That's more a factor of your hand movement than the roller mechanism, but a good roller mechanism is a critical factor in their success. All hand-held scanners ship with basic scanner drivers that provide grayscale controls, and some, such as the Logitech ScanMan Plus, have effective software for stitching images together to create whole pages, a process that can be frustrating. Caere has introduced The Typist, a hand-held unit with a bundled version of OmniPage OCR (see "Optical Character Recognition" below) for on-the-fly automated text entry. The Typist is notable because OCR generally is the domain of flatbed or sheet-fed scanners. With practice, hand-held scanners give good results, especially for small areas, and are very useful for situations where mobility is needed. An insurance investigator with a laptop would be an example. Color hand-held scanners are just being introduced to the market in the $600 to $800 range. Figure 10-10A shows the Logitech ScanMan. Figure 10-10B is The Typist.

▼ *Tip: Buy the best scanner you can afford.*

Halftoning discards a significant fraction of the data collected, so the more data you can maintain, the better your result will be. Also, work with original art. The screen that already exists in a magazine photo, for example, will cause moiré patterns in your screen.

Flatbed Scanners

Flatbed scanners are the best for flat images, DTP work, and where alignment is critical. A document placed facedown on a glass plate is scanned from below by an optical head assembly that moves along the document to scan the page. It's a good idea to have a scanner with at least the resolution of your desktop printer, so 300 dpi scanners with 256 grayscale are common. Pricing is very competitive, in the $1,400 to $2,500 range. Xerox/Datacopy (700 series), Hewlett-Packard ScanJet Plus, and Microtek MSF 300G are popular products. Other manufacturers include Abaton, DEST, AST, Howtek, and Sharp. Apple sells the Apple Scanner, which has lower resolution and grayscale, primarily useful for importing images into HyperCard, Apple's hypertextural informa-

A.

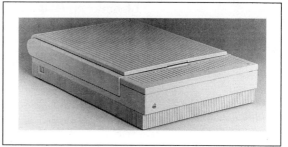

B.

C.

Figure 10-11 Three notable desktop flatbed scanners **(A)** The Hewlett-Packard ScanJet Plus with the Automatic Document Feed (ADF) mechanism is the most popular scanner for desktop publishers. It is 300 dpi 256 grayscale and comes with excellent software, including a special version of DeskPaint. *Courtesy of Hewlett-Packard.* **(B)** The Apple Scanner is a 300 dpi 16 grayscale scanner. It has received mixed reviews, particularly for its scanner control software. It comes bundled with a nice program for automatic inclusion of images into HyperCard. *Courtesy of Apple.* **(C)** The Agfa Focus S800 GS scanner is an 800 dpi 256 grayscale scanner. It has won several industry awards for excellence, and its software is highly praised. *Courtesy of Agfa Compugraphic.*

tion manger. Abaton sells a board to upgrade the Apple Scanner, but its own 300 dpi 256 grayscale unit is a better purchase if you don't already own an Apple Scanner. Agfa Compugraphic has a notable desktop flatbed model called the Focus S880 GS with 800 dpi resolution that has won several awards for excellence. It achieves this resolution through the use of an excellent bundled software package.

Flatbed scanners are not appropriate for 3D object imaging, as they have a very flat depth of focus. If you have to image small objects, look for a scanner that has its imaging head mounted for translational motion. Overhead scanners look very much like overhead projectors. An example is the grayscale Truvel TruScan TZ-3, which is a camera-based scanner with a fixed bed. This excellent scanner delivers resolution from 75 to 900 dpi with a maximum scanning area of 12 by 17 inches. Other models from Truvel are for color (TZ-3C), and a combination of the two (TZ-3BWC). Camera units have several inches of focus and, although expensive ($10,000 or more), often are among the better scanners on the market. For larger objects you will need a TV or digital camera and video capture board (see Chapter 18). The Array Scanner-One with its SpeedScan software is notable for high-resolution, fast scanning speed (two minutes at full resolution), and flexibility of setup.

Several companies make sheet-fed or roller-feed scanners that are similar to fax machines, but they are disappearing from the marketplace. Sheet-fed scanners do not always place the page accurately in the mechanism causing straight lines to appear staircased, and they can't be used for books or manuscripts. Several manufacturers are now offering removable automatic page feeders that turn their flatbed scanners into sheet-fed units. Xerox/Datacopy and Hewlett-Packard are two that come to mind. This feature is particularly valuable for optical character recognition packages where large volumes of material must be read.

Figure 10-12
Overhead scanners allow some depth of field and are often high-end units. This is the Array Scanner-One from Array Technologies setup for transmissive scanning of a 35 mm slide. *Courtesy of Truvel Division of Vidar Systems Corporation.*

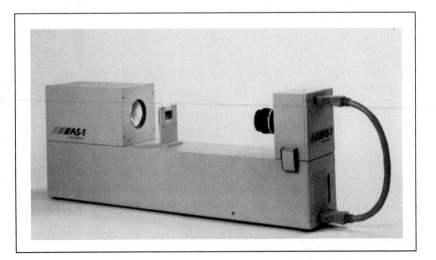

**Desktop Color
Scanners**

Eventually desktop color scanners will replace the black-and-white grayscale units in the marketplace because most color scanners can deliver good grayscale as well. High-priced color scanners have been on the market for some time and have been used successfully at large publishing houses and printing operations. In 1989 Microtek shipped the 300Z for about $2,300, and set a new price/performance point for the microcomputer market. More recently Epson and LaCie introduced $1,500 to $2,000 24-bit 300 dpi desktop color scanners, very attractive units. The Epson ES-300C also has been particularly well reviewed. The quality of these lower-priced scanners is not yet good enough to do full-color catalog work directly from a personal computer but suffices for lower-quality applications. However, the market is changing rapidly. Anyone considering a scanner purchase in the near future should consider a color model.

If you need higher-quality color scans, consider a slide scanner. As mentioned previously, slide scanners give excellent results—the best, in fact, of any scanner type. A 35 mm slide can be scanned in twenty minutes to an hour, with 1,000 lpi resolution. That level of quality is almost good enough for full-color page separations.

For those doing serious color prepress work, high-end Post-Script-based drum scanners offered by Scitex, Optronics and other manufacturers provide a level of quality suitable for commercial color publications. These types of scanners are expensive; the better ones carry price tags in the $30,000 to $140,000 range. As with other equipment, however, you don't have to buy one to use one. A significant number of color service bureaus have them, as do many traditional color shops.

Because scanners pass a lot of data to your computer, they generally require parallel ports. There is no standard scanner interface on the PC, both the SCSI and GPIB (General Purpose Interface Bus) are used. The SCSI bus is the standard for the Macintosh, and as SCSI is a preferred PS/2 I/O bus, you should purchase an SCSI scanner. Less common are serial port scanners, which use the RS-232 standard (Apple Desktop Bus) or a PC's parallel printer port. Serial connection is easy and inexpensive and tends to show up in hand-held scanners where smaller files are created, but data transfer is slow. Some scanners require the installation of an interface or NuBus board; most require external power supplies. As part of the installation process, driver software often must be installed, either as an INIT file (Mac) or in the CONFIG.SYS file with a command line placed in your AUTOEXEC.BAT file for the IBM PC.

Scanning Software

The software you use to create and manipulate your digital images is as important to the quality of your work as the film, camera settings, and processing lab are to a conventional film printing. Actually, the two processes have a lot in common. Two types of software are important: scan control software and digital image processing software. The device driver for a scanner is normally part of the scan control software package; sometimes complete application packages containing all the parts are sold with digital image editing software.

Scanner Controls

Scanner control software is usually a utility that comes bundled with a manufacturer's scanner; less frequently it is part of a larger application. Its purpose is to control the area scanned and its size, and adjust important exposure factors, then write the file to disk in an acceptable format. Often this software first requires a low-resolution scan called a *preview* from which the image is viewed, changes are applied, and the results are examined. When satisfied, the user then does the final high-resolution scan in a selected format. The most important features in this class of software are:

- Brightness: Adjusts the threshold and intensity of an image to make it either lighter or darker. High brightness washes out detail; low brightness leads to dark spots.
- Contrast: Adjusts the difference between the light and dark areas of an image, the dynamic range between white and black. Controls the tone of output, and the amount of detail and highlights that shows through.

- Automatic Exposure: A default algorithm used to adjust contrast and brightness. Normally this works quite well unless you are trying to achieve some special effect.

- Preview Mode: An initial low-resolution scan that allows you to examine and modify a scan prior to taking the final high-resolution scan.

- Scaling: Reduces or enlarges the scan size of the selected area. Ranges of 4 percent to 400 percent are common. The data collection process is the same for any scaling.

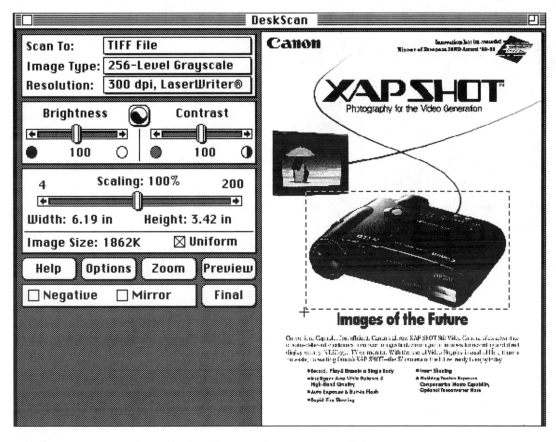

Figure 10-13 The Hewlett-Packard DeskScan package comes as a desk accessory or as an application when a larger memory partition is required. It is bundled with the ScanJet Plus scanner, Macintosh version.

A.

B.

C.

Figure 10-14 In this set of screens the image of Fozzie Bear is adjusted. **(A)** Original image, **(B)** increased brightness, **(C)** increased brightness and contrast.

- Resolution: Determines the number of dots per inch to be saved. File format determines resolution. Some file formats allow several resolution choices.

- Image Type: Scans the image in one of several ways saving different levels of grayscale, applying halftoning algorithms, or using other algorithms to create special effects, such as diffusion, which mimics a camera's filter lenses.

- File Formats: Several file formats are generally offered. If the scanner runs on a GUI, data can be saved either to the Clipboard or sent directly to a printer.

- File Sizes: Most packages calculate the image size for the selected area in the format chosen and display that number.

- Special Effects: Such effects as image negatives, mirror imaging, nonuniform scaling, and others are sometimes included.

Digital Image Processing

Digital image processing software programs allow you to work with bit-mapped images using some special tools for retouching, enhancing, and composing scanned images. Not surprisingly, certain packages such as PC Paintbrush IV Plus and Publisher's Paintbrush 2.0, are enhanced paint programs with these sets of tools. Many of these programs have scanner drivers built in, and manufacturers bundle special versions of these packages with their scanners. In this section we concentrate on the special tools and functions offered by these image editors that make them different from both paint programs and scanner controller software. Many grayscale editors on the market today sell for between $200 and $400. Sophisticated color packages cost between $500 and $2,000. These programs are the equivalent of an electronic darkroom. Five years ago these programs ran on minicomputers in science laboratories or in government research labs. Today they are yours to delight in.

Differences Between Paint and Digital Imaging Programs

Simple paint programs are ineffective for manipulating digital images because they don't contain the tools necessary to manipulate images globally or to work with a region of the image relatively. A paint program gives you individual pixel color control, but images have a range of shades that requires overall changes in brightness, contrast, noise reduction, edge enhancement, and others. These functions require specialized complex algorithms not found in paint programs. Some of these functions are similar to those found on a camera, such as exposure control; some are traditional retouching tools, such as airbrushes. Others, such as cut and paste, transparent pastes, paste a range of color values, smudges, area selection for pattern stamping, masking, and edge enhancements are tools unique to these programs.

Color image processing programs often have densitometers for measuring basic color component values; they also will do color separations, as do some paint programs. You might want to compare the list of digital image processing features with those of a paint program found in Chapter 9. Compare the screens and

Figure 10-15
Grayscale editors shown here contain sophisticated tools for adjusting color values. This is a histogram, a measure of the spectrum of gray values. Also shown is a gamma contrast slider. The gamma contrast can be adjusted on many programs as a variable gamma contrast curve.
This is a scan of a human skull from a Magnetic Resonance Imaging machine. Other medical images that benefit from enhancement are X rays. Satellite mapping can be adjusted and scaled to show landscape features. *Courtesy of MicroFrontier, Inc.*

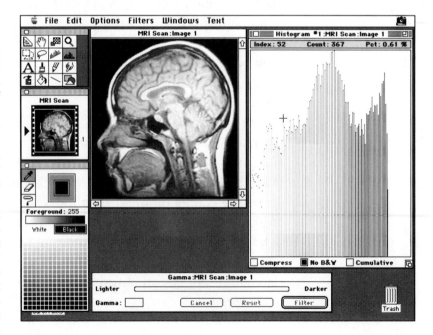

palettes of PixelPaint in color Figure C8 to the color retouching program Adobe PhotoShop in the same figure. Then note the series of special effects accomplished using color image processing programs shown in color Figure C9.

Some of the tools you should look for in an image editing package are:

- Exposure Controls: Brightness and contrast, not just for the whole image, but for regions as well. Number of grays or colors saved. For color programs each of the primary colors can be transformed separately or in combination. Gamma curves for nonlinear adjustment are often available. Histograms, or graphs showing color distributions, are also found.

- Filters: Sharpen and blur, seek a certain color value difference, and exaggerate or lower it. Despeckle or noise reduction takes white specs out of a picture replacing them with the nearest color value. Diffusion acts like a grating or a frosted glass, scattering light. Many programs have layers or maps that serve as filters to change a pixel's color value. The original image is saved as a base map, and color or gray maps are created to modify the image.

- Halftoning Options: Various screens (line densities, spot patterns, screen angles, random, dithers, etc.), diffusion patterns, and file formats are supported that permit output to various devices. Remember to check whether these programs read and write your desired file format; most offer broad support.

- Retouching Tools: Selects an area and then uses those pixels to paste onto another area. Transparent and selective pasting are often supported. Some programs have several image layers for more sophisticated manipulations. Airbrushes, smudges, and blurs are favorite tools.

- Special Effects: Posterization converts all pixels to only a selected number of color values. Pixellation turns a set of pixels into a mosaic of large single-color squares, an effect used on TV to conceal someone's identity. Solarization maps brighten and darken areas correctly, but invert middle color values so that a picture appears to be overexposed. Inversion or negative imaging is useful for certain output devices or situations. Rotations and distortions of selected images allow for moving and placing objects. Line screens such as circles and mezzotints can sometimes be found. Autotracing (raster-to-vector) conversion tools are often built in (see Chapter 9).

- Color Tools: Densitometers for color specification and color separation software (see Chapter 14). Duotones can be constructed, color can be replaced or remapped. Some grayscale editors allow for color object overlays.

Actually, there are many more tools than can be discussed here. These programs are at work in print all around you even if you have never worked with them before. Play with them once and you'll be hooked. However, they're not just for play. Figure 10-16 shows a sequence of manipulations done by Digital Darkroom on a photo to bring it up to spec. People are using these programs to create whole new business ventures. One takes old photographs and retouches them so that they look like new.

Some of the more important image processing programs and what they include are:

- **Aldus Snapshot** (Win): A grayscale editing program, with some special hardware requirements, such as a frame-grabber expansion board, an analog monitor, and a video source (a VCR or video camera). The frame-grabber takes the video source image and sends it to the analog monitor while retaining a frame in the frame buffer. So while you are using the program on your PC monitor to edit an image, the display can be seen on the analog monitor. Having an analog display presents some interesting added options, including the creation of special effects with live video. Most users work on a frozen image only. As this program has a limited toolbox, it cannot be recommended.

- **Adobe Photoshop** (Mac): This is one of the best color image processing programs on the market today. Users have commented on its ease of learning and logical complete toolbox

A.

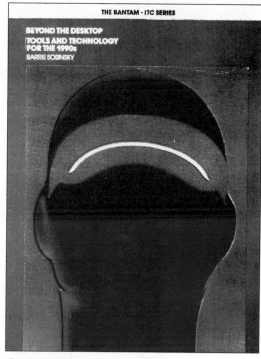

B.

Figure 10-16
In this progressive
set of frames various
manipulations enhance
the image of our cover.
(A) The original image.
(B) Cut and Paste
removes the fold lines.
(C) The despeckle filter,
fill selected areas, and
sharpen filter finalizes
the image.

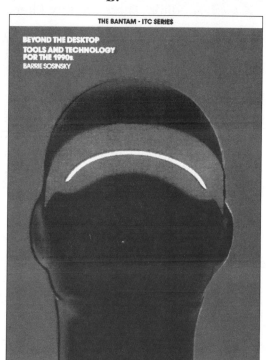

C.

and command set. It is the best-selling program in its (color) category and comes bundled with many color scanners.

- **ColorStudio** (Mac): The most complicated and complete 24-bit color image processing package on the market today and part of the Letraset Studio series. This is an impressive package with much to recommend it. It is competitive with Adobe Photoshop, but offers different features.

- **Digital Darkroom** (Mac): A full-featured grayscale editor with many special tools, plus color overlay support. An advanced paste feature allows image transfer to be manipulated in some interesting ways. Effects include transparent objects and total control of grayscale mapping of the objects manipulated. This program has a good autotrace tool and comes bundled with many scanners and often with controller software. It is one of the favored Macintosh grayscale editors.

- **Enhance** (Mac): An image analysis and enhancement application with advanced 8-bit image filtering, retouching, and painting tools that has grown into a full-featured grayscale editor. There are fifty filters, three video buffers or maps, masks, histograms, advanced paste and transformation tools, and many special effects. Enhance has been well reviewed, and it is considered the best program for technical applications sold on the Macintosh.

- **GemScan** (PC): Runs on the GEM GUI and uses the GEM .IGF bit map format. GemScan contains both paint and scanner tools. Images can be scanned as line art or as halftones, which work with a dithered image only. With halftones you can specify contrast, resolution, and the size of the halftone cells. Images can be reversed, cropped, and rotated.

- **Grey F/X** (PC): A highly recommended grayscale editor that runs in its own menued interface and has a very powerful collection of tools and features. It is a high-powered program that takes time to master but is easy to use and has good output quality.

- **Halo DPE** (PC): Includes many of the same tools as the PC Paintbrush, runs in a window, and uses the .PIC format to save files. Reads and saves files in .CUT, TIFF, or the GEM .IMG format. A number of control features are included for popular scanners.

- **Image** (Mac): A freeware program color editor that is distributed on many bulletin boards and on-line services. It was written by Wayne Rasband at the National Institutes of Health (Bethesda, MD) as a technical image analysis tool. The current version of this program is 1.29 and comes with a 65-page manual. Considering its price and the range of sophisticated tools it contains, it is competitive with commercial programs. It is worth having this program in your arsenal.

- **Image-In and Image-In-Color** (Win): Incorporates OCR, file conversion, and grayscale editing; an all-in-one package. It is the Swiss Army Knife of image processors, but is not as feature rich as Grey F/X.

- **ImageEdit** (Win): An entry from IBM that lacks many important grayscale functions. Coupled with its high price, it is not a serious contender.

- **ImageStudio** (Mac): The first important grayscale editor introduced on the Mac and pioneer of several new important editing tools. Version 1.5 has a complete toolbox with many special effects. A good clean interface and logical tools set make this a good choice for grayscale editing. It is bundled with many scanners. There is a gray map editor found as a linear graph at the lower left-hand corner of the screen that allows for quick global changes. ImageStudio requires a Macintosh II computer with more than 4 MBytes of memory. It comes with a virtual memory feature, and does file compression (3 or 4:1) in its proprietary RIFF format that allows it to write files to hard disk and retrieve the pieces when required.

- **PC Paintbrush IV Plus** and **Publisher's Paintbrush 2.0** (PC): An enhanced paint program with some basic grayscale and color tools, it comes bundled as software for many scanners sold for the PC and includes driver software. Originally developed for the Frieze graphical windows environment, it is

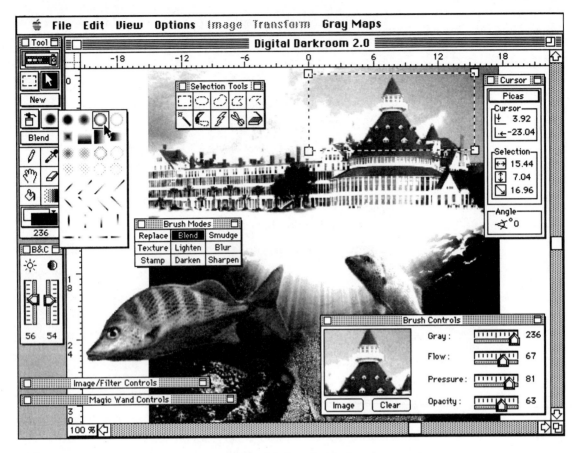

Figure 10-17 Digital Darkroom (version 2.0) is a black-and-white image processing program that allows for color overlays.

also available in a Microsoft Windows version. Offers full 300 dpi resolution with true bit-mapped editing. ZSoft recommends the use of an IBM PC AT or better. Not as good as the best programs, but its low price makes it an attractive package.

- **PhotoStyler** (Win): This just-realeased product from U-Lead has received good early reviews from the trade press. A full-powered color image editing program, it works with several graphics formats and features a full set of editing tools, built-in file compression, color separation, and customizable filters.

- **Picture Publisher** (Win): A grayscale editor that has all of the major tools: graymap editor, selection, cut-and-paste tools, retouching tools, and histograms for equalization. Flooding tools to spread a certain shade of gray, and masking tools are also included. Once an object is selected you can invert, scale, crop, or rotate it in 90 degree rotations. It is somewhat clumsy, but it is powerful.

- **Windows ColorLab I/P** (Win): A color bit-mapped editor/image processing program that supports both Extended VGA and 8514/A display standards. Several color scanners and file formats are supported.

Optical Character Recognition (OCR)

Desktop scanners enable another exciting technology called *optical character recognition*, or OCR. In OCR a computer takes a scanned bit-mapped image of a page of text, and a software program then analyzes the bit map and transforms it into ASCII text as a disk file. Using OCR it is possible for a lawyer to transform reams of court data into a single disk of data, or for you to transform Shakespeare's sonnets into words on your computer screen that you can treasure forever. OCR is at the forefront of certain forms of artificial intelligence programs, and it is developing rapidly. Five years ago these programs were $50,000 packages that ran on minicomputers. Today some very good several-hundred-dollar packages on microcomputers.

Font Recognition

Given all of the different typefaces, sizes, styles, and symbols, it can be quite difficult for an OCR program to recognize one letter from a closely related cousin. Tightly kerned (spaced) letter pairs, underlines, ligatures, unusual fonts, and italics are often difficult for OCR programs to decipher. These programs come in two flavors: *matrix matching* or *font recognition* programs are trained for a particular character set or typeface, and *feature extraction*

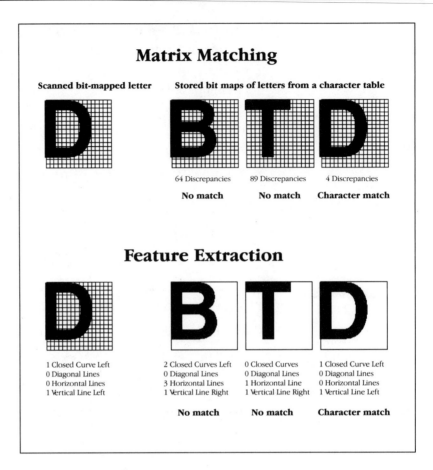

programs (also referred to as feature recognition, pattern recognition, or topological analysis), which have built-in artificial intelligence routines that take best guesses (see Figure 10-18).

Matrix matching font recognition requires stored bit maps for
comparison, and many programs allow characters to be assigned
by you. These programs are slow to set up, but fast and accurate
once they start to work. Matrix matching does, however, limit the
number of different character sets or styles that the program can
be effective with. This type of OCR software is best used on material with a limited range of fonts, such as typewriter output.

Feature extraction works by storing general information about a
character and comparing the scanned bit map to the set of rules.
For an uppercase E the rules might be: four straight lines, three
horizontal lines, one vertical line, three perpendicular intersec-

tions. These rules apply to any style of E, but the rules are given different priorities. With feature extraction, OCR can be performed on text with many different fonts and styles. Programs that do this sometimes are called omnifont packages.

Be aware that most formatting contained in the original hard copy is lost when it is converted to text file on disk. ASCII saves very little formatting information. You will have to import the file into a word processing program and reformat all the parts as needed. Figure 10-19 illustrates the sequence by which OmniPage converts a page of type into a disk file.

OCR Accuracy and Scanning

Better OCR programs often quote above 99 percent accuracy; below 95 percent is considered unusable. Even with one wrong character per 100, you will have an error every 18 words or so. A spell checker can remove perhaps half the errors. Unfortunately, the errors remaining are the ones most difficult to catch; many are real words, such as substituting *deal* for *heal*. So OCR text must be carefully proofread and cannot be used where correct text is vital, such as programming code or numeric data entry. Error rates depend on the typeface and the number of different character sets in the text. The cleanliness of your scanner and of your copy will also make a difference in the error rate. A particularly useful feature of OCR programs is that when they cannot recognize a character, they insert a place mark, usually a question mark (?), asterisk (*), or tilde (~), at the location. Then all you have to do is to search for all of the place markers to eliminate that whole class of errors.

The scanning requirements for OCR are fairly modest. A scanner with 200 dpi will do; 300 dpi is good, and any resolution greater than that is not that much more helpful because the OCR software may pick up noise. Good contrast is important, though. Most OCR packages control all of the scanner operations, parameters, and commands directly, and work with the standard grayscale file formats. Files are best saved as line art—black-and-white images. Hand-held scanners are often sold with OCR packages, or can be used with them. If you intend to do a large amount of OCR work, a scanner with a sheet feeder may speed up your work, but

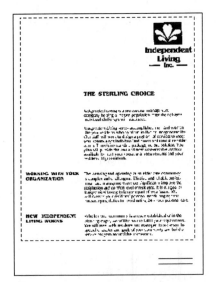

A.

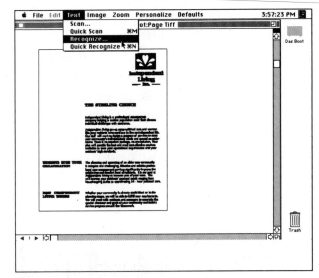

B.

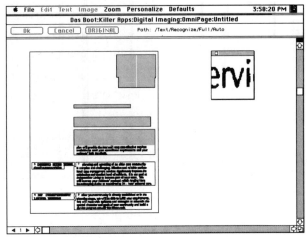

C.

Figure 10-19 **(A)** A bit map TIFF file is created from a page of two different fonts with different styles. **(B)** The file is opened in OmniPage and the Recognize command is given. **(C)** The program blocks out areas of the page separating text from graphics in a first scan.

Figure 10-19
(continued)

(D) Different fonts and styles are cataloged, and the program makes a second scan to improve accuracy. Note that as the recognition is in progress, a small dialog box shows the characters being recognized. **(E)** The final ASCII file shows almost complete recognition of the Optima font, a sans serif font. There are several errors for ITC-Benguiat Bold, a serif font that was set with an unusual kerning factor in this case. Notice the use of a tilde for questionable characters.

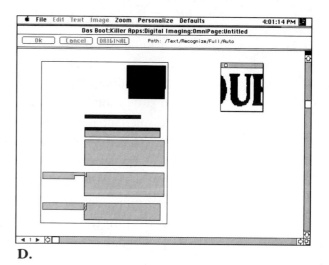

D.

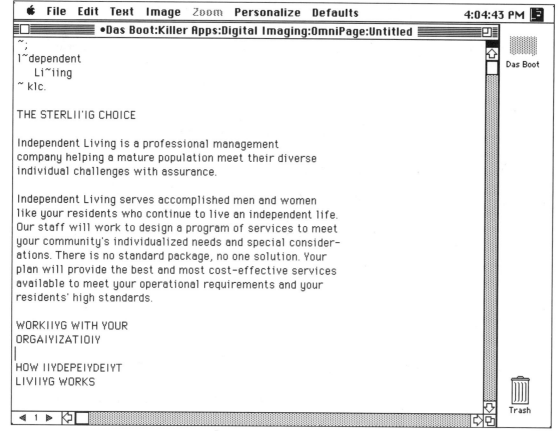

E.

be sure to check that your OCR software will support an automatic feed operation. Many OCR software programs contain scanner controls built in.

A couple of years ago OCR packages shipped with expansion boards containing added memory and powerful processors. Today, as micros have become more powerful, they are more commonly software-only packages. Some vendors sell complete systems: scanner, workstation or adaptor board, and software combined. Xerox Imaging Systems Kurzweil Model 5000 OCR ($15,950) is one example. Virtual memory will remove the memory restrictions placed on the current OCR programs and should spawn a new generation of exciting technology in this area.

Some of the better packages in OCR are:

- **AccuText** (Mac): From Xerox Imaging System, and one of the better medium-priced AI OCR packages. It comes bundled as a unit with a $2,500 sheet-fed scanner, a $2,500 memory expansion board, and about $2,000 worth of software.

- **OmniPage** (PC and Mac): An AI-based page recognition program that can recognize multiple columns of text in a variety of typestyles. This program is so powerful that it can read financial data from a newspaper listing of stock data and store the results in a spreadsheet. OmniPage provides the necessary software for controlling a scanner.

- **ReadIt!** (Mac): Cheap ($300), and suitable for limited typeface scanning, this package uses a character table for recognition. Being trainable, it has a reasonable error rate. It works with TIFF files, can control some scanners, and can work with blocks of scanned areas that you mark for analysis. Marking blocks allows you to do multicolumn text manually, which is a lot slower than the automatic systems, such as OmniPage.

- **WordScan Plus** (PC and Mac): A high-end AI program from Calera Recognition Systems that comes with a $2,500 memory expansion board for AT computers (called TrueScan). Very similar to OmniPage in features and capabilities.

Figure 10-20
The Paper Keyboard from Datacap is an automated data entry system using OCR to scan filled-in paper forms. The recognition is in progress here. The software displays original form image and recognized data during input.

- **Other Packages: ReadStar II** (Inovatic), **AutoRead** (ISTC), **SPOT** (Flagstaff Engineering), **Advantex** (Solution Technology), **Recognize** (DEST), **TextPert** (CTA), and **Catchword** (Logitech), which ships with the Scanman hand scanner. Most cost about $1,000 and are for the IBM PC.

OCR is making a whole range of new technologies possible. OCR-to-speech systems such as the Braille Reader from Kurzweil, are an exciting offshoot of artificial intelligence. With it, blind people can scan a book and have a computer read it back to them. Ray Kurzweil's book *Intelligent Machines* is a seminal work and is highly recommended.

One unique application for OCR is in automatic document processing. Applications like this one make me smile as they illustrate the power of a computer to free individuals from tedious data collection. Datacap sells a system called the Paper Keyboard that will take a paper form that you can create and scan it for data. If you fill in boxes with letters, checkmarks, numbers, and so on, the

Paper Keyboard recognizes those symbols and enters them into a database. This system, coupled with a flatbed scanner with an automatic document feeder, makes a very effective automatic data entry system. Teachers can grade tests automatically and census takers can collect numbers without losing their senses. A great time-saver for large-volume data collection.

Digital Cameras

In this decade electronic still cameras have the potential to replace film cameras in many applications because of their many advantages. A digital camera, like a conventional 35 mm camera, views the world through optical lenses; in place of film it captures images with a CCD chip and stores it on a floppy disk—which is reusable. Once the image is captured, it is digitized and can be edited, stored, transmitted through modems, displayed on the screen, and printed. The speed with which an image can be produced and transmitted is a great value to newspaper editors or others who need fast images. Still video has attracted the attention of most of the major players in photography: Canon, Kodak, Minolta, Nikon, Konica, Olympus, Polaroid, and Fuji along with the electronic giants Casio, Panasonic, Hitachi, and Sony.

Figure 10-21
The Canon XAP SHOT is one of the first still video cameras. Pictures stored to disk can be processed or input directly into Canon's color laser copier system. A microfloppy can store up to fifty images per disk.
Courtesy of Canon, Inc.

The first generation of digital cameras that have appeared don't yet have the resolution needed to compete with conventional photographs. By 1995 these devices may improve to the point that they will be popular. Actually, still video supplements film by addressing new markets rather than supplanting it. Initial digital camera models render images with half a million pixels compared to the 10 to 20 million pixels found in film, and they cost from $700 to $7,000. Their main benefit is that they require no chemical processing and are instantly available and easily manipulated. Newspapers have been early adopters because they find that they give them a speed advantage for meeting deadlines, and the resolution is within their tolerance. Some newspapers have already featured front-page color pictures produced from digital cameras.

Other properties make digital cameras unique in special applications. The Canon RC-701 camera has a very high light sensitivity that makes it ideal for use in low-light applications. Law enforcement agencies have used it for nighttime surveillance. Other digital cameras with infrared sensitivity can show how long a person has been out on a cold night (from the color of his or her nostrils), or if a car has been driven recently (by the color of the tires and engine hood). Electronic still photos taken by commercial artists also have appeared in print. This technology is likely to have future impact in desktop publishing applications where production demands require speed and integrated technology. The Canon CLC 500 integrated color printer discussed in Chapter 15 accepts input from the Canon XAP SHOT digital camera shown in Figure 10.21.

Typography

She'll wish there was more,
and that's the great art o' letter writin'.
Charles Dickens, THE PICKWICK PAPERS

Digital type has revolutionized the way we publish documents. The personal computer replaced the typewriter as a home appliance and has been transformed into a personal printing press. Sophisticated type description and handling is at the heart of this transformation in desktop publishing.

Today, more fonts are required to do increasingly complex projects. How to collect them in a logical manner and in the most cost-effective way is a question that must be answered. First, you must understand how fonts are handled by computers, how they're described, and what factors are important. In this chapter, we'll look at how computers handle type, the rendering process, utilities, and font libraries.

Font Construction

Early computers used bit maps for display, and sent nothing more than a stream of character codes to the printer. The quality of type output depended solely on the hardware installed. There was one set of characters, and with luck and perseverance (and mirrors) you could get condensed, expanded, bold, or underlined text out of a printer. All computers originally used one imaging model to display type and another model to print. Rarely could you get a page in hand with type that matched the characters displayed on your monitor. When a computer uses one model for display and another for output, two different character descriptions are required, called a *screen font* and a *printer font*. A computer must translate the description of a character into the language of the device it is driving, that is, your monitor and printer.

The Macintosh popularized an architecture by which both imaging models are merged using a page description language (PDL) to manage font descriptions. This is what has come to be know as a *graphics computer*, but some users refer to it as a bit-mapped environment. Macintosh stores the bit map of a typeface at a particular point size and makes it available to any application. Quick-Draw (the Mac's PDL) can do type scaling, styles, and positioning by applying a set of algorithms. To display and print PostScript fonts the Macintosh, until recently, required two font descriptions: one using QuickDraw for the screen and one using PostScript for the printer. A similar situation occured under Windows, another bit-mapped environment.

Now, however, both environments are able to display PostScript fonts on screen and as printed output, in any size, using a single printer font and one screen font for each style. This is accomplished with a font rasterizer. (See the discussion on rasterizers later in the chapter.)

Type on the personal computer is a wonder, and the personal computer is now the front end of complex typographical systems that are replacing conventional typesetting. A microcomputer can store a number of typefaces and any number of sizes, so it's possible to build entire type libraries. The Apple Macintosh has long since outstripped the original typeface numbering scheme Apple assigned; with only a couple of hundred type assignments. Today's scheme has tens of thousands. No longer is a character shackled to the 9 by 7 bit array matrix that the original IBM PC used. Typefaces can be anything: cursive or script, symbols, Arabic, Hebrew, Kanji, Greek, Roman, or Cyrillic. You need a basic understanding of typography to make some sense of the technological revolution of which you are a part.

Character Descriptions

A font (from the French *fondre*, meaning "to melt, cast") is made up of a complete character set of given size and typestyle or typeface (such as Roman, italic or condensed) within a type family like ITC Garamond or ITC Bookman. Computers use three types of representations to describe characters: bit-map fonts, outline fonts, and stroked fonts.

Bit-map fonts, sometimes called *raster fonts*, are memory hogs (particularly at large point sizes) and resolution specific. A character set designed for a specific resolution, a process referred to as *optimization*, can be very attractive and appear perfect when viewed in context, or when scaled at some perfect multiple of its size. Both bit-mapped and outline fonts can be optimized for specific resolution. The conversion to a bit map at a specific resolution is most precisely described as grid-fitting. Many refer to the process as font rendering. The Chicago font, which is the system font that appears on the menu bar or in the dialog boxes of the Macintosh was designed by Charles Bigelow specifically for the Mac's 72 dpi screen. It is a *sans serif* typeface that looks badly distorted at higher resolutions. Bit-map fonts are well suited to a system in which few fonts will be used, little processing is needed, and high performance is required.

Figure 11-1
The three types of font representations: (left) Bit-map font, (center) outline font, (right) stroked font.

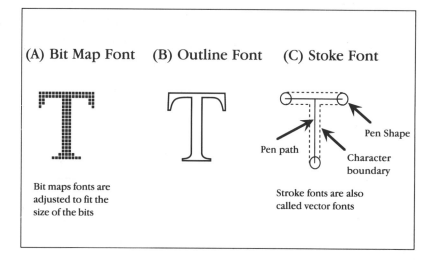

(A) Bit Map Font   **(B) Outline Font**   **(C) Stoke Font**

Bit maps fonts are adjusted to fit the size of the bits

Pen Shape
Pen path
Character boundary

Stroke fonts are also called vector fonts

Outline fonts (called *scalable fonts*) are object-oriented characters. They are compact and resolution independent. Any font described by a PDL, such as PostScript or TrueType, is an outline font. The mathematical description of an outline can vary, depending on the technology used. PostScript uses Bézier curves, True-Type uses B-spline quadratic curves; there are advantages to both. An outline font must be converted to a bit-map representation for printing. This is either at the operating system level or through the use of special software called *font rasterizers*, which can be purchased separately. Examples of rasterizers are Adobe's Post-Script (Adobe Type Manager), Bitstream's Fontware and FaceLift, Apple/Microsoft's TrueType, Agfa Compugraphic's Itellifont (licensed by H-P), Sun's Type Scaler (acquired from Folio), and Nimbus, from the German company URW, which is represented in the United States by Digital Typeface Corporation (Boston, MA). Outline fonts require significantly more processing power than bit-map ones, and because *building* a font takes time, they often benefit from the use of large RAM caches, which lets the system use previously rendered fonts. (Building refers to the process of calculating a character set from its outlines or descriptions. The resulting font is then saved in memory (cached) for later use.

Outline fonts often contain methods for optimization as a set of artificial intelligence schemes called *hints*. Hinting adjusts the shapes of letters at lower resolutions, flattening out a curve or compressing a letter stem or serif so that the font is more legible, or turning a pixel on or off so that the letter looks more symmetrical and complete. This isn't necessary at higher resolution or larger point size, where there are a sufficient number of dots to meaningfully fill the outline. Because outlines are turned into bits, the process of grid-fitting also requires hinting. When the grid doesn't match exactly a character's ideal position, that character is shifted to give a better letterform. Hinting is particularly valuable for small point sizes at lower resolutions, but loses its value at large sizes where there are many more bits than can be fitted. In order to describe fonts more compactly, many vendors also apply *encryption* schemes, which are essentially compression algorithms; encryption also serves as a barrier to piracy. Adobe's encryption algorithm is a variant of the DES standard (Data Encrypton Standard algorithm); PostScript fonts can't be compressed by utilities because they already are compressed.

Figure 11-2
Fitting an amper-
sand outline to a grid at
different resolutions.

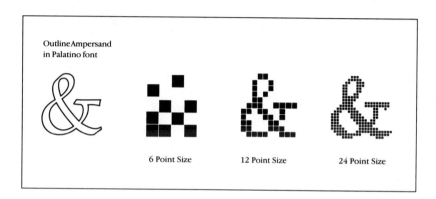

Stroke, or *vector*, fonts are named for the stroke of a pen forming the path or spine of the character. Strokes can have the properties of width, fills, patterns, line widths, line fills, line patterns, and line endings called endcaps. Strokes are resolution independent, like outline fonts, but they are even more compactly described (about 50 percent smaller), and require less computation to process. Unfortunately, few of the world's typefaces can be adequately described this way. Most faces require excessive spine description that requires more storage and processing time than stroke fonts.

Font Storage

When you buy a font from a vendor, you buy a description of a character set. It can be in the form of hardware (a printer or font cartridge), or in the form of software that is loaded into your computer. Depending on your computer system, you will need either one description or two (screen and printer fonts). Font screen processing occurs in your computer; font print processing can occur in either your computer or your printer (see Chapter 7). Fonts may be stored in:

Figure 11-3
When characters are
scaled, their shapes
change to make
them legible.

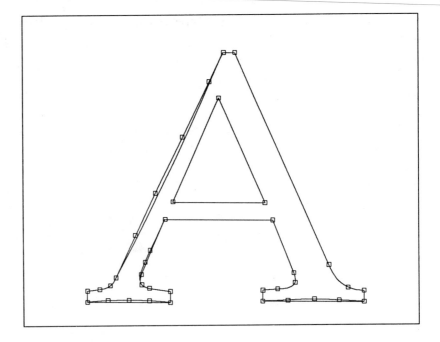

- Printer ROM: A built-in font. The Apple LaserWriter has thirty-five built in typefaces. When you buy plug-in cartridges, you are buying more printer ROM.

- Printer RAM: Your computer sends the description of the font to your printer.

- Printer Hard Drive: Some printers have one. A Linotronic ships with a hard drive of fonts. Networked printers (like a SCSI device) often allow a hard drive to be attached.

- Computer ROM: Some fonts are always stored in computer ROM. Your computer displays messages when it boots up.

- Computer System file: Macintosh can store fonts as resources attached to a system file for operating System 6, or as files stored in the System folder in operating System 7.

- Font folders: MS-DOS and MS-DOS applications, such as WordPerfect and Windows, store fonts in directories or subdirectories. Macintosh can store fonts in folders and can access those fonts using resource managers, such as Suitcase II or Master Juggler.

- Any attached volume: If there are other hard drives on a network, they too can store fonts and send them to a computer or printer for processing.

It's not absolutely critical where the font description resides, as long as your system knows where it is and how to use it. Some locations offer faster performance, others provide better and more convenient font management.

Character Use and Relationships

Describing a character is only part of the task of rendering digital fonts. There must also be a procedure or set of routines (a program) for using those characters. These routines are built into larger programs or operating systems. MS-DOS leaves this problem to the applications that run on top of it. WordPerfect and Micrografx Designer have their own font-handling technologies—different ones. When a GUI is used, then that is the application charged with font handling, as with Windows, GEM, or GEOS. Windows simplifies font handling by providing a shared set of routines and drivers for the applications that run on it. GUIs that are also operating systems, such as the Macintosh or OS/2, are where font managers reside.

Font Metrics

An application program also must know how to position characters. Character sets require descriptions regarding scale factors for small caps, super- or subscripts, styles, line spacing, and very specific intercharacter spacing. The complete descriptions of all these factors are called the *font metrics*, and they are stored in the form of a database file of numerical descriptions that accompany the object or bit-mapped description of a particular character.

A typewriter creates only *monospaced fonts* with fixed-space characters, whereas only a few digital fonts, such as Courier, are monospaced. Most fonts are *proportional*, meaning the width of a character changes depending on the context in which it's used. The ITC Garamond font used in this book is proportional, so too are the popular Times and Helvetica fonts. Font metrics include information for changing the width of proportional characters so

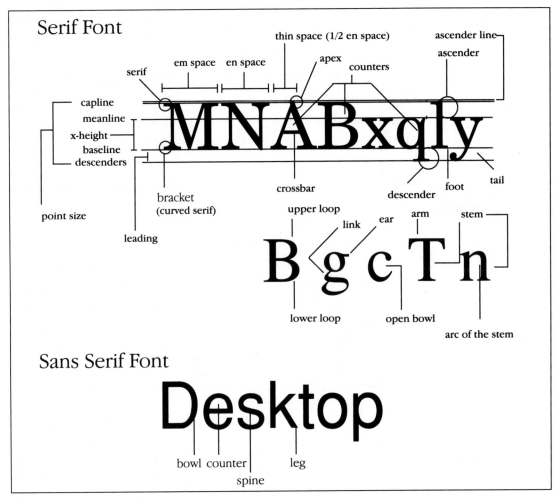

Figure 11-4 A glossary of typographic terms.

that they look better. Adjusting the set width spacing by moving letter pairs like "A V" and "T o" together is called *kerning* and makes type more readable. A PostScript font might have anywhere from 150 to 500 kerning pairs. Such pairs are a particular strength of some of the better page layout programs, such as QuarkXPress (see Chapter 12); or Edco's LetrTuck utility in which you can easily specify kerning pairs and save this information for use by Page-Maker and Ventura Publisher. There are many other kerning utilities on the market, and all of the good font editors include kerning capabilities.

Ligatures and Symbol Fonts

One complication in specifying fonts is that there is no universal set of characters. Type must deal with many nonstandard situations to improve the asthetics of the written word. Certain letter combinations such as "a e," "f i," "f l," and others look better when printed together as units called *ligatures*: fi, fl. A typographer's lettercase contained tens of ligatures, but digital type sets rarely ship with many of these. Digital foundries are just now starting to make expert type sets available for fine typography, and only for a very few of the most common fonts. Adobe, Bitstream, and Monotype offer them. There's also the problem of different symbols, countries, printers, operating systems, PDLs, and applications. All of these different combinations require different character sets. Even simple fractions are difficult to achieve in most word processors or WYSIWYG page layout programs. One strength of coded page layout systems such as TeX is that they can set fractions and do sophisticated character positioning. In order to achieve typographical effects for WYSIWYG systems, you need utilities such as ParaFont ,which can create fractions, set spacings, assign custom type styles, and build ligatures and other characters.

Figure 11-5
ITC Zapf Dingbats will supply you with a variety of useful symbols and pictures. This is the ASCII table KeyFinder from the Norton Utilities for the Macintosh.

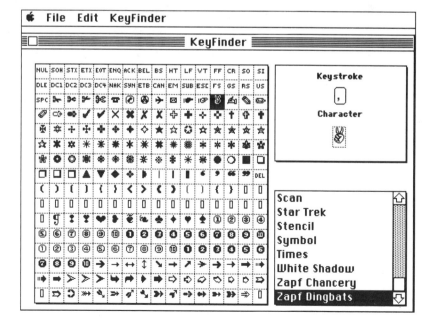

Some of the most useful font collections are picture fonts, symbols that can include everything from arrows and circles, boxes and shapes, traffic signs, map symbols, and many others. The best known are ITC Zapf Dingbats, Carta, Cairo, and Symbol. Most regular fonts have symbols squirreled away for you to find. Picture fonts exist as both outline and bit map, and they are extremely useful for a variety of applications. This list doesn't even consider all of the foreign language fonts on the market today.

▼ *Tip: If your DTP application requires a picture, you can often greatly speed up printing and display by using an outline picture font character in place of your graphic.*

History of Font Design

Worldwide there are probably about 10,000 typefaces in use today. Many were created years, decades, or centuries ago; vendors are still converting and interpreting them all into digital type. Purists judge a typeface's quality on its adherence to the original design. Some of the very old typefaces date back to Renaissance Venice, a generation after Gutenburg created the first basic lead type design. Nicholas Jenson cut one of the first Roman typefaces in 1470; Aldus Manutius invented italic type (which he called Chancery, and others called Aldine) shortly thereafter. Aldus also was the first to print Bembo type based on the typeface used in Pietro Bembo's *De Aetna* in 1494. In the very early eighteenth century, two English printers, William Caslon and John Baskerville, developed the famous faces that bear their names; their type is considered to begin the transition between old typefaces and the modern ones that originated with the face created by the Italian printer Bodoni in the late eighteenth century.

Bembo is considered to be a Venetian typeface; Caslon and Garamond are classified as old style Roman (seventeenth, early eighteenth centuries). The Venetian and old styles are recognized by serifs with large angles. The transitional Roman style (mid-eighteenth century) that includes Baskerville has increased the contrast between thick and thin strokes and has very sharp serifs. John Baskerville developed woven finish paper on which to print

Figure 11-6
Some of the famous
typefaces that have
developed throughout
printing history.

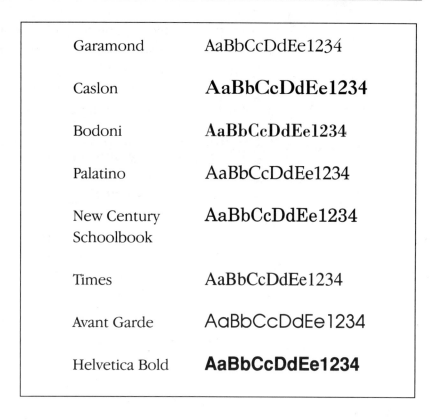

Garamond	AaBbCcDdEe1234
Caslon	**AaBbCcDdEe1234**
Bodoni	AaBbCcDdEe1234
Palatino	AaBbCcDdEe1234
New Century Schoolbook	AaBbCcDdEe1234
Times	AaBbCcDdEe1234
Avant Garde	AaBbCcDdEe1234
Helvetica Bold	**AaBbCcDdEe1234**

his typestyle and created a sensation, which is still in use today. Modern Roman (late eighteenth century), which includes Didot and Bodoni, is recognized by vertical lines and heavy contrast between thick and thin strokes. The Egyptian craze that swept Europe in the nineteenth century after Napolean's campaigns ushered in square slab serif fonts modeled after cuneiform; later in that century more fanciful display types came into use.

The twentieth century, too, has seen the creation of significant type designs. Times Roman, the dense readable serif font, was developed for the *London Times* in 1931 by Stanley Morrison to conserve print space. The calligraphic serif faces ITC Souvenir, Palatino, and Galliard look like they are drawn by a brush. ITC Bookman, Century Old Style, and New Century Schoolbook are serif text faces dating from early this century. The twentieth century is more noted, however, for the development of sans serif faces, a return to the writing style of the ancient Greeks often referred to as gothic or grotesque. Paul Renner's Futura was an early successful sans serif book font. Two other important sans serif moderns are: Helvetica and Univers, designed by Max Miedinger and Adrian Frutiger in 1957, respectively. All of the typefaces mentioned in this section have been translated into digital type.

▼ *Tip: Traditionally serif fonts are used for setting body copy. They are said to be more readable because serifs guide the eye flow. Sans serif fonts are more generally used as display type or for titles.*

Use one, perhaps two, typefaces in a document and obtain variation by using different weights and styles of the typeface throughout. But remember, limiting font variety improves printing times and lowers memory and storage space requirements.

The roots of some typefaces are lost in time. Specialists scour the great libraries of the world, and their successes read like a great novel. Adobe's Garamond, part of its Original Series, was researched from recasts of the original Garamond matrices in the collection of the Plantin-Moretus Museum in Antwerp, Belgium. Adobe's version ships with a special 144-character Expert Set of ligatures, titling caps, old-fashioned numerals, and flourished caps, among others. When Bitstream wanted to add the Palatino font to its collection, it brought in the original designer, Hermann Zapf, to supervise the creation of what was to be called Zapf Calligraphic.

As exciting as historical type design is, the noted designers of today who have crossed the threshold from lead type to CAD all say, that the best tools for creating type exist today. Most significantly, the last five years have seen an explosion of type design and production, and the democratization of this formerly arcane specialty. The creation of a new font, a task that once took years to perfect, can now be accomplished in days or weeks.

Digital Type Design

Digital type begins as a sketch by a designer; a set of drawings defines major characters and expresses the proportionality rules between them. Font foundries take these designs and digitize them. Some foundries, such as the typesetter equipment manufacturers Agfa Compugraphic, Linotype, and Varityper create proprietary fonts for specific equipment. Independent foundries, including Adobe and Bitstream, produce fonts for a variety of systems. Independent vendors usually create a digitized master file and translation software to convert these files to other formats.

Foundries use workstations to digitize type. Input comes from graphics tablets with specially designed software. By plotting control points, usually inflection points and corner points on a letterform, the entire outline of a character is created. The goal is to describe completely a character in the smallest number of points that gives the most compact description. The software provides a number of special functions for type manipulation: the ability to duplicate angles easily, scale line segments, provide grids, and so on. Designer and typographer consult on changes that the digital technology might require. Once a character is traced, its outline is stored in a master file. Translation software manipulates the outline to a format that a particular microcomputer can use and optimizes it. Some systems also perform automatic "hinting."

Don't underestimate the time needed to create a new typeface just because it's now a digitized process. It can take weeks, sometimes years. Creating twenty-six letters is not simply twenty-six times the task of creating just one. Good typography maintains consistency, standards ratios, stem weights, angles, and so on. Most faces use the M square as their basic building block—the capital letter M has the largest width and height of any character. Baseline, meanline, x-heights (literally the height of the lowercase x), ascenders, descenders, cap heights, and horizontal measurements called side bearings are often specified for character sets (refer to Fig. 11.5). Good designers also determine a complete ideal rule set *before* setting out to actually draw the letters. A professional type designer has a discerning eye that takes years to acquire. Type is an artform, and is discussed in books and magazines like varieties of fine wine. However, amateurs, too, can turn out excellent typefaces using low-cost font editors. Many people find the process of creating type to be as much fun as a good crossword puzzle.

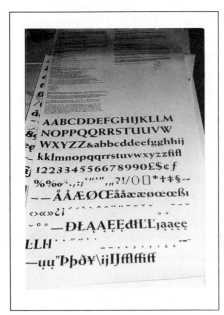

A.

B.

Figure 11-7
The process for digitizing type. **(A)** A master design is created, often by freehand, and annotated. **(B)** Graphic workstations are used to digitize the letterforms. Shown here is Dennis Pasternak Typographic Coordinator at Bitstream putting the finishing touches on a letter on a Camex workstation (Boston, MA). **(C)** The final outline shape is a combination of curves and straight lines.

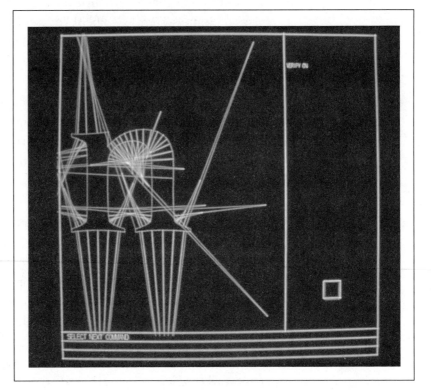

C.

Font Standards

Type 1

Fonts have been classified based on their adherence to the Adobe PostScript language. A fully encrypted and hinted font is called a *Type 1 font*. Adobe has licensed the technology for Type 1 to Linotype, Varityper, Agfa Compugraphic, and Monotype, and there are well over 1,000 different faces to choose from. Plans exist to have over 6,000 Type 1 fonts on the market in the next couple of years. This group of fonts prints well at up to 1,200 dpi and above. Their hints make subtle changes to the letterforms so that they look more legible at 300 dpi, although some type authorities think that the hinting process degrades the letterforms somewhat. Type 1 fonts are compact and relatively quick to print. Bitstream sells Type 1 fonts called Type A; it also sells a form of Type 1 fonts that are unhinted and that have been dubbed *Type 2 fonts*. (You'll also see Bitstream Type 3 fonts called C fonts and Fontware referred to as Type F.)

Adobe has recently expanded its Type 1 format to include "Multiple Master" technology. With Multiple Master, an infinite number of font line weights can be automatically derived from two or more "master" designs. This technology will give digital typographers vast new capabilities not seen since the "old days" of hot metal type. These include visual scaling at different point sizes and improved copyfitting and justification.

Type 3

Type 3 fonts do not follow the Type 1 format. Any outline shape can be defined as a Type 3 character, including your company logo or line art scanned as a 2-bit file and stored as a single keystroke. The Art Importer from Altsys on the Macintosh will take a PICT or EPS graphics file and plug it into the slot corresponding to the keystroke that will create that symbol. Sometimes Type 3 fonts are referred to as user-defined fonts. Many utilities that can convert Type 3 fonts to Type 1 are on the market today, and many graphics application packages also have this capability. Metamorphosis, also from Altsys, converts Type 3 to Type 1 fonts on the Macintosh, and vice versa. Conversion to Type 1 fonts results in an editable outline that can be modified in any program that works with Bézier graphics, which can be useful for creating type effects. The only good reason for converting fonts to Type 3 format is if you have a PostScript clone printer that can't accept Type 1 fonts.

TrueType

TrueType, originally developed by Apple and now adapted by both Apple and Microsoft, is a scalable font alternative to the Adobe Type 1 format. TrueType is built into Apple System 7 and Microsoft Windows 3.1, which precludes the necessity of using a font rasterizing utility (like Adobe Type Manager or FaceLift) for scaling screen and printer type in those environments. Additionally, a set of basic TrueType fonts is included with Apple and Microsoft operating systems. TrueType fonts can be output on both PostScript and non-PostScript printers.

Several major font vendors, including Bitstream, Linotype-Hell, Agfa Compugraphic and others, have announced TrueType font libraries, which are being brought to market now.

TrueType's main advantage, other than its built-in scaling technology, is the fact that it has an open, expandable format, which should allow type companies to easily enhance and expand its capabilities in the years to come. TrueType is a viable alternative to Adobe Type 1, albeit with a smaller selection of fonts, at least for now.

Some companies still sell bit-map font collections. Dubl-Click Software and Casady & Greene are two examples for the Macintosh. Strangely enough, there is a large shareware and freeware collection of bit-mapped fonts in the public domain. You can find them on bulletin boards and other on-line services and in the catalogs of user groups, such as the Boston Computer Society and Berkeley Macintosh User's Group, among others. Professional designers tend to work only in outline fonts, believing that they can get more sophisticated results. Bit-map fonts can be useful for non-PostScript printers, particularly dot matrix ones.

Font Editors

Font editors are programs that allow you to create new type characters. They are used for creating whole new fonts and, less frequently, for creating special type effects. If your favorite font is missing a ligature for converting, say, "I T T I" to "ITTI," you can create it and add it to your character set. Several font editors on the market today give the average user the freedom to shape digital type. The Macintosh is particularly blessed in this product category. ParaFont, mentioned earlier, is a font editor. Altsys (Plano, TX), the company responsible for developing Aldus FreeHand, has a set of products including: FONTastic, a bit-map font editor, and Fontographer, a PostScript outline editor at work in Figure 11.12. Letraset's FontStudio is another well-regarded outline font editor.

Fontographer is actually a full technical drawing environment specially created for font editing. It will import a scanned image of your character and autotrace it, thus speeding up its design. Attributes such as spacing, line strokes, fills, and so on can be assigned, and when your letterform is complete Fontographer also has a panel for the character's ASCII assignment. Fontographer also has automatic hinting and font metric assignment. You can create either Type 1, Type 3, or TrueType fonts in Macintosh, PC, or a general format with this product. It costs $495, but considering that you can become a typographer and compete with designers running $100,000 workstations, it's well worth it. Many of the smaller font vendors and public domain font creators use Fontographer.

▼ *Tip: Put your logo into Fontographer as a character. A simple keystroke will generate your graphic, and you can use font sizes for precise sizing.*

One class of font editor software is designed especially for creating special type effects. Brøderbund's TypeStyler, Letraset's LetraStudio, and Adobe's TypeAlign are examples for the Macintosh. These products enable you to create character strings and apply numerous PostScript effects to them. TypeAlign, a desk accessory, works with the Adobe Type Manager to manipulate Type 1 outline fonts. TypeAlign has a technical drawing feel to it and a limited number of type effects. LetraStudio is a full-featured draw-style application, but is pricy and requires special fonts. Even more impressive is TypeStyler, a point-and-click font modifier that uses outline fonts from almost any font vendor you can think of. It offers a template library of shapes and styles, colors, patterns, and a good set of typographical tools. Both EPS and PICT files are imported and exported. TypeStyler, illustrated in Figure 11.9, is the best program available on the market today for logo design. It's particularly easy to use, intuitive, and an excellent value.

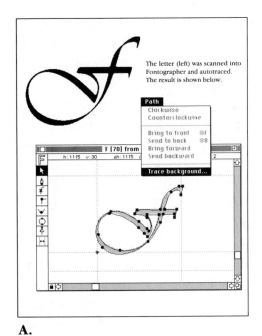

A.

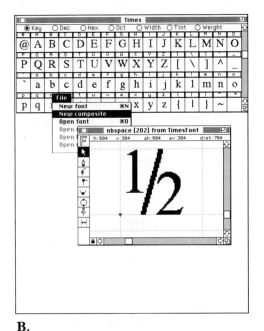

B.

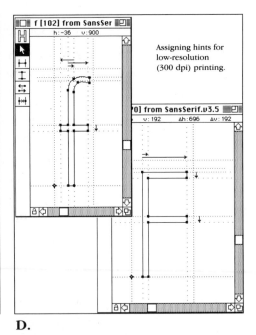

C.

D.

Figure 11-8 Fontographer is a complete font creation and editing application. Characters can be created, modified, and type characteristics assigned. **(A)** A letter is scanned in and autotraced. **(B)** Composite characters can be created for symbols, ligatures, and so on, and assigned a keystroke. **(C)** In a font metrics window, various character assignments are made, (here fill and stroke). **(D)** Fontographer adds hints for low-resolution display and printing. *Courtesy of Altsys.*

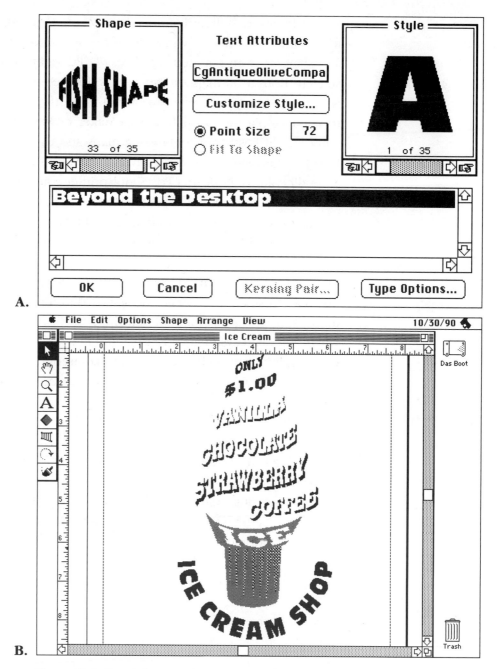

Figure 11-9 TypeStyler is an object-oriented draw program optimized for type manipulation and perfect for logo design. **(A)** Using a library of shapes and styles selected from dialog boxes, you can rapidly try out designs. A palette of tools is available to customize shapes and type. **(B)** A sample design created in TypeStyler. *Courtesy of Brøderbund, Inc.*

The Publisher's Type Foundry from ZSoft (Marietta, GA) is a font editor that runs on Windows. It creates custom fonts, logos, and symbols from scanned typefaces via PC Paintbrush, or from scratch. Both a bit-map and an outline font editor are included with the program, and you can output to PostScript printers and to major applications, such as PageMaker or Ventura Publisher. You can edit PostScript fonts to bit maps and use it to print to a LaserJet; conversely, you can convert a Hewlett-Packard font into an outline and send it to a PostScript printer using Type Foundry. A version due out soon is expected to have upgraded design tools and to allow for Type 1 font generation, but this application isn't really comparable to Fontographer yet.

Font Wars

Outline fonts are intimately related to their PDL, and for the past five years PostScript has been the standard in the microcomputer industry. Then, a turmoil, dubbed the Font Wars, began in 1989 when Sun Microsystems and Apple announced their own proprietary outline font technologies. Sun acquired a company called Folio and announced OpenFonts. Apple started development of its Royal Font technology, now called TrueType (see above). Now Microsoft has licensed TrueType for Windows (to appear in 1991) and the OS/2 Presentation Manager, and Apple has cross-licensed Microsoft's PDL, called TrueImage (see Chapter 7). That same year the PostScript type description code was broken, first by Raster Image Processing Systems (RIPS of Boulder, CO) followed shortly thereafter by Bitstream (Cambridge, MA). All of the aforementioned developments proved irresistible, and in 1990 Adobe published its encryption scheme, licensed its technology, and started selling its raster image processor to several vendors.

Font selection is something of a nightmare. Font libraries are very expensive and of course you don't want to duplicate your library. Right now, PostScript fonts are the safe play. Type 1 and Type 3 fonts look about the same at high resolutions (over 1,200 dpi), but many people find Type 3 fonts thicker and coarser at the moderate resolution of 300 dpi afforded by most laser printers because they're unhinted. The competing TrueType standard will begin to impact the market in late 1991 and will no doubt be used because it will be given away free in the Mac, Windows, and OS/2. IBM has endorsed ATM PostScript font rasterizer for its version of the Presentation Manager based on the System Application Architecture (SAA) standard. IBM PC users have trailed the market in font selection, so they will benefit from lower prices and improved standards once the market shakes out. Although the Font Wars got great press, vendors are committed to protecting their installed base and utilities will be written to smooth conversions no matter what type you buy. Renewed cooperation between Apple and Adobe suggest that Apple may not back the TrueImage PDL very aggressively.

Font Libraries

There are over twenty-five vendors selling PostScript fonts. Bitstream, founded in 1981, is the largest vendor of IBM PC compatible typefaces, with a good Macintosh selection. Most of the collection of over 1,000 typefaces are encrypted, unhinted fonts for high-resolution printing on PostScript devices. Some are unencrypted, unhinted fonts for lower-resolution PostScript laser printers. MacFontware is the modest size collection of unencrypted, unhinted fonts for the Apple LaserWriter, and PostScript clone printers. Adobe is the largest producer of Macintosh fonts. Table 11.1 lists major font vendors.

Nowadays, rarely do vendors sell single font packages. Most are starting to package collections of four or more typefaces together for special purposes, such as newspaper or advertising work. You can purchase entire font libraries from some of the type houses. Adobe sells 80 MByte hard drives with its fonts on it. Called the Font Folio, it sells for $14,200. Bitstream's library on a hard drive costs $19,995. Agfa Compugraphic sells its library on a CD ROM, and will cut you a deal on a CD ROM player if you need one. Pricing is the CD ROM and one font for $169, $975 for twenty and the CD ROM drive tossed in, and $16,995 for the entire Agfa and Adobe libraries. Typically, vendors encrypt their libraries and require a special password protection. They give you the password over the phone for any other fonts you purchase, and you make the font available to users through a control panel setting.

Table 11.1 Font Libraries and Vendors

Vendor	Library Name	Size	Format
Adobe Systems (415)961-4400	Adobe Type Library (PC, Mac)	1,000	1
Agfa Compugraphic (800)424-8937	1. Studio Series (Mac) 2 Prof. Series (Mac/PC)	100 450	3 1
Altsys Corp. (214)424-4888	Altsys Faces (Mac)	21	3
Bitstream Inc. (800)522-FONT	1. MacFontware (Mac) 2. Fontware (PC) 3. Bitstream Library (Mac) 4. FaceLift/Speedo	100 100 1,000 1,000	3 3 1 1
Casady & Greene (800)331-4321 or (800)851-1986 in CA	Fluent Laser Fonts (Mac/PC)	100	1, 3 bit maps
Dubl Click Software (818)700-9525	World Class Laser Type (Mac)	70	1 3 bit maps
The Font Company (800)442-3668	URW Typefaces Library (Mac/PC)	1,500 1,500	1 1
Image Club Graphics (800)661-9410	ImageClub Typeface Library (Mac/PC)	600	1, 3 EPS
Linotype Co. (800)633-1900	The Linotype Library (Mac/PC)	650	1
Monotype Typography (800)MONOTYP	Monotype Typeface Library (Mac)	400	1
Page Studio Graphics (602)839-2763	Pixsymbols (Mac/PC)	65	1.3
Studio231 (516)785-4222	Studio231 Typeface Library (Mac)	130	3
URW (603)882-7445	URW Typeface Library (Mac/PC)	1,250	3
Varityper (800)526-0767	Varityper Typeface Library (Mac)	300	1

Most vendors publish their typefaces in a type book or as posters. Adobe, Bitstream, Agfa, ITC, and others will supply you with these samples for free; they make very attractive wall hangings. It's also helpful to be able to scan these samples to develop familiarity with different typefaces. Adobe offers sample HyperCard stacks. Other vendors offer computer samples published in other formats.

Clearly, you need to develop a strategy for font selection. The first step is to decide which font library has the typefaces you need. If you intend to use an outside service bureau for your work, it can often be a good source of advice in this regard, as it supports a variety of customers and has experience in this area. Also, you can save yourself extra work and cost by using fonts in the bureau's collection. Most font vendors permit you to work with their screen fonts without purchasing their printer fonts. You can find them on on-line services or bulletin boards; often your service bureau will supply them. This can be an easy way to do sophisticated typography if you don't intend to do the printing yourself.

Although fonts from different vendors often have the same name, reflecting their historical heritage, it's very important to realize that the font metrics can be very different. Opening Bitstream's Baskerville in place of Adobe's Baskerville can result in a font-ID conflict and will cause problems in your layout. Your line ending and page breaks might not match once you switch back to the original font. Adobe fonts standardize on 72 points to the inch; Bitstream on the American Point Standard of 72.289 points to the inch. Keep close track of the fonts you use so that these problems don't crop up, particularly when doing work on other people's systems. Conflicts of this sort were severe in old Macintosh system software where only 256 fonts were were allowed; these conflicts prevented documents from opening, and all kinds of fonts shared the same ID numbers, even different named fonts from the same vendor.

Any good style book will tell you to limit your use of fonts to one or at most two families. By varying styles in a single typeface, you can achieve a pleasing blend of uniformity and contrast. That means collecting typeface families. A good collection of Helvetica would have black, bold, italic, normal, light, oblique, narrow (condensed), expanded, and so on. Serif faces are normally used for body copy, although many designers use them for headlines or displays. Sans serif type is more often used as display type, but some modern designers find some sans serif type attractive as body text. Use your judgment, and let the response of your audience guide you.

Working with Fonts

MS-DOS, the most widely used operating system today, contains no font handling utilities; it defers that function to application programs such as WordPerfect or Harvard Graphics. This has created something of a nightmare in the DOS world as each program adopts proprietary solutions for installing fonts; handling fonts; and working with font metrics, character sets, and other data. A page composed in WordPerfect will probably have different line breaks than the same characters typed in XyWrite. Competitive font standards cost money, time, and aggravation, and are good reasons not to choose a particular system.

GUIs such as GEM, Windows, and GEOS manage fonts, and standardize their formats between applications, simplifying your decision of what fonts to buy and how to install and use them. These are strong arguments for their adoption. Graphics computers such as the Mac, and operating systems, such as OS/2, have font managers at the system level, and they too require only one font handling process. Type handling is one function you want to have work in the background. Font conflicts and the dreaded "unexpected results" can be particularly galling when sending work out to a service bureau.

Be aware that most GIU's have limits on the number of fonts you can use. For Windows 3.0, that limit is 99; for a Macintosh it is 16. Using a font manager such as Suitcase II or Master Juggler on the Macintosh raises this limit to the hundreds or thousands.

Hard Fonts/ Cartridges

Computers can use both *hard* and *soft fonts*. A hard font is stored permanently in your computer's or printer's memory, and is often called a *resident font* or *native font*. When you insert a font cartridge into a printer, you are storing a hard font. These fonts are generally fast to work with, somewhat expensive, and not subject to technology improvements that time brings. Soft fonts, sometimes called *downloadable fonts*, are character sets loaded as software. Variations are created from a set of instructions. A point size not stored in your system would have to be created, a process called *building* a font. This takes time; how much time depends on the power of your microprocessor. However, soft fonts improve over time, whereas hard fonts lock you into a specific and aging technology. The popularity of soft fonts has led to the misconception that they afford better quality than hard fonts. This is not true (yet). A trained designer can still do a better job than an AI algorithm at adjusting the raster process and turning bits on and off.

Most printers and typesetters come with some built-in fonts. The Apple LaserWriter shipped with thirty-five resident fonts, representing eleven typefaces. That's not a very broad selection, particularly for DTP applications, so many font solutions are sold to enhance that choice. All fonts added to a LaserWriter are soft fonts, and since LaserWriters are SCSI devices, fonts can be stored on any mountable volume. The NTX can have a dedicated hard drive attached.

The H-P LaserJet printer started life with just one built-in font, 12-point Courier, so that the output would look like it rolled out of an IBM Selectric typewriter. H-P had built slots into the LaserJet to accept cartridge fonts; bit maps were stored in ROM on the cartridge. H-P initially offered over a·dozen cartridges, ranging from $99 to $399. In 1988 IQ Engineering created Super Cartridge 1, packing all of the H-P cartridge fonts onto a single cartridge; and Pacific Data Products sells a similar product called 25 Cartridges in One; both retail at $399. Jumbo cartridges are good value for the money, and these products have sold so well that H-P introduced a sixty-five-font cartridge for $300 called the ProCollection for general business printing. H-P also reorganized its cartridge line into nine functionally divided font sets. The Great Start cartridge for word processing and spreadsheets sells for $99; others cost $199. And now Bitstream has TypeCity, a super cartridge that's expandable. The base cartridge, with 35 bit-mapped fonts, costs about $379. The add-on cartridges, with 6- to 12 bit-mapped fonts each, are priced at $99 to $129.

While easy to use and fast, bit-mapped cartridge fonts have some major disadvantages. They provide limited style and sizes, work with only one printer, and are not useful for screen display. The appropriate font metrics must be built into the application or printer drivers that are normally supplied with the cartridge. Because ROM is limited, these cartridges generally contain small-size bit maps in order to maximize the number of fonts contained, which limits their use in display type applications. Soft fonts offer unlimited choices, but they are trickier to install and use, slower, and require dedicated RAM in your printer. The original soft fonts (such as H-P's Soft Fonts) were bit-map fonts that ate up valuable disk space.

▼ *Tip: Eschew font cartridges and hard fonts for soft fonts. Use the money you save to buy a faster computer—that is more important for a single user.*

In a networked printing application, hard fonts and printer performance are more important, but soft fonts allow broader access, improved type manipulation, and faster technological improvement over time. However, it is interesting to note that Bitstream's recent research into their font cartridge showed that most folks with LaserJet IIIs prefer bit-mapped cartridges because it's easier to keep a better degree of design conformity (for companies) using fixed-size fonts.

**Soft Fonts/
Font Rasterizers**

The computer industry is in transition at the moment, with bit-map fonts being replaced almost completely by scalable fonts. Scalable fonts require *font rasterizers* to build characters from outlines. A major distinction is that computer-based font rasterizers place the processing burden on your computer, not on your printer. If you're using a computer-based rasterizer, such as ATM, rather than one built into the printer (like PostScript), printing times are dependent on your CPU clock speed. Some rasterizers, such as TrueType, are part of an operating system; others are software packages that convert outline fonts to bit maps. The Adobe Type Manager (ATM) is a subset of both Display PostScript and PostScript output, creating bit maps for both; it is an add-on utility. In essence, ATM allows you to coax PostScript output out of a non-PostScript printer, but only for text. It doesn't work with graphics. ATM is available for the Macintosh, Windows, and later in 1991, for OS/2. ATM was considered to be one of the most significant products introduced in the microcomputer industry in 1990.

Figure 11-10
The Adobe Type Manager rasterizes PostScript type, smoothing out the screen display of outline fonts and improving type quality on printed output to non-PostScript printers. Shown here is 127-point ITC Bookman. **(A)** ATM on. **(B)** ATM off.

A.

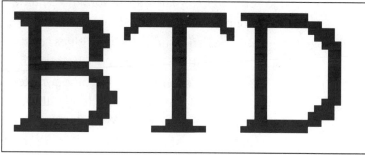

B.

Other vendors provide more limited solutions for rasterizing outline fonts to bit map for output to supported printers only, particularly on the IBM PC. Glyphix from Swfte (Wilmington, DE) provides sixteen typefaces for its utility called Font Manager. It offers font managers for many of the major MS-DOS applications (Word,

WordPerfect, PageMaker, and Ventura Publisher), and Glyphix's Font Manager can scale outlines from 6 to 60 points and output to LaserJets and compatibles. Oblique type and different type weights (such as bold or narrow) can be created. Glyphix fonts work with other MS-DOS applications. Fonts are built on-demand, and don't require storage in a font cache or as a disk file.

Bitstream's Fontware Installation Kit is a menu-driven font rasterizer for building and storing desired fonts from outlines. Sizes from 2 to 144 points in 1/10-point increments can be created from a library of over 200 Bitstream Fontware packages in fifty odd collections. Built fonts are stored in font directories, and Fontware manages these font files. Kits are available for most of the popular IBM PC DTP, graphics, word processing, and spreadsheet programs. Two major disadvantages of Fontware: It can take tens of minutes to hours to built a font, and you have to select, in advance, all of the desired sizes. Adobe PostScript PC fonts now ship with a Fontware style utility for building H-P LaserJet bit-map fonts at any size.

Hewlett-Packard and Agfa Compugraphic have a product similar to Fontware called Type Director that uses the Intellifont typefaces. It's sold for the LaserJet II and III series printers, but is being replaced by the PCL 5 technology built into the LaserJet III series. PCL 5 allows on-demand scaling and offers a resolution enhancement feature shown in Chapter 7, Figure 7-5. The LaserJet III series still supports cartridges, but now the descriptions are scalable outline fonts and not bit maps.

You're more likely to become a raster man (or woman) if you can do real-time font building. Bitstream's Speedo technology incorporated into the product called FaceLift for Windows and the Adobe Type Manager both offer on-the-fly scaling and are preferred purchases. Speedo is built into some applications, such as Micrografx Designer 3.0, and is one-fifth the size and five times the speed of Fontware. FaceLift requires Speedo fonts, available only from Bitstream, but there is a good selection of fifty-two packages of four faces each for $129 per package. Bitstream has an upgrade program for converting your Fontware typefaces to Speedo fonts.

Other scalable font generators available under Windows include ZSoft's SoftType and Atech's Publisher's PowerPak. SoftType is a collection of sixty-two typefaces with a font generator, font manager, and modifier. Users can produce hinted/encrypted Adobe Type 1 fonts on true Adobe PostScript printers and create many special effects. SoftType installs automatically into Windows and allows for immediate access through Windows applications. It also generates Windows and Ventura Publisher screen fonts. PowerPak is another font scaler. It's relatively inexpensive, but has a limited type library that's not as well designed as Bitstream's or Adobe's. PowerPak does work with a large variety of printers, including Epson and Toshiba dot matrix printers, and its low cost makes it appealing to the casual DTPer.

The best of the font scaling solutions for Windows may be Zenographics' SuperPrint. It can use Adobe, Fontware, Speedo, Nimbus Q, and Intellifonts typefaces. SuperPrint can also use LaserJet bit-map soft fonts, but only at their original size. Super-Print is a memory management champ, runs reasonably fast, and has a smaller memory partition than a LaserJet printer driver. A SuperPrint module speeds up Windows graphics printing considerably, and the version released in late 1990 also generates screen fonts on the fly.

Fonts and the IBM PC

MS-DOS has no font handling built into it. Instead, this operating system defers font handling to specific applications. That makes font installation, handling, and building a font library a difficult prospect. Access to hard fonts must be assigned within the application running. Soft fonts can be installed as part of:

- A GUI: Windows ships with a variety of fonts. Versions prior to early 1991 come with bit-map fonts; the update to version 3.0 will contain TrueType outline fonts.

- Word Processor: Many word processors ship with a selection of fonts and with utilities for installing additional ones.

- Page Layout Software: Ventura Publisher ships with some fonts, and you can install additional ones.

- Graphics Programs: Some draw and paint programs ship with a few fonts and with their own type handling technology. Designer uses the Bitstream Speedo technology; Illustrator uses PostScript and Adobe fonts.

Soft fonts also can be purchased separately from font vendors. The difficulty of installing fonts varies. Page layout programs such as PageMaker and Ventura Publisher have advanced font handling capabilities because these applications need to work with different font technologies offered for the PC. It is generally more difficult to install fonts in word processors on the PC, because most PCs were originally designed (especially the older ones) to handle just a few monospaced typewriter fonts. Additional font support, laser printer support, preview mode, and other advanced type handling procedures were add-ons and not part of the original design. Fonts must not only display on screen, but they must also be downloaded to printer memory. That means that the word processor must be aware of the font and be capable of driving the printer. GUIs simplify this process by building font and printer handling directly into the interface.

If you have an application that contains a font you want to use in another application, you can often "borrow" it for the second application. Bit-mapped LaserJet soft fonts on the PC are stored as files that are named with conventions that make their assignments obvious. Ventura stores LaserJet soft fonts using the convention TMSN3010.SFP, TMSN3012.SFP, TMS3012.SFP, TMSB3010.SFL, and TMB3012.SFP. SFP refers to Soft Font Portrait, SFL to Soft Font Landscape, and TM to Times Roman. The last two numbers in the name are the point size (10 or 12), and the letters B, N, or I refer to bold, normal, or italic styles. So, if you have an application such as WordStar 2000, you can install these fonts from Ventura. You would rename the font in the Hewlett-Packard LaserJet convention by using the following MS-DOS command:

```
COPY \ VENTURA \ TMSI3012.SFP \ WS2000 \ TR1201PN.R8P
```

After copying the font to the WordStar directory, you would use the program's standard installation procedure. This solves one-half of the problem—installing the screen font. The second half of the problem is downloading the font to the printer. Word processors ship with printer drivers that contain *printer definition files*. A monospaced font initializes the printer, switches fonts, and performs supported style operations. Proportional fonts must also download font metrics (the width table included in the font's database description) to achieve WSIWYG operation.

Word has separate printer definition files for each printer. WordPerfect contains compound files called WPRINT1.ALL and WPRINT2.ALL, and stores the width tables that are part of the font's description in WPFONT1.ALL and WPFONT2.ALL files. These files support native fonts contained in printers and the soft fonts that are supplied, as well. When you download a font in Word you generate a .PRD file from the width table. WordPerfect adds the font description to existing files. The Adobe PostScript fonts come with a downloading utility that sends the fonts to the printer through your serial port. Ventura and PageMaker easily install these fonts, but word processors are more problematic. Some, such as WordPerfect, can install the Adobe Font Metrics files (.AFM) directly, others, such as Word and XyWrite, require hacking. WordStar 2000 uses a utility called PSFONT that accomplishes the installation.

Windows standardizes font handling for any application that uses that interface. It supplies bit-map screen fonts and vector or stroke fonts. Printers' and font vendors' native, cartridge, and soft fonts are supported through Windows' printer driver files. When downloading a file to a printer, Windows checks the driver for the selected font. If it isn't found, Windows generates a raster font from the font file provided. Windows ships with a basic selection of screen fonts; certain printers also supply them. If Windows can't find a screen font for the one you have chosen to print, it substitutes a font that resembles the printer font as closely as possible.

Vendor font packages may or may not include screen fonts; consider buying font packages with both printer and screen fonts included. When you install a printer in Windows, any screen font that can be used by your printer is automatically installed. If a printer driver file doesn't supply the screen fonts, you might be able to obtain them from the printer manufacturer or font vendor. Installation programs are sometimes supplied with the font package or with the printer driver files installation program. If there is no utility for installing the font into Windows, then it is installed through the Control Panel. To do so you select the Font icon in the Control Panel to bring up the Fonts dialog box. Bit-mapped or vector screen fonts are added or removed there, bit-map fonts show individual sizes, and vector fonts show only the single size used to build any other sizes.

Fonts and the Macintosh

The Macintosh shipped in 1984 with ten bit-mapped fonts: Geneva, New York, Chicago, Monaco, San Francisco, Athens, Toronto, Cairo, London, and Venice. (It's a tradition on the Macintosh to name bit-mapped fonts after cities. Laser fonts can be anything but city names.) All were installed in the System file with the Font Mover utility supplied by Apple. Soon there were many commercial fonts on the market, spurred on by the introduction of the LaserWriter. Who would have anticipated such an embarrassment of font riches? Originally, only the fifteen fonts that could be installed in the System could appear on any applications menus. Font/DA Mover and the creation of suitcase files provided a way to work around to these limitations. Developers figured out how to make suitcase files available to the System file without installation. They provide links that make those files available to the system; using Suitcase (now version II) and Master Juggler any number of fonts (and desk accessories) can now be available.

Originally each font was assigned a FONT resource ID number; Apple created only 256 of them and reserved the first 128 for itself. That was such a limited number that even fonts from the same manufacturer conflicted. A subsequent FONT system was replaced by the current system called NFNTs, which allows font assignments from 1,025 to 32,767. The first 1,024 assignments are reserved by Apple. In the new system, font ID conflicts are much less common, but they still occur. You can minimize ID conflicts by installing all font families in the same suitcase files.

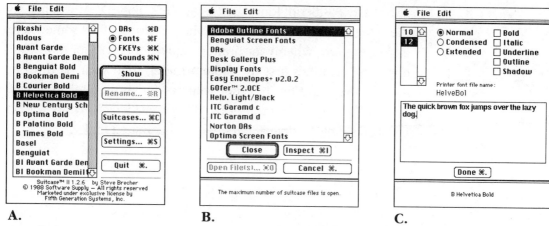

Figure 11-11 The resource manager Suitcase II allows multiple fonts to be easily used on a Macintosh. **(A)** Installed fonts are shown. **(B)** Suitcase files are opened and their location and contents are saved. **(C)** Installed fonts can be inspected.

Figure 11-12 Font/DA Mover is the Apple utility for installing screen fonts. It is headed into history as System 7 installs screen fonts directly by dragging them into the System folder.

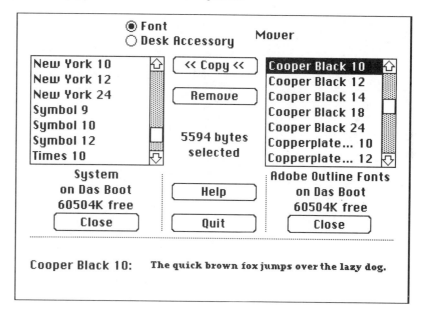

There are several methods of installing fonts on a Macintosh. In System 6, using Font/DA Mover, you can install fonts directly into the System file. Apple bit-map fonts require only a single font description, and QuickDraw uses this description to generate printer font files. Alternatively, screen fonts can be stored anywhere in their own suitcase file and opened by a resource manager, such as Suitcase II or Master Juggler. When installing third-party PostScript fonts such as Adobe's, Font/DA Mover installs the screen fonts only. You need to have a printer font somewhere in your system. When your printer requires a PostScript font, your computer searches first the System folder, then your hard drive, floppy drives, and finally, other volumes for the printer font files. System 7 changes screen font handling considerably. Fonts will be installed simply by dragging them into the System folder.

Page Composition

The give and take between me and the machine, the quick response, the color on the screen…all of it combines to give me power over the design I never had before.

Roger Black, DESKTOP DESIGN POWER

Page composition—the design and creation of a reproducible master copy, or mechanical, for each page of a publication—is central to print publishing. Traditionally, mechanicals have been constructed with waxed galleys of type, FPO stats, overlays, Xacto knives and posterboard. Now a revolution is at hand: the materials of traditional pasteup have been largely replaced with efficient, interactive page layout programs. These programs save significant amounts of time and money, while increasing a graphic artist's ability to make clean, easy modifications to the layout. This chapter surveys the wide field of page composition programs, and provides comparisons you can use to select the software best suited to your needs.

Issues

Page layout software has run on computers for quite some time now, but until recently it was in the domain of large organizations. As late as 1985 a typical typesetting system ran on a minicomputer or workstation, and the hardware and software combined could cost $50,000 or more. Early software used specialized codes to place objects on a page. Code was necessary to format text; place graphics; draw lines, boxes, bullets, and screens; place page numbers; and assemble other page elements precisely and automatically. Coding at work in word processors was discussed in Chapter 8. These coded layout systems are very powerful and are still sold today—the TeX system developed by Don Knuth at Stanford is one example.

Coded page layout software has been largely replaced on microcomputers by WYSIWYG desktop publishing software such as PageMaker, Ventura Publisher, and others. PageMaker's introduction on the Macintosh in 1985 was a watershed event, not so much because it was the first program of its type—it wasn't—but because it was commercially successful. DTP software has become popular because it is easy to learn and remember. The advantages of coded systems for typographical precision have eroded over time as even more powerful versions of graphical software have been developed. The microcomputer press today includes very little discussion of TeX systems, although TeX still has its devotees among the more powerful UNIX-based computer systems.

Figure 12-1
The original version of (1.0) PageMaker looks nostalgically simple compared to the current generation of powerful desktop page layout programs. Its effect on the microcomputer industry was dramatic. *Courtesy of Aldus Corporation.*

Features

The purpose of page layout software is to provide typographical controls for text, place graphic objects precisely, allow interaction for easy modification, and wherever possible, automate the process. Two types of approaches have been used in the design of this type of software: complete electronic documents publication production packages, and what is now classical desktop publishing software.

Document publishing programs provide complete solutions and all of the necessary tools to enable a workgroup to manage technical publications. Typically these packages contain full-featured word processors, object-oriented drawing toolboxes, and equation and table builders. They are good network solutions and contain many other tools. The intent is to create a single environment in which all phases of the page composition process can be accomplished. The fact that you can still use files created by other programs, but you don't have to, frees you from worry about file formats and other compatibility issues. Packages of this ilk offer very sophisticated features and hefty price tags (see Chapter 4). Interleaf Publisher and FrameMaker are two examples of technical publishing solutions. These two programs are among the most complex sold on microcomputers today. The documentation for Interleaf Publisher weighs fifteen pounds! Read any good manuals lately?

▼ *Tip: High-resolution bit maps can really slow down your work. Consider creating a low-resolution version of the file in black and white as a placekeeper for position only. Use a high-resolution image when you go to print.*

DTP software takes a very different approach to page composition. Software such as PageMaker, Ventura Publisher, QuarkXPress, DesignStudio, and others in this very crowded product category act as assemblers of the data you create in other programs. They import text from word processors—even formatted text in most cases—graphics from graphics programs, and then compose a page from what is essentially your own custom work environment. Text editing and graphics features, however, are generally only

Figure 12-2
Interleaf Publisher is
a complete technical
document publishing
environment with text,
graphics, image han-
dling capabilities, and
advanced features, such
as background repagina-
tion, formerly found
only in dedicated work-
stations and minicom-
puter applications.

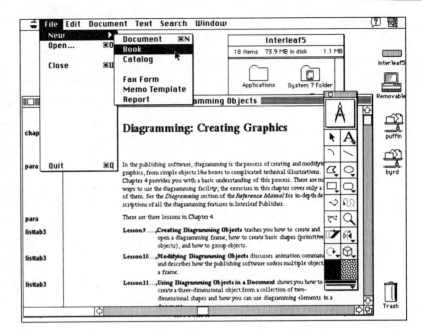

rudimentary. Any substantial changes that need to be made should occur in the creator programs. Although these programs are highly interactive and widely supported, keep in mind that the workflow often must be separated into different programs, a wide variety of file formats must be supported (and taken into account), and the resulting document must be tracked for changes.

Over the past couple of years document publishing packages and DTP layout programs have grown toward each other in sophistication and power. Their basic philosophies have stayed the same, but the packages now overlap considerably in their typographical and compositional tools. Ventura Publisher costs $795 (retail) while Interleaf Publisher costs $995, which blurs any decision based on price. A whole new generation of lower-priced DTP software has recently come to market in the $150 to $300 price range. These programs are sophisticated yet easier to use than the major packages; it remains to be seen how successful they will be. As word processors have become more powerful, many have incorporated basic page layout features in them, notably: FullWrite Professional and Microsoft Word on the Macin-

Figure 12-3
The GEM Desktop Publisher (Release 2) is a good DTP solution for IBM PC XT and AT computers. It supports most of the important features of the better packages and can import and work with other GEM graphics products for draw, paint, and image processing. *Courtesy of Digital Research.*

tosh, and Ami Professional, Word for Windows, and Legacy on the PC. Even entry-level programs, such as Microsoft Works, provide page composition solutions; however, they provide nowhere near the precision of dedicated packages.

▼ *Tip: Hyphenation and justification routines in page layout software are generally very advanced and often adjustable. You want a certain amount of hyphenation in a column, but not too much. Justification can be done in either type of application. Do not put hyphens in your text within your word processor unless they are required; let your page layout software do it.*

The most desirable features of a good page layout package are:
• Text Editing: Text is manipulated as an object and can be placed precisely on a page, then linked to columns and pages, and flowed. Some minimum duplication of word processing features is required in order to prevent switching back and forth between programs. Page layout software is often strong

Figure 12-4
Figure 12-4
Microsoft Works, the Swiss Army Knife of software, provides all the basic tools for page layout: grids, rulers, object-oriented toolbox, even linked text objects and text autoflow.
(A) A three-column grid is created as a guide for placement of objects and columns.
(B) The resulting page after all elements are in place.

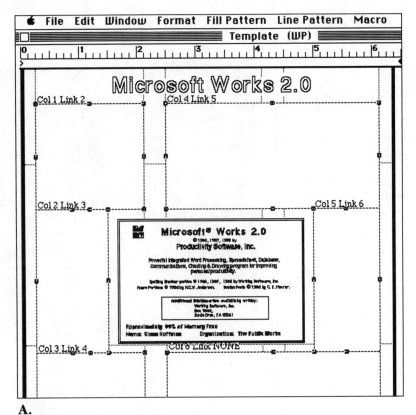

A.

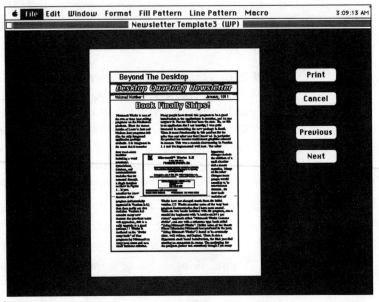

B.

in text formatting, spell checking, search and replace, has ASCII markup language, and hyphenation and justification (h&j).

- Typographical Controls: These very important elements of page composition include precision point sizes, kerning text (interletter spacing), and adjusting line spacing parameters such as leading and tracking, and are usually specified in page layout. Leading is the amount of space between lines from baseline to baseline. Tracking is the adjustment of spacing between letters and words; tight tracking produces closely spaced text, loose tracking produces text with more white space between letters and words. Some programs (such as QuarkXPress) allow you to get in and edit kerning tables in font families. It's possible to feather and card columns of text to make them align using these controls. Feathering adjusts column width, carding adjusts paragraph spacing.

- Input Graphics: For DTP packages, several types of graphics file formats (especially the standards) should be supported. File format conversion is often a strength of page layout programs. Most packages have basic draw toolboxes so that lines, boxes, screens, and other graphics elements can be added to a page.

- Precise Object Placement: Easy specification of position is a must for page layout software. This can be done precisely through dialog box entries or interactively by screen movement. Good software often includes snap-to grids, rulers, page and column margin guides, and multiple viewing modes (zoom-in and zoom-out).

- WYSIWYG Operation or Page Preview: It's important that the software display on your monitor show an accurate description of the page that will be output. This includes any page numbers, titles, headers or footers, and any other objects you may have placed. For software that isn't WYSIWYG, it's imperative that there be a page preview feature; most coded systems now ship with one. Different size views are valuable for precision work and for document overviews.

- Automation Features: Master pages are defined to contain all elements of style and formatting that repeat on each page. Style or tags are a set of formatting traits to be applied to a paragraph or text unit, and can be imported from a word processor.

- Long Document Features: Automatic page, footnote, and figure numbering are useful. Anchoring captions to figures, figures to text, lines or rules and boxes to text, and autoflow of text from page to page should be done automatically. Chapter and section numbering, automatic indexing, and table of contents generation are often included.

- Output Features: The page composition is ultimately converted to a print file in the PDL of the output device you wish to drive, often as PostScript. Some software greatly improves performance by specifying a link to any graphics file that is embedded in the page and providing a low-resolution description of that file for manipulation and placement. Printer support, printing speed, and export capabilities are important features. One feature becoming common in page layout software is color separation into process color files, or easy output to programs that do separation (see Chapter 14). Tiling pages to create larger size pages, printing crop marks for cutting the paper, and printing spot color overlays are also useful and common features.

- Workgroup Features: As projects become larger, it becomes necessary to provide features that track versions by group members over time. Some software provides project management, file management whereas others keep track of data links. This subject is discussed further in Chapter 16.

▼ *Tip: Depending on the layout program you use, you may want to format text either in your word processor or directly in the layout program. Ventura Publisher's tag system lends itself to formatting directly in the layout program. Justification, tabs, lists, and headings can be handled by the style sheet. Preformatting text within a word processor works best with PageMaker.*

It's important to specify formatting rules for authors, when to use text attributes and how to achieve them.

Graphics Effects

Certain graphics effects, especially special type effects, are particularly valuable for page design. Rotation, flipping, and scaling of graphics and text are common. It is very useful to be able to define an area to repel text, to keep free of text. This is referred to as text *run around*. Ventura Publisher frames repel text, and Page-Maker allows you to define an irregular border shape for run around, which is even more desirable. Anchoring graphics to text or text to graphics, scaling and cropping graphics are other common effects capabilities. A *step and repeat* function that duplicates objects is particularly useful, too. Some packages even offer grayscale controls such as brightness and contrast, do halftone screening, customize a screen angle, dither, and create image negatives. A basic draw toolbox would include line and shape tools, patterns and fills, and freeform lines. With these tools you can touch up graphics without ever leaving the layout package.

Color handling has become an important feature of high-end DTP packages. This reflects the extension of these programs into the professional electronic publishing market. The simplest capability is specifying spot colors, or color overlays; even basic packages aimed at the home market include this function. Some programs (DesignStudio and QuarkXPress) offer a dialog box for specifying the Pantone library of ink colors. A separate file is specified for each print color. At the higher end of the spectrum, packages such as QuarkXPress will separate a four-color file, creating four files that are linked to the central page description. See Chapter 14 for more information about color handling. Color Figure C10 shows the matching of a Pantone blue to a swatch book.

Page Management

Generally speaking, no matter what type of page layout system in which you decide to invest your time and effort learning and using, the important considerations are how well it accomplishes the basic tasks of typography and object positioning. Copy fitting a page is a crucial skill, as is good input and output technique. Your

Figure 12-5
QuarkXPress is one of
the best page layout
packages for complex
page design and is a
favored product for
full-color work. It
serves as the front end
to several proprietary
prepress systems. Ver-
sion 3.0 shows a mea-
surements palette at the
bottom of the screen,
thus allowing design
specifications to be
changed interactively
without having to access
menu commands
or dialog boxes.
*Courtesy of
Quark, Inc.*

automation requirements should be determined by the length of
the documents you construct. If you most often compose complex single pages, automation features will have less value. "Full-
page view" is a very useful page management feature that can be
found in the better page layout packages, especially if you have a
relatively small monitor. Double-page viewing, available with
larger monitors, is useful when working with facing pages. Productivity increases when you do not have to scroll about a document
and can get an overall view of your layout. If you cannot use a
large enough monitor for full- or double-page viewing, make certain that the package you use has a good system for switching to
different size views and for scrolling about. At the minimum, a
program should have a Fit in Window, plus a 100 percent and a
200 percent view. The more views the better; some programs, like
QuarkXPress even let you define your viewing magnification.

**Project
Management**

Page layout software requires extensive project management and document control. The workgroup environments in which many documents are created pose special problems. DTP programs have been among the first to adopt strategies for handling multiple users and special file handling capabilities that are part of advanced operating systems. Features to look for are project tracking, revision histories, network support, and warm and hot links to the original data files. Project tracking usually takes the form of a file listing with modification dates and times; it is most useful when several versions of files are being used simultaneously. Data linking provides a means for automatically modifying data in the original document as well as in the composed page; it's best done as a hot link automatically at the time of modification, but it can be done as a warm link when a document is closed. When several people are working on a project at the same time, it's important to be able to lock files, create read-only files, and lock elements on a page. Imagine the chaos that would result if two or more workers tried to revise a document at the same time. Database programs often employ these techniques. Network and multiple user support are considered advanced features.

▼ *Tip: Use a good naming convention to organize your files. Name files so that their project, chapter, and file format are obvious. For example, BTD12.TXT would be the twelfth chapter in* **Beyond the Desktop,** *in Text format. If you have a Macintosh, you can embed comments inside parentheses. Some translation software strips out anything inside parentheses when converting Macintosh files to PC files. Naming conventions are particularly important for programs such as Ventura Publisher, which create several files for each project. You might use this convention: BTD12.TXT (for text files), BTD12.CHP (for chapter files), BTD12.CAP (for caption files), BTD12.VGR (for Ventura graphics files), and BTD.STY (for style sheet). A style sheet typically is used for an entire publication.*

Architectures

Page layout software uses several different metaphors for page composition. PageMaker pioneered the pasteboard metaphor, which duplicates the procedure used by traditional paste-up artists. The screen has a page (or facing pages) placed over a work area of empty space (the pasteboard). Objects such as text, lines, or other graphics are placed (literally, using a Place command) on the pasteboard and remain there as you switch pages until they are moved onto a page or deleted. This approach has been so successful that many programs, including DesignStudio, have adopted it. QuarkXPress 3.0 switched to a pasteboard in 1990.

PageMaker is freeform; objects can be placed willy-nilly on a page. In fact, you're free to place objects anywhere on the pasteboard, on or off the page, in, around, or between columns. Each object is handled and described individually. That makes Page-Maker one of the best programs on the market for complex page construction. It supports master pages and text styles and tags. Any PageMaker documents can be saved as a template for later reuse under a different name.

▼ *Tip: Use the pasteboard as a shortcut for cutting and pasting between pages. If there is an element that you want to use in several places, use the Duplicate or Clone command to make a copy before you move it to the pasteboard.*

Nearly all programs offer some form of master page production, so that a user can specify which design elements will repeat on subsequent pages. In PageMaker and DesignStudio, left and right master pages can face, and when a design element is added to a master page, it appears on all pages, even those that were previously composed. QuarkXPress allows up to 127 master pages. Ventura Publisher doesn't use master pages per se, but headers and footers can be specified for left and right pages, and base frames can be created to duplicate across all frames. Ventura's treatment tends to be fairly rigid, but good for regular layouts, such as books

Figure 12-6
PageMaker 4.0 features several new tools. Shown here is the story editor, a text-only view for quick text entry and copy editing. Also enhanced are long document features and network capabilities. *Courtesy of Aldus Corporation.*

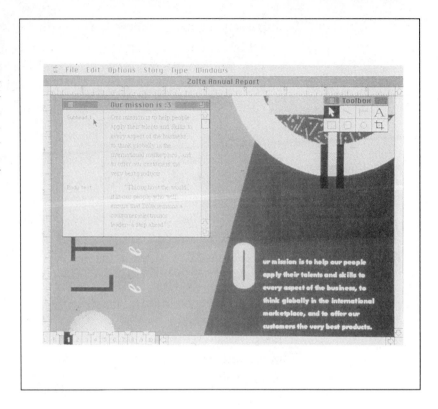

or reports. DesignStudio includes a useful feature whereby pages can be previewed in a thumbnail view, and pages can be reordered or deleted in that view.

▼ *Tip: When using facing pages and you have to delete a page, which would change all left pages to right ones (and vice versa), insert a blank page at the end of a section. Also, start all sections on the same facing page to avoid this problem.*

Another common page layout architectural feature is the frame, box, or block metaphor, which is used by Ventura Publisher, FrameMaker, QuarkXPress, ReadySetGo!, and DesignStudio. Frames are containers into which text and pictures are placed, and they can be positioned and placed anywhere on a page. Frame architecture often creates a hierarchy of nested objects and imparts a regularity that is very useful for long document construction. Frames support the use of master pages and text styles or tags, but require more extensive up-front planning than a program that treats objects individually. QuarkXPress and DesignStudio use a combination of a pasteboard with frames on the page.

File Management

One of the major differences in page layout programs is how file management is done. Two approaches are common: a file management scheme and a single file description. Ventura uses a file management scheme. Ventura files are generally very small because the page layout is stored separately from the text and graphics. It can read text in any of several word processor formats and convert draw-type graphics to a standard file format; for the GEM version, that format is the line art .GEM format; the Mac version converts to PICT. Paint files are converted to the GEM format for bit-mapped images (.IMG); for the Mac version it is the PAINT format. The unit into which each set of files is organized into a page is called the chapter file. Ventura Publisher stores links or paths to the required files as part of the page description. The program stores links or paths to all text and graphics files stored on disk. Pages are composed when the page layout is opened. Chapter files can be organized into publications, to create a long book, for example.

▼ *Tip: Don't put an entire book, newsletter, or magazine into a single file. Performance will be better if you split the publication into chapters. Don't arbitrarily divide chapters or articles into separate files. Develop a logical system or they will be harder to track as they are modified. Put any tables directly into the text file where they should appear. Whenever possible, create a single directory or folder to contain the entire project. Be extra careful not to move files once a link is created; the layout program stores the path to the file and may not be able to find it if it is moved and your file might not open.*

Figure 12-7
Ventura Publisher is a powerful DTP program for long document publishing, especially for design with many regular elements. Versions of the program now run on most major platforms, making it highly interoperable. Shown here is the screen shot from the GEM version. *Courtesy of Ventura Software, Inc.*

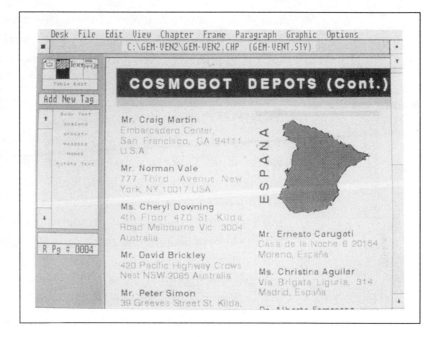

In contrast, a PageMaker document includes nearly all elements of the page in a single large file. (It does, however, link externally to high-resolution graphics.) Both types of file handling approaches have their advantages and disadvantages. Pages with linked files perform faster when opened and require less memory, but they take longer to compose, are slower to open, and are slower to print. A file saved as a compound document opens faster, is less easily corrupted, and has a unified file format, but requires more RAM and contiguous disk space to store and has slower performance when opened.

Any program that creates composite pages would become unwieldy if file sizes grow beyond a certain point. Page layout software is very susceptible to this problem, and most packages use a variety of techniques to circumvent this. It's not uncommon to find virtual memory and page swapping techniques built into this class of software. Also, when an embedded graphics file reaches a certain size, a lower-resolution image is displayed. This is particularly easy for programs such as PageMaker or QuarkXPress; they display the bit-mapped representation that is part of the EPS format.

Software

Your selection of page layout software should be guided by the work you do. Don't buy a package with a load of features that you will never use. If your needs are simple, buy a simple package. If you intend to grow into more complex projects, then invest in a more complete program. I prefer packages that integrate files from other applications, so that I can select the tools that best suit my work philosophy. Integrated packages can be very powerful but are less easily customized. However, programs such as FrameMaker and Interleaf Publisher are unique, and their powerful features may be essential to workgroups or long document projects. Page layout software is such a crowded category that it's impossible to mention all the packages or important features here. Refer to the references at the end of the chapter or to books in Appendix B for further information. Michael L. Kleper's book, *The Illustrated Handbook of Desktop Publishing and Typesetting,* contains some very detailed program descriptions.

WYSIWYG Page Layout Programs

The following are some of the more important DTP WYSIWYG page layout programs.

- Aldus PageMaker 4.0 (Mac, Win, OS/2): This is the Macintosh market leader. The PC version has the same market share as Ventura Publisher. PageMaker is the most widely supported layout program at PostScript service bureaus. It uses the pasteboard metaphor and treats objects as individual entities. It is an excellent program for complex page design, with superb interactivity and flexibility. PageMaker supports styles and can import them from Microsoft Word. It is highly praised for a logical design and toolset. PageMaker doesn't have every bell and whistle, but it is thought to be the best choice for individuals. PC users find PageMaker to be slow due to the Windows GUI—it requires an 80386 SX, or a 15 mHz 80286 PC, with 4 MBytes of RAM for adequate perfor-mance. Although it was faulted in previous versions for poor long document work, 4.0 successfully addresses many of these criticisms. Publications up to 999 pages can be tracked. This version also added a simple text editor called the Story Editor, which improved text editing capabilities. Color is not a particular strength; only spot color is supported. To read files across computer platforms, the same PageMaker version numbers are required. Aldus is noted for very strong cus-tomer support.

- DesignStudio (Mac): DesignStudio uses an upgraded version of the popular ReadySetGo! interface. It uses the block and pasteboard metaphors. DesignStudio is a solid program with no major flaws, and many users seem to like it. It ships with many advanced features, including control over h&j parame-ters, character spacing, strong typography, and good color tools. An add-on macro package called DesignScript that automates many features can be purchased.

- FrameMaker 2.1 (Mac, PC, NeXT, Sun): This is a long docu-ment publishing program. It uses the frame metaphor (hence its name) and has many advanced formatting and automation tools. For example, FrameMaker has a built-in equation editor that not only builds complex equations but can solve some of them. FrameMaker would be a good choice for technical document projects.

- GEM Desktop Publisher (PC): This is a full-featured layout program from Digital Research for the GEM GUI. It uses a block metaphor and supports the use of style sheets and tags similar to Ventura so that tags can be placed within a word processor. Headers and footers are supported, but some coded objects are required. It imports files from the library of GEM text, draw, paint, and imaging programs. It is consid-ered an alternative to Ventura for an IBM PC XT or AT when a less powerful and less structured program is required.

- Interleaf Publisher 3.0 (Mac, PC, Sun, UNIX): A full document production and processing environment that has migrated down to microcomputers. Its very large feature set and many sophisticated tools make this a higher-end package. Background repagination and very fast formatting are two examples of its advanced capabilities. It would be a good choice for long technical documentation. The Macintosh version was not particularly faithful to the Mac interface, and was criticized for that; a new version of the program is due out in late 1991.

- Publish It! (Mac, PC): A very good package that requires very little application space and runs quite quickly. Includes a good range of features for the price. A lower-priced package called Publish It Easy! is also well regarded, especially for computers with little installed RAM.

- QuarkStyle (Mac): A subset of QuarkXPress, this program is sold with a set of over seventy-five starting templates for less demanding applications and less sophisticated users. Excellent results can be obtained quickly.

- QuarkXPress 3.0 (Mac, [Win in 1992]): This is the premier program for complex page design and for color output. Quark uses the frame and pasteboard metaphors and is noted for very precise typography and color tools. XPress has a longer learning curve than PageMaker but is more useful for magazine work where complexity of design is a requirement. A good four-color separation program is included. QuarkXPress is often used as the front end of high-quality prepress stations. The Scitex Visionary Interpreter for PostScript (or VIP) uses a proprietary version of XPress for page composition. Quark has very spotty customer support but strong product development. Over 95 percent of all PostScript service bureaus support XPress.

- ReadySetGo! 4.5 (Mac): As one of the first strong page layout programs on the market, it is still valuable in applications that don't require leading edge sophistication—

color, for example. It uses a block metaphor, style sheets equipped with its own word processor, and has many good additional features.

- Personal Press (Mac): A full-featured page layout program marketed as a personal publishing package. Introduced in early 1991, the program retains the Silicon Beach philosophy of a powerful and plentiful feature set coupled with ease of use. A good choice for nonprofessional applications. Now that Aldus has bought Silicon Beach, this is considered its entry-level product.

- ProType (Mac-A/UX, UNIX, PC-Xenix): A professional typesetting program that runs on a variety of microcomputer UNIX platforms. This program is at the high end of typesetting systems that have made their way onto microcomputers. Features including networking, image processing, and strong PostScript output. The UNIX implementation may be a disadvantage, as it limits the audience on the desktop.

- Ventura Publisher (Mac, PC, Win, OS/2): This is the WYSIWYG program from Xerox that made IBM DTP respectable. The original program ran on the GEM interface as a run time version. It requires 512 KBytes of RAM, 3 MBytes disk space, and runs acceptably on an IBM PC XT or AT computer. The GEM version is a good solution for an 8086 XT computer; it is still one of the best solutions for 80286 AT PCs. The Gold Series can share files across platforms, giving it broad small computer support; interoperability makes it valuable for network publishing applications. Ventura is a program noted for long regular document processing. It has a 64-chapter limit of 100 pages each. The program is very strong in handling repeating elements and includes many advanced tools, such as automatic numbering and linkage features. Ventura is weak at composing pages where a variety of page elements must be assembled interactively. It has strong typography, mainly through dialog box selection, but has only a basic toolbox. Text can be edited directly and saved to each supporting file. Ventura style sheets are composed of individual styles called tags. Changing the style sheet forces instant reformatting of your document. You can type tags in WordPerfect (PC versions) and export them into Ventura, a powerful combination. Ventura Publisher 2.0 Professional Extension has extra features for cross referencing, variable text substitution, setting equations, table generation, vertical justification, and hyphenation control.

Figure 12-8
ProType is a UNIX typesetting program that has recently migrated down from workstations to the Mac A/UX, IBM PC Xenix operating systems. *Courtesy of Bedford Computer.*

Coded Layout Programs

Prior to 1984 and the introduction of WYSIWYG layout programs, typesetting systems required that each element of type be specified and positioned using code. Typesetting machines and computers often shared similar software for transforming text into typeset galleys. Early machines, such as the Itek Quadritek and Compugraphic MCS (Modular Composition System), eventually began to offer early word processors, including MicroPro Word-Star, as an option. Whatever the software lacked in typographic skills could be coded in using a variety of schemes. Typesetters advanced along with the computer industry in general. Some systems that emulate early typesetters are still sold, and they can be used for small design pieces, but they are notable primarily for their historical significance.

Much more useful are the coded typesetting languages that were developed for microcomputer typesetting and exemplified by the TeX system. TeX, developed by Don Knuth at Stanford as a device-independent typographical system, is particularly useful for typesetting complex mathematical equations. TeX's name was derived from the Greek letters tau, epsilon, and chi, that stands for the Greek word for art and technology. Knuth also developed a program called METAFONT for the generation of typefaces using letterform characteristics and a declarative algebraic language structure to specify various styles. The program specifies where and how a shape is drawn using a pen and eraser metaphor in a device-independent manner.

Versions of TeX migrated down to microcomputers in the mid-1980s and are widely available. As a result of this "trickle-down effect," several TeX-based programs have appeared for both the Macintosh and IBM PC. TeXtures from Blue Sky Research is a Macintosh programming environment for the TeX language that supplies a WYSIWYG screen. Other TeX programs are PCTeX, MicroTeX for the IBM PC, and MacTeX for the Macintosh. DeskSet is a typesetting program that uses the IBM PC to run Compugraphic and Varityper imagesetter; it uses the Horizon Composition Management System.

Most coded typesetting languages now contain page preview modes, so they aren't much different from specialized word processors in that regard. TeX is very powerful—almost 900 control sequences can be specified for creating a page. Any simple text editor that can create a plain ASCII file can compose a page using this system, and the placement and styles assigned can be as perfect as the device interpreting it can achieve. To obtain italic text, the code "\it" would be added; "\rm" codes for roman style. Codes such as "\par" or a blank line ends a paragraph, "\eject" specifies a page break, and so on. When using a coded language, no restrictions are imposed on the degree of control you can assign to a kerned pair or a point size. Many substitutions, such as changing the "f i" pair to the "fi" ligature, occur automatically. Many other automatic features are built into TeX—substitution of curly quote marks for straight ones, for example. TeX is also very sophisticated in assessing hyphenation and page breaks and includes a debugger for analyzing codes for logic errors.

Database Publishing

Certain publishing applications, such as telephone books, product directories, and catalogs, are data rich and don't require much formatting. Using information stored in a database—which can include pictures and graphics as well as text—and some sort of merge technique, it's possible to create very sophisticated treatments. This kind of application has given rise to the term "database publishing," and there are several approaches to creating this style of document. The least sophisticated method uses a word processing program with merge capabilities, such as Microsoft Word, and an export file in the appropriate format to create a document. Word allows the use of coded entries for data fields («field 1») and logic statements. Data values or entries from the data document up to the limit of the number of records are inserted into those placemarks. Integrated packages, such as Microsoft Works, which contain a word processor and a database module, are particularly good in this regard; version 2.0 of Works allows fairly complex database publishing projects to be undertaken.

FileMaker Pro by Claris is an example of a new category of database program with very strong graphical and typographic capabilities. All the tools necessary for database publishing come in one package, and it is a very easy and powerful system. It is the best-selling Macintosh database on the market. FileMaker is modal and allows you to create templates or graphical displays that it calls layouts. Any database file can have any number of layouts, and they can be as simple as mailing labels, data entry screens, or, more appropriate to the subject at hand, a book or catalog. Various elements can be placed on a layout: title pages, headers and footers, and repeating elements called body parts. Fields, which are like boxes that contain the data (text, numbers, dates, time, and pictures), can be placed onto layouts, along with graphics of various types. In the Layout mode FileMaker resembles a page layout program with a complete toolbox, grids, rulers, positioning devices, and other useful tools.

Headers and footers occur once a page, but body parts can occur up to the limit of the number of data records selected in the database. Data is entered in an entirely separate mode called

Figure 12-9
FileMaker Pro is a graphical database that excels at database publishing. Shown here is a product catalog with text, pictures, and graphics.

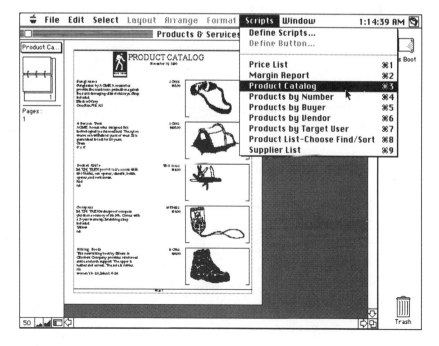

Browse, and by using Find and Sort functions, all or part of the data set can be selected for output. A combination of data and layout is specified as a report, and there is a unique scripting language for automating all of the steps involved in creating a publication. A preview mode shows the result, and FileMaker can output to any Macintosh device. The results obtained are quite impressive. I've seen catalogs of shareware programs, pictorial screen shows of an art museum collection, and complete auto parts catalogs displayed and printed with FileMaker. The main advantage of database publishing is that the document can stay live and change right up to the time it's needed (again).

Another example of a database publishing system is the dbPublisher system sold for MS-DOS computers. The program is a report generator and typographical publication tool that creates a master file with stored paths to data documents. The program is compatible with many databases, spreadsheets, word processors, and graphics programs. It composes pages from the current versions of the required documents. dbPublisher has some very sophisticated tools: It offers the SGML (standard general markup language), style sheets/templates, many DTP pagination and layout tools, strong typographical tools, sophisticated database report generation capabilities, text and graphics handling, database logic and functions, and report writing. Even relational databases can be tackled, as can bar codes, statistics, and data handling. A complete description of this powerful and versatile program is not possible here. dbPublisher is aimed at the professional market, and it is difficult to learn, but very complete. Datashaper, from ElseWhere, preformats tab-delimited text files from any database for loading into PageMaker (Mac).

Filevision IV for the Macintosh is an integrated object-oriented draw/imaging and database package in which thirty-two graphical layers can be shown, each with its own associated database. Every object on a layer is represented by a record in the database that corresponds to that layer. The program can import and modify virtually any type of image that can be created on the Macintosh, and it can manage graphics libraries, track and manage projects, store templates, and perform a number of graphics tasks that can be exported into DTP packages. Filevision is a unique program that can be of particular value in applications requiring a combination of graphics and analysis.

There is now a product that couples ORACLE RDBMS, dBASE III and IV, and ASCII files with Aldus Pagemaker 3.01 or 4.0 running under Windows. It is called PageAhead, and it can be used to create professional quality catalogs, directories, and other reports. The interface features a spreadsheet with over 60 features for database publishing, including heading control, text replacement, style replacement, capitalization control, and typographical sorting.

Package Design

Although most packages are three-dimensional, the materials used to construct them are normally assembled in two dimensions. For a design agency or packager, the initial stage in production is to create a mockup or a prototype of the package, actually a 3D comp. All of the tools that have been discussed in this book can be assembled and applied to the process. The process is dramatic and can be the difference between a design team being successful and winning a contract, or failing.

A logo design, for example, can be generated in a draw or paint package. Patterns for backgrounds can be created using the pattern tile feature in a draw package such as Illustrator or by scanning an image and modifying it in a color image processing program such as ColorStudio or Photoshop. The actual mechanical outline of a box would be generated as a precision draw file or as a CAD file. Finally, all of these elements are assembled in a page layout program and output to a color printer or proofing device, and then assembled as a cardboard model. To speed up the process a designer might even bypass constructing a model and create a file in a 3D modeling program such as Swivel 3D, in which changes can be made on the fly.

The Creative Systems division of Scitex has put together the Scitex Cornerstone Design System, with all the elements you need to design packaging. It includes a Mac IIfx, 24-bit color setup and related hardware, and a collection of software that includes Illustrator or FreeHand, Photoshop, QuarkXPress, Microphone II,

StuffIt, a special CAD program from Lasercomb used for package design, and other goodies. These applications are tied together with the SuperCard-based interface that provides program access, expert advice, project management, job cost tracking, and billing. (SuperCard, a HyperCard clone from Silicon Beach, has an expanded feature set that allows hypertextural linkage of subject matter). You could choose these products yourself if you were a power user, but Scitex provides invaluable training and support for the entire portfolio.

Advertising Software

Packages that create advertising for magazines and newspapers are a special type of page layout software. Very simple applications are sold that allow a user to construct an ad for submission as original copy. You can use your standard page layout software for ad creation, but it's hard to get an overview or concept flow. ExpressPage (discussed in Chapter 15) enables you to create thumbnails, roughs, and comps and import them into PageMaker (PC); as such it's very useful for ad creation. More complete systems sold to newspapers or the telephone company for its yellow pages are complete turnkey workstation-based solutions. Many in the latter category that started on the UNIX workstation are now found on 80386 PCs and Mac IIs. This kind of software is characterized by many typefaces and styles, variable line spacing and measurements, and high graphics-to-text content. Often, advertising software must track constant change and keep the material live right up to print time. The high code-to-text ratio of these systems makes it very operator intensive; using them requires a high level of skill.

Multi-Ad Creator and AdWriter are two programs for the Macintosh that specialize in creating full-page advertisements. As the single page is the basic building block of print advertising, many organizations find that they can get by at this level of sophistication; they don't require a complete publication management system. These programs contain a full set of tools for text and graphics, and templates for specific ads can be stored. Precision

Figure 12-10
Multi-Ad Creator is a complete single ad composition environment with specialized tools, including bursts, border editors, an extensive clip-art library, a pasteboard, and many other goodies. It is a special-purpose page layout program.

placement and movement tools are also included. Multi-Ad Creator is the more complete of these two products and has been well reviewed. It contains most of the features detailed below for the DisplayAdSpeed package. Multi-Ad Services sells a variety of ancillary products, including a large and growing clip art collection and the Multi-Ad Custom Ad-Planner System that coordinates production, inventory, distribution, fulfillment, and market services for organizations.

DisplayAdSpeed from DTI is an advertising layout program that runs on a Macintosh. It creates ads by formatting text and graphics from dialog boxes; no code is written, and the program is structured to position multiple ads on a page and to do page management. DisplayAdSpeed is highly interactive and will input text from other computer systems (PCs and mainframes) and programs and do optical character recognition from scanners. Both bit-mapped and object graphics are supported, and an on-line CD ROM library of graphic images, including sunbursts, borders, and logos is included.

DisplayAdSpeed is meant to be a complete solution for creating and managing ad space. It is also intended to be compatible with editorial space and has a page production management system built in that minimizes lost space by intelligently composing pages. By using networked workstations to run the program printers, databases and printers can be shared. A color separation utility is part of the package, as is specific color assignment. PostScript output is supported.

Ad design and newspaper production is a large software category. Thousands of people in the print and news industry use this class of software daily, and many of the packages now run on personal computers. Typically this is an active area for value-added resellers, but some companies specialize in complete software/hardware solutions. Camex (Boston, MA) sells workstation-based solutions, such as Breeze on the Sun platform and AdStylist for the Macintosh, that are higher-end ad design and production systems. The company also sells software for photo and graphics production, pagination systems, imagesetters, gateways for imagesetters, editorial page layout software. A gateway is a computer (generally a PC or workstation) that takes files created on PCs and reformats them so that they can be used on proprietary systems or on more powerful computers.

Templates

Templates are layout documents or dummy publications that can be used as starting points for similar documents. They serve several important functions. They can save you a lot of time—much of the work in page layout can be set up in advance and then stored in a template. Templates also help you maintain consistency in your work; if you start from the same place, a document will look the same. This is particularly valuable for newspapers, magazines, and books, where a "look," or a "style," is imperative. Templates also capture the talent of an expert designer in a form that anyone can use. In fact, only by using templates can you take advantage of the savings in time and cost that desktop publishing promises. If you don't use them, you may end up spending more time and money than if you went back to the posterboard.

To create a template, you usually work with a document until it's in the form you want and then save it. It is more efficient if you leave out elements that are going to change from page to page. This cuts down on the file size and prevents you from having to do this maintenance every time you work with the file anew. It's also helpful if the program allows you to use *placeholders* to show what elements go where. Write "`Chapter Header`" as a text object in the correct format where it is supposed to occur, or consider using greeked text as a placeholder. Greeked text actually looks more like Latin. The phrase: "Beyondus the Desktopum locutus imaginatum expandus indefinato…" is duplicated and used *ad infinitum* in the correct point size and formatting. The greeked text can be selected and replaced by either a text file or text on the Clipboard. The term "greeking" is less accurately applied to the conversion of text to symbolic bars and boxes to indicate positioning of text on your screen. At certain point sizes (particularly small ones) greeking improves file performance measurably. For graphics or text objects consider drawing shapes as placeholders, such as rectangles with crossed lines in them, and then label them to make their purpose obvious. Ultimately you will delete the placeholders and substitute real text and graphics in their place.

As PageMaker creates compound PostScript files of all page elements, it's nearly an ideal format for creating templates. PageMaker files can be saved as templates. When they are reopened as untitled files to be saved under new document names, they contain all of the elements of the saved file. Some programs and System 7 on the Macintosh save files in a "stationary" format; when they are reopened, the original document is saved intact and an untitled document is opened.

▼ *Tip: Develop a standard style, a style sheet, and a set of design rules and then write them down for reference. A standard style will aid you in creating a template, which will, in turn, save you hours of redesign work and give your product a polished, professional appearance. Use template chapters (Ventura Publisher) or master pages (PageMaker or QuarkXPress) to reuse settings from one issue of a publication to another.*

Figure 12-11
PageMaker ships with a set of templates, and other commercial sets are available. This is: **(A)** The Fit in Window view of a newsletter template. **(B)** A 100 percent view of a template using greeked text as placeholders.

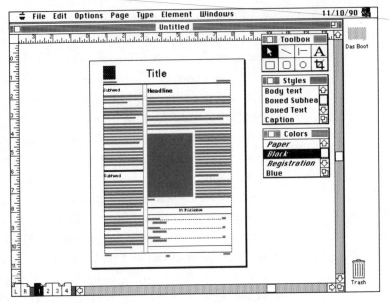

A.

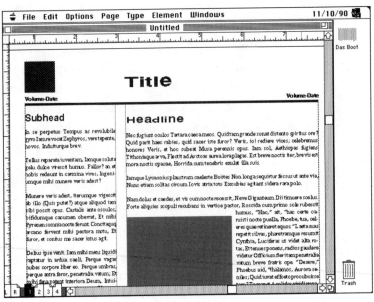

B.

Many elements can be saved in a template. These include:

- Page Size and Orientation: Some programs let you specify single-sided or double (facing) pages, and others let you create as many pages as you need using these master pages. You can often insert or delete extra pages later.

- Columns and Margins: A grid system should be part of your template, including both left and right pages, title pages, and any other master pages (or base frames) that are required.

- Style Sheets: Tremendous time savers. Titles, headings, body text, and lists can be stored and, where appropriate, displayed.

- Headers and Footers: Store symbols for dates or page numbers, letterheads, logos, rules, and other repeating elements in headers and footers.

- Page Numbers: Ideally, your program should automatically number pages as you create them.

- Logos or Other Graphical Elements: You can supply formats, sizes, captions, and other important features of graphics. Lines or rules, screens, and boxes are commonly placed on a template.

Obviously, the more elements you can define in a template, the more useful it will be. Ideally, define a template that includes all the elements that are needed. That's difficult, of course, because some elements change from job to job, or issue to issue, so consider using the pasteboard (if your package uses one) to store additional elements that users may need.

Most layout programs ship with sets of starter templates, and many manufacturers sell templates from commercial libraries. Templates are so valuable that you might consider hiring a professional designer to help your organization put some together. Many companies designate one person as an official designer, and he or she is the only one who can make changes to templates. He or she is also responsible for maintaining a template library.

Common Problems

Printing complex layouts can be problemmatical. It's a good idea to create some sample dummy pages or a template that contains all of your fonts and representative graphics and try to print them. Pay attention to how long it takes to laser print and you'll get a good idea of the cost of creating mechanicals on an imagesetter. If your pages take too long to print, you might want to reduce the number of fonts used in them. This procedure should shake out any problems with fonts that your service bureau or printing device has. It should also make it possible to spot major differences between the draft printer and the final printing. You may wish to refer back to Chapter 11 for more information about fonts and to Chapter 7 for information about printers.

If you intend to send work out, you might want to contact your service bureau before you buy software. Not all programs are fully supported, and file compatibility is a problem. DTP software can input a wide variety of graphics and text formats but will not open a file created by another DTP package. Most DTP software is written as PostScript, but some PC software can do a good job on an H-P LaserJet printer, particularly when there is restricted use of graphics. Create a laser proof of your pages prior to high-resolution output in order to spot any formatting or type errors. If you switch a publication from one printer to another, say, from a PostScript printer to a non-PostScript printer, many changes may distort your final output. Page breaks, line breaks, margins, and other features may change. So be particularly careful what output devices you use, and use the right device driver software.

Managing style sheets can also be a problem. They can become Byzantine, and Ventura Publisher is notorious in this regard. However, it supports a vigorous third-party aftermarket for add-on products, particularly for the GEM version, which has been on the market for over four years now. VPToolbox allows you to print out style sheet summaries and to copy tags from one style sheet to another. It also shows a list of all the files contained in a chapter or Ventura publication. Corel Systems (the publisher of CorelDRAW) publishes a group of utilities for Ventura: Styler to print summaries of style sheets, Vpshow to document all linked files, Vpdelete to delete an entire chapter, Vpcopy to move a chapter to another disk, Psprint to allow standard text files to be printed to a PostScript printer, and Tabin to import ready-made tables into Ventura from Lotus or a word processor.

Alignment of objects is crucial to good results in page layout. Everything on a layout should align to something else. That's the point of having columns and grids and placing nonprinting, snap-to guides on a layout. Use them along with justification commands to align text and other objects. A pixel or two of misalignment on a low-resolution monitor can be very noticeable on a high-resolution printout.

Lack of legibility of text showing through screens is another commonly encountered problem. Reverse type (white on a black background) can be very dramatic, but it is hard to read. Black-and-white combinations tend to look gray. Type itself also can be screened, and certain combinations of screened type and screened backgrounds should be avoided, especially light type/light screen, dark type/dark screen, and situations where the type and screen are similarly shaded. Contrast is what you seek, preferably dark type on light screens. You can see this graphically illustrated in Figure 12-12.

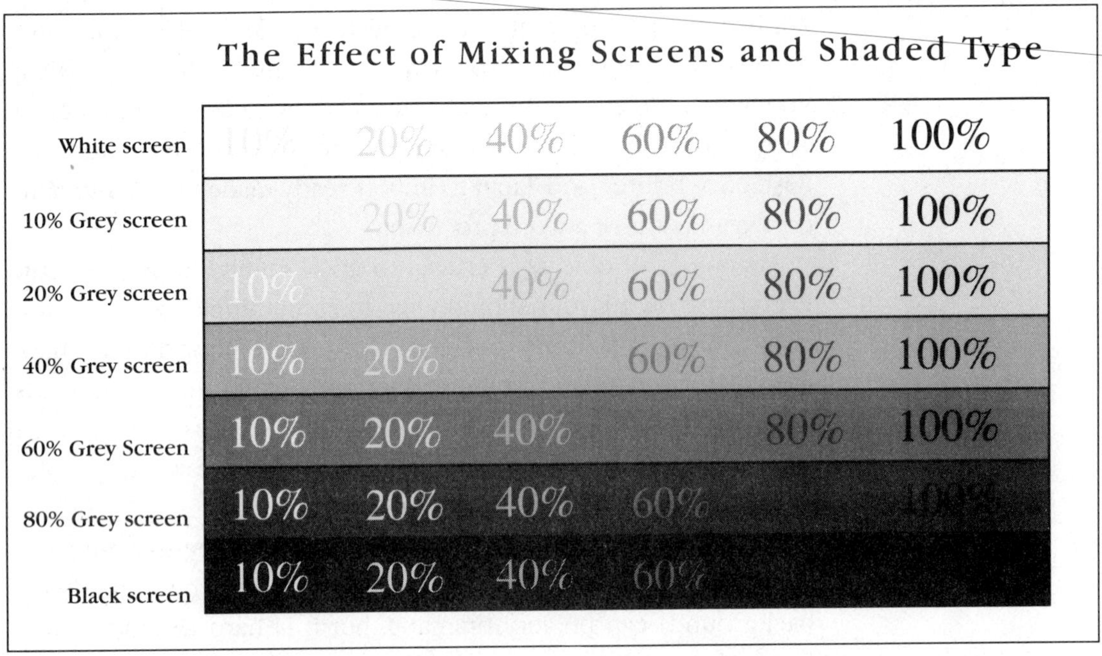

The Effect of Mixing Screens and Shaded Type

White screen	10%	20%	40%	60%	80%	100%
10% Grey screen		20%	40%	60%	80%	100%
20% Grey screen	10%		40%	60%	80%	100%
40% Grey screen	10%	20%		60%	80%	100%
60% Grey Screen	10%	20%	40%		80%	100%
80% Grey screen	10%	20%	40%	60%		100%
Black screen	10%	20%	40%	60%		

Figure 12-12 Various screen shadings and type fills drastically alter readability.

Transferring Data

Therefore is the name of it Babel;
because the Lord did there confound the language of all the earth.

Genesis 11:9

Once again we touch on file formats, used by programs to save and transfer data. Chapter 2 introduced the topic and explained the basic data types: ASCII text and bit-map and object graphics. Some understanding of these basic concepts is necessary in order to discuss programs. Chapter 8 and Chapter 9 also covered some of this material. This chapter takes a more in-depth look at file formats and some of the important issues that must be considered when using them.

How Programs Store Data

Data is saved in a file as bits of information, 1 or 0, and bits are grouped into words called bytes. Characteristically, data is saved or transmitted as 7- or 8-bit binary codes. Text, graphics, or a combination of data types may be saved; text characters or symbols can be saved as ASCII code, and graphics as a bit map or a mathematical equation representing an object that can be coded in a variety of forms depending on the programming language. Text can also be saved as graphics, but it's wasteful to save a bit map or object for each character. Applications save letters and symbols in ASCII and compare them to a table of master characters stored elsewhere. ASCII code consists of 256 characters, the first 127 of which are standard for all machines and software. Characters 0 to 31 are keys for line spacing, carriage returns, tabs, and other control characters. Numbers 32 to 127 consist of the alphanumeric characters that compose words. This part of ASCII is called *standard ASCII* and uses a 7-bit byte; it is a constant in all computers and software packages. ASCII was defined in the days of CP/M (Control Program for Microprocessors), which was used prior to MS-DOS's introduction when many computers used 7-bit bytes. The 7^2 combination gave 128 possibilities. Newer operating systems with 8-bit bytes extended ASCII to 256 characters, or 8^2. Numbers from 128 to 255 (the eighth bit) are called *extended ASCII*, and they are not standard. Extended ASCII is used to create formatting.

When you use a word processor, additional code is added in the file to specify formatting characteristics for each character string. Paragraphs can be formatted using other extended ASCII characters. WordPerfect uses one set, Word uses another, WordStar uses yet a third; because they are not universal, they are called *native formats*, and there are hundreds. A translation utility is necessary in order to read a native format with another piece of software; sometimes these utilities are built in. This is what enables one program to read another program's file.

You can, however, save a file as *ASCII text*, and when you do, all

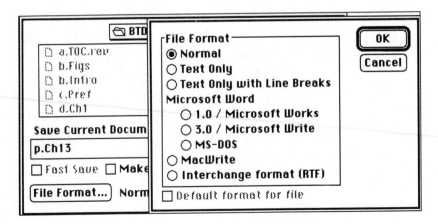

Figure 13-1
Most good word processors can save a file as ASCII text in several native formats and in some interchange formats. If they have versions on other platforms, they may also save files in the format of that second computer to ensure interoperability.

of the extended ASCII symbols are stripped out. You are left with standard ASCII and all of the formatting is removed. You can then read the file with another program, but you will have to reformat your document. MS-DOS batch files are text files, and they write only in the standard ASCII code. If you use the TYPE command in DOS to read a batch file, you see clean text; but specify TYPE for a WordPerfect file and your screen goes beserko. You get all of those strange and wonderful characters that look like they are off an Anazazi petroglyph (rock wall painting). DOS reads only ASCII, but several DOS shells, such as PC Tools Deluxe, come with file viewers that translate various native formats.

In order to circumvent the problem of native formats, some manufactures with clout, such as IBM and Microsoft, have created *interchange formats*, in which only standard ASCII characters are written and the file is specified in such a way that all formatting is contained. (The term "interchange format" is often (and less accurately) applied to any format that is in common usage between platforms, such as the graphics standards TIFF and EPS.) Using an interchange format can save most, but not all, of your formatting work. When a file must be output, the ASCII code is translated to a file in the appropriate page description language. You saw an example of this in Figure 8.7 where a Microsoft Word file was saved in the Rich Text Format (RTF).

Adequately representing graphics is a much more complex matter, as shown in Chapter 9. Representation can be bit map or object; again, often it is both. The underlying representation of a graphic can be a simple pattern of 1 and 0 (the bit map), or a combination of extended or standard ASCII code written in a programming language. A PostScript file is a text file, but it also is written in its own page description language and interpreted by a PostScript interpreter. PostScript is a rich graphics language that can be used to describe simple characters and many graphics effects. In essence, PostScript is Adobe's interchange format. EPS, a version of PostScript, is an object graphic with a corresponding low-resolution bit-mapped representation of that object. That EPS bit map can be saved either as QuickDraw on the Macintosh or as TIFF on both the Macintosh or PC. The format depends on the program and operating system involved, and the Save As option must be chosen. PICT, the draw standard on the Macintosh, also can save both objects and bit maps. To further complicate matters, there are now officially two types of PICT, three types of TIFF, and two forms of EPS files.

File Formats

The format a program uses to save data should not be regarded as just "value added." It is an important buying consideration. It's valuable to have a program that provides file compression or enhanced performance through some sort of disk swapping technique; it's critical in some cases. Also important is the ability of a program to import and export data to other applications. Eventually you may want to use the data you create in another context, such as text or a graphic in a page layout program, or a PC file created on your killer PC laptop with your Macintosh (or *vice versa*). Therefore, when you are thinking about purchasing an application, what file formats it supports should be a primary consideration. Unfortunately, it is difficult information to come by. The blurb on the box may say "1001 formats supported," but sloppy programming or poor interpretation of format standards can yield unexpected results or undocumented features when you go to print a file.

There has been a proliferation of file formats on microcomputers, and I suppose (ultimately) this is all to the good. New formatting standards keep programmers employed, and competition yields improved results that benefit users. "Survival of the fittest" whittles the number of standards down to perhaps twenty significant file formats. Sometimes the best of the bunch manage to rise to the top. In this state of confusion your best bet is to invest in applications that support the standard file formats. It's fine to use proprietary formats, but the application *must* have at least one standard to which it reads and writes, permitting you to use data outside of the program. Text standards are: WordPerfect, Word,

MacWrite, and WordStar native formats; RTF and DCA interchange file formats. Graphics standards are: PostScript, EPS, TIFF, PAINT, and PICT. Be aware that there are multiple versions of many of these standards, and choose the one best suited to your purpose.

Five text file formats are the most important:

- *ASCII* (All), or American Standard Code for Information Interchange, is a generic character set. Standard ASCII has 128 characters and is a nearly universal standard. Extended ASCII is a 256-character set; the lower 128 are the original set and the upper 128 are symbols and control codes. Upper characters are not standard. Generally, system software recommends using the upper character set.

- *Native Formats* (All) are the implementations of extended ASCII by individual software packages.

- *Interchange Formats* (All) are specifications of unofficial standards for exchanging text in standard ASCII. Chapter 8 describes the word processing interchange formats Document Content Architecture (DCA) and Microsoft's Rich Text Format (RTF). There are two other common formats: SYLK and DIF. SYLK, for Symbolic Link, is a Microsoft format used for transferring database and spreadsheet information. SYLK can contain significant text formatting information (font, sizes, etc.). DIF, or Data Interchange Format, is a simpler file format for transferring database and spreadsheet data without formatting.

- *Bit-Mapped Text* (All) saves characters as a graphic representation of bits. Unless a program has a translation utility that allows a bit-mapped graphic to be recognized as a character, it has no ASCII representation. Bit-mapped text can be saved in any of the bit-mapped formats, such as PAINT, TIFF, and .PIC. Much more common is the conversion of ASCII into bit maps by font rasterizers (see Chapter 11).

- *Object-Oriented Text* (All) represents characters as outline shapes. Most software converts ASCII into objects using a PDL, and then displays or outputs it using a font rasterizer.

They can be converted through rasterization into bit maps for display and output using a page description language or a special utility designed for text description. PostScript, GEM, HPGL, and SLD are pure object formats.

Three bit-map formats are the most important:

- *PAINT or .PNT* (Mac, PC) is a simple bit-map format, also called the MacPaint format. So much graphic art is in PAINT that many programs on the IBM PC use it. Those files are normally given the .PNT suffix. MacPaint is a black-and-white (1-bit) format that has a 72 dpi resolution, matching the classic Macintosh screen. There is a nominal 8-inch horizontal by 10-inch vertical limit to page size. Most paint programs can save in this format, but files that contain additional information, such as SuperPaint II's 300 dpi laser bits, PixelPaint's color bit maps, and Digital Darkroom's grayscales, are translated to this lower resolution standard and lose all additional information. If an image is wider than 8 inches, the right side is deleted.

- *TIFF or .TIF* (Mac, PC) is a versatile bit-map format that allows various resolutions, grayscales, and colors. It has no object descriptions. It is the most commonly used format for digital or scanned images. There are three different types of TIFF in use: *Monochrome TIFF,* which is a 1-bit black-and-white representation; *Grayscale TIFF,* which is used for 8-bit gray images (256 grays) and is common today for page layout work; and *Color TIFF,* which is a 32-bit color image. TIFF is the standard file format for bit-mapped images, but its conversion is notorious for introducing subtle changes in the image. RIFF (Raster Image File Format) is a compressed format of TIFF used by Letraset.

- *PICS* (Mac) is an animated bit-map format that is a collection of PICT or PICT2 images stored in a playback order. PICS is used by MacroMind Director, Studio/1, and SuperCard, and it's used in output by such 3D modeling programs as Super 3D, Swivel 3D, and DynaPerspective. PICS produces huge file sizes, depending on frame size, number of stored (not played) frames, and color depth. PICS is sometimes compressed, although that is not part of the format specification.

There are two important object-oriented formats:

- *PostScript* (Mac, PC, NeXT, others). It is a text file description of an image and is purely object oriented. PostScript has commands to describe shades or screens, blends, grayscale values, certain patterns, and colors. Many files allow a pure PostScript file to be written as an option; PageMaker (Mac) will create one if you hold the Command-F keystroke while clicking the OK button in the Print dialog box. PostScript files may be read and used by any program that can read text and work with that language. Also, the PostScript file can be downloaded to a printer using a simple utility program. PostScript files cannot be previewed normally; although you can change the text in the file, the image isn't easily edited.

- *Computer Graphics Metafile* (CGM). The CGM (PC) object-oriented format is excellent for non-PostScript printers. CGM exports files to PageMaker and Ventura Publisher. This format supports a wide range of colors in vector patterns.

There are two combined bit-map/object formats:

- *EPS* (Mac, PC, NeXT, SUN, others) is the most popular format for storing object-oriented graphics. EPS can store bit maps, but that produces huge files. EPS comes in two forms: *ASCII EPS* (text) and *Binary EPS* (hexadecimal). Most draw programs save in the ASCII EPS. An ASCII EPS file contains two versions of the graphic: A resolution-independent description for PostScript output (see Figure 2.13) and a low-resolution bit-map preview image that doesn't require PostScript interpretation. For the Mac, that representation can be QuickDraw or TIFF; for the PC, it's TIFF. This low-resolution image allows for rapid display, manipulation, and modification of the image on screen. EPS files often cannot be edited (even by the creator application), but can be transformed. Binary EPS is similar to ASCII EPS, has files half the size of

ASCII EPS, and color separates well in programs that don't accept TIFF files, such as the Adobe Separator. Only Photoshop and ColorStudio save in Binary EPS.

- *PICT* (Mac) is the original Macintosh file format; objects and bit maps are encoded in QuickDraw. Original PICT saved in eight colors. The newer PICT2 saves as 8-bit PICT with 256 colors, or as 32-bit PICT in one of 16.8 million colors. PICT allows resolutions of greater than 72 dpi to be saved. It is suitable for low-resolution bit maps and medium-quality line art; both can be in the same file, although you won't be able to know which until you open it. The Mac Clipboard supports all PICT formats, but applications have problems with PICT2 color translations. PICT2 is well supported by Mac presentation programs but poorly supported by page layout programs.

In keeping with MS-DOS file naming conventions, files can have up to an eight-character name with up to a three-character suffix for the format. Native formats are most likely to have a name derived from the application that creates them: .WP for WordPerfect, .WS for WordStar, .XYW for XYWrite, and so on.

File Naming Conventions

The Macintosh uses a different format naming convention. The files are assigned two four-letter codes: a file type and a creator type. The file type is what the Macintosh uses to launch the creator application when a file is opened, and is registered with Apple. The creator type is whatever the programmer desires. A Microsoft Word document has a file type of WBDN and a creator code of MSWD, whereas the application itself has the file type of APPL and the creator code of MSWD. The APPL indicates the the file is an executable program.

Some of the more common file formats are described in Table 13.1. New formats are added all the time. This list does not account for workstation, minicomputer, or mainframe formats, nor is this list complete for the Mac and PC.

Table 13-1 File Formats

Format	Type	Platform	Description/Applications
.BIT	BM	PC	For Bit Map, Lotus Manuscript's native format.
.BMP	BM	Win	For Bit Map, MS Windows format.
.CGM	OO	PC	For Computer Graphics Metafile. Used by Lotus Freelance, Harvard Graphics, Zenographix's Pixie, and Aldus PageMaker (PC).
.CLP	BM	Win	For Clipboard. MS Windows format.
.CUT	BM	PC	Media Cybernetics' Dr. HALO native format.
.DB2 or .DB3	Text	PC, Mac	For dBASE. The native formats used by Ashton or Tate's dBASE II (.DB2) and dBASE III (.DB3), respectively.
.DCA	Text	All	For Data Content Architecture. IBM's interchange format for text.
DIF	Text	All	For Document Interchange Format. The Lotus 1-2-3 interchange format for text used in spreadsheets and databases. Used by many programs.
.DOC	Text	Mac, PC	For Document. Microsoft Word's native format. Used for other word processors.
.DRW	OO	Win	For Draw. Micrografx programs native format.
.DXB	OO	PC	Binary (compiled) form of .DXF.
.DXF	OO	Mac, PC, Sun, etc.	For Data Exchange Format. Developed by AutoDesk for AutoCAD. The standard file description for CAD files. Many Mac CAD packages ship with translation for .DXF.
.EPS	BM/OO	Mac, NeXT, PC, Win	For Encapsulated PostScript. Used by Aldus, Adobe, and others. The standard format for object or raster graphics.
.GEM	OO	PC	For Graphics Environment Manager file. Used by Digital Research products and Ventura Publisher (GEM) for object graphics.

Table 13-1 File Formats *(continued)*

Format	Type	Platform	Description/Applications
.GIF	BM	PC	For Graphics Interchange Format. Used by CompuServe for color graphics files.
HPGL	OO	PC	For Hewlett-Packard Graphics Language. Used by H-P plotters. Often the .PLT extension is used for HPGL files.
.HSG	BM	PC	For HotShot Graphics. HotShot Graphics native format.
.IFF	BM	Amiga	For Image File Format. The Commodore Amiga standard file format.
.IMG	BM	PC	For Image file. Used by GEM programs and Ventura Publisher for bit-mapped graphics. Widely supported.
.MAC or PAINT	BM	Mac, PC, etc.	For MacPaint format. Used by many PC programs and all Mac paint programs. Some PC programs use the alternate .PNT suffix.
.MSP	BM	PC	For Microsoft Paint. Two versions exist, one for each Windows version.
.PCC	BM	PC	ZSoft's Paintbrush Clipboard format.
.PCL	BM/OO	PC	For Printer Control Language. Used by H-P LaserJet printers.
.PCX	BM	PC	ZSoft's PaintBrush native format. Widely supported.
.PCT PICT	BM/OO	PC, Mac	For Picture. Used by most Macintosh graphics software, this format is encoded using the QuickDraw PDL.
.PCT PICT2	BM/OO	PC, Mac	For Picture 2. Used by color Macintosh graphics software, this format is encoded in the QuickDraw PDL. Exists in either 8-bit or 32-bit forms.

Table 13-1 File Formats *(continued)*

Format	Type	Platform	Description/Applications
.PIC	BM/OO	PC	For Picture. Used by Lotus 1-2-3 (OO), Dr. HALO, PC Paintbrush+, Pictor, and Grasp (all bm). There are several implementations, including a .PIC format for Micrografx Draw, Draw Plus, Designer, Graph, and Graph Plus.
PICS	BM/OO	Mac	For Pictures. Used by several 3D graphics and multi-media programs on the Macintosh.
.PIX	BM	PC	For Picture. Versions exist for Inset, the screen capture utility, and for some of the PC video capture boards.
.PLT	OO	Mac, PC	For Plot. AutoCAD plot file.
.PNT or PAINT	BM	Mac, PC	For MacPaint format or the PAINT file type. Used by PC programs and Mac paint programs. Some PC programs use the .PNT suffix.
.PUB	BM/OO /Text	Mac, PC	For Publication. Used as the file extension for Aldus PageMaker files. Includes references or hooks to original graphics files, and multi-chapter Ventura Publications.
.RLE	BM	PC	For Run Length Encoded. Used by CompuServe and CCITT 3 Fax.
.RND	OO	Mac, PC	For Render files. Used by AutoShade, it consists of polygon definitions.
.RTF	Text	Mac, PC	For Rich Text Format. The Microsoft interchange format for text.
.SCX	BM	PC	RIX, EGA Paint, and other RIX software.
.SLD	OO	Mac, PC	For Slide format. Used by AutoCAD as a native format.

Table 13-1 File Formats *(continued)*

Format	Type	Platform	Description/Applications
SYLK	Text	Mac, PC	For Symbolic Link. A Microsoft text interchange format for spreadsheet and database data. Used by many programs, especially on the Macintosh.
.TGA	BM	Mac, PC	For Targa file format. Used by Targa video capture boards.
.TIF or TIFF	BM	Mac, PC, NeXT, etc.	For Tagged Image file format. Developed by Aldus and Microsoft. The most popular PC/Mac bit-map file formats.
.TXT or TEXT	ASCII	All	For Text. Specifies an ASCII text file. The universal standard.
.WKS	Text	PC	Used by Lotus 1-2-3 Release 1A (.WKS), or the alternative .WK1 for Release 2.
.WP	Text	Mac, PC	For WordPerfect. WordPerfect's native format. Sometimes written .WPF.
.WS	Text	PC	For WordStar. WordStar's native format.
.XYW	Text	PC	For XYWrite. XYWrites's native format.

Key: BM = bit map or raster graphics; OO = object-oriented or vector graphics.

Windows is a bit-mapped environment, obvious by its native file format and Clipboard. However, it is still possible to save files in an object format. To do so, go into the printer menu of the Control Panel, select a PostScript printer, and then click the Configure button to go to Setup. Click the Options button and in the Option dialog box select the Print to Encapsulated PostScript option. Enter the name of the File in the File Text box, giving it an .EPS suffix; then click the Header button and Send the Header to the File. Finally, click the OK buttons to close all dialog boxes. Save your document to preserve this setting.

Format Conversions

Because ASCII is a universal standard, it can be opened from most applications without change. Native formats that use extended ASCII require that all of the formatting marks specified by the upper ASCII characters be converted to the ones used by your current application. Not all formatting conventions are included in all applications, so the conversion process doesn't always preserve all formatting. Nevertheless, most major applications contain several filters to convert from other major applications on your computer, or to convert from their versions. Some vendors have started to make their translation technology available to third parties so that that an extensive set of filters can be written. The Apple File Exchange, discussed below, and the Claris XTND technology are two examples of this trend.

Figure 13-2
The Claris XTND technology (a set of external commands) was first incorporated into FileMaker Pro and will be found in all Claris products. It enables third-party vendors to write translation filters that can be directly incorporated into their applications by dragging their files into the Claris system folder.

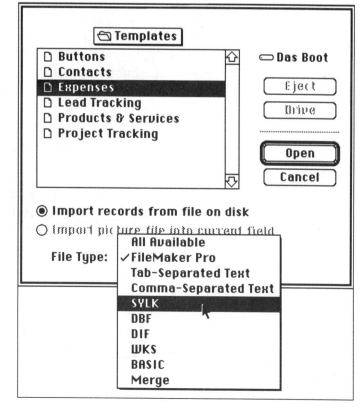

Some applications make file translation so easy that you forget to appreciate the process involved. If you create a file in PICT format, another program that reads PICT may open the file, changing it in the process. Some imaging programs open a PICT and convert it to something that they can use, say TIFF. In the process all object description is discarded. This may have been what you intended, but if it isn't, you have a problem. Software vendors take a lot of flak for these kinds of problems, and tend to put warnings in their programs or write better translators into future versions. Programs such as PageMaker, Photoshop, CorelDRAW, Micrografx Designer, and others build up tremendous file translation capabilities over time. A solution to format conversion may be sitting right there on your shelf.

In the early days of the plug-and-play Macintosh, formats weren't much of a problem. You could have any format you wanted as long as it was PICT or PAINT. (A third format, called the style format, is used internally for formatted text on the Macintosh Clipboard.) This is no longer the case, and Mac users are now subjected to the same kind of alphabet soup that PC users are accustomed to. Format proliferation on the PC has always been a problem and has led to a variety of stand-alone utilities for file conversion, such as Micrografx XPort, Xenographic's ImPort (and ImPort for Windows), Halcyon Software's DoDOT, Inset System's HiJaak, Computer Presentation's ImagePrep, and The Graphics Link Plus from HSC Software. Some of these packages offer screen capture (DoDOT, HiJaak, TGL+), others, such as ImagePrep, do file compression, but most are advertised for their conversion prowess. DoDOT, TGL+, and HiJaak (in that order) are the best at converting bit-map formats on the PC. XPort is the best program for object-oriented format conversion. Compare that to the most popular Macintosh screen capture utility, Mainstay's Capture, which saves files only as PICT, TIFF, or to the Clipboard.

Files can be written to disk using a Save command; with the Open command they can be read. A program must fully support a file's format in order to fully edit a file. Some programs, such as page layout software, can open a file using a Place command, Get

Picture command, or some similar phrase. A placed file can be either displayed or transformed in certain limited ways, including scaling or cropping. Just remember, whenever you use a program different from the creator application, you can run into problems. Even simple processes can yield unexpected results. If, for example, you prepare a PICT file in the color paint program, Pixel Paint (Mac), with a full 256 colors, and then import it into MacDraw, the result is a substantially different picture. MacDraw supports only eight colors, and translates each color in the original PICT file to the nearest color. Also, 8-bit PICT saves a custom palette of 256 colors that different applications can ignore or misread. The lesson is, you can't take anything for granted where file formats are concerned.

Things get really hairy when you do file conversions between formats. You can always convert objects to bit maps or vice versa, but you suffer some loss of detail. We addressed the compromises in Chapter 9. The important point to note is to always save the original file format, as it's the one that will contain the most detail and image data. If you throw the original file away there will be no way to retrieve it. The conversion from objects to bit maps is generally more precise than the reverse process. Bit-map graphics converted to objects through edge detection algorithms generally result in a collection of shapes that add tremendous complexity to a file. Consider a bit-mapped circle shape: when converted to an object representation, you may end up with a multitude of small line segments. Some bit-mapped shapes result in many polygons. Rarely is the true perfect shape recognized by the computer.

Color Conversions

Converting images with few colors to formats with many colors doesn't produce additional colors, only the original image with the ability to add more colors. Image quality suffers considerable degradation when a format with many colors is converted to one with fewer color values. Keep in mind that in order to see 32-bit images, you need software, a monitor, and a video card that's set up for it. If you have an 8-bit monitor, a program can display only an 8-bit image that is an approximation of what may be stored in the file. The example above converted an 8-bit PICT to only eight colors. Less obvious is when a 32-bit color is converted to an 8-bit image. The image can look similar, but the conversion may affect shading, hues, and other subtle properties that can be a problem for color matching on screen.

Language usage for full-color images has yet to be standardized. Full color, or true color, is often referred to as 24-bit color (16.8 million colors). Due to the 32-bit bus that many microcomputers are using, there are 8-bits of extra information that are used for other purposes, so many applications and documentation refer alternatively to 24-bit color. This topic is discussed further in Chapter 14.

Conversion from 32-bit PICT2 to monochrome TIFF yields truly ugly and unusable results. Some programs solve this problem by mixing or dithering the available colors in patterns that simulate the original colors, with concomitant resolution loss. Others use a matching algorithm to map the colors to the more limited color palette, also producing poor results. How good a job you can do is dependent on the programs involved.

It would be nice to have a table that listed all of the options available to convert one file format to another, and which programs read or write which formats, but a complete listing would require several pages to define and would be subject to perpetual change. New program versions can dramatically alter the efficiency of a particular program or conversion routine. The best way to find out how to convert files is to experiment on samples, but remember to always save the original files.

File and Disk Conversions

Moving files between computers involves two steps: *file transfer* and *file translation*. File transfer can be accomplished by a disk swap over a network, through an asynchronous direct modem-to-modem connection using telecommunications software, or by use of a null modem connection that hooks Macs to PCs via their serial ports.[1] Several approaches will allow a Macintosh to talk with an IBM PC, and there are both hardware and software solutions. For users on SneakerNet, there are disk drives that can mount other computer's disks and software that can translate their files. Networks that connect PCs and Macs, such as TOPS, transfer files and may have translation routines built in.

Modem transfer is slow; two 2,400 bps modems transfer only about 800 KBytes per hour, so this is not a practical solution for graphics files. Null modem connections are better; serial ports offer about 57,600 bps (connecting Macs and PCs of 12 MHz 80286 or better), and that rate allows roughly 19 MBytes per hour transfer. AppleTalk is even faster at 230,400 bps, with a transfer rate of 77 MBytes per hour. TOPS is faster still at 770,000 bps, and Ethernet is the fastest common solution at 2 to 10 Mbps. These transfer rates don't include compressed files, so it's possible to do significantly better.

The Macintosh SuperDrive (1.44 MBytes) reads 3 ½-inch PC formatted disks from within the Apple File Exchange (AFE). Apple sells a 5 ¼-inch drive for Mac that enables you to read 5 ¼-inch IBM PC disks. SuperDrive will not recognize a DOS disk from the Finder, although you can automatically mount DOS disks using DOS Mounter, from DYNA, which allows you to launch an application on the Macintosh that can read a DOS file. It does this through a process called *extension mapping*. The three-letter PC suffix is mapped to the four-letter creator code. PageMaker 4.0's (PC) .PUB suffix maps to ALD4, the PageMaker 4.0 creator application on the Mac; and using DOS Mounter you can assign this mapping to anything you want. You could, for example, manually map a Lotus 1-2-3 .WKS file to Excel's XCEL extension. But, although PageMaker (Mac) can open a variety of PC word processor files, it requires them to have the correct three-letter extension: .WP for WordPerfect, .XYW for XYWrite, and .DCA for the DCA interchange format.

---

[1] Refer to the BLAST products in the "Software" section in Appendix C. An ImageWriter I cable (Apple part M1050) can function as a null modem cable when coupled with a gender changer adapter. For PS/2s with 25 pin male connectors, use Radio Shack part 26-1495; and for the Mac use a DB-9 to DIN-8 adaptor, Apple part M0199. To create your own cable, see "Inside the Apple Macintosh," by Jim Heid and Peter Norton.

Figure 13-3
The DynaFile external floppy disk drives provide a complete hardware/software file translation solution for Macintosh and NeXT computers. Models read 5 ¼-inch and/or 3 ½-inch IBM PC formatted files and mount them on the Macintosh desktop.

Translators

To use files from the IBM PC on the Mac (or vice versa), a *translator* program is necessary. Some vendors call these utilities filters, a common term in the mainframe world. Translators preserve character identity and formatting, and there are several utilities on the market for this purpose. Apple supplies AFE as part of its system software, which comes with two translators for text. One converts MS-DOS or ProDOS (Apple II) to text, and the second converts DCA or RFT to MacWrite. AFE also removes unwanted line feed codes from PC text files. An alternative to this FDHD-SuperDrive/ AFE combination is the DynaFile floppy disk drive, an SCSI device. It both mounts (using DOS Mounter) and reads DOS files directly into either 3 ½-inch or 5 ¼-inch format. The Graphics Link Plus is another PC/Macintosh translation utility, and heavyweight applications, such as Adobe Photoshop, also are often good at translating a range of cross-platform formats.

Other Macintosh file transfer utilities include DataViz's MacLinkPlus/PC and Travelling Software's LapLink Mac III. The MacLinkPlus/Translators package can be purchased separately and used with AFE directly simply by copying it into the AFE folder.

Figure 13-4
The Apple File Exchange (AFE) ships with the Macintosh system software. It offers file translation from the IBM PC disks read with the SuperDrive disk drive. Shown here are the additional MacLinkPlus/Translators installed in AFE.

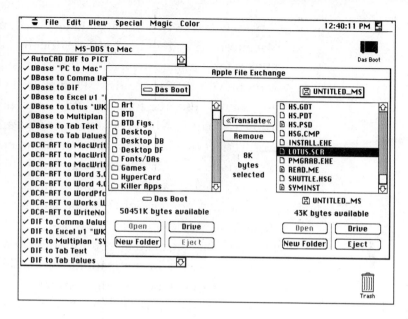

DataViz offers over 150 translators for word processor text conversion, spreadsheets, databases, and graphics applications, including translators for Mac-to-Wang, Mac-to-Sun, and Mac-to-NeXT computers. MacLinkPlus/Translators in combination with the AFE is a great solution, but for $30 more MacLinkPlus is a stand-alone application that also allows you to transfer files directly from a PC with either the serial cable it supplies, or by modem. LapLinkMac is another application that supplies a serial cable, but it translates files on the PC first, and then transfers them—two separate steps. It's a less powerful solution designed for Macintosh users with PC laptops. Software Bridge from Systems Compatibility is a set of Apple File Exchange filters in 380 combinations that are supposed to give excellent file translations.

Emulators

Emulators, programs that put another operating system in a partition on your hard drive, offer yet another solution to file transfer. They also can be purchased as hardware in the form of add-in boards. Orange Micro's Mac86 and Mac286 NuBus boards for the Mac II series provide MS-DOS emulation that is directly mountable on the Macintosh desktop. The Amiga has emulators available on which both PC and Macintosh operating systems can be run.

SoftPC and SoftPC AT are MS-DOS software emulators for a Macintosh. They require 2 MBytes for the smaller version and 4 MBytes for the standard version; the AT version emulates an 80286 with the VGA display standard. PC files read by the Macintosh AFE are given a resource fork by SoftPC, and directories are turned into HFS folders. When you create a WordPerfect document using WordPerfect running in SoftPC, that document is directly compatible with the PC version *without* any translation required. Printing can be either to an Epson FX-80 (ImageWriter) or a PostScript (LaserWriter) printer. SoftPC's one limitation is that it cannot, in its current version, emulate expanded memory, only extended memory. This means that you cannot run Windows in it. Emulators, no matter how compatible, also suffer from performance issues. Their operation is akin to running an operating system on top of an operating system. Soft PC works best with a fast 68020 or 68030 Macintosh.

Other Transfer Programs

MacChuck is a program that allows a Macintosh to control a PC by remote. Using a serial cable connection to communicate, Mac-Chuck loads programs on both computers. The Macintosh user sees a representation of the PC's monochrome or CGA display on screen, and can enter any valid PC command from the Mac keyboard. Programs can be launched, DOS commands executed, and files transferred. Text cut in MacChuck can be copied to the Clipboard, and MacChuck supports text transfer as ASCII, binary, or in the MacBinary (Macintosh only) formats, and can copy files back and forth. It has some utility for print capture, whereby a PC program can print to disk with the Macintosh volume serving as the disk; you can capture a PC screen with the Macintosh Command-Shift-3 FKey; and last, it offers DOS file redirection so that a PC program can be output to the Macintosh. These functions are useful for DTP applications.

AnyPC from Compatible Systems offers yet another solution for transferring files from the IBM PC to the Mac. Although there are many file formats on the PC, nearly all programs can write print files in the language of the IBM Graphics Printer. AnyGraph creates a print-to-disk file and translates it to the MacPaint standard. When in a PC program, this TSR (terminate-and-stay-resident) program opens and you then can create a print file. As the Graphics Printer format has higher resolution than MacPaint, no detail is lost, although you are limited to 72 dpi resolution. The file, which now has an .ANY suffix, is then transferred onto a disk to a Macintosh and translated using the Macintosh version of AnyGraph. AnyPC also has a text transfer utility called AnyText that works similarly. The same company offers a product based on AnyPC called QuickShare that connects a PC and Mac together through the SCSI port on the Mac and an AT bus board on the PC.

The easiest way to translate files transferred from one computer to another is to use programs that have a version on each; this is the promise of interoperability realized. Microsoft Word or WordPerfect for text, Adobe Illustrator for object-oriented draw graphics, Excel for spreadsheet analysis or charts, and Aldus PageMaker or Ventura Publisher for page layout have versions on both the Macintosh and IBM PC. They can read their own formats if you mount the volume containing the file. Usually, the transfer works transparently, opening the file with all formatting and elements intact.

Be aware that program version numbers affect their translation ability. Word for Windows 3.1 can read Macintosh Word 4.0 native files correctly, but the reverse is not true. To translate from Word 4.0 on the Macintosh to the Windows version you must save a file in the Rich Text Format (RTF) for correct translation. RTF format is also useful for importing a Word file into PageMaker (Mac or PC). WordPerfect 2.0 (Mac) ships with the ability to match ASCII characters in various fonts from WordPerfect 5.1 (DOS), and the translator marks characters that can't be matched with a box. These are programs from the same manufacturers! PageMaker's text translation performance is much better.

▼ *Tip: Because translating text can present serious problems, especially when converting between different programs, create a text file that contains all of your file's ASCII symbols in the order in which they are numbered. Then do the file translation and examine the resulting file for any mismatches. If you find any, you*

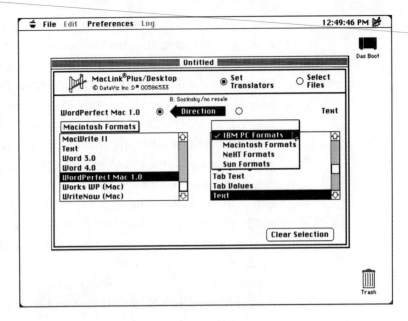

Figure 13-5
The MacLinkPlus
Desktop application
translates any of over
150 file formats between
the Macintosh and IBM
PC, NeXT, and Sun
computers. It is the
easiest solution for
file translation.

can do a change and replace operation in the result-
ing file to clean it up. Whenever possible, try to match
exactly the fonts in your export file to fonts that exist in
the importing program and that will be used on your
printer. This too can help to minimize translation
errors.

On the PC side, MacLinkPlus/PC can translate Macintosh text,
spreadsheet files, and several graphics formats. PC DataBridge,
form DataViz (the companion for MacLink Plus) is used in Windows 3.0 and contains over 150 translators. A version of the program is bundled with the TOPS networking software and is
responsible for file conversion on that network. The PC market
has a number of dedicated file translation utilities, such as Micrografx XPORT, which is valuable for object-oriented graphics. However, it deletes bit maps from Macintosh PICT files. HSC Software's
The Graphics Link Plus is a good choice for bit-map graphics. It
can apply several halftone options and autotrace to improve
images. File translation is a common feature of screen capture util-

ities (see Chapter 9). HiJaak from Inset Systems and HSC Image-Tools from HSC Software are examples, and they are useful for bit-map conversions.

Translating Graphics Files

Translating graphics files between platforms is a particular problem. The Macintosh PICT format saves images as both object and bit-map graphics in QuickDraw, the PDL of the Macintosh. As QuickDraw is not supported on the IBM PC, many programs will have trouble with either or both components of PICT. Opening a PageMaker file created on the Mac in PageMaker (PC) results in blank boxes in place of the image. FreeHand, ImageStudio, Digital Darkroom, and Photoshop all open and convert PICT files. Translating graphics from a native IBM PC format to a Mac also causes disappearing graphics; Macintosh programs don't recognize the draw commands for Windows or the OS/2 Presentation Manager.

▼ *Tip: Files saved as TIFF on the IBM PC often can't be opened on a Macintosh because the Mac requires a four-letter Finder file type code to be opened. The Macintosh file system uses this code to place the file name in a standard file Open dialog box. Some networks update PC files when they see the .TIF extension and add the file type, as does MacLinkPlus/PC, LapLink Mac III, and the DOS Mounter, but direct transfer and communications software usually does not. MacLink Plus/Translators used with the Apple File Exchange correctly translate PC.TIF files. To add the TIFF file type code to PC files on the Mac, use DiskTools II (see Figure 4.8) or DiskTop; they allow you to change the Finder file attributes.*

Judicious conversion of graphics to more well-supported file formats often can solve many problems. EPS and TIFF are the two best-supported formats, EPS is recommended for draw graphics and TIFF for bit-map graphics. Keep in mind that text characters saved in TIFF format are translated to their bit-mapped representation and that limits your resolution for output along with your ability to resize the graphic. These files are large also. EPS, therefore, is the desired solution whenever possible, but it too has its problems. EPS cannot be altered once saved, unless you use the creator application. Also, EPS displays the low-resolution, bit-mapped representation of the image on screen, and some programs cannot interpret EPS files for display if their bit map is saved in the wrong format. (This occurs because Macintosh programs save the EPS bit-map component as QuickDraw, and PC programs as TIFF. On the PC, Macintosh EPS won't appear on screen if they don't have a TIFF component. Mac Aldus FreeHand, Adobe Illustrator, and Letraset ImageStudio save EPS bit maps as TIFF, but for Illustrator you must select the IBM PC option in the Save dialog box. Preview an IBM PC EPS file using a program like CorelDRAW that uses an EPS file with a TIFF representation; always create this type of file to avoid problems.) You may see a shaded box in place of your graphic, but chances are that the file will print properly.

Telecommunications

Telecommunications is a term usually applied to any data transfer done over phone lines, most often with a modem. This distinction separates the topic from general networking, although there is considerable overlap between the two. It's a big subject with an extensive lexicon that easily could fill a book this size. Handshaking, baud rates, parity, protocols, and a hundred other terms describe the variables involved in the process. They intimidate, and keep many people from reaping the wealth of rewards available, although modern software does much to shield the user from the complexity of the process. Some software ships with a set of macros or scripts that require only that a button be clicked to log onto a service. In the sections that follow we focus on using the telecommunications process for transferring data rather than on a full explanation of the details involved.

You can telecommunicate in real time by typing on your keyboard what will appear on another person's screen, while he or she types what you see. Some software has what's called a *buffered keyboard*, which allows you to type and edit a block of text and then download it in real time. Connecting to an information service or bulletin board also allows real-time communication. Most sessions involve either file transfers where data is moved from your computer to the storage device of the host, or files are transferred onto your hard drive from a service. Only the status of the transfer is shown once you select the desired information for transmittal.

Standards

The first step in establishing a telecommunications session is to make the physical connection between your computer and another using your modem, which is a serial port (RS 232) device or an add-in board that connects into a phone line (see Chapter 6). Sending data to a distant computer is called *uploading*, receiving it is called *downloading*. In order to send or receive information in a form that can be used, you must set several software parameters, including:

- Speed: Your modem determines the maximum transfer rate (quoted in bps or baud), but software can set a lower speed. With an 8-bit byte, a 2,400 baud modem transfers about 240 characters per second, or about as many words per minute as the number of bps.

- Data Characteristics: Software allows you to set the manner in which your data is handled. The important settings are: *character width* or *data bits* of a byte, usually 7 or 8 bits (most common because they allow extended ASCII transfer); *stop bits*, set either at one, one and a half, or two. It is a bit that signals the end of a byte; *parity*, even, odd, or no parity; it is a simple form of error detection. For a single-parity bit, a system can detect a 1-bit error in the received signal. Even parity is when the system sums the bits in a byte, and if the sum is even, the parity bit transmitted is 0; if the sum is odd, then a 1 is transmitted. This keeps the sum of the byte always even. Odd parity works similarly with an odd result. A mark or space is sometimes transmitted for no parity. Parity errors result in a request for the data block to be retransmitted; *duplex* describes the direction of data flow at any moment. It is set either as full (both directions) or half (one way) duplex. In full duplex a computer monitors data received and sent at the same time; this mode of operation is called *sliding windows*. *Echo*, set on or off, is a technique where data is returned for error checking. The wrong setting results in double signals appearing on screen. Echo is too slow to be turned on in the half-duplex mode. *Handshaking* is a method for telling a faster system when to pause so that the slower system can catch up. A signal such as XOFF (X stands for transmit), DC3, or Control or Command-3 is sent to pause transfer, and a signal such as XON, DC1, or Control or Command-q is sent to resume transfer.

It's not important that you understand or remember these settings, just that you set them when first communicating. Most software allows you to save them in your file or as a script.

- Protocols: These comprise a set of agreements made concerning how data is transferred. They include the size of data blocks, advanced error checking methods, and prevent transmitted characters from being interpreted as commands. The ISO has established various protocols for the seven layers of hardware and software involved in a data transfer session. From the user's point of view, the critical considerations are the protocols involved in the upper two layers, the session layer and application layer. Important protocols include: Text (ASCII), Binary (Macintosh files), XModem, YModem, ZModem, Kermit (mainframe communications), and others.

Figure 13-6
An asynchronous transmission scheme for a data byte. Typically, the data string is bracketed by control bits; the start bit tells the modem to save the incoming data, the parity bit is for error checking, and the stop bit resets the modem's clock. A specified number of bytes comprises a block, which can have additional data error checking schemes that are defined by the transfer protocol.

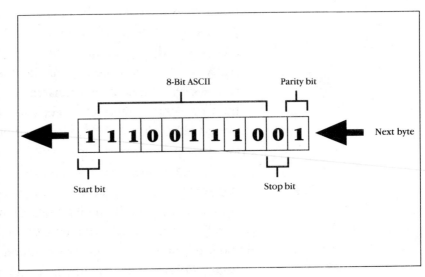

To establish a telecommunications session, you would do the following:

1. Connect and turn on your modem and launch your communications software.

2. Set the modem speed and data characteristics to those recommended by the service you are calling, or for a direct modem transfer, to those decided by both parties.

3. Dial the service and wait for the connection to be established.

4. Use the software to navigate the service, to leave messages, or to pick them up.

5. To download a file, select a file, choose a protocol, then issue a Receive File command.

6. To upload a file, select a file, choose a protocol, then issue the Send File command.

7. To end the session, first log off, then give the Hang Up command.

8. Save the session settings as a file or a script depending on your software (optional).

9. Quit your communications software.

▼ *Tip: If random characters appear on your screen, you may have a noisy line. If you can read through it, continue. If not, or if transferring a file, hang up and reestablish the connection. Completely indecipherable text may also indicate mismatched baud rates, or data bits (7, 8) so try changing the rates (without disconnecting) and see if that helps. With Call Waiting, an incoming phone call disconnects a session. Some phone companies offer a disable feature for Call Waiting. Dial *70 (with a tone phone) or 1170 (with a pulse phone) prior to dialing your number. When you hang up Call Waiting is turned back on. If this service isn't available, you will get a message that the call can't be completed as dialed.*

For two computers not in close proximity (Mac or PC) and for which a direct connection is not practicable, you can do a *direct modem transfer* to exchange data. This is a form of telecommunications session where one computer (the *guest*) calls up another computer (the *host*) by modem and uses the phone lines for the connection. Both users have their telecommunications programs active, and match speed, protocols, bit size, and other settings. Okyto is one software program aimed at users wishing to do Macintosh-to-Macintosh file transfers. A direct modem transfer usually incorporates these:

1. The guest chooses the Dial command from his telecom program, and the host has his program on the Auto-Answer command setting.

2. Both parties will see something like **CONNECT 2400** on their monitors.

3. Each person types a few lines to ensure a reliable connection was made, such as:

   Guest: "`Hello, HAL, Let's transfer your files today.`"

   Host: "`Thanks, Dave, I'm glad to be on the mission with you.`"

4. The guest chooses the desired protocol and then gives the Upload (or Send) File command, and selects the file.

5. The host then chooses the same protocol and issues the Download (or Receive) File command, and the transfer is accomplished.

6. Some final comments like: Host: "`I enjoyed that, Dave!`" are exchanged, and both parties hang up, disconnecting the session.

On-Line Services

Doing a direct modem transfer can be very inconvenient. For example, when I want to download a file or transfer a message to my editors in London before leaving at 5:00 p.m. (EST), one of them has to be there to take the call at 11:00 p.m. (GMT). This cuts into valuable pub time. If I want to transfer that message at 3:00 a.m. Boston time, forget it! It's much easier to leave that message from where it can be uploaded later. That's where commercial telecommunication services come in. An on-line service is a sophisticated database in which a variety of activities such as messages, file transfers, commercial services including shopping, and so on, can take place by many users concurrently.

On-line services share a lot of technology with the airline reservation systems that pioneered the concept. In the early 1960s IBM built the SABRE (Semi-Automatic Business Research Environment) system for Eastern Airlines. It revolutionized the airline industry. Some 2,000 terminals connected by a time-share to a mainframe in Briarcliff Manor, New York, gave travel agents the sense that they were querying the system for flight information directly. When you log onto a system such as CompuServe or Prodigy, a similar system is at work. Several thousand users can be on at the same time, and through conferencing, you can actually "talk" with some of these folks, but the feeling is that you are communicating directly with the service.

The services available on-line are extraordinary, and increase as time goes by. You can find forums (conferences) from companies, magazines, user groups, and special interest groups there. Forums are either interactive or message-board based and cover the gamut of subjects that have been discussed in this book: DTP, CAD/CAM, graphics, and others. You can access shopping, banking, weather, news, games you play with others, and many special databases. If you want to do a search on some arcane surgical procedure, you probably can find a medical database that allows you to do key word searches and article retrieval. Not every service is on-line yet, however. You can't find TV listings on a service, but you can have food delivered to your door and charge it to your credit card. Some of the features of on-line services are included in Table 13.2. Services charge some combination of a sign-up fee plus hourly or monthly fees with discounting for off-peak-hour connections.

Two different approaches are used for connecting to on-line services: graphics-based or text-based software. Text-based software is generally a generic telecommunications package—anything from the communications module in Microsoft Works, to White Knight, Microphone II, ProComm, or a host of others discussed at the end of this chapter in "Software." In that case, logging onto a commercial service isn't much different than connecting to your favorite local bulletin board. There are just more choices. Transferring files or messaging is no different from the procedure you would use on your BBS. Recently companies have found that GUI software improves learning time and increases billable on-line hours. Many are proprietary packages included in the sign-up price. (One example is the America Online software, provided free with sign-up information, which runs on Macintosh and Windows environments.)

Graphics interfaces have the feel of well-developed database systems. CompuServe is an example of a text-based service and graphical interface software can be purchased for it. CompuServe Information Manager (CIM), and Navigator are both available. CIM is useful for beginners connecting to the system, while Navigator is valuable for veteran users who know exactly what they want, and need to get on-line and off-line quickly. Both are useful for automating specific tasks, such as conferencing. When you connect to a service with interface software, the sequence for file transfer varies but is generally much easier to accomplish.

Be aware that not all graphical software is an improvement. Early adopters of the IBM/Sears service Prodigy found the bit-mapped environment slow and somewhat ugly. Prodigy is fairly inexpensive and has attracted a wide audience, but that's because the service is underwritten by a number of advertisers whose wares are hawked on the bottom third of the screen. (Hooks to Prodigy are included as part of the IBM PS/1 computer's software and hardware.) The original version of the software ran on PCs, and in 1989 the Macintosh version was introduced—it ran only in MultiFinder. I object particularly to the tracking of users navigating the system while checking out ads and features; I think it's intrusive.

Figure 13-7
(A) Text-based CompuServe, as accessed by Microphone II.
(B) It is much easier to move around CompuServe using graphical software. Shown here is Navigator.

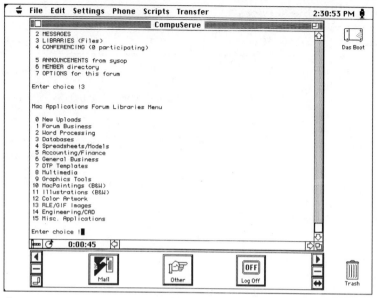

A.

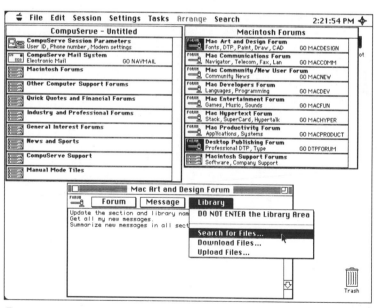

B.

Table 13.2 On-Line Services

Statistics	AOL	BIX	CS	Connect	Delphi	GEnie	Prodigy
Platforms Supported	Mac, Win	All	All	All	All	All	Mac, PC
Phone Numbers (All Area Code 800)	227-6364	227-2983	848-8199	456-0553	544-4005	638-9636	776-3449
Access Network	N	Tymnet	Prop.	Tymnet Acunet	Tymnet Acunet	Prop.	Prop.[A]
Start/Month cost ($)	0/5.95	0/13.33	39.95/1.50	99.95/6	49.95[B]/0	29.95/0	49.95/9.95
Hourly cost P/OP ($)	10/5	6/2[C]	12.80/12.80	10/5	17.40/7.20[D]	18/10	0/0
Interface	graphic	text	text	graphic	text	text	graphic
Proprietary software	Y	N	N[F]	Y	N	N	Y

Features							
Airline reservations	Y	N	Y	N	Y	Y	Y
Banking	N	N	N	N	N	N	Y[D]
Bulletin Boards	Y	Y	Y	Y	Y	Y	Y
Companies on-line	N	Y	Y	Y	N	Y	N
Conferencing (chat)	Y	Y	Y	N	Y	Y	N
E-Mail/file transfer	Y/Y	Y/Y	Y/Y	Y/Y[E]	Y/N	Y/Y	Y/N
Encyclopedia	Y	N	Y	N	Y	Y	N
Fax (cost in $)	1	N	0.75	0.80	1.25	N	N
Games (interactive)	Y	Y	Y	N	Y	Y	Y
Movie Reviews	Y	N	Y	N	Y	Y	Y
News/Weather	Y/Y	Y/N	Y/Y	Y/Y[E]	Y/Y	Y/Y	Y/Y
Real time seminars	Y	Y	Y	N	Y	Y	N
Shopping	Y	N	Y	N	Y	Y	Y

Table 13.2 *(continued)*

Features	AOL	BIX	CS	Connect	Delphi	GEnie	Prodigy
Software libraries	Y	Y	Y	Y^E	Y	Y	N
Stocks (B/Q)	N/Y	N/N	Y/Y	N/Y	N/Y	Y/Y	Y/Y
U.S. Mail (cost in $)	2	N	1.50	2	N	1	N
# of Members	50,000	35,000	555,000	17,000	100,000	195,000	400,000

Ratings							
Cost Factors	Good	Excellent	Good	Fair	Excellent	Excellent	Excellent
Downloading Files	Excellent	Good	Fair	Excellent	Good	Fair	N/A
Getting Connected	Good	Fair	Excellent	Fair	Excellent	Excellent	Good
Navigating	Excellent	Good	Poor	Excellent	Good	Good	Good
Using Interface	Excellent	Good	Fair	Excellent	Good	Good	Poor

Key: AOL = America Online. BIX = Byte Information Exchange. CS = CompuServe. GEnie = GE Network for Information Exchange. P/OP = Peak hours/Off-peak hours. Y = Yes. N = No. A = Not available in all areas. B = Includes two nonprime hours. C = Tymnet Charges. D = $160 yearly plus Tymnet charges. A flat-fee Tymnet program is available for $20 per month. E = Extra cost. F = Graphics software (extra price): CompuServe Information Manager and the Navigator. Stock (B/Q) = Stock brokerage services/Stock Quotes. N/A = Not available. Ratings consider how new users will find the system. Experienced users will not have difficulty.

Source: Adapted from *MacWorld* magazine, September 1990, p. 198.

When deciding what network to use for transferring information, the size and distribution of the service is of vital importance. CompuServe is an information giant with links to several continents including Europe, Asia, and Africa. Connect also provides gateways to other networks that give it a global reach. In the United States, most services (excluding Prodigy) have wide area coverage, and nearly all provide for local phone access to the network.

MCI Mail is an electronic mail service that offers instant letter services (letters are transmitted, printed, and then delivered), fax or telex dispatch, and electronic bulletin boards. It's great for publication managers who want to receive files electronically from writers and correspondents. In fact, publications such as *Publish* and *Desktop Communications* make heavy use of MCI Mail. It can also send documents to CompuServe and access the Dow Jones News/Retrieval database. Desktop Express and Lotus Express are communications packages specifically sold for MCI mail. Files can be sent to other users who have the package. SuperGlue also ships with Desktop Express so that you can print images from any program. Desktop Express is graphical with icons for log on, an address book, mail management, the MCI print center, a text editor for memo writing, entry to Dow Jones, and a pull-down menu interface. Desktop Express is expensive and slow, but it comes with one year of MCI free and may be valuable for image file transfers. AT&T Mail and EasyLink from Western Union are two other electronic mail systems to consider.

▼ *Tip: Because the cost of on-line services is set by the connect time and modem speed, a higher speed modem saves money. Rarely will a 2,400 baud connection cost twice that of a 1,200 baud connection. Find and use software that lets you create scripts and macros, and prepare your messages and files off-line. Don't pay for the time you spend writing and thinking.*

Other information services that may be of use to you include:

- *Accu-Weather Forecaster* turns a Macintosh into a weather station by accessing the nation's largest private weather service. Price includes software that allows charts, narratives, and graphs to be downloaded. Great for sailors, farmers, and flyers.

- *Dialog* is an on-line information retrieval system with access to over 320 databases focused on business, science, and technology. With 175 million records, there are directory listings of companies, people, associations, corporate financial statements, journal abstracts, and complete text from over 630 magazines, journals, and newsletters. News from the wire services are constantly updated.

- *Dow Jones News/Retrieval* is an on-line service aimed at the business user. The E-Z Online software package connects you to up-to-date news and financial data, business facts, and figures. You can define custom business reports from more than fifty databases.

- *InfoMaster* is a database system from Western Union that provides access to business information. It also provides connect support to several other services.

- *Lexis/Nexis* is a service for news, business, and legal information. Lexis is a specialized legal research database. Nexis is the general and business news and information service.

- *NewsNet* covers over thirty industries and professions with more than 400 newsletters, daily services, and news wires. Articles are full text and can be fully searched and retrieved.

- *TeleMax* includes communications software and on-line services for corporate users and consumer communications. It includes electronic mail, bulletin board systems, file transfer, shopping, electronic publishing services, games, financial services, and support. File transfer includes documents, graphics, even spreadsheets that can be sent directly to someone's mailbox. The interface is written in Apple Macintosh's HyperCard.

- *USA Today Sports Center* provides on-line services for sports and games information. Users can compete in fantasy sports leagues, get sports news, talk with *USA Today* editors, trade memorabilia, and get expert advice. Clipping services are available for teams.

- *Westlaw* offers legal research services. There is a comprehensive law database with case law, statutory law, and administrative law from both federal and state sources. Access to over 2,000 legal databases and a variety of research tools includes a gateway to eight other on-line services.

Software

Communications software can be very simple, such as the communications module in Microsoft Works, or full-featured, as Microphone II is. What you use should be determined by what you need; it's very easy to buy more telecommunications software than you need, but unlike other software categories, this is not necessarily a bad thing. Good telecom software allows you to use the basic features of the program and grow into the more advanced features. In this section we look at some of the major packages that you might want to consider and the features that make them valuable. Many on-line services, such as Prodigy, America Online, and others, ship with proprietary software that serves as the entry to the system, but these are not addressed here because they are part of the service. Still others, such as CompuServe Navigator, Dow Jones' Desktop Express, and Lotus Express for MCI Mail are available at retail outlets.

Good telecom software reduces the number of parameters required in a session to the absolute minimum. You may have to throw the switches for all the different settings in a session, but you should have to do it only once. The software should allow you to save it either as a macro or script. Ideally, you should issue a command and have the software dial and log on for you. More advanced software will navigate a bulletin board system or service and do various file transfers and message uploads and downloads automatically. The more time you spend communicating, the more valuable this can be. Good software saves you money, and if you are a heavy user of on-line services, a package can pay for itself over time.

The most important features in communications software are:

- Automation: Autodial, redial, and autoanswering are useful. Your service might be busy, so an auto-dialer redialing the number until it connects is a great convenience.

- Buffered Keyboard: Places the keystrokes you type into a buffer that can be downloaded as a unit. Allows you to edit a conversation off-line while the other party is sending a message.

- Ease of Use: There should be a basic mode from where you make your choices for communications settings, dial, and go. Text capture and file transfer should be simple. A program that is too complex for a novice will waste time and energy.

- Filters: File translation utilities are often built into communications software so that garbage characters can be removed.

- Macro or Scripting: A scripting language is a valuable method for saving connect time by doing autologons and navigation chores. Some software ships with a complete development environment valuable for constructing front-ends to services and bulletin boards. An "automatic scripting" mode can save the operations you do in a script automatically.

- Terminal Emulation: A terminal emulator turns your PC into a "dumb terminal" so that it can display characters sent to it. Even basic software does TTY (teletype) and DEC VT100 or VT200 terminal emulation.

- Timer: Time is money, and it's valuable to know how long a session has been going on.

- Wide Protocol Support: Text, Binary, XModem, and YModem should be supported. ZModem is an extra. Protocols can affect data transfer rate and reliability and are very valuable. Kermit and IRMA are the two most widely used microcomputer protocols for mainframe access.

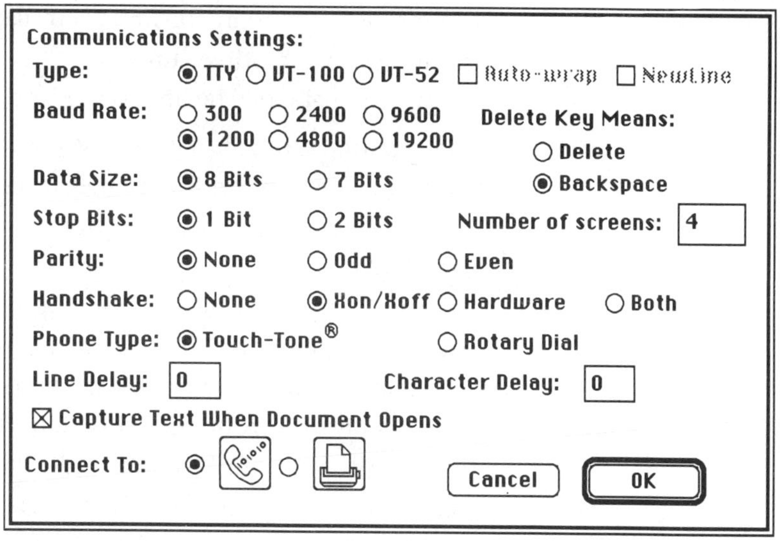

Figure 13-8
Even simple telecom software, such as the module in the integrated package Microsoft Works that ships with many laptops, offers a good collection of settings for connecting to an on-line service or bulletin board.

Communications Settings:

Type:	⦿ TTY ○ VT-100 ○ VT-52 ☐ Auto-wrap ☐ Newline
Baud Rate:	○ 300 ○ 2400 ○ 9600 **Delete Key Means:**
	⦿ 1200 ○ 4800 ○ 19200 ○ Delete
Data Size:	⦿ 8 Bits ○ 7 Bits ⦿ Backspace
Stop Bits:	⦿ 1 Bit ○ 2 Bits **Number of screens:** [4]
Parity:	⦿ None ○ Odd ○ Even
Handshake:	○ None ⦿ Xon/Xoff ○ Hardware ○ Both
Phone Type:	⦿ Touch-Tone® ○ Rotary Dial
Line Delay:	[0] **Character Delay:** [0]

☒ Capture Text When Document Opens

Connect To: ⦿ 📞 ○ 🖨 [Cancel] [OK]

Some of the important communications software on the market includes:

- *Crosstalk MK 4* (PC), *Crosstalk for Windows 1.0* (Win), *Crosstalk XVI 3.71* (PC) are full-featured packages from DCA/Crosstalk Communications. They include most protocols, good terminal emulation, log on scripts for several services, a "Learn Script" mode, and a full scripting language. DCA also sells several products for micro-to-mainframe connection based on the IRMA protocol.

- *DynaComm* (Mac, Win) is a complete package with automatic logon, scripting, terminal emulation, transfer protocols, and function key support. The script is a high-level programmable language.

- *MacBLAST* (Mac), *MS/DOS BLAST* (PC), others, stands for Blocked Asynchronous Transmission. This family of products, based on the BLAST protocol from the Communications Research Group, allows you to do file transfers among Macintosh, IBM PC, minis, micros, and mainframe computers under some thirty operating systems including VAX/VMS, PDP, Data General, Unix, Prime, Xenix, and others. Text, graphics, binary (MacBinary) files can be transferred; the programs offer standard terminal emulation. The BLAST programs offer scripting, automatic file compression, on-line help, automatic dialing and logon, and modem support.

- *Microphone II* (Mac, Win) is the most powerful telecommunications package on the market today with a wide range of protocols, a point-and-click scripting module, and full access to XCMDs (external commands) and XFCNs (external functions). At the simplest level Microphone is very easy to use and offers a complete terminal package, but it can also serve as a sophisticated telecommunications interface design package. Use it as a front-end to bulletin board and on-line services, with custom buttons and dialog boxes, automated scripts and many other features. It comes with a "Watch Me" script writer, free subscriptions, and canned scripts to several on-line services. Version 1.5 is often bundled with third-party modems.

- *Microsoft Works* (Mac, PC) offers a simple communications package that is quite adequate for connecting to a service or bulletin board. For the occasional user, this program has all of the necessary features to get you going. What's lacking is a scripting or macro environment and advanced protocols.

- *ProComm Plus* (PC) is the most popular telecommunications package on the PC. The ProComm version is shareware. It is easy to learn and use and has a compete features set. There is a centralized dialing directory, a powerful script language, keyboard macros (it uses the Alt-key combinations), context-sensitive help, and a large set of protocols.

- *Qmodem* (PC) is an easy-to-use program aimed at novices. It contains context sensitive help, redialing, batch uploads, many protocols including ZModem, and it's easily set up and configured.

- *Smartcom II* (Mac, PC) is a software package that comes bundled with the Hayes Smartcom modem and can check modem parameters and report incorrect settings. It can store twenty-five macros for each phone number, contains a text editor for sending messages, has full text support, and includes a large number of protocols for file transfer. Smartcom is also sold as a stand-alone package.

- *VersaTerm* (Mac) is a text and graphics communication program that allows terminal emulation for DEC VT100, VT220, Data General D200, and Tektronix 4014 terminals. It provides mainframe connection, file transfers, and database access. Most protocols (except ZModem) are provided. VersaTerm has autodial, full macro language support, and is the preferred package for mainframe communications.

- *White Knight* (Mac) is Scott Watson's commercial version of the shareware Red Ryder telecom software. It has gone through more versions than a dog has fleas, sometimes changing versions through the course of a trade show. White

Knight is very powerful with a fuller range of protocols than any other package. Its interface is a little quirky, the scripting language is high level, contains a debugger, and once compiled it runs very quickly. Contains a customizable filter for translating any version of ASCII. A good choice for all levels of users who want a very complete feature set at a reasonable price.

- *ZTerm* (Mac) is the current Macintosh shareware favorite. It gets its name from the fast and most modern transfer protocol, ZModem, which it implements along with several other protocols and terminal emulation. Its main limitation is a lack of scripting language, but otherwise the program is very complete.

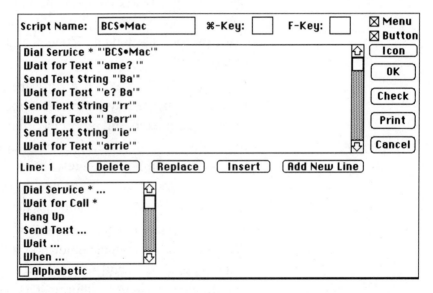

Figure 13-9 For dedicated users, a scripting language is very useful. It can streamline a session or serve as a front-end to services or bulletin boards. The macro language often can automate all features, create routines, buttons, and so on, all with the power of a high-level programming language. Future generations of software will ship with even more powerful object-oriented programming approaches that will make development of communications environments easy. Shown here is the Script dialog box from Microphone II with a "Watch Me" mode, a debugger, and many other features.

Working With Color

*The painter of the future will be a colorist such as there has
never yet been.*

Vincent van Gogh

Color is an important and developing segment of computer publishing technology. It serves the integral function of ordering
related elements such as icons, menus, and other items, and is
obviously central to graphics and color prepress. In the 1990s
color will steadily replace both black-and-white (achromatic) and
single-color (monochromatic) systems for input, display, and output devices. Meanwhile, photographic-quality digital color on the
desktop is in development now and soon will be in use like its
cousin, digital sound.

Still, microcomputer-based color has many challenges related to
calibration among different devices, image manipulation, and the
compression and portability of large color files. This chapter will
explain color theory as it relates to computers and publishing, will
discuss emerging standards for color definition and manipulation,
and will survey the field of color tools for your desktop.

Understanding Color

Color is the mental perception of light received by the eye. Light,
however, can be quantitatively described in terms of wavelength,
intensity, and other variables, while color is much more subjective.

In order for a computer to work with colors, they must be described numerically. That is, every color must be reduced to a binary representation.

Researchers are attempting to quantify color perception by matching the human visual response or sensation of color to various types of light input. For example, a yellow light may be simulated by a mixture of red and green lights, and many other mixtures besides, including such factors as light intensity (brightness) and purity of color (saturation) (see Color Figure C2). Psychophysicists categorize colors in terms of the components that lead to their observation by people, and then attempt to create a numerical model of color generation based on several measurable variables. These models, or colorimetric systems, serve as the basis for describing and working with color in computers.

Absorptive Versus Reflective Color

Color can be produced by light that is emitted by a light source or transmitted through an object (the same thing), or reflected by a surface. These processes produce color in two different ways, as illustrated by Color Figure C2. Emitted light can be thought of as *additive mixing*. As shown in the lower set of overlapped colors, red light + blue light = yellow light; blue + green = cyan; and so on. When all three primary colors are combined, white light results. The RGB (Red, Green, Blue) model is best suited for describing this type of mixing. It is the color model of choice for light emission, and thus for CRT monitors. In fact, as discussed in Chapter 5, RGB is exactly how CRTs produce color, and it is no accident that these color phosphors were selected.

The second effect, reflected light, is shown in the color overlays for subtractive color in Color Figure C2. Here, cyan, magenta, and yellow (CMY) are the complementary colors for each of the three primary colors; that is, white − red = cyan light; magenta is the complement of green, and yellow is the complement of blue. Creating a color in this manner is called *subtractive mixing*, and in theory, mixing equal parts of C, M, and Y gives *black* (K). This is so because the body is absorbing light, while white reflection occurs for an intrinsically colorless object, and a black body absorbs all visible colors. The CMYK (Cyan, Magenta, Yellow, Black) model commonly is used for reflective technologies such as printing and would also be appropriate for reflective displays such as LCDs. You can see the effects of various colored lights' transmission or absorption in the reflective process in the six panels in Color Figure C2.

A description of all possible colors is called a *color space*, and the numerical method used to represent it is called a *color model*. Every computer that assigns color must use a model for input, display, and output. The Macintosh Color Wheel, shown in Color Figure C1, is one implementation of the description of all possible colors. It is based on the RGB model, which breaks down all colors into their red, green, and blue components. If you know the component's numbers, they can be entered in the text boxes, or you can use the scroll bar to adjust intensity and click the color of your choice. The Windows Control Panel Color module works similarly.

Some Colorful Language	Light is a very narrow part of the electromagnetic spectrum, and the measurement of light's speed and its theoretical description is one of the underpinnings of modern physics that every high school student learns. Light has both wave and particle (photon) properties and is described by its wavelength. Visible light is found in the 3,800 to 7,000 angstrom (Å) range (an Å is equal to 10^{-8} meters or 10 nanometers) with the shortest wavelengths below 4,600 Å detected by the eye as violets and blues; from 4,900 to 5,400 Å, as green; and the longest, above 6,100 Å, as oranges and reds. Light can be described also by its intensity of strength and its spectral purity or sharpness. A single wavelength of light would be 100 percent pure and monochromatic—the type of light produced by lasers and other special devices, such as emission spectra of pure elements or compounds. Most light sources are broadband and have a wide spectral distribution. Light from the sun appears white and is very broadband, especially when compared to the narrow window detected by the eye.

The relation of light to color was recognized well before Newton's time. Moisture in the air can split white light into all of the visible colors, forming a rainbow. A similar distribution could be

Figure 14-1
The visible spectrum
and the electromagnetic
spectrum.

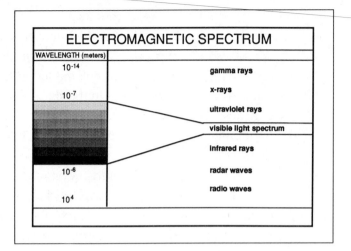

created with a glass prism. Newton studied the splitting and rejoining of color light and devised a circular model based on hues. Most models use the variables of wavelength, which is perceived as color or hue (H); spectral purity, referred to as saturation (S); and intensity, which is described as lightness (L). Quantitative measurement of these three factors is one measure of color space called the HSL model, and Color Figure C1 shows how it can be directly translated numerically by an internal lookup table to the RGB model.

Color Models

Most color models use a system of three variables to describe color. Furthermore, all models use three-color specification. This system has some foundation in physiological terms because the eye has three different color receptors. Some computer color models, including RGB, use absolute measurements such as component colors or brightness, whereas perceptual color models, such as the color space measures developed by the Commission Internationale L'Eclairage in 1931 (see CIE Color Space below), perceive color using psychometric parameters as defined by a statistical group of observers. The essential point is that some color spaces are device specific—RGB—whereas others are device *independent*—the CIE system. RGB space refers to the control of hardware, the electron beams on your CRT, and not color vision. Because different monitors require different voltages, each RGB space is unique. Perceptual and physical descriptions of light are not correlated. This is an important and active area of computer research.

CIE Color Space

The international standard xyY, established in 1931 by the Commission Internationale L'Eclairage (CIE), is the preeminent perceptual model for color specification. Originally intended for creating mixtures of pigments and lights, this model has been extended for use in display and print because it is the one system that allows for device independence, and hence, color matching. One of the advantages of CIE space is that numerical interpretation of color, based on real color matching data, is possible. Vendors in the personal computer industry, including Adobe, RasterOps, Tektonics, Letraset, Kodak, and others, have just begun to adopt the CIE system in an attempt to standardize a unique color scheme. PostScript Level 2 is based on the CIE standard. CIE undoubtedly will be discussed substantially in the trade press in the next couple of years.

CIE recognizes that many combinations of colors can be mixed to create other colors, and it sets about constructing a color space based on vision data. In the original 1931 experiments, light of a specific color was matched to a combination of three primary light sources by a human subject on a 2-degree test circle. There are limitations to the colors that can be mixed to create other colors. For example, a mixture of primary colors can never exactly duplicate a color of a single wavelength. A CIE color space is three-dimensional and appears as a rounded cone, but the diagram shown most often (see Figure 14.2) is a parabolic slice of the CIE color space. It shows pure spectral hues on the outside, where the eye's color gamut (color limit) defines the boundary, and whites at the center, where colors are mixed. Lines drawn through the center of the diagram would connect the colors required to create white light, and any mixture of two colors would exist on those lines. People who are color blind do not have the ability to view colors along these specific CIE lines.

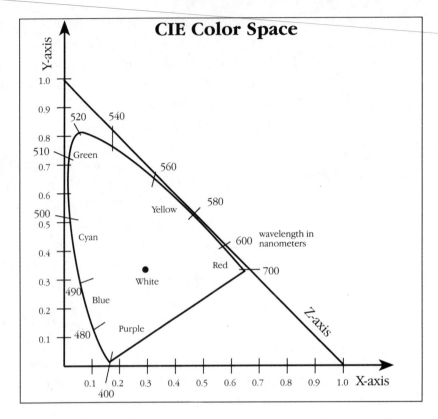

Computers necessitate that color measurements be accurate over large areas, such as monitors. The CIE model redefined the standard in 1964. Most hardware vendors still specify the 1931 CIE space, although the 1964 Large Field CIE color space is more appropriate for many viewing purposes. The conversion tables from CIE to computer RGB and HSL models also are widely known. CIE space is nonlinear and requires that phosphors and ink colors be measured for mixtures to be matched. It is not particularly sensitive to brightness factors, and only hue and saturation are modeled. Thus, the colors of a chocolate bar and a red lipstick appear very close together on a CIE diagram. However, extensions of the CIE model such as UCS (Uniform Color Space), CIELUV, CIELAB, and others have appeared to address some of these concerns.

RGB Color Space and Displays

The RGB model, based on combinations of red, green, and blue light to compose all colors, is used for light emission and CRT displays. Additive mixing in this model synthesizes white light, whereas combining pairs of primary colors produces the secondary colors of CMY. When light intensity is varied, a full palette of colors can be achieved. Most often, RGB space is depicted by a cube where each of three opposing corners on the main axes is a primary color (see Figure 14.3). The remaining corners are the three secondary colors, and black and white (at the origin). Grays are found on the white/black axis; red is opposite to cyan, green to magenta, and blue to yellow.

RGB colors may be quantified and then translated to the HSL color model for a particular device. Axis are normalized to 1, and colors are a vector sum of components. RGB values are not, however, related in a linear fashion to phosphor intensity on a monitor, and therefore require a lookup table for display. The values determined for each monitor are unique. RGB is the current standard for computer graphics, and conversion has been determined for most of the other color models. RGB emphasizes hardware implementation of color at the expense of color perception. Put another way, RGB space is perceptually nonuniform.

Figure 14-3
The RGB model representation. Each axis is normalized to one unit, and any color can be represented by vector addition.

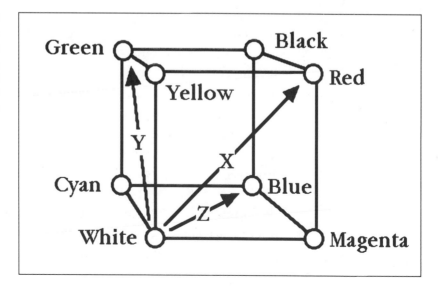

Two other models—HSL for hue, saturation, and lightness; and HSV (the V stands for value)—are mappings of RGB space into transformations that attempt to model perceptual color. These models are limited by hardware and are not specifically related to color perception. HSL is represented by a cylindrical coordinate system transformed onto a cube. The resultant shape is a double hexcone. HSV takes RGB space and tilts the cube onto its back corner. These models are sometimes used in paint programs because they yield easy-to-use controls, but they require more complex mathematics to describe composite colors. Both systems also yield unique monitor calibration values.

The CMYK Model and Printing

The CMYK system, which uses the colors cyan, magenta, yellow, and black as its component colors, is the model of choice for subtractive color mixtures. Color paints and dyes printed on surfaces form thin films that act like colored filters, trapping or absorbing some colors and reflecting others. An inked surface appears yellow when it reflects long-wavelength or blue light and short-wavelength or red light while absorbing middle-wavelength or green light (see Color Figure C2). The print industry use process inks that are transparent to about two-thirds of the incident light. Printers identify process cyan as that ink which absorbs only red light; process magenta absorbs green light, and process yellow absorbs only blue. Process inks minimize the loss of lightness and saturation. Artists, on the other hand, use opaque inks and have a color scheme based on RGB.

Four-color printing uses a screening technique to break up colored pictures into a halftone screen, because printing inks used are basically opaque (see Color Figure C5). A similar process is used in digital imaging to create grayscale images (see Chapter 10). Each area of the picture is converted to colored dots of a certain size and shape so that the overall visual appearance re-creates the original picture. The pattern of dot intersection is often referred to as a rosette. Screening algorithms are a proprietary process created by equipment vendors and are often part of page

Figure 14-4
(A) The HSL model
representation.
(B) The HSV model
representation.

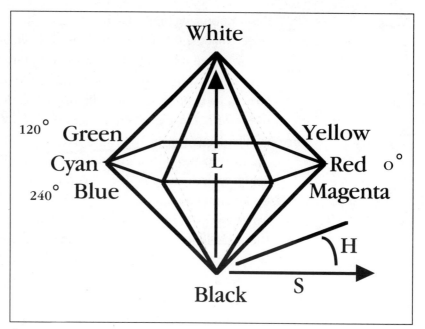

A.

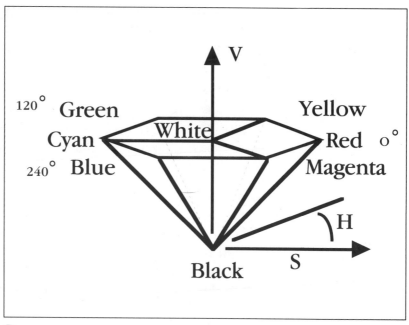

B.

description languages. Each process color is offset (screened) by a selected angle so that, as much as possible, ink dots don't overlap. Ideally, screening angles would be separated by 90 degrees each, but there are too many colors to allow this. A compromise of around 60 degrees each for the darker black, magenta, and cyan is used, with the perceptually lighter yellow maintaining a much smaller angle (particularly in respect to cyan).

Print cyan, yellow, and magenta, and, in theory, you would achieve black. In practice, it is difficult to achieve pure black in this manner. Current process dye technology doesn't absorb all wavelengths of light, and often brown is the result. Furthermore, there is a limit to the amount of ink that can be applied to a sheet of paper, particularly glossy paper. By using black ink instead, you can get a good black and reduce the amount of ink necessary on the paper.

Creating grays (especially dark shades) is another example of how color mixing is important. You can create gray by mixing the correct amounts of cyan, yellow, and magenta together, or alternatively, by mixing black ink with the white of your paper. In the first case you get extensive ink coverage (and probably smearing); in the latter case you achieve the same effect with less ink. This principle of creating grays by removing complementary colors equally and replacing them with black ink is called gray component replacement (GCR). A similar process called undercolor removal (UCR) removes CYM in nongray dark areas and replaces those three colors with black ink for the same reasons.

▼ *Tip: The hardest colors to achieve in a four-color printing process are the shades of gray from white to black because they require balanced ink coverage. When proofing a print, always look at these colors first. Other important colors are the so-called memory colors: the flesh color of a face, the green of the grass, the blue of the sky, and so on; other colors are less important to inspect.*

The Pantone Library

In 1963, Pantone, Inc. (Carlstadt, NJ), the ink manufacturing giant, developed a system of 747 color standards that it calls the Pantone Matching System (PMS). This system is meant for use in spot color applications where each color is printed as a layer with a separate impression. Spot color prints can be laid down as a blanket or can be screened to lower the amount of ink coverage required. Printers often refer to a Pantone ink as the "fifth color" because it is not specified by CYMK halftones. This also means that you will pay more for Pantone inks than for process colors because they involve additional preparation. Printers will try, however, to match Pantone colors with CYMK if requested to hold down costs. The higher cost of Pantone inks means that they tend to be used infrequently in large print runs, and are found more often in small shops where precise colors are desired—typical microcomputer applications.

PMS uses up to eleven inks in combination to provide this library of colors. These specifications take into account different types of paper, coated or uncoated, along with some other variables. And although no conventional four-color process can simulate exactly Pantone inks, Pantone and many other licensed manufacturers have been fairly successful in re-creating them as four-color inks for print or as three-color phosphors for on-screen use. Pantone colors have been mapped to CIE, RGB, and CMYK space. Many programs, such as Letraset ColorStudio, Adobe Illustrator, Aldus FreeHand, PixelPaint, and QuarkXPress, now have Pantone selection dialog boxes; Quark's is shown in Color Figure C9. Some Pantone color mappings are approximate; usually a program will warn you when this is the case. To date, only 736 colors are offered on computers—the high-intensity fluorescent and metallic colors have yet to be translated. Printer manufacturers, including QMS and Océ, also are implementing the Pantone system.

Pantone swatch books, such as the *Pantone Color Formula Guide,* are available at most graphics arts stores, and single pages are also available (see Color Figure C10). For computer implementations of Pantone refer to *Color Matching*, by Michael and Pat Rogondino, which supplies 10,000 swatches of color output with the CMYK color percentage specifications that created them. Also, see *Pantone Process Color Simulation Guide* from Pantone itself. This approach bypasses the problem of color matching, but is really only a starting point. You need a lot more colors to do serious prepress process color matching. Color Curve Systems (Minneapolis, MN) offers 2,185 graduated colors based on the CIE space, but this system has yet to be translated to CMYK and microcomputer software.

How Digital Color Is Formed

Computers store a binary description of a pixel's color in memory. In this sense, storing color information is exactly the same as storing grayscale information for a pixel. The size of the data stored in memory has a direct impact on the number of colors that can be displayed. Color Figure C4 shows the effect of increasing color values for both grayscale and color pictures in print. In order to reduce the size of stored color information, color values are compared to a palette of color values for output.

Bits and Colors

Images are created in memory as a description called a frame buffer. A frame buffer doesn't store explicit color values for each pixel, but its data points to the addresses in memory where that information is stored. In order to translate a frame buffer to a bit map that can be used by a monitor, the buffer is sent to a color lookup table (CLUT) for processing. The CLUT is a software matrix of all possible color values, with rows corresponding to a color's value and columns corresponding to the state (R on, G off, B on) of each color primary. A frame buffer might use 8 bits to produce 256 combinations of RGB, but if those 256 combinations are used as pointers to addresses chosen from a table of HSL values, the possible colors would be nearly limitless, while the data describing it would be quite compact. CLUTs typically are part of an application. Device drivers, those pieces of software responsible for color input and output, also come with video lookup tables. Once the frame buffer is remapped by the CLUT, the resulting bit map is

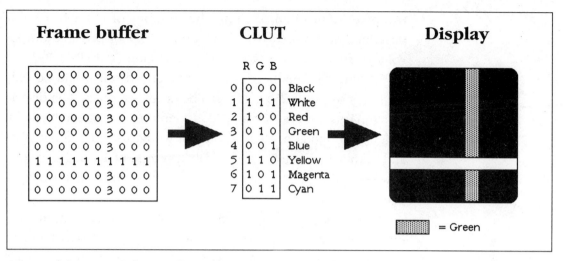

Figure 14-5 Mapping a frame buffer to a bit map by using a CLUT as a color reference.

sent to a digital-to-analog converter (DAC) to generate the appropriate electrical signals. The levels from the DAC normally determine color value, not RGB assignments.

Pixel depth usually doesn't match the width of the CLUT, which means that mapping of colors within the available color gamuts and other customizations, such as special shadings or color effects, can be accomplished. A CLUT can use a custom palette that is appropriate to the image you want to create. Additionally, when a display is capable only of processing a small number of colors per bit map, the CLUT can make the translation from a larger data set stored in memory. A computer storing 16.8 million colors in memory, but capable of displaying only 256 at a time, applies a sampling algorithm to create a custom CLUT. Vendors produce color samples to work within the pixel depth in order to limit the image processing time so that your computer's speed doesn't drop to a crawl, but speed and resolution are always a tradeoff in the computer game.

▼ *Tip: To improve the speed of your computer system, set your monitor to display only a few colors.*

The threshold level for photorealism or museum-quality printing is reached at the 16-bit per pixel level, $2^{16} = 65,536$ colors. If the pixel depth is 8 bits and the number of planes of color described is three (RGB), then the number of possible output voltages from the DAC would be 16.8 million ($2^{(\text{bits per pixel by bit planes})}$), but the number of colors referenced still would be only 2^8. That's why only 256 colors can be described on an 8-bit display system. This kind of display is considered to be medium-resolution (VGA) standard. High resolution would use 24 bits per pixel and output 16.8 million colors from a palette of 1.1 billion colors. Low resolution (CGA) typically uses 4 bits per pixel, a 4,096 color palette with a 16-color display.

Colors are great, but computers often use techniques for improving the apparent color palette at the expense of resolution, such as dithering or mixing colors into superpixels that the mind can average to other colors. The Amiga uses a special technique called "hold and modify," or HAM, to improve its color performance and to display all 4,096 colors in its palette. Here, all the different sets of colors are polled rapidly with each screen refresh and then updated as needed. A special chip called "Denise" is responsible for this process. As a result, the Amiga is blessed with some excellent, low-priced hardware and software for creating stunning color graphics, modeling, and animation software, even though, on the face of it, the Amiga has a restricted palette and modest color handling capability.

Calibrating Color Displays

Computers form color images on a CRT screen by using three energy beams to raster scan the screen. Turning on and off at pixel locations, the three sets of colored phosphors are excited. Red, green, and blue phosphors combine to create additive light emission. When a color value is assigned, a pixel is mapped by the CLUT, and the DAC outputs the voltages that generate the desired composite colors. Not all monitors use the same phosphors, and therefore RGB values result in different colors on each monitor. Every monitor has a different range of colors, called its color gamut, which is affected by the phosphors used, including the brightness and contrast settings.

Figure C1
The Macintosh Color Wheel (or Color Picker)

A unique color may be specified using the RGB or HSB models.

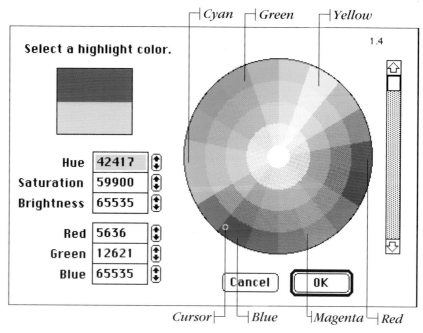

Figure C2
Color Theory

Subtractive colors are composed from light reflected from an object.
Additive colors are composed of light emission or transmission from an object.

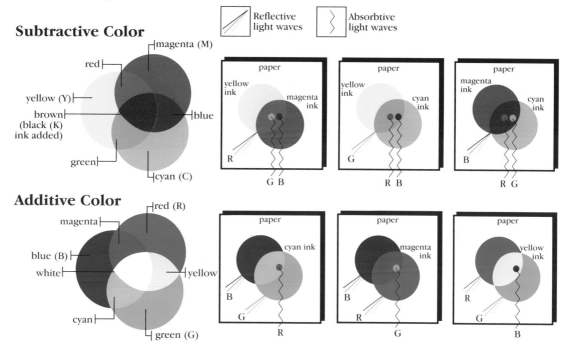

Figure C3
Desktop Color Separation

(A) In the first step, a color slide is scanned by transmission or a color print is scanned by reflection. (B) Software is used to perform color correction and image manipulation, then separates the digital file into its cyan, magenta, yellow and black color components. (C) Four film negatives for each printing ink color are created on an imagesetter. (D) Printing plates are created from the negatives by a commercial printer. (E) Lastly, each ink is applied to the paper to create the final printed image.

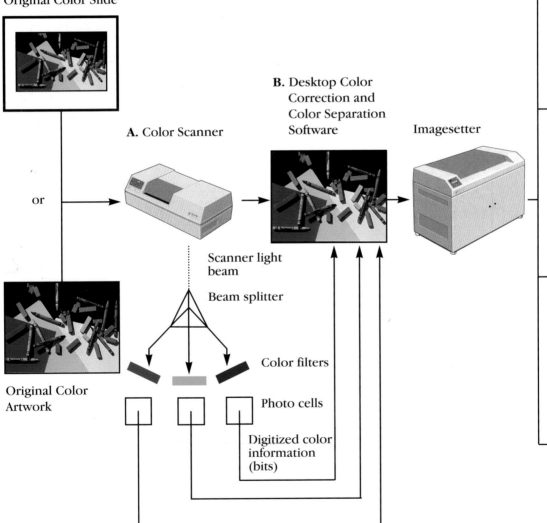

Original Color Slide

or

Original Color Artwork

A. Color Scanner

B. Desktop Color Correction and Color Separation Software

Imagesetter

Scanner light beam

Beam splitter

Color filters

Photo cells

Digitized color information (bits)

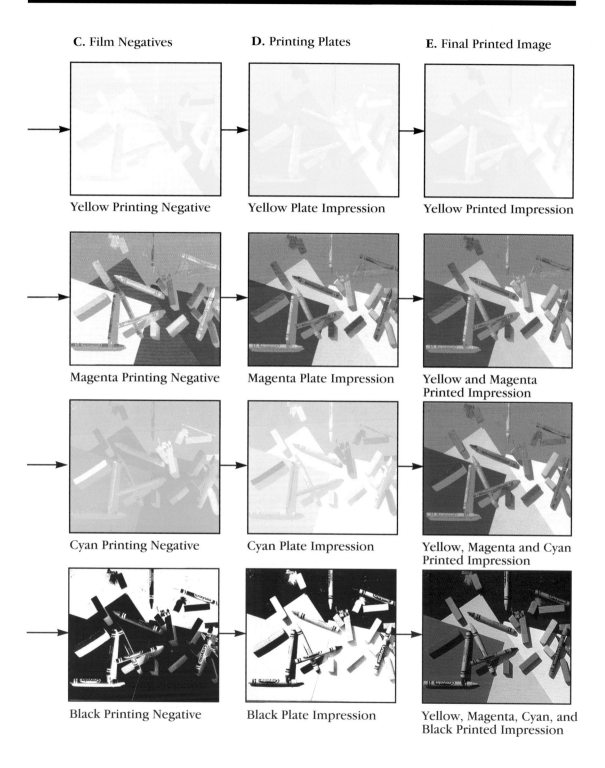

C. Film Negatives

D. Printing Plates

E. Final Printed Image

Yellow Printing Negative

Yellow Plate Impression

Yellow Printed Impression

Magenta Printing Negative

Magenta Plate Impression

Yellow and Magenta
Printed Impression

Cyan Printing Negative

Cyan Plate Impression

Yellow, Magenta and Cyan
Printed Impression

Black Printing Negative

Black Plate Impression

Yellow, Magenta, Cyan, and
Black Printed Impression

By saving different levels of data for each pixel, you can restrict or enhance the number of greys or colors in a picture.

2 bit Black and White

4 bit Color

4 bit, 16 Grey Levels

8 bit Color

8 bit, 256 Grey Levels

24 bit Color

Halftone screen angles for four color process negatives generated by programs such as Adobe PhotoShop® and Letraset ColorStudio® use 45° for black, 90° for yellow, 108.4° for cyan, and 161.6° for magenta. This is considered the optimum setting for most high-resolution Postcript imagesetting devices. Traditional printer halftone screen angles are different. The halftone process is a proprietary computer algorithm that evaluates the colors in a particular location and simulates those colors with a pattern of primary ink color spots. These spots are offset at various angles to that they don't overlap. The eye views the output recreating the original pattern from the simulated one.

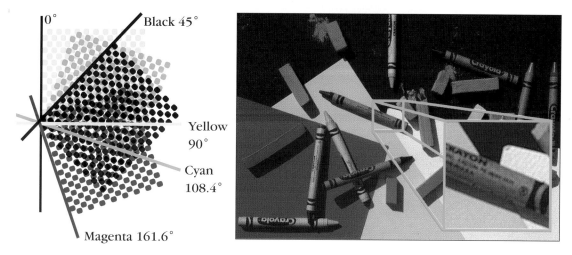

Figure C6
Determining
and Matching
Color Gamuts

A color gamut is the range of colors that may be created or viewed. Computers can create all colors and monitors can display most colors. Output devices allow yet a smaller subset of colors, while the human eye has the smallest gamut. This figure doesn't address color sensitivity, which for the human eye is non-linear for different colors.

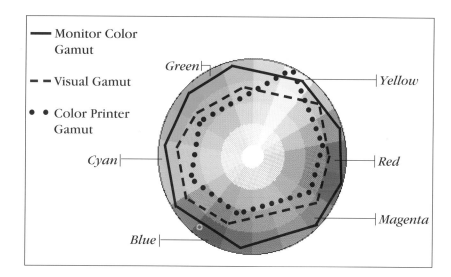

Paint programs with special tools are being applied to digital images to recreate an electronic darkroom on your desktop.

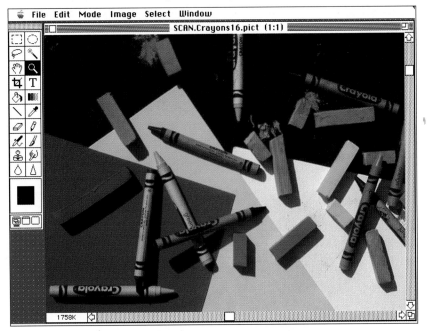

Color paint programs off a complete artist's development environment for spectacular effects and realistic applications.

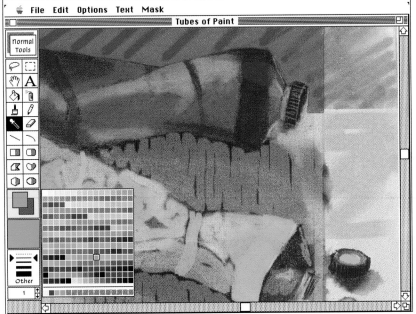

© 1990 Illustrations: Donna Merrell Chernin

Figure C9
Special Color Effects

Using color paint programs or digital image processing an artist can create spectacular new effects. Here Adobe Photoshop® was used to create four effects. (A) Posterization applies an algorithm to limit color values. (B) Diffuse reduces edges by averaging adjacent pixel color values. (C) Twirl applies an algorithm to smear colors in a circular pattern. (D) Find edges defines the edges of the image, and Impressionist reads in the colors from the last saved version of the image, then smears together the colors of the pixels beneath.

A. Posterization

B. Diffuse

C. Twirl

D. Find Edges and Impressionist

The Pantone® Matching System (PMS) mixes inks using standardized color formulas. A color can be exactly specified by a corresponding number. This system, most useful for spot color applications, shows up as color panels or dialog boxes in many programs. For the most accurate representation of a PMS color ink, Pantone, Inc. produces color specifier books containing small swatches of inks printed on both coated and uncoated papers.

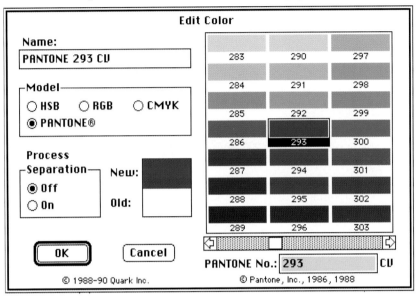

Quark XPress® Pantone® color dialog box.

Pantone® Color Matching Systen
Color Specifier (swatch book).

A set of voltage corrections, called a gamma curve, is used to translate the output value of a monitor so as to adjust its brightness level. Computers interpret the transition from white to black, or from light colors to dark colors, in a linear fashion, but the human eye responds logarithmically. Gamma correction measures the evenness of transition across the color space and compensates for any mismatch. Gamma curves are properties of individual monitors, and along with the color gamut, can change with the age of the monitor, temperature, humidity, and several other factors.

You can calibrate a monitor in hardware or in software so that the colors displayed are true and reproducible. The Barco Calibrator monitor uses a sensing cup device to measure the luminence of colors in a test pattern and uses hardware to self-adjust calibration circuitry to adjust the excitation voltages. The RasterOps True Color Calibrator Display System uses its sensor to adjust the voltage lookup table in the monitor's video card, but this is an expensive solution and opinion is divided about its utility for all but supercritical work by color scientists. Less expensive solutions that are more appropriate for average users are coming to market. An ordinary high-resolution monitor can be calibrated using the same sensing cup arrangement, but the settings are saved in software as a gamma correction table.

The SuperMac SuperMatch system and the Radius Precision-Color Calibrator take the software approach. SuperMatch uses the Tektronix TekColor memory-resident control panel device (CDEV), which replaces the Macintosh Color Wheel. The TekColor CDEV is based on the CIE model, while the Color Wheel is based on the RGB color space. SuperMatch TekColor calibration can be matched to the TekColor calibrations on printers to achieve good color matching. Radius has licensed the Pantone Matching System, and the CIE-to-RGB conversion routines determined by Pantone will yield very accurate Pantone ink colors on a calibrated screen. Both the D50 indoor light and D65 daylight illumination can be achieved. D50 mimics a press sheet seen in a printing plant. This system also achieves print color fidelity to Pantone inks. Undoubt-

Figure 14-6
The PrecisionColor Calibrator is a display calibration device for the Radius Color Display Systems for the Macintosh. Radius has licensed the Pantone Matching System for calibrated matching of PMS inks to their display on screen.

edly, display calibration will become much cheaper and more pervasive over the next couple of years as full color boards become common on IBM PCs using Windows.

Color Matching

The recent implementation of 32-bit QuickDraw on the Macintosh and Microsoft's 24-bit color standard on Windows 3.0 has propelled the issue of obtaining color fidelity to the forefront in microcomputers. This issue is important to designers, and in color prepress applications as well. Color matching is a complex problem that requires as many as three separate calibration procedures for the three different devices involved:

- Input: Obtain correct color data from your input device (scanner).
- Display: View the same colors your data intended on your monitor or display. Your monitor must also simulate the color temperature you wish to achieve in output. The American National Standards Institute (ANSI) specifies a 5,000 degree K color temperature for its viewing standard.

- Output: Match the colors on your output device (printer) to the colors on your original artwork or the colors created on your monitor.

Even if you obtain light of the same color (hue) in hard copy that you had on your monitor, the fact that the former is reflective and the latter is absorptive light mixing means that the overall light intensity probably is different—lower for reflective light. A yellow light on your monitor will be much brighter than the yellow on paper simply because more emitted light is entering your eyes. It is also difficult to match saturations (spectral purity) between display and hard copy. Inks reflect a broader spectrum of light than phosphor emissions, and thus subtractive mixing always appears less saturated. You can increase the specular reflection of an inked surface by using glossy paper—it reproduces the colors from a CRT more accurately. Any system of color matching attempts to account for basic, inherent mismatches, but generic problems also must always be dealt with. Mismatched color gamuts always limit the fidelity of a color match, and matching color gamuts to monitors where different phosphors are used is always more difficult than matching gamuts to printers.

Consider also that lighting conditions play a critical role in color matching. If you are in a studio where the ambient light varies during the day, you either will have to create a standard light viewing area or run through your calibration procedure before any analysis. Artificial lighting with a specified brightness can alleviate this problem somewhat, and it's particularly important for your monitor, because it's not easily portable.

For best color matching ink jet printers give better results than other technologies, even dye sublimation printers. Ink jet inks are better balanced than process inks. The $7,000 Tektronix ColorQuick CSQ and the $50,000 Iris (Bedford, MA) ink jet printers are notable.

Pantone matching is a good approach, but it still results in varying degrees of quality. The original Pantone RGB specifications were done on a Mitsubishi monitor and don't match the popular Sony Trinitron screens used on a Macintosh. New specifications for Sony monitors have just appeared. About 10 percent of Pantone inks fall outside a typical monitor's color gamut anyway, so they have to be approximated. Also, the specifications for Pantone are printed in a YMCK order, which doesn't match the print world's CMYK order, and screen angles are not specified. All these factors result in subtle color differences. Pantone is addressing them, but for now, its swatches work exactly only when a printer uses Pantone inks. Pantone process ink simulations in computer color programs yield a much less accurate match, and many are now outdated. Don't assume your program uses the most up-to-date values. Compare its CMYK values to the latest official Pantone specification.

Because each device may use a different color model, there arises the additional problem of translating between models. Many factors, such as the nature of your input medium (film or paper), the light temperature of your screen, the viewing light, the nature of the inks used, the quality of your output medium (absorbent versus glossy paper), and a dozen others also come into play. No one translation routine is sufficient. Obviously, some standards must be defined in order to limit the variables and achieve specific results. These standards are being vigorously developed by the computer industry and undoubtedly will begin to affect the average user over the next few years.

Most color matching schemes are based on CIE space. Tektronix (Beaverton, OR), long a leader in workstation technology, has developed TekColor for the Macintosh based on the CIE UCS color space. A Tekcolor CDEV replaces the Color Wheel CDEV, using an HVC (hue, value, and chroma) mapping of CIE. A user picks a hue, and then is presented with the TekColor 2D leaf or slice of the color space. There the user can see the range of available colors of the monitor and printer and make a match. TekColor still requires screen calibration, but it simplifies the color matching process. It is supposed to work well with the color specifications in PostScript Level 2, released in mid-1991. The Kodak Prophesy prepress system uses the CIELUV description. Primary system software vendors, such as Apple and Microsoft, have been slow to adopt perceptual color models for color matching.

Figure 14-7
Tektronix's TekColor
matching system is
based on the HVC
model, similar to CIE
space. Any device, such
as a monitor or printer,
is mapped for its color
gamut and identical col-
ors can be compared.
When there is no over-
lap, similar colors
can be assigned.

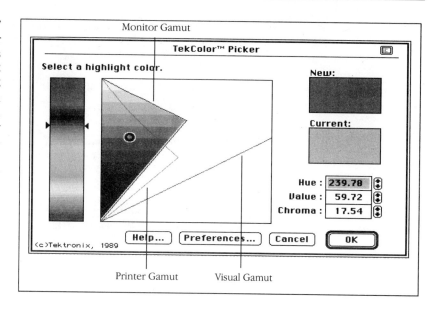

One final caveat about color matching: No matter how careful you are in calibration, and even if you are able to get perfect sepa-rations, proofs, or color prints, once you take your masters to a printer you still may run into trouble. Printing ink, although sub-ject to rigorous controls, still varies by lot, and your printer can work only within the limits of the materials. If color matching is vital to your work, choose a printer capable of and very experi-enced in doing museum-quality printing. It is also a good idea to be present at the start of a press run to check a proof yourself.

Color Separations

Because printing ink is opaque, color can be printed as a solid color, a single screened color, or as a blend of screened colors. Four-color printing requires that the image be converted to four separate halftones for each CMYK printing ink. A specialized piece of software, called a color separation program, takes the colors on your screen and converts them into a form that your printer can use. Pages or files are transformed into a set of four files, one file for each of the process colors. Some applications use a master or the original file as an index that links all of the separation files together. Be aware that color separation can yield a set of four 10

MByte files from a master file of 2 MBytes in size. Some separators will yield additional files for each spot color specified. The result is a set of printed sheets on either film or paper, called negatives, that serve as a printer's plate impression. The process of separation is illustrated in Color Figure C3.

▼ *Tip: When sending out separated files for imagesetting, make sure you send all related files on disk. One of the most common mistakes is to send the separated files without the master file (when the separator produces one), just as one of the most common mistakes in page layout is to send the layout file without linked images.*

Color separation takes into account many variables and either manually or automatically specifies:

- Color control: Separators have algorithms to break down composite colors to process colors. Even spot or Pantone ink colors can be separated. Output is specified in your file as areas of color in a certain percentage. A separator does *not* specify the density and size of printed dots.

- Dot gain: The generation of halftone dots is accomplished by the RIP in the printer (a PostScript process) or halftone separations are created from the master copy by your printer's photographic screen. Separators often allow you to gain compensation by adjusting the density of color in your file.

- Screen specifications: Imprecise screen angles yield moiré patterns that can be removed with fine-angle adjustment. Knowing the screen density (lines per inch) and the paper type enables a separator to adjust the image density appropriately.

- Registration: Precise placement is required to re-create the original continuous tone (contone) image. As little as one-half a dot width off in placement of a print impression can yield fuzzy pictures or moiré patterns. Separation software prints registration marks as circles with crosshairs to aid in alignment and cropping.

- Trapping: If registration is not perfect where two colors abut, you can get a white line when printed. Trapping is the process where the two areas are extended slightly so that they will overlap. Trapping can be done manually by the designer, but higher-end color separation software will also build traps for you. Trapping problems can also occur in printing when not enough ink is printed on top of another ink layer.

- Undercolor removal (UCR) and gray component replacement (GCR): These are both methods for removing cyan, yellow, and magenta inks equally, and replacing them with a smaller quantity of black ink. The net effect is better contrast, and less ink used, resulting in less smearing, hence less dot gain.

- Image adjustments: Tone, contrast, and color saturation often can be modified from within color separation software. Some software has internal densitometers to measure color density on screen, and many allow you to calibrate imagesetter-separated output to measurements made with a real densitometer. Softening and sharpening filters and many tools found in image editors often are included.

- Output options: Images can be negative or positive with emulsion up or down. Masks also can be created to indicate "for position only," or FPO.

PostScript separation works by screening pictures into machine spots of up to 256 pixels on an imagesetter. At 2450 dpi, a spot could be as large as 0.1045 inch and would represent a 100 percent screen, whereas one imagesetter dot would comprise only a 1 percent screen. Spots can be many shapes: round, elliptical, square, cross, line, or custom shapes. Smaller than 50 percent dots appear as black on a white background; larger than 50 percent appear as white dots on a black background; and at the 50/50 interface, black and white appear as equal-size squares that are a PostScript artifact or defect most viewers perceive as banding. Some imagesetters produce spots that are dense and well defined, and in the trade they are referred to as "small spots" or "hard spots," which are preferable to those that produce fuzzy dots. PostScript separation also is subject to banding when graded screens are used; this is more pronounced in darker colors, grades over longer distances, and lower resolutions or screen frequencies. Refer to Agfa Corporation's "An Introduction to Digital Color Prepress" for an excellent description of PostScript screens.

Separation Software

Separation software is on the leading edge of desktop publishing technology. In this rapidly changing, complex area, packages range from $200 up to $50,000 to $1,000,000 for workstation solutions, such as Scitex systems. In the sections that follow we focus on desktop separation packages. Higher-end prepress systems are described in Chapter 15.

There are many color separation programs on the market; some are stand-alone packages, such as Aldus Preprint, while others are built directly into application software, such as Aldus FreeHand, Adobe Photoshop, and QuarkXPress. Most desktop color separation software is based on PostScript, which is not nearly as mature as the high-end prepress processing systems. These systems use proprietary processes and require trained operators. PostScript Level 2 undoubtedly will bridge some of the gap between the two. The goal of desktop color separation packages is to bring this sophisticated, arcane discipline into the hands of the average user. Software is largely automated, and the range of controls over the variables mentioned in the previous section are condensed into a narrow set of windows.

Color separation software is changing so rapidly that it is hard to rank this category. PostScript Level 2's 1991 introduction probably will change this category completely. For now, you can find good separation within:

- *Adobe Photoshop* (Mac): Separates files using a PostScript program based on Adobe Separator. Photoshop (and ColorStudio) accepts many file formats, but is not as sharp as Preprint or XPress.

- *Adobe Separator* (Mac, PC): A separate application that is bundled with Adobe Illustrator.

- *Aldus FreeHand* (Mac): Separates files from within the application with good results.

Figure 14-8
Aldus PrePrint desktop separations program features an Auto enhance tool for color-correction analysis and adjustment that automatically optimizes highlights, midtones, and shadows. Preprint color separates entire PageMaker publications, including TIFF images.

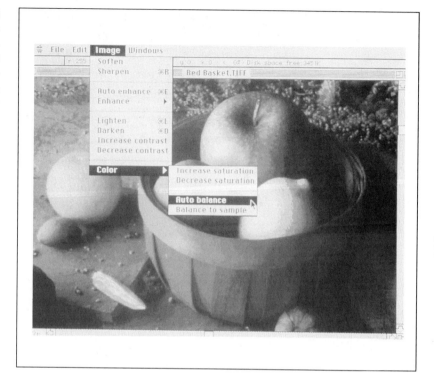

- *Aldus Preprint* (Mac): Accepts files from PageMaker and other programs and it works with PageMaker Color Extensions. Preprint produces good results but has minor problems with TIFF and with printing in its current version. Incorporates the Aldus Open Press Interface (OPI) file format, which consists of PostScript comments that provide information about placement, size, and cropping of color TIFF images. Using OPI as a standard format, you can link to high-end prepress systems.

- *ColorSep/PC* (Win3): Another full-page separation program, published by Ozette Technologies. Handles complete page layouts rather than single images.

- *CorelDRAW* (Win): Effective at separating drawn objects, less so for paint or digital images.

- *Image-In-Color* (Win3): Created in Germany in coordination with Agfa-Compugraphic, it also includes optical character recognition and autotracing capabilities.

- *Letraset ColorStudio* (Mac): An image editing program that produces excellent results. It has a unique facility to handle Pantone colors, decomposing them into CMYK. It can also take CMYK and translate it to the nearest Pantone color. Impressive for packaging applications.

- *Micrografx Designer* (Win): Effective at separating drawn objects, less so for paint or digital images.

- *PhotoMac* (PC): An image editing program with separation. Results are fair, requiring correction.

- *Publisher's Prizm* (Win3): A full-page separator from Insight Systems.

- *PhotoStyler* (Win3): This powerful manipulation and separation program developed by U-Lead, now marketed by Aldus. It's similar to Photoshop, with many of the same capabilities. It works with TIFF, TGA, EPS, and other graphics formats.

- *QuarkXPress* (Mac, NeXT, Win, OS/2): Has a reputation as one of the best applications for handling color. Its separation utility was determined to produce the best results in a recent publication comparing output.

- *SpectrePrint Pro* (Mac, PC): A high-price package from Prepress Technologies that gives very sharp separations, among the best for desktop programs. A cheaper entry, called SpectrePrint II, is also available. Packages exist for PageMaker (SpectreSep PM) and QuarkXPress (SpectreSeps QX).

Printing Color Separations

Even correctly and precisely prepared film separations may not print properly. Printing presses tend to stretch paper in the direction the paper flows, and paper shifts horizontally. Shifts of just a few thousandths of an inch can cause registration problems that affect color printing in particular. White lines, misalignment of type fills, and other printing defects can result. In addition, background and foreground colors composed of common process colors that aren't trapped properly will show through. Thus, a letter that is 80C/60M/40Y on a background of 20C/60M will show a line of 20C/60M.

Trapping   In the past, these were issues for printers, but desktop separation packages have shifted the responsibility to designers and users. As mentioned in brief previously, trapping is the solution to registration problems and can be accomplished in several ways. Traditionally trapping was done by a professional camera operator in a separation house by slightly overexposing one film separation while underexposing another. The overexposed film produced a color spread, while the underexposed film provided a color choke, causing different abutting colors to overlap slightly.

Desktop separation programs don't generally use chokes and spreads to trap. Rather, a trap is created by drawing a line where colors meet in one of the separations to overprint the color below. Half the line overlays one region, while the other half falls into the second area. When a color is used as a fill, trapping is particularly important. In prepress terminology, a line overprints a trap, while a fill knocks out (or eliminates) a background. Adobe Illustrator, Adobe Photoshop, Aldus FreeHand, and QuarkXPress enable the user to create traps for type and objects of various widths.

▼ *Tip: To trap two colors where the common colors would show through, create a line with a different color. To trap two colors with common colors, use the highest percentage of each color. To trap a black created as a process mixture of CYM, use a 100 percent black stroke to knock out the object to be trapped. To trap a line of any shape, create a thicker line than the original line overprints. When overprinting uncommon colors, if there are no similar colors, the foreground image adds its color to the background. When overprinting similar colors, the largest percentage of color shows through in the trap.*

UCR and GCR are processes where black ink replaces the CYM process inks. Although most programs accomplish these effects in the background, some programs, such as Adobe's Photoshop, are beginning to offer control over these settings. Generally they are hidden as settings called black levels with these choices: none, light, medium, heavy, and maximum. When images have small areas of black, increasing black ink can improve contrast without

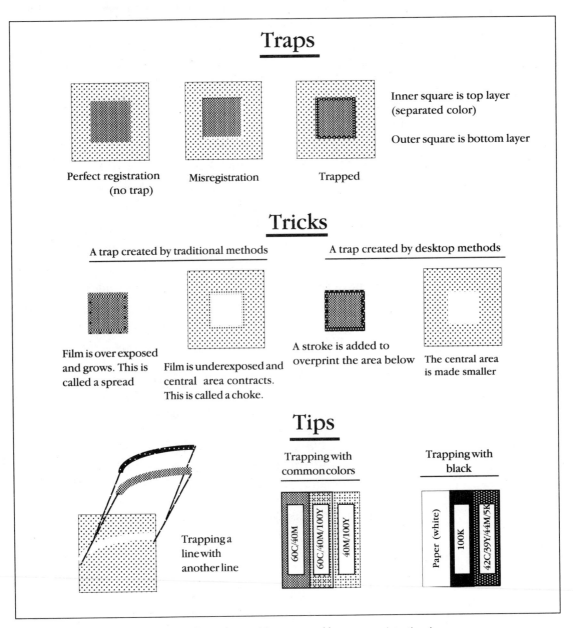

Figure 14-9 (Top) Trapping is used to solve problems caused by poor registration in printing. (Center) In traditional printing a trap is set by using a spread and a choke. Desktop separation uses special techniques, such as overprinting, to eliminate misprints. (Bottom) Lines can be trapped by using thicker lines below, common and uncommon colors, and composite blacks with real black.

color loss. Images with large black areas may suffer not only significant loss of colors but also lose contrast in shadow areas. UCR is helpful in reducing misregistration by hiding the process colors that would otherwise show through. One caution, however: Excessive use of UCR can cause poor and abrupt color transitions from light to dark. Using black ink can also save a lot of money in ink charges, but the most important reason for using these techniques is to avoid excessive inking of paper. In high-speed printing there is little time for the ink to dry, and web presses require that no more than 250 to 260 percent total ink coverage (TIC) be attempted. The current SWOP (Specifications for Web Offset Publications) recommends a maximum 300 percent for coated paper. The best way to address this problem is to ask your printer for advice.

When the screening pattern is well constructed and the screen angles are correct, the printed result is the illusion of color and pattern. A poorly aligned screen can yield a moiré pattern that destroys this illusion. PostScript and the Adobe Emerald RIPs are noted for this problem. Reduce the problem of moirés in PostScript screens by choosing colors carefully. Black areas require the densest rosette pattern and are a particular problem. Other dark areas, such as browns, grays, and purples, also are more prone to moiré patterns. Reducing the amount of black used in UCR and GCR also helps to eliminate moirés. Another solution is to use other halftoning hardware and software products, and to always experiment and proof. PostScript Level 2's finer control over screening angles will also help in this matter.

From Prepress to Print

Some said, "John, print it"; others said, "Not so."
Some said, "It might do good"; others said, "No."
John Bunyan, PILGRIM'S PROGRESS

The 1990s find the print industry in the midst of a revolutionary change in how design and production are coordinated. The personal computer has placed new tools in the hands of many people, thereby democratizing the design process and fusing disparate disciplines. Designers still like to retain complete control over all phases of their work, but now maintain it from their desktops. Often, however, that control is the result of great cost or complexity. That complexity associated with today's computer technology is a sign of the industry's immaturity and dynamism. The years to come will produce standards that will unify and simplify design and production tasks, making the entire printing process transparent to the DTP user. This chapter is about the technologies available today at the interface of computers and graphic arts reproduction, an area known as prepress.

The Master Copy

The print industry has been profoundly affected by the conversion from long- to short-run production. In long-run production, the goal of a design project is to create a prototype from which all copies are duplicated. For print work that prototype is a master copy, which that can be as simple as a laser printout or as complicated as a set of color separations. For many projects, except photographic images and color, today's desktop computer tools are sufficient to create acceptable master copy, although desktop printing is not yet economical or of high enough quality for long-run production. It would be prohibitively expensive and slow, for example, to print a newspaper on a desktop laser printer or print a four-color magazine on an ink jet printer. In these cases, traditional offset printing achieves both economy of scale and the requisite quality level. Your printer has the equipment to transfer a master photographically to a photosensitive aluminum plate or drum as a screened set of dots. Ink adheres to the latent image, and that image then transfers to a rubber blanket on a cylinder, which finally contacts to paper. Be aware that in offset printing, when the plate is made up, no changes can be made to your document without creating a new plate.

On the other hand, when you want highly economical reproduction for smaller quantities, short-run production is the method of choice. Indeed, you do short-run production when you run copies off on a photocopy machine; and xerography has the same engine found in your laser printer, another short-run production tool. Electronic printing is advancing to the stage where master copies can be refined, processed, and printed entirely in digital form, and the implications of this are staggering. A document composed in memory can remain "live," ultimately eliminating the need for a physical master copy entirely. Duplication can be achieved with rapid turnaround, and with a high level of customization. The entire process can be thought of as a complex version of a mail merge: The same newspaper can be produced in "individualized" formats; a college student can walk over to a machine in a bookstore and download a printed copy of a class manual with material suitable for personal study. This "on-demand printing" is the promise of some leading edge duplication technologies coming to market.

Duplication Technologies

Copiers

Copier or duplicating technology is sometimes called reprography. Prior to 1940, copies were made primarily as photostats. Then Gevaert and Agfa introduced several processes based on diffusion transfer, and 3M introduced a process called thermography that used heat to copy. Xerox's introduction of the 914 Copier, in 1960, which used electrophotography, revolutionized the quick copy market and supplanted most other methods in popular use. Electrophotography is the electrostatic transfer of toner (magnetic dry ink) first to a charged photoconductive surface and then to paper. It is the electronic equivalent of the offset printing press. Xerography is used mostly for single-color print jobs on plain paper copiers as short-run printing, but it is rapidly expanding to full-color copying and to high-speed, long-run printing.

▼ *Tip: As most copiers duplicate at 300 dpi, a laser print may be sufficient for master copy.*

You can use the higher resolutions on more expensive equipment to create an oversize master copy and then photocopy in the reduction mode. In other words, you use the photocopier's reduction mode to get an enhanced resolution picture.

Anyone who has seen the computer programmer/trainer or the ten-pound, spiral-bound manual that comes with the modern-day copier knows that a revolution is occurring in plain paper copying. Copiers enlarge/reduce, count, collate, print duplex, staple and bind, and image from microfilm to paper or film output. Perhaps the next generation of copiers will make coffee and lunch as well.

Full-Color Copiers

The Sharp CX-7500, Seiko Mead Cycolor 3000, and Canon CLC 200 are three examples of a generation of full color copiers currently on the market and meant for the office. They cost from $12,000 to $30,000. The Xerox 9500 series and Kodak Ektaprint 250 copiers are complete publishing solutions with binding and finishing capabilities. They can print in quantities in the hundreds; add an optional feeder mechanism, and they can print in the thousands. Xerox, Kodak, and Canon are introducing new, intelligent computer-based copiers that will displace today's quick print market.

**Canon Color
Laser Copier 500**

In 1989, Canon introduced the $49,000 Canon Color Laser Copier 500 (CLC 500), a four-color copier based on the electrophotographic (CMYK toners) process. The CLC 500 is a harbinger of the future, one of the best examples of what might be termed "convergent technologies." It's really much more than a copier, as it accepts both analog and digital input from a variety of electronic sources: PostScript files from computers, slide scanners, TV tuners (NTSC), VCRs, motion video cameras, still video cameras (the Canon XAP SHOT camera), or video floppy disks on a still video player. The CLC 500 gives 400 dpi, 24-bit continuous tone, which although not quite color matched, produces acceptable output for comp work. The versatility of this print and duplication platform

Figure 15-1
The Canon CLC 500 is a full-color, multi-input copier/printer.

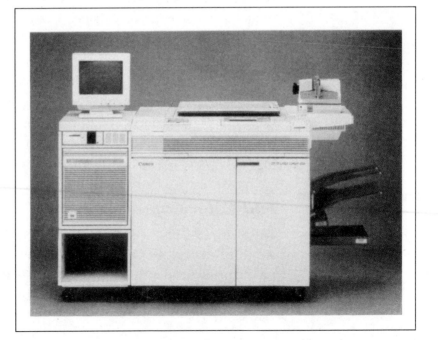

as a PostScript device makes it an interesting and valuable graphics output device for a large organization (it can be networked) or for a service bureau.

To fully configure a CLC 500, you need a $10,500 Adobe-licensed PostScript Intelligent Processing Unit (PS-IPU) and more memory; these improvements bring the cost of the unit to about $83,000. Rated at five copies per minute for three- or four-color output at letter size, (ledger size at three cpm), the CLC 500 produces output for about 20 to 40 cents per page. There is very little lost margin on a copy, only about eight mm on the leading edge and two mm on the three other edges. In addition to a scanner for hard copy reproduction, the CLC 500 has a digitizing tablet with stylus for precision drawing. Combined with an assortment of third-party software, the CLC 500 can function as a versatile CMYK and RGB color graphics environment. A $2,990 version of Freedom of the Press for the CLC 500 translates PostScript output into the Canon format, and PostScript interpreters from Adobe and EFI are also available. The PostScript type results have been well reviewed.

Using the CLC 500 with a PostScript interpreter you can create many interesting and useful effects. One image can be added to another, type features can be assigned, textures can be simulated, image mosaics or step and repeat patterns can be created; and images can be slanted, squeezed, mirrored, or tapered. Some color conversion and correction also can be done, and the CLC 500 can color separate multipage images. Pictures can be scaled from 50 percent to 400 percent. Another notable feature of the CLC 500 is digital recognition of type versus pictures, which means type can be printed in black toner without halftoning while using CMYK PostScript halftones for pictures on the same page. Non-Adobe interpreters, such as Freedom of the Press, stick to continuous tone even for text, which suffers a bit, though art looks great. The Adobe interpreter uses color halftones, hence color is only a bit better than that of 300 dpi wax transfer printers. Monochrome text is better (at 400 dpi). The CLC 500 doesn't look much different from the average company copier and it doesn't require any special installation, but it is remarkable technology for short-run prototype or production work.

Xerox DocuTech Production Publisher

In late 1990, Xerox introduced the most advanced copying and electronic digital printing reproduction system on the market today. The DocuTech Production Publisher was the culmination of a seven-year project headed by Bill Lowe, one of the executives at IBM who was in charge of the effort that resulted in the IBM PC. To describe DocuTech Production Publisher as simply a copying machine is a vast understatement. It is, in effect, a graphics super-computer with over a gigabyte of internal disk storage. This $220,000 system provides 135-pages-per-minute laser printing at 600 dpi resolution. The associated scanner can image 23 ppm also at 600 dpi, and image processing software is built in. An attached workstation with a GUI page layout package incorporates text and images into pages, sending halftone screened output to a print queue controller. Sophisticated print job software is also included.

Xerox has been responsible for many watershed events in computing and the DocuTech Production Publisher may represent one of those events. Using this system to do on-demand printing (with no waste), a customer can turn around a short- to medium-run print job in a few hours, in from 15 to 25 percent of the time it would take to get an offset print job back. And, while the system is printing one job, other jobs can be created and modified, ticketed and added to the print queue. Copies still have the associated 2 to 5 cent Xerox click charge per page, but the DocuTech Production Publisher can do duplex (both sides) page printing at sizes up to 11 by 17 inches (tabloid size), create impositions, and fold, cut, and bind documents into signatures or booklets—all automatically.

The DocuTech Production Publisher can be networked, via Ethernet or Novell Netware server. It can accept and store Interpress, PCL, and PostScript files created off line for further manipulation, storage, or printing. The software allows networked users to specify such print options as paper stock, number of prints, single- or double-sided printing, print queue position, and storage in memory. Lower-priced and less capable versions of the DocuTech Production Publisher, an Adobe PostScript interpreter, links to desktop computers and DTP software, and color are all slated for introduction into the system in 1991–92.

Figure 15-2
(A) The DocuTech Production Publisher is a copier/printer that processes, assembles, and modifies documents. The equivalent of a graphics supercomputer, this machine is capable of printing tabloid-size paper, and folding and binding at the rate of 135 ppm.
(B) The DocuTech Production Publisher has a scanner, laser printer, and icon-based interface. Paper follows a "race track" inversion path allowing for duplex printing. *Courtesy of Xerox, Inc.*

A.

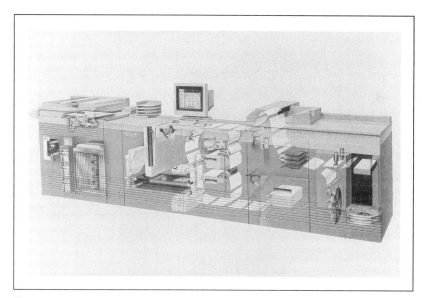

B.

The DocuTech Publisher is impressive technology. It is nearly ideal for literature, proposals, technical manuals, directories, books, and other document creation and production as well. It was tested and well received at many large corporate sites, print shops, and high-volume copy centers. These are high-profit markets, and it remains to be seen whether Xerox will address the general consumer mass market through service bureaus successfully. Xerox, after all, could have been the IBM or Apple Computer of today if it had commercialized the graphics computers it created fifteen years ago at PARC.

Several other manufacturers are active in computer-generated graphics printing. One is the LionHeart document management system from Eastman Kodak. It accepts PostScript files from microcomputers on Ethernet, IBM Token Ring, and AppleTalk networks, and can print at up to 92 ppm using a Kodak Ektaprint 1392, model 24, 300 dpi laser printer. LionHeart contains print server software but has many fewer document modification tools than the DocuTech Production Publisher; it is more like a fast printer.

From Separations to Print

The goal of electronic publishing is to create a completely digital master copy. That goal is achieved by electronically combining type, drawings, and images. As mentioned in Chapter 3, only higher-end computer systems can achieve full electronic production, and only at a cost. For the average user working from the desktop, the best and most cost-effective approach still is to combine both computer and traditional methods in a mechanical construction.

In the traditional approach, an artist takes all the elements of a page and places them individually on a posterboard. The desktop method uses the computer-generated page for most elements (type and drawn images primarily) and indicates positioning for images. Sometimes, a piece of red plastic, called rubylith, is then placed manually where the photo should go. Other times, photographs are imported and stripped in electronically. Tissue paper may be overlaid with written instructions for the printer. All overlays and elements are carefully positioned and aligned. Crop marks (circles with crosshairs) assure element alignment. A completed mechanical accounts not only for a single page, but for all pages needed for the printing plate, and in the correct imposed

Figure 15-3
(A) The LionHeart's print menu for IBM PCs and compatibles. **(B)** LionHeart's Page Setup (top) and Print (bottom) dialog boxes for the Macintosh. *Courtesy of Eastman Kodak, Inc.*

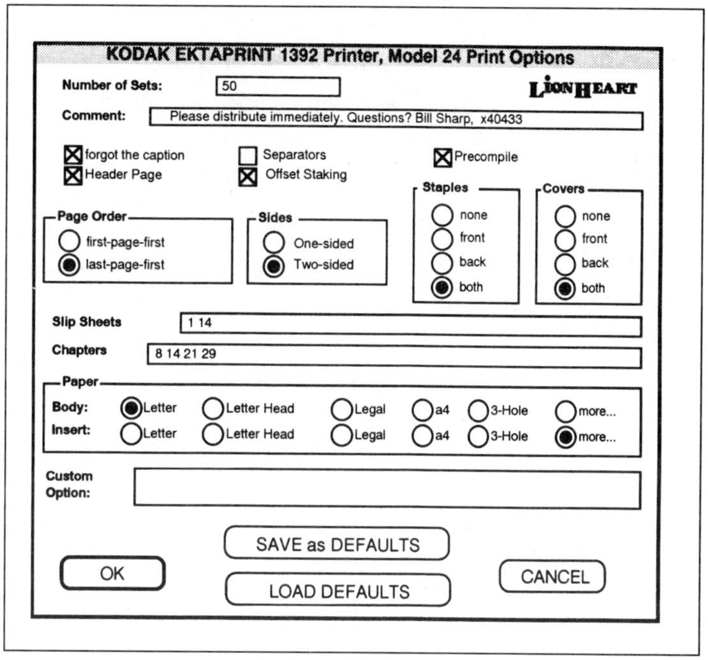

A.

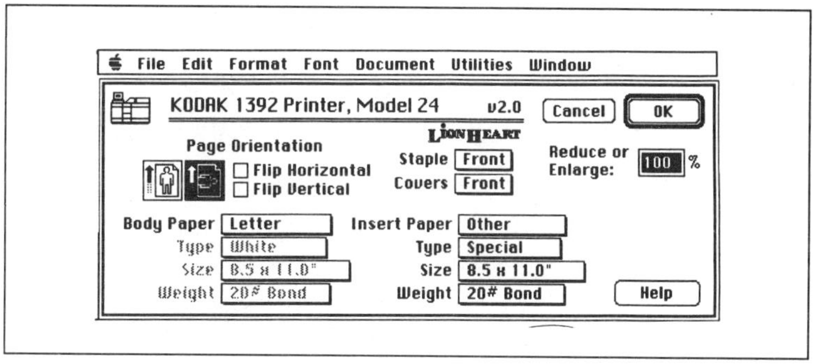

B.

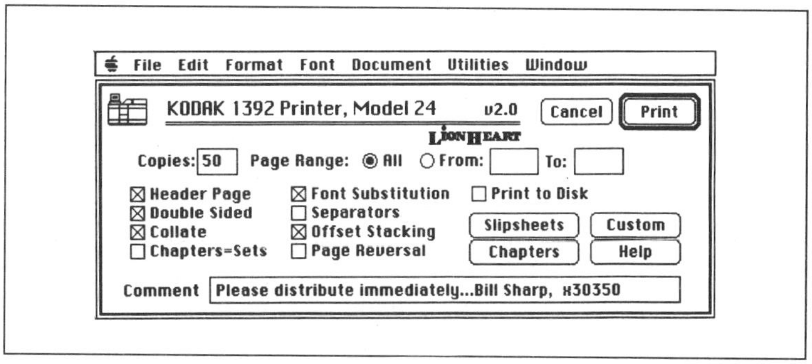

order. This process is laborious and subject to human errors and omissions. The 1990s will see more and more printers using master copies and separations created entirely by digital methods in place of mechanicals.

Electronic Imposition and Signature

Master pages or mechanicals are the design segment of the printing process. If a page were the same size as the printing press, you could create a plate directly from the master. But normally, the page is smaller than the plate, and a printer duplicates the page and then gangs two or more pages together on a plate to reduce print time. And, when a multipage print job is requested, a special page setup is required, called a signature. Once printed, pages can be folded, trimmed, and bound (see Figure 3.8). A signature often constitutes sixteen pages of a publication arranged by a process known as imposition, so that they appear in the right order when bound.

Further preparation is usually needed to complete a printing plate. Flats are photographed and the film from which the plates are made are positioned on a mylar flat in a process called stripping. Stripping involves cutting windows for picture elements and creating separated color films. Some commercial printers use automated cameras to strip and impose print jobs, although many still do them by hand. Stripping is a production bottleneck and the cause of many errors. It is one of the setup procedures that consumes much of a printer's time and adds to print cost. You can save money by submitting your own impositions to a printer. Some printers won't accept them, because they consider this to be their domain, or because they have special printing requirements.

Eventually all the high-end desktop page layout programs will do imposition and create signatures, but now none of them do. Some programs on the market can help you create impositions. Some are part of more complex packages for color separation; others are part of special purpose, higher-cost layout packages. If you do a lot of print work or are a printer, these packages can save you money. They are not for the casual user.

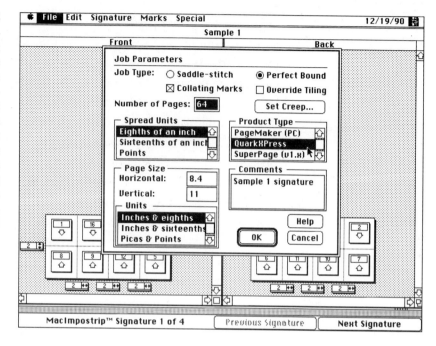

Figure 15-4
Impostrip is an automated signature layout program that can take master pages created in other page layout programs and position them correctly on a printing plate. Impostrip automates one of the most labor-intensive parts of the printing process and accounts for numerous variables. *Courtesy of ULTIMATE Technographics, Inc.*

ULTIMATE Technographics (Montreal, Canada) offers the ULTIMATE Electronic Prepress System, a set of prepress software modules. This system, which uses an IBM PC, consists of a text editor based on XyWrite, a file format converter, a page layout system (called the ULTIMATE Professional Publishing System), automatic pagination, a table generator, color separator, color masking, and imposition. It is also networkable. The imposition module called Impostrip is available separately for the Macintosh as Mac Impostrip. This module creates film or print signatures from the Professional Publishing System or other page layout packages. It can add appropriate margins for the gripper of the press, lap margins for a collator, and paper fold thickness margins. The program adjusts for different types of bindings and can account for paper grain and fold direction. Proofs are scaled down to a PostScript laser printer size, and output is to a PostScript imagesetter as positive or negative film, RC paper, or to silver master plate material. Larger output can be broken up as tiles or proportionately reduced as master copy for subsequent camera enlargement.

Proofing

Lithographic printing (from the term lithography, or "writing on stone") requires that several technologies work together properly, particularly in color printing. When a job is on press it is usually too late to correct errors due to poor separation, color balance, traps, and so on, so proofs are pulled to catch these problems. Often proofs called bluelines (or blues), which are photoprints (negative or positive), are used to check for position, scratches, broken type, and other imperfections. Color, however, cannot be checked on a blueline. Traditionally, color proofs are done on a proofing press using ink and paper. The results, while accurate, are slow, expensive, and don't allow for interactive control because they occur late in the design cycle. This has created a market for "off-press" color proofs.

Today there are several options for color proofing:

- Color laser proofs: Rough color comps can be produced from 300 dpi color printers. Ink jet printers are the best for color matching. The most lifelike or photographically realistic are dye sublimation printers, and the most readily available are thermal transfer and color dot matrix printers. Color laser copiers, such as the Canon CLC 500, are another alternative.

- Photographic proofs: Systems such as Recoprint and Double-Check are available that use photographic dyes to simulate printing inks. The color image is contone (not halftone) and the color match is good. Cost is moderate, cheaper than overlay or contract systems.

- Overlay proofs: Overlays are sheets of actetate film that are colored CYMK and Pantone inks. When registered and combined, the image is shown. Color positioning shows up well, but quality is moderate. The Color Key system is an example of this type of proof.

- Contract proofing: These are the most accurate nonpress proofs, made directly from film negatives. They are based on separate layers of colorants or toner laminated to a single base. Examples are Agfaproof, Matchprint, and Chromalin. They are called contract proofs because both customer and printer sign off on them.

- Press proofs: These are actual printed samples from a press. They account for such variables as press or dot gain, paper type, grain effects, and so on. Press proofs are the closest match possible, but they can still vary due to conditions such as weather, paper inconsistencies, ink batch variation, and other factors.

▼ *Tip: Don't be afraid to criticize a proof if it isn't to your liking. Using such words as brighter, darker, richer, less red, and more detail, can help a printer correct your work and bring it up to your expectations.*

The graphics art community uses a standard language for this type of conversation; and you can find it described in the *Pocket Guide to Color Reproduction* by Southworth, referenced in the bibliography.

Overlays and laminates are popular proofing systems. 3M's Color Keys are overlays of four CMYK acetate sheets on a white sheet of underlying paper. Color Keys cost about $20 to $60 for each letter-size page. DuPont's Chromalin and the similar 3M MatchPrint are single, laminated, sheet color proofing systems. Laminates show better registration and generally give more accurate color matches, but they are more expensive to correct. If a yellow in a laminate is too dark, the entire process must be redone, whereas an overlay might only require a single sheet be replaced. Laminated proofs cost from $30 to $90 for a letter-size page. As in all color work, a standard viewing light is required. A color separation house uses proofs extensively to check its work, and the final proof is a de facto contract that matches customer expectations to what the printer will attempt to duplicate. This makes the accuracy of proofing a central issue in printing.

Proofs based on computer-data generated photographic film are becoming more popular, but they are continuous tone (contone) images. They lack the dot structure typical of process printing and are not representative of either texture or color. A color correction to a contone would result in a different density on a separated film, but what would change on a printed page is the size, shape, and concentration of halftone dots. The color contone print created by a DuPont 4CAST printer (by dye sublimation) looks photographic but doesn't accurately show the results you would obtain in print. All dye sublimation printers also suffer from some color matching problems due to the dyes used. Color ink jet printers such as the $75,000 Iris 3024 or the $8,000 Tektronix Phaser CQS, give the best results due to more balanced dyes and halftone patterns created by using opaque colorants.

"Soft proofing" on a color monitor offers broad appeal to the lay public, but its success hinges on the issues of color calibration, gamut matching, RGB/CYMK conversion, and color temperature matching, issues discussed in the previous chapter. Proofing on a monitor still is a very limited and inaccurate solution.

Prepress

A Definition

Prepress is the process of combining all of the elements on any page to produce master copy. This book has discussed many of the automated hardware and software tools that create the type effects, screens, color, and numerous other elements that are making documents more sophisticated. Many are brand new and would not be possible without the modern computer and associated peripheral devices. Integrating these elements is one of the gifts of computers to the printing industry. When industry gurus describe prepress systems, they are generally referring to turnkey systems that synthesize all elements of a page with a low- or medium-resolution page description to create a high-resolution master.

A prepress system might include the following:

- Microcomputer or Workstation: Popular prepress systems are built around DEC, Apollo, or Sun UNIX workstations, or Macintosh II or IBM PC 80386 computers. Designs can be prepared on the desktop as the front end of the process, transferred and reformatted to a gateway system (a computer that can interpret files for use by another computer or device) or assembly station, and finalized on the complete prepress system—this is called a prepress link. A high-resolution monitor is part of a prepress package.

Figure 15-5
The demo room at Optronics (Chelmsford, MA) where the color plates for *Beyond the Desktop* were produced. A well-stocked prepress operation contains many of the stations shown here. *Courtesy of Optronics, Inc.*

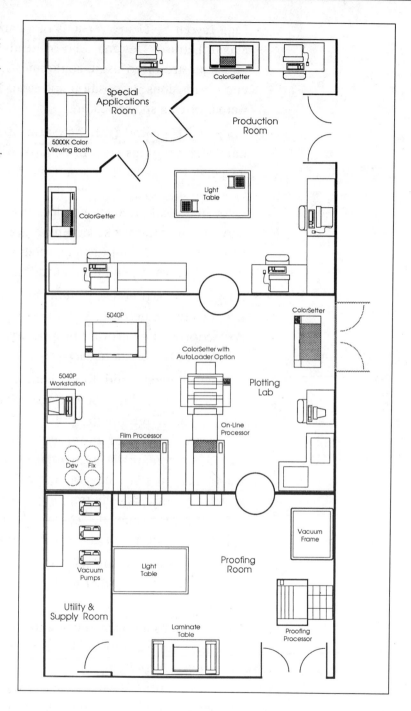

- Page Layout Software: Versions of QuarkXPress, Aldus Page-Maker, Letraset DesignStudio or ReadySetGo!, and Ventura Publisher are often used, sometimes incorporating proprietary extensions. Imposition and signature creation in software is often a special feature.

- Scanners: High-end (generally drum)scanners are a critical part of a prepress system because they provide quality images for processing. A scanner can cost from $60,000 to $250,000 and provide 4,000 dpi and from 16 to 32 bits of color information. Many vendors use PostScript and some provide proprietary screening algorithms. Programs for image retouching, airbrushing, rotation, montaging, cloning, masking, and sharpening are included.

- Imagesetter: A prepress system often ships or outputs to a high-quality imagesetter. As with scanners, vendors often use PostScript RIPs or provide proprietary color screening algorithms for even better quality.

- Color Correction and Tools: Long ago, prepress vendors solved many of the problems associated with RGB/CMYK conversion. High-quality color separation is one of the important features of a prepress system, and the film produced is automatically stripped at high resolution and registration. Prepress systems offer special techniques for color matching, automatically trapping colors, correcting moirés, and addressing other defects. Nearly perfect colors, beyond "pleasing or good enough" quality can be achieved.

- Proofing Systems: Many systems output to contone printers, ink jet printers, and other devices that are part of a prepress system.

Prepress systems are experiencing the same downsizing trends typical of the entire computer industry. Some vendors, such as CyberChrome, are building systems entirely from off-the-shelf components. If it sounds like this technology is coming to a desktop near you, it is. A major problem yet to be worked out is an open page specification that would allow any application to write files to be exchanged between microcomputers and prepress systems; digital data exchange specifications (DDES) are currently being established.

Color Electronic Prepress Systems

Color electronic prepress systems (CEPS) have been on the market for a dozen years now, the first appearing in 1979 from Scitex. They are responsible for most of the magazines and color reproductions that we see today. The Scitex Response, from Scitex America (Bedford, MA); Hell ChromaCom, from Hell Graphics Systems (Port Washington, NY); and Crosfield Studio, from Crosfield Electronics (Glen Rock, NJ), are CEPS that range from $500,000 to $1,000,000. These three manufacturers have 89 percent of a market, estimated to be around 2,500 installations. CEPS systems are complex enough to require trained operators, and they cost $200 to $400 per hour to use.

A line of CEPS aimed at the corporate market range from $125,000 to $350,000. Vendors including Aesthedes (Torrence, CA), DuPont Design Technologies (Santa Clara, CA), Xyvision Design Systems (Wakefield, MA), Crosfield Lightspeed (Boston, MA), and Unda (New York, NY) produce them. Many prepress systems serve in specialized industries. Atex is one such system networked as an editorial and production process by many news publications. Atex Design Software runs on several types of PCs and can lay out type and other elements, but has no color and limited desktop capabilities. Xyvision sells a package design prepress system.

High-End Prepress Links

The merging of microcomputers and workstations has led to prepress systems based on Mac II, IBM PC 80386, and Sun SPARCstation computers, and to prepress links to desktop computers offered by Scitex, Crosfield, and Hell: Scitex supplies a Mac II with a souped-up version of QuarkXPress that enables an independent designer to create a page on a desktop setup called a Visionary Primary Design Station. Images are scanned at low resolution and manipulated by the designer. Layout, color specification, and proofing are done at the Design Station and then the files are transmitted by modem to a Visionary Gateway System. Design Stations costs $31,000 ($13,600 for additional stations), and the Visionary Gateway costs $80,000. At the gateway, text, graphics, and layout are converted to the file format of the high-end Scitex Response system. The system performs a final high-resolution scanning of images using information contained in the original layout file and then color separates it.

Crosfield Lightspeed has created a prepress link called the Lightspeed Color Layout System. Each $43,000 station ships with a Mac II, color monitor, color scanner, and color thermal transfer printer and proprietary StudioLink software for detailed color work. Files are sent via ½-inch tape (optional) to a high-end prepress system (Crosfield, Hell, or Scitex) for high-resolution scanning and color separation. Another, the $61,000 Design System 20, is a bridge station between the Mac II and a prepress system. Crosfield is offering PostScript in the form of the Scripter/PS interpreter and links to Ventura Publisher and ReadySetGo!, but the Color Layout System is limited by having no prepress link for photographs. Hell Graphic's ScriptMaster can import any PostScript file and reformat it for the Hell ChromaCom 2000 prepress system. Designs can be developed on either a Macintosh or IBM PC using any PostScript application including PageMaker, QuarkXPress, ReadySetGo!, Interleaf Publisher, and other page layout programs. Files are sent to the ScriptMaster, which acts as a gateway to the ChromaCom system.

Some prepress systems are being developed from the desktop up, most with PostScript as the common thread. Kodak has introduced the Prophecy Color Workstation, a Sun SPARC IV UNIX system with a slide scanner that does closed-loop color calibration. Prophecy uses an open network architecture to process files and output to a proofing device or to an imagesetter. CyberChrome (New Haven, CT) also has a system based on PostScript color separation using QuarkXPress on a Mac II. The $200,000 CyberChrome 36B Electronic Color Prepress Imaging System takes PostScript files and processes them in a production environment where all devices are on a linked AppleTalk/Ethernet network. Output is to a commercial imagesetter. CyberChrome yields very good quality at a

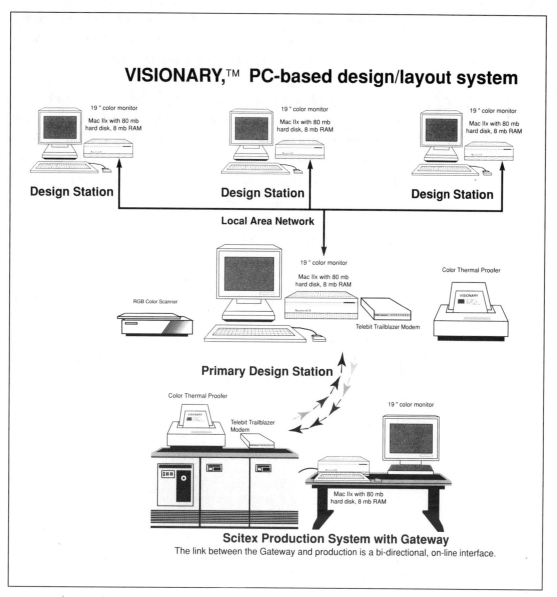

Figure 15-6 The Scitex Visionary system links a desktop design station to a high-end Scitex Response prepress system through a gateway. High-end prepress links may represent the immediate future of prepress until the end of the decade when newer, more powerful desktop computers and peripherals are introduced. *Courtesy of Scitex America, Inc.*

much lower cost than higher-end CEPS. The ULTIMATE Electronic Prepress System described earlier is a complete desktop prepress system that lets users work with their own hardware.

Prepress Costs

The considerable cost of prepress is due to the machine time needed for high-resolution image manipulation necessary for duplicating what was done on the desktop. In order to link the final image to the one in a design, Aldus has proposed a standard called the Open Prepress Interface (OPI) that has been adopted by most vendors. Images scanned at a prepress bureau are saved both in high-resolution form and as a low-resolution TIFF file. The TIFF file is incorporated into the design, and any changes made are saved as a set of PostScript comments. When the file is returned for processing, the prepress system automatically notes the name, position, size, and cropping of images from the embedded PostScript comments, removes the TIFF file, and replaces it with the high-resolution image suitably changed. Only color balance and slight touch-up is done prior to separation. Scitex uses a similar image linkage (non-OPI) in Visionary and has introduced the Visionary Interpreter for PostScript (VIP) for complete PostScript page description.

In theory, low-resolution/high-resolution image linkage works well, but in practice, unless certain characteristics (scaling, rotation, screen ruling, and other factors) are known in advance, the images often require rescanning for high-resolution placement. This is both inflexible and expensive, and it reduces much of the cost advantage of CEPS. For many jobs, particularly small complex pieces with several images, it is still usually cheaper to have type and object artwork imageset, and the images in them manually stripped. Longer pieces with regular design features are the best candidates for CEPS. Beyond the cost factors, CEPS offer much faster turnaround, improved design control, and the opportunity to reuse artwork. In addition, work on proprietary screening solutions yields much better results than PostScript-based separations. These proprietary solutions also provide for photographic special effects that are not available via traditional methods.

▼ *Tip: Moiré patterns are a common problem in prepress caused by imperfect separations.*

You can reduce these patterns by using a CMYK pattern of 100 percent one color plus a screen of a second color; moiré patterns are typically not found in a two-screen pattern. Problems arise in three- and four-screen patterns. Using fewer screens also saves you money. For three-screen patterns, avoid browns, purples, and dark grays. Also use CMY to generate grays, not black. Consider creating a swatch book of your most common colors to test for moiré patterns in output for large or complex print jobs.

The evolving prepress links to high-end systems are still too expensive to impact the market for individual users. Their main effect has been to increase the number of seats in front of the console at organizations with full prepress systems in-house, thus lowering costs, improving efficiency, and facilitating workgroup solutions, although some extension into smaller organizations has also occurred. Many vendors see prepress links improving and becoming a major factor in the printing industry. Others (myself included) expect to see color prepress as desktop technology in the 1990s, as both hardware and software are downsized, improved, and simplified. The prepress system of today is the dinosaur of tomorrow. Design and production will meld as a front end to commercial printing at the back end. Printers will act like a black box, accepting data files specially formatted for a specific printing press or print process.

The Print Job

Most desktop publishers assume their job is done when they hand their masters to a printer and state the number of copies that they want. Approaching printing with this attitude will yield variable results at best. An understanding of the factors involved in printing will help you get better results for less money. Some knowledge of the setup, makeready (press preparation) work, and printing press that will be used is necessary for you to do your job properly. Your printer should be able and willing to give you suggestions and to quote competitive pricing. An early visit to a printer, or better yet, several printers, will alert you to options, choices, and potential problems—all before the fact.

▼ *Tip: The "5-50-500 Law" states, "A change that costs $5 to fix on a mechanical costs $50 to fix on a blueline and $500 to fix on a press." The latter is probably an underestimate.*

Earlier we talked about electronic printing, duplication, and reproduction. There, the designer has direct control over the production within the limits of the equipment. Some of these methods have replaced traditional printing, and their market share is increasing. But traditional print methods still represent the lion's share of printing and will for some time to come. The production aspect of traditional printing falls outside the realm of computer technology, but it is worth digressing here to explain some of the important considerations necessary to achieve the print results you have strived so hard to obtain. Several references for printing, working with printers and graphic arts services, and understanding factors in print quality and production control are given at the end of this chapter.

Brøderbund's DTP Advisor is a computer program aimed at smoothing the printing process for the desktop publisher. This set of connected HyperCard stacks for the Macintosh is both a tutorial on design and printing and a resource for creating projects. It separates each part of the process and explains its importance to you. Then it instructs you to fill out a set of project management forms to organize your involvement with writers, photographers, and the print shop. There are type specification sheets, cost estimate worksheets, and print specification and project definition forms. While this product has received good reviews, it is being discontinued due to its limited commercial success. It is too bad, because the limited success says more about the strength and weakness of HyperCard as a software medium than it does about DTP Advisor. Other good HyperCard products, including Danny

Figure 15-7
Screens from The DTP
Advisor. **(A)** The pro-
gram menu with topics
list. **(B)** Defining your
project by audience.
*Courtesy of
Brøderbund, Inc.*

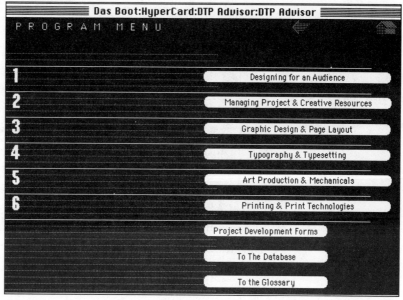

A.

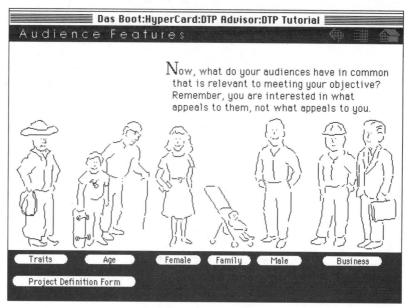

B.

Goodman's personal information manager, Focal Point II, also are disappearing. However, you may be able to find DTP Advisor in a discount bin if you search around.

At the Print Shop

Three major print technologies are in use today: offset, letterpress, and silkscreen printing. Each has limitations in delivering print at a certain quality and cost. In addition, each offers size, color, and image reproduction restrictions. Each print method specializes in achieving certain special effects.

Offset Lithography In this print technology, a flexible aluminum plate with the image on it is wrapped around the plate cylinder. The image is a photo emulsion and accepts oil-based ink while rejecting water. The plate is dampened, then inked by a roller, and the plate cylinder transfers (offsets) that ink to a smooth rubber-coated blanket cylinder. The image is finally printed from the blanket to paper with the impression cylinder providing the pressure to ensure smooth ink coverage. It's called offset printing because the plate doesn't touch the paper. (See Figure 15.8).

Offset presses are either sheet-fed or web. Sheet-fed presses print on sheets using one side; a perfecting press prints on both sides. Up to 10,000 impressions per hour with up to six colors can be printed. A web press uses paper rolls and prints on both sides of the paper simultaneously. Web presses operate at up to 40,000 impressions an hour and can print up to eight colors. The size of web presses allows for signature printing, but the size and speed of the press also limits the types of paper that can be used. Sheet-fed offset printing is common in all kinds of print shops, whereas web printing is found generally in large commercial printers. Offset printing is fast, flexible, cheap, and can use process colors effectively.

Letterpress Printing This print method uses a raised form to transfer ink to paper. It is the original technology used in printing. It can also be used for scoring paper for folding, die-cutting, embossing, and foil stamping. You can tell letterpress forms by an edge of heavy ink formed by ink spreading under pressure and by the form debossing (pressed into) the page. Letterpresses are sheet fed (see Figure 15.9), rated at 5,000 impressions per hour, printing up to four colors. Letterpress works well for medium-quality printing where custom features are important: business cards, timetables, tickets, packaging, directories, and so on. Letterpress formerly was used for all forms of printing, but offset is more economical for color photo reproduction and is used more often now.

Silkscreen Printing Silkscreen printing, a form of stencil printing, is done by forcing ink through a mesh that is open only where the image is to be inked through. Silk or synthetic nylon mesh is used and the area to be blocked is taped, painted, or sealed with a photoactive polymer. The screen is placed, ink is applied with a blade and forced through the screen onto the painted surface (see Figure 15.7). Automated silkscreen presses have been built with speeds of up to 5,000 impressions per hour at low cost.

Silkscreen allows for very heavy ink coverage of any size or type of surface. It is used by sign painters, on mugs, T-shirts, or electronic circuit boards. Silkscreen is highly flexible; it can use inks, glues, circuit boards, and scratch-'n'-sniff coatings. Silkscreened inks tend to look opaque and flat; silkscreening is often combined with other printing.

Print shops offer additional effects that can also enhance your final printed product:

- Varnishes: Varnishes can be applied to give a reproduction either a gloss or dull effect; they can be washed over an entire sheet, placed in spot areas, or printed on specific areas, such as logos, for dramatic effect. It's a good idea to print dull varnish on gloss paper and gloss varnish on dull paper for best contrast and maximum effect.

- Coatings: Marcote is a plastic that is sprayed onto a page after printing, making it impervious to liquids. Marcote is used on drivers' licenses and ID cards. Ultraviolet (UV) coatings are also available. They are applied after printing and

Figure 15-8
(A) Offset lithography is commonly used in high-speed process printing. Shown here is a web press.
(B) Letterpress is used for many custom print jobs.
(C) Silkscreen printing is used for special surface and effect printing. These are illustrations from the demos included with The DTP Advisor. *Courtesy of Brøderbund, Inc.*

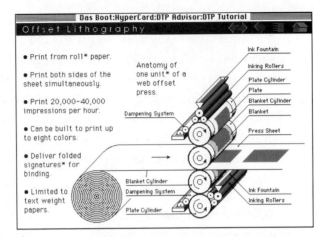

A.

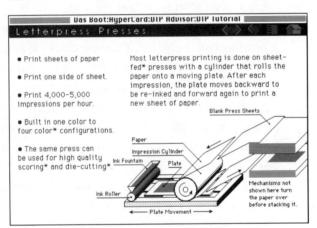

B.

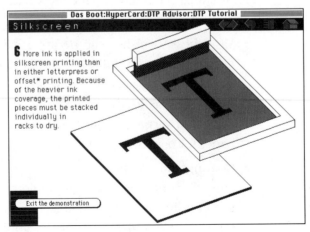

C.

cured by UV light. These coatings are liquid, tight, hard, and durable, but because they are put on after printing they add significantly to the cost of the job. Plastic can also be heat-laminated to a page.

- Embossing: This effect is achieved when a surface is raised or depressed (debossed) by a die, which is often heated. The embossed area can be preprinted for greater effect. A plain emboss is called blind embossing. A foil can be applied to an emboss, called foil stamping. Metallic, opaque colors, and clear plastics also can be applied, and this effect works well on dark paper.

- Die-cutting: A sharp die is used to cut a shape out of a page, in order to create irregular shapes or pieces or windows, such as those used in envelopes for return addresses.

- Scoring: A dull edge is used to impress a thin line in a paper to make folding easier. This is particularly important for heavier paper weights, such as cover sheets.

Paper

The paper you choose also can affect which printing method is best for a project. Papers come coated, uncoated, dull, or polished to a high gloss (smooth). Coated paper reflects light like a mirror (specular reflection), whereas uncoated paper has diffuse reflection. Most high-gloss paper is coated, and this is the best stock for reproducing photographs. Manufacturers grade their paper according to weight, fiber content, grain direction, durability, reflectance, opacity, and brightness. Higher-opacity paper exhibits less "show-through." Brightness is a measure of the amount of reflected light, affecting the color or white point of the paper. Table 15.1 lists the more common types of papers and their applications. For a more complete listing of paper types, see *Getting It Printed*, by Mark Beach, Steve Shepro, and Ken Russon, listed in the reference.

Table 15.1 Printing Papers

Grade	Size (inches)	Weight (#/½M/or ream)	Applications
Coated cover	20 by 26	65 to 100	White, some colors. Medium to high quality. Excellent color reproduction. Business cards, tickets, posters, book covers.
Uncoated cover	20 by 26	65 to 100	White, some colors. Medium to high quality. Textures available. Modest color reproduction.
Coated text	25 by 38	60 to 100	White, some colors. Medium to very high quality. Excellent color reproduction.
Uncoated text	25 by 38	50 to 80	White, most colors. Medium to high quality. Textures available. Modest color reproduction.
Offset	25 by 38	50 to 100	White, most colors. Low- to medium-quality lithography printing. Magazines and newspapers.
Book	25 by 38	50 to 100	White, most colors. Low- to medium-quality letterpress printing. Books, brochures, magazines, newspaper inserts.
Bond	17 by 22	16 to 24	White, most colors. Low to medium quality. Business paper, forms, copier stock.

Ink, too, reacts to paper type. For example, uncoated paper can accept more ink, because ink absorbs into the paper (poor "hold-out") and spreads out (large "dot gain"). Coated paper has good hold-out and small dot gain, but accepts less ink and surface ink appears brighter and sharper. The order for hold-out decreases from high gloss to gloss, dull, and finally, matte coatings. Antique and vellum finishes are uncoated papers. Every manufacturer provides sample books of available papers that your printer can show you. Good printers will actively help you select the best paper for your print job.

Binding

Your printer can suggest many different types of bindings for any given job. These include spiral, comb, Velo, stitched, glued, or stapled bindings. Several types of folds are also possible: parallel, accordion, roll-over, right angle, and others. The type of binding or fold you choose is often the last detail you think about, but remember, the right margins and design details must accept the binding or fold you want. So don't forget to ask up front.

Pricing a Job

Many factors affect the pricing of a print job. Often printers have you fill out a printing specification form that details all your requirements. Consider creating your own print specification form before you ever set foot in a print shop. Ask the printer or print representative for recommendations on paper, inks, and print techniques that will result in quicker turnaround, better results, or cost savings. Good printers are forthcoming with this information—it is their "value added." The most important factors are:

- Quantity: Print runs often have substantial price breaks at 500, 1,000, 5,000, and 10,000 copies. Beyond that the cost of the materials limits further price breaks. Always get 10 percent more copies than you need, because reprinting is expensive. Some pricing is for an exact number of copies and some is for an approximate number.

- Number of colors: Paper color is the one color you don't pay for, it's part of the paper's price. Two color printing is about one and a half times as expensive as one color. Three-color printing is normally not cost effective; four colors is better. Some presses have four, six, and eight ink colors available in a press run, and they allow process colors, plus spot colors, to be printed. Clear varnish costs the same as any color and gives a good, high-quality effect.

- Paper: Often the largest portion of the print cost is the paper used.

- Photographs: When your printer color separates and strips in photographs for you and they are not part of a master set of separations, the number and sizes of photos are a pricing factor.

- Bleeds/Solids: A bleed is a printed image that extends into the margins. Heavy ink coverage is difficult to work with and will require extra time for press washings. They add to the cost of the job.

- Print schedule: The turnaround time is important and a rush job costs extra. Part of a good quote will give a time estimate (many don't), and variation of about 25 to 50 percent is normal.

You may be surprised to find that printers quotations often vary by as much as 50 percent. Shopping pays. Some of this variation is due to differences in skill levels, equipment, and demand at one printer versus another. Printers either quote based on formulas or custom price a job. Quick print shops most often formula price and stick to that pricing regardless of how the job progresses. Specialty printers who do envelopes, direct mailers, fliers, and forms will also quote from price lists. The advantage of formula pricing is that you always know how much it is going to cost you and roughly what you are going to get. The disadvantage is that your print options are constrained within narrow limits. Custom pricing delivers up to 10 percent more than the amount you wanted, and you are charged for the "overs."

▼ *Tip: A good printer will try to save you money and meet your deadlines and budget by suggesting alternatives.*

The lowest-priced printers are not always your best bet, because they may cut corners to produce your job, fit you in to *their* schedule, or compromise quality. Often the professionalism of the quote itself is a good selection criteria.

Commercial printers usually try to estimate a custom price for each print job. Very high-quality (museum grade) printers also use this approach. A custom price is a quote; it considers how fast you need turnaround, special print options and different quality levels, along with other factors. Many printers will not quote an estimate on specifications alone, but require a look at the mechanicals. Every print job is unique and every firm has a different set of skills and equipment for achieving a desired result. If your job is large, you should solicit quotes; for very large jobs you may want to hire a print broker to place your print job. Often he or she can add valuable experience and save you money.

Working with Your Printer (Who Was That Guy?)

A good approach to selecting printers is to ask to see samples of their work. Most are happy to show you samples. The design of the samples was not the printer's responsibility, so ignore that. The print *quality* is the issue here. It might even be a good idea to look at the samples upside down. The factors that you are looking for are:

- Personality and reputation: Can you work with and do you trust this person? Does this shop have a good reputation among clients? Does the printer deliver on time? The best printing isn't useful if it is delivered late. Good printers are always busy because clients always return with regular work.

- Equipment: Does this printer have the necessary equipment to do the quality of work you require? Ask the printer to show you around the shop. If it is a disorganized mess, move on.

- Registration: Do abutting colors line up properly?

- Print defects: Are there spots or dots (called hickeys) in solid colors, or are there streaks inside solid color areas?

- Color quality: Are the colors in photos natural, do they look right?

Many print jobs are done through brokers, printing salespeople, or representatives. These people may be employed by a print shop, or be independents, but they work for *you*. It is their responsibility to provide good estimates, confirm schedules, and move print jobs through production. If the rep is only interested in writing the job, move on. And remember, a rep is only as good as the support he or she receives from the printer. Often, however, delays occur that are outside a rep's control, and you have to decide whether you can live with the results. One advantage to using print brokers is that they can work with other print shops; however, print brokers also require larger print jobs so that they can draw adequate commissions.

The first time I had a job printed, the printer laser-printed my disk file and pasted up the pages. (Imagesetting the pages would have required little additional work or cost.) I was promised a two-week turnaround, which turned into eight weeks. The printer assumed I wanted a "good enough" job and didn't bother to ask me. Be careful of terms in the quotation such as "commercially acceptable," which means your printer will make the quality determination. These were all details that I didn't ask about, for at the time I wasn't even aware they existed. Good DTPers cultivate a long-term relationship with a good printer, who in turn will find ways to save you money and time. In the end, you have to trust your intuition.

Network/Workgroup Publishing

A team effort is a lot of people doing what I say.
Michael Winner, British film director

Picture this. You get home from a hard day at the Engulf & Devour Corporation. Today, 50,000 direct mail pieces for the *Compleat John Wayne Video Library* were mailed. After a good supper, you settle in to work on a direct mail piece for the CD of *Tiny Tim's Greatest Hits*. You fire up your computer, launch your word processor, and write the perfect copy. After scanning in some photographs, drawing the artwork, and picking some nice type, you launch a page layout program and blend it all together. You've taken special care to make sure the colors are right, so you print a comp, review it, and then print a set of color separations to take into work the next day. It's even still early enough to catch Monday Night Football and watch the NY Giants beat the Washington Redskins.

The preceding should sound ridiculous to you. Very few people have all of the technical skills necessary to accomplish the tasks described. It would take days to design a Tiny Tim mailer by yourself. No one person who could write perfect copy could draw, scan, layout, and separate a design using the dozen or so software packages and hardware equally as well as skilled individuals can. As DTP becomes more sophisticated, most complex projects are tackled by teams of individuals electronically connected on networks, each skilled at one task or another. The results are everywhere to be seen: national magazines, newspapers, books—and yes, even junk mail.

Working in groups makes sense. Large organizations have used computers for many years to aid in their work flow, project development, and production. Until recently, many of these tools were minicomputer or mainframe systems with dumb terminals, called host-based computing. Today these systems are run on distributed networks based on powerful PCs and servers. Networked software improves the work in progress by incorporating electronic mail (E-mail), scheduling, project management, and quality assurance while providing each worker with the best tools available.

In this chapter we examine some of the hardware and software that is available to create workgroup solutions. These products have been dubbed "groupware," and include office automation and integrated office solutions. Groupware for personal computer users often integrates networking hardware and software packages such as Apple's AppleShare, TOPS, Novell NetWare, Microsoft LAN with LAN Manager, 3Com 3+, and Banyon Vines with off-the-shelf, add-on software. You can wire up your own network for as little as a few hundred dollars, adding nodes as you require, and then use the best applications that you can find, upgrading as you go along. Most networks start in a small workgroup environment and average 63 computers with a cost of several hundred dollars per node. Most important, you preserve your investment in equipment and training by using what you currently have as a building block.

Connecting a Workgroup

Systems for connecting workgroups vary greatly in sophistication and scope. One trend is the development of small modular applications that install on a distributed network and can add both scope and capability over time. An example would be messaging software which could be expanded into a complete bulletin board and central file storage system. These act like the "glue" that binds similar applications together into projects; some are system software, others are system extensions. They provide connections, but few application facilities. Another class of solutions provides a bundle of applications capabilities, plus allows you to choose the additional applications you need. Office automation software falls into this category. A third class includes the all-in-one proprietary solutions like LotusNotes or the Odesta Document Management System that provide a total work environment. Total solutions tend, however, to be niche systems aimed at larger users within a specific industry; many are provided as customized packages by value-added resellers.

Important Features

The best way to decide what type of system to install to connect a workgroup is to define what the goal of the organization is. A workgroup is delineated by a project or department, not by geography. List the capabilities you need. Some of the specific features might include:

- Scheduling: This includes tracking and prioritizing tasks, calendars, and reminders. Some software tracks the whereabouts of your employees by an electronic version of the pegboard. CE Software's In/Out is one such program for the Macintosh.

- E-mail: E-mail can go beyond one-to-one correspondence to full conferencing. A standard index, called the Message Handling Service (MHS), is an interchange format (like ASCII) that has been defined to allow different E-mail programs to exchange messages. It is supported by Da Vinci E-mail, Higgins, and cc:Mail, among others.

- Document management: This is an aspect of project tracking that organizes and uses information in new, intelligent ways. A document can be changed and kept live at all times for the group to work with.

- Ease of use: Getting at the information contained on the system easily, and learning the system without extensive training is very important. On-line context-sensitive help systems are a common feature.

- Security and privacy: Who sees what message or documents. Some combination of file locking, passwords, access groups, encryption, and other common security features should be built in.

- Network configuration: Although most workgroups begin as local area networks (LANs), good solutions allow for upgrades to wide area network (WAN) connections that provide for more complete enterprise-wide computing.

The advantage of networking personal computers is that you can build a system one step at a time, starting with as few as two computers and ending up with thousands, as required.

Licensing Considerations

When a software vendor sells you a product, it normally comes with a license to install that product on a *single* computer CPU. This restriction has caused some controversy among industry analysts due to the large number of individuals who have two or more personal computers, say a laptop and a desktop system. Once you break the packaging on a product, you are normally bound by the fine print of the license, but few companies today would hold you to the single CPU rule. Most interpret their license to be for single user, not single CPU, use. But groupware and networking software provides some unique licensing problems, because theoretically, each node is a user requiring a purchased copy.

Many computer users ignore the license and use bootlegged copies. Many vendors live with this problem and recoup by charging more for their products and locking users into regular meaningless upgrades—the benign approach. Some have installed sensing codes in the software that search for other copies of unregistered programs and refuse to load the programs when it finds them—the passive-aggressive approach. Still others support the Software Industry Association's program for punishing individuals or companies with unregistered software. It works something like this: Someone reports the use of illegal software. The association threatens a suit if all unregistered copies of that software are not destroyed, and/or the licensing fees are paid for the use of the software desired. This is the aggressive approach and it is a fair system, except that it tends to affect larger installations more than smaller ones. It can also be a problem when an organization is going through financial difficulties.

Some software is available with licenses for multiple copies. Typically, they come in 2-, 5-, 10-, 50-, and 100- packs and cost per installation is much less than for single user cost, often from 10 to 50 percent less. In a large installation these multipack licenses may be all that you need, but these licenses grant you the right to install the program on only the specified number of machines, and only once. It is not a floating grant. For blanket licenses, vendors sell what is called a site license, which allows an organization to make an unlimited number of copies of the software for use on a LAN. Often the vendor also supplies multiple (but fewer) copies of the documentation.

Hardware

Network Types

A computer network generally is considered to be two or more computers connected together by a cable. A Macintosh computer comes with AppleTalk built in, so a case can be made that a Laser-Writer connected to a Mac is a network, but this is not correct. Each computer on a network is called a node, and software assigns each a unique address or number. Networks are constructed to include shared resources such as high-speed printers, large storage devices, networked modems (called net modems), and other peripherals. Initially, many networks are built to allow for the amortization of these expensive resources among a workgroup.

Servers Devices on the network that aid in providing information sharing, E-mail, and other services are called servers, and they require special software. There are file servers, printer servers, E-mail servers, and so on. Complete systems are often called network operating systems. A file server can be any or all computer(s) on a network or a workstation or a larger computer. There are distributed LANs (peer-to-peer) where each PC can act as both a server and a workstation. A centralized LAN (peer-to-host) uses one central computer as a server and the connected PCs don't share information directly with each other.

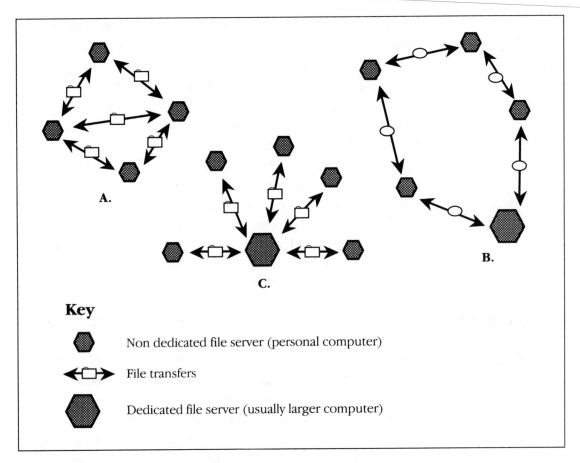

Key

⬡ Non dedicated file server (personal computer)

◄☐► File transfers

⬡ Dedicated file server (usually larger computer)

Figure 16-1 Network types: **(A)** Distributed Local Area Network (LAN) with nondedicated file servers. **(B)** Distributed LAN with dedicated file server. **(C)** Centralized LAN with dedicated file server.

AppleShare, Novell NetWare, TOPS, 3Com 3+, and DynaNet are examples of server software. Whereas Macs have AppleTalk built in, PCs require special add-in boards (network interface cards, or NICs) to connect to networks. For the PC, LANtastic for small distributed networks and NetWare 386 centralized or dedicated servers for large sites are highly recommended. Network components consist of hardware—all computers, shared devices, media (physical conductors), and connections; and software—user applications and network control software.

Network Architecture Computer networks have a design plan that is called their architecture. Two networks can have the same components and still have a different architecture. The architecture affects what communication protocols are in effect and the topology or arrangement of components to one another. For example, LANs typically are found in a limited area, often a single building or site. A LAN's speed is generally determined by the connections used, and often it is quite high. WANs, on the other hand, are computers connected across a long distance by telephones, satellites, and other special links. The highest level of integration is a set of networks called an internet system. Internet devices require special connection devices, such as modems, bridges, routers, and gateways (see "Connecting Networks" below). Most of the software to be described is sold for LANs, although many offer support for WANs and internets through the purchase of additional packages.

Data Transmission and the OSI Model

Most modern networks transmit data in bundles of specific sizes and formats called packets. Packets include data, the addresses of sender and receiver, plus additional information about the type or purpose of the transmission. Often, error-sensing data is included also. Packet construction depends on the type of network, and its format is determined by the network's protocol. The labeling attached to a packet describes where it is sent. Networks that can route packets are packet switching networks; those that route data by bundling packets together for transmission and using dedicated lines (such as the phone company or on-line services), are circuit switching networks.

Every communication session is governed by a set of rules called protocols. The International Standards Organization (ISO) has established a model called the Open Systems Interconnection (OSI), a hierarchy of protocols governing both hardware and software designs. Each layer in the hierarchy handles data in a specified manner and interacts with the next higher and lower layer.

Hardware layers are low-level functions; software layers are high-level functions. From higher to lower, the layers for the OSI model are:

7. Application: The software used to provide network services including user applications and file server software.

6. Presentation: Responsible for data format conversion, this software is often either a network driver that is a Chooser RDEV on the Mac or a part of the CONFIG.SYS file on the IBM PC.

5. Session: Manages the sequencing of interaction between communicating network devices. NetBIOS is a session-level protocol. Two sequencing methods, carrier sensing and token passing, are used in LANs. Carrier sensing detects whether the media is transmitting a signal, and if not, transmits. When (by accident) two signals pass through at the same time, protocols such as collision detection or collision avoidance detect transmission errors and retransmit the signal. Carrier Sense Multiple Access with Collision Detection (CSMA/CD), used by Ethernet, is one of the most widely used access methods. Token passing is a method for activating one node on a network at a time (the "token" is passed); that node alone has access to the cable. When transmission is completed, the token is passed in sequence to the next computer. ARCnet and Token-Ring use token passing.

4. Transport: Composed of all devices/software that ensure reliability and continuity of the communication transaction process.

3. Network: Composed of switching devices controlling addressing and routing of data to each node.

2. Data Link: Composed of circuits and devices that orchestrate the coordination and timing of access to the network media.

1. Physical: Includes connections to the network, media (wires), and any device that generates the electromagnetic signals.

The applications and communication services described in Chapter 13 require that a user purchase software that works only on the application and presentation layers. Connecting a network requires the purchase of both hardware and software that uses all seven layers. To intelligently discuss networking you must be aware of the different layers and where each device fits in. Refer to one of the books on networks listed in the references for more information on protocols.

Connecting Networks

Every computer network has some restrictions on wiring length and on the number of nodes it can support. Cable length can be extended by inserting devices called repeaters into the network. They act as signal amplifiers, often increasing the maximum number of nodes available. Repeaters are simple hardware devices, and have no effect on network software. The three devices most commonly used for connecting networks are bridges, routers, and gateways.

Figure 16-2
Network connection devices. **(A)** Repeaters **(B)** Bridges **(C)** Routers **(D)** Gateways

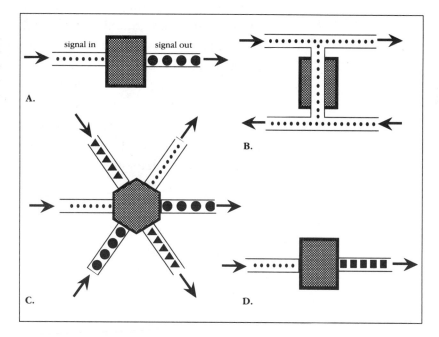

Bridges are hardware devices that connect networks by reading a data packet's destination and selectively filtering or transmitting that data in the appropriate sequence. Bridges act like traffic cops, working at the physical and data link level. Networks connected by bridges remain physically separate but appear as a single network to the rest of the internet.

Routers are used in internets to allow networks to maintain separate identities. The router works at the physical, data link, and network levels and has both software and hardware components. A router's software component selects the most efficient data path.

Gateways are the hardware/software package with the widest range of capabilities. They operate at all seven levels of the network. Gateways not only make networks larger, but connect dissimilar networks and perform complete data format translation. You often will find gateways to commercial on-line services for your network, allowing mail to be up- and downloaded.

Network Topology

When wiring a network, the major problem workgroups face is that topology often is dictated by physical surroundings—where phone connections, computers, and wiring conduits are located. Many companies design their entire buildings around the type of network they desire. Needless to say, if you make a mistake in planning, it can end up costing you a great deal of money later on.

Topologies can be either logical or physical. Token Ring and ARCnet both use token passing as their carrier method, but each uses a different physical arrangement (star-wired ring and bus, respectively). There are three important physical topologies for personal computer networks in use today:

- Bus topology: The bus is a reliable and effective configuration that rarely uses a central controller. It uses a length of main cable with devices branching off it and has two termination points. Failures usually are caused by disconnections on the cable. AppleTalk and Ethernet are two bus networks.

- Ring topology: This layout connects devices around a daisy chain as offshoots off a closed loop. Data are sent as packets around the ring from node to node until they find the correct recipient. Data often travel only some of the segments of the loop, and software controls which code transmits on which segment at any given moment.

- Star topology: This network is defined as a radiating set of spokes from a central controlling device. The controller can be an amplification device (active hub) or it can simply split the signal (passive hub); it can be a computer with special software or a dedicated routing device called a switch. PhoneNet can use the telephone wiring installed in your office as a star network with the telephone control box as its hub.

Figure 16-3
Some network topologies. **(A)** Bus **(B)** Ring **(C)** Star **(D)** Star-wired ring

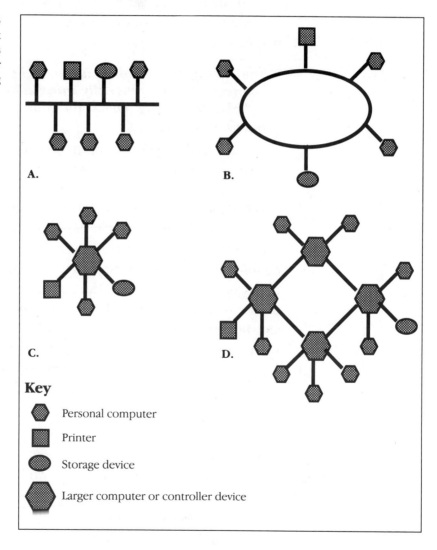

Key

- Personal computer
- Printer
- Storage device
- Larger computer or controller device

Three types of media networks are in common use today: twisted pair, coaxial, and optical fiber wiring. Their cost, bandwidth, maximum length, and immunity to interference increase in order from twisted pair, to coaxial, to optical fiber wiring. Their ease of connection and installation decrease in that order. Reliability for each is high, and optical fiber is extremely reliable but installing optical cabling can be very difficult. Improvements have blurred the boundaries for rating between media, and it is now possible to find twisted-pair wiring rated for 10 Mbps Ethernet transmission, once possible only on coaxial cabling.

▼ *Tip: Wiring on networks is generally very reliable, but connections are generally unreliable. If your network is behaving badly, check all connectors before checking the wiring.*

Systems on the market enable networks to be constructed without wires, using instead radio waves or infrared (IR) beams. The IR beam is pointed at the ceiling and the reflected radiation connects to other computers. The PhotoLink TR system is available for the Macintosh with a transmission distance of about 70 feet; to connect to PCs you would have to use TOPS software. Radio wave out-of-sight connections can reach up to one-quarter mile outdoors or 200 to 300 feet indoors. The ARLAN 450 and LAWN transceivers are two examples of radio wireless networks. Radio and IR devices are becoming increasingly popular for offices where networks must be reconfigured often, for they provide great flexibility. Wireless networks have a throughput of up to several hundred bps.

Network Standards and Architectures

Computer vendors have implemented their own proprietary networks in order to provide design advantages to their customers, and the proliferation of dissimilar networks has led to the development of several networking standards. Standards are promulgated by vendors and by official standards organizations to allow the development of compatible networking products. Standards can cover a range of protocols, and vendors can adopt all or some of them. Be aware that partial adoption can lead to incompatibilities in systems using supposedly identical protocols. Some important networking standards are:

- System Network Architecture (SNA): Developed by IBM as the standard network for all IBM computers. SNA uses twisted-pair wiring and is slow speed.

- NetBIOS (Network Basic Input/Output System): is an application programming interface (API). It operates at the OSI session level and was part of the IBM original PC LAN standard. NetBIOS is the standard for PC network communications, a session-level protocol.

- AppleTalk: A set of protocols developed by Apple for the Macintosh computers. These networks use a bus topology, twisted-pair wiring, have a 32-computer limit, are inexpensive to implement, and are slow speed (320 bps).

- Ethernet: The current industry standard for high-speed network transmission (10 Mbps), with a 1,024 node limit in a bus topology. It was developed by Xerox and DEC and originally ran on coaxial cables. Ethernet specifies protocols for both connection and transmission. Novell and 3Com sell Ethernet LANs; they are incompatible with one another.

- Transmission Control Protocol/Internet Protocol (TCP/IP): The network standard used by the U.S. government (DARPA), universities, and Ethernet. IP is a physical layer protocol, TCP is an OSI transport layer protocol. The Government Open Systems Interconnection Profile (GOSIP), introduced on August 15, 1990, is the new federal standard that updates TCP/IP.

- X.25: An international standard recommended by the CCITT. It specifies an interface for packet switched networks.

- X.400: Another CCITT standard for international E-mail transform. It is used by MCI Mail and CompuServe.

- Integrated Services Digital Network (ISDN): A new standard for very high speed transmission that allows for wide area networks (WANs) spanning thousands of miles. Optical cables are used, and the transmission speed is fast enough to transmit voice, data, text, images, and possibly even radio and TV. ISDN is the future of networking and is discussed in more detail in Chapter 19.

Networks are complicated beasts, and new technology is always being introduced. If you work hard and read a lot, you can just about stay a few months behind. But simple, distributed networks are easy to set up, particularly for the Macintosh where networking capabilities are built in. It you are planning a large network, find and use a consultant to help you set up your network.

Software

Once you have decided on and connected the type of network you desire, you install the software that makes it functional. This choice of software involves the establishment of file servers (either dedicated or nondedicated), print servers, and E-mail systems. File servers offer the possibility of sharing files and applications across a network. Print servers allow users to send to print simultaneously by queuing the files (spooling) in the server until the printer becomes free. It is possible to share a printer on a network without printer server software, but it's inefficient, because it ties up all computers until the printer executes the print file. Most commercial network packages include both file and print servers.

E-mail, Bulletin Boards, and Conferencing

Most networks are established with E-mail services that allow users to send messages and files to each other. These E-mail applications, which can be part of the network installation or purchased as individual applications, use either a mail server system or a direct delivery approach. Normally, E-mail capabilities are the first level of groupware applications created when establishing a workgroup; they are also the most valuable. The packages listed below were selected for their E-mail capabilities. More complete office systems are listed in the next section.

- cc:Mail (Mac, PC): A powerful, easy-to-use E-mail LAN package that allows for low-price entry and good upgrades. It has text, DOS, and graphics file transfers along with screen capture and graphics editing.

- Da Vinci eMail (PC): A complete E-mail system with many features. It uses MHS and is very easy to learn. It comes in a DOS or Windows version.

- DynaMail (Mac): A basic E-mail package for AppleTalk. There is memo and phone message forms, and a message can enclose one file. Compression routines make this package slow.

- InBox Plus 3.0 (Mac): This package from TOPS is a good E-mail system and runs on either AppleShare or TOPS. Memo and phone messages are sent to mailboxes; there are passwords and storage boxes. Easy to set up.

- Microsoft Mail 2.0 (Mac): A strong package for Mac and VAX servers, Mac LANs, and internets. It has a good interface, is simple to run and use, uses custom forms, and contains an efficient database engine.

- QuickMail 2.2.2 (Mac): Currently the best E-mail package for the Mac. It has many powerful tools and is very configurable. Messages allow multiple file enclosure, and there are custom forms. QuickMail requires some time to learn and has some disk de-fragmentation and larger disk storage space requirements.

Many companies, service bureaus, universities, and individuals find that they can create a group identity by establishing their own electronic bulletin boards (BBS). These services have been around for many years, even before the on-line services made them popular. It would be almost impossible to list the tens of thousands of BBSs in the world; they come and go with blinding frequency. There are commercial packages on which you can create your own BBS using a personal computer. They provide messaging services, file libraries, and file transfers. The most popular are:

Second Sight, TeleFinder, and WWIV Mac BBS for the Macintosh; RBBS-PL, The Bread Board System, The Major BBS, Tpost, and Wildcat for the PC. Many organizations find that a BBS improves their response time to customers and in general promotes a higher level of service. Refer to Russ Lockwood's article cited in the References under "Network—Software" for a case study.

Using a program called Aspects from Group Technologies, real-time document conferencing is possible on up to sixteen Macintosh computers connected by modems or on a LAN. Graphics or text documents are loaded into memory on each machine, and cursor movement and edits are transmitted almost simultaneously. The conference initiator serves as the moderator and manages access privileges. Aspects has word processing and graphics modules, and sessions can be like brainstorming on a conference chalkboard. Object- and paragraph-locking ensures that only one user can make modifications at a time.

Office Automation

Office automation software initially was written to distribute clerical tasks using a minicomputer or a mainframe and associated dumb terminals. Groupware is more often based on LANs, but due to the explosion of PCs in the marketplace, today there is often very little difference between office automation and groupware products. AT&T's Rhapsody and IBM's OfficeVision are modern office automation packages that allow you to use third-party software while maintaining a consistent interface—two important features of groupware. Groupware either integrates existing software or offers a proprietary solution. Each approach has benefits and drawbacks. Integration lets you use the combination of features best suited for your work, often with software and hardware you are already familiar with. Hence, there's less training involved and more opportunity to upgrade whenever the technology improves. Proprietary solutions are harder to modify but offer features that are better suited to specialized tasks.

WordPerfect Office 3.0 (Mac, PC) is a collection of one of the more complete proprietary automation packages offered. It is modular and you can add nodes to a network of WP Office at any time. It comes with the Shell, a menuing program, which along with the File Manager, organizes your programs and manages your files and directories. The Calendar is a scheduling program for appointments, to-do lists, and memos. The Editor is a simple text editor, while the Calculator provides four calculation modes. WordPerfect Office PC can be attached to other PCs on a LAN using either the WP Office LAN 3.0 product or standard NetBIOS networks. WP Office LAN includes a Mail E-mail program and a Scheduler for coordinating meetings and events with other people on the network. WordPerfect sells systems that provide for multiple LAN connections through an Async Gateway, EasyLink Gateway, or MHS Gateway for WAN support.

Some of the software packages available for office automation are:

- Higgins (PC): Offers E-mail, document management, group scheduling, and project tracking.

- Intuitive Network Total Office (INTO) (PC): Provides E-mail, scheduling, data management, phone messaging, text editor with search and retrieval, word processor, spreadsheet, graphics, and calculator.

- The Microsoft Office (Mac): A combination of Mail, Word, Excel, and Powerpoint sold on disk or CD ROM together. Good value for the money.

- Office Minder 1.10 (PC): Contains E-mail, scheduling, project management, and terminate and stay resident (TSR) capabilities.

- OfficeVision/2 (PC): An office automation system with a strong E-mail component, Standard Query Language (SQL) front end, and phone dialer. Best for IBM host environments.

- Office Works LAN (PC): Provides E-mail with telex and fax, phone messaging, document and people tracking, and has limited application launching.

- Right Hand Man (PC): A memory-resident program that contains E-mail, scheduling, and conversation modules.

- Synchrony (Win): Includes E-mail with conversation tracking, calendars, group scheduling, and hypertext document linking capabilities. Supports both LAN and WAN. Synchrony works with Novell NetWare or NetBIOS and includes Message Handling Service (MHS) on WANS. Windows Dynamic Data Exchange (DDE) protocol is supported.

- The Coordinator 2.1 (PC): Includes E-mail, calendars, and The Conversation Manager, a module for sorting mail and tracking E-mail conversations.

Wang Freestyle   Office automation is becoming increasingly sophisticated and is enabling the use of systems that create electronic documents. In 1989, Wang Labs unveiled its Freestyle system that combines an IBM PC computer with graphics tablet, voice input, fax board, and icon-based DOS software for creating a composite document that can be stored or forwarded for further use. Fully developed Freestyle stations cost about $12,000, but the system can be attached to a NetBIOS network. Freestyle documents can be used on ordinary IBM PCs with a $249 software package called Freestyle/Light. Freestyle integrates with the Wang VS Office Systems and with Wang Integrated Image Systems (WIIS). You can draw a handwritten note on a spreadsheet using the graphics tablet, mention some changes, attach a report, and then send it to a colleague for real-time playback. Freestyle is as close to the paperless office system as exists at the moment.

Other voice E-mail systems allow you to create, play, and transmit verbally annotated documents (such as Artisoft's LANtastic and VoxLink's VoxMail), but what makes Freestyle innovative is that it combines several peripherals to allow full, real-time multimedia presentation of documents. A similar solution for Macintosh users can be had at a fraction of Freestyle's cost in a program that Farallon is introducing, called Annotator. Annotator works with the MacRecorder sound digitizer, adding voice and markup and comment facilities similar to those found in Freestyle. Using these systems you can create multimedia presentations, storyboard displays, liven up meetings and demos, and use all of your favorite applications.

Figure 16-4
The Wang Freestyle
Desktop, iconic-GUI
software for managing
documents and infor-
mation. *Courtesy of
Wang Laboratories, Inc.*

Freestyle creates a virtual desktop on your screen. Anything that can be displayed on your screen is converted for use and storage to a bit-mapped TIFF representation of a page. The program accepts digitized image input from scanners or outside facsimile devices. It can be launched with a touch of the pencil on the graphics tablet (it has an eraser function as well!), and documents can be minimized to an icon. When you exit Freestyle, you are returned to the point you were at in the application before entering Freestyle. Freestyle is not groupware per se because it lacks document management by an underlying database, but it is a considerable extension of the office system into new areas, and a very noteworthy product.

Groupware

Groupware defies description; it is as much a set of capabilities as it is a product category. It is an outgrowth and expansion of office automation systems. Terms such as shared object management, task flow automation, and interactive conferencing are often used in the press to describe some of its objectives. Groupware can provide communication and services between one-to-one, one-to-many, many-to-one, and many-to-many. You can add groupware capabilities to almost any mix of hardware and software, and solutions range from a simple network with an E-mail package (one-to-one) to an entire set of computers with full conferencing software.

The definition of groupware diverges from automation tools when it starts to include capabilities for information management. Groupware provides organization to an environment, prioritizing and assigning tasks, and classifying information. Many packages use a relational database as the engine to power the automatic cross-referencing of data for the workgroup. Each piece of information or document can be attached to a project and supplied to a user as the response to a request or query. How much capability a system has can be programmed by an overlying macro language, or built up over time. Many of the most important advances of personal computer system software in the 1990s are aimed at bringing the benefits of this concept to the average user. Groupware is a rapidly developing category of sophisticated software.

New networking solutions, integrated with groupware software, are providing workgroup publishers with the chance to interact in innovative ways with remote colleagues, and without the headaches of playing phone tag. You can work anywhere, connect to a network, download old work while uploading new work. There are products that allow remote access to a network, usually incorporating either a modem package or a gateway. Shiva Corporation's NetModems come with dial-in access for Macs, and the Shiva DOS Dial-In package allows PCs to call into a network. Infosphere's Liaison software for the Mac also allows remote access. Many E-mail services, such as CompuServe or MCI Mail (see Chapter 13), integrate to office mail programs, including Microsoft Mail, CE Software's QuickMail, InBox, cc:Mail, and WordPerfect Office;

many others provide a gateway feature that unites the network with a service. Automatically, at specified intervals, mail is sent and retrieved.

Still another new class of groupware software aimed at network users is appearing that allows even more active collaboration between groups of users. With Farallon's Timbuktu and Micro-com's Carbon Copy Mac, you can control a Macintosh or set of Macintosh computers from your own Macintosh. These products are showing up in classrooms for computer training because they enable a teacher to train many students by controlling their com-puter screens from a central station. Even more impressive is Tim-buktu/Remote by which you can perform the same function by calling up a network using a modem by phone. Carbon Copy Mac can be used similarly. These products require a 9,600 baud modem for reasonable performance.

Object-Oriented Programming Environments Not all groupware products are canned solutions. Hewlett-Packard's NewWave application is a construction kit for creating complex document links and integration. This product won numerous industry awards in 1989, and the techniques it introduced are likely to become part of operating systems and GUIs in the future. NewWave is an extension of the macro programming language concept, but uses object-oriented graphical programming in place of code. The concept is harder to explain than to use. NewWave runs on top of Windows, and adds additional capabilities to docu-ments created with other applications.

NewWave binds applications and data together into an Object. When you double-click on the icon for that Object, that file auto-matically loads. Another element of the program called an Agent records a set of tasks or procedures into a script or macro for play-back later. Double-click an Agent and the macro runs, even across applications, and at any time—prompting you for information, if needed. A NewWave Document can integrate several different types of files into a compound file, hot-linking data to its use in another file. Change a number in a Lotus 1-2-3 spreadsheet, and the dependent graph created in Micrografx Graph Plus is instantly updated. Double-clicking that graph in a Samna Ami word processor file and the data from 1-2-3 is displayed for editing. Building a composite document is as easy as combining Objects into a NewWave Document; you simply drag icons into folders. With a feature called Bridges, you assign an icon to any file. Another feature called Object Storage lets you assign an icon to a network disk or volume and make it available across a LAN.

Figure 16-5
H-P NewWave is an object-oriented programming environment that runs on top of Windows. It allows users to combine off-the-shelf applications into a fully integrated network solution. *Courtesy of Hewlett-Packard Company.*

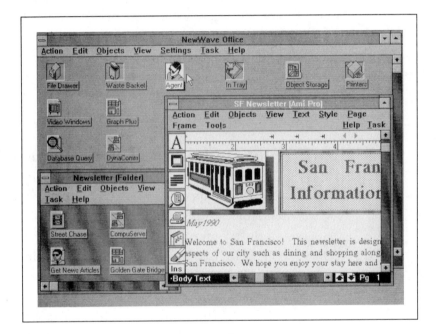

NewWave is hot stuff, and will undoubtedly serve as a platform for groupware in the future. It is compatible with all of the major PC networks, and there are plans to extend the system to OS/2 Presentation Manager and UNIX. Although you can use all DOS programs on NewWave, currently about 100 products fully conform to the NewWave guidelines and are fully enabled by the system. Most of these are in the office products area: E-mail systems, telecommunications packages, word processors, graphics, spreadsheets, databases, and project management areas. There are also some language products and application generators that are

NewWave-able, but no special DTP groupware programs have adopted this environment. Bridges to over twenty major programs, such as PageMaker 3.0, have been written. Some of the more interesting applications appearing for NewWave are multimedia products. Object-oriented programming will become the standard basis for creating computer presentations in the 1990s (see Chapter 18).

Figure 16-6
(A) The Links command keeps one version of a PageMaker file live while permitting a user to archive older versions. **(B)** A Book command structures a long document and allows a user to order and print a job correctly. These functions are essential to production in a workgroup.

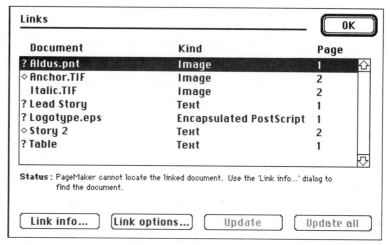

A.

B.

The concept of adding object-oriented programming to system software has been an ongoing topic of conversation at both Apple and Microsoft. DOS has a batch file capability that allows complex repetitive functions to be programmed, but the approach is non-graphical. An AppleScript may appear in Macintosh System 8.0, similar to the object-oriented HyperTalk programming language. Both Windows and Macintosh System software continue to add some automatic data linkage capabilities to all of their new versions. New capabilities for managing workgroup process flow are also in development. Page layout, because it uses so many elements, is becoming a proving ground for groupware features. PageMaker 4.0 on the Mac has introduced a system that tracks the live versions of documents using the Links command and then orders them into a structured compound document using the Book command (see Figure 16.5). Potentially, these improvements may enable the average or power user to "write" workgroup applications suited to his or her own needs before the decade is out.

High-End Groupware Lotus Notes is a complete networked, groupware application that is a stand-alone package rather than a development environment. It uses Windows or OS/2 as the client to an OS/2 server and runs on NetBIOS compatible networks such as 3Com 3+, IBM PC LAN, and Novell NetWare. It provides WAN support and comes as a $62,500, 200-node installation package. Lotus has described the system as a document management and group communication package. Actually, it is much more. It is a complete office management system that comes with a correspondence editor, an E-mail system, file import/export capabilities, distributed database document management software with hypertextural linked information, and a data security system. With Lotus Notes you can work with your traditional software, and it is customizable through the use of a set of programming extensions and can be adapted to most workgroup enterprises.

Lotus Notes is software that is much more than the sum of its parts. None of its modules is notable in its features, but the combination creates an effective groupware environment. Information organized in a Notes database can be indexed and viewed in various ways, retrieved, organized, and shared with other users with GUI-based software applications. Notes is "noted" for its ability to create custom applications and specialized databases. Some templates shipping with the program include: Client Tracking, Document Library, Status Reporting, and Service Request Tracking. It is being used by large organizations, such as Reuters, for news dispatch dissemination, and by banks and other financial institutions. It represents the latest stage in groupware and, with significant development effort, could be the basis for a distributed electronic publishing system.

Document Management Systems   Computer publishing requires extensive document and file management capabilities, particularly for large publishing efforts such as newspapers or magazines. Articles must be tracked through copy editing and typesetting, photos and drawings must be monitored as they are produced, and printing and distribution must be supervised. All these elements comprise what is basically a database problem, and in the 1970s several vendors addressed it by developing proprietary systems for copy flow and production. One of the most successful was the Atex Magazine Publishing System (Bedford, MA), a PC-based system that provides a word processor, copy editor, copy flow, and page layout modules. The system then expanded to Mac II computers to incorporate the graphics found on that platform. Atex is customizable and designs and installs major networked/workgroup installations; it is not a do-it-yourself solution. However, more and more commercial publications are shying away from this closed, proprietary, single-vendor approach in an effort to get the best new tools available. The result is that multiplatform, open system, electronic publishing is gaining favor even though this approach requires stronger document management type software. Odesta (Northbrook, IL) has adapted its popular Double Helix relational database for this task. Odesta Database Management System (ODMS) is a custom application built on top of that database. It provides advanced document management capabilities including access control and security, version control and revision tracking, plus a relational document tree structure. It also provides a framework through which a network of client Macintosh computers using popular software can be managed in a multiuser network with either a powerful Macintosh or a DEC VMS Vax computer acting as the host. Connections to Windows, OS/2, and UNIX clients are planned for the near future. ODMS is marketed to large commercial accounts, or through VARs.

Figure 16-7
The Odesta Document Management System, shown here running on a DECwindows client, offers compound document tracking for complex electronic publishing projects. *Courtesy of Odesta Corporation.*

ODMS is a modular system. When you scan a picture, the name and details of the file created are recorded by a program called the Image Filer, which is a database of pictures. You can view a thumbnail of your image before opening it. If you altered that scanned image in a photo retouching program, the next time you viewed the data record for that image, ODMS would also show you an icon, allowing you to launch that application and open the file if you choose to. Once you quit the retouching program, your file is reclaimed as a new version. Any application available on the desktop can be used in this manner. For example, the Copy Desk is used on ODMS for the text files of magazines and newspapers. The computer functions in the familiar way, but underlying the process is the concept that the image or text file is data contained in a field in a database file residing in a server elsewhere on the network. This is transparent to the user. ODMS replaces the wall of clipboards that many publications use to track their production.

As a database, ODMS has special tools for creating an audit trail for documents. They can be attached to project definitions that provide the bases for a relational database file. Searching is done using the Standard Query Language. Files and versions are time stamped, and live versions can be used while older versions are archived. An outlining module is useful for creating long, technical documentation, and ODMS has found favor with organizations that do this type of work. Complex document management is a "fourth wave" solution for large publishing efforts, and ODMS is a unique product that can be designed from the ground up.

WriteOn, an integrated suite of magazine planning, production and administration modules, was to be available through Linotype (Hauppage, NY) in the second half of 1991. Developed in the Netherlands, the package works on any standard Macintosh network with off-the-shelf word processing and layout software. A PC module will allow the use of MS-DOS workstations in the system.

WriteOn's base module, called Planning, allows managing editors to map an unlimited number of magazine pages, including specification of ad pages and limits, editorial elements, assignments, signatures, and impositions. The Production module tracks page and document status and controls page elements and authorization levels. The administration module generates up-to-the-minute reports on ad costs, paper decision, production progress, and assignments.

P.Ink Press is a QuarkXpress-based magazine and newspaper management system slated for release by Time Warner in the latter part of 1991. Developed in Germany for newspapers, the product works with P.Ink's SQL database on LocalTalk/Ethernet networks. Time Warner is developing a prototype magazine version of the product for *Entertainment Weekly*, to be followed by separate newspaper and magazine editions for both large, commercial publications, and for staffs in corporate communications and small business. Time Warner will distribute the large installation versions directly and through value added resellers, while Quark, Inc. will sell the mass-market edition. Features include text editing and processing, editorial management, page makeup, bookkeeping, ad management, and wire-service links.

Meanwhile, North Atlantic Publishing Systems (Carlisle, MA) plans to release three new document management products in 1991. Editorial Copy Management System (ECMS), a tracking system with a XyWrite-based front end, and Publication Locking, an editorial and art file locking system to be published as a QuarkXtension, were both slated for May release. Publication Administrator, another Quark-based document tracking system for page makeup, editorial, and art staffs, will be released later in 1991. Linking to Acius's 4th Dimension database, it is designed to work with all of North Atlantic's other products, including ECMS, Publication Locking, CopyFlow and CopyBridge.

Managing Editor Software (Elkins Park, PA) plans a release of Ad Director, an extension to its Page Director publication management system for the Macintosh. Ad Director includes expanded capabilities for managing ad placement and tracking for commercial magazines.

The IBM PC also has workgroup document management systems. Saros Corporation's FileShare system works with IBM PCs using a Microsoft/Sybase SQL Server. Sybase is a relational database, the server is an OS/2 LAN Manager. It can be customized and tracks files in many ways. Another company called Boss Logic is developing a Sybase SQL server for the NeXT. The North Atlantic Publishing Systems' CopyFlow and CopyFlow Reports systems link the DOS word processor XyWrite to QuarkXPress on the Macintosh. Profound, by Wang Informatics, is yet another document and file management system that can be used from within most single PC applications.

Production Considerations

Desktop applications in workgroup production can cause difficulties at several steps in the process. Tracking, discussed above, is one problem, but even if you are using a single, live version of your documents, you still must maintain control over multiple users making changes at the same time. It is impractical to create a new, live version every time a document is opened for viewing, or for some very minor change. Also, it is desirable to have a system in place that allows multiple users to edit at the same time.

Copy editing is a major bottleneck in workgroup publishing. It's not always practical to set up a full-blown document management system, particularly when all the participants aren't connected on a network. Several products are available that enable many people to work concurrently on an electronic document. MarkUp from Mainstay is one such product for the Macintosh. Users can comment and review documents even if they don't own the creator application(s), but no reviewer can make changes to the original document; only the coordinator can. Each reviewer uses a run-time version of the product called MiniMarkUp to indicate suggested changes using standard graphics tools for highlighting, deleting, and commenting. Each set of comments is placed in a separate transparent layer (overlay). MarkUp allows the use of color (or simulates it on a black and white screen), and contains a toolbox of standard proofreader's copy marks.

MarkUp has a simple underlying database of files and provides a basic, integrated document management. The process of editing is controlled by a manager who assigns reviewers and sends out copies. Reviewers can work on editing concurrently, signing off and returning their copies when done. Each copy can be password protected, and MarkUp keeps a journal of all editing sessions that take place. The manager then assembles the final copy using or rejecting all of the comments provided, and MarkUp can be used to store the version history of a project. MarkUp can be used on an AppleShare, TOPS, or Apple Filing Protocol (AFP) network. Best yet, MarkUp works with all of the applications you already have.

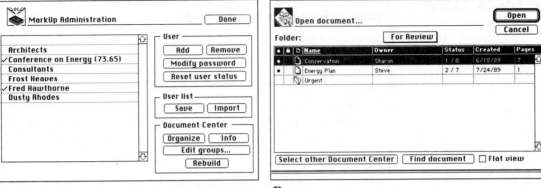

A.

B.

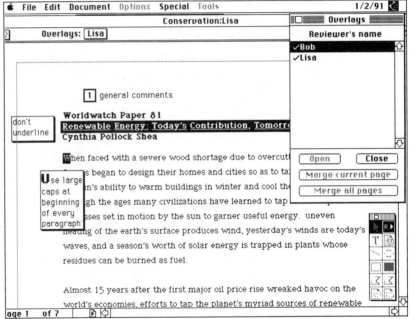

C.

Figure 16-8 (A) MarkUp has a system of passwords and access groups.
(B) MarkUp projects are organized by a Document Center. **(C)** Each reviewer's editing goes into a transparent overlay in MarkUp, leaving the original document for final edit by the manager.

File Sharing

Workgroup file sharing for electronic publishing has the same problems associated with it that networked databases do. You need to limit access to a file to those who have the right to view or edit it. This involves setting up privileges and password-protecting each group. While a live document is being used by someone in the group, it is important to restrict access to others who might want to use it at the same time. You don't want simultaneous changes. Databases solve this problem by providing file and record locking mechanisms that limit access to work in progress. File sharing requires that a manager be appointed to oversee work flow. Complete document management systems can minimize the amount of time a manager must spend on such work, or reduce the overall requirements of the position, but they rarely eliminate the need for such a person entirely.

Data Archival

One problem a document management system solves is tracking project components. As old versions of documents are retired and replaced by updated live versions, a project acquires a history that must be annotated. Data archival or storage can be an organization nightmare, but one that can be solved by using file attributes to track a creation and modification date. Both Macintosh and IBM PC files have attributes that can be used for this purpose (see Chapter 4). However, unless you are very organized, your project files still may end up located at several different places on your system. What's required is a combination archival, search, and retrieval software.

MarcoPolo from Mainstay is another groupware product for project organization. It organizes projects within a special-purpose database called a MarcoPolo Document Center, compressing files not in use and indexing their contents to provide a rapid search and retrieval. You can find information based on content (keyword), author, title, commentary, and archival dates automatically. MarcoPolo supports many file formats, text and graphics, even E-mail messages, and will search an 80 MByte hard drive in seconds.

▼ *Tip:Complex project management threatens any data backup and archival or storage system.*

Therefore, it is imperative to pay special attention to your backup procedure, creating multiple, regular backups of your projects to ensure protection against data loss. Also consider investing in an uninterruptible power supply (UPS) for protection against blackouts or brownouts.

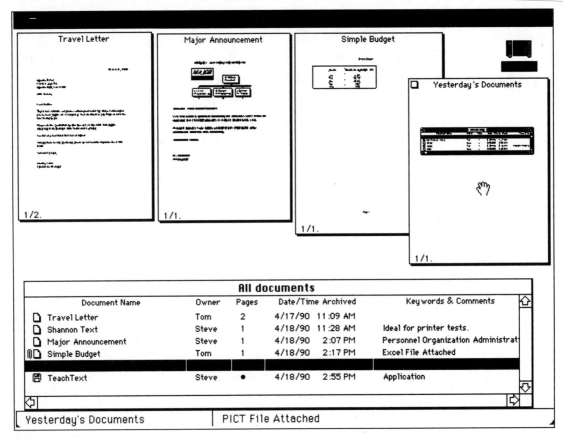

Figure 16-9 MarcoPolo organizes project documents in a database for indexing, search, and retrieval.

MarcoPolo is a basic document management system geared to the individual user. Documents are grouped into projects, and when a desired document is located, it is displayed in miniature on your screen. You can flip pages, move live documents about on your desktop, and then double-click to bring up the actual size. The Document Center that organizes a project can be shared with other users, a form of electronic publishing and distribution. MarcoPolo also allows users to open documents without having the creator application(s), and you can embed your searches with a document for other users to use. MarcoPolo is useful for separating E-mail messages by content or can be used to distribute electronic documents throughout a company.

Using Service Bureaus

Never argue with people who buy ink by the gallon.
Tommy Lasorda, manager, Los Angeles Dodgers

In the late 1980s an industry of service bureaus specializing in desktop publishing services was born. Ranging from small shops and medium size companies to large franchises, there are now more than 1,000 PostScript service bureaus in the United States according to Adobe, the developers of PostScript. (The Adobe and other service bureau directories are listed in the references at the end of the book.) Recently various service bureau user groups and trade associations, such as the Service Bureau Association, Professional PostScript Alliance, New York PostScript Users Group, and others have been formed. They can be a valuable source of names. Organizations such as the Typographer's International Association and the National Composition and Prepress Association also have service bureaus as members and are a good source of information.

If you look in the yellow pages of the phone book under the heading *Desktop Publishing*, both service bureaus and other design services are offered. The Boston phone book lists some 111 companies, some of which are individuals offering design services. Perhaps forty of those shops are places you can go to get various output capabilities, which is the focus of this chapter. You can also find service bureaus listed under the categories "Typesetting" and "Printing," although those categories generally list more traditional organizations.

Service bureaus have diverse origins. Some began as cottage industries in people's dining rooms. Others became service extensions of the corner copy shop, and still others were formed by printing companies. A number of service bureaus specialize in CAD/CAM, solid model prototyping, music and video production, and other niches not discussed in this chapter. Here we focus on computer-based publishing, this diversity means that a wide range of expertise is available to you. Often bureaus promote a specialty, perhaps design, process color, presentation materials, or printing, for example. Your goal should be to select the service bureau whose capabilities, style, and pricing match your specific needs.

About 75 percent of service bureaus currently doing DTP work use Macintosh computers as the base for their business; maybe 40 percent are strictly IBM PC-based. Perhaps 25 percent of the shops use both Macs and PCs. Many service bureaus don't use IBM PCs at all, but this will probably change rapidly over the next year or two. It is still extremely rare to find a DTP service bureau that offers Amiga, NeXT, or Sun SPARCstation work, although Commodore Amigas are common at service bureaus dedicated to music or video production. The quality of DTP software and hardware being written for the NeXT computers suggest that they, too, will make inroads into service bureaus in 1991.

The basic approach to selecting a service bureau shouldn't be much different from the way in which you would go about choosing a physician, a professional designer, or a printer. You may need extensive direction or only initial guidance. Ask other desktop publishers for recommendations and do some comparison shopping. Obviously, the more complicated a project, the more expertise will be necessary from the service bureau. Some bureaus offer full production (print) capabilities.

The size of a service bureau should not be a factor in your choice. Some small shops are excellent, and, conversely, some large shops are mediocre. The right equipment is not a guarantee that you'll get excellent results either, especially with complex projects involving process color, for example. The experience of a bureau's staff with the equipment used on your type of project is what's important. Ask to see samples of a bureau's work, and call references as an additional safeguard.

Typical Services Offered

Some shops allow you to walk in and do-it-yourself on rented equipment. Some are extensions of copy shops. The least expensive service bureaus are high-volume, low-price imagesetting shops. However, intense competition in imageset page prices have led to many organizations broadening the services that they offer. A "full-service" operation might include 24 hour black-and-white imagesetting, scanning, film separations, color proofs, hardware and software sales, technical support, and sometimes medium or long run print jobs. Most of this chapter is concerned with high-resolution output because that is the most common need for DTP work.

Because service bureaus staff experts in very specialized areas, often they also are active in training. Training is also available from computer dealerships, but it is generally on basic equipment and software. Service bureaus offer some of the better classes on general computer technology with a special view toward DTP and design. Topics include computer equipment, common and specialized software packages, graphics, layout, prepress, and other related technologies.

Some standard prices for services are:

- Media conversion: Both disk and file format conversions. Prices range from $15 to $25 a file and $60 to $90 per disk, depending on the time required to convert.

- Laser print: Paper or transparency 8 ½ by 11 inch, 50¢ to $2.

- Imagesetter output: 8 ½ by 11 inch, paper, $7.50 to $15; 8 ½ by 11 inch, film: $15 to $30.

- Photo scan: Hourly rates, $30 to $150, depending on the quality of the equipment used; less for black and white, more for better color work.

- Separation: Four-color (desktop) and four films, $80 to $250; four-color film, $60 to $140.

- Computer-generated slides: 35 mm, $15 to $30 each.

- Proofs and overlays: Chromalin, 8 ½ by 11 inches, $75; Matchprint, $50 to $65; Fujifilm Color Art, $65; Color Key, $20 to $40.

- Color prints: QMS ColorScript, $10 to $20; DuPont 4 CAST, $25 to $50.

- Layout, artwork, designer services: Hourly rates, $50 to $100.

- Optical Character Recognition (OCR) services: Page, 8 ½ by 11 inches, $2 to $4.

There are a number of specialized service bureaus for large-size color output. ReproCAD (Lafayette, CA) has a national network of service bureaus to print color graphics up to 42 inches wide by 12 feet long using its Megachrome service. It is currently available in New York at National Reprographics, in San Francisco at Blue Print Service Company, in Los Angeles at Blair Graphics, in Chicago at RiteWay Reproductions, in Seattle at Waterfront Reprographics, and in Dallas at Carich Reprographics. Over sixty other sites are planned. A Megachrome graphic can include any EPS graphic, bit-mapped images, and line art. Documents are printed at 400 dpi resolution on a four-color electrostatic plotter manufactured by Versatec (Santa Clara, CA). These printers can be used for banners, renderings and site plans, large flip charts, in-store displays, and meeting signage. Output can be on bond paper, film, or vellum. A 30-by 40-inch Megachrome print costs $100.

Renting Equipment

Renting is a great way to try out software and hardware that you are thinking of buying, or that you can't afford at the moment. Fees for renting equipment are charged on an hourly basis and determined by the type of equipment used. Usually, minimum rentals of thirty minutes to one hour are required. Be aware, however, that service bureaus have different policies regarding how much support they give to clients renting their equipment. Initial setup generally is free, with additional instruction or consultation charged at a rate ranging from $40 to $80 an hour.

One nice way to learn about software packages and new hardware is to test drive them at a service bureau. Some service bureaus will allow you to spend some time with the documentation on-site before you begin your work. If you have never used a scanner, for example, you can get a taste for the technology by using one there.

Standard prices for equipment rentals are as follows:

- Low-end computers: Mac Classic or IBM PC 286 (AT), $8 to $12 per hour; Mac SE/30, $12 to $15 per hour.

- Personal workstations: Mac II series or 80386 PC, $15 to $25 per hour.

- Black-and-white scanners: ScanJet Plus, $20 to $30 per hour.

- Color scanners: Microtek 300Z or Epson ES-300C, $25 to $50 per hour.

Output devices such as printers, plotters, imagesetters, and slide recorders are usually networked, and you are charged per each piece of output. So, shop around, because prices vary substantially.

Sometimes you may require more time on equipment than a service bureau can grant you, or perhaps you may need to work with computer equipment at another site. Some equipment rental companies specialize in computer and electronic equipment for longer-term needs, with rental/leasing programs that can range from one day to years and include end-of-lease purchase options. One such leasing company is GE Rental/Lease (Latham, NY), a division of General Electric. Offering personal computers, laptop computers, monitors, printers, modems, plotters, add-in boards, scanners, large-screen monitors, projectors, and other accessories, the company also has a line of industrial and electronic equipment. Check your city's *Yellow Pages* under "Computers—Renting and Leasing" for a rental company near you. And remember, rentals and leases are good business write-offs and make sense for many special situations. But, also remember, they are not cheap, and for the average individual over the long haul, they don't make sense. For the price of a three-month lease you could pay off 60 percent of the purchase of the computer; the price of a six-month lease would pay off the entire cost. For example, an IBM 33 MHz 80386 computer or a Mac IIci might cost $1,000 to $1,200 per month or $400 per week to rent, but would cost $4,000 to $6,000 to buy.

Preparations/Questions

Most people go to a service bureau to get print or film high-resolution output to be used in future projects. This can be as simple as going into the shop to rent time on a computer to get a 300 dpi laser print. More often, however, an imagesetter's higher resolution is required. As explained in Chapter 7, imagesetting is a photographic process. A latent image is created, and, using light-sensitive materials and chemical developers, that image is transferred to film or paper. Unfortunately, it is not yet simply a matter of dropping off files to be output at a service bureau in the same manner that you would drop off film at a photo shop. As discussed earlier, preparing master copy is much more complicated than running film through a set development process. Issues such as file and font management, screen angles, the output format required by your printer, and many other factors come into play. Therefore, before you head for your nearest service bureau, find out the answers to the following questions.

Should an Application or PostScript File be Provided?
Some bureaus prefer one format over the other. With an application file, the service bureau staff can open it and look for problems. About 25 percent of all files that service bureaus work with require some modification. Troubleshooting takes time and money, but it also can guarantee that the file will be output successfully. I prefer to go to shops that take the trouble to check out my files. A PostScript file can limit the costs involved because all needed imagesetter settings, linked images, and downloadable or

soft fonts are included. Printing to disk puts all the onus on you for the successful output of the file, but in highly repetitive work it can be useful. A PostScript file can be a great convenience for lay-out software, such as Ventura Publisher, where the document is composed only when printed. Ventura Publisher has a print-to-disk format called a .COO file that is much easier to create and send off to a service bureau.

Are You and the Service Bureau Using the Same Application and System Versions? Different versions may cause problems (see below). Never assume that you are both using the same version numbers—ask! This is most important. Shops are familiar with some software packages and not others—an important selection criterion for you. You and the bureau you choose must be in sync.

How Do You Send or Transfer Your File? Should you modem-in your file, or bring in a floppy disk, a removable cartridge disk, or another medium (see Chapter 6). Always ask about disk formats, because they are not all compatible. Bernoulli disks, for example, are made and sold by a single vendor, so there is only one format, whereas SyQuest and Ricoh drives are sold through OEMs and come with proprietary software. Find out if your service bureau can mount your disk, and if there is any doubt, bring in the device driver software to help out. For MS-DOS this is a .SYS file and a line added in the CONFIG.SYS file that calls up the routine. For Macintosh it is an INIT file added to the System folder.

File compression utilities are handy for sending files off to a service bureau, particularly when telecommunicating. Most service bureaus have a good collection of software: StuffIt, Disk Doubler, and Compactor are the most common for the Macintosh; Zip and ARC are the standards for the PC. Try to use the latest version of the software, but again, don't assume you and the bureau have the same versions. Compression programs often come with additional license-free software to send with your files to expand, extract, or decompress them.

▼ *Tip: Don't send your only copy of a file to a service bureau! You may need to work with that file, and disasters happen. Back up your data. It is also a good idea to send a backup copy of your files with your submission for the same reason.*

What Output Devices Does the Bureau Have? More established service bureaus have newer, faster, and higher resolution devices. Although Linotronic images from Linotype are common, many vendors have entered the fray with other competitive products (see Chapter 7). Ask about resolution and page output size options. The current image processor from Linotype is called RIP30, which supplants the previous RIP4. Current versions are faster and have higher resolution. Newer imagesetters also produce more accurate film separations due to better mechanical film transport mechanisms and full page buffering. The best imagesetters found today in service bureaus include the Linotronic 330 and 530, Optronics Colorsetter, Scitext Dolev PS, Compugraphic Selectset 5000, and the Varityper 5300. In general, imagesetters with helium-neon lasers are preferred in the industry to those with infrared lasers. They are believed to have greater sensitivity, and there are more sources of helium-neon paper than infrared paper.

What Fonts Are Available? Make sure you and the service bureau have the same fonts. Most font software licenses permit the use of a font on a single output device; you aren't legally allowed to use it to print elsewhere. Check the license agreement that comes with each font for details and ask the service bureau about its rules.

If a service bureau doesn't have the fonts you use, you may need to supply them, although most good service bureaus have a font junkie who, given the chance, will order your favorite font. And, if you become a regular customer and you use a certain font often, a good shop will generally buy it. But, most likely, the service bureau will have fonts that you want to use but don't currently own. Font foundries allow screen fonts to be distributed freely. Often you can find screen fonts on special-interest DTP forums or the forums run by font vendors on on-line services. You set up your document properly by using your service bureau's screen fonts and then the bureau prints it using the appropriate printer fonts.

What Rates Are Charged? Rates depend both on equipment and human factors, and they vary widely and often are negotiable. Many shops do have a minimum charge of $20 to $25. A single, letter-size page can cost from $5 to $15 based on volume. Charges can be by the page, by the minute, or a combination. Pages that take longer than five, ten, or fifteen minutes to print due to complex graphics are often surcharged, as are any special services requiring special setup. High-resolution output takes longer than low-resolution output and uses more expensive equipment, and is priced accordingly. Film is more expensive than paper, but that expense can save you additional charges from a commercial printer. Make sure to ask what type of film is required. PostScript file printing is cheaper than application file printing.

Turnaround time is also a factor in charges. One to two days is typical. If you need faster turnaround, rush charges are assessed and can run from 50 percent to 300 percent more. Always ask for a printed rate sheet from the service bureau when shopping around.

What Are Business Hours? Some bureaus are staffed by shifts up to twenty-four hours, others work only a standard eight-hour day.

What Support Is Offered? Self-service operations offer support only when you have a problem. More complete bureaus will troubleshoot your files and build the cost into overall service charges.

What Is the Service Bureau's Experience? The specific technical competence of the staff as it relates to your project's requirements is an important consideration. This includes design, software, and hardware. If you are interested in process color work, for instance, look for a staff with such a computer specialist.

Before submitting work to a service bureau, it is a good idea to create a checklist of items for which you need to account. Good service bureaus often have such forms already available. Ask for one and use it! Your submission should include the following:

1. File information. Include all file names, applications used (with version numbers), file formats, and font families and styles used in each document.

2. Page setup. Note the number of pages and copies to be generated. Specify page dimensions and any enlargement or reduction requirements.

3. Output options. Be clear about the form in which you want your output. In addition, note at what resolution, line screen, and screen angle your document is to be printed. Crop or registration marks should be clearly identified. Paper can be coated or uncoated, film can be positive or negative (acetate), emulsion up or down, and right reading or wrong reading. Paper output is best for when you will want to make small additional changes with traditional tools (pens, knives, etc.). Film negatives are best for a totally digital page, computer illustrations or halftones, or for spot or process color separations. The most common printer specification is right reading, emulsion down. For color work, describe whether it is spot or a process color separation. List all layers of color to be printed.

4. Deadline. Specify your deadline for work completion and how the work should be returned to you.

▼ *Tip: Always specify the lines per inch your graphics and screens should print at, in addition to specifying the resolution.*

If your line screen is finer than the printing program defaults allows, you may lose fine detail, particularly on higher-quality printing.

MicroPRINT
214 Third Avenue ♦ Waltham, MA 02154
Fax 890-7541 ♦ Modem 890-1513 ♦ (617) 890-7500

02184

PostScript Imagesetting
Weekdays 7:30–7:30 ♦ Saturday 9:00–5:00 ♦ Closed Sundays
Modems 890-1513 ♦ 890-8277 ♦ 290-0791 ♦ 24-hour BBS 890-2630

Color Comps ♦ Color Keys ♦ On & Off-site Mac Rentals ♦ Disk Conversions ♦ Electronic Stripping

Client	Delivery	200% (<5 Hr)	100% (<24 Hr)	24 Hr (Except weekends)

First Name   Last Name
Company
Street Address
City   State   Zip
Phone (Day)   (Evening)

Call when ready
Customer pickup
Courier delivery
Ask about our Delivery Savings!
Federal Express
___ for ___
Customer FedEx Number

Received ___ Day ___ Date ___ Time ___ AM PM
Due ___ AM PM

Qty   Page Price   Rush
___ @ ___ x ___ = ___
___ @ ___ x ___ = ___
___ @ ___ x ___ = ___
___ @ ___ x ___ = ___

Cash/Check   Account   Subtotal ___

Stuffit | Archive | **Computer** | **Received Via**

Mac   IBM PC
Disk Name: Laser Proofs

Courier Drop-off FedEx
Instructions Attached

Pickup # ___
Delivery # ___
Job # ___   Subtotal ___
PO # ___   Tax ___
Check   Cash   Total Price ___

Resolution (dpi)	Screens (lpi)	Density	Film Emulsion	Custom	Graphics

3386   2540   1270
635   QMS Color

133 | 133 | 100
3386 | 2540 | 1270   PAPER
DEFAULT
180 | 150 | 110
3386 | 2540 | 1270   FILM

Normal
Higher ___

Positive   Up
Negative   Down

Kern Track (PM4)
Data (XPress)

EPSF   Tiff   Pict

Zeppo Groucho Harpo Calvin   3386 2540 1270 ___   Norm Higher ___   LPI / APD: ___   Oper: ___   System: ___

File Name	Program	Pages	Size	Paper	Film	Crops	Color Separations
___	___	___	8.5x11 11x17	Paper	Film	Crops	
___	___	___	8.5x11 11x17	Paper	Film	Crops	
___	___	___	8.5x11 11x17	Paper	Film	Crops	
___	___	___	8.5x11 11x17	Paper	Film	Crops	

Aachen Bold (34)
Akzidenz Grotesk (96)
Am. Typewriter (10)
Americana (68)
Antique Olive (82)
Antique Olive 2 (107)
Arnold Bocklin (90)
New Aster (99)
Avant Garde Cond (124)
Avenir 35,55,85 (79)
Avenir 45,65,95 (80)
New Baskerville (18)
Bauhaus (87)
Belwe (52)
Bembo (161)
Benguiat (11)
Berkeley Old Style (106)
Bauer Bodoni (98)
Bauer Bodoni 2 (111)
Bodoni (26)
Bodoni 2 (118)
Bookman 2 (146)
Brush Script (33)
Bundesbahn pi (156)
New Caledonia (66)

Candida (102)
Carta (35)
Cascade (110)
Caslon 224 ITC (157)
Caslon 540 & 3 (53)
Caslon Open Face (72)
Caxton (133)
Lino Centennial (74)
Century (141)
Century Cond (142)
Century Expanded (70)
Century Old Style (22)
Charlemagne (120)
Cheltenham (24)
Cheltenham 2 (140)
Cheq (171)
Clarendon (64)
Clearface (22)
Cochin (86)
Concorde (84)
Cooper Black (32)
Copperplate Gothic (113)
Corona (43)
Cushing ITC (170)
Dom Casual (91)

Eras (56)
European. Border pi (155)
Eurostile (44)
Eurostile 2 (130)
Excelsior (45)
Fenice ITC (173)
Fette Fraktur (90)
Folio (93)
Franklin Gothic (23)
Franklin Gothic #2 (103)
Freestyle Script (34)
Friz Quadrata (11)
Frutiger (73)
Futura et al (39, 46, 47)
Galliard (17)
Adobe Garamond (100)
Garamond Cond (139)
Garamond Expert (101)
Garamond ITC (9)
Garamond 2 ITC (150)
Garamond 3 (77)
Simoncini Garamond (148)
Stempel Garamond (75)
Gill Sans 1 (152)
Gill Sans 2 (162)

Glypha (12)
Glypha 2 (164)
Gothic 13 (85)
Goudy Old Style (20)
Goudy Extra Bold (54)
Helv. Comp (50)
Helv. Cond (14)
Helv. Inserat (90)
Helv. Ltr/Black (13)
Helv. 25,95 (59)
Helv. 35,55,75 (60)
Helv. 45,65,85 (61)
Hiroshige (89)
Hobo (33)
Impressum (97)
Italia (51)
Janson Text (55)
Kabel (57)
Kaufmann (63)
Korinna (19)
Kunstler Script (115)
Leawood ITC (159)
Letter Gothic (27)
Life (83)
Linoscript (94)

Lithos (121)
Lubalin (8)
Lucida Math (154)
Lucida Roman (36)
Lucida Sans (48)
Machine (10)
Mathematical pi (158)
Maximus (135)
Medici (110)
Melior (16)
Memphis (49)
Meridien (112)
MICR (58)
Minion (143)
Minion Expert (144)
Minister (129)
Mistral (109)
Neuzeit S (137)
News Gothic (30)
Novarese (114)
Nuptial (110)
OCR A & B (58)
Olympian (169)
Optima (6)
Orator (33)

Park Avenue (25)
Parisian (108)
Peignot (65)
Post Antiqua (92)
Present Script (90)
Prestige Elite (28)
Quorum (132)
Raleigh (128)
Reporter (109)
Revue (34)
Rockwell 1 (151)
Rockwell 2 (163)
Sabon (88)
Sassoon Primary (172)
Serif Gothic (69)
Serifa (71)
Serpentine (153)
Shannon (166)
Shelley Script (136)
Snell Roundhand (147)
Sonata (21)
Souvenir (7)
Souvenir 2 (117)
Stempel Schneidler (125)
Stencil (33)

Stone Informal (42)
Stone Sans (41)
Stone Serif (40)
Symbol ITC (167)
Syntax (134)
Tekton (123)
Tempo Heavy Cond (85)
Tiffany (31)
Times New Roman (145)
Times Ten (62)
Trade Gothic (126)
Trade Gothic Cond (127)
Trajan (120)
Trump Mediaeval (15)
Umbra (108)
Univers 45,55,65,75 (37)
Univers Cond (38)
Univers Extd (168)

Universal News/Math (78)
University Roman (34)
Utopia (104)
Utopia Expert (105)
VAG Rounded (95)
Versailles (138)
Walbaum (81)
Weidemann (131)
Weiss (76)
Wood Types (122)
Wood Types 2 (160)
Zapf Chancery (165)

LaserWriter Plus
(Avant Garde, Bookman, Courier, Helvetica, Helvetica Narrow, New Century Schoolbook, Palatino, Symbol, Times, Zapf Chancery, Zapf Dingbats)

Apple | Adobe | NFNT

Other Typefaces

12/1/90   ACCOUNTING

Figure 17-1 A good submission checklist cites all disks, files, and fonts used and output options. This is an imagesetting spec sheet from MicroPrint (Waltham, MA), a full-service PostScript bureau. *Courtesy of MicroPrint.*

Always submit a laser print (hard copy) of your document to the service bureau with your files. Without hard copy, it's impossible for the service bureau staff to tell if your job printed correctly on the imagesetter. If you don't have a laser printer, rent some time on a copy shop's or the service bureau's laser printer to print and check your document.

Output Problems

Most output problems can be avoided by advance planning, but first you must have some understanding of the important factors discussed in this book, and then develop good communication regarding your work and needs with both your printer and the service bureau—in that order. The people in service bureaus are desktop publishing pioneers and are great to talk to when you run into problems. Chances are that any problem you run into that is caused by incompatible programs, file formats, PostScript errors or omissions, or other hardware or software factors, the service bureau has already encountered too, and knows the solution.

Always consider the size of the files you are creating and using. Small files can usually be brought in on floppy disks, or sent in by modem. A removable Bernoulli, SyQuest, or Ricoh cartridge disk may be necessary to work with large files, however. Color scans are particularly data intensive. Chapter 6 discussed various input and storage devices. Check to see whether your service bureau can mount your disk on its equipment or will allow you to bring in your storage device, if needed.

Applications/ File Format Considerations

Most service bureaus have a large collection of the most popular and current versions of applications. Obviously, problems occur when different versions of software are used, so if you are using an uncommon program, or an older or *newer* version of a program, you also may have some difficulty finding compatible services. Brand-new versions of software are often "buggy." So wait about three months, and use the maintenance upgrades that come along, if possible. One of the rationales for learning and using programs that are industry leaders is that they are well supported in service bureaus. But if you must (or desire to) use a program not commonly found, bring your copy of the program along, or capture the output as a PostScript language file, and send *that* to the bureau, as recommended above; most service bureaus will install it on their computers temporarily. Doing so does stretch the concept of the software license, however, so remember to remove the program when you are done. Consider how embarrassing it would be to have personalized software running on public equipment if you don't.

Often, newer program applications can be used in place of older versions, but you should be aware of one problem. Once you open a file within the newer version of a program, that file is probably permanently changed to the new file format. You will not generally be able to reopen the file within the older version of the application, which is another good reason to always work on and submit duplicate files.

As mentioned, most service bureaus use either Macs or IBM PC compatibles. If you are working on another platform you can still use service bureaus, but it is more problematical. One approach is to supply files in PostScript descriptions saved in text format (see Figure 2.14). Most applications (especially graphics) allow for this type of file format. Raw PostScript files often can bypass many application-specific printing problems. You can use them to customize files, and they can speed up considerably the rasterization of a file. But not all service bureaus can use PostScript files in this manner, so ask before trying this approach. Also, note that sending files by modem eliminates the need to mount the disk, which can be a problem if the disk is from a different type of system.

▼ *Tip: When you send your layout files and all supporting graphics file to a service bureau they may be unable to print a graphic due to some incompatibility. Tell them to suppress or delete the problem graphic, and then have your printer strip those graphics in manually. It will add an additional step, but your work will not be delayed.*

Font Problems

The fonts used in documents are the source of many file handling problems and therefore deserve careful attention. If a font that isn't loaded on the computer at the time of output is used in a document, another font is automatically substituted. More insidious is font ID conflicts caused by identically numbered or named fonts with different font metrics from independent vendors.

Service bureaus have many of the same problems with fonts that you do (see Chapter 11). Printing a font not only requires that it be loaded in your computer, but that you have both screen font (for display) and printer font (for output). Many computers and laser printers have built-in fonts. The complexity of font handling may not occur to the uninitiated until they move to another computer system. Missing fonts are replaced by default fonts (such as Courier) to make their substitution obvious. When a font is substituted, the job must be redone with the fonts installed, for which you will be charged. If possible, provide a laser print of any document you want imageset so font problems can be identified immediately.

▼ *Tip: Consider supplying a Suitcase file of all screen fonts for each Macintosh document sent to a service bureau and, if needed, printer fonts.*

Supplying a Suitcase is particularly valuable when you customize the kerning or tracking of fonts used, because the customization can't be duplicated easily by a service bureau. IBM PC font handling is more problematical because fonts need to be installed in the applications used. Submit all fonts used on disk in a couple of subdirectories. Windows 3 has a ninety-nine-font limit, and if you exceed it, you will start to see unexpected results.

Font ID conflicts were a particular problem with the older Apple Macintosh FONT format and numbering scheme. There were only 256 FONT numbers available, 128 of which were reserved by Apple, and conflicts and substitutions occurred often. The new NFNT format has a much larger number of registered fonts (about 32,000), and conflicts based on font ID numbers on the Macintosh occur much less frequently. Apple registers fonts by vendors and assigns blocks of nonconflicting numbers to them. Most Macintosh programs use the NFNT ID numbers, but some programs still use font names. The FONT and NFNT are compatible with one another, so problems are rare.

Font conflicts also can occur when fonts bearing the same name come from different vendors. The font metrics of Palatino by one vendor are different from those of another, and substitution will lead to incorrect line endings, changes in leading, and other typographical problems. You can minimize these problems by specifying the exact font, including vendor, that was used. Older versions of fonts also cause problems, so upgrade to the newest versions.

Page Setup Problems

In order for a document to be composed properly, it must be created using the printer driver for the desired output device. Changing printer drivers changes various parameters of a page due to resolution differences—margins, line endings, even character shapes are affected. Change printer drivers from a dot matrix to a laser printer, or vice versa, and you will see what I mean. Or, if you compose your document using a laser printer driver and then expect to have it print properly on an imagesetter, you may be in for some surprises. Find out what imagesetter will be used at the service bureau and then use the appropriate printer driver. Your service bureau should supply you with a list of its drivers upon request, and sometimes a service bureau will customize that driver to get better print output or to solve some special setup need.

Most larger DTP layout programs supply customized drivers for many high-end output devices. Aldus PageMaker, for example, has drivers known as APDs for most of the common printers and imagesetters, plus many other output devices, such as slide recorders, plotters, and so on. These drivers take control over the output device and modify output. Sometimes it improves the process, while other times it changes the calibration of the output device and throws off tints and colors. A good service bureau is aware of these potential problems and can circumvent them or solve them.

▼ *Tip: Never format a long document without using the exact printer driver or device driver of your ultimate output device.*

In programs that allow you to specify output resolution, including Windows 2, be sure to use the correct specification. Imagine your chagrin if you lay out a complex book, take it into a service bureau, and watch as all of your page elements are repositioned. It's a common, major error.

Some DTP layout programs provide setting options such as crop marks, registration marks, special sizes, different image polarities (positive or negative), and different emulsion orientation (emulsion up or down). Depending on how savvy your service bureau is (and many aren't) it may be able to guide you on the use of these options. A discussion with your printer should answer most of these questions.

Quality control is important, and sometimes mistakes are made in the final output. Halftones created at inappropriate screen frequencies or screen angles also cause printing dilemmas. A halftone meant for lithography on newsprint can't handle a 150-lines-per-inch screen, for instance, as the paper is too coarse and absorbent. Screen angles determine how well process colors are positioned. Poor control of screen angles leads to moiré patterns. Traditional printers' gauges enable you to check screen frequency and angle to make sure the service bureau output your job correctly. They are available at most graphic supply stores. A line gauge is a series of accurately spaced lines on a transparent sheet (see Figure 17.2A) with line spacings indicated. When you place the gauge over a printed pattern you see a star-shape interference pattern where the line frequencies match (see Figure 17.3A). One version of the Half-Tone Screen Finder costs $2.95, but often they are given away as gifts by printers. More difficult to obtain is a screen angle gauge, which works similarly (Figure 17.2 [13]). Overlapping the angle gauge on a pattern provides a circle interference at the angle that was printed (Figure 17.3B). Printers' gauges are accurate to within 2 degrees and 3 lpi, satisfactory for finding gross errors.

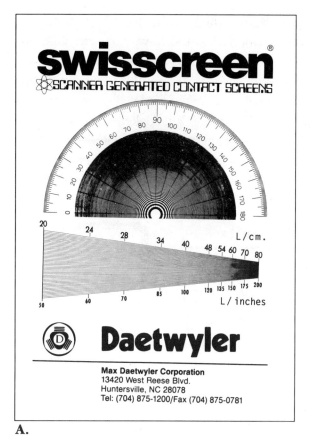

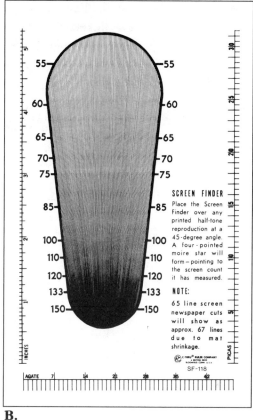

A.

B.

Figure 17-2 **(A)** A printer's screen line gauge, **(B)** A printer's screen angle gauge. Overlapping the screen line gauge onto a print sample shows a star-shaped interference pattern at the printed line frequency. Overlapping the screen angle gauge on a print sample shows a circle-shaped interference pattern at the printed screen angle. *Courtesy of Daetwyler Corp.*

Graphics Problems

Linked Files Perhaps the most common problem service bureaus have is locating missing graphics files. Check to see that all your files are clearly named and logically grouped. For complex, linked file schemes, consider submitting a print-to-disk file.

Applications use two different techniques to place graphics into documents. Either they incorporate the graphics directly into the file, or they provide a link to the graphics document composing the page only when called upon to print. Sometimes both approaches are used. For example, Aldus PageMaker, version 3.0, incorporates encapsulated PostScript files, but writes a link to any

TIFF file larger than 64 KBytes. When a PageMaker file is opened, a linked TIFF file will be displayed as the low-resolution TIFF but printed as the high-resolution TIFF. This means that if you submit the PageMaker file without also including all linked files, your pages will not print correctly. The linked files will be missing, and blank boxes will appear in their place. PageMaker 4.0 is even more complex in that you specify whether graphics are linked or incorporated through dialog box selections. And QuarkXPress, Aldus FreeHand, and Ventura Publisher all use linked files exclusively.

Figure 17-3
The PageMaker 4.0 Link Options dialog box (Element menu) allows you to specify whether text or graphics elements are included in the page layout file or linked. Linked files are separate, and the page is composed in memory when opened or printed.

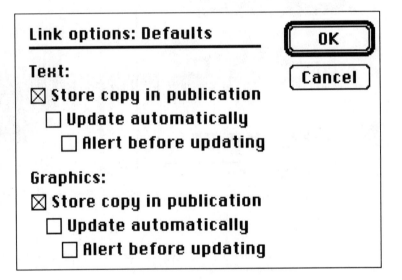

Tints and Calibration   Imagesetting is not a perfect science yet, and discrepancies between tint specification and actual output are common. This is a particular problem for process color work where color matching is important. A good service bureau calibrates imagesetter output on a daily basis using a densitometer on a ramped series of tints, and for process color work measures each film. Keep in mind, however, that even if a bureau is careful about calibration, certain software, such as Adobe Photoshop, QuarkXPress, and Aldus PrePrint, uses its own printer drivers and can change the calibration settings for an individual print job.

Calibration involves determining the blackness, or Dmax value, of the type, a measure of the density of the film; the dot value which is the percentage of tint, and both positive and negative dots can be measured; and the size and shape of the dots. Even a 2 percent shift in the dot value can dramatically shift the colors in a color print, and uncalibrated imagesetters can vary by as much as 30 percent from their specified values. Film is calibrated using a transmission densitometer, and paper is calibrated with a reflection densitometer. Film is much more sensitive to change than paper.

Imagesetter output can be adjusted to compensate for drift or change by customizing the settings in the printer driver or in the RIP. Technical Publishing Services sells the Color Calibration Software system, and Kodak sells the Kodak Precision System for this purpose, whereby a test ramp is created and measured, and the uncalibrated numbers are entered into the software (see Figure 17-4). A curve similar to the gamma curve used in scanner calibration adjusts the RIP, and the ramp is then measured again after calibration. The Color Calibration Software can adjust gray value, dot gain, maintain page geometry, and work in conjunction with Page-Maker, QuarkXPress, Aldus FreeHand, Adobe Illustrator, and others. Legend has it that dedicating one imagesetter to film work and another to paper improves results, as does dedicating a film processor to a single imagesetter, since settings don't have to be changed often.

Other adjustments can be made to the chemical film processor as part of regular maintenance. By changing the temperature and quality of the chemical bath used to develop the film, closer tolerances can be maintained. A "deep tank processor" using more chemicals and a replenishing mixture offers more consistent results and is worth asking about. Be on the alert for some processing devices that recycle mixtures until significant image degradation results—these systems are to be avoided. One good, alternative system is to use separate, conventional developers for paper and film.

One problem with imagesetter tints that cannot be corrected is that darker tints always appear to be darker than expected and lighter tints are lighter. An 85 percent tint might look 100 percent black when output. So always ask for an imageset proof before

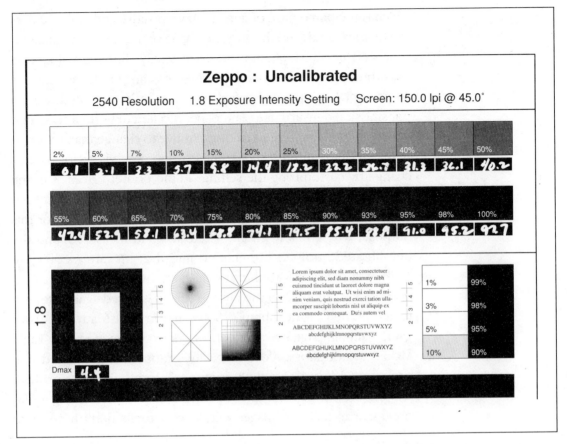

Figure 17-4 The test ramp (film) used by the Kodak Precision Software for imagesetter calibration. *Courtesy of MicroPrint (Waltham, MA).*

completing your design work. Many bureaus offer a free page, and you may wish to test several bureaus with the same page as part of your selection process.

▼ *Tip: Construct and run a couple of test pages for every project with all of the important graphics elements (fonts, graphics, screens, etc.) for high-resolution output. Most problems likely to arise will show up with this test.*

Always laser print all layers of a separation to see if they print correctly. You won't be able to spot problems with trapping, but you will find gross errors.

The problems of variability associated with obtaining accurate tints makes using service bureaus for color separation particularly contentious. Whereas the experience of color prepress and separation houses (color prep bureaus) is extensive, few service bureaus have much experience in this area. It is rare to find a bureau that is even adequately equipped for these tasks. Prepress setups can cost from $150,000 to $500,000 (see Chapter 15), outside the range of most small shops. Most organizations that use color desktop prepress for production have very tightly established procedures that an individual will have more difficulty reproducing. There are also the perceptual differences of color that were discussed in Chapter 14.

Print Efficiency Some output problems are caused by the construction of a file, especially if you use a PostScript blend of, say, one hundred steps or more for fills, create complex patterns or tiles, or require many intermediate steps between objects. A significant computer processing bottleneck can result, and pages that take a long time to print on a laser printer will also take a long time to print on an imagesetter, and you will be charged for that. It's not even that uncommon to find pages that are so complex that the imagesetter can't print them at all. In such cases, if you're lucky, the computer will indicate a PostScript error such as a rangecheck, VMerror (for virtual memory error), invalid command fill or cureto, or invalid operator errors. If you're not so fortunate, the imagesetter will just sit there blinking at you until you reset it. There isn't any way to solve this problem absolutely, but you can use laser print proof time as a guideline.

You can generate a difficult print file easily by doing a raster-to-vector conversion on a complex TIFF file and by specifying the maximum sensitivity of paths. All those complex shapes are transformed into large numbers of line segments that require calculation. Simplifying the shape by decreasing the number of points on a shape path reduces the number of segments and improves printer performance. Most PostScript programs have a dialog box in which a flatness tolerance and a preference for the trace gap distance can be set. You also can improve performance by using many simple shapes in place of a single complex object. Another factor that affects print times is the number of downloadable or soft typefaces that are used. Rendering and rasterizing them can take a considerable amount of time, so limiting their number and variety improves performance.

Virus Prevention

As long as there have been computers, people have written programs to control or damage other people's data or equipment. Some stories are legendary, such as the bank programmer who wrote a program that checked every morning at boot-up if he was still on the payroll, and erased all files if he wasn't. The day he was gone, so were all the bank records. After the bank reconstructed the files from backups, six months later the same program erased the files once again.

People write computer viruses as technical challenges, elaborate jokes, and out of sheer maliciousness. It is far easier to write a virus than you can imagine, considerably easier than writing most of the software described in this book. Viruses are rampant on personal computers, both PCs and Mac, because of the spread of public domain and shareware software.

Taking a disk to, or getting a file back from, a service bureau represents one of the highest risks of contracting a virus. Think of working with files at a service bureau as the computer equivalent of group sex. Only large networks offer similar risks, and networks are normally managed by knowledgeable management information systems (MIS) people. But there is a simple, easy way to prevent computer viruses. Buy or obtain one or two good antivirus utilities that are regularly upgraded to account for new strains, and use them. Make sure you stay on the upgrade path. The best virus utilities have monitoring components as either a TSR program on the PC or an INIT on the Macintosh. Full applications called vaccines can detect all viruses and remove or deactivate them. The current preferred antivirus programs for the Macintosh are the SAM (Symantec Antivirus for the Macintosh), Rival, and Virex (all commercial); Disinfectant (freeware); and VirusDetective (shareware). Two good PC antivirus programs are Norton Antivirus and Virex PC, both commercial. This is a crowded product category in which good new products, like the viruses they protect against, constantly are being introduced. In fact, virus makers and antivirus makers are playing a game reminiscent of "Spy versus Spy."

▼ *Tip: Using a locked disk when printing at a service bureau can often reduce the risk of infection by a computer virus.*

And One More Thing...

One final word to the wise about approaching service bureaus. It's fine to know about imagesetter calibration, "deep tank processors," and tight management of screen frequency and screen angles. But if you ask about all these things when they aren't important, the good folks at service bureaus are going to think you just arrived from another planet. Most shops try to make a very complex process as easy as they can for their customers, and most of their output is good. They wouldn't stay in business otherwise, because their business is built by word of mouth and sustained by repeat customers. Of course, personalities come into play, and you won't always be able to work well with some people and organizations. So ask around and let a good shop lend you its expertise. If the results aren't quite right, give yourself enough margin to experiment and try again. And by all means, shop around until you find a service bureau you like.

PART IV

Emerging Technologies

Multimedia

The world's a global village, the computer is its glue,
Because even as you're watching it, it is watching you.
                                        Dave Ross, CHIP TALK

Multimedia is the creation of any document that engages two or more of the natural senses. Birthday cards containing microchips that "sing" "Happy Birthday" when opened are multimedia displays. When you get cash from an automatic teller machine (ATM), buy a train ticket from a machine, use a kiosk at a toll road rest stop to ask questions or watch an animated display, you are experiencing computer multimedia at work, whether you are aware of it or not. Interactive terminals have received wide acceptance, and their potential is so widespread that they have attracted most of the heavyweights of the computer industry: IBM, Apple, Commodore, Intel, Sony, Phillips, and many, many others.

NYNEX, the New York-based baby Bell, is in the phone directory business and has been for one hundred years. As a natural extension of its business, NYNEX Information Resources introduced *FACETS of New York*, a magazine and related set of videoguide kiosks. Placed at booth locations at the Javits Center in New York City during PC Expo '90 were the Product Locator, an electronic, interactive terminal, and VideoGuide, an interactive terminal version of *FACETS* magazine. Terminals were comprised of Macintosh computers programmed in MacroMind Director and equipped with a Mass Microsystem's ColorSpace NuBus video graphics display card and a Mac 'N Touch touch screen. (Apple uses a similar system based on HyperCard to aid MacWorld Expo attendees.) The NYNEX VideoGuide, JumboTron (a 252-square-foot video screen), VideoWall (a portable 25-square-foot multiple monitor video display), and Backlit Signs appeared throughout the exposition. Such information kiosks are a new electronic medium that can print maps or coupons, track interest in a product, and be instantly updated.

Figure 18-1
VideoGuide is an interactive, information terminal that is part of the *FACETS of New York* multimedia package developed by NYNEX. It provides touch-screen access to a directory of services, with high-quality sound and video. *Courtesy of NYNEX Information Resources Company.*

Computers are uniquely suited to mix sight and sound to create living documents. When computers are used as servo controllers with programmed feedback, touch can be added to the sensations, which is particularly valuable for simulations. Airlines train pilots with these technologies. A university researcher studying enzymes uses a touch feedback system to check for good fit between enzyme and substrate. One game, the x-rated *Leather Goddesses of Phoebos,* even has a scratch 'n sniff strip for creating smells at predetermined times. Virtual reality results when several of the senses are mixed to create an extremely realistic simulation; this active area of research is described in Chapter 19. Computer projects in multimedia have focused on:

- Training and education.
- Sound and video production.
- Presentations, designs, and simulations.
- Art and entertainment.
- Advertising.

Multimedia receives tremendous trade press because it is a new frontier in communications using desktop computers. Depending on whom you talk to, multimedia is either a passing fad or a watershed technology that will be as revolutionary as desktop publishing was. Some predict that future PCs will serve as the central controlling devices linking TV capabilities with high-quality sound, thereby replacing all of the separate entertainment devices in homes today. Animated visualizations, digital teleconferencing, and new forms of electronic publishing that produce compound documents will be possible. But multimedia is a moving target, highly dependent on the capabilities of the computer. It actually is more a set of enabling technologies or a platform than it is a defined market segment, as new techniques and technologies are being introduced at a dizzying pace. In this chapter we'll survey this emerging technology and attempt to put it in perspective.

The Value of Multimedia

Two important, related concepts make many computer multimedia projects unique as information mediums: interactivity and nonlinear access. A computer program can be written in such a way that the user determines the operation of the program, what is displayed and when. Implicit to interactivity is the concept of nonlinear access. When a user selects an action or event, interactivity is greatly enhanced by directly displaying the result without any intermediate steps.

Many studies have established the value of involving several of the senses in communication. Compare the amount of information you retain from a speech to the amount you can recall when slides or other visual aids also are used. Chances are, you remember more in the latter case. It's an old saw that people remember 20 percent of what they hear, 40 percent of what they see, and 60 percent of what they eat, that is, interact with. Part of this is because a compound presentation is more interesting, but part is due to the fact that there is more than one way to learn the material being presented. Hence, multimedia applications are easier to understand and learn, and therefore are more memorable.

Interactivity and nonlinear access may mimic the way the human mind remembers and thinks, whereas print media are linear and sequential. As Vannevar Bush, a noted computer pioneer, stated in 1945: "The human mind does not work that way. It operates by association. With one item in its grasp, it snaps instantly to the next that is suggested by the association of thoughts, in accordance with some intricate web of trails carried by the cells of the brain." Bush believed that one day desk-size computers would be programmed to respond to users in the same manner as the human mind, a process called free association. For example, say you are trying to remember the name of the movie you saw a month ago—*Desktops from Outer Space*. You bought a new desk for your office, that jogs your memory.

The mind can reach back across space and time to retrieve information and make connections in both logical and illogical sequences. These connections are rarely random, often, in fact, they are highly prescribed and channeled. If one link is suspect, the mind can evaluate other links as a check. Patterns of links are more important than any one single link. Redundancy is one of the great strengths of the human mind. Using a multipath approach is the best and most common way to learn and retain information.

Knowledge Networks/Hypermedia

On a computer, it may be more difficult to develop the web of paths and links necessary to provide nonlinear access than to create a sequential system, but the results are generally worth it. Constructing linked information systems is a specialized type of database management problem, requiring search engines and relational definitions. This type of application now is called hypertext or, more generally, hypermedia, after the work of computer visionary Ted Nelson who popularized the concept in the '60s and '70s. (Nelson, an *Autodesk Fellow* [honorary researcher] currently is helping to create a hypertextural information file server called Xanadu [described in Chapter 19] that is an extension of his earlier ideas. Xanadu is a new form of electronic storage and publishing system, and the first commercial prototype will be released soon by a subsidiary of Autodesk.)

Hypermedia can be defined as multimedia that has an interactive component to it. Examples of hypermedia available today include electronic encyclopedias, interactive maps, and games. Custom software, called expert systems, that are built around if-then-else equations use hypertextural construction. The 1990s will usher in a new generation of interactive hypermedia applications using optical storage devices and innovative video and sound compression techniques. When you consider that recorded knowledge is approximately doubling every eight years, it is clear that we must find new ways to learn and to retrieve information. I predict hypermedia will change the manner in which we learn, become the next great publishing medium, and will provide valuable new forms of educational tools. Although it's exotic now, in a few years hypermedia will be *de rigueur*.

Hypermedia stores information in blocks called nodes, which can contain text, graphics, sound, video, or anything that can be represented or controlled by a computer. Nodes are linked and can be accessed in a window. They can be general purpose (contain anything), a type (contain specified information), or a composite. Links can be hierarchical, connect nodes of like attributes, reference an association, or be a cluster of two or more equally associated nodes. A good system organizes nodes and links for efficient system operation, sort, search, and retrieval. Most hypermedia applications ship with a global system map or browser to show overall location, and then mark a trail as you navigate the system to aid you in finding previously viewed information.

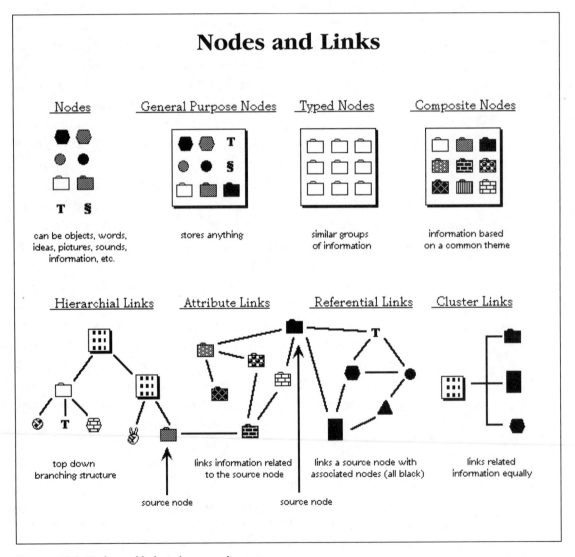

Figure 18-2 Nodes and links in hypermedia systems.

One class of software is specifically designed for authoring multimedia projects based on the hypermedia concept (see "Authoring Software" below). This software is like a conductor directing all the elements of a multimedia orchestration. The first popular hypermedia application on a personal computer was Bill Atkinson's HyperCard for the Macintosh. Released in 1988, and described more fully subsequently, HyperCard uses a card metaphor to organize general-purpose nodes. Collections of cards, composite nodes, are called stacks. Fields containing information are typed nodes, and other objects, such as buttons, can have multiple actions associated with them (sound, visual effects, messages, etc.) that represent composite nodes. Cards are numbered sequentially by creation order, and navigation is accomplished through links by buttons with a general-purpose search (Find command), and through a set of Go commands.

HyperCard has spawned a tremendous quantity of custom programming by average users, but few commercially successful products. Its flexibility makes commercial products expensive and difficult to support. Stacks created by HyperCard 1.0 can't even be opened by version 2.0. HyperCard is distributed free by Apple as system software, and in order to better support the product, Claris now sells a commercial package with full documentation. HyperCard's primary value is as a multimedia developers' tool, and its success has been expanded on by SuperCard (Mac) and Plus (Mac, PC), and translated into Toolbook (Windows 3).

Many Macintosh programs ship a HyperCard stack as a training tool or help facility. One hypertext program that predates HyperCard, Owl International's Guide, is often used to provide context-sensitive, on-line help systems. Context-sensitive help allows you to link words or ideas to their explanation, and it is one of the more ubiquitous and useful examples of hypertext applications. HyperCard 2.0 offers "hot text," in which you click on the text to go to a card with further explanation or association.

Object-Oriented Programming

The elements used in multimedia—text, graphics, sound, voice, music, video, and so on, are all extremely memory intensive. This fact causes a major bottleneck for computer-generated multimedia

Figure 18-3
(A) The Home stack from HyperCard 2.0 contains a card with buttons linking important stacks, a top-down approach.
(B) The Go Recent command in HyperCard 2.0 saves the path followed in memory. To go back to it, click on a card.

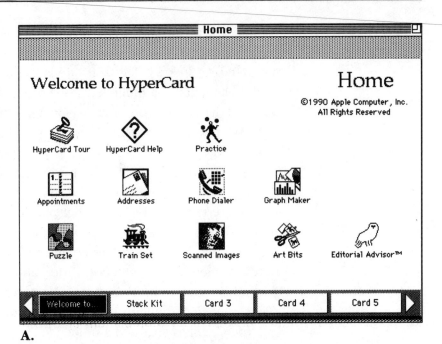

A.

B.

and is being addressed on several fronts. Manipulating these elements in their raw data form would be unweildy, so multimedia authoring programs reduce elements to objects or, as they are called in animation programs, actors. Objects can be grouped in classes, and only certain actions can be performed on each class.

Text can be translated, but not resized, for example. Object-oriented programming (OOPs) defines a hierarchy of object classes so that user-generated actions or events (called messages) can be handled in a logical manner. HyperCard defines a hierarchy of button, field, card, stack, Home stack, and up to global so that any action requiring response is passed up to the lowest appropriate object that can act on the message.

OOPs is not new. It was one of the developments arising out of work at Xerox PARC in the 1970s. Alan Kay, now an Apple Fellow, was one of the primary developers of a programming language called SmallTalk. SmallTalk V (Mac, PC) is now in commercial release and has been used to create a few applications. All multimedia authoring systems are using OOPs to some extent, and it has many advantages. In fact, many industry pundits think that OOPs is the programming wave of the future because it is easier to learn than such structured programming languages as C, Pascal, BASIC, or others. Objects can be saved and reused, and the flexibility of the construction of OOPs languages mean that there are often several effective ways to accomplish the same goal.

OOPs are high-level languages, and as such require much less code to create the same effect than a structured language. But OOPs programs are generally slower to execute than structured coded languages because the environment has substantial overhead. This is similar to the performance rationale of a GUI system compared to a command line interface (CLI) system. Manufacturers including Borland, Microsoft, AT&T, and others are modifying their programming languages to include object support, indicated by the plus signs in C^+ and C^{++}, or the object in Object Assembly or Object Pascal. Apple used C^{++} to program System 7.0.

HyperCard ships with an underlying programming language called HyperTalk. Every object in HyperCard has an underlying script (see Figure 18-5). Users don't need to know HyperTalk to use HyperCard, however, because most objects can be cut, pasted, copied, linked, and created with the underlying scripts either intact or created automatically by the program. HyperTalk's many special effects, such as dissolves or wipes, sounds, links, and other

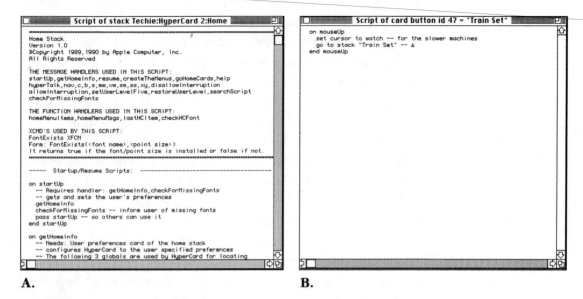

A.

B.

Figure 18-4 Every object in HyperCard has a script. **(A)** Some are complex such as the script for the home stack (left). **(B)** Others are simple, such as the button that sends you to the Train Set stack (right).

actions required by multimedia presentations, can be scripted. A product called ADDmotion can be included with HyperCard 2.0 to do animation. It allows for path-based sprite animation (see below). Graphics and sound capabilities are an integral part of HyperCard. A set of external program routines (in any language) called up by named commands opens up the entire Macintosh environment to HyperCard. External functions (XFNs) summon toolbox routines; external commands (XCMDs) also can be summoned, and they act as device drivers controlling videodisk players, CD ROM drives, and other peripheral devices.

Animation

There are two basic approaches to computer-based animation: hypermedia software and the more traditional frame-by-frame animation software. With time, the line separating these approaches blurs; animation software on personal computers is a very dynamic product category.

Classic Animation   Animation means "to bring to life," and most people associate it with motion. Beyond a certain frequency the mind isn't capable of separating one image from the next in a sequence, an effect called the persistence of vision. That frequency has, as its lower threshold, sixteen frames per second, and achieves smooth animation at from twenty-four to thirty frames per second (the speed of videotape). Any time-varying alteration can produce animation: position (motion dynamics), shape, color, transparency, texture (update dynamics), even changes in lighting, viewing position, and other factors.

Most of us are familiar with animation used in cartoons and films. Traditional character-based animation was developed as an industry by the Walt Disney studio between 1925 and 1930 as a two-dimensional (2D) drawing technique, and the screening of the first Mickey Mouse cartoon was an industry landmark. The noted director Ray Harryhausen is credited most often with clay-based three-dimensional (3D) model animation, sometimes called stop-action animation. The best example of his work can be seen in *The Seventh Voyage of Sinbad*. Claymation's most recent expression is the acclaimed California Raisin commercials. Both two- and three-dimensional animation finds expression in computer software today.

Conventional two-dimensional animation follows a well-established execution sequence. The story is written or conceived and then a storyboard is created. A storyboard is a set of sketches drawn on static slides showing important scenes in sequence. A soundtrack is recorded, followed by the production of a more detailed layout. Artists then draw key frames, with scenes at either extreme or average positions from which intermediate frames can be interpolated. (Interpolation is the time-dependent motion of a constrained object along a specified path, and when done well is mathematically complex.) Creating intermediate frames is called inbetweening or, more simply, tweening. A trial film called a pencil test is made; and pencil test frames are used to create cels, sheets of acetate film that are either hand or photocopied. Each frame may be composed of multiple film overlays. Once all frames are drawn, animation occurs by rapid viewing of the sequence. Every minute of a Mickey Mouse cartoon requires 1,440 frames. This type of animation is called cel or key frame (or frame) animation, a name also given to computer software that uses this technique.

A three-dimensional model-based animation uses a similar scheme—figures are created and manipulated slightly to create the next frame. The advantage of real-life three-dimensional models is that many details such as lighting, coloring, and range of motion can be accurately displayed. But creation of the model is a limiting factor. For example, for speech, a set of models must be made with a full range of facial expressions. Model-based animation works particularly well with scenes in which the background remains static and only a foreground element, or sprite, changes. Sprites can be used in any animation and are especially important in computer-based animation because they keep file sizes manageable. Sprites also are used regularly in programming video games.

Desktop Animation

Many of the new techniques in desktop-based animation incorporates three-dimensional modeling and rendering software. Objects are drawn and described in a three-dimensional modeling program such as AutoCAD, Super 3D, Swivel 3D, or MacroMind Three-D, as wireframes or smooth-surface models, and assigned ranges of motion. A standard file format is written—PICS (Mac), .DFX (PC), and so on, and that file is imported into a rendering program. Rendering is the process by which drawings are translated into realistic objects using mapping, shading, ray tracing, and autotracing. Mapping takes a two-dimensional surface texture like marble and wraps it onto a three-dimensional surface.

Rendering is highly processor intensive, with the creation of the three-dimensional model again causing a bottleneck for computer animation. Pixar's MacRenderMan, which has the potential to become an industry-standard rendering program (its RIB file format is written by many programs) is extremely slow on a personal computer. A Mac IIfx with 8 MBytes of RAM can take twelve hours to render a 32-bit color scene; the Levco RenderMan Accelerator board can reduce that time to an hour. Some programs, such as DynaPerspective and StataVision 3d, are modeling and rendering programs combined. For broadcast-quality rendering, Symbolics offers the MacIvory program on a special $50,000 Mac IIfx-based system.

Figure 18-5
The fully rendered spinning image of the ABC logo was created on a Mac II using StrataVision and DynaPerspective. *Courtesy of DynaWare and ABC: '89-'90 ABC Network Master Graphic. Producer: Marks Communications, Inc. Creative Director: Harry Marks. Designer: Dale Herigstad.*

Computer-assisted animation has caused a revolution in the entertainment industry—nearly all of the steps in a sequence can be done on computers. In fact, animators were one of the early adopters of computer technology, minicomputers, and workstations. Hewlett-Packard's first product was sold to Disney. Personal computers as yet don't have the processing power or storage space to render scenes realistically or interpolate complex tweening for professional animation smoothly, but they are making progress. Macintosh-based animation was used to create the creature in the movie *The Abyss*, and many commercials are created with Commodore Amigas, Macs, and PCs. Personal computers are now used as prototyping stations in the film industry for the more advanced animation work done on powerful computers.

Authoring Software

Authoring software is any program that is used to create, read from peripheral devices, combine, edit, and produce multimedia or hypermedia presentations. This is a broad definition that covers a wide range of capabilities, and new programs constantly are re-creating the way in which multimedia is utilized. To summarize, the representative approaches are:

- Multimedia macro recorders: Exemplified by MediaTracks and ScreenRecorder from Farallon Computing (Berkeley, CA). ScreenRecorder is a macro recorder that saves all screen activity in a file that can be played back for future use. Media-Tracks also allows sound to be added and sequenced. This is a simple concept, easy to use, and great for training applications, but limited in scope.

- Hypermedia programs: Authorware, Ask*Me 2000, Guide, HyperCard, SuperCard, Plus, and Toolbook are hypermedia authoring applications. These programs allow for visual effects, sound (more so on the Mac than PC), and intelligent data manipulation. One of their main strengths is their underlying programming language, which permits the description of a wide range of actions. Animation is generally limited in hypermedia, and these programs are best used in electronic publishing applications.

- Animation software: Exemplified by Animator, FilmMaker, MacroMind Director, and Authorware, these programs allow for classic frame or cel two-dimensional animation. They are great for simple sequences, flying logos, and corporate identity advertising. Good programs are easy to edit on and often will animate accelerated motion, collision deformation, and other subtleties.

- Assembly or integration software: These programs take elements created by other programs and sequence them into full multimedia presentations. MacroMind Director, Media-Maker, and Ask*Me 2000 are examples of this approach.

- Modeling and rendering programs: Such software as DynaPerspective, StrataVision 3d, RenderMan, Super 3D, Swivel 3D, and others create three-dimensional models that can be rendered and animated. They are being used to do limited animation work and as prototyping stations for larger computers.

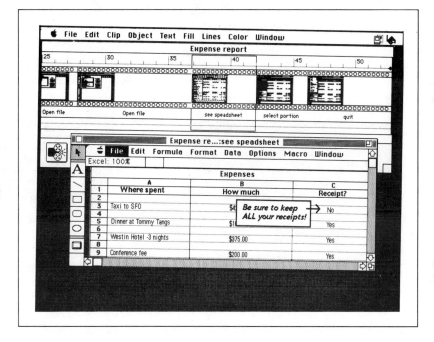

Figure 18-6
MediaTracks records screen activity into executable files on the Mac. Here, an Excel spreadsheet has a cell annotated with voice input using MacRecorder. Each frame can be edited individually and sequenced. *Courtesy of Farallon Computing, Inc.*

Representative Authoring Software is listed here.

- AmigaVision (Amiga) from Commodore. This hypermedia package comes bundled with the Amiga and is widely used and supported. It has a built-in database, accepts a wide range of graphics and animation files, and can run laser disks.

- Animation Works (Amiga, Mac). A low-priced animation package with good capabilities.

- Animator (PC). The most popular animation program on the IBM PC. Somewhat less capable than MacroMind Director, but Animator produces good sprite-based animation.

A.

B.

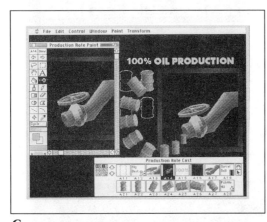

C.

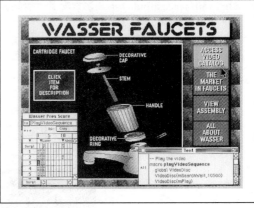

D.

Figure 18-7 MacroMind Director 2.0 is one of the most complete authoring and animation programs available for the personal computer market. It includes: **(A)** an Overview module for document organization; **(B)** a Score timeline for adding sound; **(C)** a 32-bit paint program; and **(D)** the Lingo scripting language.

- Ask*Me System 2000 (PC). A hypermedia authoring environment for DOS. You can add sound to video, work with .PCX images (even Animator files), create databases, and build run-time applications and hypertext systems. Ask*Me uses a complex and proprietary authoring language called Statos. This is mainly a developer's tool.

- Authorware (Mac). A high-end object-oriented authoring program with frame-based animation and object animation. It has a visual mapping approach that eliminates the need for scripting. Interactive multimedia applications are created by arranging objects along a flow line. Objects can be program events such as interactions, decisions, and calculations, or sounds, displays, animation, or video. Logic is graphically displayed and editable. There are animation templates, and over one hundred functions and variables. The Farallon MacRecorder is included to allow for digitized sound input.

- FilmMaker (Mac). An animation program with a wide range of capabilities that is somewhat easier to use than MacroMind Director. FilmMaker can render 8-bit color with mapping, dithering, and antialiasing capability. Sound and motion can be added to create sequences.

- Guide 2.0 (Mac). A hypertext system that is widely used for information management and presentation. It uses features of a word processor and outliner to create cross-referencing and annotation. It is often used as a context-sensitive, on-line help system for other programs or projects.

- HyperCard 2.0 (Mac). The most widely used authoring system. Its HyperTalk language provides a rich medium for organizing information. Version 2.0 adds compiled script for faster execution upon loading. This is a great authoring tool for beginners and intermediate users, it offers a rich library of books, training tools, and shareware and commercial stacks. However, its animation capabilities are limited.

- MacroMind Director (Mac). The most popular and capable midpriced animation program for the Macintosh. Director can create, record, store, and play back animation. The program ships with a full 32-bit color paint program and accepts a wide range of graphics, video, and sound files. Sound is matched to picture using a score metaphor. Director supports MIDI devices, accepts PICS files, and often is used for playback of sequences created in other three-dimensional programs. Its scripting language is called Lingo, and animation is normally sprite-based. The program can be sluggish, making the MacroMind Accelerator NuBus board a necessity for complex scenes. MacroMind Windows Player allows a Mac

Director file to be played on the PC. This is a very capable program with a long learning curve. VideoWorks II was its predecessor and was used for simple animation. Apple used VideoWorks to produce the introductory disks that came bundled with each Macintosh.

- MediaMaker (Mac). An authoring program developed by the MultiMedia Corp. of the British Broadcasting Corp. It allows a multimedia presentation to be assembled from a variety of sources and devices, and is simple enough to be used casually. MediaMaker builds a database of elements and assigns them a picture icon. The items are sequenced and then printed to tape. This is a great tool for assembling training films or simple animation with good results. A unique product.

- MediaTracks (Mac). This program allows users to record Macintosh screen action into "tapes" that can be run back. An earlier product called ScreenRecorder (a desk accessory) is now bundled with it. Editing and playback are accomplished using an interface that works just like a common VCR. Tape animation with text, graphics, and buttons can be added. Farallon sells a Multimedia Pack that includes the MacRecorder digitizer for sound input. This program is invaluable for creating simple training aids.

- Plus 2.0 (Mac, Win, OS/2). An enhanced version of Hyper-Card 1.x. Plus's main attraction is that it runs on several platforms. Stacks created on a Mac can be run on a PC, or vice versa. It adds color and resizable windows but is not as well regarded as SuperCard.

- Studio/1 (Mac). A black-and-white paint program with path-based and tweening animation capabilities.

- SuperCard 2.0 (Mac). An enhanced version of HyperCard. SuperTalk, its scripting language, is based directly on Hyper-Talk. It supports color and variable screen sizes, multiple screens, and many other features. SuperCard accepts standard graphics files and compiles animations for increased speed. However, the program is a sluggish performer. Macintosh developers favor SuperCard, and the program creates stand-alone run-time applications that don't require additional site licenses.

- Storyboard Live! (PC). From IBM. This program can animate sprite graphics and combine text, video, and audio from an XT on up. The interface is clunky, but some neat effects are possible with this package.

- Toolbook (Win3). A hypertext authoring system similar to HyperCard. A very capable system, but it lacks HyperCard's support for sound because the PC doesn't support sound (it has a single voice to the Mac's eight voices). It is still possible to convert HyperCard stacks to Toolbook books using a utility called ConvertIt! from Heizer Software.

Fun and Games

There is a simple rule for evaluating the quality of a particular computer or authoring system for multimedia potential: Examine the best games currently available. Game developers write software that taxes the quality of graphics, sound, and animation techniques on a platform, and many design compromises that they make are compromises you may want to make, unless you plan to invest in exotic add-on equipment. As a software reviewer I am constantly amazed by how large and sluggish many business programs are compared to game programs. Games are written to get the biggest bang for the buck, and are among the most successful software programs on the market today. For example, take a look at F-19 Stealth Fighter or Microsoft Flight Simulator on the PC.

Colony was a *MacWorld Magazine* Hall of Fame game winner, and its evaluation gives insight into what a reasonable multimedia application might look like. I lost three weeks of my life to Colony during the Christmas season of 1989. Colony was written by David Alan Smith, a researcher in virtual reality programming, as an exercise to determine what is possible on a personal computer. In Colony you become a Space Marshall and answer an SOS from a colony overrun by alien creatures. The game is a shoot-'em-up. You explore the underground colony as you attempt to retrieve cryogenically frozen kiddies, restore your damaged spacecraft, and destroy the aliens. Each level contains traps, dead ends, and mazes with many objects to examine and understand. The game is complex and somewhat convoluted. I needed the hint book and a session with tech support at Mindscape to finally solve it, but it is a great game.

The construction of Colony says a lot about how to develop an interactive multimedia program. You navigate through space cleanly, fire your weapon with a mouse click, and sound accompanies most actions. The spaceship and colony are constructed as a floorplan, a graphical database. The construction is entirely analogous to walk-through architectural programs such as Virtus Walk-Through 1.0. Certain objects such as airlocks, doors, elevators, forklifts, teleporters, and so on, are represented by dialog boxes when you encounter them. This decreases the interactivity of the game, but also the size of the program and its memory allocation. Had Colony been written for a more powerful computer, all of these objects could have been fully interactive. Colony runs on a Mac Classic, and a color version runs on a Mac II. (Note: 32-bit QuickDraw crashes the program.)

HyperCard also has games written for it, and some are quite good. Bomber is one that re-creates a World War II bombing run over Germany. You operate from the cockpit of the bomber and monitor gauges for gas, engines, and other variables. The Manhole and Cosmic Osmo, both published by Activision, are HyperCard stacks. Cosmic Osmo ships on CD ROM as a 100 MByte of data and provides a compelling interactive display of sounds and music, animation, puzzles, and characters that is delightful.

Multimedia Hardware

The kinds of multimedia projects you can undertake are largely predicated by the capabilities of the computer equipment. Not surprisingly, therefore, manufacturers stress different approaches to multimedia that paint their computers in a favorable light. The three major PC platforms for multimedia are the Macintosh, IBM PC, and Commodore Amiga. In the sections that follow, the focus is on the general capabilities of these systems. Multimedia is very equipment intensive, and major differences are apparent when we examine the high-performance graphics necessary for animation, high-quality audio, and video. Some of these differences are radical and are underpinned by the design philosophy of each manufacturer. These differences are found in the capabilities of: the operating system; the ability to read/write from such peripherals as video disk players, CD ROM drives, optical disk drives, and video cameras; authoring system software; file format standards; and third-party add-ons.

Macintosh

Apple regards multimedia as a natural extension of desktop publishing and refers to it as desktop media, including in that definition the entertainment, training, and presentation markets. The authoring software for melding elements into multimedia documents is a particular strength of the Mac. The Macintosh has a standard set of protocols and drivers called the Apple Media Control Architecture (AMCA) for applications to follow. HyperCard is the first step on the road to what John Scully (Apple's CEO) calls "the Knowledge Navigator." The Navigator concept envisions a portable computer with a multimedia database incorporating artificial intelligence. Agents built into the software would search for, store, and filter information, using past work as a guideline.

The main advantages of the Mac are its high-quality color display and output. Macs drive noninterlaced analog RGB monitors that require an encoder to be synchronized with TV video. Genlocking boards—boards that synchronize video signals and allow for overlays—and many digital, video-effect NuBus cards are available that can turn the Mac into an impressive video production and editing station. One difference between the Mac and other PCs is that all graphics run through the System software's QuickDraw routines. Add-in coprocessor boards from such companies as Radius and Raster Ops started appearing in 1990 to accelerate screen display, and Apple put this capability on board for the Mac IIfx and in the Apple Graphics Display Card 8•24 GC. The Macintosh also has a very active video add-in, third-party market.

The Mac supports eight-channel stereo sound and has a very impressive third-party market for sound hardware and software. Apple sells a MIDI controller, and other vendors' MIDI devices make the Macintosh a music industry computer standard. The Audiomedia board from Digidesign and the Deck program allow 16-bit, CD-quality audio and sound effects to be added to multimedia presentations. The low-priced voice recognition system from Articulate Systems called The Voice Navigator is a unique input device. For sound input, Farallon's MacRecorder, a low-priced sound digitizer, is available. Some of the newest Macs also come with microphones.

IBM PC

Although IBM PCs have strong processing power and good new video standards (VGA, 8514/A , and XGA), it is the least capable multimedia personal computer right out of the box. However, it has the best third-party add-on support and is the biggest segment of the multimedia market. Windows and OS/2 offer better memory management, multitasking, standard file formats, and device support and are more actively supporting multimedia developers than MS-DOS. However, multimedia on the PC is a more complicated and expensive proposition than on other personal computers due to a lesser degree of standardization.

The PC is a one-voice machine. To add sound, an audio capture board, such as the Sound Blaster, must be purchased. The best come with a digital sound processor (DSP) chip and MIDI and sound digitizers are readily available. Interlaced RGB PC monitors require an encoder for NTSC or PAL TV or video I/O, a genlock device for video overlays, and character generators for titling. Video Charley from Progressive Image Technologies combines these three features for $750. Video capture and TV video in a window are well supported on the PC. Most of the programmable videodisk players sold are for the PC, and this platform is strong in video authoring. Intel's DVI technology, one of the leading real-time compression technologies, may make the PC the preeminent video mastering platform in the next year or two (see "Sound and Video Compression").

The PC multimedia hardware market is vibrant, but moderate-priced authoring software lags somewhat behind the Macintosh. HyperCard and its clones, are more fully developed than programs like Toolbook on the PC, and this is probably due to more open hardware standards. Animation programs including Autodesk's Animator, look primitive when compared to MacroMind Director. Both IBM and Microsoft are actively interested in multimedia, and the next couple of years should see considerable growth in this market. IBM has been aggressive about introducing new software. Microsoft has a new division for multimedia publishing with a PC focus, and Bill Gates has championed the use of CD ROM. The IBM view of multimedia on the PC begins with authoring software, and seeks to integrate it into large storage devices using digital video compression to achieve full-motion video.

Commodore Amiga

The Amiga, introduced in 1985, pioneered desktop video; the Amiga 2000 received the 1988 National Association of Broadcasters Most Useful Video Product award. The success of the Amiga (1 million sold) is largely attributable to its impact on the desktop video market. In addition to the multitasking operating system, the Amiga ships with a set of coprocessor chips specifically designed to speed up graphics, video, and I/O. Commodore stresses these advantages by emphasizing the video market. This platform is blessed with good low-cost equipment, mature authoring software, and a vigorous third-party market. Shareware video clips on the Amiga exist in the same way that clip art is ubiquitous for the Macintosh.

The Amiga was designed with most multimedia support right in the hardware. Angus, a graphics coprocessor chip, has blitter circuitry that updates only the area on the screen that changes, thus greatly increasing screen performance. The Denise chip supports animation sprites (a graphic object that can be called and quickly relocated on the screen, like a spaceship or Pacman character on a video game) with simple program calls. Paula, the I/O coprocessor, improves the four-channel stereo sound and video performance. Paula also includes sound and speech synthesizing support, and a full set of English phonemes. There are third-party MIDI devices that connect to the serial port and an active market of music and sound peripherals. But processing hardware isn't the Amiga's only advantage. Commodore also has designed the display system for the video world by allowing switchable noninterlaced, interlaced, and overscan video modes.

Overscan expands the picture past the edge of the display, thus eliminating the border at the edge of the monitor. The Amiga ships in two versions, one to match the U.S. NTSC and the other to support the European PAL standards, and that video design compatibility greatly simplifies TV or VCR I/O—you don't need to translate back and forth from RGB monitors. Genlocks are cheap on the Amiga, often as little as $200. The Amiga is a particular favorite in professional video studios that create animation design, titling, or character generation overlays. Two professional character generators for the Amiga are the Broadcast Titler and Pro Video Gold.

A unique product for video on the Amiga is the Video Toaster ($1,595), a device that creates broadcast-quality video and animation. It pushes, pulls, slips, tumbles, mosaics, fisheyes, and does a hundred other special effects in real time. It includes a genlock, frame grabber and storer, a four-input switcher for frame dissolves, paint program, character generator, and Chroma/FX color processor for many special color effects. The Video Toaster slices, dices... it's the equivalent of a set of boards that cost tens of thousands of dollars on other computers. There isn't anything like the Video Toaster on other PCs—it is nothing short of phenomenal. If video's your game, you owe it to yourself to have a look at this product.

Animation software on the Amiga is reasonably priced, mature, easy to learn, and uses the standardized .IFF format. Three of the best are Commodore's AmigaVision (which comes bundled with the Amiga), The Director, and Animation Works. Draw 4D is a well-regarded modeling and animation package. When you consider the cost of the Amiga, its true multitasking operating system, and its sophistication, it is not difficult to understand why it is the choice of many video professionals. All that is lacking is high-end color and a compression scheme for full-motion video.

Sound

Digitized Sound

Sound is a perception caused by vibration against the eardrum. It is a time-dependent phenomenon sensitive to fluctuations in air pressure. Your voice is what results when your mouth forms an air pocket and propels it outward. The diaphragm in your ear detects the motion and then generates electrical signals that the mind interprets. Electrical devices such as speakers and microphones work similarly. Sound waves are an analog waveform, with loudness a function of pressure represented by the amplitude. Pitch is the frequency of the repetitive motion measured by the number of peaks per second. The difference between a frequency and double that frequency is an octave. The phase of a wave shows where the sound is coming from. Square waveforms sound harsh, sine waves sound sweet, and complex waves sound rich and full. A waveform can be manipulated by computer programs.

In order to represent sound, an analog-to-digital conversion must be done. Because, aside from video displays, many computers don't have A/D circuitry, an additional device called a sound digitizer must be used. Sound digitizers are microphones that are constructed to generate the electrical signals a computer can recognize. The process of digitizing sound is called sampling. A sound's waveform is examined at periodic intervals and its amplitude is measured. If the frequency of the sampling is fast enough, the sound is well represented. Musical sampling is not unlike the video sampling used in cel or frame animation. However, sound has a greater physical persistence than video, as new notes can be played as others are dissipating.

The quality of sound in digital audio is dependent on the sampling rate, the number of bits saved per sample (called the sam-

Figure 18-8
(A) An idealized sinusoidal sound waveform.
(B) Sampled sound at 3-bit resolution (2^3 or 8 levels).
(C) Sampled sound at 5-bit resolution (2^5 or 32 levels).

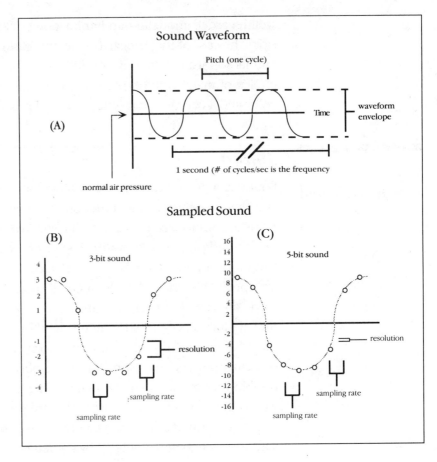

pling resolution), and the qualities of the audio circuitry used. Most computers use medium-quality "speakers" that require additional amplification. Good, small speakers (some with self-amplification), similar to the type sold at Radio Shack with miniplugs are often used. The human ear is far more forgiving of sound quality than the human eye is of visual quality. It is hard for most people to discern sound quality beyond that of FM.

A professional digital recording uses a sampling rate of 44.1 KHz, and the Mac II can record at that rate. At that rate the highest sound a human can hear (about 22 KHz) can be accurately recorded because recording a sound frequency requires a sampling rate of twice the frequency (called the Nyquist frequency). A sound file recorded at 22 KHz would be twice as large as the file of the same sound measured at 11 KHz, but it would sound measurably better. Sound files are large, and are often compressed, but compression lowers the quality of sound in playback. (See "Sound and Video Compression" below.)

Sampling resolution determines how accurately changes in loudness can be measured. A 16-bit sample would allow a loudness resolution of 65,536 levels of sound to be recorded. The rounding off of sound amplitude is called quantization, and it introduces sampling errors into sound as noise. Macintosh computers sample at 8 bits, allowing 256 loudness levels to be measured. By adding a sampling board such as the DigiDesign's Sound Accelerator with the Motorola 56001 digital signal processing (DSP) chip, higher sampling resolution and CD-quality sound can be achieved.

The most popular sound capture add-in board for the IBM PC is Sound Blaster from Creative Labs (San Francisco, CA). It adds 8-bit sampling; 11-voice FM-quality sound; sound sampling; microphone input; a joystick I/O port; MIDI interface; 4 watt-per-channel amplifier; and a text-to-speech synthesizer to an IBM PC (XT on up), PS/2 (25/30), Tandy computers, and compatibles. Sound Blaster ships with the FM Intelligent Organ (play it on-screen); the funky Talking Parrot; and VOXKIT, a development toolkit. Sound Blaster has the largest library of compatible software (games and music especially) for the PC. Until a universal standard sound capture board arrives from IBM, this is the one to get. Other PC sound boards with MIDI adapters include the LAPC-1 and the MPU-IMC (for PS/2), both from Roland.

Farallon Computing's MacRecorder is a sound digitizer for the Macintosh; the microphone that ships with the Mac IIsi is another. MacRecorder's SoundEdit software allows you to save sounds in standard formats. There are sound file formats and two types of sound resource formats on the Macintosh. An snd resource can be saved as part of the resource fork of a Macintosh file, the System file (available through the Control Panel or resource managers such as Suitcase II), a HyperCard stack, or an application. There are many sound editing and management programs and whole libraries of digitized sounds in the public domain to be found on bulletin boards and the on-line services.

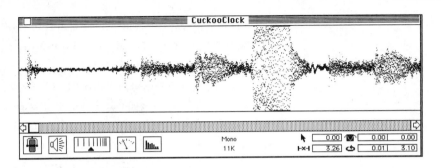

Figure 18-9
A sonogram (or spectograph) showing a real waveform using the Farallon SoundEdit software from MacRecorder. The digitized sound was a cuckoo clock playing. SoundEdit can mix four channels and edit sound.

Voices Versus Music

The terms voice, music, and speech have very different meanings when applied to computer-generated sound. A voice is a channel, or for stereo, a pair of channels that can be a separate sound track. An eight-channel computer can have eight-monaural or four-stereo channels, or any combination. Music is more generally ascribed to sound with a regular, well-described waveform where individual sounds can be represented as notes, which relate mathematically to other notes on the musical scale. The sound a note makes will differ depending on the device used to generate it, but it is the mathematical regularity that makes it identifiable as music. Speech is a very different proposition, for the sound that composes speech is highly nonregular and complex.

Computer-generated speech and automatic speech recognition (ASR) are very active areas of research. All computer manufacturers are interested in these technologies and are developing projects in education, special needs (handicapped), and improved I/O devices. (Chapter 19 discusses future aspects of speech and voice recognition.)

Speech Generation Speech generation is a very different problem from speech recognition. To generate speech, a set of several dozen basic sounds called phonemes are created. The quality of the phoneme set determines how well a computer "speaks." The Amiga ships with phonemes hardwired, and Apple has a system patch (INIT) called MacinTalk (current version 2.0). An improved MacinTalk ships with Macintosh System 7.0. Humans speak about three words per second and average about six phonemes per word. In order to be computer spoken, text must be translated into phonemes, a process now done manually,, although translation programs, currently in development, will automate it. Speech-generation programs are complex, and their difficulties are similar to those faced by the developers of grammar checkers.

Phonemes					
IY beet	IH bit		EY made	AY hide	
EH bet	AE bat		OY boil	AW power	
AA hot	AH under		OW low	UW crew	
AO talk	UH look				
ER bird	OH border		Q kitten (glottal stop)		
AX about	IX solid		DX pity (tongue flap)		
			RX car LX call		
R red	L yellow		(postvocalic R and L)		
W away	Y yellow		QX = silent vowel		
M men	N men		UL = AXL IL = IXL		
NX sing	S sail		UM = AXM IM = IXM		
SH rush	Z has		UN = AXN IN = IXN		
TH thin	DH that		1-9 stress marks		
J judge	/H hole		. sentence terminator		
/C loch	B but		? sentence terminator		
P put	D dog		– phrase delimeter		
T toy	G guest		, clause delimeter		
ZH pleasure	F fed		( ) phrase delimeters		

Figure 18-10 (A) The Talking Moose; and **(B)** A set of phonemes used by the Moose.

Programs on the market combine speech and animation using phoneme sets, where speech is synchronized to lip motion. One delightful program is Steve Hall's Talking Moose, a Macintosh cult classic that started life as shareware and is now a commercial product. The Moose comes on either at random or at predetermined times and speaks humorous phrases or reads the names of dialog boxes. Of a more serious nature is Bright Star's HyperAnimator (for HyperCard), and the more complete interFACE (interactive facial animation construction environment). interFACE goes beyond simply matching lip motion to phonemes to create a full development environment using actors and agents where animation matches digitized sound to lip motion. Actors also can be imported. Animated "talking heads" can be applied in training, communications, advertising, demos, kiosks, advanced storyboards, telecommunications, and live databases.

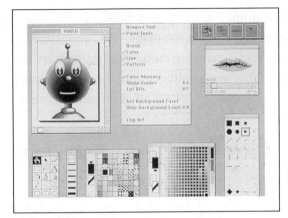

A.

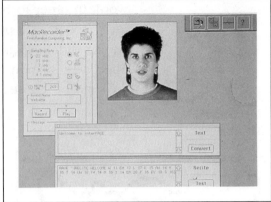

B.

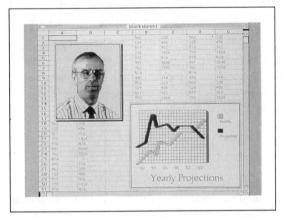

C.

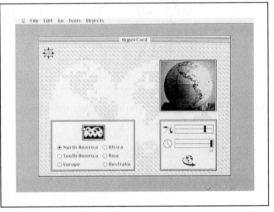

D.

Figure 18-11 interFACE animates speech. **(A)** Animated images (actors) are created in the Dressing Room, a paint and animation environment. **(B)** Speech Sync records and synchronizes animation to digitized sound. **(C)** A talking agent explains data inside an Excel spreadsheet. **(D)** interFACE brings animation into HyperCard. *Courtesy of Bright Star Technologies.*

Speech-Recognition Speech is a composite of many sounds with different frequencies. Speech-recognition programs break apart the speech waveforms into bands and apply a pattern-recognition algorithm based on segmentation and labeling to each. ASR (automatic speech recognition) can be done quite successfully by using a trainable system. A set of spoken words is saved by the computer and speech input is compared to these stored patterns. A number of commercial products including the Voice Navigator II from Articulate Systems (Cambridge, MA) are now entering the personal computer market. They represent a new form of computer input where hand input is impractical or impossible, such as with the handicapped or with surgeons in an operating room. Some remote applications include phone-in or network command of remote computers. Demonstrations of this technology are quite impressive.

Generalized ASR is a much more difficult and complex proposition that involves significant processing horsepower. Systems are being developed at research organizations, including MIT, Carnegie-Mellon, Dragon Systems (Newton, MA), AT&T Bell Labs, IBM, Unisys, SRI, and Bolt, Beranek, and Newman. Often, parallel processing is used as a front end; high accuracy rates have been possible only for trained systems. A generalized recognition technology is probably fifteen years away on larger computers, twenty years away on personal computers.

The MIDI Interface

The Musical Instrument Digital Interface (MIDI) is a universal standard created in 1929. It specifies protocols for wiring and connectors that enable computers and instruments to communicate. It is similar to a LAN protocol and does not transmit sound or music per se. MIDI actually transmits a simple signal called a channel message that indicates that an event took place.

When you press middle C on an electric keyboard for a certain time period, a signal is sent. Keystroke velocity, aftertouch, pitch blend, modulation wheel, foot pedal, and sound changes also can be recorded. A playback signal to a music synthesizer is then translated and sent to a speaker. The quality of the sound changes when a different digitizer or speaker is used, but the signal's recording would remain the same. MIDI also can transmit system messages to control overall instrument settings. MIDI can create a network of instruments that can be played from a single device. MIDI also lets you use a computer to record and play back music, in essence, create a music studio. Some companies sell MIDI music sequences, the equivalent of music clips for use in your own multimedia projects.

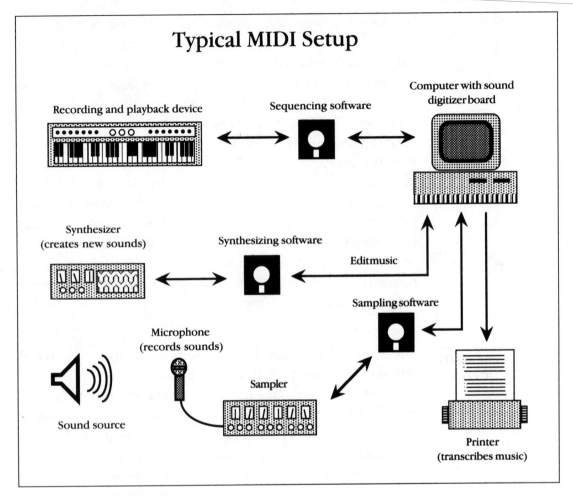

Figure 18-12 Components of a typical MIDI setup.

MIDI allows up to sixteen channels of simultaneous instruments, and communication is at 31.25 Kbits/sec. This frequency is fast enough so that a chord sounds like a chord and not the separate notes comprising the chord. MIDI adaptors are serial port devices and simple hardware connectors. Apple sells an adaptor with a single MIDI In and MIDI Out connection. More sophisticated Mac MIDI adapters include Mark of the Unicorn's MIDI Time Piece and J.L. Cooper Electronics' SyncMaster. Roland also sells a line of MIDI adaptors for the PC and Amiga that include the

CM-64 LA/PCM Sound Module, PC-101 Data Keyboard, CF-10 Fader, CN-20 Music Entry Pads, and MCB-1 MIDI Connector Box. Connecting MIDI systems can be intimidating to beginners, but HookUp! (Hip Software) is an object-oriented control software that allows you to link devices by drawing connections in order to create multimedia sequences. Higher-end MIDI adaptors have multiple I/O connectors that write the The Society of Motion Picture and Television Engineers (SMPTE) Time Code which allows a MIDI sequence to be synchronized and played back as the audio track of a film or videotape. Timecode Machine (Opcode) is one converter program for the Macintosh that writes SMPTE code on a soundtrack.

Sound Editing Systems

Programs called sequencers let you record and play back MIDI data. With such a program, you actually can write a musical piece for up to sixteen MIDI instruments or record the notes played on each of the instruments. The sequence of notes can be edited and then played back just as if your computer were an elaborate digital musical instrument. Software called patch editors (or editor/librarian programs) can store thousands of different sounds and change a synthesizer's sound settings, adjusting the instrument's sounds as needed. It might take 100 MBytes to store ten minutes of digital stereo sound, but a ten minute MIDI sequence uses only 30 KBytes or so. Some of the popular sequencers are Performer (Mark of the Unicorn), Vision (Opcode), Media Tracks Pro (Passport), Cubase (Steinberg/Jones), and Deluxe Recorder (Electronic Arts). Musical pieces that once cost $100,000 to record can now be done with computers for a few thousand dollars—less as time goes by.

▼ *Tip: Whenever possible in multimedia projects, use MIDI commands and a sequencer in place of sampled recorded sound. Music recorded this way gives greatly compacted sound files and quality at the level of your playback devices.*

In addition to music sequencers, some very sophisticated music processors can turn a computer into a symphony. A scoring program enables you to write and print music using conventional notation. (The Adobe Sonata font is used in most of these programs.) A scoring program is to composers what a word processor is to writers. Many scoring programs actually write the notation as the instruments are played, although some require cleanup due to slightly misplayed notes. This cleanup process has given scoring programs the unfortunate reputation of being difficult to learn. Still, it is an astonishing capability that has been the fantasy of most musicians. Scoring programs for the Mac include Professional Composer (Mark of the Unicorn), NoteWriter and Encore (Passport Designs), and Deluxe Music Construction Set (Electronic Arts).

A new generation of software/hardware is appearing on the scene that promises to create the ultimate music workstation. Sound Tools from DigiDesign (Menlo Park, CA) turns a Macintosh into a two-track, 16-bit, CD-quality recording module that can be controlled from Opcode's Vision sequencer. Sound Tools consists of a DSP NuBus card, an A/D converter, and software. It signals the beginning of the professional-quality home recording studio that can do music editing, audio postproduction, and produce master recordings.

Video

In the same way that desktop publishing has turned the personal computer into a print shop, desktop video may make the personal video studio a reality. The ultimate goal is to create print-to-video applications. Presently, standards are not good enough or cheap enough to compete with professional broadcast-quality standards, but for some projects such as overlays, character generation, and animation, the results can be quite respectable. Overlays are produced when a computer-generated image is put on top of an image from a camera or videotape; character generation (or titling) overlays text on the screen. Chances are that the weather charts you see on television were created on a personal computer, as are most titles, many commercials, and trailers.

In general, still video applications are more advanced than full-motion video due to the extreme amount of data that must be moved in the latter case (see "Sound and Video Compression" below). But when you consider that an hour-long, industrial-quality film might cost from $10,000 to $100,000, the potential savings of desktop video is substantial. While "broadcast-quality" video still is only a laudable goal, desktop video does produce a quality level sufficient to address this market. A major hurdle to overcome is the creation of an easy-to-use, plug-and-play computer system (hardware and software) that simplifies the overall video creation process.

General Issues

There are three issues important in computer video: design, storage, and delivery. Design is an authoring software problem; storage involves memory, compression, and file format issues; and delivery is a hardware problem that immediately affects your choice of computer and peripherals. Moving a video signal both in and out of your computer in a format that a TV or video film can use involves two conversions. First, a digital-to-analog conversion (DAC) in the computer-to-analog RGB display must be made, then analog RGB must be converted to the U.S. or Japanese National Television System Committee (NTSC), the European Phase Alternating Line (PAL), or the alternate European SECAM standards using an encoder. The RGB-to-NTSC conversion is called encoding; the reverse process is decoding. NTSC is an interlaced mode with a horizontal scan rate of 15,750 Hz (525 lines, 30 frames per second). Only the Commodore Amiga directly supports I/O of NTSC and PAL. Its DAC circuitry is built into the computer.

NTSC is a thirty-five-year-old standard that was modified in the 1950s to allow for compatible color. This was accomplished by adding an additional signal for chrominance (color) to the original luminance (brightness) signal used in black-and-white pictures. S-Video (separated video) is the signal format that puts chroma and luminance on separate signal lines instead of a single composite line. Nonetheless, this standard is of lower image quality than computer video, and no doubt will be replaced by High Definition Television (see Chapter 19) later in this decade.

Figure 18-13
Character generation
and overlays. Putting
text on top of video
signals is called
compositing.

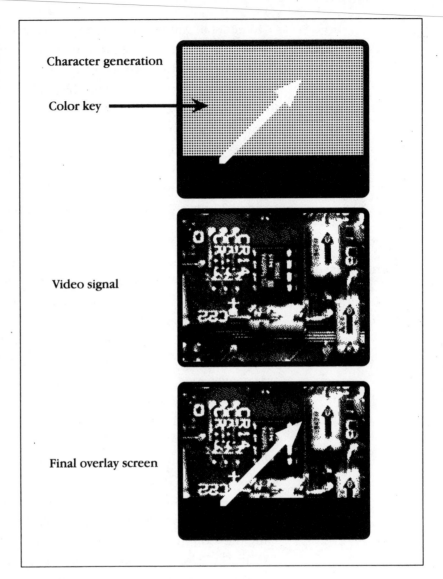

Character generation

Color key

Video signal

Final overlay screen

▼ *Tip: Monitor flicker is a significant problem in designing text and graphics for an NTSC video screen.*

Avoid dithered patterns, single or odd-numbered pixel lines, highly saturated colors (reds and oranges), high contrasts (black next to white), and fonts smaller than 18 point. Always use antialiasing to soften edges, particularly for sharp vertical lines.

Avoid cross-hatching or banded, dark, vertical lines because they result in fringing effects. Also, always design your screen so that the important areas occur in the middle 80 percent of the screen as overscan will reduce effective screen size.

Overlaying an image requires a device called a genlock (short for synchronization generator lock), which synchronizes the computer's output with the video signal. Overlays assign a color key (or chroma key) so that a selected color drops out of the foreground image in order for the background image to show through. Genlocks cost from $200 (for the Amiga) to $1,500, with $600 to $800 the typical price for an average unit for the Mac and PC. Genlocking refers only to the synchronization, but most units are a combination of both genlock and encoder. If you don't want overlay, you need only an encoder. Video Quill is a character-generating program for the Macintosh. Broadcast Titler and Pro Video Gold are choices for the Amiga.

Video Capture

Video digitizers can produce images and save them in the common graphics files such as PICT2 or TIFF for the Mac, or .TIF or .TGA (Targa) format for the PC. Low-cost video capture boards, including Koala's MacVision, can be bought for less than $500. Some of the better products are TrueVision's NuVista boards for the Macintosh and TARGA boards for the PC. Because video digitizers acquire images using a video camera, the resolution of the images obtained is always a constant set by the hardware. Focus and lighting are also important issues. Digitizers create images with a fixed array of CCD's (light-sensitive transistor diodes) and are limited in resolution by the size of each CCD in the array. Scanners, by translating their array of CCDs across an object, minimize some of this limitation.

With video digitizers halftones must be produced at the input end because you are dealing with real objects instead of photographs. Therefore, the halftones created with video systems are usually not of the same quality as those created with scanners, and

Figure 18-14
(A) The VideoLogic DVA-4000/Mac control panel can set audio and video attributes for an incoming signal.
(B) Using a graphic of a TV created in MacroMind Director (note Director's floating palettes) and a high-resolution video signal from a camcorder displayed as an inset (motion video), the appearance of a live TV show is created.
Courtesy of Video-Logic, Inc.

A.

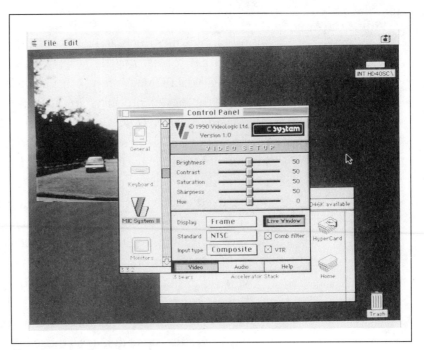

B.

nowhere near the quality produced on systems writing light images to film, although digitizing hardware is steadily improving in quality and decreasing in cost. In addition, still video can be very slow—as much as two minutes per image, or as fast as a fraction of a second, depending on whether or not a coprocessor has been included.

Still video boards with camera input are being supplanted by real-time, full-motion video boards. A complete motion video board would contain an encoder, genlock, extra RAM, and coprocessors. These components control peripheral devices, digitize still video images, control the fade or transparency of an image, and offer special visual effects and audio controls. Most video boards include controlling software for these functions, but while some are full screen, others only allow video within a specific window. The PC choices are the M-Motion Video Adapter/A, VideoWindows, and VideoLogic DVA-4000. In a crowded field, good choices for Macintosh video boards are the ColorBoard 364, WTI-Moonraker, Video Explorer, ColorSpace, and the VideoLogic DVA-4000/Macintosh NuBus boards. The Video Toaster (previously discussed) is the video board of choice for the Amiga.

TV in a Window

There are a number of ways to put a TV on your computer monitor. Most users place the TV inside a small window, although it is possible to make a TV signal full-screen size. The price for these systems varies considerably, from around $350 up to $2,500. DAK Industries sells one for $99. These systems have a surprising range of uses for training and for people who must watch TV while they work. One notable product in this area is RadiusTV, which displays live video or TV (RGB or NTSC) using a Macintosh. You can capture images as PICT files, create special effects, and digitize sound input. A notable capability of this system is the ability to capture closed caption information as a disk file or ASCII text. By searching the file for a keyword, you can bring up the video images associated with the captions. Refer to the article by Don Steinberg in the references for information about IBM PC TV input systems.

Video Editing Systems

A complete desktop video editing setup costs around $10,000 and would include:

- Computer: A Macintosh with 68030 cpu or an IBM PC 80386 cpu with minimum 16-20 MHz clock speed and 4 to 8 MBytes RAM. Video is extremely processor intensive, so spend the extra money on more powerful hardware.

- Storage: Desktop video makes tremendous demands on memory and storage, so a large, fast hard drive is essential. An 80-MByte, 28-millisecond drive should be the minimum, and drives of 150 to 300 MBytes, with access times of 12 to 15 milliseconds, are often used.

- Genlock/Encoder: Necessary to record to a VCR. The quality of equipment has a dramatic effect on film quality. Video is edited by rerecording onto tape, unlike film, which is cut and spliced, so an edit controller can be helpful.

- VCRs: A VCR used for film recording must be capable of genlocking, and one with a "flying" erase head results in cleaner editing. An accurate frame counter is also useful on a VCR, as is the ability to connect to an external film editor. Overlays and editing require two VCRs, sometimes three. SuperVHS and 3/4- or 1-inch reel-to-reel tape gives better-quality results.

- Input devices: A camera or camcorder, lights, lenses, and other accessories typical of a video studio are useful. Professional cameras or camcorders write the SMPTE Time Code.

Many video jobs have been done with only a VCR, genlock, and computer. If you don't want to go to the trouble of trying to build your own system, Avid Technology's Avid1/Media Composer and Digital F/X are professional video editing systems for the Macintosh.

Videodisks

Videodisks look like large CDs. They can store sound, text, still pictures, and full motion video with a ten-year lifetime. Videotape still is more prevalent than videodisks in the recording market, but it does not work well in multimedia applications due to its linear access. Lengthy searches for material destroy interactivity. Computer-controlled videodisks (similar to audio CDs) can deliver

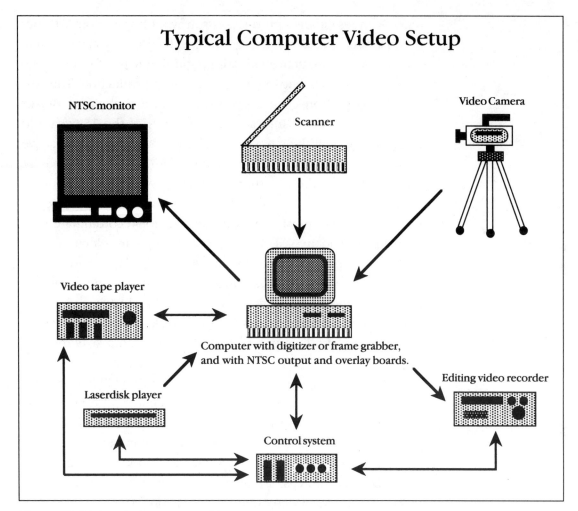

Figure 18-15 A typical computer video setup.

better picture quality while offering the advantage of fast random-access searches. Videodisks are not simply moving pictures, although they can be. Most take advantage of the interactivity of the medium by creating an authored hypermedia application as a front end for search and retrieval purposes.

3M's (Minneapolis, MN) Optical Laserdisc Mastering Service or Pioneer Electronics (Carson, CA) can transfer computer output to laserdisc. A single, sample disk called a check disk can be made for about $100 to $125, and a single distribution-quality disk for about

$360. A thousand-disk production run would cost about $10 per disk. Pioneer specializes in large-run production. If you were commissioning an interactive videodisk, you might pay from $50,000 to $250,000 for a twenty-minute to one-hour production. The cost benefits of in-house desktop production are obvious. Belser Knowledge Services' Interactive, a division of the 150-year-old Belser Verlag publishing house, specializes in authoring interactive optical laserdisk systems. The standard format for Pioneer, Sony, Mitsubishi and others is the LaserVision format in which most commercial disks are encoded, but there are other proprietary formats. The two most common methods for recording are constant linear velocity (CLV) and constant angular velocity (CAV), both of which can be read by any videodisk player. CAV is preferred for interactive media applications. It stores one frame per revolution, and allows slow motion forward and backward, freeze frame, and rapid frame searches. A CAV disk can store thirty minutes per side of full-motion video, a CLV disk about sixty minutes per side.

A videodisk player such as the Pioneer LD-V 4200 has an average seek time per video frame of three seconds, the LD-V 8000 one of 0.5 seconds. These players, along with the Sony LDP 1200, are called Level 3 players because they are computer ready and come with an RS-232 connector. Some Level 3 players are genlocking and overlay devices, useful only if you do not intend to include this capability in your computer, which is preferred because computers generate crisper text. Level 2 players offer remote keypad control and interactivity but not computer I/O. Level 1 players are simple playback devices. Level 1 and 2 players can be found in consumer electronics stores, Level 3 devices in computer equipment retailers. Good playback devices deliver around 400 horizontal lines per frame. Some authoring programs can control video disk players using an ASCII command set. If you are interested in this capability, check to see which models are compatible.

Videodisk is a very exciting computer technology. There is a small but growing market of several hundred professionally created interactive videodisks primarily in the educational market. Costing $50 to $100 each, the leaders in this field include the Voyager Company (Santa Monica, CA), ABC News Interactive (New York, NY), the Optical Data Corp., and WGBH (Boston, MA). The range of topics addressed is very broad. Example titles are "The Louvre Gallery of Art" (Voyager); "The St. Louis Zoo" (Oxford Scientific Films); "Guernica" (Bob Abel); "In the Holy Land" (ABC); films such as *Blade Runner* and *Casablanca* (Voyager); the training course *Make the Telephone Work for You* (Interactive Instructional Systems); and the game "Frame Up" (Imedia International). (See the *VideoLogic Guide* referenced at the end of this chapter.)

CD ROM as a Publishing Medium

Compact Disk Read Only Memory (CD ROM) is the oldest desktop optical technology. It is an optical storage technique where a laser beam permanently writes a series of pits onto a metallic surface covered by plastic or glass material. CD ROM differs from videodisk in that it is more often used for music and still-frame video display. It does not address motion video applications. Probably 250,000 CD ROM drives have been sold (ten PC drives for each Mac drive), with several thousand titles in the current commercial catalog. Recently, a couple of dedicated CD ROM bookstores have appeared.

The standards are the High Sierra and International Standards Organization (ISO). These formats enable a disk to be shared between Macs and PCs on a network, using one data set and two independent data headers and drivers. Sony, Phillips, and Matsushita are actively working on a technology called CD-I (for compact disk interactive) that is High Sierra compatible. CD-I doesn't require a computer for playback, only a low-cost decoder or player, and is aimed at the consumer electronics market.

CD ROM can store and display text, visual information, even audio CD sound, and is a superb distribution medium because of the density of information it can contain. A 4.75-inch disk can store 650 MBytes of data and has a 100-year lifetime. The density of information requires a sophisticated search engine in order to make good use of the format. Most CD ROMs come with hypertextural applications as front ends. Very sophisticated authoring software packages ($10,000 to $50,000) are available that can completely tag data on a CD ROM. These packages are offered as services and fall outside the scope of PC-based software. Accessing CD ROMs presents the same problem as accessing a very large database on a host computer using a client station on a microcomputer. CD ROM access times are slow (75 to 150 milliseconds) and data structures can be complex. Good keyword searching is required, and if you are doing logic extractions, good inference engines, too.

Many reference works have appeared on CD ROM including *Bartlett's Familiar Quotations*, *Compton's Encyclopedia*, *Roget's Thesaurus*, *The World Almanac*, the *U.S. Zip Code Directory*, entire encyclopedias, shareware and public domain collections, and large technical documentation. Boeing reduced a shelf's worth of 747 maintenance manuals to a CD ROM, and Digital Equipment Corp. puts its entire VMS operating system (for its minicomputers) on a disk. There are clip art CD ROMs, and the *Whole Earth Catalog* has appeared as a HyperCard CD ROM stack. The *Whole Earth* disk shows scanned photos, page diagrams of how-to books, and sixty-second samples of recordings the company sells.

CD ROM-based tools are a compelling reason for owning a computer. The products available for technical professions, writers, and businesses are outstanding. Lotus's MarketPlace, a listing of statistics on individuals and households, was a useful tool for the direct mail industry. Unfortunately (depending on how you look at it), Lotus withdrew the product due to consumer concerns over privacy. Many directory listings are published on CD. For example, NYNEX has put all of the residents of New England on a single CD ROM that is used by law enforcement agencies, credit departments, marketing, and other organizations needing rapid name retrieval. CD ROM is also excellent as a publication medium for technical journals. For example, doctors who have a hard time keeping up with the medical literature can use Aries Systems Corp. (Andover, MA) Medline and CANCERLIT databases on CD ROM.

A 100 disk pressing can cost $2,000 to $3,000; with most of that cost paying for the master. Copies cost between $1 and $2. 3M's

A.

B.

C.

D.

Figure 18-16 Compton's Multimedia Encyclopedia is an award-winning CD ROM for the IBM PC that fulfills the promise of this technology. In addition to storing the entire encyclopedic text, it also includes pictures, charts, maps, and graphs. It has animation, video sequences, sixty minutes of sound clips, and a very sophisticated search engine. The *Merriam-Webster Intermediate Dictionary* is included, and words are hot-linked to their definitions. **(A)** The main screen provides eight different types of entry and searches. The Picture Explorer is a database of associated pictures. **(B)** A Mayan temple. **(C)** Peru Andes scene. **(D)** Saturn. *Courtesy of Britannica Software, Inc.*

Optical Recording Dept. will create an evaluation disk and ten copies for $650. The mastering system for creating CD ROMs is starting to show up in service bureaus. CD Publisher ($32,000) from Meridan Data is one such mastering system, and the company provides services on a contract basis. Optical Media Interna-

A.

B.

Figure 18-17 **(A)** *The Whole Earth Catalog* CD ROM (now out of print). **(B)** Hyper-Card search engine provides entry to images, product information, and sound clips. Here a mountain chickadee sings to you. *Courtesy of Brøderbund, Inc.*

tional (Los Gatos, CA) manufactures and sells the TOPix CD-R system for about $150,000; it allows for data capture, editing, indexing, formatting, encoding, and output of CD ROM disks.

Pundits have thought for some time that 1991 might be the year of the CD ROM. There are compelling titles in the marketplace, and it's a great distribution and storage medium with strong industry standards. Impediments have been slow access speeds (even slower than floppy disks) and high-cost equipment. The Fujitsu FM-Townes (available only in Japan), HeadStart Technologies (a division of Phillips Corp.), and Tandy 2500XL computers are shipping with an internal CD ROM drive, a likely trend. The FM-Townes was built to be a packaged computer-based multimedia platform. One school of thought believes that read/write optical drives will supplant CD ROM, but the nonvolatile nature of CD ROM and its archival quality suggest to me that in the 1990s CD ROM will become a dominant computer publishing medium.

Figure 18-18
The NYNEX Fast Track CD ROM is a listing of all the names, addresses, and phone numbers for residents of New England. *Courtesy of NYNEX.*

Sound and Video Compression

A 32-bit image on a 640 x 480 pixel monitor requires 921 KBytes per frame. A 600-MByte disk stores only 21 seconds of 30 frames per second of video, or about 13 minutes of high-quality recorded sound. This, in a nutshell, is the bottleneck in making motion video and sound practical. While it's true that faster processors and I/O bus structures are a continuing trend, what's really needed is some way of reducing the amount of data that must be processed. Therefore, data compression is the most promising approach. Most vendors are seeking to develop symmetrical compression systems where the same device that compresses the file decompresses it. Expect to see compression chips in the next generation of computers. DSP and video compression chips are already in the NeXT computer.

Sound compression is already built into most record and playback media, accounting for CD storage of a little more than an hour of sound instead of the thirteen minutes quoted above. Algorithms compressing sound from 3:1 to 8:1 are common, and most sound digitizing software writes files in this compressed format. Further compression is possible, but the problem isn't as severe as video compression by almost two orders of magnitude.

The proposed Joint Photographic Expert Group (JPEG) standard for high-quality video image compression is being developed for random-access video. Software has already appeared for static images with compressions of 15:1 over a minute (see Chapter 6). JPEG ultimately may yield 100:1 compression. The CL-550 processor from C-Cube Microsystem is a hardware JPEG implementation that can compress files from 20:1 to 35:1 and possibly up to 200:1 in real time. JPEG will be applied to color image storage, electronic cameras, and color scanners and printers. JPEG doesn't use interframe compression and doesn't address audio compression so it isn't a motion video compression format. The Moving Picture Expert Group (MPEG) is developing standards for a symmetrical compression system, and chips should appear in early 1992. JPEG and MPEG are international standards and have the potential to be accepted in the same manner as CCITT standards are for fax.

Digital Video Interactive (DVI) compression for audio/video, developed initially by GE and RCA, is being actively developed by Intel and promulgated by IBM. DVI is a set of programmable chips that reduce areas of like color (called region coding) to a single small digital representation. It also does interframe compression by coding only the parts of a moving picture that change. DVI sacrifices some color content and focus for compression. It can squeeze files to 1 percent of their initial size and deliver an hour of full-motion video from a standard CD ROM. Without DVI, 74 minutes of high-quality audio and 90 seconds of video on a CD are possible. With DVI, 44 hours of audio, 650,000 pages of text, and 72 minutes of video can be stored on a CD. The first authoring programs for DVI include Authology:Multimedia ($4,500) from CEIT Systems (San Jose, CA) and Mediascript ($1,500) from Network Technologies.

Initial development of DVI suffered from asymmetrical compression, as different systems are needed to record and play back. Recording video required a parallel-processor system and a PC with a $1,000 playback board to read it. Additionally, DVI requires the use of the Intel Compression Service, a $250-per-minute mastering process. In 1989 RCA announced a symmetrical compression scheme. Today a PC with the ProMedia 750 board ($5,000) can both compress and decompress files. This real-time video is of lower quality than the production-level video that Intel masters because it doesn't use interframe compression. Nonmastered files are larger, but they can be stored on a hard drive and are good for moderate-quality work. Intel expects to offer a symmetrical system by 1993 for a few hundred dollars, and has announced support for the MPEG standard in DVI.

One Final Note...

In this chapter we have addressed new communication methods that are at the front of computer presentation and publishing. Many media projects, such as slide shows, hypertext, and sound capture, are easy to accomplish; some, such as interactive full-motion video, are more difficult and time consuming. The relative cost and effectiveness of the various-computer based multimedia methods are shown in the graph in Figure 18-19.

Figure 18-19
The relative costs versus effectiveness of various multi-media projects.

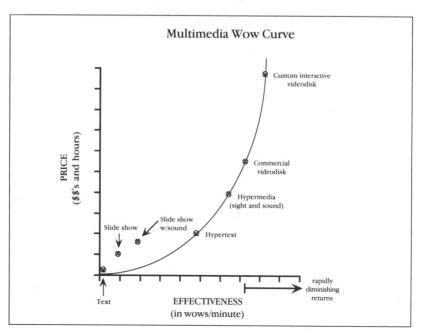

A Look Ahead

And in today already walks tomorrow.
Samuel Taylor Coleridge

There has never been a decade in the history of printing and publishing where production technology has changed as rapidly and with as much impact as it will in the 1990s. Computers have changed the way writers write, editors edit, artists draw, photographers photograph, layout is laid out, printers print, and how they all work together. Advances to come will make the publishing industry even more visual, individualized, immediate, graphically interesting, and interconnected. Publishing will expand into electronic media, with an attendant rise in availability and access.

In this chapter we focus on the changes likely to occur over the next ten years. Many of them are right around the corner. The obvious trends are toward tools that increase productivity and creativity, lower costs, give better visualization, are easier to use, allow for collaboration, conform to universal standards while retaining backward compatibility, and improve mobility. All of the successful tools will ultimately address these needs.

In 1991 the important advances are being made in graphical user interfaces, type and page description standards, display and storage technologies, color prepress, the mobile office, and voice and expert systems. The year 2000 will see huge, instantly accessible image databases, better voice and image recognition, multimedia applications with true 3D, interactive electronic publishing, and even more mobile systems.

We are also in the midst of what could be termed an "image revolution." More powerful hardware allows richer computer display environments to be available and gives rise to new publishing enterprises based on image management. Just as newspapers have been challenged by TV, print will be challenged by multimedia. Eventually, and without much fanfare multimedia will evolve into "virtual reality," which will allow publishers and corporate communications to surround the user in a computer-generated environment. But wait, let's not get too far ahead of ourselves. Let's first take a look at some more immediate trends.

Computer Hardware Advances

Advances in computer publishing are based on hardware and software. A new generation of computers is introduced every five years and new software, every three years. With each innovation comes improved performance and a decrease in equipment size. The sections that follow look at the trends in logic and memory, display, storage, input, and system software to predict their impact on publishing. Ten years from now desktop PCs still may come in the same size box and cost about the same in real terms. But there the similarity abruptly will end. They will be supercomputers whose power is hard to comprehend today. Laptops will be the size of a Walkman, and there will be new types of personal computers.

Tablet computers are new, and the first models are already here. These "pen-based" PCs, downsized to the size of a memo pad, add a new metaphor to computing that will create a revolution in forms management, office design, and new publishing opportunities. In the 1990s, the development and dominance of the microprocessor will continue. Any device in publishing that can be made with embedded intelligence will be, because doing so will be inexpensive.

Processing Speed

In the years ahead the processing speed of desktop computers will increase dramatically, allowing fast, efficient compression, manipulation and publication of large photographic-quality graphic images. The late Gordon Moore (Intel) drew a famous curve called Moore's Law that predicts this doubling effect. The relationship has been extended to chip clock speeds, where doubling takes place roughly every five years. Predictions are that today's 2 to 15 MIPS desktop/workstation computers will be replaced by computers operating in the 2-billion-instructions-per-second (BIPS) range at 200 MHz by the year 2000.

Figure 19-1
Moore's Law, and
Intel's CPUs.

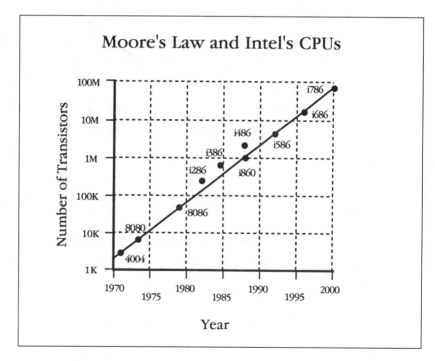

Computer Architecture

The current mix of computer architectures is Intel 80x86 microprocessors (50 percent), Motorola 68000 (10 percent), RISC (2 percent), and proprietary chips (40 percent). This mix is unlikely to change much in the next five years because companies want to adopt standards, and most equipment choices are based on available software. In publishing enterprises there is a trend to using heterogeneous computer environments. Shops with networked PCs, Macs, Suns, NeXTs, and other UNIX computers are becoming the norm. Electronic publishers want to use the best tool for each job. What's required is strong interoperability and interconnectivity (see below). Figure 19.2 illustrates the overall market for PCs.

Figure 19-2
The penetration of
PCs and applications
into the marketplace.
*Courtesy of Portia
Isaacson, BIS Cap
(Norwell, MA).*

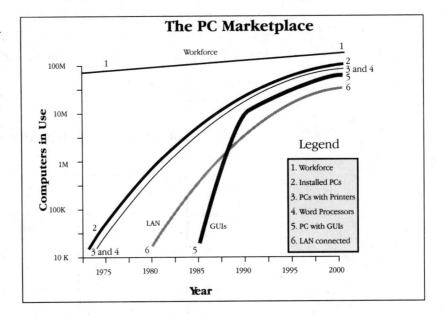

New chip technology is very expensive. A fabrication plant manufacturing 4 MByte DRAM chips or a 32-bit CPU costs $350 million. The implication of this enormous cost is that most computer chips are commodity items. The same CPU chips used in large computers also will be used in your PC. Higher system performance just will use more chips, making future PCs into miniature mainframes. This trend will also simplify programmers' tasks by standardizing the instruction set.

The 32-bit CPU will be dominant architecture for the next ten to fifteen years, when it is replaced by 64-bit CPUs. The address space of a 32-bit CPU is 4.3 by 10^9 (billion) bits, so there really isn't much incentive to go to larger byte sizes. A 64-bit CPU addresses an 18.5 by 10^9 (quintillion) bit byte, an almost inconceivably large number. Larger addresses buy higher-level languages that can be used by less well trained programmers, making for, in a sense, more friendly computing.

Integration

Integration means more power in the same place for less cost, and it will have an important role to play in desktop computers, peripherals, and electronic print. In 1990, where a PC might use seventy different chips, by 1993 an entire PC will be built on a single chip. This will turn the PC into a very low-cost item by minimizing the labor necessary for its construction. The first example of this technology is Advanced Micro Device's Am286LX/ZX IP, an integrated processor IBM PC AT on a chip. By the year 2000, a PC will be sold for the price of a cheap radio and available in office supply and consumer electronics stores. They will be as ubiquitous as digital watches. When they break, they will be recycled.

Integration is less dramatic for desktop computers where increased functionality uses specialty chips for graphics, sound, or speech. There is always a better video standard, or special function that will defy compact packaging. Nonetheless, vendors are building specialty chips for integrated functions. National Semiconductor's NS32G by 320 chip was designed to integrate imaging functions needed for control of scanners, laser printers, fax machines (even Group 4), intelligent terminals, and solid state phone answering. This technology, if commercialized, would replace the clutter of separate peripherals with a single control box and software.

Displays

Display technology is important in electronic publishing for improved image management. Clear trends can be seen in the migration of workstation display technology to the personal computer in increasing screen resolutions and video memory. More video memory increases the number of video frame buffers that can be stored and manipulated, resulting in improved color and new video techniques and effects. Specialized graphics coprocessors will allow complex and rapid real-time three-dimensional rendering and will be available as powerful add-in boards. But these coprocessors always will be specialty items because, given a fast enough CPU, video processing can be done without offloading. Also, as future PCs will be multi-CPU machines, dedicated video coprocessors may not be required.

Many experts believe that the CRT slowly will be replaced by very large, high-resolution, color, flat-panel display technology by the year 2000. Just what kind of flat panel may become commercially viable is unknown, but some candidates include active matrix LCD, thick-film cadmium sulfide/cadmium cyanide LCDs, transistors, LEDs, and virtual projection devices. New display technologies such as stereo 3D and High Definition Television (HDTV) are part of a video revolution, with desktop video being the desktop publishing of the '90s.

HDTV High Definition Television (HDTV) provides a much higher-resolution, more graphically rich display than is widely available today. Experts expect HDTV to become common by the late 1990s. The technology actually dates back to the 1960s when the Japanese broadcaster NHK began to experiment with it and led an industry-wide research consortium. A prototype was shown in 1979. Sony introduced a model in 1984, and Japanese programming to support this new format is appearing. The NHK standard is called MUSE; the European one is called Eureka-95; and the recently chosen U.S. standard created at the Sarnoff Labs is called ACTV-1.

HDTV monitors currently use interlaced display technology, which allows more information to be transmitted in a narrower bandwidth, but results in more "flicker" and less sharpness than interlaced displays. A 27-inch model sells for around $4,000. A 1920 by 1035 pixel 27-inch monitor uses 6 MBytes of video RAM. Size is not a specification of the HDTV standards. Image compression (encoding) and decompression (decoding) are important to this technology. The use of fiber optic cable for data transmission would allow images to be used without compression and is being considered by manufacturers. Since high-quality computer monitors are *non*interlaced, it is anticipated that there may be two separate HDTV standards. Computer graphics require better displays, so HDTV should have greater initial impact as a computer product than in the consumer electronics arena. In fact, there really is not much immediate demand for better-quality TV in the consumer market—perception of image quality is not that discriminating.

Stereo Three-Dimensional TV Stereo three-dimensional monitors have been available as $50,000 options on workstations for a few years from Tektronix (Beaverton, OR) and StereoGraphics (San Raphael, CA). Early adopters include mechanical, architectural, engineering, and construction CAD users; and medical, remote handling, manufacturing inspection, promotions, and entertainment users seeking better visualization. Stereo viewers should begin to appear on personal computers by the late 1990s as they become less expensive to manufacture.

Figure 19-3
StereoGraphics CrystalEyes stereo three-dimensional viewing system. *Courtesy of Stereo-Graphics Corporation (San Rafael, CA).*

Memory and Storage

The key to digital document processing and image management is computer storage. The magnetic and magneto-optical disk drives we use today will soon be regarded as mechanical dinosaurs, and will be replaced by more reliable, cheaper, and faster solid state memory devices. A disk drive is to a solid state memory device what the vacuum tube or a relay switch was to the transistor.

Conventional disk drives will continue to dominate primary storage until around 1995, when magneto-optical erasable drives will become competitive in cost and speed. Solid state devices (nonmechanical) should be serious players by the year 2000. Storage capacities for desktop computers are increasing at about 100 percent per year, so in the year 2000 desktop computers will ship with a gigabyte of storage.

Solid state semiconductor memory cards have appeared in video games, such as the Sega system, and in palmtop computers, such as the Poqet. Memory cards are just a packaging technique that can contain any kind of semiconductor. As technology improves, so too do memory cards. ROM cards, which are dense and cheap, can store from 512 KBytes to 16 MBytes of data, with 64 MBytes just around the corner. Read/write formats such as RAM, erasable programmable ROM (EPROM), and electrically erasable programmable ROM (EEPROM) are more expensive and problematical. Flash memory, which has the density of DRAM, is finding use in electronic still photography and in laptops. Once written, flash memory does not require a power source to retain data; power is used for erasure and write only. Flash memory is still quite expensive and requires more downsizing to be really useful in computer memory applications, but it may be a factor several years from now.

Experimental systems based on holographic light storage in crystals are being developed at the Microelectronics and Computer Technology Corporation (Austin, TX), Bellcore (Livingston, NJ), and Stanford University. The storage device called a holostore has random access, superconductor performance hundreds of times faster than any present technology, and capacities projected up to 100 gigabytes. Prototypes of crystallites with 500 pages of information and transfer rates of 800 MBytes/sec have been demonstrated. Holostores may sound like science fiction, but their ability to access ultra-large files very quickly may make them a potential solution to full-motion interactive video applications, high-quality video, and rapid visualization technology.

New Computer Forms

Powerful portable PCs have long been a goal for the computer industry. They allow people to work in remote locations and will change the office structure of tomorrow. In the late 1960s Alan Kay crystallized the thinking of many by describing the Dynabook, a notebook with a 1 million pixel screen, eight processors, and both wireless and cabled networking. Kay's concept probably will become a reality in the laptops of the mid-1990s. Kay's other versions of the Dynabook were a head-mounted display and a computer wristwatch, both also possible. Some predict the fusion of portable computers with cellular phones, faxes, and wireless networked to other computers.

Grid's GridPad, Scenario's DynaWriter, Toshiba's PenPC, Sony's Palmtop, Go Technology's PenPoint, and the new computer from the Active Book Company (Cambridge, England) are examples of a new type of pen-based portable computer. Dubbed pen- or stylus-based, or slate computers, they are expected to find a market in applications where portability and ease of use are required. They are perfect for note taking, as personal information managers (PIMs), and mobile forms-based data entry. Nearly all Japanese computer manufacturers are working on this form of computer because the Kanji character set doesn't lend itself to keyboard entry. The computer industry is excited about this technology. It is expected that slate computers will introduce millions of computer-phobic people to the new technology. Whole office systems will be built around them, so it pays for electronic publishers to watch these developments.

The PenPoint goes beyond the traditional concept of a notebook computer by containing a proprietary 32-bit, object-oriented, multitasking operating system that addresses the unique needs of a strictly pen input system. The goal of PenPoint is to empower new users by employing natural everyday motions and metaphors. PenPoint's notebook user interface (NUI) contains a set of gestures or pen motions for important commands. You click on buttons to navigate, mark an X to delete text, and insert new text with a caret symbol. Data entered by pen (block printing, not cursive) is analyzed by a handwriting recognition system and matched to a vocabulary by a set of AI rules that can be specified by each application. The PenPoint uses a notebook metaphor with documents organized as separate pages, and the file system is a strict superset of the MS-DOS file system. Documents can be embedded live inside other documents, and a Hypertext system is supported.

Figure 19-4
PenPoint's GUI concept: notebook, pages, tabs, and a table of contents manipulated by a set of gestures.
Courtesy of Go Corporation (Foster City, CA).

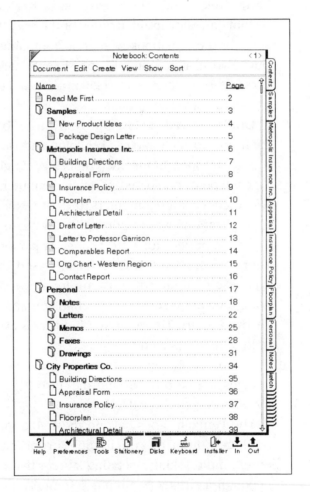

The PenPoint is not yet available but will be introduced in 1992 through developers, VARs, and other computer vendors. Many important software and hardware companies have signed licenses to use the operating system and announced hardware/software product support. Stylus computers may have significant commercial impact in the mid-1990s as a niche product, but eventually will be supplemented by the much more important voice input and natural language recognition systems that will come early in the next century.

Compound Technologies

Systems Packaging

Computer systems are going through the same integration that is appearing at the board level. The Canon Navigator is an all-in-one computer-based office system. It combines an IBM PC XT, mouse, 40 MByte hard drive, with a scanner, Canon BJ-10e BubbleJet printer, fax machine, telephone, answering machine, and eight commercial software packages. The Navigator is for companies and individuals who want a capable desktop office system without having to configure their own. Canon supplies a DOS shell to launch each system function from an icon. There is software for scheduling, phone logs, clocks, and so on. The system is available

Figure 19-5
The Canon Navigator Desktop Office is a complete desktop office package. *Courtesy of Canon, Inc. (Lake Success, NY).*

from office supply stores and consumer electronic or computer catalogs. Other integrated systems are the GLC/SBS from Cumulus Computer Corp. (Cleveland, OH) and The Home Office from US Integrated Technologies (Richmond, CA).

Hydras

You often see discussions in the computer trade press about integrated peripheral devices called hydras. The combination of copier, laser printer, scanner, and plain paper fax machine is a natural one that saves construction costs by sharing common components. Purchased separately these units might cost $7,500, but the combination would cost about $2,500. This is the idea behind the Canon CLC 500 (Chapter 15). Some argue that when one part of the device goes down it would cripple the entire system. However, integration generally brings better performance, and good engineering would minimize inconvenience by making parts modular and replaceable. Within the next couple of years these devices should begin to appear in large numbers on the market.

Beyond the GUI

Clearly Graphical User Interfaces (GUIs) are the wave of the '90s, and improving computer performance increases their capabilities. But the GUI metaphor is fifteen years old, and it is tired technology. When you ferret your way into the second of a set of nested dialog boxes or manually update the data in several places, you are experiencing the limitations of the technology. GUIs are meant to teach you about the capabilities of your system, but anything hidden is not intuitive.

To choose and display options in a feature-rich environment, you have to use more of the senses. Multimedia interfaces, dependent on display technology and image content, will become more important. Xerox PARC has developed an interactive three-dimensional interface with color and real-time animation. Called the Information Visualizer, it uses a standard screen to create three-dimensional representations of data and structure. A database might be represented by a room of walls, with data located by rotating that structure. The Visualizer has a virtual large screen with intelligent windows of working program sets and other structures, including hierarchical trees. Apple Computer also has developed an interface called the SonicFinder that associates sounds with actions.

Portability and Interoperability

The Mac, PC (Windows, GeoWorks, OS/2 PM), UNIX (Motif, X Windows), and others all have GUIs that compete for your attention. Although similar, each has software or system features that excel at one task or another. Users want to use any computer, the available computer, or the one with the best toolbox. And when that step in the process is complete, they want to take their work and use it on any other computer seamlessly. Portability and interoperability are results of open standards, and are a clear trend.

It is difficult to predict what operating system may come to dominate because it is not just a technical issue. Marketing, user resistance, and happenstance play a role. It may even be a moot point. The day is approaching when vendors will build transparent system software. GeoWorks, for example, ships with a GUI based on the Open Systems Foundation's (Cambridge, MA) OSF/Motif standard. Future versions of GeoWorks are planned that will allow other GUIs to be chosen as an option. Someone familiar with Page-Maker on Windows could choose that GUI, while another user could choose Motif. A PC could look like a Sun, Mac, or NeXT computer. The operating system takes care of all of the details of redrawing and implementing the interface. When this happens, the whole electronic publishing process will become infinitely easier.

Dynamic Links

The sharing of data between documents is referred to as *dynamic linking*. Macintosh System 7 Interapplication Communications (IAC), Windows, or OS/2 Presentation Manager's Dynamic Data Exchange (DDE), or the Hewlett-Packard NewWave routines are dynamic links. Whereas a "warm link" requires a user to manually update shared data (like the Subscribe and Publish commands in System 7), a "hot link" makes those changes automatically. Among the many uses are updating multiple documents in workgroup publishing, and coordinating and updating information in large database-intensive publications such as telephone books and catalogs. The Links feature in PageMaker, as well as P.INK Press, WriteOn and other document managers, already use a form of dynamic linking. Interleaf is developing a prototype "active" document facility that searches for information and uses a set of rules to determine when and to whom to send out documents.

Data Highways

Network operating systems will be written so that object-oriented GUI network operating environments will extend the desktop across the entire system. Other important achievements will include hardware and software that allow for easier network installation, reconfiguration, and management; all are currently major headaches for large installations. These developments probably will happen within the next three or four years.

A major problem in the current technology is the bandwidth of data transmission. It is just too slow. To work with large image or sound files, new networks must be built. Data transmitted as light has tremendous bandwidth. Optical data transmission networks are practical and are being installed. Integrated Services Digital Networks (ISDN) is a two-part solution: The digital network consists of ISDN lines, equipment, and software; and the integrated services refer to applications and services that can be developed by the movement of voice, data, and images over the same physical interface.

ISDN has begun to be installed widely in Europe and Japan. Currently there are 100,000 miles of fiber optic cabling in American phone networks. ISDN is a major investment and appears to be too expensive now for general use, although costs are coming down. In a recent project it cost $5,000 to fiber wire a home. The number of different standards also have slowed its growth. The consensus is that broadband ISDN will be installed in the United States in the late 1990s using government funding. When that happens, ISDN will be hardwired into every computer that is made because it will make digital video and high-quality sound transmission more practical.

Open Page Description Standards

The microcomputer industry has always been plagued by competing standards and the barriers they create between hardware systems and applications. With the development of multi-platform networking systems, such as TOPS and Novell, and with communications protocols like Ethernet, or standardized database query languages like SQL or Apple's Data Assess Language (DAL), our machines have become a bit more accomplished at talking to one another—as long as they speak within the limits of ASCII or the same application.

The next challenge, especially for publishers, is to create standards by which any publication can be read and edited on every publishing system with complete formatting intact, regardless of whether or not those systems share the application under which the publication was created. This type of standard is now developing, and should appear on the market long before the end of the decade.

A consortium of hardware and software companies, including Sun, IBM, Apple, Aldus, and Quark, are already working on such a standard, called Publishing Interchange Language (PIL). Initially, documents created under this format will be readable, but not editable, on different systems. Later versions expected in the next few years also will allow document editing.

Meanwhile, Adobe is working to expand PostScript into a universal, editable medium for describing any type of document on any system. At first, machine-specific utilities will be needed to view and modify an "editable PostScript" document on a particular system. Before the end of the decade, however, this capability could be built into all publishing systems, creating a technology that could truly match paper as a transportable, universal communications medium.

"Now we use computers to create paper," Adobe CEO John Warnock told *PC Week*. "We should be able to use them to communicate and replace many traditional paper functions. To do this, we need to break out of the ASCII jail."

True Colors

Now there is considerable momentum toward establishing a full digital printing press—not a Boston Celtic defense, but evolutionary electronic publishing technology. Manufacturers are currently experimenting with high-speed imaging of presses directly from a page description file without any intermediate chemical processing. In essence, a printing press would become a very large, high-speed laser printer. That would obviate the need for a printing plate and eliminate the need for any chemical processing of images onto film. When you consider that this portion of the publishing process accounts for over 30 percent of the cost of printing and perhaps 75 percent of the time, the benefits are clear. The full digital press should be a reality by 1995.

Increasingly stringent environmental restrictions are part of why there is so much interest in the full digital press, but the trend also addresses a need for improved flexibility in the printing process. As more and more short-run works are produced, even high-speed presses aren't always fast enough. Given a choice, most publishers prefer to customize their product as much as possible.

Before the full digital press can become a reality, a satisfactory solution must be found to the color prepress issues (see Chapter 14). As a color comp is the essential element in the contract between a customer and a printer, accurate color printer output matched to the final printed output of a full digital press would eliminate the need for any other intermediate steps. Accurate color printer output is very close to becoming a reality with the cooperative efforts of Adobe (PostScript Level 2), Electronics for Imaging (Color Portability), and other vendors. They are working to establish a color description model that can be used to define and implement consistent color on any input, output, or display device.

Electronically Produced Publications

The universal introduction of the personal computer into the graphic arts was one of the major publishing industry developments of the 1980s. In the 1990s this trend will continue. It wasn't all that long ago that a completely computer-generated book was a novelty. In 1984 using a 128K Macintosh, Peter Gillis and Mike Saenz released the first computer-generated comic book called *Shatter*. The unique (albeit crude) look made it one of the best-selling comics of the year. *Batman: Digital Justice*, a 1990 issue from DC Comics by the artist Pepe Moreno, advances this art form even further to create an exceptionally beautiful and unique work. *Batman* was created using a Macintosh II (see Fig. 19-6 and 19-7). Illustrations were done using CAD programs, vector drawing programs, three-dimensional modeling, and paint programs such as Studio/8 and Photoshop. The entire book was laid out in QuarkXPress, and printing negatives were made from over 200 MBytes of files.

Meanwhile, more and more commercial magazines and newspapers are embracing desktop-based electronic production. Time, Inc.'s *Entertainment Weekly* was one of the first, and *Time* magazine will soon follow. *USA Today* depends heavily on electronic composition using "off the shelf" software. *Playboy*, *Popular Science*, and of course *Publish*, *Macweek*, and *Desktop Communications* are produced using the new tools. The *San Francisco Examiner* and scores of other newspapers are produced "on the desktop," and *The New York Times* will soon follow.

Hyperpublishing

The 1990s are going to see a lot of experimentation in the publishing community as people attempt to identify new forms of creativity and expression as well as new business opportunities. Electronic literature is just beginning. Publishers who put data on a CD-ROM and sell it for hundreds of dollars are beginning to think in terms of the *experience* of accessing information by non-serial methods. By editing data and making it interactive, the whole process is enriched. Publishing and multimedia are on a collision course; what's coming will be known as *hyperpublishing*.

More and more, magazines are taking a compound approach to disseminating information. IDG Communications has a *MacWorld* magazine forum on America Online, and Ziff-Davis, publisher of

Figure 19-6
The cover of *Batman: Digital Justice* is the best example of a computer-generated comic book.

several publications (*PC Magazine, PC/Computing, MacUser,* and others), has set up industry forums on CompuServe. You enter these forums just as if they were a separate on-line service. PC MagNet for *PC Magazine*, and ZMac for *MacUser* readers offer extended services: bulletin boards, software libraries, libraries of printed articles (both current and past), and an editorial forum used by the magazine editors. Through these services, readers become part of the ongoing process of creation by supplying the editors with instant feedback; a readership community is also created. IDG and Ziff-Davis have also used their material to launch companies in the computer book trade.

Figure 19-7 A sample page spread from the book. *Courtesy of DC Comics (New York, NY) © 1990. All rights reserved.*

David Bunnell's launch of the magazine/information service for the biological technology industry called BioWorld is one example of what he calls "interactive publishing." Perhaps a better term would be a hypermedia publication. BioWorld is an on line publishing and conference service (*BioWorld Online*), a daily subscription fax newsletter (*BioWorld Today*), a consulting service (BioWorld Advisory Service), a monthly magazine (*BioWorld Magazine*), and a newsletter (*BioVenture View*)—with the emphasis on the electronic components of the service.

Bunnell says:

The day is coming when readers, not publishers, will do the printing—making the printed word a more economical, timely, and effective medium. Publishers will deliver their magazine over a modem. Interactive publishing offers timeliness and efficiency. News no longer arrives at the newsstand or the mailbox days after the fact. Instead it is delivered in seconds to the subscriber's personal computer. The printed word doesn't come any hotter off the press. The reader can use an on-line database management facility to electronically skim through literally thousands of pages of information, extracting only what is of immediate interest. Electronic letters to the editor enables subscribers to communicate with authors and readers, bringing publishers and readers closer together. As soon as the information is on-line, it's instantly available worldwide. Yet unlike radio or TV, or even magazines, interactive publishing places no limits on the depth of a piece. Interactive publishing combines the benefits of the electronic and printed media.

The customization of published information for individual needs has been called *narrowcasting*, as opposed to broadcasting. A person requests or receives just the information in which he or she is interested. Computers have made publishing newsletters infinitely easier and can provide the tools needed to personalize them for each subscriber. Narrowcasting transfers the trends seen in short-run production and manufacturing to communications.

Electronic Photo Albums

The photography industry sees the 1990s as a decade of transition to digital technology. Film won't disappear as a medium, however. Because of its quality and resolution, it will probably not be duplicated digitally for twenty years. But new markets in electronic photography have compelling benefits for electronic publishing, and vendors are releasing products that address these markets. The benefits include instant access to images, great enhancement and editing tools, and convenient storage and distribution. In Chapter 10 we discussed the new class of cameras for still-frame photography based on CCD sensors that write data to disk. They are of much lower quality than 35 mm film, but their "instant" development makes them very attractive to newspapers. Industry analysts think that they may account for 50 percent of camera sales by the year 2000. There are 250 million 35 mm cameras in use today, and they account for 85 percent of the 50 billion photos taken annually.

Eastman Kodak has created a system that couples the quality of film with the density of CD-ROM. Called the Photo-CD system, it was developed jointly with Philips Corp., and is scheduled for introduction in 1992. Standard 35 mm photographs are used. A photofinisher scans the film using a $100,000 Photo-CD Transfer Station, which includes a high-resolution scanner, Sun SPARCstation, image processing software, Photo-CD writer, and a thermal printer. Kodak sells the Prism XL electronic previewing station so that images can be viewed and edited prior to writing to disk. Images are returned on a CD disk album that can store up to 100 images in a jeweled case for a price that is anticipated to be under $20 per disk for twenty-four images. Thumbnail photos are included that show the CD's contents. To add more images to a disk, you can return it with more film. To play back Photo-CDs on a computer, you can use a CD ROM XA (extended architecture) drive; use a CD-I player or a Kodak Photo-CD (ca. $500) player to play back to any TV set.

Just how well the Photo-CD system will be received by the consumer market is unknown. The moderate quality and resolution of the images make it a good medium for the commercial market, and it should be an important advance for desktop publishers, for anyone doing presentations, or for multimedia applications. Photo-CD provides "electronic negatives," where each image is stored as 18 megapixels with compression. That means that it is sixteen times the density of current TV standards, four times the density of the proposed HDTV standards, and goes well beyond today's electronic still cameras. The quality is high enough to result in very good prints to be made into second generation prints.

The Digital Document

The digital document is a collection of information that has several important implications for the future of communication. Viewing or printing the document is like taking a snapshot in time. Unlike the written form, digital documents can contain many information types (text, images, sound, and so on), exist in multiple places on a network, are linked to or depend on other documents for their content, stay live, have intricate structure and nonserial access, and be accessed and modified by a group of peo-

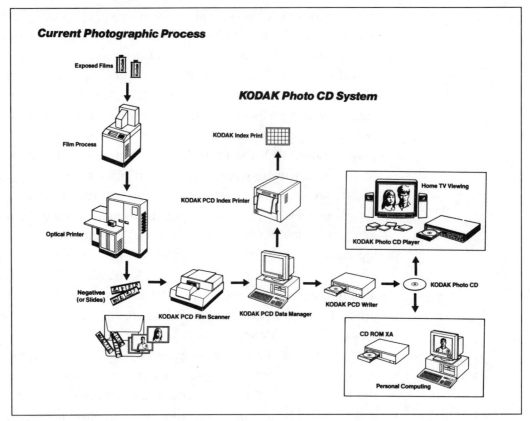

A.

B.   **C.**

Figure 19-8 (A) Eastman Kodak's new photographic system called Photo-CD takes scans of 35 mm film and writes them to a CD. Using a Kodak Photo CD player, images can be displayed on any TV set or on a computer. **(B)** The Photo-CD Transfer Station. **(C)** A Photo-CD disk and player. *Courtesy of Kodak, Inc.*

ple. The term Intelligent Document Management (IDM) has been used to describe the ensemble of electronic imaging disciplines that enable this technology.

In order to be useful as electronic information, digital documents must be refined (see Figure 19-9). If you scan a newspaper, you get a bit-map file that is merely a collection of unrelated information. The image by itself is meaningless; your understanding of that image is what imparts knowledge. To refine the bit map further, an optical character recognition program might be used to process the document to get ASCII code, and any nontextural images might be indexed. Now the file has more meaning. Proofing software to turn ASCII into text and using indexed images to create relationships provide further refinements. To create more

Figure 19-9
Information
refinement of a
digital document.

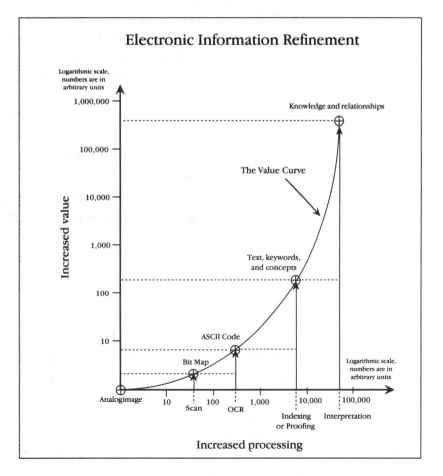

useful information, an artificial intelligence program would interpret the text, indexed images, and create the relationships. Thus human knowledge is transferred to the computer, which now meaningfully organizes the document.

Though IDM sounds pretty abstract, it is important. If electronic data is tagged with indexing and artificial intelligence, then communication can be done in new ways. When you fax your federal income tax return to the Internal Revenue Service, a bit map arrives. The IRS interprets it, and processes your check, issues a refund, or becomes your pen pal. Even more powerful systems are possible if the form itself has intelligence. The Electronic Data Interchange Standard (EDI) protocol, also known as ANSI standard X.12, lets businesses exchange data in a standard format. Purchase orders, invoices, and tax forms are processed with it. EDI specifies that a document have a header and trailer and a group of data elements that are identified by a reference. When a system reads an EDI communication, it sees the tag for the element (say a name field or social security number) and knows the data type, description, length range, and other standard attributes. The document is never bit mapped, and is thus small and easily communicated.

EDI is used by over 18,000 organizations worldwide, from the U.S. Government to Sears to Levi Strauss and on down, with software ranging from $500 to $6,000. EDI also can make a small company look big. For more information about EDI contact Data Interchange Standards Association, Inc. (Alexandria, VA) or the consulting organization EDI, Spread the Word! (Dallas, TX).

The Paperless Office

Computers were supposed to reduce paperwork, but in reality they are printing engines that have created mountains of paper. Most people consider the paperless office as likely as the paperless bathroom, but that is changing. There is certainly tremendous incentive for change. One survey claims that American business produces 1 trillion pages of paper a year, enough at letter size to more than cover the earth. A four-drawer file cabinet costs $25,000 to fill and $2,160 a year to maintain. Some 3 percent of all documents are lost, costing $120 to recover each one. An executive spends four weeks a year searching for documents.

Enter the digital document and Document Image Processing or DIP, aka the paperless office. The confluence of technologies of computers, scanners, deep storage on optical media, video terminal display, printers, and faxes can be implemented by single users or small businesses. Larger systems can be networked with mainframe systems with jukebox laser disk storage devices in the tens or hundreds of gigabyte range. Companies that have installed these systems as a replacement for paper, microfilm, or microfiche have reported tremendous cost and efficiency gains. The '90s will bring improvements that make PC-based DIP systems affordable and essential office technology. DIP systems will have particular impact on the publication process. The document management systems discussed in Chapter 16 are the first expressions of this trend.

DIP is not without its difficulties. Knowledge refinement of a digital document requires the creation of new methods for retrieval. Indexing documents for content, importance, and relationship is a complex task that will require the creation of a new type of computer specialist, the knowledge engineer. The creation of the algorithms and procedures for indexing is at the highest level of information refinement. Because these systems will contain so much information, automated systems will be required for effective search and retrieval; these will probably require expert systems software with artificial intelligence techniques.

HyperMedia Database Publishing

Thirty years ago Ted Nelson conceived of a knowledge-networked database he called "Xanadu" that would be a repository of all human achievements. Documents, books, images, animation, or music would be reduced to data that anyone could access from a personal computer. Xanadu would be a new form of compound electronic publishing, with broad implications for the way we think and learn about subjects. Xanadu is the beginning of computer experiments in shared memory and group consciousness. The Xanadu Hypermedia Information Server program developed by Nelson and others at the Xanadu Operating Company (now a subsidiary of AutoDesk, Sausalito, CA) is about to become a reality. Xanadu will run on Suns, 80386 PCs, Macs, and NeXT computers.

Users would navigate Xanadu through a sophisticated electronic file system that links related information, has version dating and comparison, allows commentary (like Post-It! notes), and has a search-and-retrieval engine. If you were researching the explosion of the volcano on the island of Krakatoa in 1883, you might do a keyword search to bring up a listing of relevant subjects, then use that cross-listing to find articles, photos, or even movies on the subject. An article in *Scientific American* on the cold summer of 1884 might be there for you to use, or a documentary from PBS's *Nova* series. Everything would be hyperlinked so that you could include all the information in your written work (Nelson calls this "transclusion"). You could draw on these resources as part of Xanadu, and the system would award royalties to authors and publishers. You might read other people's commentary, add your own, and receive royalties for your work as well. Publishing your work would be as simple as clicking a Publish button on the Xanadu network.

Public Access Xanadu, or PAX, will open in August 1991. Nelson calls it a "licensed and franchised storage and forwarding service run along the lines of McDonald's" with Silverstands where billions and billions of documents are served. PAX will license franchises to storage vendors who will provide the services and support. PAX provides the overall structure. Fees would be charged for connect time, storage, and publication; a monthly bill would credit any royalties that are due you. Xanadu's operating system would serve as the back end, managing the system, and vendors would provide specialty software to access the information. Nelson's concept is explained more fully in his self-published book *Literary Machines*.

Virtual Reality

Virtual reality is the extension of multimedia to create a simulated environment. In a virtual reality condition, objects are created and manipulated so that the user can understand, learn, and relate to them. For example, wandering around a virtual room you might bang into a wall, have to exert force to move a chair, or have an object that you release appear to drop to the floor. Vendors are inventing and experimenting with new classes of input devices such as data gloves or suits with sensors in them; three-dimensional joysticks; flying mice; and visors that project simulated three-dimensional space. Eventually, when computers support full speech recognition, holography, eye tracking, tactile feedback, and other effects, they too will be applied. Multimedia, desktop video, improved visualization software, and others all point in this direction. More and more computers will ship with standard peripherals such as microphones, cameras, and more sophisticated input devices that will enable this technology.

The extension of the desktop metaphor to three-dimensions has been dubbed "cyberspace." The word was coined by science fiction writer William Gibson in his book *Neuromancer* to describe a fantasy world where people used electrodes daily as part of "consensual hallucination." Cyberspace subsumes users *into* the computer interface to make them part of the program experience. This approach dramatically improves the amount of information that can flow, along with the quality and quantity of the responses, creating a new form of information and communications medium.

Virtual reality has some very important and serious applications with tremendous implications for education. NASA has developed the Virtual Interface Environment Workstation (VIEW) at the Ames Research Center (Mountain View, CA) that includes a heads-up three-dimensional display, data gloves, voice controller, and gesture recognition software. NASA believes that virtual reality systems will allow astronauts to perform hazardous space operations using robots. Aircraft and fighter pilots train in million-dollar simulators for the same reason. In a virtual reality environment, an intern could practice delicate surgery in cyberspace, architects could "walk" through their buildings, and an engineer could travel into a microchip to get a feeling for how the design works. Even the games played in cyberspace would be remarkable. You could play a simulated game of squash with an opponent who was your exact equal, or with an opponent in another city (or on another planet).

Or, you could fly around in a programmer's interpretation of the body of a pterodactyl through a simulated prehistoric landscape.

AutoDesk (Sausalito, CA), VPL Research (Redwood City, CA), several universities, and a number of small companies in the San Francisco area are specializing in virtual reality work. VPL sells a set of goggles called EyePhones ($9,400), gloves called DataGloves ($8,800), and a full-length DataSuit (ca. $100,000) for total immersion into cyberspace. Datasuit contains fifty motion sensors, 300 feet of fiber optical cable. A good research setup for virtual reality might cost over $250,000. VPL has licensed a scaled-down version of the DataGlove to Mattel, Inc., which is selling it under the name of "Power Glove" for Nintendo systems. Most systems allow for good three-dimensional input by providing software that lets commands be entered in a language of motion gestures. This could result in an important solution to three-dimensional manufacturing workstations for prototyping work. It is not inconceivable that a desktop manufacturing workstation would couple cyberspace input and modeling software, a three-dimensional scanner, and a three-dimensional printing device as a single platform. Perhaps by the year 2000 a holographic printer also will become available as a mainstream device.

All of these new technologies will change the landscape of our lives. Electronic publishers will be in the forefront, on the cutting edge, creating new art forms. New tools and new skills will put tremendous power at our reach. Just beyond the desktop.

How this Book was Produced

Beyond the Desktop was written in Microsoft Word 4 (Mac). Line art was created and manipulated with SuperPaint 2.0a and Aldus FreeHand. Digital Darkroom and Adobe Photoshop were used for image manipulation. These choices were based on my familiarity with these programs as well as their positions in the Macintosh marketplace. Scans were made with a H-P ScanJet Plus, and a LaserWriter NTX was used for printing manuscript pages. Screenshots were accomplished with Capture on the Macintosh and Hot-Shot Graphics on the PC. Some files were created under MS-DOS with a Toshiba T3100SX laptop and an H-P Vector Tower 386. All PC files used for the book were translated using MacLinkPC Plus and the Apple File Exchange.

At the outset of the project, sample text pages representing all possible text formats were sent to Nancy Sugihara, who created the interior design.

The style sheet for the manuscript utilized 12 MS Word styles; all the remaining styles to be used in page layout were to be defined by the compositor. Styles created in MS Word were: Title, Part, Chapter Header, Section Header, Subsection Header, Subsubsection Header, Body, Body2 (reduced type size), Bullets, Tip Header, Footnote, and Normal. MS Word 4 adds other styles including

Headers and Footers, and Page Numbers. Once you index a document you get additional styles such as Index 1, 2, 3, etc.

In order to facilitate document management inside MS Word, each chapter was named according to the convention "a.TOC," "b.Pref," "c.Intro," "d.Ch.1," "e.Ch.2," and so on. Then, when the folder containing the book was opened in the Macintosh Open standard file dialog box, the files appeared (alphabetically) in order from the beginning (at top) to the end (at bottom). Also, all of the chapter and section files were added to the Work menu in Word. Figure 1 shows how convenient this construction of the Word Work menu is for rapidly opening and closing files.

Figure A.1
Setting up a Word 4 Work menu for a multi-chapter book. Note hidden text indexing with dotted underlining.

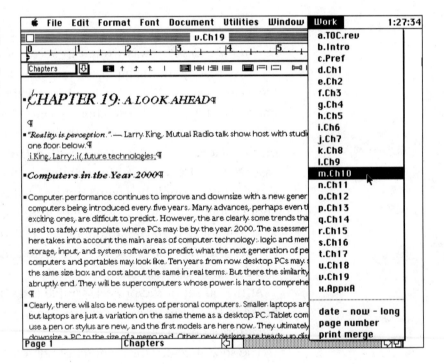

After the writing was finished, each chapter was indexed using Word's indexing feature. Indexing is done by using hidden text and enclosing it within special formatting codes. You can index words, have nested and hierarchical indexes, index ranges, and have index entries that are cross references. All are hidden text entries. Word collects the index entries using an Index command on the Utilities menu and appends them at the end of the document with page numbers attached. It was our intention to preserve the hard work done with style-sheet formatting and indexing within whatever layout program was used.

Two leading Macintosh layout programs, Aldus PageMaker and QuarkXPress, were considered for page composition and typesetting. We chose QuarkXPress for several reasons. They include: strong typographical tools, multiple master pages, and good figure status tracking tools. Overall, QuarkXPress allows a greater flexibility of design than any of the layout programs on the Macintosh market. Quark's great strength in the area of color handling was put to good work in the composition of the color pages.

QuarkXPress 3.0 imports Word style-sheets well, but requires the use of the Sonar Bookends XTension (Virginia Systems Software Services, Inc., 5509 West Bay Court, Midlothian, VA 23112, Tel. (804)739-3200) to create a table of contents and an index. The Index module is sold for about $120, and the Table of Contents module retails for $99.

Figure A.2
A set of facing pages in QuarkXPress.

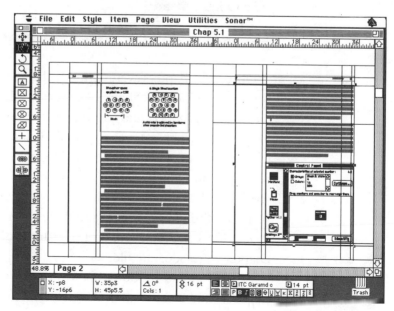

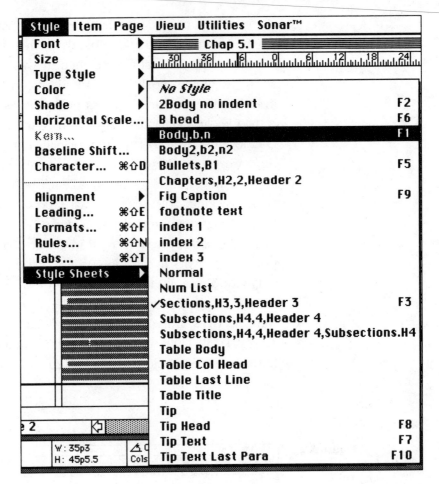

Figure A.3
The styles created in
QuarkXPress duplicated
those created in
Word, plus additional
layout elements.

Once the chapters were written, the laser pages and disk files were sent to Bantam. Figures were sent as laser pages; photos and slides were scanned and printed at low resolution to be used as FPO "stats." The book was copyedited, and Donna Chernin set up the page templates. All of the style names created in Word were recreated in Quark so that they imported properly; additional styles for the other book elements were also created. The template for the chapters contained three master pages (C = Part Page, B = Chapter Page, and A = Interior Facing Pages). Each chapter was a separate file.

No one should lay out a book without running test pages. Test pages should include all of the different elements to be used in a layout, some simple lines, and various screens to test the image-setter output. We used a Varityper 4300 at 1270 dpi with a 120-line screen setting. We used PageWorks in Cambridge, MA, as our service bureau for output. Donna ran a test chapter with figures through a LaserWriter NTX to test the different file formats. These tests were timed, the rationale being that there is a rough correlation between how long it takes to print a laser page and an image-set page. It's a good thing we ran these tests because we discovered several file format incompatibilities that had to be resolved with file format conversions. In some cases this necessitated that figures be redrawn.

The final layout put boxes where slides and halftone reproductions would be placed, but imported a large number of PICT files as camera-ready art on the page mechanicals. All laser proofs went back to the publisher for final approval before imagesetting. The pages were output to paper, which was then sent to the printer. The printer used these pages to make negative film, onto which the halftone negatives were stripped. The printer then made blue-lines (proofs) of the pages, which were approved by the publisher before the final print run.

Creating the Color Plates
by Donna Chernin

My involvement with this book began with an introduction to the author through the Boston Computer Society's Macintosh Users Group's electronic bulletin board. We discussed the scope of the color plates: how many pages and figures, what information the figures were to convey, what style illustration we'd use, and software and hardware requirements. The main objective was to use existing computer technology to create the pages, without having to resort to any traditional techniques such as stripping. We also wanted to use figures that were different from anything we had seen, and which showed common techniques, such as color photo separation, along with some of the special effects available only from the desktop.

My toolbox was a Macintosh IIcx, with 8 MBytes of RAM, an 80 MByte internal hard disk, and a 13-inch Sony color monitor. The page layout software was QuarkXPress with ITC-Garamond as the principal font. Black-and-white proofs were output to an Apple Laserwriter IINT, and color laser proofs were produced on a QMS ColorScript 100.

Figures C1, C6, C7, C8 and the top of figure C10 (QuarkXPress Pantone Color Dialog Box) were 32-bit PICT screen captures. They were brought into Photoshop, converted from RGB to CMYK color mode, then saved as "Desktop Color Separation" EPS files to create the color separations. PhotoShop creates five files, one EPS file each for C, Y, M, and K, and one preview PICT (either 1 bit/pixel or 8 bits/pixel) that displays in the page layout program. We chose the 8 bit/pixel PICT file format to display color, which was then imported and resized, and labels created in QuarkXPress. Each illustration was "grouped" so it could be moved around with labels, lines, and graphics.

Figure C3 shows all the steps involved in desktop color separation using a color slide as the original image. The image of the crayons was photographed using Ektachrome 100 film for color slides, on a very hot August day in Barrie's backyard. We worked fast because the crayons were melting! The slide was then scanned at 300 dpi using the Optronics ColorGetter by Bob Janukowitz at Optronics (Chelmsford, MA) in their demo room. Optronic's scanning software, ColoRight, was used for some minor color correction to enhance and adjust the colors in the image. Aesthetics play a role in how color is perceived and presented, and a good operator is still required for ultimate success in color work. This is something that has *not* changed with the advent of desktop color.

For the full 32-bit color work Figure C3 required, we used a faster machine with a lot more memory. This included: a Mac IIfx, 8 MBytes of RAM, a RasterOps TrueColor Monitor with the 24L RasterOps Color Card, a 160 MByte internal hard disk, a 600 MByte MicroNet external hard disk, with a 44 meg PLI tape backup. The files for this color file eventually grew to 135 megabytes at one time. The scanned image, saved as a 4 MByte TIFF file, was opened in Adobe PhotoShop, sharpened, color corrected, converted from RGB to CMYK color mode, and finally saved as five EPS files using Desktop Color Separation algorithm.

Creating the right side of the Figure C3 was a challenge. To create the look of a color separated photo, the original scanned TIFF image was brought into Adobe PhotoShop and converted from RGB to CMYK color mode. The image on the screen first displays the black printing plate. Then, to get the Magenta Printing Plate Impression, we selected the entire image, and deleted the black printing plate. Next, we displayed the cyan printing plate, selected and deleted it, then displayed the yellow printing plate, and selected and deleted it also. The only plate left was magenta. Other plates were created in a similar manner. The image was saved as five EPS files. To create the Magenta Film Negative, the magenta printing plate image was remapped using the invert function in PhotoShop. Thanks are due to Steve Guttman at Adobe for his help with this process.

Figure C4, which demonstrates how different levels of data can restrict or enhance a grayscale or color image was also done in Photoshop. The crayon image was remapped using the posterize function, setting the number of gray or color levels to illustrate the desired effect.

Figures C2 (Color Theory), the left side of C5 (Four Color Process Halftone Screen Angles), and the bottom of Figure C10 (The Pantone Matching System) were all created in Aldus FreeHand. Since our final pages were going to be separated from QuarkXPress, we had to make sure that we used process colors to define our colors and fills. QuarkXPress will not separate spot colors or PMS colors created in FreeHand.

Figure C9 (Special Color Effects) was by far the most fun to create. The illustrations use a combination of traditional drawing techniques with the latest digital image manipulation software. One of my original charcoal drawings was scanned in on a Sharp JX scanner at 150 DPI, then colorized and manipulated in Super-Mac PixelPaint and Adobe Photoshop. This digital image was then manipulated again using the posterize, diffuse, twirl, find edges, and impressionist filters in PhotoShop to create the final images shown in the figure. The features in many paint and image manipulation programs now allow an artist to create effects that have never before been possible.

Film separations and color proofs were made from QuarkXPress. The Optronics ColorSetter was used as the imagesetter. C, Y, M, and K were printed directly from their Quark files, which took about 15 to 20 minutes each and resulted in four 35 MByte files. These files were transferred separately over a UNIX network to the ColorSetter, and processed as two film pieces (four pages each). This took 10 to 14 minutes for each eight-page separation; the entire process took less than an hour. To check the results a Chromalin Proofing System was used.

Finally, the film separations were sent to the printer, who made the plates and printed the pages. The color pages were completed early in the production process, which is very rare. Admittedly, the time savings due to the new technology was not significant due to the technological complexity of the pages. But the fact remains that we could not produce some of the figures traditionally. The color pages speak for themselves. Color from the desktop is an exciting and economical alternative to traditional color work, but careful consideration of a project's budget, scheduling, and expertise of designers, illustrators, and technical personnel play a large part in the decision of which method to use.

Tell Us What You Think...

We would like to have your comments regarding the production techniques we've described here. If you would like to share good shortcuts you have found we will try and include them in future work. Contact Barrie Sosinsky via CompuServe (72020,2311) or America OnLine (Screen Name: BASman), or through Bantam Electronic Publishing. Donna Chernin, who produced the color plates and laid out the book, can be reached at: DMC & Company, 169 Central Street, Acton, MA, 01720, or via CompuServe (70451,1760).

References

Chapter 1

Computer Art

"A Painting Revolution", by Barbara Robertson, *Computer Graphics World*, April 1991, p. 34.

"Great Graphics", by Joe Matazzoni, *MacWorld Magazine*, March 1991, p. 144. Mac Masters Art Contest winners.

"Macintosh Masterpieces (Is it MacArt Yet?)", by Joe Matazzoni, *MacWorld Magazine*, August 1988, p. 74. The annual *MacWorld Magazine* art contest winners.

"Peter Max Sings the Electric Canvas", *MacWeek Magazine*, May 17, 1988.

"StereoLithography Proves Viable Medium for Fine Art", by Susan D. Harper, *Computer Graphics Review*, May 1989, p. 55. Creating artwork using CAD and laser drive polymerization.

Design Projects

"Class Ads", *Publish!,* April 1989, p. 64. Programs to create and layout advertising.

"Clement Mok: A Master of Macintosh Design", by Karen Sorenson, *MacWeek Magazine*, October 25, 1988, p. 56.

"Logos from Letters", by Deke McClelland, *Publish!,* April 1990, p. 68. Using Illustrator and Coral draw to create letter designs.

"The 3rd Annual Desktop Design Awards", by James Martin, *Publish!,* January 1990, p. 47. The annual *Publish!* magazine design awards.

How Technology Has Changed

"Brave New World", by Jerry Borrell, *MacWorld Magazine*, May 1989, p. 19. How MacWorld came to be desktop published.

"Is it Time to Telecommute", *Byte Magazine*, May 1991, p. 121. An editors roundtable on the subject.

"Making Telecommuting a Reality", by Carol Ellison, *PC/Computing,* July 1990, p. 174. Three books reviewed.

"Teaching the Electronic Palette", by Susan Katz, *MacWeek Magazine*, October 25, 1988, p. 78. Learning design with personal computers in schools.

"The Complete Home Office", by Preston Gralla, *PC/Computing*, October 1990, p. 186.

"The World of Macintosh Visualization", by David Peltz and Neil Kleinman, *Computer Graphics Review*, July 1990, p. 17.

Prototyping

"Computers and Architecture", by Donald P. Greenberg, *Scientific American*, February 1991, p. 104.

"Designing Assemblies", by Rick Cook, *Computer Graphics Review*, November 1990, p. 42. Solid modelling complex design pieces.

"Designing Made Easy", by Gary Pfitzer, *Computer Graphics World*, October 1990, p. 102. How PCs are used by designers in the carpet, garment, wallpaper, and gift wrapping industries.

"Desktop Prototyping", by Lamont Wood, *Byte Magazine*, May 1991, p. 137. Solid 3-D modelling.

"Introduction to Modeling", by Doug Houseman and Anna O'Connell, *MacWorld Magazine*, November 1990, p. 160.

"Milling Around", by Richard Wolfson, *MacUser Magazine*, July 1988, p. 188. Creating a solid model from a CAD file using EZ-Mill on the Macintosh.

"Practical Prototypes", by Terry Wohlers, *Computer Graphics World*, March 1990, p. 73. Building prototypes from 3D CAD .

"Smart Prototypes", by Debra Rosenberg and Audrey Vasilopoulos, *Computer Graphics World*, June 1990, p. 99. Using CAD to create solid model prototypes in plastic.

Chapter 2

Bus Architecture

"Bus Wars", by Winn Rosch and Ben Meyers, *PC Magazine*, June 26, 1990, p. 113. ISA, EISA, and MCA bus architectures tested and reviewed.

"Cashing In on the Micro Channel", by Winn L. Rosch, *PC Magazine*, October 30, 1990, p. 101. A review of non-IBM MCA machines.

"EISA vs. MCA", by Patrick Honan and John Blackford, *Personal Computing,* June 29, 1990, p. 144. PC bus structures.

"Guide to SCSI / Understanding the Small Computer System Interface", by NCR Corp., 1990, Prentice Hall, New York, NY.

Choosing Hardware

"Benchmarks at a Glance", by Standford Diehl, *Byte Magazine*, November 11, 1990, p. 75.

"Buyer's Guide: Computers for the Year of Windows", *Home Office Computing*, November 1990, p. 51.

"Mac vs. PC", by Jim Heid, *MacWorld Magazine*, March 1991, p. 120. The two platforms compared, hardware and software.

"PC vs. Mac: The Great Debate", by Bill Crider and Steve McKinstry, *Publish!*, November 1988, p. 48. Factors influencing a purchase.

"Rating High-End Workstations: Beyond MIPS and MFLOPS", *Computer Graphics Review*, September 1989, p. 54. Benchmarking graphics.

"Running the Tech Doc Race", by Bob Weibel, *Publish!*, February 1991, 74. Comparing the Sun SPARCstation to the Mac IIfx for heavy duty publishing.

Computerizing an Office

"Computer Power for your Small Business", by Nick Sullivan, 1990, *Home Office Computing*, 248 pages, $22.95. Tel. (800)325-6149.

"Home Ergonomics", by Thom Hogan, *MacUser Magazine*, December 1990, p. 293. Creating a computer station.

"The Digital Designer", by Alyce Kaprow, *Publish!*, August 1989, 70. Case studies of design firms computerizing their operations.

"The Home Office Computer Book", by Steve Rimmer, 1991, Sybex, 2021 Challenger Dr., Alameda, CA 94501.

GUIs

"A Guide to GUIs", by Frank Hayes and Nick Baran, *Byte Magazine*, May 1989, p. 250. Review of 12 GUIs.

"Graphical User Interfaces: A Window to the Future - Part I", by Kenneth Wadeland, *Computer Graphics Review*, November 1989, p. 42; Part II, by Kenneth Wadland, *Computer Graphics Review*, January 1990, p. 36.

"Looking at the Graphical User Interface", by Bill Nicholls, *Byte Magazine*, November 11, 1990, p. 161. A general look at GUIs for IBM users.

"PC GUIs Go Head to Head", by Stan Miastkowski, *Byte Magazine*, November 11, 1990, p. 82.

"The Dilemma Facing Graphical User Interfaces", by David Burdick, Kathleen Hurley, and Rikkie Keizner, *Computer Graphic Review,* February 1990, p. 52.

"VLSI Trends Predict the Future in Computer Graphics", by Stephen Roe, *Computer Graphics Review*, March 1990, p. 44.

"What's in a Window?", by Matt Zeidenberg, *MacWorld Magazine*, November 1987, p. 137. GUI workstations.

"Windows Wars", by Kenneth M. Sheldon, Janet J. Barron, and Ben Smith, *Byte Magazine*, June 1991, p. 124. Features and comparisions of GUIs.

"Sorting Through the GUIs", by Joel Orr, *Computer Graphics World*, June 1990, p. 83.

Operating Systems

"Looking Back, Looking Ahead: CP/M, DOS, OS/2, and Windows", by Rachel Pred, *PC Today*, December 1990, p. 20. A comparison and short history.

"The Object-Oriented Amiga Exec", Tim Halloway, *Byte Magazine*, January 1991, p. 329.

"Understanding Computers", The Time-Life Library of Books, volumes: *Computer Languages* p. 73, *Revolution in Science* p. 73, The *Software Challenge* 26, *The Computerized Society* p. 8, *Software* p. 19, 73, and 88.

Chapter 3

Comparison of Traditional to Desktop Methods

"Is Desktop Publishing Worth It?", by J.E. Arcellena, *MacWorld Magazine*, October 1988, p. 107. Compromises needed to do DTP from a desktop computer.

"PDR Computer Impressions", by Jonathan Altman, *MacWeek Magazine*, October 25, 1988, p. 62. Typsetting vs. DTP in a mixed technology type shop.

"Planning Pays Off", by Michael Roney, *Publish!*, November 1990, p. 101. How Dunn & Bradstreet brought in desktop publishing.

"Real World BookMaking", by Barrie Sosinsky, *The Desktop Publishers Journal*, July 1991. The story of how this book was produced. See also the appendix at the back of this book.

"Traditional vs. Desktop", by Howard Fenton, *Pre- Magazine*, May 1990, p. 36. Comparing traditional and DTP at the typesetting levels.

Copyright Issues

"Copyrights and Wrongs", by Brad Bunning, *Publish!,* April 1990, p. 76. Computer legalities from the viewpoint of a copyright lawyer.

"Law and the Computer", by Michael C. Gemignani, 1983, Van Nostrand Reinhold, 115 Fifth Avenue, New York, NY 10003.

Electronic Publishing

"Desktop Entrepreneurship", by Donna Barron, *Publish!,* November 1989, p. 53. Establishing a business plan for a DTP operation.

"Desktop Publishing: Five Years Old and Still Going Strong", by Pamela Pfiffner, *MacWeek Magazine*, January 16, 1990, p. 26. History of DTP on the Macintosh.

"Smart Tips for Desktop Publishing", by Maria Hoath, *Personal Computing*, May 1990, p. 107. Strategies for making desktop publishing more efficient.

"Technology Solutions", *Publish!*, Summer 1991. A special supplement to the magazine with 70 case studies of computers in business.

"The 1991 Buyer's Guide to Desktop Publishing Products", *Publish!,* October 1990, p. 71. The fourth annual buyer's guide with a listing of over 1400 products.

"What's Happening to Desktop Publishing. Part Two: Working With Photography and Prepress Color", by Jerry Borrell, *Macworld Magazine*, July 1991, p. 23.

Chapter 4

Computer Graphics Setup

"Buyer's Guide: Computers for the Year of Windows", *Home Office Computing*, November 1990, p. 51.

"Buying Smart", by Shelley Zulman, *MacUser Magazine*, January 1991, p. 174. Where and how to buy your gear.

"Laying Out the Future", by Matt and Mary Page, *Byte Magazine*, November 11, 1990. An agency looks at hardware and software choices.

"System Solutions", by Steve McKinstry, *Publish!,* May 1990, p. 71. Building a Macintosh hardware system for desktop publishing.

"The Desktop Publishing Supplement", by Leslie Simons, *Home-Office Computing*, July 1990, p. 56. Style, hardware, and software selections for someone just starting out.

"Hard Choices", by Bill Crider, *Publish!,* June 1990, p. 92. Setting up shop on a PC to do DTP.

DOS

"286 Memory to the Max", by Doug Van Kirk, *PC/Computing*, November 1990, p. 194. Software memory managers for IBM PC ATs.

"386 Multitasking Environments: Making DOS Work Overtime", by Brian Carr, *PC Magazine*, July 16, 1990, p. 191.

"Making DOS Manageable", by Lincoln Spector, *PC World*, July 1990, p. 119. DOS shells.

"Super DOS", by Brett Glass, Chris Devoney, and Dale Lewallen, *PC/Computing*, October 1990, p. 104. Various programs and utilities for extending DOS.

"Task Switchers: The Hot Key to Fast Application Access Time", by M. David Stone, *PC Magazine*, October 30, 1990, p. 175. Task switching software for the PC, particularly valuable for lower end equipment.

"Type "M" for Menuing Software", by Bruce Brown, *PC Magazine*, January 15, 1991, p. 345. DOS menu utilities.

"Ultimate Utility Shelf", by Bill Howard, *PC Magazine*, June 26, 1990, p. 165. Review of 33 of the best PC utility programs.

Macintosh

"Apple Computer's Graphics Strategy, by Tom Kucharvy, *Computer Graphics Review*, March 1990, p. 12. Apples move into multimedia.

"Beating the System", by Michael Swaine, *MacUser Magazine*, June 1990, p. 251. Upgrading a Macintosh to System 7.

"Chasing the IIfx: Accelerators", by Winn L. Rosch and the MacUser Lab Staff, *MacUser Magazine*, August 1990, p. 84. Upgrading Macintoshes and benchmarks.

"Getting Started with System 7", by Jim Heid, *Macworld Magazine*, July 1991, p. 269.

"Here Comes System 7.0", by Lon Poole, *MacWorld Magazine*, August 1989, p. 124.

"The Macintosh Family Evolves", by Lon Poole, *MacWorld Magazine*, December 1990, p. 168. This article is followed by three more articles on the Mac Classic, Mac LC, Mac IIsi.

"The Macintosh Interface: Showing Its Age", by Don Crabb, *Byte Magazine*, June 1989, p. 235.

"The New Macs on the Block", by Owen Lindeholm and Jeff Bertolucci, *Byte Magazine*, November 1990, p. 147.

"Three Cheers for the Three New Macs", by Rik Myslewski with the Editors and MacUser Lab Staff, *MacUser Magazine*, December 1990, p. 90. The current line up on Macintosh computers compared.

"Tools of the Trade", by Robert C. Eckhardt, *MacWorld Magazine*, March 1991, p. 130. The best Macintosh utilities.

OS/2 and the Presentation Manager

"OS/2 2.0: It's a Family Affair", by Jon Udell, *Byte Magazine*, April 1990, p. 119.

"Presentation Manager Goes Beyond OS/2", by Thomas Kurcharvy, *Computer Graphics Review,* September 1989, p. 10. Presentation Manager on DOS and UNIX.

Other Platforms

"Amiga Insight", by Michael Brown, *Boston Computer Currents*, October 1990, p. 46. Desktop publishing on the Amiga.

"Fast New Systems from NeXT", by Nick Baran and Owen Linderholm, *Byte Magazine*, November 1990, p. 165. NeXTstation, color NeXTs, NeXTdimension, and NeXTstep 2.0 detailed.

"NeXT WEEK: The NeXT Computer as a Publishing System, *MacWeek Magazine*, April 13, 1990, p. 25. Supplement with several articles.

"Next on the Agenda", by Bruce F. Webster, *MacWorld Magazine*, January 1991, p. 160. New NeXT offerrings reviewed.

"Sizing Up the Cube", by Tom Thompson and Ben Smith, *Byte Magazine*, January 1990, p. 169. Review of the NeXT computer.

"Son of SPARCstation", by Tom Yager and Ben Smith, *Byte Magazine*, December 1990, p. 140. New SPARCs and SPARC clones.

"Sun Makes SPARC's Fly", by Henry Bortman, *MacUser Magazine*, July 1989, p. 220.

"Technical Publishing Software", by Paul Kinnucan, *Computer Graphics Review*, January 1990, p. 42. Advanced integrated workstation desktop publishing packages.

"The Amiga Option", by Jeff Evans, *Publish!*, January 1989, p. 68. Desktop publishing on the Amiga

"The Next Wave", by Rodney Stock and Barbara Robertson, *Computer Graphics World*, August 1990, p. 82. New graphics workstations redefine the state of the art in hardware acceleration.

"Two Power Systems form Sun", by Nick Barran, *Byte Magazine*, May 1989, p. 108.

"What's NeXT?", by Bruce Webster, *MacWorld Magazine*, January 1989, p. 108. The NeXT computer reviewed.

PC Hardware

"14 SX Systems: Big Deals in Small Boxes", by T.J. Byers, *PC World Magazine*, August 1990, p. 108.

"20 MHz 386SXs: The New Entry Level Machines", by Bruce Brown, *PC Magazine*, November 27, 1990, p. 101.

"33-MHz 386s: At the Peak of Their Careers", by Bill O'Brien, *PC Magazine*, January 15, 1991, p. 237.

"33-MHz 386s: Mainstream Muscle", by Alfred Poor, *PC Magazine*, December 25, 1990, p. 101.

"33-MHz 486 PCs: Maximum Performance", by Jim Seymour, *PC Magazine*, February 1991, p. 103.

"33-MHz 486s: Ultimate PC Power", by Lincoln Spector, *PC World*, March 1991, p. 128. Five machines reviewed.

"486 EISA: Born to Blaze", by Steve Apiki and Stanford Diehl, *Byte Magazine*, May 1991, p.216. Review of 19 systems.

"486/25: Entry to 486 Power", by Bruce Brown, *PC Magazine*, June 25, 1991, p. 239. A review of 32 systems.

"Affordable Desktop", by John Edwards, *ITC Desktop*, No.5, p. 47.

"Bringing It All Home: Five New PCs Your Family Can Live, Work, and Play With", by Mitt Jones, *PC Magazine*, January 15, 1991, p. 521.

"Can You Afford A No-Name Clone?, by Marina Hirsch, *PC World Magazine*, August 1990, p. 164.

"Computer Equipment Delivered to Your Door", by Henry F. Beechhold, *Home-Office Computing*, July 1990, p. 47. Buying mail-order PC clones discussed with five vendors highlighted.

"Easy-to-Upgrade PCs", by John Dickenson and Doug Van Kirk, *PC/Computing*, November 1990, p. 96. Seven upgradeable PCs reviewed.

"How to Buy a Tailor-Made PC", by Carol Ellison, *PC/Computing*, March 1991, p. 88.

"IBM at a Glance", by Nick Baran, *Byte Magazine*, November 11, 1990, p. 60.

"IBM Personal System/2 Reference Guide", by IBM Corp., October 1990, US Marketing & Services, Dept. ZW1, 1133 Westchester Avenue, White Plains, NY 10604.

"IBM's Half-Step Towards Home", by Eric Bender, *PC World Magazine*, August 1990, p. 79. The IBM PS/1 introduction.

"IBM's PS/1 Removes the Hassles and Delivers Decent Performance for Beginners", by Gus Venditto, *PC Magazine*, August 1990, p. 33.

"The Cheapest 386SXs Ever", by Alfred Poor, *PC Magazine*, August 1990, p. 95. Review of 21 machines under $1850.

"The First 24 486/25 PCs: Giant Step or Stepping Stone", by Jim Seymour, *PC Magazine*, September 11, 1990.

"Tracking the 486: Real Work, Real Workstations", by Russ Lockwood, *Personal Computing*, August 1990, p. 74.

Windows

"41 Utilities for Windows 3.0", by Tom Unger, *PC Magazine*, February 26, 1991.

"Making Windows Work", by Jeffrey H. Lubeck and Bruce D. Schatzman, *Byte Magazine*, February 1991, p. 293. Tips on installing and running Windows sucessfully.

"The Future of Windows, OS/2 PM", by Gina Smith, *PC/Computing*, May 1991, p. 50. Good brief overview of future trends.

"Three's the One", by Jon Udell, *Byte Magazine*, June 1990, p. 122. Review of Windows 3.0.

"Tips, Tricks, and Hints for Windows 3.0", by Don Willmott, *PC Magazine*, February 26, 1991.

"Window 3.0 Under the Spotlight", by William Hall, *PC Magazine*, September 11, 1990, p. 97.

"Windows 3.0: Once You Try It, You'll Be Hooked", by Paul Bonner, *PC/Computing,* July 1990, p. 66.

"Windows 3: The PC to Be Your Best?", by Fred Davis and Lee Thé, *MacUser Magazine*, September 1990, p. 222.

"Windows Made Over", by Judy Getts, *PC World Magazine*, May 1989, p. 151.

"Windows: A PC World Supplement on Windowing Environments", edited by Robert Luhn, *PC World Magazine*, February 1990, p. 145. Windows applications.

"Windows 3.0 Quiets the Critics", by Roberta Furger, *PC Magazine* July 1990, p. 80.

"Windows Makes the Grade", by Robert Luhn, *PC World Magazine*, July 1990, p. 75. Windows 3.

Chapter 5

Display Standards

"1,024-by-768 Coprocessed Graphics Adapters: High Resolution and Speed", by Alfred Poor, *PC Magazine*, June 25, 1991, p. 103. A review of 13 PC video boards.

"1024 Display Systems", by Winn L. Rosch, *PC Magazine*, April 10, 1990, p. 97.

"1024 Graphics Adaptors", by Alfred Poor, *PC Magazine,* April 10, 1990.

"A Bevy of Boards: The Uses and Limits of Graphics / Add-In Boards", by William White and David Brambert, *Electronic Publishing & Printing*, October 1989, p. 32.

"A VGA on Every Desk", by Stanford Diehl and Howard Eglowstein, *Byte Magazine*, March 1990, p. 126.

"Accelerated Color", by Christine Whyte, *Publish!*, February 1991, p. 63. Five 24-bit color boards with graphics accelerators for the Macintosh reviewed.

"Apple's 32-Bit QuickDraw Covers the Spectrum", by Tom Thompson, *Byte Magazine*, May 1989, p. 99.

"Boosting Video Performance Under Windows 3.0", by David Stone, *PC Magazine*, February 26, 1991.

"Buyer's Guide: Look Sharp with a Super-VGA Board", by Eric Knorr and Matt Lake, *PC World Magazine*, May 1990, p. 174.

"Color Graphics in Bloom", by David Ushizima, *MacWorld Magazine*, April 1988, p. 173. 32-bit boards for the Macintosh.

"How to Put 16 Million Colors to Work", by Tom Thompson and Ben Smith, *Byte Magazine*, December 1989, 32-bit boards for the Macintosh.

"New Views for PC's", by Bob Weibel, *Publish!,* February 1990, p. 44. Life beyond VGA.

"Super VGA: Monitors With More", by Winn L. Rosch, *PC Magazine*, May 15, 1990, p. 97.

"The Mac In Living Color", by Helmut Kobler, *Publish!,* February 1990, p. 48. Apple's 32-bit QuickDraw.

"VGA Boards Raise the Standards", by T.J. Byers, *PC World Magazine*, July 1989, p. 108. Six super-VGA boards reviewed.

"Windows in Technicolor", by Richard Jantz, *Publish!*, February 1991, p. 53. Five 24-bit graphics cards for Windows reviewed.

General

"Computer Images", from Understanding Computers, Time-Life Books, 1986.

"CRT Displays: The People's Choice", by Paul Kinnucan, *Computer Graphics Review*, July 1990, p. 16.

"Do-It-Yourself Screen Tests", by Kelli Wiseth, Paul Yi, and the MacUser Lab Staff, *MacUser Magazine*, February 1991, p. 198. How to test display quality.

"Full View", by Bob Weibel, *Publish!,* June 1990, p. 75. Choosing a large monitor.

"Presenting a Professional Image", by John Battelle, *Publish!,* February 1991, p. 66. Presentation display devices.

"Stars of the Big Screen", by Bill Crider, *Publish!* October 1988, p. 72.

Monitors—Greyscale

"Grading the Greys", by Owen W. Lindemayer and the MacUser Lab Staff, *MacUser Magazine*, October 1989, p. 182. Eleven greyscale monitors for the Macintosh reviewed.

"Greyscale Enters the Mainstream", by Richard Jantz, *PC World Magazine*, November 1989, p. 132.

"Monochrome Monitor Mania", by Bob Eckhardt, *MacWorld Magazine*, April 1990, p. 132. Mac greyscale monitors reviewed.

"Solving the Monitor Mystery", by Robert C. Eckhardt, *MacWorld Magazine*, May 1991, p. 132. Review of 38 monochrome and greyscale monitors.

"The Golden Age of Gray Scale", by Owen W. Linzmeyer and the MacUser Labs Staff, *MacUser Magazine*, October 1990, p. 150.

"The Golden Age of Greyscale", "A Study in Black and White", by Rik Myslewki and the MacUser Lab Staff, *MacUser Magazine*, April 1990, p. 182. A review of 19 b & w displays for the Macintosh.

Monitors—Color

"A Guide to Professional Graphics Displays", by Paul Kinnucan, *Computer Graphics Review*, October 1989, p. 30. High resolution monitors reviewed and listed for several platforms.

"Color Monitors Put to the Test", by Robert Eckhardt, *MacWorld Magazine*, July 1990, p. 146. A review of 16 color monitors for the Macintosh.

"Fast Color", by Cheryl England Spencer, *MacWorld Magazine*, January 1991, p. 136. Several 24-bit Mac display accelators reviewed.

"In Living Color", by Winn Rosch and the MacUser Lab Staff, *MacUser Magazine*, May 1990, p. 32 (of the Buyer's Guide). Eighteen color Macintosh monitors evaluated

"Macintosh Color Displays", by Karen Moody Serlin, *Computer Graphics World*, November 1989, p. 69.

"Picture-Perfect Portraits: Full Page Displays", by Kelli Wiseth, Paul Yi, and the MacUser Lab Staff, *MacUser Magazine*, February 1991, p. 176. Ten full page displays reviewed.

"Presentation Monitors", by Alfred Poor, *PC Magazine*, May 14, 1991, p. 347. Nine 25- to 35-inch monitors reviewed.

"Screen Tests", by Adrian Mello, *MacWorld Magazine*, August 1989, p. 148. Mac color displays.

"The 16 Million Color Question", by Cheryl England Spencer, *MacWorld Magazine*, January 1991, p. 152. Twelve 24-bit Mac monitors reviewed.

"The Perfect Image: True-Color Displays", by Andrew Eisner and the MacUser Lab Staff, *MacUser Magazine*, May 1991, p. 4 (Buyer's Guide). Twenty 24 bit color monitors for the Macintosh reviewed.

"True Color for Windows", by Adam Bellin and Pier Del Frate, *Byte Magazine*, December 1990, p. 281. Recent 24-bit color boards and options for Windows and DOS.

"True Colors", by Aileen Abernathy and the MacUser Labs Staff, *MacUser Magazine*, October 1988, p. 236. Color displays for the Macintosh.

What's Coming Up

"Boosting PC Graphics Performance", by Paul Kinnucan, *Computer Graphics Review*, September 1989, p. 40. Graphics accelerator boards for the PC and Mac, review and listed.

"Buyer's Guide: Displays that Outshine VGA", by T. J. Byers and Eric Knorr, *PC World*, December 1990, p. 209, a good treatment of advanced displays and graphics standards with many products specified.

"LCDs and Beyond", by Nick Barran, *Byte Magazine*, February 1991, p. 229.

"The Forthcoming New Era in High-Resolution Graphics", by Thomas Kurcharvy, *Computer Graphics Review*, July 1989, p. 16. The IBM 8514A standard and the AT vs. MCA. bus.

"XGA: A New Graphics Standard", by Jake Richter, *Byte Magazine*, February 1991, p. 285.

Chapter 6

Connections

"A Beginner's Guide to Daisy Chains", by Thom Hogan, *MacUser Magazine*, August 1990, p. 243. The voodoo of SCSI chains, that you do so well.

"Guide to SCSI / Understanding the Small Computer System Interface", by NCR Corp., 1990, Prentice Hall, New York, NY.

"SCSI: An Interface Whose Time Has Come", by Robert Kane, *PC Magazine*, October 16, 1990, p. 341. The implementation of SCSI for the PS/2 models of IBM PCs.

"SCSI: The I/O Standard Evolves", by Bruce Van Dyke, *Byte Magazine*, November 11, 1990, p. 187. SCSI and the IBM PC.

Fax Modems

"Designing for Fax", by Kathleen Tinkel, *MacUser Magazine*, May 1991, p. 201.

"Distributing Text and Graphics via FAX Boards", by Paul Kinnucan, *Computer Graphics Review*, May 1990, p. 34.

"E-Mail FAX: Costly Alternative" by Daniel J. Rosenbaum, *PC World Magazine*, June 1989, p. 168. Five services for file transfers reviewed.

"Fast Full-Featured Fax Modems", by Owen W. Linzmayer and the MacUser Labs Staff, *MacUser Magazine*, May 1991, p. 105. Six Macintosh fax modems reviewed.

"Fax Boards and Fax Gateways", by Susan Lusty, *PC World*, March 1991, p. 182. PC Fax equipment.

"Fax Facts", by Brett Glass, *Byte Magazine*, February 1991, p. 301. A good technical introduction to fax technology.

"Fax Line Managers: The Electronic Call Director", by Frank J. Derfler, Jr. and R. Dennis Boatner, *PC Magazine*, December 11, 1990, p. 351. Devices for managing phone, voice phone, modem, faxes and other devices on a single phone line.

"Fax Modem Influx", by Steve Swartz, *MacWorld Magazine*, August 1990, p. 168.

"Mac FAX: Not Ready for Prime Time", by David Kosiur, *MacWorld Magazine*, March 1989, p. 138.

"Plain-Paper Fax Devices", by Frank J. Derfler, Jr., *PC Magazine*, February 26, 1991, p. 313.

"Powerhouse Fax Boards for Less than $500", by Preston Gralla, *PC/Computing*, Decmeber 1990, p. 272. Twelve add-in boards for the IBM PC reviewed.

"Sending Faxes Easily Without Buying a Board or a Machine", by Peggy Wallace, *PC/Computing*, November 1990, p. 348. Using your modem and a dial up service to send faxes.

"Speed, Price, Convenience: FAX Boards Deliver", by Mike Byrd, *PC Magazine*, August 1990, p. 303. Eighteen PC boards under $500 reviewed.

"The Collision of PC and FAX", by Paul Saffo, *Boston Computer Currents*, October 1990, p. 48. The future and PC Fax options.

"The Expert's Edge", by Thom Hogan, *MacUser Magazine*, June 1990, p. 261. Experiences using a FAX modem.

"The FAX Factor", by Gordon McComb, Owen W. Lindemayer, and the MacUser Labs Staff, *MacUser Magazine*, August 1989, p. 148.

File Compression (see also Ch. 10)

"First Image Compression Products Hit the Market", by Lisa Picarille, *Publish!*, January 1991, p. 56.

"Getting Your Bytes Worth", by Steve J. Vaughan-Nichols, *Byte Magazine*, November 1990, p. 311. File compression.

"Putting the Squeeze on Graphics", by Nick Baran, *Byte Magazine*, December 1990, p. 289. Image compression technologies.

"Some Assembly Required: Loss Data Compression", by Steve Apiki, *Byte Magazine*, March 1991, p. 309. Huffman and LZW compression algorithms explained.

"The Big Squeeze", by Charles Seiter, *MacWorld Magazine*, January 1991, p. 128. An excellent general introduction to file compression methods and products.

"The Big Squeeze", by Johna Till Johnson, *Personal Computing*, June 29, 1990, p. 139. File compression utilities for the PC.

"Too Big to Fit on a Floppy", by Kathleen Tinkel, *MacUser Magazine*, February 1991, p. 232. Strategies for dealing with big files.

Input Devices

"Achieving Magic With Graphics Tablets", by Paul Kinnucan, *Computer Graphics Review*, March 1990, p. 26. A comprehensive overview and survey of graphics tablets.

"Getting Started with Input Devices", by Jim Heid, *MacWorld Magazine*, November 1990, p. 301.

"Input/Output", from Understanding Computers, Time-Life Library of Books.

"Mice and Trackballs: Choices for the New Generation of Applications", by Mary Kathleen Flynn, *PC Magazine*, August 1990, p. 211. Input devices for PCs, also discusses light pens and graphics tablets.

"Opening Doors for the Disabled", by Joseph J. Lazzaro, *Byte Magazine*, August 1990, p. 258. Adaptive computer input technology for the disabled.

"The Keyboard Conundrum", by Deborah Branscum, *MacWorld Magazine*, October 1990, p. 87. A discussion of the problems that can arise from poor keyboard input, and the alternative technologies available.

"The Mouse That Roared", by Roger Alford, *Byte Magazine*, November 1990, p. 395. The history, anatomy, and physiology of the mouse.

Modems

"9,600-bps Modems: Breaking the Speed Barrier", by Mike Byrd/PC Labs, *PC Magazine*, December 11, 1990, p. 307.

"Choosing A 2400 bps Modem", by Steve Schwartz, *MacWorld Magazine*, May 1990, p. 330.

"Modem Business", by Steven E. Turner, *Byte Magazine*, November 1990, p. 353. The Bell and CCITT standards.

"Sorting Through the Modem Maze", by Robert Hollis, *MacWeek Magazine*, April 3, 1990, p. 48.

Modems: 9,600 and Counting", by Gordon McComb, Rik Mykewski, and the MacUser Labs Staff, *MacUser Magazine*, January 1990, p. 180.

Storage Devices

"Back it Up!", by Ben Templin, *MacUser Magazine*, June 1988, p. 171. Tape backup.

"Buyer's Guide: 80 MByte Upgrades", by Susan Lusty and Lincoln Spector, *PC World*, September 1990, p. 204. Hard drives for the PC.

"DAT's a Solution", by Karina Lion, *Byte Magazine*, November 1990, p. 323. Using Digital Audio Tape for computer backup devices, and gigabyte storage solutions.

"Erasable Optical Drives", by John Rizzo and the MacUser Labs Staff, *MacUser Magazine*, November 1990, p. 102.

"Erasable Opticals: New Light on Data", by Charles Seiter, *MacWorld Magazine*, March 1990, p. 152.

"Expansion Made Easy", by Tom Negrino, *MacWorld Magazine*, May 1991, p. 124. Removable cartridge drives.

"Gigabytes On-Line", by James J. Burke, and Bob Ryan, *Byte Magazine*, October 1989, p. 259.

"Gigabytes: The 1,000-Megabyte Solution", by H.B.J. Clifford, Stephen Satchell, and the MacUser Labs Staff, *MacUser Magazine*, July 1991, p. 140.

"Letting in the Light", by John Rizzo, *MacUser Magazine*, November 1989, p. 132. Optical storage on the Macintosh.

"Magneto-Optics Reach Critical Mass", by Ric Ford, *MacWeek Magazine*, January 16, 1990.

"Massive Storage for Multiple Platforms", Steve Apiki, Stan Wszola, Rick Grehan, and Tom Yager, *Byte Magazine*, November, 1990, p. 172. Fifteen large hard drives reviewed.

"MegaFloppies", by Stephen Satchell, *Byte Magazine*, October 1990, p. 301. Four new technologies disk drives coming to market.

"Memory and Storage", from Understanding Computers, Time-Life Library of Books, 1987.

"Midrange Hard Drives, Just Right", by Cheryl England Spencer, *MacWorld Magazine*, March 1991, p. 136.

"Moving Up to a Big, Fast Hard Drive", by Owen Linzmayer and the MacUser Labs Staff, *MacUser Magazine*, December 1990, p. 114.

"Optical Horizons", by Jon Zilber, *MacUser Magazine*, June 1988, p. 157.

"Optical Outlook", by Charles Seiter, *MacWorld Magazine*, June 1991, p. 140. Twenty optical drives for the Macintosh reviewed.

"Optical Storage Primer", by David Harvey, *Byte Magazine*, November 11, 1990, p. 121.

"Portable Secure Unlimited-Storage Cartridge Devices", by Seve Costa, and the MacUser Lab Staff, *MacUser Magazine*, February 1991, p. 206. Thirty removable hard drives reviewed.

"State of the Art: Magnetic vs. Optical", *Byte Magazine*, November, 1990, p. 272-339. A series of articles exploring present and future storage technologies.

"The High and the Mighty", by Robert C. Eckhardt, *Macworld Magazine*, July 1991, p. 184. Reviews of 66 hard drives over 300 MBytes large.

Chapter 7

Color Printers

"Color for the Desktop", by Rich Cook, *Byte Magazine*, November 11, 1990, p. 175. General article on color printers.

"Color on the Page", by Phillip Robinson and the MacUser Lab Staff, *MacUser Magazine*, May 1990, p. 57 (Buyer's Guide). Macintosh color printers evaluated.

"Color Page Printers", by M. David Stone, *PC Magazine*, December 25, 1990, p. 339. Four color printers reviewed.

"Color Printers Here and Now", by Charles Seiter, *MacWorld Magazine*, February 1991, p. 168. Fourteen printers reviewed.

"Easy Hard Copy: Color PostScript Printers", by Paul Yi and the MacUser Labs Staff, *MacUser Magazine*, May 1991, p. 38 (Buyer's Guide). Five Macintosh printers reviewed.

"Hot Wax and Cold Ink", by Cheryl Spencer England, *MacWorld Magazine*, February 1990, p. 162. Review of Macintosh color printers by type.

"In-House Color Printing", by Roger C. Parker and Pamela Pfiffner, *Publish!*, April 1991, p. 42. Reviews of under $10,000 color printers, and some case studies of their uses.

"Printing a Rainbow", by Ron Risley, *MacWorld Magazine*, January 1989, p. 134. Macintosh color printers.

"The Debut of Dry Silver Color", by Jim Thurlow, *Computer Graphics Review*, February 1990, p. 40. New / old continuous tone output.

"The Technology Cornucopia in Color Printers", by Paul Kinnucan, *Computer Graphics Review*, July 1989, p. 26. Review and listing of color printers by type for Macintosh and PC.

"Winning Colors", by Wes Nihei, *PC World Magazine*, May 1990. Six PC color printers reviewed.

Film Recorders

"Film Recorders at the High End", by Gregory MacNicol, *Computer Graphics World*, August 1990, p. 102.

"Film Recorders Receive Mixed Ratings", by Paul Kinnucan, *Computer Graphics Review*, April 1990, p. 24.

"Film Recorders", by Alfred Poor, *PC Magazine*, May 14, 1991, p. 305. Four desktop film recorders reviewed, and the technology described generally.

"Film Recorders: Creating Images with a Rainbow of Colors", by Paul Kinnucan, *Computer Graphics Review*, May 1989, p. 28. Review and listing of film recorders for Macintosh and PC.

"Film Recorders: The Marketplace Myths", by Gregory MacNicol, *Computer Graphics Review*, July 1990, p. 62.

Page Description Languages

"A Guide to PostScript For Non-Postscript Programmers", by Luisa Simone, *PC Magazine*, April 30, 1991, p. 343.

"Clones: The PostScript Impersonators", by Helmut Kobler with Bob Weibel, *Publish!*, November 1989, p. 58.

"Desktop Tutorial: Word 4 and PostScript", by Gregory Wasson, *MacUser Magazine*, September 1989, p. 245. Using PostScript to create effects within Word 4 on the Macintosh.

"PostScript Insider Secrets", by Don Lancaster, *Byte Magazine*, July 1990, p. 293. Tweaking PostScript to improve your output.

"Six PostScript Tricks for Word Processors", by Gregory Wasson, *MacUser Magazine*, August 1990, p. 230.Special printing effects using PostScript and word processors.

"The Evolution of PCL", by Roger C. Alford, *Byte Magazine*, June 1991, p. 325.

"True Stories", by Bob Weibel, *Desktop Communications*, January-February 1991, p. 54. TrueImage laser printers.

"Unraveling the Upheaval Underway in PostScript", by Bruce Anderson, *Computer Graphics Review*, March 1990, p. 20. Trends in the page description and font standards.

"Where are the Clones?", by Brita Meng, *MacWorld Magazine*, August 1988, p. 103. PostScript interpreters.

Printers and Imagesetters

"Beyond Desktop Publishing: When a Laser Won't Cut It", by Michael Antonoff, *Personal Computing*, July 27, 1990, p. 90.

"Beginner's Guide to Printers", by John G. Stephenson, 1991, Sams, Carmel, IN.

"Blazing Printers", by Barry Zuber, *Publish!*, October 1990, p. 52. Industrial strength laser printers.

"Fit to Print", by Henry Bortman, Aileen Abernathy, and the MacUser Labs Staff, *MacUser Magazine*, September 1989. p. 178. Review of 16 PostScript Macintosh printers.

"Fonts Unlimited: Seven Smart Lasers for Under $3000", by Daniel Miles Kehoe, *PC World*, September 1990, p. 161.

"Going Beyond the Lino: The Imagesetter Explosion", by Steve Roth, *MacWorld Magazine*, February 1990, p. 140.

"Hewlett-Packard Laser Printer Power Pack", by Steven Bennett and Peter Randall, 1990, Brady Books, New York, NY.

"Imagesetters: The Latest and the Greatest", by J. Scott Finnie, *MacWeek Magazine*, February 27, 1990, p. 38.

"Laser Lite: Apple's New Personal LaserWriters", by Henry Bortman, *MacUser Magazine*, September 1990, p. 212.

"Laser Printer Handbook", by D. Meyers, 1989, Dow Jones-Irwin, Homewood, IL.

"LaserWriters for Less", by Jim Heid, *MacWorld Magazine*, August 1990, p. 128. A review of the Apple Personal LaserWriters

"Looking at Lasers", by Bruce Webster, *MacWorld Magazine*, June 1988, p. 119. What to look for in a laser printer.

"Low Cost Laser Printers", by Joseph Devlin and Daniel Grotta, *Personal Computing*, May 1990, p. 124. A review of 10 printers under $2000.

"Macintosh Printer Secrets", by Larry Pina, 1990, Hayden Books, Carmel, IN. Good introduction to Apple dot matrix with many repair secrets and tips.

"Name and Address for Less: Envelope Printers Cut Your Costs", by Alfred Poor, *PC Magazine*, January 29, 1991, p. 185.

"Page Printers Revisited", by Jim Heid, *MacWorld Magazine*, October 1990, p. 184. Low priced Mac lasers.

"Personal Best: Two New Apple Printers", by Henry Bortman and Jon Zilber, *MacUser Magazine*, May 1991, p. 91. The Apple StyleWriter and Personal LaserWriter LS reviewed and compared to other Apple Printers.

"Personal Page Printers Arrive", by Jim Heid, *MacWorld Magazine*, May 1991, p. 142. Personal laser printers reviewed.

"Personal PostScript Printers", by Bruce Fraser and the MacUser Lab Staff, MacUser Magazine, March 1991, p. 116.

"Picking A Personal Personal PostScript Printer", by Bruce Fraser, *MacWeek Magazine*, November 6, 1990, p. 47.

"Plain-Paper Printers Get Serious", by Larry Stevens, *Publish!*, May 1991, p. 85. New 1,200 dpi laser printers reviewed.

"Printers: 7th Annual Special Issue", by Bill Howard and the PC Magazine Staff, *PC Magazine*, November 13, 1990. Over 121 printers: lasers, ink jets, and dot matrix printers reviewed. Awesome, and a great place to start when considering a purchase.

"Printing from Mac to LaserJet", by John Rizzo, *MacUser Magazine*, May 1991, p. 120.

"Printing Without Postscript", by Charles Seiter, *MacWorld Magazine*, June 1990, p. 172. Macintosh QuickDraw printers.

"The Business Type", by Bob Weibel, *Publish!,* August 1990, p. 48. Review of the Hewlett-Packard LaserJet III.

"The LaserJet Handbook", 2nd Ed., by Steven Bennett and Peter Randall, 1990, Brady Books, New York, NY.

"When Laser Printers Can't Cut It", by Stanford Diehl and Howard Eglowstein, *Byte Magazine*, December 1990, p. 156. Over 27 dot matrix and page printers reviewed.

Training Tools for Laser Users", by Bruce Brown, *PC Magazine*, April 30, 1991, p. 253. A review of 17 books and 4 videotapes on laser printer technology. A good place to start learning about the subject. The review focuses on PC technology, but the products reviewed are more generally useful.

Plotters

"Hardware Survivors: Desktop Plotters Face the Competition", by Winn Rosch, *PC Magazine*, March 27, 1990, p. 133.

"Surveying Electrostatic Plotters", by Paul Kinnucan, *Computer Graphics Review*, October 1989, p. 42. Reviewed and listed.

Utilities

"Add-In Laser Boards", by Edward Mendelson and Robin Raskin, *PC Magazine,* April 24, 1990, pl. 161. Enhancing the resolution of a laser printer.

"Buyer's Guide: More Power to Your Printer", by Matt Lake and Wes Nihei, *PC World Magazine*, May 1989, p. 166. PC printer tools.

"Extend Your Printer's Reach Without a LAN", by Roger C. Alford, *Byte Magazine*, May 1991, p. 277. Printer sharing devices.

"PS I Love You", by Gregory Wasson, *MacUser Magazine*, August 1988, p. 158. PostScript programming utilities for the Macintosh.

Chapter 8

General

"As the Word Turns", by Dan Shafer, *MacUser Magazine*, November 1988, p. 104. Various word processor modes analyzed.

"The Writer's Toolbox", by Janet Ruhl, 1989, Prentice Hall, New York, NY. A guide to selection and setting up computers for a writer.

"Word Processors that Build Characters", by Howard Eglowstein, Stan Wszola, and Tom Thompson, *Byte Magazine*, September 1990, p. 132. Macintosh and PC GUI word processors reviewed.

"Word Processors: Can One Fit All?", by Steve Morgenstern, *Home Office Computing*, December 1990, p. 39. A good introduction to the factors important in word processing with references to 22 programs.

"Word Processors: The Best and the Brightest", by Edward Mendelson/PC Labs, *PC Magazine*, December 11, 1990, p. 107. A good thorough review of PC word processors and writing tools.

Word Processors—Macintosh

"The Complete Guide to Word Processing", by Charles Spezzano, *MacUser Magazine*, February 1990, p. 94. Reviews of ten Macintosh word processors.

"Word Processor Olympics", by Robert C. Eckhardt, *MacWorld Magazine*, September 1990, p. 172. Six top Mac word processors compared.

"Words, Words, Everywhere", by Charles Seiter, *MacWorld Magazine*, September 1989, p. 180. Reviews of eight Macintosh word processors.

Word Processors—PC

"Advanced Word Processors. Familiar Faces, New Features", by George Beinhorn, *PC World Magazine*, July 1989, p. 96. Review of eight PC word processors.

"The Graphical Advantage: Tomorrow's Word Processors Today", by Edward Mendelson, *PC Magazine,* July 1990, p. 95. A thorough review of PC word processors that run on Windows.

"Word Processing Buyer's Guide", by Patrick Honan and Joseph Devlin, *Personal Computing*, August 1990, p. 74. Ten leading PC word processors reviewed.

"Word Processing in Windows", by Lamont Wood, *Byte Magazine*, April 1990, p. 57.

Utilities

"Beyond Word Processors", by Cheryl England Spencer, *MacWorld Magazine*, February 1989, p. 188. Mac word processor utilities.

"Buyer's Guide: 38 Tools for Great Writing", by Matt Lake and William Rodarmor, *PC World Magazine*, July 1989, p. 178.

"Finishing Touches", by Linda Iroff, *MacUser Magazine*, July 1990, p. 216. Creating tables of contents and indexes using several different Macintosh word processors.

"The Missing Link", by James Cavuoto, *Computer Graphics World*, July 1989, p. 149. PC annotation software.

"Comparison: Grammar Checking Programs", *MacWeek Magazine*, June 12, 1990, p. 3. Five Mac grammar programs reviewed.

"Finishing Touches", by Linda Iroff, *MacUser Magazine*, July 1990, p. 216. Using Word, WordPerfect, Nisus, and Full Write Professional on the Macintosh to generate table of contents and indexes.

Chapter 9

Autotracing

"The Elements of Auto-Tracing", by Salvatore Parascandolo, *MacUser Magazine*, August 1990, p. 206. How to get the best results from auto-tracing.

CAD Software

"Choosing A CAD Package: Let Your Need Be Your Guide", by Phillip Robinson, *MacWeek Magazine*, February 23, 1990, p. 31. Macintosh CAD; "CAD Heavyweights Seek to Capture the Mac Market", by Phillip Robinson, *ibid.*, p. 46.

"Hands on CAD", by David Peltz and the MacUser Labs Staff, *MacUser Magazine*, July 1989, p. 152.

"Introduction to Modeling", by Doug Houseman and Anna O'Connell, *MacWorld Magazine*, November 1990, p. 160.

"Mac CAD Takes Off", by Phillip Robinson, *MacUser Magazine*, August 1990, p. 114. Review of Mac packages and features.

"Macintosh CAD/CAM Book", Greco/Anders, 1989, Scott, Foresman & Co., Glenwood, IL.

"Making Plans", by Doug Houseman and Ann Marie O'Connell, *MacWorld Magazine*, July 1990, p. 172. Review of 19 2D Macintosh CAD programs.

"The Apple Engineering/Scientific Solutions Guide (Winter 1989/90)", Apple Computer, Tel. (800)538-9696, ext. 600. A list of important CAD applications (and many other scientific products) and specialized solutions for the Macintosh.

"The Emergence of Smart CAD Software", by Phillip Robinson, *Computer Graphic Review*, July 1990, p. 55.

Clip Art

"Clip Art", by Luisa Simone, *PC Magazine*, May 14, 1991, p. 203. PC clip art libraries reviewed. A great place to start looking for PC clip art.

"Clip Artistry", by Aileen Abernathy and Salvatore Parascandolo, *MacUser Magazine,* November 1990, p. 168.

"Dover Pictorial Archive Book Catalog, Dover Publications, 31 E. 2nd Street, Mineola, NY 11501. Traditional clip art books costing between $5 and $10 each.

"First Class Clip Art", by Tony Lane with David W. Hopkins, *Publish!,* September 1990, p. 68.

"Is it Art Yet?", Marjorie McCloy and Janet McCandless, *Publish!,* July 1989, p. 46. Where to get clip art.

"Mac Art Mart", by Efert Fenton, *MacWorld Magazine*, October 1990, p. 194. Review of 50 Mac art collections.

"Picture This", by Michael Antonoff, *Personal Computing*, August 1990, p. 98. How to use clip art.

Creating Slides

"Creating Slides Gets Easier, Better:, by Donna Z. Meilach, *MacWeek Magazine*, March 28, 1989, Macintosh slide making.

"From Screen to Slides", by Cheryl England Spencer, *MacWorld Magazine*, July 1989, p. 108. Making slides on the Macintosh.

"Graphics on the Slide", Gregory Wasson, Jeff Pittelkau, and Aileen Abernathy, *MacWorld Magazine*, November 1989, p. 156.

"In House Slidemaking", by Gregory MacNicol, *Publish!*, June 1991, p. 85.

"Slide Rules", by Richard Scoville, *Publish!*, March 1989, p. 51.

"Slide Services", by Kellyn S. Betts, *PC Magazine*, May 14, 1991, p. 277.

"Step by Step Slide", Franklin Tessler, *MacWorld Magazine*, September 1988, p. 149. A guide to creating slides on the Mac.

"The Microcomputer Approach to Preparing Visual Presentations by William L. Coggshall, *Computer Graphics Review*, April 1989, p. 38.

Draw Software

"Draw Partner", by Steve McKinstry, *MacWorld Magazine*, August 1989, p. 140. Object oriented drawing programs on the Macintosh.

"Drawing the Lines", Salvatore Parascandolo, *MacUser Magazine*, April 1990, p. 92. Review of seven Macintosh draw programs.

"Tools for the Talented: Five Illustration Packages", by Luisa Simone, *PC Magazine*, September 11, 1990, p. 241. The leading drawing programs for the PC thoroughly reviewed.

"Well Rounded Drawing", by Steve Roth, *PC World Magazine*, July 1989, p. 164. Review of five Bèzier curve PC drawing programs.

"Your Draw", by Steve Cummings, *Publish!*, July 1989, p. 61. Review of five PC draw programs.

Equipment

"Color LCD Technology", by Victoria Von Biel, Jeff Pittelkau and the MacUser Labs Staff, *MacUser Magazine*, February 1990, p. 230. Review of LCD panels.

"For that Special Effect: Color LCD Panels, by Steve Bass, *PC World*, November 1990, p. 183.

"Liquid Glass", by Jeff Pittelkau and Diane Wilde, *MacUser Magazine*, January 1989, p. 213. Review of LCD devices.

"Presentation Monitors", by Alfred Poor, *PC Magazine,* May 14, 1991, p. 347. Nine 25- to 35-inch monitors reviewed.

"Producing Large Screen Graphics at Small Screen Prices", by Paul Kinnucan, *Computer Graphics Review*, February 1989, p. 30. LCD projection panels.

Forms Generation Software

"Fill in the Blanks", by Bill Schnieker, *Publish!*, June 1988, p. 62. Mac and PC programs reviewed.

"Forms of Intelligence", by Jim Morton, *MacWeek Magazine*, July 1988, p. 113. Review of Macintosh forms software.

"In Good Form", by Ben Templin, *MacUser Magazine*, January 1990, p. 137. Review of three Mac programs.

"Self-Fulfilling Forms", by Aaron Marcus, *Publish!,* August 1990, p. 57. Review of Smart-Forms and perForm.

"The Best in Forms Software", by Michael Goodwin and Luther Sperberg, *PC World Magazine*, July 1989, 110. Five PC programs reviewed.

General

"Endurance Tests: Graphics", by Lori Grunin, *PC Magazine,* May 15, 1990. Review of some of the best PC graphics products.

"Getting Started with Paint and Draw Software", by Jim Heid, *MacWorld Magazine*, July 1990, 253.

"Image-Creation Software: Paint and Draw", by Alyce Kaprow, *Pre- Magazine*, May 1990, p. 20. An overview of technical issues and available software.

Paint Software

"Brushes with Color", by Efert Fenton, *MacWorld Magazine*, May 1989, p. 151. Survey of Macintosh color paint programs.

"Color Paint Revisited", by Bert Monroy, *MacWorld Magazine*, March 1990, p. 144.

"Digital Palettes", by Salvatore Parascandolo, *MacWorld Magazine*, October 1989, p. 93. Five Mac 8-bit color programs reviewed.

"Live and In Color", by Efert Nielson, *MacWorld Magazine*, February 1988, p. 149. An introduction to color paint programs on the Macintosh.

"Paint for the Pros", by Tom Thompson and Rick Grehan, *Byte Magazine*, June 1991, p. 258. Eight 24-bit programs reviewed.

"Paint Roundup", *MacWorld Magazine*, September 1988, p. 150.

"Painting Programs: The Fine Art of 32-Bit Color", by Darryl Lewis, Kelli Wiseth, and the MacUser Lab Staff, *MacUser Magazine*, March 1991, p. 134. Four 32-bit paint programs reviewed.

"Two-Tone News", by David Pogue, *MacWorld Magazine*, December 1989, p. 154, Review of seven Macintosh b & w paint program.

Presentation Graphics Software

"A Wealth of Software for Presentation Graphics", by Paul Kinnucan, *Computer Graphics Review*, February 1990, p. 16. Survey and listings of PC and Mac software.

"Buyer's Guide: Business Graphics Software", by Joseph Devlin and Jon Pepper, *Personal Computing*, February 1990, 119.

"Buyer's Guide: Business Graphics", *Personal Computing*, February 1990, p. 119. PC presentation software.

"Getting to the Point", by Brita Meng, *MacWorld Magazine*, April 1988, p. 137. Tools of presentation graphics on the Macintosh.

"Graphics Power for the Rest of Us", by Mike Smith-Heimer and John Walkenbach, *PC World*, November 1990, p. 164. Eight leading presentation product for the PC reviewed.

"Here's the Pitch", by David Pogue, *MacWorld Magazine*, March 1990, p. 166. Macintosh presentation graphic programs reviewed.

"Mac Desktop Presentation Software", by Lawrence Stevens, *Byte Magazine*, April 1989, p. 203.

"Picking the Best Presenter", by Phillip Robinson, *MacWorld Magazine*, May 1989, p. 166. Five Mac programs reviewed.

"Polished Presentations", by Richard Jantz and Michael Smith-Heimer, *PC World Magazine*, November 1989. Review of seven PC programs.

"Power Presentations", by Peter Polash, Kathleen Tinkel, and Howard Bornstein, *MacUser Magazine*, October 1990, p. 191. Hardware, software, services, and some technique reviewed in three articles.

"Presentation Graphics", by Luisa Simone, *PC Magazine*, May 14, 1991, p. 107. Fourteen packages for the PC reviewed.

"Presentation Power Will Light Up Your PC", *PC Magazine*, June 1991, p. 40. Nine PC software packages reviewed.

"Presentations That Persuade", by Michael Antanoff, *Personal Computing*, July 27, 1990, p. 60.

"Top of the Charts", by David Foster, *MacWorld Magazine*, July 1990, p. 156. Macintosh graphing programs reviewed.

Screen Capture Utilities

"Hold It! Screen Capture Software Saves the Moment", by Robin Raskin, *PC Magazine*, April 24, 1990, p. 257. PC screen capture utilities.

"Shooting Gallery", by Dave Valinis, *MacUser Magazine*, October 1989, p. 235. Macintosh screen capture utilities.

Chapter 10

Digital Cameras

"The Picture Perfect Mac", by Thom Hogan, *MacUser Magazine*, January 1991, p. 245.

"The Still Video Picture", by Phillip Robinson, *Computer Graphics World*, February 1990, p. 69. Digital cameras.

Digital Image Processing

"A Digital Portrait Montage", by the editors of Verbum, *MacUser Magazine*, October 1990, p. 214. Special effects from digital image processing programs.

"Between Black and White: Six Grey-Scale Editors", by Alfred Poor, *PC Magazine*, October 16, 1990, p. 237. Six major PC packages reviewed.

"Bridging the Photo-Retouching Gap, by Barbara Robertson, *Computer Graphics World*, October 1990, p. 52. Higher-end systems for digital image processing that can be used for prepress applications.

"Grey Scale Contrasts", by Joe Matazzoni, *MacWorld Magazine*, April 1990, p. 124. B & W image processing programs on the Macintosh.

"It's Magic", by Connie Guglielmo, *MacWeek Magazine*, October 25, 1988, p. 26. Restoring old photos with the Mac II and Digital Darkroom, a case study.

"Paint Programs Pass the Screen Test", by Jesse Berst, and Scott Dunn, *PC World Magazine*, March 1990. Four PC paint programs used as image editors.

"Photo-Retouching Technology: Friend or Foe?", by Barbara Robertson, *Computer Graphics World*, November 1990, p. 92. The effect of image processing on the world of photography.

"Reality Transformed", by Brita Meng, *MacWorld Magazine*, August 1988, p. 82. Macintosh image processing programs.

"Some Light Magic", by Barrie Sosinsky, *The Desktop Publishers Journal*, June 1991. A review of digital image processing technology.

"What a Color Retouching Program Can Do for You", by Ken Milburn, *MacUser Magazine*, October 1990, p. 172.

File Compression (see also Ch. 6)

"Image Compression Squeezes to the Fore", by Rick Cook, *Computer Graphics World*, September 1990, p. 3.

"JPEG Emerges as Standard for Compressing Image File Formats", by Steve Rosenthal, *MacWeek Magazine*, March 27, 1990, p. 31.

"Putting the Big Squeeze on Bulky Color Files", by Eric Holsinger, *Publish!,* May 1990, p. 30.

Optical Character Recognition

"Character Analysis", by Ben Templin, *MacUser Magazine*, September 1988, p. 295. OCR on the Macintosh.

"Character Witness", by Phillip Robinson and the MacUser Labs Staff, *MacUser Magazine*, July 1990, p. 120. AccuText and OmniPage reviewed.

"Easy Reading", by Phillip Robinson, *Byte Magazine*, May 1989, p. 203. Review of two leading PC OCR programs.

"Getting Started with OCR", by Jim Heid, *MacWorld Magazine*, October 1990, p. 297.

"OCR Software Moves into the Mainstream", by Lori Grunin, *PC Magazine*, October 30, 1990, p. 299. A review of several of the top packages for the IBM PC, and some overall principles.

"OCR Teaches Your PC to Read", by David Dejean, *PC/Computing*, August 1990, p. 94. Setting up OCR on a PC.

"Strength of Character (Recognition)", by Matthew Lake, *Publish!*, January 1991, p. 62. Ten products reviewed.

"Tame the Paper Tiger", by Stanford Diehl and Howard Eglowstein, Byte Magazine, April 1991, p. 220. A review of 14 OCR packages for the PC and Mac.

"Text Without Typing", by Brita Meng, *MacWorld Magazine*, October 1990, p. 176.

"The Reading Edge", by Brita Meng, *MacWorld Magazine*, February 1989, p. 170. Review of eight Macintosh OCR packages.

Scanners

"A Handful of Scanners", by Phyllis Neumann, *PC World Magazine*, August 1990, p. 134. Hand scanners for the PC.

"Affordable Color Scanners", by Joe Matazzoni, *MacWorld Magazine*, June 1991, p. 132. Fifteen under-$15,000 scanners for the Macintosh reviewed.

"An Inside Look at Scanners", by Owen W. Linzmayer, Bruce Fraser, Ron Hipschman, and the MacUser Labs Staff, *MacUser Magazine*, September 1990, p. 132.

"Capturing Color" by Steve Roth, *MacWorld Magazine*, July 1989, p. 134. Color scanners for the Macintosh.

"Color Scanners: Pick from a Growing Field", by Jim Ronga and Luther Sperberg, *MacWorld Magazine*, August 1990, p. 152.

"Desktop Scanners Capture A Growing Market", *Computer Graphics Review*, April, 1990, p. 38.

"Grey Expectations", by Aileen Abernathy, Peter Riss and the MacUser Lab Staff, *MacUser Magazine*, June 1989, p. 170. Greyscale scanners for the Macintosh.

"Hand-held Scanners — The New Generation", by Mikkel Aaland, *Publish!*, September 1990, p. 58.

"Keep it in Color", by Peter Vanags and Keith Baumann, *Publish!*, March 1990, p. 68. Color scanners for the PC and Mac.

"One in the Hand", by Steve Cummings, *MacWorld Magazine*, June 1991, p. 154. Hand-held scanners for the Macintosh reviewed.

"Scanners: Capturing A Brighter Image", by Paul Kinnucan, *Computer Graphics Review*, November 1989, p. 28. Scanner survey with product guide for several computer platforms.

"Scanning the Horizon" by Henry Bortman and the MacUser Lab Staff, *MacUser Magazine*, June 1989, p. 106. Color scanners for the Macintosh.

"Shades of Grey", by Jim Morton, *MacWorld Magazine*, January 1988, p.110. Macintosh greyscale scanners.

"Shopping for Scanners", by Steve Roth, *MacWorld Magazine*, May 1989, p. 124. Choosing a Macintosh b & w scanner.

"The Big Scan", by Eric Holsinger and Bob Weibel, *Publish!*, March 1990, p. 56. Grey scale scanners.

"The Incredible Importance of Scanners", by David Biedney, *MacWeek Magazine*, October 25, 1988. A survey of scanner types for the Macintosh.

The Scanning Process

"A Halftone Handbook" by Joe Matazzoni, *MacWorld Magazine*, October 1988, p. 116.

"A Touch of Grey", by Stephen Beale, James Cavuoto, and Aileen Abernathy, *MacUser Magazine*, February 1989, p. 257. Primer on digital halftoning.

"Grade-A Gray Scale", by Steve Roth, *MacWorld Magazine*, October 1990, p. 202.

"How to Get a Good Scan", by Peter Vanags, *Publish!*, November 1989, p. 82.

"Optimizing Halftones" by Stephen Beale and James Cavuoto, *Computer Graphics Review*, May 1990, p. 77.

"PC Scanners: Not Just for High-End Users Anymore", by Roger Alford, *PC Magazine*, October 16, 1990, p. 403. An excellent introduction to scanning and scanners.

"The Art of Scanning", by Robert Virkus, *MacUser Magazine*, May 1990, p. 4 (Buyer's Guide). Scanning in color.

Chapter 11

Font Construction

"Font Wars", L. Brett Glass, *Byte Magazine*, August 1990, p. 289. An analysis of Adobe Type 1 and TrueType construction techniques, strengths, and future potential.

"Fonts on the Fly", by Michael Antonoff, *Personal Computing*, May 1990, p. 96. Font scaling.

"Smooth Characters", by Allen Matsumoto, *Publish!,* March 1990, p. 82.

"The ABC's of Digital Type", by John Collins, *Byte Magazine*, November 1989, p. 403.

"The Future of Type?", by Henry Bortman, *MacUser Magazine*, July 1991, p. 187. Adobe's Multiple Master font technology described.

Font Libraries

"Buying Macintosh Laser Fonts", by Mary Jane Westmoreland and Ric Ford, *MacWeek Magazine*, July 31, 1990, p. 77. Contains a good listing of Mac PostScript fonts and vendors.

"Font Buyer's Guide", by Allen Matsumoto, *Publish!,* October 1989, p. 52. PostScript font listings.

"Font Woes", by Henry Bortman, *MacUser Magazine*, January 1990, p. 245. Mac font organization.

"Fonts by Number", by Steve Bobker, *MacUser Magazine*, July 1989, p. 187. How the Macintosh handles fonts.

Font Standards

"Battle Royal", by Efert Fenton, *MacWorld Magazine*, April 1990, p. 146.

"Fazed by Fonts":, by Tom McMillian, *Computer Graphics World*, October 1989, p. 115.

"Font Fear?" by Bob Weibel, *Publish!,* July 1990, p. 59. A review of font standards.

"The Truth About TrueType", by Pauline Ores, *Desktop Communications*, January-February 1991, p. 49.

General

"Dazzling Design Tools", by Steve Cummings, *Boston Computer Currents*, October 1990, p. 20. Recent innovations in type tools and general desktop publishing.

"Font Basics and Beyond", by Thom Hogan, *MacUser Magazine*, July 1990, p. 231.

"Fonts from A to Z" by Steve McKinstry, *MacUser Magazine*, September 1989, p. 120. Font primer.

"The Type Explosion", by Clay Andres, *MacWeek Magazine*, October 25, 1988, p. 16. Fonts and faces for the Mac.

"Times & Helvetica", by David Barlow and James Felici, *The Desktop Publishers Journal*, May 1991, p. 12. A short treatsie on type history.

"Type Renaissance", by Alex Brown, *Macworld Magazine*, July 1991, p. 202. Typography and the Mac.

Typographic Tools

"Enhancing PostScript Fonts" by Efert Fenton, *MacWorld, Magazine* May 1989, p. 134. Font editing software for the Macintosh.

"Font Creation Software Shifts Into High Gear" by Dennis Klatzkin, *MacWeek Magazine*, May 8, 1990, p. 58. Fontographer and LetrStudio on the Macintosh.

"Font Foundries for the Mac", by Allen Matsumoto, *Publish!*, July, 1990, p. 119. Fontographer, FontStudio, and ParaFont reviewed.

"True Conversions", by Jim Schmal, *Publish!*, July 1991, p. 33. Font type conversions utilities.

"Twisting, Shouting Type", Eric Taub, *MacUser Magazine*, December 1990, p. 211. Type Align, TypeStyler, and LetraStudio for the Mac reviewed.

"Typographic Horizons Expand", by Paul Kinnucan, *Computer Graphics Review*, April 1989, p. 22. Manipulating digital type.

Working With Fonts

"Capturing Font Outlines", by Gregory Wasson, *MacUser Magazine*, August 1990, p. 210. Nine ways to capture editable outlines .

"Easy Fonts for Great Looking Documents", by George Campbell, *PC World Magazine*, January 1991, p. 122. Review of font rasterizers, and how to buy fonts.

"Color Fonts", by Jan V. White, *Electronic Publishing & Printing*, December 1989, p. 25. How to use color with fonts, and a listing of font utilities.

"Creating A Font Outline", by the Editors of Verbum Magazine, *MacUser Magazine*, December 1990, p. 224. Turning artwork into a PostScript font.

"Fine Print" by David Holzgang and Salvatore Parnscandolo, *MacUser Magazine*, August 1989, p. 169. How to use fonts from a service bureau.

"Fit to Print", by Efert Nielson, *MacWorld Magazine*, April 1988. Fine points of typesetting.

"Font Basic and Beyond", by Thom Hogan, *MacUser Magazine*, July 1990, p. 231. Hints about using the Adobe Type Manager on the Macintosh and handling fonts for various printers.

"Fonts Made Easy", by Ross Smith, *PC World Magazine*, June 1990, p. 158. PC font installation and history. Good introduction.

"No More Jagged Fonts", by Dale Lewallen, *PC/Computing*, November 1990, p. 134. A summary of Windows 3 font rasterizer options.

"Working with Fonts", by Efert Fenton, *MacWorld Magazine*, May 1991, p. 152. Setting up and managing fonts on a Macintosh.

Chapter 12

Desktop Packaging

"One-Stop Packaging", by Efert Fenton, *MacWorld Magazine*, November 1990, p. 184.

"Scitex Unveils Package Design System", by Carolyn Said, *MacWeek Magazine*, April 10, 1990, p. 27.

Features

"Easy on the Eyes: Hyphenation and Justification" by Robert Virkus, *MacWeek Magazine*, March 28, 1990, p. 52.

Page Layout Software—Macintosh

"A New Leaf", by Gregory Wasson, *MacUser Magazine*, May 1988, p. 158. Interleaf Publisher.

"Coming of Age", by Gregory Wasson, *MacUser Magazine*, October 1987, p. 156. A review of JustText coded page layout program for the Macintosh.

"How to Choose the Best Macintosh Page Layout Program", by Kate Hatsy Thompson, *Publish!*, January 1990, p. 66.

"Layout Superstars Face Off", by Diane Burns, *Publish!,* October 1990, p. 58. Quark XPress compared to Aldus PageMaker.

"Layouts for Less", by Gregory Wasson, *MacUser Magazine*, July 1991, p. 110. Five-low priced Mac programs reviewed.

"Page-Layout Contenders", by Jim Heid, *MacWorld Magazine*, April 1989, p. 108. Macintosh page-layout programs reviewed.

"Page-Layout Playoffs", by Robert Virkus, *MacUser Magazine*, January 1990, p. 104. Three Macintosh DTP programs reviewed.

"Page-Makeup Roundup", by Steve Cummings, *MacWorld Magazine*, April 1988, p. 162. Review of Macintosh DTP programs.

"Picking a Publishing Program", by Steve Roth, *MacWorld Magazine*, May 1990, p. 230. Three Macintosh page-layout programs reviewed.

"Three DTP Powerhouses Face Off", by Rick LaPage, *MacWeek Magazine*, October 30, 1990, p. 45. DesignStudio, PageMaker and Quark XPress compared.

Page Layout Software—Other

"The NeXT Alternative", *Publish!*, June 1990, p. 66. FrameMaker on the NeXT computer.

"The Amiga Option", by Jeff Evans, *Publish!*, January 1989, p. 68. Desktop publishing on the Amiga

"Technical Publishing Software", by Paul Kinnucan, *Computer Graphics Review*, January 1990, p. 42. Advanced integrated workstation desktop publishing packages.

Page Layout Software—PC

"Desktop Publishing Light", by Jesse Berst, *PC World Magazine*, August 1990, p. 125. Low-priced page-layout software for the PC.

"Five Desktop Publishing Programs Especially Suited for Page-Layout Beginners", by Joey Latimer, *Home Office Computing*, November 1990, p. 80.

"Is the Typesetter Obsolete?", by Stanford Diehl and Howard Eglowstein, *Byte Magazine*, October 1990, p. 152. Seven high-end WYSIWYG page layout programs for the Mac and PC reviewed.

"The Easy Road to Low End Packages", by George Beinhorn, *PC World Magazine*, November 1989, p. 152. PC DTP programs under $200.

"The PC Page Layout Personality Profile Quiz", by Christine Whyte, Rick Altman, Margery Cantor, and Bill Crider, *Publish!*, January 1990, p. 58.

"Software Strategies", by Steve Cummings, *Publish!*, July 1989, p. 103. Choosing a DTP package on the PC.

Templates

"Flexible Frameworks", by Michael Sullivan, *Publish!*, September 1990, p. 74. Setting up a layout grid in DesignStudio.

"Publish Your Database", by Jim Heid, *MacWorld Magazine*, February 1991, p. 184. Database publishing using layout software.

"Strong Foundations", by Sandi Baker, Carl Ballay, and Angie Martinson, *Publish!*, September 1990, p. 81. Setting up templates in Ventura and PageMaker on the PC.

Chapter 13

File Conversion

"A File Transfer Primer", by Charles Seiter, *MacWorld Magazine*, April 1989, p. 118. Moving PC files to the Macintosh.

"Connecting to DOS", by Henry Bortman, *MacUser Magazine*, September 1988, p. 108. The Mac-PC file transfer.

"Getting Started with Data Exchange", by Jim Heid, *MacWorld Magazine*, August 1988, p. 295.

"Hassle-Free Foreign Exchange, by Jim Heid, *Publish!*, December 1990, p. 93. Tips for Mac/PC file exchange.

"Hold It! Screen Capture Software Saves the Moment", by Robin Raskin, *PC Magazine*, April 24, 1990, p. 257. PC screen capture utilities and their graphic file translation abilities.

"MacDOSsier", by Jim Heid, *MacWorld Magazine*, July 1990, p. 164. File exchange and conversion from Mac to PC and vice versa.

"Matching Up File Translators", by Dale Coleman, *MacWeek Magazine*, November 6, 1990, p. 58.

"Object to Object: Vector File Conversion Utilities", by Luisa Simone, *PC Magazine*, January 29, 1991, p. 243. Four utilities reviewed, along with some discussion of file formats.

"PC to Mac and Back", by John Rizzo, *MacUser Magazine*, October 1989, p. 143. File conversion.

"The Mac/PC File Exchange Cookbook", by Bob Weibel and Erik Holsinger, *Publish!*, December 1990, p. 103. Recipes for specific file exchanges.

"The MS DOS-Mac Connection", by Cynthia Harriman and Bill Hodgson, 1987, Brady Books, New York, NY,

File Formats

"An Image is Worth 2048 Bytes", by Jake Richter, *Personal Workstation*, June 1990, p. 36. File formats and format conversions.

"Getting From Here to There", by Rick Cook, *Desktop Communications*, May/June 1991, p. 52. A primer on file formats.

"Graphics Formats", by Gerald Graef, *Byte Magazine*, September, 1989, p. 305.

"MacUser Guide to File Formats", by Salvatore Parascandolo and Aileen Abernathy, *MacUser Magazine*, September 1990, p. 266.

"Putting It Graphically", by Salvatore Parascandolo, *MacUser Magazine*, March 1989, p. 189. File format primer.

"The ABCs of Mac Graphic File Formats", by Lonnie Guglielmo, *MacWeek Magazine*, January 30, 1990, p. 19.

"The True Story Behind Text Files", by Lynn Schwebach, *PC Today*, November 1990, p. 69. An explanation of the ASCII code and word processor file formats.

File Transfer

"Graphic Examples", by Salvatore Parascandolo, *MacUser Magazine*, April 1989, p. 189. Exchanging graphics between programs on the Macintosh.

"Moving Pictures", by Steve Roth, *MacUser Magazine*, September 1988, p. 164. Converting graphics files on the Macintosh.

"Smooth Moves", by Brita Meng, *MacWorld Magazine*, February 1988, p. 194. Exchanging graphics files between programs on the Macintosh.

On-Line Services

"Life On-Line" , by David Pogue, *MacWorld Magazine*, September 1990, p. 198. A week hole'd up in a NYC apartment connected only by modem to the world.

"The World At Your Fingertips", by Daniel J. Rosenblaum, *Publish!*, June 1988, p. 52. A guide to on-line services.

Telecommunications

"Calling Information", by Larry Loeb, *MacWorld Magazine*, June 1990, p. 156. Communications programs for the Macintosh reviewed.

"Communications", from the Understanding Computers Series, Time-Life Books, 1986, New York, NY. Good general introduction.

"Conquer the E-Mail Frontier", by Don Steinberg, *PC/Computing*, June 1991, p. 190. Interservice communication.

"Great Communicators" by Brita Meng, *MacWorld Magazine*, February 1988, p. 140. Seven Macintosh communications programs reviewed.

"Improving Information Access", by Mike Byrd, *PC Magazine*, April 30, 1991, p. 101. Seventeen PC asynchronous communications software packages reviewed.

"Reach Out and Publish", by Janet McCandless, *Publish!,* June 1988, p. 52. Using modem, fax, and on-line services to aid in publishing.

Chapter 14

Color Matching

"All the Colors of Space", by Bruce Webster, *MacWorld Magazine*, February 1991, p. 103.

"Color In, Same Color Out?", by Phillip Robinson, *Computer Graphics World*, February 1991, p. 93.

"Color Matching: Making Light of It", by Barrie Sosinsky, *The Desktop Publishers' Journal*, January/February 1991, Vol. 2, #1, p.21.

"Color Page Printers", by David Stone, *PC Magazine*, December 25, 1990, p. 339. Reviews of four color printers and factors involved in color fidelity discussed.

"Color WYSIWYG Comes of Age", by Frank Vaughn, *Byte Magazine*, December 1990, p. 275. Obtaining color fidelity on screen and in print.

Color Models

"Between the Lines: True Color", by Aileen Abernathy, *MacUser Magazine*, March 1990, p. 233. Calibrating color on your monitor.

"Breaking the Color Barrier", by Rebecca Hansen, *Computer Graphics World*, July 1990, p. 38. An article spotlighting the difference between color perception and color generation.

"Desktop Color Publishing", by Tom McMillan, *Computer Graphics World*, January 1990, p. 36. Color calibration.

"Four Color Fundamentals", by Helene Eckstein, *Publish!,* May 1989, p. 44. Color models, spot color, and process color.

"Pantone: panacea or placebo?", by Steve McKinstry, *MacUser Magazine*, May 1990, p. 341.

General

"A Brief Glossary of Color", by Nicholas H. Allison, *Aldus Magazine*, November/December 1990, p. 45. Color terminology defined.

"Add Color Impact to PC Publishing", by Sharyn Venit, *PC/Computing*, December 1990, p. 114. Various technologies discussed.

"An Introduction to Digital Color Prepress", Agfa Corporation, Agfa Compugraphic Division, 200 Ballardvale Street, Wilmington, MA 01887.

"An Introduction to Rendering Color on Video Displays", by Charles Petzold, *PC Magazine*, December 11, 1990, p. 483.

"Buyer's Guide: Color, Techniques and Technologies", *MacUser Magazine*, May 1990, p. 199. Several articles covering input, processing, and output on th Macintosh.

"Color on the Horizon", by Jim Cavuto, *Computer Graphics World*, February 1991, p. 88. Color DTP and magazine production.

"Color Transformations", *MacUser Magazine*, May 1990, p. 12. Using Photoshop and ColorStudio to do color digital image processing.

"Computer Graphics: Principles and Practice", 2nd Ed., by James D. Foley, Andries van Dam, Steven K. Feiner, and John F. Hughes, Addison-Wesley, Reading, MA, Chapter 13, p. 563-604, "Achromatic and Colored Light."

"Low Cost Color Reaches the Desktop", by Mary Jane Westmoreland, *MacWeek Magazine*, February 6, 1990, p. 33.

"The Full Color Desktop" by Keith Baumann and Jake Widman, *Publish!,* May 1989, p. 50. The effectiveness of PC and Mac color tools for correction and separation.

"The Persuasive Palette: When Color Works", by Christopher O'Malley, *Personal Computing*, February 1990, p. 111. Printer and software.

Separations

"Angling for Color", by Bruce Fraser, *Publish!*, June 1991, p. 74. Color screening technology described.

"Color Separations Explained", by Steve Roth, *MacWorld Magazine,* February 1989, p. 198; part 2, March 1989, p. 128.

"Color Separations: Where are we today?", by Laslo Vespremi, *MacWeek Magazine*, March 28, 1989, p. 48.

"Deciphering Screen Angles", by Jock Baird, *The Desktop Publishers Journal*, May 1991, p. 34. New techniques for better quality color output.

"Do-It-Yourself Color Separation", by Keith Baumann, *Publish!,* September 1989, p. 59.

"Electronic Color Stripping", by Tobin Koch, *MacUser Magazine*, April 1990, p. 265. Using PhotoMac to strip a page in Quark XPress.

"Mechanical Color Separation Skills for the Commercial Artist", by Tom Cardamone, 1980, Van Nostrand Reinhold, New York, NY.

"Prepress Techniques", by Steve Guttman, *Desktop Communications*, January-February 1991, p. 33.

"Selecting A Color Separator", by Steve Roth, *MacWorld Magazine*, March 1989, p. 128.

"Separating UCR and GCR", by Keith Baumann, *MacUser Magazine*, April 1991, p. 205.

"Separation Anxiety", *MacUser Magazine*, May 1990, p. 20 (Buyer's Guide).

"Separation Anxiety: Desktop vs. High End", by Keith Bauman, *MacWeek Magazine*, March 27, 1990, p. 40; also, "Color Sep Shops Expand Markets", by Steve Hannaford, p. 42.

"Setting Traps", by Steve Roth, *MacWorld Magazine*, May 1991, p. 159. Color separation techniques for registering abutting colors.

"Prepress: Cures for Poor Registration", by Steve McKinstry, *MacUser Magazine*, July 1990, p. 175. Using traps to eliminate misregistration.

Chapter 15

Formats

"An elegant format: Editable PostScript", by Gary Cosimini, *MacWeek Magazine*, December 18, 1990, p. 64. Universal page file formats.

"Prepress: The OPI Option", by Keith Baumann and Aileen Abernathy, *MacUser Magazine*, October, 1990, p. 219. The Aldus (Open Prepress Interface) OPI for transmission of TIFF images from design to prepress.

General

"A Glossary of Color Prepress Terms", by Robert Virkus, *Publish!*, November 1990, p. 78.

"A Snapshot in Color", by Peggy Thompson, *Aldus Magazine*, November/December 1990, centerleaf. Color prepress state of the art.

"Add Color Impact to PC Publishing", by Sharyn Venit, *PC/Computing*, December 1990, p. 114. Various technologies discussed.

"An Introduction to Digital Color Prepress", Agfa Corporation, Agfa Compugraphic Division, 200 Ballardvale Street, Wilmington, MA 01887. An excellent visually-oriented introduction to the prepress process. A free brochure.

"Prepress Progress Report", by Joe Matazzoni, *MacWorld Magazine*, October 1990, p. 168.

Prepress Links

"Closing the Gap", by Robert Virkus, *Computer Graphics World*, October 1989, p. 66.

"Color Prepress on the Desktop", by Robert Virkus, *MacWeek Magazine*, October 25, 1988, p. 46.

"Color Shops Prep for PostScript", by Steve Hannaford, *MacWeek Magazine*, December 18, 1990, 56.

"From Computer to Page", by Peter Johnson, *Computer Graphics World*, January 1990, p. 28. A review of color pre-press.

"Joining Prepress Society", by Steve McKinstry and Robert Virkus, *Publish!*, November 1990, p. 62. Prepress links.

"Prepress", by Keith Baumann and Aileen Abernathy, *MacUser Magazine*, November 1990, p. 211. Prepress links.

"The Coming Marriage of Design and Production: A CGR Staff Report", *Computer Graphics Review*, June 1989, p. 30. Desktop links to color pre-press.

"The Prepress Connection", by Steve Roth, *MacWorld Magazine*, October 1989, p. 146.

Printing

"Getting It Printed" by Mark Beach, Steve Shepro, and Ken Russon, Coast to Coast Books, Portland, Oregon, 1986. A book by printers on printing. How to work with printers and graphic arts services to assure quality, stay on schedule, and control costs. Not much concerned with the role of computers in this technology.

"Graphics Designer's Production Handbook, by Norman Sanders and William Bevington, 1982, Hastings House Publishers, New York, NY.

"Pocket Pal", International Paper Company, 6400 Poplar Avenue, Memphis, TN 38197, 14th Ed., 1989, $6.95. A concise and informative handbook to graphic arts production. A classic.

"The Chicago Manual of Style", The University of Chicago Press, 13th Ed., 1982, Chicago, IL. Style, technology, printing, all rolled into one. A companion volume for electronic publishing exists.

"The Graphics of Communications", 5th Ed., by Russell N. Baird *et. al.*, 1987, Holt, Reinhart & Winston, New York, NY.

Proofs

"Proof Positive", by Keith Baumann, *MacUser Magazine*, July 1990, p. 183. Getting a proof prepared for a printer.

Chapter 16

Groupware

"A Look Forward" by James Cavuoto, *MacWeek Magazine*, October 25, 1988. Desktop publishing moves to the networks.

"Beyond the GUI: Wang Freestyle", by Charles Petzold, *PC Magazine*, September 12, 1989.

"Down to Business: The Growth of Groupware", by Wayne Rash, Jr., *Byte Magazine*, November 1990, p. 89.

"Groupware: Tomorrow's Software Today", by Jackie Fox, *PC Today*, November 1990, p. 27.

"Odesta DMS: Making a Multiuser Application from Standalone Software", by George Alexander, *The Seybold Report*, Vol 19,#9, January 29, 1990.

"Sky High Notes", by David DeJean, *PC/Computing*, March 1990, p. 114. Lotus Notes reviewed.

"Team Work" by James A. Martin, *Publish!*, December 1988, p. 38. Workgroup publishing issues.

"The Electronic Office: Who will have one, how it will work, where you fit in", by Russ Lockwood, *Personal Computing*, May 1990, p. 74. Products, software, and case studies for a PC based office.

"The National", by Michael Roney, *Publish!*, February 1991, In Press. A case study of the multi-platformed electronic publishing system set up at the sports newspaper *The National* (now defunct).

"Windows Rides A New Wave", by John Lussmyer, *Byte Magazine*, April 1990, p. 171. H-P's NewWave environment.

Network—General

"Communications", Time-Life Books, from the Understanding Computer Series, 1986, New York, NY.

"Ethernet", by Richard Seifert, *Byte Magazine*, January 1991, p. 315.

"Five Ways Networks Pay Off", by Sharon Fisher, *PC World*, March 1991, p. 193.

"Getting Started with a Network", by Jackie Fox, *PC Today*, November 1990, p. 13.

"Getting Started with Networks", by Jim Heid, *MacWorld Magazine*, December 1990, p. 291.

"Is DOS-Based LAN for You", by Jackie Fox, *PC Today*, December 1990, p. 55.

"Managing the DOS and Mac Mix", by Charles Rubin, *Personal Computing*, February 1990, p. 88.

"Network Management", *Byte Magazine*, March 1991, p. 154 - 217. A series of six articles on various LAN issues.

"Networking for the Novice", by Brita Meng, *MacWorld Magazine*, December 1990, p. 202. AppleTalk / Macintosh networking solutions.

"Wired: Network Publishing's Good, Bad, and Ugly", by Jack Powers, *Electronic Publishing & Printing*, June / July 1989, p. 24.

Network—Hardware

"Being There: Remote Networking", by Bob Weibel, *Publish!*, December 1988, p. 52.

"Buffered Printing-Sharing Devices", by M. David Stone, *PC Magazine*, April 30, 1991, p. 283. Nine printer sharing products under $150 reviewed.

"Connectivity Made Simple", by Christopher O'Malley, *Personal Computing*, March 1990, p. 93. Low cost connectivity solutions for sharing peripherals, E-Mail, and file transfer without installing a LAN.

"Distributing Text and Graphics via Fax Boards", by Paul Kinnucan, *Computer Graphics Review*, May 1990, p. 34.

"Making Do with DOS", by Frank Derfler, Jr., *PC Magazine*, May 29, 1990, p. 153.

"Networking Buyer's Guide", *MacUser Magazine*, June 1990, p. 134. Networking solutions for large networks.

"Special-Function Servers", by Frank J. Derfler, Jr., *PC Magazine*, January 15, 1991, p. 375.

"The LAN Survival Guide", by Frank Derfler, Jr., *PC Magazine*, May 29, 1990, p. 97. Several articles about PC LANs.

"The Next Wave: LANs without Wires", by Frank Derfler, Jr., *PC Magazine*, May 29, 1990, p. 295.

"Unraveling the LAN Mystery", by Jackie Fox, *PC Today*, November 1990, p. 19.

"Wide Area Information Transfer Systems", by Mike Byrd and Frank Derfler, Jr., *PC Magazine*, March 27, 1990, p. 249.

"Work Groups or Work Teams?", by Kurt VanderSluis, *MacUser Magazine*, October 1990, p. 234. Different schemes for setting up a Macintosh network.

"Zero Slot LANs", by Kimberly Maxwell and Patricia McGovern, *PC Magazine*, April 24, 1990, p. 187. Small work group networking solutions.

Network—Software

"Building Workgroup Solutions: LAN E-Mail Systems", by Frank J. Derfler, Jr., *PC Magazine*, November 27, 1990, p. 225.

"Building Workgroup Solutions: LAN Memory Management Software", by Frank J. Derfler, Jr., M. Keith Thompson, and R. Dennis Boatner, *PC Magazine*, January 29, 1991, p. 203.

"Building Workgroup Solutions: Voice E-Mail", by Frank J. Derfler, Jr., *PC Magazine*, July 1990, p. 311.

"Building Workroup Solution: LAN Backup Software", by R. Dennis Boatner, *PC Magazine*, January 29, 1991, p. 273.

"Can You Do Better Than Netware", by Robert Lauriston, *PC World Magazine*, March 1991, p. 157. PC LANs reviewed.

"DOS LANs Grow Up", by Frank J. Derfler, Jr., *PC Magazine*, June 25, 1991, p. 167. A review of 13 DOS LAN networking systems.

"E-Mail for LANs", by Patrick Honan and Joseph Devlin, *Personal Computing*, June 29, 1990, p. 154. Survey of 10 PC E-Mail programs.

"E-Mail: A Postal Inspection, by David Kosiur, *MacWorld Magazine*, June 1990, p. 156. Survey of Macintosh software.

"Getting Bigger Groupware", by Wayne Rash, *Byte Magazine*, December 1990, p. 93. High-end solutions.

"LAN E-Mail: Spreading the Network News", *PC Magazine*, September 26, 1989.

"LAN Fax Gateways: Can They Eliminate Fax Machines Bottlenecks?", *PC Magazine*, April 10, 1990.

"Mail Call", by Michael Miley and the MacUser NetWorkShop Staff, *MacUser Magazine*, July 1990, p. 92. Five Macintosh E-Mail programs reviewed.

"Managing Networks", by Dave Kosiur, *MacWorld Magazine*, February 1991, p. 160. AppleTalk network management.

"Organizing the Global Office", by Eric Bender, *PC World Magazine*, July 1989, p. 164, Office Vision for Presentation Manager.

"The Corporate BBS", by Russ Lockwood, *Personal Computing*, March 1990, p. 62.

"Workgroup Software Worth Waiting For", by Robert J. Lauriston, *PC World Magazine*, June 1990, p. 122. LANs.

Chapter 17

Selecting A Service Bureau

"At Your Service Bureau", by Efert Fenton, *MacWorld Magazine*, October 1989, p. 154.

"At Your Service", by Mard Naman, *Publish!*, November 1990, p. 85. How to choose a color service bureau. A profile of ten nationally ranked color service bureaus.

"Beyond the Laser Printer", by Kathleen Tinkel, *MacUser Magazine*, January 1991, p. 197. Imagesetters and service Bureaus.

"Fine Print" by David Holzgang and Salvatore Parascandolo, *MacUser Magazine*, August 1989, p. 169. How to use fonts from a service bureau.

"Getting It on Film", by Keith Baumann, *MacUser Magazine*, May 1990, p. 351. Using film calibration as a criteria for selecting a service bureau.

"Selecting A Service Bureau", by Nichole J. Vick, *Aldus Magazine*, November/December 1990, p. 22. Finding a service bureau.

"Service with a Style", by James A. Martin, *Publish!*, February 1991, p. 81. Case study of the Stat Store, NYC.

"Shopping for a Service Bureau", by Henri Froissart, *MacWeek Magazine*, February 27, 1990, p. 38.

"Your Neighborhood Service Bureau", by Stephen Hannaford, *MacWeek Magazine*, October 25, 1988, p. 30. Choosing the right one.

Starting A Service Bureau

"Clients from Hell", by Jonathan Littman, *Publish!*, June 1991, p. 68. Service bureau horror stories.

"Setting Up Shop", by Kristi Coale, *MacUser Magazine*, October 1988, p. 275.

Service Bureau Listings

"2nd Annual Service Bureau Directory", Electronic Publishing & Printing,. Send $7.50 to Ms. Jean Miller, Electronic Publishing & Printing, Dept. SBD, 29 N. Wacker Drive, Chicago, IL 60606.

CompuServe, Adobe Forum. Type Go Adobe, enter the Service Bureau library, and then download the file SRVBUR.TXT

"TypeWorld PostScript Services Directory", TypeWorld, P.O. Box 170, Salem, NH 03079, (603)898-2822. Listing 1000 of service bureaus, who to contact, and what platform they support. Specific output devices, programs supported, and the number of fonts in each bureau is also mentioned. Price is $19.95 plus $3.95 postage and handling.

Viruses

"An Ounce of Prevention", by Robert R. Wiggins, *MacUser Magazine*, March 1989, p. 79.

"Know thy Viral Enemy", by Ross M. Greenberg, *Byte Magazine*, June 1989, p. 275.

Chapter 18

Authoring Software and Animation

"3-D Reading with the Hypertext Edge", by Henry Fersko-Weiss, *PC Magazine*, May 28, 1991, p. 241. Eight PC packages reviewed.

"Authoring, Modeling, and Animation", by Lon McQuillen, *MacUser Magazine*, February 1991, p. 52 (buyer's guide). Software and techniques for the Macintosh.

"Desktop Animation Becomes a Reality", by Paul Yarmolich, *Computer Graphics Review*, July 1990, p. 10. RenderMan arrives on the Mac for rendering figures.

"Desktop Multimedia: You Ain't Seen Nothing Yet", by Eric Bender, *PC World Magazine*, March 1990, p. 191. PC hypermedia programs.

"HyperCard for Graphic Artists", by Andrew Goodman, *MacWeek Magazine*, October 25, 1988, p. 68.

"Media Integration:Authoring Software Makes It Happen", by Lori Beckmann, *PC Today*, June 1991, p. 21.

"Playing Author", by Jack Sculley and Inge Hutzel, *Computer Graphics World*, February 1990, p. 58. Multimedia authoring software compared.

CD-ROM and Optical Storage

"An Introduction to Rewriting Optical Disk Technology", by Winn L. Rosch, *PC Magazine*, December 11, 1990, p. 439. A good general introduction to optical storage technology.

"CD-ROM Drives: Is it Time for CD-ROM?", by Rik Myslewski and the MacUser Lab Staff, *MacUser Magazine*, June 1991, p. 150.

"Getting Started with CD-ROM", by Helmut Kobler, *Publish!*, March 1991, p. 44. Drives and published titles.

"Gigabytes On-Line", by James J. Burke, and Bob Ryan, *Byte Magazine*, October 1989, p. 259.

"Letting in the Light", by John Rizzo, *MacUser Magazine*, November 1989, p. 132. Optical storage on the Macintosh.

"Magneto-Optical Drives: Fulfilling the Promise of Rewritable Optical?", by M. David Stone, *PC Magazine*, June 11, 1991, p. 281.

"Miles of Files", by Bob Weibel, *Publish!*, July 1989, p. 55.

"Optical Horizans", by Jon Zilber, *MacUser Magazine*, June 1988, p. 157.

"Sizing Up CD-ROM", by Russ Lockwood, *Personal Computing*, July 27, 1990, p. 70.

"The Brady Guide to CD-ROM", by Laura Buddine and Elizabeth King, Brady Books, 1990, New York, NY.

Equipment

"Digital Video Interactive", by Brett Glass, *Byte Magazine*, May 1989, p. 283.

"From RGB to NTSC: The Scan Converter Way", by Rober Marius, *Computer Graphics Review*, August 1989, p. 21.

"From VGA to NTSC: Putting Your PC on Tape", by Lori Grunin, *PC Magazine*, July 1990, p. 197.

"How To: Getting Started with Desktop Video", by Jim Heid, *MacWorld Magazine*, September 1990, p. 319.

"Interactive Video Comes to PC Graphics", by Bob Brannon, *Byte Magazine*, November 1989, p. 46, Intel's Digital Video Interactive (DVI) technology.

"Mac TV Tools", by Lon Poole, *MacWorld Magazine*, September 1989, p. 208. The Macintosh as a video workstation.

"Making the Video-Computer Connection", by Bruce Anderson, *Computer Graphics Review*, July 1990, p. 48. Still video imaging as a useful midway point on the road to full multimedia.

"Multimedia and Video", by Lon McQuillin, *MacUser Magazine*, February 1991, p. 4 (buyer's guide). Equipment for the Macintosh.

"Multimedia: DVI Arrive", by Greg Loveria and Don Kinstler, *Byte Magazine*, November 11, 1990, p. 105

"State of the Art Briefing Center" by Stuart Silverstone, *MacWeek Magazine*, March 28, 1989, p. 44. Apple Computer's Maryland center.

"The 4 Multimedia Gospels", by Phillip Robinson, *Byte Magazine*, February 1990, p. 203. The four main platforms.

"The Amiga: A Multimedia Marvel, by Jackie Fox, *PC Today*, June 1991, p. 47.

"The Audio Visual Connection: Turnkey Multimedia from IBM", by Alfred Poor, *PC Magazine*, May 5, 1990, p. 157.

"The Outlook of PC-Based Video Digitizers", by Jon Peddie, *Computer Graphics Review*, June 1989, p. 52.

"The Quest for Mac Video Input", by Clay Andres, *MacWeek Magazine*, July 31, 1990, P. 59. A review of video boards for the Mac.

Examples

"Alternative Publishing: CD-ROM and Other Technologies Take Off", by Phillip Murray, *Electronic Publishing & Printing*, August / September 1989, p. 44. Telepublishing, video-tex, CD-ROM, DVI, and compact-disk interactive discussed as print alternatives.

"Animation Across the Airwaves", by Peter Sorensen, *Computer Graphics Review*, November 1990, p. 80. Television as a showcase for computer special-effect techniques.

"Batman Meets the Computer", by Gary Pfitzer, *Computer Graphics World*, August 1990, p. 131.

"Creating Interactive Brochures", by Stuart Silverstone, *MacWeek Magazine*, March 6, 1990. Designer Clement Mok uses HyperCard for multimedia projects.

"Exploring the Unknown", by Audrey Vasilopoulos, *Computer Graphics World*, October 1989, p. 76. Modelling and rendering animation using a Macintosh to create visual sequences for the movie "The Abyss".

"LIFEmap: A Museum Exhibit That's Off the Wall", by Carol S. Holtzman, *Macintosh-Aided Design*, February 1991, p. 14. Multimedia interactive journey through time at the California Academy of Sciences.

"Macs in Hollywood", by Lori Beckmann, *PC Today*, June 1991, p. 65.

"Made for the Stage", by Stephen Porter, *Computer Graphics World*, August 1990, p. 60. Using computer generated actors in film as movie stars.

"Making Multimedia Work for You", by Steve Rosenthal, *MacWeek Magazine*, February 30, 1990, p. 22.

"PC/Computing's Top 20 CD Hits", by David Harvey, *PC/Computing*, June 1991, p. 104.

"Peeking Behind the Interface", by Karen A. Frenkl, *Publish!*, July 1991, p. 58. Case studies of multimedia projects: kiosks, CD-I, computer generated commercials.

General

"A 3-D Animation Primer", by Gregory MacNichol, *Publish!*, May 1991, p. 44. A good general introduction to computer based multimedia technology.

"Amiga 3000, AmigaVision Heat Up Multimedia Market", by Gary Pfitzer, *Computer Graphics World*, June 1990, p. 29. Evaluating hardware/software on the Amiga.

"But Can it Sing and Dance?", Rick Cook, *Computer Graphics World*, July 1989, p. 78. Multimedia on the Amiga.

"How To/Getting Started with Multimedia", by Jim Heid, *MacWorld Magazine*, May 1991, p. 225. A general intro with emphasis for the Macintosh.

"Interactive Learning", by Denise Caruso, *Publish!*, April 1990, p. 75. Multimedia products in the education market.

"Making Sense of Multimedia", by Bruce Anderson, *Computer Graphics Review*, February 1990, p. 32.

"Multimedia in Business: The New Presentations", by Ross Lockwood, *Personal Computing*, June 29, 1990, p. 116. Applications and hardware needed to create multimedia presentations.

"Multimedia is the Message", by Don Steinberg, *PC/Computing*, September 1990, p. 134. An introduction to multimedia on the PC with a bevy of examples.

"Multimedia: About Interfaces", by John J. Anderson, *MacUser Magazine*, March 1989, p.88. A primer on approaches.

"Multimedia Today: Four Paths Towards the Future", p. 92. Examples.

"Multimedia: The Next Frontier for Business?", by Robin Raskin, *PC Magazine*, July 1990, p. 151. A very complete and up-to-date introduction to hardware/software needed to do multimedia projects on the PC.

"PC Animation Hugs the Inside Lane", by Gregory MacNicol, *Computer Graphics World*, July 1989, p. 58. Software and hardware for the PC.

"Spotlight on Animation", by Gregory MacNicol, *Computer Graphics World*, June 1991, p. 49. A two-part review of computer animation, high-end to low-end.

"The Main Event", by Nick Arnett, *Publish!*, February 1990, p. 66. Multimedia on the PC and Mac.

"VideoLogic Guide to Multimedia Development Tools and Resources", VideoLogic, Inc., 245 First Street, Cambridge, MA 02142, Tel. (617)494-0530.

"When Worlds Collide: Demystifying Multimedia", by Jackie Fox, *PC Today*, June 1991, p. 7.

Issues

"Multimedia and Education", by Tom McMillan, *Computer Graphics World*, October 1990, p. 68.

"Multimedia: Is it real?", by Suzanne Stefanac and Liza Weitman, *MacWorld Magazine*, April 1990, p. 116. Macintosh multimedia issues.

"Recording High-Resolution Computer Graphics", by Carroll Cunningham, *Computer Graphics Review*, August 1989, p. 30.

"Tailoring your multimedia images and sound to fit big screens", by Steve Rosenthal, *PC World Magazine*, July 1990, p. 24.

Sound

"Digital Audio at Last", by Christopher Yavelow, *MacWorld Magazine*, February 1991, p. 160. Technology for the Macintosh, software and hardware.

"Equipping Your PC for High Quality Sound Production", by John Walkenbach, *PC Today*, June 1991, p. 32.

"First Steps in the Sequence", by David Pogue, *MacWorld Magazine*, June 1991, p. 146. Sequencing software on the Macintosh.

"How to Get Started With MIDI", by Jim Heid, *MacWorld Magazine*, August 1990, p. 249.

"Macworld Music & Sound Bible", by Christopher Yavelow, 1991, IDG Books Worldwide, San Mateo, CA.

"Making Music", by Bruce F. Webster, *MacWorld Magazine*, March 1991, p. 85. Setting up a MIDI system on a Mac.

"Multimedia and Audio", by Ken Gruberman and Lon McQuillen, *MacUser Magazine*, February 1991, p. 38 (buyer's guide). Sound on the Macintosh, software and hardware.

"Sound Advice", by James Bradbury, *MacUser Magazine*, May 1990, p. 284.

"Sounds of Success", by Dean Friedman, *Byte Magazine*, September 1990, p. 429. Professional sound programs, MIDI, sequencers, keynote recorders, etc.

"The MIDI Manual", by David Huber, 1990, Sams, Carmel, IN.

"The Spoken Word", by Kai-Fu Lee and Alexander G. Hauptmann, Alexander I. Rudnicky, *Byte Magazine*, July 1990, p. 255. Voice input technology and voice recognition: assessment and future.

Video Production

"Coming Soon to a Monitor Near You", *MacWeek Magazine*, September 1988, p. 142. Producing professional quality video-tapes on the Macintosh.

"Desktop Video Studies", by Rick Cook, *Byte Magazine*, February 1990, p. 299.

"Desktop Video: The Hidden Revolution", by Jon Leland, *PC Today*, June 1991, p. 23.

"Mac Video, Take II", by Peter S. Marx and Franklin N. Tessler, *MacWorld Magazine*, February 1991, p. 178. Hardware for the Mac.

"Prime-Time Video", by Peter S. Marx and Franklin N. Tessler, *MacWorld Magazine*, September 1990, p. 206. Video digitizers for the Mac.

"The Mac/TV Connection: Desktop Video", by Paul Yi and the MacUser Labs Staff, *MacUser Magazine*, July 1991, p. 124.

"Video Meets PC", by Gregory MacNicol, *Computer Graphics World*, February 1991, p. 55. PC video editing systems.

Chapter 19

Artificial Intelligence

"AI Metamorphosis or Death", by Jane Morill Tazelaar, *Byte Magazine*, January 1991, p. 236. The State-of-the-Art section spotlighting the field of AI with eight articles following it.

Automatic Data Exchange

"Future Documents", by Martin Heller, *Byte Magazine*, May 1991, p. 126. Microsoft's OLE technology and HP's NewWave are described, as is their use in the creation of compound documents.

"Hot Links to Go", Michael Vose, *Byte Magazine*, November 1990, p. 373. Dynamic data exchange between Windows and OS/2.

"Live Data Exchange Between Applications", by Bud E. Smith, *Personal Workstation,* June 1990, p. 54. New GUI's and API's let applications work together seamlessly.

Data Transmission Technologies

"Coming Soon to a Mac Near You: ISDN", by Stephan Somogyi, *MacUser Magazine*, October 1990, p. 227.

"Data Superhighways", by Tom Kiely, *Computer Graphics World*, December 1989, p. 40. ISDN.

"Data Transmission in the '90s", by Melene Follert, *Pre- Magazine*, May 1990, p. 42. What the options are for moving print sized files electronically.

"Developing Trends in High-Speed Networked Graphics Data Transmission", by Patrick Naughton and Greg Schechter, *Computer Graphics Review*, June 1990, p. 46.

"Technical Introduction to ISDN", by Apple Computer, 1990, 20525 Mariani Avenue, Cupertino, CA 95014-6299, Tel. (408)996-1010.

"The Future of Network Operating Systems", by Barry Nance, *Byte Magazine*, February 1991, p. 268.

Display Trends

"3-D Graphics, from Alpha to Z-Buffer", by Ron M. Brinkmann, *Byte Magazine*, July 1990, p. 271, The effect of expanding computer memory on graphics and display technology.

"Graphics Go 3-D", by Steve Upstill, *Byte Magazine*, December 1990, p. 253. Creating 3-D figures on-screen.

"HDTV Sparks a Revolution", by Andrew Lippman, *Byte Magazine*, December 1990, p. 297. Discussion of the many proposed display standards.

"HDTV: Is it Worth the Hype", by John Webster, *Computer Graphics Review*, June 1990, p. 26.

"In Search of the Miracle Hologram", by Arielle Emmett, *Computer Graphics World*, February 1991, p. 44.

"Ray Tracing for Realism", by Andrew S. Glassner, *Byte Magazine*, December 1990, p. 263. Creating photo realistic images with computed lighting effects.

"Seing the Future in 3-D: Stereoscopic Viewing", by Carl Machover, *Computer Graphics Review*, August 1989, p. 60.

"Stereo 3D", by Phillip Robinson, *Computer Graphics World*, June 1990. Equipment and technology for 3D computing.

"Telltale Gestures", by Paul McAvinney, *Byte Magazine*, July 1990, p. 237. 3D applications needed for 3D input.

Electronic Publishing Trends

"Batman: Digital Justice", $24.95, DC Comics, Inc., 666 Fifth Avenue, New York, NY 10103, Tel. (212)484-2885.

"Catch the Wave of DIP", by David Harvey, *Byte Magazine*, April 1991, p. 173. Document image processing.

"Data Interchange Standards Association, Inc., 1800 Diagonal Road, Suite 355, Alexandria, VA 22314, Tel. (703)548-7005. Ask for the X12/DISA Information Manual, ASC X12S.

"EDI, Spread the Word!", P.O. Box 811366, Dallas, TX 75381, Tel. (214)243-3456. Ask for the "EDI Yellow Pages International."

"Fast Fax Publishing", by Rusty Weston, *Publish!*, July 1991, p. 71. Publishing case studies with fax as the distribution method.

"HyperTED", by Steve Ditlea, *PC/Computing*, October 1990, p. 200. Ted Nelson and Xanadu.

"Managing Gigabytes", *Byte Magazine*, May 1991, p. 153. A state of the art section of six articles on using and managing large databases.

"Practically Paperless", by David A. Harvey and Bob Ryan, *Byte Magazine*, April 1991, p. 185. Document image processing case studies.

"Smart Documents", by Ellen Beal, *Computer Graphics World*, May 1991, p. 53. "Active" documents and their use in electronic publishing applications.

"The Dark Side of DIP", by Christopher Locke, *Byte Magazine*, April 1991, p. 193. Data retrieval from documents.

"The Paperless Office", by Bob Ryan, *Byte Magazine*, April 1991, p. 157.

"The World of Documents", by Gerald P. Michalski, *Byte Magazine*, p. 159. Intelligent document management.and the Electronic Data Interchange ANSI standard.

Future PCs

"Computing With Light", by H. John Caulfield, *Byte Magazine*, October 1989, p. 231.

"Destination Laptop", by Doug Gephardt and Mark C. Klonower, *Byte Magazine*, February 1991, p. 239. AMD's "AT on a chip."

"Multiprocessing", *Byte Magazine*, June 1991, p. 196. A set of six articles on the state of the art in multiprocessor technology.

"Notebook PCs Set the Portable Standard", by Paul Schmidt, *Byte Magazine*, November 11, 1990, p. 153. The shape (thin!) of portable PCs in the mid-1990s.

"Portable Chips", by Owen Linderholm, Byte Magazine, December 1990, p. 313.

"The PC's Future: "You ain't seen nothing yet", by Stanley Klein, *Computer Graphics Review*, June 1990, p. 8.

General Trends

"A Talk with Intel", *Byte Magazine*, April 1991, p. 131. An interview with three lead Intel engineers on the future of the 80x86 CPUs.

"Byte's 15th Anniversary Summit", *Byte Magazine*, September 1990, p. 218. An collection of essays and panel discussions by 63 of the leaders and pioneers in the field of computer hardware and software.

"Chips for the 90's and Beyond", Janet J. Barron, *Byte Magazine*, November 1990, p. 342. Weird laboratory stuff.

"Dynabook Revisited with Alan Kay", by Bob Ryan, *Byte Magazine*, February 1991, p. 203.

"Forecasting the Future in Computer Graphics", by Stephen Roe, *Computer Graphics Review*, May 1989, p. 46.

"Home Office: All-in-one PCs", by Marty Jerome, *PC/Computing*, March 1991, p. 278.

"Hydras: An Idea Whose Time Has Come? Or a Monster in the Wings?", by John Dvorak and Jim Seymour, *PC/Computing*, February 1991, p. 65.

Input Devices and Interfaces

"An Easier Interface", by Mark A. Clarkson, *Byte Magazine*, February 1991, p. 277. Xerox PARC's new animated 3D GUI.

"Divide and Conquer", by David P. Wright and Christopher L. Scofield, *Byte Magazine*, April 1991, p. 207. Automatic handwriting recognition.

"Fascinating Rhythm", by Joel N. Orr, *Computer Graphics World*, August 1990, p. 117. Tuning computers input and output into a user's body rhythm. Fascinating.

"Merging Man and Machine", by Daniel Gross, *Computer Graphics World*, May 1991, p. 47. Future interface technology from Japan.

"Opening Doors for the Disabled", by Joseph J. Lazzaro, *Byte Magazine*, August 1990, p. 258. Adaptive computer input technology for the disabled.

"Pen-Based Computing: Get the Point?", by Bill Machrone, *PC Magazine*, April 30, 1991, 75.

"Sign Here, Please", by Gale Martin, James Pittman, Kent Wittenburg, Richard Cohen, and Tom Parish, *Byte Magazine*, July 1990, p. 243. Interactive tablets and handwriting recognition.

"Smoke and Mirrors", by Bill Buxton, *Byte Magazine*, July 1990, p. 205. Looking beyond GUIs to new computer interfaces and input technologies.

"The Multilingual Edge", by Peter M. Benton, *Byte Magazine*, March 1991, p. 124. Machine translation of human languages.

"The Point of the Pen", by Robert M. Carr, *Byte Magazine*, February 1991, p. 211. Go's Pen-Point computer.

"The Spoken Word", by Kai-Fu Lee and Alexander G. Hauptmann, Alexander I. Rudnicky, *Byte Magazine*, July 1990, p. 255. Voice input technology and voice recognition: assessment and future.

"Touch-and-Feel Interfaces", by Andrew Reinhardt, *Byte Magazine*, February 1991, p. 223. New laptop input devices.

Memory and Storage

"Crystal Clear Storage", by Tom Parish, *Byte Magazine*, November 1990, p. 283. Holographic data storage.

"Entering a New Phase", by Bob Ryan, *Byte Magazine*, November 1990, p. 289. Phase change storage media.

"Flash Memory: Is it a Flash of Genius or A Flash in the Pan?", by Gina Smith, *PC/Magazine*, March 1991, p. 56.

"Giga-Storage", by Richard A. Peters, *Byte Magazine*, May 1991, p. 201. Large storage devices and schemes.

"Memories in My Pocket", by John Reimer, *Byte Magazine*, February 1991, p. 251. Future silicon based memory options.

"Paper, Magnets, and Light", by Robert R. Gaskin, *Byte Magazine*, November 1989, p. 391. The history of data storage devices.

"State of the Media", by David Harvey, *Byte Magazine*, November 1990, p. 275. Magnetic disks vs. optical.

"Store Data in a Flash", by Walter Lahti and Dean McCarron, *Byte Magazine*, November 1990, p. 311. Flash memory integrated circuits.

"The Once and Future King", by Bob Ryan, *Byte Magazine*, November 1990, p. 301. Prospects for hard disk drives.

Virtual Reality

"Artificial reality: don't stay home without it", by Doug Stewart, *Smithsonian*, January 1991, p. 36.

"Living in a Virtual World", by Scott Fisher and Jane Morrill Tazelaar, *Byte Magazine*, July 1990, p. 215. Virtual reality computer systems

"Reach Out", by Gary Stix, *Scientific American*, February 1991, p. 134. The use of touch in virtual reality simulations.

"Reality Check", by Dwight B. Davis, *Computer Graphics World*, June 1991, p. 49. The state of virtual reality technology.

"The Wizards of the Media Lab", by Janet Baron, *Byte Magazine*, December 1989, p. 353.

"What's Wrong with Reality", by Gregory MacNicol, *Computer Graphic World*, November 1990, p. 102. Virtual reality: boon or boondoggle?

Bibliography

Books

Art/Graphics

Fenton, Erfert, and Christine Morrissett. *Canned Art for the Macintosh*. Berkeley, Calif.: Peachpit Press, 1990. A compilation in pictures of over 15,000 images and a guide to clip art collections.

Foley, James D., Andries van Dam, Steven K. Feiner, and John F. Hughes. *Computer Graphics, Principles and Practices*, 2d ed. Reading, Mass.: Addison-Wesley, 1990. A classic college textbook on all aspects of graphics and theory.

Kerlow, Isaac Victor, and Judson Rosebush. *Computer Graphics for Designers and Artists*. New York: Van Nostrand Reinhold, 1986. An introduction to the principles and practice of computer graphics.

MacNeill, D. *Mastering Graphics on the Macintosh*. Greensboro, N.C.: Compute! Publications, 1990.

Prusinkiewicz, Przemyslaw, and Aristad Lindenmayer. *The Algorithmic Beauty of Plants*. New York: Springer-Verlag, 1990. Spectacular computer-generated artwork.

Richmond, Wendy. *Design & Technology: Erasing the Boundaries*. New York: Van Nostrand Reinhold, 1990. A very interesting and diverse collection of case studies of the impact of using computers for graphic design.

Truckenbrod, Joan. *Creative Computer Imaging.* Englewood Cliffs, N.J.: Prentice Hall, 1988. Many special effects shown using computers.

Ward, Fred. "Images for the Computer Age." *National Geographic Magazine,* June 1989, p. 719.

White, Jan V. *Designing for Magazines,* 2d ed. New York: R. R. Bowker, 1982.

————. *Editing by Design,* 2d ed. New York: R. R. Bowker, 1982.

————. *Graphic Design for the Electronic Age.* New York: Watson-Guptill Publications, 1988.

————. *The Grid Book.* Paramus, N.J.: Letraset U.S.A., 1988.

————. *Mastering Graphics.* New York: R. R. Bowker, 1983.

Williams, Robin. *The Mac Is Not a TypeWriter.* Berkeley, Calif.: Peachpit Press, 1990. A small style guide, useful for any computer.

Will-Harris, Daniel. *Desktop Publishing with Style.* South Bend, Ind.: And Books, 1987. Design with some technology for DPT on IBM PCs.

Wilson, Adrian. *The Design of Books.* Layton, Utah: Gibbs Smith, 1967.

Xerox Corporation. *Xerox Publishing Standards.* New York: Watson-Guptill Publications, 1988.

Artificial Intelligence

Kurzweil, Raymond. *The Age of Intelligence Machines.* Cambridge, Mass.: MIT Press, 1990. A seminal book by one of the pioneers in the field of artificially intelligent machines. Lavishly illustrated; a wonderful blend of history and science.

Color

Kuehni, Rolf. *Color: Essence and Logic.* New York: Van Nostrand Reinhold, 1983. An introduction to color theory, perception, and reproduction.

Molla, Rafiqul. *Electronic Color Separation.* Montgomery, Va.: Printing and Publishing Co., 1988.

Southworth, Miles. *Color Separation Techniques,* 2d ed. Livonia, N.Y.: Graphic Arts Publishing, 1979. A treatise on color reproduction technology and theory. Mostly concerned with traditional methods rather than digital ones.

————. *Pocket Guide to Color Reproduction: Communications and Control,* 2nd ed. Livonia, N.Y.: Graphic Arts Publishing, 1989.

Thorell, L. G., and W. J. Smith. *Using Computer Color Effectively: An Illustrated Reference.* Englewood Cliffs, N.J.: Prentice Hall (Hewlett-Packard), 1990. An excellent introduction to all aspects of computer color and theory.

Desktop Publishing—Design

Beach, Mark. *Editing Your Newsletter.* Portland, Ore.: Coast to Coast Books, 1988.

Black, Roger. *Roger Black's Desktop Design Power.* New York: Bantam Books, 1991. The third book in the Bantam-ITC series by the well-known designer.

Dover Pictorial Archive Book Catalog. Mineola, N.Y.: Dover Publications, annual. Traditional clip art books costing between $5 and $10 each.

Gosney, Michael, John Odam, Jim Schmal. *The Gray Book.* Chapel Hill, N.C.: Ventana Press, 1990. Achieving special effects in black and white.

Groff, Vern. *The Power of Color in Design for Desktop Publishing.* Portland, Ore.: MIS Press, 1990. A design book that concentrates on color usage and techniques.

Lichty, Tom. *Design Principles for Desktop Publishers.* Glenview, Ill.: Scott, Foresman, 1989.

Marshall, George R., and Ken Frieldman. *The Manager's Guide to Desktop Electronic Publishing.* Englewood Cliffs, N.J.: Prentice Hall, 1990.

"The 1991 Buyer's Guide to Desktop Publishing Products." *Publish,* October 1990, p. 71. The fourth annual buyer's guide with a listing of over 1,400 products.

Parker, Roger C. *Looking Good in Print.* Chapel Hill, N.C.: Ventana Press, 1988. A guide to basic design for desktop publishing. Many before-and-after case studies.

————. *The Make Over Book: 101 Design Solutions for Desktop Publishing.* Chapel Hill, N.C.: Ventana Press, 1989.

Rech, Rolf F. *Typography and Design for Newspapers.* Indianapolis: Design Research International, 1989.

Seybold, John, and Fritz Dressler. *Publishing From the Desktop.* New York: Bantam Books, 1987. An outdated look at publishing by a pioneer in the field.

Shushan, Ronnie, and Don Wright. *Desktop Publishing by Design.* Redmond, Wash.: Microsoft Press, 1989. A substantial book with many useful resources. A 1989 computer trade book award winner.

Chicago Guide to Preparing Electronic Manuscripts for Authors and Publishers. Chicago: University of Chicago Press, 1987.

The Waite Group. *Desktop Publishing Bible.* Carmel, Ind.: Howard Sams and Co., 1987. A good introduction to both design and technology on microcomputers, both PC and Macintosh. The technology is getting somewhat dated, but there is still much valuable material to be gleaned here.

Electronic Publishing—General

"The Apple Guide to Desktop Publishing." *Apple Computer,* Summer 1989. Desktop Media Collection: Publishing.

Berst, Jesse. *Managing Desktop Publishing.* Thousand Oaks, Calif.: New Riders, 1989. The technology and style issues for managing a DTP project. Focuses mainly on the PC, but is broadly applicable with many useful concepts.

Burnes, Diane, S. Venit, and Rebecca Hansen. *The Electronic Publisher.* New York: Simon & Schuster/Brady Books, 1988. Good design primer relating design issues to microcomputer technology. The focus is on the process involved.

Harris, Robert. *Understanding Desktop Publishing.* Alameda, Calif.: Sybex, 1991. A design handbook for PC users.

McClelland, Deke, and Craig Danuloff. *Desktop Publishing Type & Graphics.* Cambridge, Mass.: Harcourt Brace Jovanovich, 1987.

McKenzie, Bruce G. *The Hammermill Guide to Desktop Publishing in Business.* Memphis: Hammermill Papers Business/International Paper Company, 1989. A good beginners' introduction to electronic graphic arts production, a blend of design and technology.

Moreno, Pepe. *Batman, Digital Justice.* New York: DC Comics, 1990. Holy microchips, Batman! Conceived and executed on a Macintosh, the caped crusader fights on against the nets and the Joker (now a computer virus) in the first completely microcomputer-generated comic book novel.

Sitarz, D. *Desktop Publisher's Legal Handbook.* Ill.: Nova, 1989.

Electronic Publishing—Technology

Barry, John A., Frederick E. Davis, with Phillip Robinson. *Desktop Publishing IBM Edition.* Homewood, Ill.: Dow-Jones Irwin, 1988.

Bove, Tony, Cheryl Rhodes, and Wes Thomas. *The Art of Desktop Publishing,* 2d ed. New York: Bantam Books, 1987. A smorgasbord of microcomputer products and techniques, with much useful discussion on putting it all together. Somewhat dated.

Kleper, Michael L. *The Illustrated Handbook of Desktop Publishing and Typesetting*, 2d ed. Blue Ridge Summit, Pa.: Tab Books, 1990. An encyclopedic review of hardware and software on the PC and Mac relating to DTP. Covers history, technology, and the basics. This book is tremendous in scope and deserves a place on your bookshelf, if only as a reference work. A CD ROM version is available. My only criticism is that the book lacks focus. However, there are gems in there as well as the kitchen sink.

Lanyi, Gabriel, and Jon Barrett. *IBM Desktop Publishing*. Blue Ridge Summit, Pa.: Windcrest Books, 1989. A good solid treatment of hardware and software for IBM PCs and clones.

Makuta, Daniel J., and William F. Lawrence. *The Complete Desktop Publisher*. Greensboro, N.C.: Compute! Publications, 1986. A good treatment of DTP technology, mainly IBM PC based. Also deals with some style issues.

Digital Imaging

Beale, Stephen, and James Cavuoto. *The Scanner Book*. Torrance, Calif.: Micro Publishing Press, 1989. A good general introduction to theory, software, hardware, and projects that digital imaging affords. A good place to start.

Busch, David D. *The Complete Scanner Handbook for Desktop Publishers, PC Edition.* Homewood, Ill.: Dow-Jones Irwin, 1990. A Macintosh edition is available by the same author.

Glover, Gary. *Image Scanning for Desktop Publishers*. Blue Ridge Summit, Pa.: Windcrest/Tab Books, 1990.

Holzmann, Gerald J. *Beyond Photography, the Digital Darkroom*. Englewood Cliffs, N.J.: Prentice Hall, 1988. Some of the theory of digital imaging.

Jensen, John R. *Introductory Digital Image Processing: A Remote Sensing Perspective*. Englewood Cliffs, N.J.: Prentice Hall, 1986.

Roth, Steve, Chris Dickman, and Salvatore Parascandolo. *ScanJet Unlimited*. Berkeley, Calif.: Peachpit Press, 1989.

Future Technologies

Buddine, Laura, and Elizabeth King. *The Brady Guide to CD-ROM*. New York: Brady Books, 1990.

Cutala, Al. *Technology Projection Modeling of Future Computer Systems*. Englewood Cliffs, N.J.: Prentice Hall, 1990.

Hsu, Jeffrey, and Joseph Kusnan. *The Fifth Generation: The Future of Computer Technology*. Blue Ridge Summit, Pa.: Windcrest/Tab Books, 1987. A look at hardware and software innovations that will shape the next generation of computers.

Nelson, Theodor. *Literary Machines*. Sausalito, Calif.: Mindful Press, 1981. Send $25 to Mindful Press at 3020 Bridgeway #295. Digital documents and information networks.

Graphical User Interface Theory

Apple Computer. *The Human Interface Guidelines: The Apple Desktop Interface*. Reading, Mass.: Addison-Wesley, 1988. The guidelines for the Apple Macintosh interface.

Bolt, Richard. *The Human Interface: Where People and Computers Meet*. New York: Van Nostrand Reinhold, 1984.

Laurel, Brenda, ed. *The Art of Human-Interface Design*. Reading, Mass.: Addison-Wesley, 1990.

History

Juliussen, Egil, and Karen Juliussen. *The Computer Industry Almanac*. New York: Brady Books, 1990.

Kidder, Tracy. *The Soul of a New Machine*. New York: Avon Books, 1981. A Pulitzer Prize-winning account of the development of the Eagle minicomputer at Data General. Burnout and triumph in the high-tech industry.

Levy, Steve. *Hackers: The Heroes of the Computer Revolution*. New York: Bantam Doubleday Dell, 1984. An entertaining introduction to the beginning of the computer industry, when men were men, machines were big, and Chinese food was served late into the night.

Nelson, Ted. *Computer Lib/Dream Machine*. Redmond, Wash.: Tempus Books, 1974, rev. ed. 1987. Before the first personal computer even shipped, Ted Nelson spelled out the principles for interactive systems, hypertext, image synthesis, and computer education in a visionary book that is a cult classic.

Smarte, Gene, and Andrew Reinhardt. "15 Years of Bits, Bytes, and Other Great Moments." *Byte Magazine*, September 1990, p. 369. Wow, great fun.

IBM PC

The Cobb Group: Lori L. Lorenz and R. Michael O'Mara. *Windows 3 Companion*. Redmond, Wash.: Microsoft Press, 1990.

Dvorak, John and Nick Anis. *Dvorak's Guide to DOS and PC Performance.* Berkely, Calif.: Osborme/McGraw Hill, 1991.

Glossbrenner, Alfred and Nick Anis. Glossbrenner's Complete Hard Disk Handbook. Berkeley, Calif.: Osborne/McGraw Hill. 1990. The best PC hard disk management book available.

IBM Personal System/2 Reference Guide. White Plains, N.Y.: IBM Corp., IBM US Marketing and Services.

InfoWorld Product Guide, vols. 1 and 2. New York: Brady Books, 1990. A compilation of hardware and software product reviews that appeared in 1989 for IBM PCs and clones.

Lorenz, Lori and Michael O'Mara. *Windows 3 Companion.* Redmond, Wash.: Microsoft Press, 1990.

Nelson, Kay Yarborough. *The Little Windows Book.* Berkeley, Calif: Peachpit Press, 1990. A good short introductory text.

Norton, Peter. *Inside the IBM PC and PS/2,* 3d ed. New York: Brady Books, 1989.

Person, Ron, and Karen Rose. *Using Microsoft Windows*, 2d ed. Carmel, Ind.: Que Corporation, 19 .

Seymour, Jim. *Jim Seymour PC Productivity Bible.* New York: Brady Books, 1991.

Somerson, Paul. *PC DOS Power Tools,* 2d ed. New York: Bantam Books, 1990. As good as it can get for DOS users.

Stinson, Craig, and Nancy Andrews. *Running Windows.* Redmond, Wash.: Microsoft Press, 1990.

The Windows Shopping Guide. Beaverton, Ore.: White Fox Communications. A product guide with a summary of all Windows-based products. Updated twice yearly.

Wolverton, Van. *Running MS DOS,* 5th ed. Redmond, Wash.: Microsoft Press, 1991. The definitive introduction to MS-DOS, a four million seller.

Macintosh

Aaker, Sharon Zardeko. *The Macintosh Bible,* 3d ed., ed. Arthur Naiman. Berkeley, Calif.: Goldstein and Blair, 1990. Tips, tricks, and traps for the Macintosh from the masters.

———. *The Macintosh Companion: The Basics and Beyond.* Reading, Mass.: Addison-Wesley, 1991. Basic introduction.

Apple Computer. *Technical Introduction to the Macintosh Family.* Reading, Mass.: Addison-Wesley, 1989. An excellent overview of the internal workings of the Macintosh.

————. *Programmer's Introduction to the Macintosh Family.*

————. *Guide to the Macintosh Family Hardware,* 2d Ed..

Danuloff, Craig, and Deke McClelland. *Encyclopedia Macintosh.* Alameda, Calif.: Sybex, Inc., 1991. A valuable general reference to the Macintosh.

Danuloff, Craig. *System 7 Book.* Chapel Hill, NC: Ventana Press, 1991.

Heid, Jim. *Macworld Complete Mac Handbook.* San Mateo, Calif.: IDG Books Worldwide, 1991. The best introduction to Macintosh hardware and software.

Heid, Jim, and Peter Norton. *Inside the Apple Macintosh.* New York: Simon & Schuster/Brady Books, 1989.

LeVitus, Bob. *Dr. Macintosh.* Reading, Mass.: Addison-Wesley, 1989. Tips and techniques.

Lu, Cary. *The Apple Macintosh Book,* 3d ed. Redmond, Wash.: Microsoft Press, 1988. Good, but dated.

Poole, Lon. *Macworld Guide to System 7.0.* San Mateo, Calif.: IDG Books Worldwide, 1991.

McClelland, Deke. *Painting on the Macintosh.* Homewood, Ill.: Dow-Jones Irwin, 1990.

Nelson, Kay Yarborough. *The Little System 7 Book.* Berkeley, Calif.: Peachpit Press, 1991.

The Macintosh Buyer's Guide. Vero Beach, Fla.: Redgate Communications, 1991. A listing of products, hardware, and software for the Macintosh. Published quarterly.

Rose, Carla and Frank Rose. *The First Book of the Mac.* Carmel, Ind.: Sams, 1991. A nice beginners' introduction to the Mac.

Rose, Frank. *West of Eden: The End of Innocence at Apple Computer.* New York: Penguin, 1990. A history of the early days of Apple Computer up to about the time of Steve Jobs leaving.

Multimedia

Anderson, Carol, and Mark D. Ljaov. *Authoring Multimedia.* Glenview, Ill.: Scott, Foresman, 1990.

Bove, Tony, and Cheryl Bove. *Que's Macintosh Multimedia Handbook.* Carmel, Ind.: Que Corporation, 1990.

Brand, Stuart. *The Media Lab: Inventing the Future at MIT.* New York: Viking Press, 1987. A chronicle of several months at the think tank for media technology at MIT.

Brown, Michael. *Desktop Video Production.* Blue Ridge Summit, Pa.: Windcrest/Tab Books, 1991. Using the Commodore Amiga and Macintosh computers to create video productions. Considers hardware, software, and project management issues.

Efreim, Joel Lawrence. *Video Tape Production and Communication Techniques.* Blue Ridge Summit, Pa.: Tab Books, 1972.

Martin, James. *Hyperdocuments and How to Create Them.* Englewood Cliffs, N.J.: Prentice Hall, 1989.

Roncarelli, Robi. *The Computer Animation Dictionary.* New York: Springer-Verlag, 1989.

Wilson, Stephen. *Multimedia Design with HyperCard.* Englewood Cliffs, N.J.: Prentice Hall, 1990.

Networks/Communication

Apple Computer. *Inside Appletalk.* Reading, Mass.: Addison-Wesley, 1989.

———. *Speaking of Networks.* Reading, Mass.: Addison-Wesley, 1990 .

———. *Understanding Computer Networks.* Reading, Mass.: Addison-Wesley, 1989. The best introductory book for a beginner.

Banks, Michael. *Understanding FAX and Electronic Mail.* Carmel, Ind.: Howard Sams, 1990. A beginner's introduction.

Bove, Tony, and Cheryl Rhodes. *The Well-Connected Macintosh.* Cambridge, Mass.: Harcourt Brace Jovanovich, 1987.

Durr, Michael, and Mark Gibbs. *Networking Personal Computers,* 3d ed. Carmel, Ind.: Que Corporation, 1989. A general treatment, more geared toward larger computers and large networks.

Harriman, Cynthia. *MS DOS-Mac Connection.* New York: Brady Books, 1988. Good general coverage, but getting a bit dated.

Heid, Gilbert. *Understanding Data Communications,* 3rd Ed. Carmel, Ind.: Howard Sams, 1991.

Michel, Stephen. *IBM PC and Macintosh Networking.* Carmel, Ind.: Howard Sams, 1990.

Needleman, Raphael. *Inforworld: Understanding Networks.* Englewood Cliffs, N.J.: Prentice Hall, 1990.

Rue, Jim. *The ABC's of On-Line Services.* Alameda, Calif.: Sybex, 1991. An overview of computer telecommunications.

Schatt, Stan. *Understanding Local Area Networks.* Carmel, IN: Sams, 1990.

Stallings, William. *The Business Guide to Local Area Networks.* Carmel, In: Sams, 1990.

PostScript

Adobe Systems. *PostScript Language Tutorial and Cookbook*. Reading, Mass.: Addison-Wesley, 1985.

Braswell, Frank. *Inside PostScript*. Berkeley, Calif.: Peachpit Press, 1989.

Kunkel, Gerald. *Graphic Design with PostScript*. Glenview, Ill.: Scott, Foresman, 1990.

Roth, Stephen, ed. *Real World PostScript*. Reading, Mass.: Addison-Wesley, 1988.

Smith, Ross. *Learning PostScript: A Visual Approach*. Berkeley, Calif.: Peachpit Press, 1989.

Thomas, Barry. *A PostScript Cookbook*. New York: Van Nostrand Reinhold, 1988.

Presentations

Meilach, D. *Dynamics of Presentation Graphics*. Homewood, Ill.: Dow Jones-Irwin, 1990.

Rabb, Margaret Y., ed. *The Presentation Design Book*. Chapel Hill, N.C.: Ventana Press, 1990. An introduction to the special design issues required by presentations.

White, Jan V. *Using Charts and Graphs*. New York: R. R. Bowker, 1984.

Printing

Beach, Mark, Steve Shepro, and Ken Russon. *Getting It Printed*. Portland, Ore.: Coast to Coast Books, 1986. A book by printers on printing. Discusses how to work with printers and graphic arts services to assure quality, stay on schedule, and control costs. It's not much concerned with the role of computers in this technology.

International Paper Company. *Pocket Pal,* 14th ed. Memphis: International Paper, 1989. A concise and informative handbook to graphic arts production. A classic.

The Chicago Manual of Style, 13th ed. Chicago: University of Chicago Press, 1982. Style, technology, printing, all rolled into one. A companion volume exists for electronic publishing.

Service Bureaus

Electronic Publishing & Printing. *2nd Annual Service Bureau Directory.* Send $7.50 to Ms. Jean Miller, Electronic Publishing & Printing, Dept. SBD, 29 N. Wacker Drive, Chicago, Ill. 60606.

TypeWorld. *TypeWorld PostScript Services Directory.* Lists 1,000 service bureaus, whom to contact, and what platforms are supported. Also mentions specific output devices, programs supported, and the number of fonts in each bureau. Send $19.95 plus $3.95 postage and handling to TypeWorld, P.O. Box 170, Salem, N.H. 03079.

Type

Adobe Systems. *Font & Function.* Mountain View, Calif.: Adobe Systems. Adobe's semiannual type library with examples of uses and interesting discussions. Free by calling Adobe at (800) 29-ADOBE.

Beaumont, Michael. *Type: Design, Color, Character, and Use.* Cincinnati: North Light Books, 1987.

Biggs, John R. *Basic Typography.* New York: Watson-Guptill Publications, 1968.

Collier, David. *Collier's Rules for Desktop Design and Typography.* Reading, Mass.: Addison-Wesley, 1990. A typographic *Pocket Pal.*

Cook, Alton, and Roger Fleury. *Type and Color, a Handbook of Creative Combinations.* Rockport, Mass.: 1989.

Fenton, Erfert. *The Font Book,* 2nd ed. Berkeley, Calif.: Peachpit Press, 1991. Creating and managing a Macintosh font library.

Labuz, Ronald. *Typography and Typesetting: Type Design and Manipulation Using Today's Technology.* New York: Van Nostrand Reinhold, 1988. History, technology, and application of typographic principles.

Magazines

AmigaWorld. IDG Communications, 80 Elm Street, Peterborough, N.H. 03458. Covers the Amiga market broadly from a user's perspective.

Bioworld. IO Publishing. 217 South B Street, San Mateo, Calif., 94401. Biotechnology hypermedia magazine.

Byte Magazine. 1 Phoenix Mill Lane, Peterborough, N.H. 03458. Technical reviews and features for all manners of computers. An industry authority with leading edge coverage.

Computer Graphics Review. 730 Boston Post Road, Sudbury, Mass. 01776. A qualified subscription magazine where some of the most insightful articles on graphics may be found. Technology tends to be reviewed at an expert level.

Computer Graphics World. 1 Technology Park Drive, P.O. Box 987, Westford, Mass. 01886. A magazine devoted to the leading edge computer graphics problems.

Design Graphics World. 6255 Barfield Road, Atlanta, Ga. 30328.

The Desktop Publishers Journal. National Association of Desktop Publishers, P.O. Box 1410, Boston, Mass. 02205. A society for DTPers; annual fee, $95.

Electronic Publishing & Printing. 29 N. Wacker Drive, Chicago, Ill. 60606. An industry trade publication with good coverage.

Folio. 6 River Bend, PO Box 4929, Stamford, Conn. 06907. A DTP journal.

InfoWorld. 1060 Marsh Road, #C-200, Menlo Park, Calif. 94025. A weekly news magazine giving general industry coverage.

ITC Desktop. 2 Dag Hammarskjold Plaza, New York, NY 10017. A DTP journal focused on aspects of type.

Macintosh-Aided Design. Auerback Publishers, 210 South Street, Boston, Mass. 92111. Aimed at design and engineering professionals using the Macintosh. Glossy and well produced with many interesting articles.

MacUser Magazine. Ziff-Davis Publishing Co., 950 Tower Lane, 18th fl., Foster City, Calif. 94404. One of the better Macintosh consumer-oriented trade publications with excellent product reviews.

MacWeek. 525 Brannan Street, San Francisco, Calif. 94107. The insider's power tool for the Macintosh. It is a very well written, insightful, and timely magazine. This author owns just one Mac the Knife coffee cup. So far.

MacWorld Magazine. 501 Second Street, San Francisco, Calif. 94107. Monthly coverage of matters mostly Macintosh, reviews, and in-depth articles with excellent industry coverage.

Media Letter. P.O. Box 142075, Coral Gables, Fa. 33114. A multimedia newsletter.

New Media Age. PO Box 1771, Riverton, N.J., 08077-9771. An industry trade magazine that surveys multimedia technology on several computer platforms.

PC Letter. 3 Lagoon Drive, Suite 160 Redwood City, Calif. 94065. Stewart Alsop III is the premier microcomputer industry guru, and this is his rag. Read by all the movers and shakers in the personal computer industry before they shake and move; Alsop has great insight.

PC Magazine. 1 Park Avenue, New York, NY 10016. One of the best industry journals with excellent reviews and editorials and leading edge coverage. *PC Magazine* is to the PC what *The Chicago Manual of Style* is to writers, definitive.

PC Week. 110 Marsh Drive, #103, Foster City, Calif. 94404. A PC user's power tool. Fast-breaking industry news.

PC World. 501 Second Street, #600, San Francisco, Calif. 94107. A PC magazine aimed at the user, not overwhelmingly technical.

PC/Computing. 4 Cambridge Center, Cambridge, Mass. 02142. A good magazine for general PC coverage.

Personal Computing. See *PC/Computing*, which replaced it.

Personal Publishing. 191 S. Gary Avenue, Carol Stream, Ill. 60188. Reviews and articles on DTP, Mac, and PC. A very useful and valuable magazine for DTP.

Publish. PC World Communications, 501 Second Street, San Francisco, Calif. 94107. Good balanced reporting of both Mac and PC DTP. Probably the most popular magazine on DTP.

RELease 1.0. New York, N.Y. Ester Dyson's newsletter is one of the most widely read insider commentaries in the business. A good place to look for trends and announcements before they happen.

Seybold Report on Desktop Publishing. 6922 Wildlife Road, Malibu, Calif. 90265. The Seybolds are gurus to the DTP community, and many industry announcements take place at their semiannual conferences This report is technical and in-depth with excellent insight for the experienced DTPer.

Typeworld. PO Box 170, 35 Pelham Road, Salem, NH 03079.

Verbum: Journal of Personal Computer Aesthetics. Verbum, P.O. Box 15439, San Diego, Calif. 92115. A journal of computer art, principles, and practices.

VideoMaker. 381 East 4th Street, Chico, Calif. 95928. Covers desktop video production.

The Weigrand Report P.O. Box 647, Gales Ferry, Conn. 06335. A highly respected Macintosh newsletter with a desktop publishing focus.

Product Index

Note: *Prices listed are 1991 retail, and subject to change, as are program version numbers. Always shop around for the best prices.*

A

Above Disk
Above Software
2698 White Road, Suite 200
Irvine, CA 92714
(800)344-0116 or (714)851-2283
Memory management utility.
$119 V. 4.0 PC.
Also, **Above Utilities for DOS**, utilities package, $119.

AccuText
Xerox Imaging Systems/Datacopy Products
1215 Terra Bella Avenue, Mountain View, CA 94043
(415)965-7900 or (800)821-2898
OCR package. $995 Mac.

AccuWeather Forecaster
Metacomet Software
PO Box 31337
Hartford, CT 06103
(800)345-9111
Software access for the AccuWeather information service.
$89.95 V. 1.08 Mac.

ActionMedia 750
Intel Corporation
3065 Bowers Avenue
Santa Clara, CA 95051
(408)765-8080
DVI compression boards. $5,000 PC.

ADDmotion
Motion Works
1334 W. 6th Avenue, Suite 300
Vancouver, BC V6H 1A6 Canada
(604)732-0289.
HyperCard animation program.
$295 Mac.

Adobe Illustrator
Adobe Microsystems
1585 Charleston Road
Mountain View, CA 94039-7900
(415)961-4400
Technical drawing program. $495 Win3, V. 3.0 Mac.

Adobe Photoshop, see **Photoshop**

Adobe Streamline
Adobe Microsystems
1585 Charleston Road
Mountain View, CA 94039-7900
(415)961-4400
Raster-to-vector autotrace application. $395 Mac, PC.

Adobe Type Library
Adobe Systems
1585 Charleston Road
Mountain View, CA 94039-7900
(415)961-4400
The entire library on a hard drive is available for around $7,000. Individual fonts cost $95 to $370.

Adobe Type Manager
Adobe Systems
1585 Charleston Road
Mountain View, CA 94039-7900
(415)961-4400
Font rendering utility. $99 V. 2.0 Mac, Win3, OS/2.

AdStylist
75 Kneeland Street
Boston, MA 02111
(617)426-3577
Ad production page layout software. Mac, Camex.

AdWriter
Mycro-Tek, Incorporated
9229 East 37th Street North
Wichita, KS 67226
(800)835-2055
Display ad page layout software.
 Mac.

After Dark
Berkeley Systems, Inc.
1700 Shattuck Avenue
Berkeley, CA 94709
(415)540-5536
Great funky screen saver. $39.95
 Mac, Win.

Aldus FreeHand
Aldus Corporation
411 First Avenue S., Suite 200
Seattle, WA 98104
(206)622-5500
Technical drawing program. $595
 V. 3.0 Mac.

Aldus PageMaker
Aldus Corporation
411 First Avenue S., Suite 200
Seattle, WA 98104
(206)622-5500
Page layout program. $795 V. 4.0
 Mac, $795 Win3, $795 OS/2.

Aldus Persuasion
Aldus Corporation
411 First Avenue S., Suite 200
Seattle, WA 98104
(206)622-5500
Presentation graphics program.
 $495 V. 2.0 Mac, $595 V. 2.0
 Win.

Aldus Preprint
Aldus Corporation
411 First Avenue S., Suite 200
Seattle, WA 98104
(206)622-5500
Color separation program. $495
 V. 1.0 Mac.

Am286LX/ZX IP
Advanced Micro Devices
901 Thompson Place
PO Box 3453
Sunnyvale, CA 94088
(408)732-2400 or (800)222-9323
IBM PC AT on a chip.

America OnLine
Quantum Computer Services,
 Incorporated
8619 Westwood Center Drive
Vienna, VA 22182
(800)227-6364
HyperCard-like on-line service.
 $5/hour for connect time. Mac,
 Win, DOS.

Ami Professional
Samna Corporation
5600 Glenridge Drive, Suite 300
Atlanta, GA 30342
(404)851-0007
Word processor. $495 Win3.

Amiga, see **Commodore Amiga**

AmigaVision
Commodore Business Machines,
 Incorporated
1200 Wilson Drive
West Chester, PA 19380
(215)431-9100
Multimedia authoring program.
 $149 Amiga.

Animation Works
Gold Disk Software Incorporated
5155 Spectrum Way, Unit 5
Mississauga, Ontario L4W 5A1
 Canada
Animation program.
$ V. 1.0 Mac, Amiga.

Animator
Autodesk, Incorporated
2320 Marinship Way
Sausalito, CA 94965
(800)445-5415 or (415)332-2344
Multimedia authoring system,
 $299. Autoshade shading pro-
 gram, $500.

AnyGraph
Compatible Systems Corporation
2900 Center Green Court S.
PO Drawer 17220
Boulder, CO 80308
(303)444-9532
PC-to-Mac graphics file translation
 utility. $95 Mac to PC.

AnyText
Compatible Systems Corporation
2900 Center Green Court S.
PO Drawer 17220
Boulder, CO 80308
(303)444-9532
PC-to-Mac text file translation util-
 ity. $95

AppMaker
Bowers Development
PO Box 9
Lincoln Center, MA 01773
(508)369-8175
Interface builder. $295 Mac.

ARC
System Enhancement Association
21 New Street
Wayne, NJ 07470
(201)694-4710
PC telecommunications file com-
 pression standard. $50 V. 6.02
 DOS.

ARLAN 450
Telesystems SLW, Incorporated
85 Scarsdale Road, #201
Don Mills, Ontario, Canada M3B
 2R2
(416)441-9966
Wireless radio LAN. $15,000.

Array Scanner-One
Array Technologies
7730 Pardee Lane
Oakland, CA 94621
(415)633-3000
High-end color scanner. ca.
 $25,000 Mac, PC.

Art Importer
Altsys
269 Renner Road
Richardson, TX 75080
(214)424-4888
Font utility. $149 V. 2.0 Mac.

Artline
Digital Research
Box DRI
70 Garden Court
Monterey, CA 93942
(408)649-3896
Strong drawing program on GEM
 interface. $595 V. 2.0 PC.

Arts & Letters
Computer Support Corporation
15926 Midway Road
Dallas, TX 75244
(214)661-8960
Presentation program. $695 V. 3.0
Win3. Includes Arts & Letters
Graphics Editor draw program.
Arts & Letters Composer
$395.

Artus
Trony GmbH
Kufsteiner Strasse A2
D-A000 Berlin 62,
West Germany 30 853 6077
Digital image processing pro-
gram. $500–$600 Win3.

Ashlar Vellum
Ashlar, Incorporated
1290 Oakmead Parkway,
Suite 218
Sunnyvale, CA 94086
(408)746-3900
2D CAD. $995 V. 1.0 Mac, $1995
Win3. A 3D package is planned.

Ask*Me System 2000
Innovative Communications Systems, Incorporated
2534 26th Avenue S.
Fargo, ND 58103
(701)293-1004
DOS-based multimedia authoring
system. V. 2.01 PC.

Aspects
Group Technologies, Incorporated
000 N. Taylor Street, Suite 204
Arlington, VA 22203
(703)528-1555
Groupware document conferencing software. $299 per user Mac
V. 1.0.

AT&T Mail
Room 1813
5000 Hadley Road
S. Plainsfield, NJ 07080
(800)367-7225
On-line service. See also **MailFax**.

Atari 1040ST^E
Atari
1196 Borregas Avenue
Sunnyvale, CA 94089-1302
(408)745-2000
$2,395 PC.

Atex Design Software
Atex Magazine Publishing Systems
32 Wiggins Avenue
Bedford, MA 01730
(617)275-8300
Networked magazine production
system.

Audiomedia
Digidesign, Incorporated
1360 Willow Road, Suite 101
Menlo Park, CA 94025
(415)688-0600
Recording, editing, and playback
system.

Authorware Professional
Authorware
8500 Normandale Lake Boulevard, 9th floor
Minneapolis, MN 55347
(612)921-8555
Multimedia authoring system.
$8,000 V. 1.6 Mac.

AutoCAD
Autodesk, Incorporated
2320 Marinship Way
Sausalito, CA 94965
(415)332-2344
3D professional CAD package.
$3,000 V. 10 Mac. PC, OS/2.

Autographix, Incorporated
100 Fifth Avenue
Waltham, MA 02154
(800)548-8558 or (617)890-8558
Slide imaging service. A network
of twenty-two worldwide
centers.

Avid1/ Media Composer
Avid Technology, Incorporated
3 Burlington Woods, Suite 330
Burlington, MA 01803
(617)221-6789
Video editing and production system. $60,000–$80,000.

B

BackFAX
Solution Incorporated
30 Commerce Street
PO Box 783
Williston, VT 05495
(802)865-9220 or FAX (802)865-
9224
Fax software. $245 V. 1.02 Mac.

Barneyscan
Barneyscan Corporation
1125 Atlantic Avenue
Alameda, CA 94301
(415)521-3388
A 35mm desktop color slide scanner.

Belser Knowledge Services
54 West 21st Street, Suite 309
New York, NY 10010
(212)727-3888
Multimedia videodisk authoring
service.

Bernoulli Box
Iomega Corporation
1821 W. 4000 S.
Roy, UT 84067
(801)778-3000
Removable 44 MByte hard car-
tridge disk drive. $2,199 Mac,
PC.

BLAST
Communications Research Group
5615 Corporate Boulevard
Baton Rouge, LA 70808
(504)923-0888 or (800)242-5278
Telecommunications package and
file transfer utility. **MacBLAST**,
$195 Mac; **MS/DOS BLAST**,
$195 PC.

Bomber
Inline Design
70 W. 95th Street, Suite 26F
New York, NY 10025
(212)222-4837
HyperCard simulation game.
$39.95 V. 1.3 Mac.

The Bread Board System
eSoft, Incorporated
15200 E. Girard Avenue, Suite 2550
Aurora, CO 80145
(303)699-6565
Bulletin board system. $299.95 (1 user), $895 (16 users), $1,495 (32 users). PC.

Broadcast Titler
Innovision Technologies
1933 Davis Street, Suite 238
San Leandro, CA 94577
(415)638-8432
Character generator. $299.95 Amiga.

C

C-Cube CL550 Processor
C-Cube Microsystems, Incorporated
339-A West Trimble Road
San Jose, CA 95131
(408)944-6300
JPEG image compression microchip.

CA-Cricket Draw
Computer Associates International, Incorporated
40 Great Valley Parkway
Malvern, PA 19355
(800)531-5236
Draw program. $295 V. 1.2 Mac, Win3.

CA-Cricket Graph
Computer Associates International, Incorporated
40 Great Valley Parkway
Malvern, PA 19355
(800)531-5236
Charting and graphing package. $195 V. 1.2 Mac, Win3.

CA-Cricket Presents!
Computer Associates International, Incorporated
40 Great Valley Parkway
Malvern, PA 19355
(800)531-5236
Presentation package. $495 V. 1.2 Mac, Win3.

Calibrator
Barco, Incorporated
1000 Cobb Place Boulevard
Kennesaw, GA 30144
(404)590-7900
Calibrated color display system $7,600. Display $6,700, sensor (Optisense) $795, software (CalibratorTalk) $1,950.

Canon CLC 500
Canon USA, Incorporated
1 Canon Plaza
Lake Success, NY 11042-1113
(516)488-6700
Color laser copier that accepts input from a variety of sources. $49,000 base, $83,000 complete.

Canvas
Deneba Software
3305 NW 74th Avenue
Miami, FL 33122
(305)594-6965
Draw program. $395.95 V. 3.0 Mac.

Capture
Mainstay
5311-B Derry Avenue
Agoura Hills, CA 91301
(818)991-6540
Screen capture utility. $79.95 V. 3.0 Mac.

Carbon Copy Mac
Microm Software Division
55 Federal Road
Danbury, CT 06810
(617)551-1999
Remote control and file transfer software. $199 (1 user) Mac.

cc:Mail
cc:Mail, Incorporated
2141 Landings Drive
Building T
Mountain View, CA 94043
(800)448-2500 or (415)961-8800
Electronic-mail application. $695 (25 users). PC V. 3.1, $495 (25 users) Mac V. 1.1. $595 additional 75 users. **cc:Mail Gateway** $1,295.

Charisma
Micrografx, Incorporated
1303 Arapaho
Richardson, TX 75081
(800)733-3729 or (214)234-1769
A graphing and charting presentation package. $495 Win.

Claris CAD
Claris Corporation
5201 Patrick Henry Drive, Suite 58168
Santa Clara, CA 95052
(408)727-8227
2D CAD package. Mac market leader. $899 V. 2.0 Mac.

Click Change
Dubl-Click Software, Incorporated
9316 Deering Road
Chatsworth, CA 91311
(818)700-9525
Macintosh interface modifying software. $59.95 Mac.

CM-64
RolandCorp US
7200 Dominion Circle
Los Angeles, CA 90040
(213)685-5141
Sound module and MIDI adapter. $1,395 PC, Amiga.

Colony
Mindscape, Incorporated
3444 Dundee Road
Northbrook, IL 60062
(708)480-1948 (order) or (415)883-3000 (general)
Adventure game. $39.95 Mac. Color version $15 additional.

Color Calibration Software
Technical Publishing Services
2205 Sacramento
San Francisco, CA 94115
(415)921-8509
Postscript imagesetter calibration software. $695 V. 2.0.3.

Color Display System
Radius
1710 Fortune Drive
San Jose, CA 95131
(408)434-1010.
19 inches.

Color MacCheese
Delta Tao Software, Incorporated
760 Harvard Avenue
Sunnyvale, CA 94087
(408)730-9336
A full 32-bit color paint program.$99 Mac.

ColorBoard 364
RasterOps Corporation
2500 Walsh Avenue
Santa Clara, CA 95051
(800)468-7600 or (408)562-4200
Color graphics board. $1,995 Mac.
   ColorBoard 264 $745

ColorGetter, see **Optronics ColorGetter**

ColorSetter, see **Optronics ColorSetter**

ColorSpace FX
Mass Microsystems
810 W. Maude Avenue
Sunnyvale, CA 94086
(800)522-7979 or (408)522-1200
Video processor board. $3,499.95 Mac. **ColorSpace IIi** and **Plus/SE** are for other Macintosh models.

Colorsqueeze
Eastman Kodak Company
Rochester, NY 14560-0519
(800)445-6325 xt. 110
Color file compression utility.$179 Mac.

ColorStudio
Letraset USA
40 Eisenhower Drive
Paramus, NJ 07653
(201)845-6100
Color digital image processing program. $995 V. 1.1 Mac.

ColorWriter 400
Synergy
Billerica MA.
$120,000.

CommGate
Solution Incorporated
30 Commerce Street
PO Box 783
Williston, VT 05495
(802)865-9220 or (802)865-9224 fax
Gateway from E-Mail to MCI Mail. $245 V. 1.02 Mac.

Commodore Amiga
Commodore Business Machines, Incorporated
1200 Wilson Drive
West Chester, PA 19380
(215)431-9100
Personal computers: 2000, $2500; 2500, $3,799.

Compactor, see **Compact Pro V**

Compact Pro V. 1.30
Bill Goodman
109 Davis Avenue
Brookline, MA 02146
File compression utility. **Extractor** is the decompression utility. $25 V. 1.20 Mac.

Compton's Multimedia Encylopedia
Britannica Software, Incorporated
345 Fourth Street
San Francisco, CA 94107
(800)533-0130
CD-ROM disk. $795 PC.

Compugraphic Selectset 5000
Agfa Compugraphic
90 Industrial Way
Wilmington, MA 01887
(508)658-5600
Imagesetter.

CompuServe
CompuServe Information Services
PO Box 20212
5000 Arlington Centre Boulevard
Columbus, OH 43220
(800)848-8199
World's largest on-line subscriber service. $13/hour connect charge.

CompuServe Information Manager
CompuServe Information Services
PO Box 20212
5000 Arlington Center Boulevard
Columbus, OH 43220
(800)848-8199
Fax service. Text is 75¢ for the first 1,000 characters, 25¢ for each additional 1,000 characters. No graphics.

CompuServe Navigator see **Navigator**

Connect Business Information Network
Connect, Incorporated
10161 Bubb Road
Cupertino, CA 95104
(408)973-0110 or (800)262-2638
On-line service. $149.95 with $10 (prime time) or $5 (off peak) connect charges. V. 1.5 Mac.

ConvertIt!
Heizer Software
PO Box 232019
Pleasant Hill, CA 94523
(800)888-7667
HyperCard-to-Toolbox conversion utility. $199 Mac/PC.

The Coordinator
Action Technologies, Incorporated
1145 Atlanta Avenue, Suite 101
Alameda, CA 94501
(800)624-2162
Groupware system. V. 2.1 PC.

CorelDraw
Corel Systems Corporation
1600 Carling Avenue
Ottawa, Ontario, K1Z 8R7 Canada
(613)728-8200
Excellent object-oriented draw program for the PC with sophisticated type manipulation support. $595 V. 2.0 Win3, V. 1.0 OS/2.

Cornerstone
Scitex America Corporation
8 Oak Park Drive
Bedford, MA 01730
(617)257-5150
Desktop packaging development system, hardware and software collection. ca. $15,000 Mac.

Correct Grammar
Lifetree Software
33 New Montgomery Street, Suite 1260
San Francisco, CA 94105
(415)541-7864
Grammar checker or proofreader. $79 Mac.

Cosmic Osmo CD ROM
Activision
3885 Bohannon Drive
Menlo Park, CA 94025
(415)329-0500
HyperCard game. $79.95 Mac.

Crosfield Studio 800 and 9500 Series
Crosfield Electronics, Incorporated
65 Harristown Road
Glen Rock, NJ 07452
(201)447-5800
Color electronic prepress systems. See also **Lightspeed Color Layout System.**

Crosstalk XVI
DCA/Crosstalk Communications
1000 Alderman Drive
Alpharetta, GA 30201-4299
(404)442-4000 or (800)241-6393
Telecommunications software.
$195 V. 3.71 PC; **Crosstalk for Windows,** $195 V. 1.0 Win; **Crosstalk MK 4,** $245 V. 1.1, PC.

CrystalEyes
StereoGraphics Corporation
2171-H E. Francisco Boulevard
San Francisco, CA
(415)459-4500
Stereo 3D viewing system. Requires stereo-ready monitor and graphics board. $1,995. Total system ca. $10,000.

CrystalPrint Publisher
Qume
500 Yosemite Drive
Milpitas, CA 95035
(408)942-4000
LCD PostScript clone printer. $4,499. Personal non-PostScript printer: $1,995. CrystalPrint Series II.

Cubase
Steinberg/Jones
17700 Raymer Street, Suite 1001
Northridge, CA 94107
(818)993-4091
Music sequencer. $579 V. 2.0 Mac, Amiga

The Curator
Solutions Incorporated
PO Box 783
Williston, VT 05495
(802)865-9220
Art cataloger. $139.95 Mac.

Cyberchrome 36B Electronic Color PrePress Imaging System
CyberChrome, Incorporated
5 Science Park
PO Box 9565
New Haven, CT 06536
(203)786-5151
PostScript color electronic prepress system.

D

Da Vinci eMail
Da Vinci Systems Corporation
PO Box 17499
Raleigh, NC 27619-7449
(800) DA VINCI
$445 (8 users) to $1145 (site) DOS/Win3. E-Mail system.

Daetwyler Printers' Gauge
Max Daetwyler Corporation
310 Oser Avenue
Hauppauge, NY 11788
(516)231-3232
Gauge for determining line screen and screen angle.

Data Interchange Standards Association, Inc.
1800 Diagonal Road, Suite 355
Alexandria, VA 22314
(703)548-7005
Ask for the X12/DISA Information Manual, ASCX12S.

DataProducts LZR 1260i
Dataproducts Corporation
6200 Canoga Avenue
Woodland Hills, CA 91367
(818)887-8800
A 300 dpi laser printer. $5,995 Mac.

dbPublisher

Digital Composition Systems, Incorporated
1715 North Western Avenue
Phoenix, AZ 85021
(602)870-7667
Database publishing system. PC.

DECAdry

Alvin & Company
PO Box 188
Windsor, CT 06095
(203)243-8991
Color laser paper, many designs. Boxes of 10 or 100 available.

Delphi

General Videotex Corporation
3 Blackstone Street
Cambridge, MA 02139
(617)491-3342 or (800)544-4005
On-line information service.

DeltaGraph

DeltaPoint, Incorporated
200G Heritage Harbor
Monterey, CA 93940
(800)367-4334 or (408)648-4000
PostScript graphing and charting package.$195 V. 1.5 Mac. All computers.

Deluxe Music Construction Set

Electronic Arts
1820 Gateway Drive
San Mateo, CA 94404
(415)571-7171
Music scoring program. $129 V. 2.5 Mac.

Deluxe Recorder

Electronic Arts
1820 Gateway Drive
San Mateo, CA 94404
(415)571-7171
Music sequencer. $149.95 Mac.

Designer, see **Micrografx Designer**

DesignStudio

Letraset USA
40 Eisenhower Drive
Paramus, NJ 07653
(201)845-6100
Page layout program. $795 Mac.

DeskDraw/DeskPaint

Zedcor, Incorporated
4500 E. Speedway, Suite 22
Tucson, AZ 85712
(602)881-8101 or (800)482-4567
Desk accessory draw/paint package. Great DTP companion. $129.95 V. 3.0 Mac.

DeskJet 500

Hewlett-Packard
19310 Pruneridge Avenue
Cupertino, CA 95014
(800)752-0900
Excellent low-cost ink jet printers. Has some built-in typefaces. Adobe Type Manager support. Mac model requires SCSI interface. $729 PC, Mac or **DeskWriter** $995

DeskSet

G.O. Graphics
18 Ray Avenue
Burlington, MA 01803
(617)229-8900
Typesetting program. $995 PC.

Desktop Express

Dow Jones & Company, Incorporated
PO Box 300
Princeton, NJ 08543
(609)520-4641
GUI communication software for MCI Mail. $149 Mac, PC.

DeskWriter, see **DeskJet**

DESQView V. 2.26

Quarterdeck Office Systems
150 Pico Boulevard
Santa Monica, CA 90405
(213)392-9851
Multitasking windowing environment. $129.95. **DESQView 386,** $219.95.

Dialog

Dialog Information Services, Incorporated
3460 Hillview Avenue
Palo Alto, CA 94394
(415)858-2700 or (800)334-2564
On-line information system. All computers.

Dicomed

DuPont & Fujifilm Electronic Imaging Company
11401 Rupp Drive
Burnsville, MN 55337
(800)888-7979
Slide imaging service.

Digital Darkroom

Silicon Beach Software, Incorporated
9770 Carroll Center Road, Suite J
San Diego, CA 92126
(619)695-6956
Grayscale digital image processing program. $395 V. 2.0 Mac.

Dimensions

Artbeats
Box 20083
San Bernadino, CA 92406
(714)881-1200
Pattern and texture clip art. $79.95 Mac, PC (3 800 KByte disks-EPS).

Director

MacroMind
410 Townsend, Suite 408
San Francisco, CA 94107
Multimedia authoring package. $695 V. 2.0 Mac, V. 1.0 Win3

The Director

The Right Answer Group
Box 3699
Torrence, CA 90510
Multimedia authoring program. $69.95 Amiga.

Disinfectant
John Norstad
Academic Computing and Network Services
Northwestern University
2129 Sheridan Road
Evanston, IL 60208
Bitnet: jln@nuacc
Internet: jln@acns.nwu.edu
CompuServe: 76666,573
AppleLink: A0173
Virus detection, prevention, and elimination utility. Available from most on-line services. Free V. 1.8 Mac.

DiskDoubler
Salient Software
124 University Avenue, Suite 103
Palo Alto, CA 94301
(415)852-9567
File compression utility. $79 V. 3.0 Mac.

DiskTools Plus
Fifth Generation Software
10049 Reiger Road
Baton Rouge, LA 70809
(504)291-7221 or (800)873-4384
File management utility. $49.95 Mac.

DiskTop
CESoftware, Incorporated
1854 Fuller Road
West Des Moines, IA 50265
(800)523-7638 or (515)224-1995
File management utility. $99.95 Mac.

DisplayAdSpeed
Digital Technology International
500 West 1200 S.
Orem, UT 84058
(801)226-2984
Display advertisement page layout system. Mac.

Distributed Publishing System
Intergraph Corporation
Huntsville, AL
$4,000.

DocuTech Publisher
Xerox Corporation
Long Ridge Road
Stamford, CT 06904
(800)DOCUTECH or (203)968-3000
Advanced 600 dpi 135 ppm document processing and publishing system. $220,000.

DoDOT
Halcyon Software
10297 Cold Harbor Avenue
Cupertino, CA 95014
Screen capture utility. $129 PC.

DOS Mounter
Dyna Communications
50 S. Main Street, 5th floor
Salt Lake City, UT 84144
(801)531-0203
Mounts DOS-formatted floppy disks automatically on a Mac. $89.95 V. 2.0 Mac.

Dow Jones News/Retrieval Membership Package
Dow Jones & Company, Inc.
PO Box 300
Princeton, NJ 08543
(609)520-4641
On-line information service. All computers supported. $29.95 Mac.

Dr. DOS 5.0
Digital Research
PO Box DRI
70 Garden Court
Monterey, CA 93942
(800)443-4200
DOS operating system. $200.

Draw 4D
Adspec Programming
PO Box 13
Sallem, OH 44460
Modeling program. $249.95 Amiga

DrawPerfect
WordPerfect Corporation
1555 North Technology Way
Orem, UT 84057
(801)222-5800
A menued draw program that integrates well with the WordPerfect word processor. DOS.

Dreams
Innovative Data Design, Incorporated
2280 Bates Avenue, Suite A
Concord, CA 94520
(415)680-6818
Good mid-end 2D CAD package. $500 V. 1.1 Mac.

DTP Advisor
Brøderbund
17 Paul Drive
San Raphael, CA 94903-2101
(800)521-6263 or (415)492-3200
Graphics art advisor and project management system. $79.95 Mac.

DynaComm
Future Soft Engineering
1001 S. Dairy Ashford, Suite 203
Houston, TX 77077
(713)496-9400
Telecommunications package. $295 Mac, Win.

DynaFile
Dyna Communications
50 S. Main Street, 5th floor
Salt Lake City, UT 84144
(801)531-0203
Disk drive and software for Macintosh/PC translation. $650 V. 2.8 Mac, $650 V. 1.0 NeXT.

DynaMail
Dyna Communications
50 S. Main Street, 5th floor
Salt Lake City, UT 84144
(801)531-0203
E-Mail software. $295 (5 users) V. 1.01 Mac .

DynaNet
Dyna Communications
50 S. Main Street, 5th floor
Salt Lake City, UT 84144
(801)531-0203
Network operating software. $795 to $3,995 PC, Mac.

DynaPerspective

DynaWare Corporation
1163 Chess Drive, Suite J
Foster City, CA 94404
(415)349-5700
3D CAD visualization software.
$995 V. 2.0 Mac, PC.

E

EasyLink

Western Union Corporation
1 Lake Street
Upper Saddle River, NJ 07458
(201)818-5000
Fax service. Text 55¢ for first
1,250 characters, 35¢ each additional 1,250 characters. Graphics 55¢ for 30 seconds, 35¢ for
additional 30 seconds.

EDI, Spread the Word!

PO Box 811366
Dallas, TX 75381
(214) 243-3456
Ask for the EDI Yellow Pages
International.

Editorial Advisor

Petroglyph
123 Townsend Street, Suite 345
San Francisco, CA 94107-1907
(415)979-0588
Expert on-line style guide in
HyperCard 2.0 format. A Windows 3 version is under development. $149.95 Mac.

Edsun Continuous Edge Graphics

Edsun Laboratories, Incorporated
564 Main Street
Waltham, MA 02154
(617)647-9300
VGA graphics enhancement chip.
PC.

Encore

Passport Designs
625 Miramontes Street
Half Moon Bay, CA 94019
(415)726-0280
MIDI composing and composing
software. $595 Mac.

Enhance

Micro Frontier, Incorporated
7650 Hickman Road
Des Moines, IA 50322
(512)270-8109
Grayscale image editor. $375 Mac.

Epson ES-300C Color Scanner

Epson America
20770 Madrona Avenue
Torrence, CA 90503
(800)922-8911 or (213)782-0770
Color scanner. $1.995 Mac, PC.

Excel

Microsoft Corporation
1 Microsoft Way
Redmond, WA 98073
(206)882-8080
Graphical spreadsheet and
database. $395 V. 2.2 Mac,
Win3, OS/2.

Exposure

Preferred Publishers, Inc.
5100 Poplar Avenue, Suite 617
Memphis, TN 38137
(901)683-3383
Screen capture and graphics
editor. $99.95 Mac.

Expressionist

Alan Bonadio Associates
814 Castro Street
San Francisco, CA 94114
(415)282-5864
Mathematical equation editor.
$129.95 V. 2.0 Mac.

ExpressPAGE

Carberry Technology
600 Suffolk Street
Lowell, MA 01854
(508)970-5358
Creates comps, roughs, and
thumbnails for page layout software. $395 Win.

F

F-19 Stealth Fighter

Microprose
180 Lakefront Drive
Hunt Valley, MD 21030
(800)879-PLAY or (301)771-1151
Arcade game, flight simulator.
$69.95 PC.

FaceLift

Bitstream, Incorporated
215 First Street
Cambridge, MA 02142
(800)522-FONT
Font rasterizer. $99 Windows.

FACETS of New York

NYNEX Information Resources
Company
100 Church Street
New York, NY 10007
(212)513-9411
Interactive information kiosks.

Fax Dispatch

MCI Mail
1150 17th Street NW, Suite 800
Washington, DC 20036
(800)444-6245 or (202)833-8484
On-line fax service. Text is 50¢ for
the first half page, 40¢ for each
additional half page. No
graphics.

FAXGate Plus

Solution Incorporated
30 Commerce Street
PO Box 783
Williston, VT 05495
(802)865-9220 or
(802)865-9224 fax
Fax network software. $395
(5 users) V. 1.01 Mac.

FileMaker Pro

Claris Corporation
5201 Patrick Henry Drive
Box 58168
Santa Clara, CA 95052
(408)987-7000
Database with strong database
publishing capabilities. A Windows version is rumored. $299
V. 1.0 Mac.

Filevision IV
Marvelin Corporation
3420 Ocean Park Boulevard, Suite 3020
Santa Monica, CA 90405-3395
(213)450-6813
Integrated drawing and database program. $495 Mac.

FilmMaker
Paracomp
1725 Montgomery Street, 2nd floor
San Francisco, CA 94111
(415)965-4091
Animation program. $695 V. 1.0 Mac.

FirstApps
hDC Computer Corporation
6742 185th Avenue NE
Redmond, WA 98052
(206)885-5550
Utilities for Windows. $100 V. 1.0 Win3.

Flight Simulator
Microsoft Corporation
1 Microsoft Way
Redmond, WA 98073
(206)882-8080
Arcade game. $59.95 V. 4.0 PC.

Focus Color Scanner
Agfa Compugraphic
90 Industrial Way
Wilmington, MA 01887
(508)658-5600
Desktop color scanner. $7,995 scanner, $695 software.

FONTastic Plus
Altsys
269 Renner Road
Richardson, TX 75080
(214)424-4888
Bit-map font editor. $99.95 V. 2.0 Mac.

Fontographer
Altsys
269 Renner Road
Richardson, TX 75080
(214)424-4888
Outline font editor. $495 V. 3.2 Mac.

FontStudio
Letraset USA
40 Eisenhower Drive
Paramus, NJ 07653
(800)343-8973
Typeface design utility. $595 Mac.

FontWare
Bitstream
215 First Street
Cambridge, MA 02142
(800)522-3668
Font rasterizer. $25; $129 per typeface PC.

FormBase
Ventura Software, Incorporated
101 Continental Boulevard
El Segundo, CA 90245
(213)536-7000
Forms management and database program. $495 V. 1.1 Win.

4CAST
DuPont Imaging Systems
Dye sublimation printer. $45,000.

FrameMaker
Frame Technologies
1010 Rincon Circle
San Jose, CA 95131
(408)433-3311
Long technical document publishing package. $995 V. 2.1 Mac, PC, NeXT; $2,500 Sun.

Freedom of the Press
Custom Applications, Incorporated
900 Technology Park Drive, Building 8
Billerica, MA 01821
(508)667-8585 or (800)873-4367
PostScript emulation (interpreter) software. Wide printer support for non-PostScript printers, excellent output quality. $495 V. 3.0 Mac. Professional version ($1,495) supports varying levels of color. A $98 version called **Freedom of the Press Light** supports fewer output devices but most common laser printers.

FreeHand, see **Aldus FreeHand**

FullWrite Professional 1.1
Ashton-Tate
20101 Hamilton Avenue
Torrence, CA 90502
(213)329-8000
Word processor. $395 Mac.

G

GEM Collection
Digital Research
PO Box DRI
70 Garden Court
Monterey, CA 93942
(408)649-3896

GEM Desktop Publisher
Digital Research
PO Box DRI
70 Garden Court
Monterey, CA 93942
(408)649-3896
Page layout program. Release 2.

GEM Scan
Digital Research
PO Box DRI
70 Garden Court
Monterey, CA 93942
(408)649-3896
Scanner control and image processing software.

Generic CADD
Generic Software, Incorporated
11911 North Creek Parkway S.
Bothell, WA 98011
(800)228-3601
2D CAD package $595 V. 1.0 Mac, Level 3 PC. Low-end packages available on the PC.

GEnie
General Electric Information Services
401 N. Washington Street
Rockville, MD 20850
(301)340-4000 or (800)638-9636
On-line information services. All computers.

Genigraphics Corporation
2 Corporate Drive, Suite 340
Shelton, CT 06484
(800)638-7348
Slide imaging service.

GEOS
GeoWorks
2150 Shattuck Avenue
Berkeley, CA 94704
(415)644-0883
A GUI for DOS. $195 PC.

GE Rental/Lease
General Electric Company
15 Avis Drive
Latham, NY 12110
(800)GE-RENTS or (518)783-4400
Equipment rental company.

GLC/SBS
Cumulus Computer Corporation
23500 Merchantile Road
Cleveland, OH 44122
(216)464-2211
Integrated computer system.
$2,195 PC.

Glyphix
SWFTE International
PO Box 219
Rockland, DE 19732
Font rasterizer. $99.95.

GOfer
Microlytics, Incorporated
1 Tobey Village Office Park
Pittsford, NY 14534
(800)828-6293 or (716)248-9620
Text search and retrieval utility.
$79.95 V. 2.0 Mac.

**Graphic Utilities,
Incorporated**
PO Box 332
Cheney Grove Industrial Park
Fort Fairfield, ME 04742
(800)669-4723
Hundred percent waterfast black
ink for the H-P
DeskJet/DeskWriter printers.
$20.95 per twin pack Also, 80
percent waterfast inks in black,
red, blue, green, and brown.
$19.95 per twin pack.

**Grammatik Mac, Grammatik
Windows, Grammatix IV**
Reference Software International
330 Townsend Street, Suite 123
San Francisco, CA 94107
(415)541-0222
Electronic Proofreader. V. 2.0 $99
Mac, Win3, PC.

The Graphics Link Plus+
HSC Software
1661 Lincoln Boulevard, #100
Santa Monica, CA 90404
(213)392-8441
Screen capture and file conversion utility. $149 PC.

Great Start Cartridge
Hewlett-Packard
19310 Pruneridge Avenue
Cupertino, CA 95014
(800)752-0900
Font cartridge for LaserJets, $99
each.

Grey F/X
Xerox Imaging Systems, Inc.
535 Oakmead Parkway
Sunnyvale, CA 94086
(800)248-6500 or (408)245-7900
Grayscale image editor. $495 PC.

**GRID GRIDCASE 1450sx or
1550sx**
GRID Systems Corporation
47211 Lakeview Boulevard
PO Box 5003
Fremont, CA 94537
(800)222-4743
Portable 80386 laptop computer.

Guide
Owl International, Incorporated
2800 156th Avenue SE
Bellvue, WA 98007
(206)747-3203
Hypertext system. V. 2.0 $295
Mac, PC.

H

Hammerlab Scan Do
Hammerlab Corporation
938 Chapel Street
New Haven, CT 06510
(203)624-0000
Digital image processing program
and scanner driver. $195 Win3.

Harvard Graphics
Software Publishing Corporation
1901 Landing Drive
PO Box 7210
Mountain View, CA 94039
(415)962-8910
Presentation program. $495 V. 2.3
DOS.

Hell ChromaCom
Hell Graphic Systems, Incorporated
25 Harbor Park Drive
Port Washington, NY 11050
(516)484-3000
Color electronic prepress system.

Helo DPE
Media Cybernetics
8484 Georgia Avenue, Suite 200
Silver Spring, MD 20910
(301)495-3305
Image editing software. $295 PC.

Higgins
Enable Software, Incorporated
North Way 10 Executive Park
Ballston Lake, NY 12019
(800)888-0684
Groupware system.

HiJaak
Inset Systems
71 Commerce Drive
Brookfield, CT 06804
(800)828-8088
Screen capture utility and a
graphics package for file translation. $199 V. 2.0 PC.

The Home Office
US Integrated Technologies
3023 Research Drive
Richmond, CA 94806
(415)223-1001
Integrated computer system.
$3,195 PC.

HookUp!
HIP Software
656 Bair Island Road, Suite 304
Redwood City, CA 94063
(415)361-1710
MIDI connection software. $149
   Mac.

HotShot Graphics
Symsoft, Incorporated
444 First Street
Los Altos, CA 94022
(800)344-0160 or (415)941-1552
Screen capture and editing utility.
   $249 V. 1.7 PC, Win, OS/2.

HyperAnimator
Bright Star Technologies
1450 114th Avenue SE, Suite 200
Bellevue, WA 98004
(206)451-3697
Voice/animation software for
   HyperCard. $199.95 V. 1.5.2
   Mac.

HyperCard
Claris Corporation
5201 Patrick Henry Drive
PO Box 58168
Santa Clara, CA 95052
(408)987-7000
Hypertextural development system. Offered free by Apple
   without documentation. $49 V.
   2.0 Mac.

I

Illustrator, see **Adobe
Illustrator**

Image
Wayne Rasband
National Institute of Health
Bethesda, MD
Contact the author at: Internet,
   BitNet:wayne@helix.nih.gov or
   at CompuServe:76067,3454.
   Free V. 1.29 Mac.

ImageEdit
IBM Corporation
Old Orchard Park Road
Armonk, NY 10573
(203)783-7000
Digital image processing pro-
   gram. $495 Win3.

Image-In
Moniterm, Incorporated
5740 Green Circle Drive
Minnetonka, MN 55343
(612)935-4151
Digital image editing program
   with OCR support. $795 Win3.

ImagePrep
Computer Presentations, Incorporated
1117 Cypress Street
Cincinnati, OH 45206
(513)281-3222
Screen capture, file conversion,
   and image compression package. $295 V. 3.0 Win.

ImageStudio
Letraset USA
40 Eisenhower Drive
Paramus, NJ 07653
(201)845-6100
Black-and-white digital image pro-
   cessing program. $495 V. 1.5
   Mac.

ImPort
Zenographics
4 Executive Circle
Irvine, CA 92714
(714)851-6352
File translation utility for the PC.
   A Windows version called
   ImPort for Windows is sold.

Impostrip, see **ULTIMATE
   Electronic Pre-Press System**

In/Out
CE Software, Incorporated
1801 Industrial Circle
PO Box 655580
West Des Moines, IA 50265
(515)224-1953
Electronic people tracker. $199
   (5-users) Mac.

InBox Plus
TOPS
950 Marina Village Parkway
Alameda, CA 94501
(415)769-9669
E-Mail software. $995 (100 users).
   V. 3.0 Mac.

InFormed Designer
Shana Corporation
#105, 9650 20th Avenue
Edmonton, Alberta, Canada
   T6N 1G1
(403)463-3330
Form design tool. $295 Mac.
   miniManager is its database
   data entry system. V 1.2.

interFACE
Bright Star Technologies
1450 114th Avenue SE, Suite 200
Bellevue, WA 98004
(206)451-3697
Voice/animation software.
   $499.95 Mac.

Interleaf Publisher
Interleaf
10 Canal Park
Cambridge, MA 02141
(617)577-9800
$999 V. 3.5 Mac, PC.

INTO
Benchmark Associates, Incorporated
7400 West Detroit Street
Chandler, AZ 85226
(602)961-7519
Office automation system. $1,499
   (5 users), $3,899 (25 users) PC.

J

JustText
Knowledge Engineering
GPO Box 2139
New York, NY 10116
(212)473-0095
Coded page layout system for
   writing PostScript code. $195
   Mac.

K

KaleidaGraph

Synergy Software (PCS Inc.)
2457 Perkiomen Avenue
Reading, PA 19606
(215)779-0522
Data analysis and graphing. $249 Mac.

KaleidoSCAN

Impact Research
1230 Big Rock Loop
Los Alamos, NM 87544
(800)356-2464
Color imaging package for grayscale scanners. $149.95 Mac.

Key Caps

Apple Computer, Incorporated
20525 Mariani Avenue
Cupertino, CA 95014
(408)996-1010
Part of the system software, a desk accessory.

Kodak LionHeart

Eastman Kodak Company
901 Elmgrove Road
Rochester, NY 14653-6304
(716)253-0058
High-speed digital copier system.

Kodak Precision Software

3435 Greystone Drive, Suite 107
Austin, TX 78731
(800)258-2227
Imagesetter calibration software for true Adobe RIPs. $795.

Kodak Prophecy System

Kodak Electronic Printing Systems
23 Crosby Drive
Bedford, MA 01730
(617)275-5070
Color electronic prepress system.

Kodak XL7700

Eastman Kodak Company
343 State Street
Rochester, NY 14650
(716)724-4000
A color sublimation printer. $24,895.

Kurtzweil 5000 OCR

Xerox Imaging Systems/Datacopy Products
1215 Terra Bella Avenue
Mountain View, CA 94043
(415)965-7900 or (800)821-2898
OCR package, scanner, and hardware. $15,000 Mac.

L

L*View MultiMode

Sigma Designs
46501 Landing Parkway
Fremont, CA 94538
(800)933-9945 or (415)770-0100
Multi-resolution display system. $1,995.

LANtastic

Artisoft, Incorporated
575 East River Road
Tucson, AZ 85704
(602)293-6363
Voice E-mail for the PC. Voice adapter $149, software $495, Low-cost LAN, $349 per node.

LAPC-1

RolandCorp US
7200 Dominion Circle
Los Angeles, CA 90040
(213)685-5141
Sound add-in board. $595 PC.

LapLink Mac III

Travelling Software, Incorporated
18702 N. Creek Parkway
Bothell, WA 98011
(800)343-5414 or (206)483-8088
File translation utility. $189.95 Mac.

Laserdisc Mastering and Production Service

3M Optical Recording Department
3M Center Bldg. 233-5N-01
St. Paul, MN 55144
(612)733-2142
Videodisk production and manufacturing.

LaserJet II and III

Hewlett-Packard
Customer Information Center
19310 Pruneridge Avenue
Cupertino, CA 95014
(800)752-0900
Laser printers. LaserJet IIP with PostScript $2,685; IID $3,595 2-bin printer; IIID 2-bin printer, LaserJet III $2,395, LaserJet III with PostScript $3,585.

LaserMax 1000 Personal Typesetter

LaserMax
7150 Shady Oak Road
Eden Prarie, MN 55344-9890
(612)944-9696
A 1000 dpi laser printer. $7,995 Mac.

LaserPaint

LaserWare, Incorporated
PO Box 668
San Raphael, CA 94915
(800)367-6898
Graphics program, draw/paint with image editing. $495 Mac. LaserPaint Color II version $595.

LaserWriter IISC

Apple Computer, Incorporated
20525 Mariani Avenue
Cupertino, CA 95014
(408)996-1010
300 dpi laser printers. $4,499 IINT, $5,995 IINTX.

LaTeX
Addison-Wesley
Jacob Way
Reading, MA 01867
(617)944-6795
TeX-based coded page layout
    software. Mac.

LAWN
O'Neill Communications, Incor-
    porated
100 Thanet Circle, #202
Princeton, NJ 08540
(609)924-1095
Radio LAN. $495.

Layout
Michael C. O'Connor
Letronic System Design Co
Macintosh interface modifying
    software. V. 1.9 shareware Mac.

**Leather Goddesses of
    Phoebos**
Mediagenic
3885 Bohannon Drive
Menlo Park, CA 94025
(415)329-0500
X-rated game. $19.95 Mac, PC.

Legacy
NBI, Incorporated
3450 Mitchell Lane
Boulder, CO 80301
(800)624-1111 or (303)444-5710
Word processor. $495 Win3.

LetraStudio
Letraset USA
40 Eisenhower Drive
Paramus, NJ 07653
(800)343-8973
Display type customization utility.
    $495 Mac. Typefaces are $75
    each; package contains four
    bundled faces.

**LetrTuck (PC), LetrTuck+
    (Mac)**
Edco Services, Incorporated
12410 North Dale Mabry Highway
Tampa, FL 33618
(813)962-7800
Font kerning utility. $99 PC, $147
    Mac.

Letterhead
Brøderbund
17 Paul Drive
San Raphael, CA 94903-2101
(800)521-6263 or (415)492-3200
Electronic stationery. $99.95 Mac.

Lexis/Nexis
Mead Data Central
PO Box 933
Dayton, OH 45401
(800)227-4908
On-line information service. $50
    session software V. 1.5 for Mac.

Liasion
Infosphere, Incorporated
4730 SW Macadam Avenue
Portland, OR 97201
(800)445-7085
Software bridge for remote access
    to networks. $295.

**Lightspeed Color Layout
    System**
Crosfield Lightspeed
47 Farnsworth Street
Boston, MA 02210
(617)338-2173
Prepress link system.

Linotronic 200P,300, and 530
Linotype Company Corporation
425 Oser Avenue
Hauppauge, NY 11788
(518)434-2000 or (800)633-1900
PostScript imagesetters. $25,000
    to $125,000.

Lotus Freelance
Lotus Development Corporation
55 Cambridge Parkway
Cambridge, MA 02142
(617)577-8500.

Lotus Notes
Lotus Development Corporation
55 Cambridge Parkway
Cambridge, MA 02142
(617)577-8500
Groupware system. $62,500 Win,
    OS/2.

Lotus 1-2-3
Lotus Development Corporation
55 Cambridge Parkway
Cambridge, MA 02142
(617)577-8500
Spreadsheet.

Lumena
Time Arts, Incorporated
1425 Corporate Center Parkway
Santa Rosa, CA 95407
(707)576-7722
Paint program with texturing.
    $795 PC, Lumena Visa $3,995,
    Lumena 16/32 $24.95.

M

M-Motion Video Adapter/A
IBM Corporation
(800)IBM-2468
MCA-bus motion video board.
    $2,250 PC.

Mac N' Touch
MicroTouch Systems, Incorpo-
    rated
55 Jonspin Road
Wilmington, MA 01887
(508)694-9900
Touch screen monitor. Pricing
    depending on size and configu-
    ration.

MacBLAST, see BLAST

MacBravo
Schlumberger Technologies
4251 Plymouth Road
PO Box 986
Ann Arbor, MI 48106-0986
(313)995-6171
Professional 3D CAD package for
    Macs. Several modules sold:
    Detailer $1,995. Facilities
    $4,900. Modeler $1,495.

MacChuck
Vano Associates, Incorporated
PO Box 12730
New Brighton, MN 55112
(612)788-9547
Mac-to-PC remote control pro-
    gram and file translation pro-
    gram. $99.95 V. 1.5 Mac to PC.

MacConnection
14 Mill Street
Marlow, NH 03456
(800)MAC-LISA
The best direct mail organization in the world for the Macintosh.

MacDraft
Innovative Data Design, Incorporated
2280 Bates Avenue, Suite A
Concord, CA 94520
(415)680-6818
Good low-end 2D CAD package. $299 V. 2.0 Mac.

MacDraw II
Claris Corporation
5201 Patrick Henry Drive
PO Box 58168
Santa Clara, CA 95052
(408)987-7000
Draw program. MacDraw Pro $399 due second quarter 1991. V.1.1 $395 Mac.

Mac86
Orange Micro, Incorporated
1400 N. Lakeview Avenue
Anaheim, CA 92807
(714)779-2772
NuBus MS-DOS emulation boards for the Mac II. $699 Mac. Also Mac286 $1,599.

MacEZ-CAM
Bridgeport Machines, Incorporated
500 Lindley Street
PO Box 32
Bridgeport, CT 06606
(203)367-3651 or (800)243-4292
$11,475. System includes EZ-Turn, EZ-Mill, and a Macintosh II. Available modules include: EZ-Turn $3,000, EZ-Surf Plus $6,000, and EZ-EDM $3,000; package pricing offered.

MacImage (bundled with the JetReader scanner)
Xerox Imaging Systems/Datacopy Products
1215 Terra Bella Avenue
Mountain View, CA 94043
(800)821-2898
Scanner driver software. $695 Mac.

MacInker
Computer Friends
14250 NW Science Park Drive
Portland, OR 97220-9891
(800)547-3303 or (503)626-2291 in Oregon
Computer ribbon reinker. $45 for ImageWriter, $75 for universal MacInker.

Macintosh Computers
Apple Computer, Incorporated
20525 Mariani Avenue
Cupertino, CA 95041
(408)996-1010

MacIvory Animation and Paint System
Symbolics, Incorporated
1401 Westwood Boulevard
Los Angeles, CA 90024
(213)478-0681
Rendering program. $19,900 Mac. With Mac IIfx system $48,900.

MacLinkPlus/PC
DataViz, Incorporated
5917 Main Street
Trumbull, CT 06611
(203)268-0300
File translation utility. $199 V.4.5 Mac. MacLink Plus/Translators, $169 V.4.5 Mac: can be used with the Apple File Exchange. PCLinkPlus for Windows 3 exists.

MacPaint II
Claris Corporation
5201 Patrick Henry Drive
PO Box 58168
Santa Clara, CA 95052
(408)727-8227
Paint program. $125 Mac.

MacProof
Lexpertise USA, Incorporated
175 East 400 S., Suite 100
Salt Lake City, UT 84111
(800)354-5656
Grammar checker or proofreader. $195 Mac.

MacRecorder
Farallon Computing, Incorporated
2000 Powell Street, Suite 600
Emeryville, CA 94608
(415)596-9000
Sound digitizer/microphone and SoundEdit and HyperSound software. $249 V. 2.0 Mac.

MacRenderMan
Pixar
1001 W. Cutting Boulevard, Suite 200
Richmond, CA 94804
(415)236-4000
Rendering program. $795 V. 1.0 Mac.

MacroMind Director
MacroMind, Incorporated
410 Townsend Street, #408
San Francisco, CA 94107
(415)442-0200
Animation program. $695 V. 2.0 Mac. **MacroMind Accelerator** $195. **MacroMind Windows Player** $75.

MacroMind MediaMaker
MacroMind, Incorporated
410 Townsend Street, #100
San Francisco, CA 94107
(415)442-0200
Authoring program. $495.

MacroMind 3D
MacroMind, Incorporated
410 Townsend Street, #408
San Francisco, CA 94107
(415)442-0200
3D animation, rendering, and image manipulation program. $1,495 Mac.

MacTeX
FTL Systems, Incorporated
234 Eglington Avenue, Ste. 205
Toronto, Ontario, Canada M4P 1K5
(416)487-2142
$750 Mac.

MacVision
Koala Technologies Corporation
70 N. 2nd Street
San Jose, CA 95113
(408)287-6278
Video capture board. $499.95
Mac.

MacWrite II
Claris Corporation
5201 Patrick Henry Drive
PO Box 58168
Santa Clara, CA 95052
(408)987-7000
Word processor. V.1.1 Mac.

Magellen 2.0
Lotus Development Corporation
55 Cambridge Parkway
Cambridge, MA 02142
(800)343-5414
DOS shell. $139.

MailFax
AT&T Mail
Room 1813
5000 Hadley Road
South Plainfield, NJ 07080
(800)367-7225
Fax service. 55¢ for first half page,
40¢ each additional half page.
Graphics, same price.

The Major BBS
Galaticomm, Incorporated
4101 SW 47th Avenue, Suite 101
Ft. Lauderdale, FL 33314
(305)583-5990
Bulletin board system. $59 (2
users); $659 (8 users); $1,259 (32
users); $1,559 (64 users). PC.

Management Graphics
MGI
1401 E. 79th Sreet #6
Minneapolis, MN 55425
(612)854-1220
Slide imaging service.

The Manhole
Activision
3885 Bohannon Drive
Menlo Park, CA 94025
(415)329-0500
HyperCard game. $79.95 Mac.

MarcoPolo
Mainstay
5311-B Derry Avenue
Agoura Hills, CA 91301
(818)991-6540
Search-and-retrieval software.
$299 (1 user); $499 (2 users);
$999 (5 users). Mac.

Markup
Mainstay
5311-B Derry Avenue
Agoura Hills, CA 91301
(818)991-6540
Group editing software. $245 (1
user); $495 (2 users); $995 (5
users). Mac.

Mass-11 Draw
Microsystems Engineering Corporation
2400 West Hassell Road
Hoffman Estates, IL 60195
(708)882-0111
DOS drawing program. $695 V.
6.0 DOS.

Master Tracks Pro
Passport
65 Miramontos Street
Half Moon Bay, CA 94019
(415)725-0280
Music sequencer. $495 V. 4.0 Mac,
PC. Amiga.

MasterJuggler
ALSoft, Incorporated
PO Box 927
Spring, TX 77383
(713)353-4090
Font and resource management
utility. $89.95 Mac.

Math Type
Design Science, Incorporated
6475-B East Pacific Coast Highway, Suite 392
Long Beach, CA 90803
(213)433-0685
Mathematical equation editor.
$249 Win.

MCI Mail
1150 17th Street NW, Suite 800
Washington, DC 20036
(800)444-6245 or (202)833-8484
On-line service with strong E-mail
capabilities. See also **Fax Dispatch**.

MediaTracks
Farralon Computing, Incorporated
2000 Powell Street, Suite 600
Emeryville, CA 94608
(415)596-9000
Records screen activity. $295 V.
1.0 Mac. **MediaTracks Multimedia Pack** $495. Includes
ScreenRecorder DA.

MegaChrome
ReproCAD
(415)284-0400
Large-format color prints.

Metamorphosis Professional
Altsys
269 Renner Road
Richardson, TX 75080
(214)424-4888
Font conversion utility. $149
V. 1.0 Mac.

Micrografx Designer
Micrographx
1303 Arapaho Road
Richardson, TX 75081
(214)234-1769 or (800)733-3729
Excellent high-level draw/illustra-
tion/drafting package. $695 V.
3.01 Win3.

Micrografx XPORT
Micrographx
1303 Arapaho Road
Richardson, TX 75081
(214)234-1769 or (800)733-3729
File translation utility. $199 PC.

microLaser

Texas Instruments Incorporated
Information Technology Group
PO Box 202230
Austin, TX 78720
(800)527-3500
A best-buy 300 dpi PostScript
laser printer. PS17 $2,499 PC,
PS35 $2,849.

Microphone II

Software Ventures Corporation
2907 Claremont Avenue
Berkeley, CA 94705
(415)644-3232
Telecommunications package.
$295 V. 3.0 Mac, Win3. Version
1.5 ($149) is sometimes bun-
dled with modems.

microPrint

214 Third Avenue
Waltham, MA 02154
(617)890-7500
PostScript service bureau.

Microsoft Mail

Microsoft Corporation
1 Microsoft Way
Redmond, WA 98073
(206)882-8080
V. 3.0 Mac $125 (1–4 users). **Mail
Server** $395, $1,495 (20 users),
PC Workstation, $125.

**Microsoft Mouse, Microsoft
Paintbrush**

Microsoft Corporation
1 Microsoft Way
Redmond, WA 98073
(206)882-8080
The 400 dpi mouse comes with
Paintbrush or with a Windows
driver. $125.

The Microsoft Office

Microsoft Corporation
1 Microsoft Way
Redmond, WA 98073
(206)882-8080
Mail, Excel, Word, and Powerpoint on disk. $895 Mac. $949
on CD-ROM.

Microsoft Word, see **Word**

MicroStation

Intergraph
1 Madison Industrial Park
Huntsville, AL 35807
(800)345-4856
3D CAD package. $3,300 V. 3.5.1
Mac.

Microtek 300 Series

Microtek Lab, Incorporated
680 Knox Street
Torrence, CA 90502
(213)321-2121
Grayscale and color desktop
flatbed scanners. 300Z color
scanner $2,195 Mac. 3002 color
scanner PC.

microTeX

Addison-Wesley
Jacob Way
Reading, MA 01867
TeX-based page layout system.
$295 PC.

MIDI Time Piece

222 Third Street
Cambridge, MA 02142
(617)576-2760
MIDI adapter. $495 Mac.

Mishu

Xanatech, Incorporated
20 Fresh Pond Place
Cambridge, MA 02138
(617)492-7463
Chinese word processor with
complete set of modules. $249
Mac, Desk accessory alone ver
sion 2.0, for $89.

Mitsubishi S340

A 150 dpi color sublimation
printer. ($14,000).

More

Symantec Corporation
10201 Torre Avenue
Cupertino, CA 95014
(800)441-7234 or (800)626-8847
(CA)
Outlining, writing, and desktop
presentation package. $395 V.
3.0 Mac.

MPU-IMC

RolandCorp US
7200 Dominion Circle
Los Angeles, CA 90040
(213)685-5141
Sound add-in board for MCA bus,
IBM PS/2 computers. $350 PC.

MS-DOS

Microsoft Corporation
1 Microsoft Way
Redmond, WA 98073
(206)882-8080.
V. 4.1 PC.

MS/DOS BLAST, see **BLAST**

MultiClip

Olduvai Corporation
7520 Red Road, Suite A
S. Miami, FL 33143
(305)665-4665
Clipboard enhancement utility.
$99 Mac.

Multi-Ad Creator

Multi-Ad Services, Incorporated
1720 W. Detweiller Drive
Peoria, IL 61615-1695
(309)692-1530
Advertising page layout system.
$995 V. 2.5 Mac.

MultiSync Monitors

NEC Technologies, Incorporated
1255 Michael Drive
Wood Dale, IL 60191
(708)860-9500
High-resolution monitor. 2D, 3D,
4D, and 5D monitors are very
popular and recommended for
PCs.

Mx6 Controller

LaserMax
7150 Shady Oak Road
Eden Prarie, MN 55344-9890
(612)944-9696
A high-resolution printer controller for the Apple Laser-
Writer (400 X 400 or 800 X 800
dpi). $2,795 to $5,095.

N

National Reprographics, Incorporated
44 West 18th Street
New York, NY 10011
(212)366-7073
Megachrome large-format color printing service.

Natural Images
Artbeats
Box 20083
San Bernadino, CA 92406
(714)881-1200
Landscape and pattern EPS clip art. CD-ROM available. $99.95 Mac, IBM (5 800 KByte disks-EPS).

Navigator
CompuServe, Incorporated
5000 Arlington Centre Boulevard
Columbus, OH 43220
(614)457-0802 or (800)848-8199
Automated access software for CompuServe on-line information service. $99.95 Mac.

Navigator HD-40
Canon USA
1 Canon Plaza
Lake Success, NY 11042
(516)488-6700
Integrated computer system. $2,495 PC.

NEC Silentwriter
NEC Technologies
1414 Massachusetts Avenue
Boxborough, MA 01719
(508)264-8000
LC 890XL $3,995, Silentwriter2 290 $3,995.

NetModem
Shiva Corporation
1 Cambridge Center
Cambridge, MA 02142
(617)252-6300
Networked modem device. V.32 9600 baud modem $1,995, V2400 $599.

NetWare 386
Novell, Incorporated
122 East 1700 S.
Provo, UT 84606
(800)453-1267 or (801)429-5900
LAN network operating system. V. 3.0 $7,995 (unlimited users). **Advanced NetWare 286** V. 2.15 $3,295 (100 users). NetWare for Macintosh also available.

NewWave
Hewlett-Packard
3000 Hanover Street
Palo Alto, CA 94304
(408)447-4391
Object-oriented application and document shell for Windows. $195 V. 3.0 Win3.

NewWave
Hewlett-Packard
3000 Hanover Street
Palo Alto, CA 94304
(408)447-4391
Object-oriented application and document shell for Windows. $195 V. 3.0 Win3.

NeXT Computers
900 Chesapeake Drive
Redwood CIty, CA 94063
(800)848-NeXT
Computer/workstation. **NeXT-Station** $4,995 black and white, $10,100 color; **NeXTCube** $7,995 black and white, $11,790 color.

Nikon LS-3500 (with Nikon ColorScan software)
Nikon, Incorporated
623 Stewart Avenue
Garden City, NY 11530
(516)222-0200, ext. 365
High-resolution 35mm film scanner.

Nisus 2.11
Paragon Concepts
Highland Drive, Suite 312
Solana Beach, CA 92075
(619)481-1477
Word processor. $395 Mac.

Norton Antivirus
Peter Norton Computing
100 Wilshire Boulevard, 9th floor
Santa Monica, CA 90401
(800)365-1010
Virus detection and vaccine. $129 V. 1.0 PC.

Norton Commander 3.0
Peter Norton Computing
100 Wilshire Boulevard, 9th floor
Santa Monica, CA 90401
(800)365-1010
DOS shell. $149 PC.

Norton Utilities for the Mac
Peter Norton Computing
100 Wilshire Boulevard, 9th floor
Santa Monica, CA 90401
(800)365-1010
Hard disk management utility. $129 Mac.

Notes
Lotus Development Corporation
55 Cambridge Parkway
Cambridge, MA 02142
(617)577-8500
Networked integrated application. $62,500 (per 100 nodes) (!) Win3.

NoteWriter II
Passport Designs
625 Miramontes Street
Half Moon Bay, CA 94019
(415)726-0280
Music publishing program. $495 Mac.

NS32GX320 chip
National Semiconductor
2900 Semiconductor Drive
PO Box 58090
Santa Clara, CA 95052
(408)721-5000

NuVista+
Truvision, Incorporated
7340 Shadeland Station
Indianapolis, IN 46256
(317)841-0332 or (800)858-8783
Video capture board. $2,995 to $4,500 Mac. Price depends on added RAM. Also TARGA boards for the PC.

NYNEX Fast Track
NYNEX Information Resources
  Company
100 Church Street
New York, NY 10007
(212)513-9411
CD-ROM phone listing database.

O

Oasis
Time Arts, Incorporated
1425 Corporate Center Parkway
Santa Rosa, CA 95407
(707)576-7722
Paint program with texturing.
  $795 Mac.

**Odesta Database Management
  System**
Odesta Corporation
4084 Commercial Avenue
Northbrook, IL 60062
(312)498-5615
Groupware system.

Office Minder
Advanced Concepts, Incorpo-
  rated
4129 N. Port Washington Avenue
Milwaukee, WI 53212
(800)222-6736
Groupware software for V. 1.10
  PC.

Office Works
Data Access Corporation
14000 Southwest 119th Avenue
Miami, FL 33186
(305)238-0012
Office automation software. $695
  (6 users); $1,995 (unlimited
  users) PC.

OfficeVision/2
IBM Corporation
(800)IBM-2468
Office automation software.
  Release 1.1, $750 per node for
  OS/2, $210 per user for DOS.

Okyto
The FreeSoft Company
150 Hickory Drive
Beaver Falls, PA 15010
(412)846-2700
Mac-to-Mac file transfer utility.
  Sometimes bundled with White
  Knight. $39.95 Mac.

Omnipage
Caere Corporation
100 Cooper Court
Los Gatos, CA 95030
(408)395-7000 or (800)535-7226
OCR package. $795 Mac V. 3.0
  $695 Win3. Also **OmniPage
  Professional.** $995 Win.

OnLocation
On Technologies
1 Cambridge Center
Cambridge, MA 02142
(617)225-2545
Text location utility. $99.95 V. 1.2
  Mac.

Optronics ColorGetter
Optronics
7 Stuart Road
Chelmsford, MA 01824
(508)256-4511
Color scanner. ca. $60,000.

Optronics ColorSetter
Optronics
7 Stuart Road
Chelmsford, MA 01824
(508)256-4511
Imagesetter. ca. $80,000.

OS/2
Microsoft Corporation
1 Microsoft Way
Redmond, WA 98073
(206)882-8080
An operating system touted as
  the next generation of PC software. $295 V. 1.2 PC. V. 2.0 due
  out in 1991.

Outbound Laptop System
Outbound Systems, Incorporated
4840 Pearl East Circle
Boulder, CO 80301
Apple Macintosh compatible
  portable computer. $2,995 Mac.

P

PacificPage
Pacific Data Products
9125 Rehcold Road
San Diego, CA 92121
(619)552-0889
PostScript cartridge for the H-P
  LaserJet II. $695 PC. The Pacific
  MacPage cartridge is also avail-
  able for the LaserWriter NT.

PageAhead
PageAhead Software Corporation
2125 Western Avenue, Suite 300
Seattle, WA 98121
(206)441-0340
Database publishing software.
  $795 v. 1.0 Win.

PageMaker, see **Aldus Page-
Maker**

PageDirector
Managing Editor Software
8208 Brookside Road
Elkins Park, PA 19117
(215)635-5074
Publication management software
  for QuarkXPress. V.1.5 Mac,
  $895–$1495.

PaintJet
Hewlett-Packard
19310 Pruneridge Avenue
Cupertino, CA 95014
(800)752-0900
Color ink jet graphics printer.
  $1,395 Mac or PC.

Pantone Inks
Pantone, Incorporated
55 Knickerbocker Road
Moonachie, NJ 07074
(201)935-5500
Ink manufacturer.

Paper Keyboard

Datacap, Incorporated
5 West Main Street
Elmsford, NY 10523
(914)347-7133
OCR data entry system. $895 V.
1.2 Mac, Win3.

PaperCatalog

PaperDirect
57 Romanelli Avenue
South Hackensack, NJ 07606-9904
(800)A-PAPER
Laser printer, copier, and DTP
paper and envelopes.

ParaFont

Design Science
6475B Pacific Coast Highway,
Suite 392
Long Beach, CA 90803
(213)433-0685
Font customization utility. $99
Mac, Win.

Parlance

Xyvision
101 Edgewater Drive
Wakefield, MA 01880
(617)245-9004
High-end page layout program.
$100,000 (2 nodes including
DEC workstations).

PCConnection

6 Mill Street
Marlow, NH 03456
(603)446-7741
The best direct mail organization
in the world for the PC.

PCLinkPlus

DataViz, Incorporated
5917 Main Street
Trumbull, CT 06611
(203)268-0300
File translation utility. MacLink-
Plus/PC for the Macintosh
exists. $199 PC.

PC Paintbrush Plus IV Plus

ZSoft Corporation
450 Franklin Road, Suite 100
Marietta, GA 30067
(404)428-0008
A black-and-white paint program.
Can also be used as a scanner
driver and image editing program. $199 PC. Also **PC Paint-
brush IV** $99.95. **PC Paint-
brush Plus for Windows**
$149.

PC Tools Deluxe 6.0

Central Point Software
15220 N.W. Greenbrier Parkway
#200
Beaverton, OR 97006
(503)690-8090
DOS shell. $149.

PCTeX

Personal TeX
20 Sunnyside Avenue, Suite H
Mill Valley, CA 94941
(415)388-8853
TeX-based page layout program.
$249 PC.

perForm Pro

Delrina Technology, Incorporated
1945 Leslie Street
Don Mills, Toronto, Ontario
Canada M3B 2M3
Forms generation and management package. Forms design
and management package.
$495 Win3. A cheaper version is
available for $295.

Performer

Mark of the Unicorn
222 Third Street
Cambridge, MA 02142
(617)576-2760
Music sequencer. $495 V. 3.4 Mac.

Personality

Preferred Publishers, Incorporated
5100 Poplar Avenue, Suite 617
Memphis, TN 38137
(901)683-3383
Macintosh interface modifying
software. $59.95 Mac.

Personal LaserWriter NT

Apple Computer, Incorporated
20525 Mariani Avenue
Cupertino, CA 95014
(408)996-1010
A 300 dpi PostScript laser printer.
$3,299 Mac. The SC is a Quick-
Draw model. Model LS, True-
Type Printer $1,299.

Personal Press

Silicon Beach Software, Incorporated
9770 Carroll Center Road, Suite J
San Diego, CA 92126
(619)695-6956
Page layout program. $299 V. 1.0
Mac.

Persuasion, see **Aldus
Persuasion**

Phaser PX

Tektronix Graphics
Printing, Imaging Division
Howard Vollum Park
PO Box 1000, MS-63-583
Wilsonville, OR 97070
(503)627-7111
Color printer. Also CQS model.
$7,995.

PhoneNet

Farallon Computing, Incorporated
2000 Powell Street, Suite 600
Emeryville, CA 94608
(415)596-9000
Connects AppleTalk and EtherNet
networks over telephone
wiring. Many confgurations.

PhotoLink

Photonics Corporation
200 E. Hacienda Avenue
Cambell, CA 95008
(408)370-3033
Infrared LAN connection devices.
$1,195 (4 nodes).

PhotoMac
Avalon Development Group
Distributed by Data Translation, Incorporated
100 Locke Drive
Marlboro, MA 01752
(800)522-0265 or (508)481-3700.
$695 Mac.

Photoshop
Adobe Systems, Incorporated
1585 Charleston Road
PO Box 7900
Mountain View, CA 94039-7900
(415)961-4400
Color digital image processing program. $895 V. 1.0 Mac.

Picture Publisher IV
Micrografx, Inc.
1303 East Arapahoe Road
Richardson, TX 75081
(800)733-3729
Grayscale image editing program. $595 Win3. **Picture Publisher Plus 2.5.** $695 color and grayscale.

Pioneer Communications of America
Industrial Division
1058 East 230th Street
Carson, CA 90745
(213)513-1016
Videodisk production and manufacturing.

Pioneer LD-V 4200 and 8000
Pioneer Communications of America
Industrial Division
1058 East 230th Street
Carson, CA 90745
(213)513-1016
CD-ROM players. DRM-600 (6 disk) $1,295.

PixelMaster
Howtek, Incorporated
21 Park Avenue
Hudson, NH 03051
(603)882-5200
Crayon-based thermal transfer color printer.

PixelPaint
SuperMac Technology
485 Potero Avenue
Sunnyvale, CA 94086
(408)245-2202
Color paint program. $395 V. 2.0 Mac-8-bit color. **PixelPaint Professional** $699 V. 1.0 Mac-24-bit color.

Pizazz Plus
Application Techniques, Incorporated
10 Lomar Park Drive
Pepperell, MA 01463
(800)433-5201
Screen capture and editing utility. $149 V. 1.3 PC.

Plus
Spinnaker Software Corporation
201 Broadway
Cambridge, MA 02139
(617)494-1200
Hypermedia authoring tool. V. 2.0 $495 Mac, Win3, OS/2. Unlimited run-time license $495.

PopChar
Shareware virtual keyboard utility. V. 1.1 Mac.

PostScript Cartridge
Adobe Systems, Incorporated
1585 Charleston Road
Mountain View, CA 94039-7900
(415)961-4400
PostScript interpreter for H-P LaserJet II. $495 PC.

PowerPoint
Microsoft Corporation
1 Microsoft Way
Redmond, WA 98052
(206)882-8080
Presentation package. $495, Mac, Win3.

PrecisionColor Calibrator
1710 Fortune Drive
San Jose, CA 95131
(408)434-1010
$695 Radius.

Presentation Manager
Microsoft Corporation
1 Microsoft Way
Redmond, WA 98052
(206)882-8080
GUI shell. OS/2.

Presentation Team
Digital Research
Box DRI
70 Garden Court
Monterey, CA 93942
(800)443-4200
Presentation package. V. 2.0.

Printer Control Panel
LaserTools Corporation
1250 45th Street #100
Emeryville, CA 94608
(800)767-8004
Print driver for converting PostScript files for non-PostScript printers. $149 PC.

Print Shop
Brøderbund
17 Paul Drive
San Raphael, CA 94903-2101
(800)521-6263 or (415)492-3200
Print utility. $59.95 PC, Mac, Apple II.

The Private Eye
Reflection Technologies
240 Bear Hill Road
Waltham, MA 02154
(617)890-5905
Miniature virtual display. $795 PC. Available from PCConnection for $499 with video board for IBM PCs.

Pro Video Gold
Shereff Systems, Incorporated
15075 SW Koll Parkway, Suite G
Beaverton, OR 97006
(503)626-2002
Character generator. $299.95, Amiga.

ProCollection
Hewlett-Packard
19310 Pruneridge Avenue
Cupertino, CA 95014
(800)752-0900
Font cartridges for LaserJets. $300.

ProComm
Datastorm Technologies
PO Box 1471
Columbia, MO 65205
(314)443-3282 or (314)875-0595 fax
$35(shareware) V. 2.4.3 PC. For $50 you get a bound manual. Available on-line. Telecommunications software.

Procomm Plus
Datastorm Technologies
PO Box 1471
Columbia, MO 65205
(314)443-3282 or (314)875-0595 fax
Telecommunications software. $89 V. 1.1 PC.

Prodigy Interactive Personal Services
Prodigy Services Company
445 Hamilton Avenue
White Plains, NY 10601
(800)222-6922, ext 205
On-line information services. $49.95 Mac, Win.

Professional Composer
Mark of the Unicorn
222 Third Street
Cambridge, MA 02142
(617)576-2760
Music scoring program. $495 V. 2.3 Mac.

ProFound
Wang Informatics Legal and Professional Systems, Incorporated
2111 East Highland Avenue, Suite 400
Phoenix, AZ 85016
(800)333-4785
Document and file management system.

Project
Microsoft Corporation
1 Microsoft Way
Redmond, WA 98052
(206)882-8080
Project management software. $695 V. 3.0 Mac, Win3.

ProType
Bedford Computer Corporation
23 Industrial Drive
Londonderry, NH 03053
(603)668-3400
Typesetting package for A/UX, Xenix, and other UNIX platforms. $3,995 Mac, PC. ProType Plus at $11,995 imports images and does math.

PS/1 and PS/2 Computers
IBM
Old Orchard Road
Armonk, NY 10504
(800)IBM-2468

Publish It!
Timeworks, Incorporated
444 Lake Cook Road
Deerfield, IL 60015-4919
(312)948-9200
Page layout software. **Publish It! Easy 2.0** $249.95, $395 Mac, PC.

The Publisher
ArborText
Ann Arbor, MI
$1,995 per node, 30 nodes

Publisher's Paintbrush IV
ZSoft Corporation
450 Franklin Road, Suite 100
Marietta, GA 30067
(404)428-0008
$285 PC.

Publisher's Powerpak
Atech
5962 La Place Court
Carlesbad, CA 92008
(619)438-6883
Font rasterizer. $79 Win.

Publisher's Type Foundry
ZSoft Corporation
450 Franklin Road, Suite 100
Marietta, GA 30067
(404)428-0008
Type editing and creation application. $545 PC.

Pyro!
Fifth Generation Software
10049 Reiger Road
Baton Rouge, LA 70809
(504)291-7221 or (800)873-4384
Macintosh screen saver. $24.95 Mac.

Q

Q & A Write
Symantec Corporation
10201 Torre Avenue
Cupertino, CA 95014
(800)441-7234 or (800)626-8847 (CA)
Word processor. PC.

QEMM-386
Quarterdeck Office Systems
150 Pico Boulevard
Santa Monica, CA 90405
(213)392-9851
Expanded memory manager. $99.95 V. 5.0.

Qmodem
Forbin Project
PO Box 702
Cedar Falls, IA 50613
(319)232-4516 or (319)233-1725 fax
$30 (shareware) V. 4.2 PC. Send $49.95 for disks. $79.95 with disks and bound manuals. Available on-line. Telecommunications software.

QuarkStyle
Quark, Incorporated
300 S. Jackson, Suite 100
Denver, CO 80209
(303)934-2211
Page layout program and template set. A subset of QuarkXPress. $295 V. 1.0.1 Mac.

QuarkXPress

Quark, Incorporated
300 S. Jackson, Suite 100
Denver, CO 80209
(303)934-2211
Page layout program. $795 V. 3.0
Mac. Windows, OS/2, and NeXT
versions are expected in 1991.

Quattro Pro

Borland International, Incorporated
1700 Green Hills Road
Scotts Valley, CA 95066
(408)438-8400
Graphical spreadsheet. PC.

QuicKeys

CE Software, Incorporated
1801 Industrial Circle
PO Box 655580
West Des Moines, IA 50265
(515)224-1953
Macro and keyboard remapping
utility. $99.95 V. 2.0.1 Mac.

QuickMail

CE Software, Incorporated
1801 Industrial Circle
PO Box 655580
West Des Moines, IA 50265
(515)224-1953 or (800)523-7638
E-Mail software. $185 (1 user);
$339.95 (5 users); $499.95 (10
users); $2,299.95 (50 users).
Mac V. 2.2.2.

R

Radius Color Display System

Radius, Incorporated
1710 Fortune Drive
San Jose, CA 95131
(800)227-2795 or (408)434-1010

Radius Pivot

Radius, Incorporated
1710 Fortune Drive
San Jose, CA 95131
(800)227-2795 or (408)434-1010
Configurable monitor. $995 monitor, $695 interface.

RadiusTV

Radius, Incorporated
1710 Fortune Drive
San Jose, CA 95131
(800)227-2795 or (408)434-1010
TV in a window. $2,795 Mac.

Random House Electronic Encyclopedia

Microlytics, Incorporated
1 Tobey Village Office Park
Pittsford, NY 14534
(800)828-6293 or (716)248-9620
Disk based encyclopedia.

ReadIt!

Olduvai Corporation
7520 Red Road, Suite A
S. Miami, FL 33143
(305)665-4665
Pretrained and trainable OCR
package. $495 Mac, $249 Personal Version Mac, $495 V. 2.0
PC.

ReadRight for Windows

OCR Systems
1800 Byberry Road, Suite 1405
Huntingdon Valley, PA 19006
(215)938-7460
OCR package. $595.

ReadySetGo!

Letraset USA
40 Eisenhower Drive
Paramus, NJ 07653
(201)845-6100
Page layout program. $295 V. 4.5a
Mac.

Redux

Microseeds Publishing, Inc.
7030-B W. Hillsborough Avenue
Tampa, FL 33634
(813)882-8635
Backup utility. $99 V. 1.62 Mac.

RenderMan Accelerator

Levco
6181 Cornerstone Court E., Suite
101
San Diego, CA 92121
(619)457-2011
NuBus board, graphics accelerator for MacRenderMan. $5,500
Mac.

Right Hand Man

Future Soft, Incorporated
3131 North I-10 Service Road
#401
Metairie, LA 70002
(800)368-3542
Groupware system. $189. $495 (5
users); $899 (10 users); $1,275
(15 users); $3,500 (50 users);
$6,500 (100 users). PC.

RightWriter

Rightsoft, Incorporated
4545 Samuel Street
Sarasota, FL 34233
(813)923-0233
Grammar checker or proofreader.
$95 PC, Mac.

Rival

Microseeds Publishing, Incorporated
7030-B West Hillsborough Avenue
Tampa, FL 33634
(813)882-8635
Virus detection, prevention, and
elimination utility. $99 V. 1.62
Mac.

S

SAM

Symantec Corporation
10201 Torre Avenue
Cupertino, CA 95014
(800)441-7234 or
(800)626-8847 (CA)
Symantec AntiVirus for the Macintosh is a virus protection, detection, and elimination program.
V. 2.0 $99.95 Mac.

ScanJet Plus

Hewlett-Packard
16399 W. Bernardo Drive
San Diego, CA 92127
(619)487-4100
The leading selling grayscale
desktop scanner. For good reason. $2,195 Mac, $1,895 PC.

ScanMan Plus
Logitech
6505 Kaiser Drive
Freemont, CA 94555
(415)795-8500
64 Grayscale handheld scanner. $499 Mac, $299 PC. Also Catchword OCR package $149.

Scitex Dolev PS
Scitex America Corporation
8 Oak Park Drive
Bedford, MA 01730
(617)275-5150
Imagesetter.

Scitex Response
Scitex America Corporation
8 Oak Park Drive
Bedford, MA 01730
(617)275-5150
Color electronic prepress system.

Scitex Visionary
Scitex America Corporation
8 Oak Park Drive
Bedford, MA 01730
(617)275-5150
Prepress link system. Visionary Interpreter for PostScript. V. 3.0. V.I.P. for Mac and V.I.P./2 for IBM PS/2 and AIX operating system also available.

Scrapbook Plus
Eikon Systems
989 E. Hillsdale Boulevard, Suite 260
Foster City, CA 94404
(415)349-4664
Clipboard and file conversion utility and picture librarian. $149.95 V. 2.1 Win3.

Second Sight
The Freesoft Company
150 Hickory Drive
Beaver Falls, PA 15010
(412)846-2700
Bulletin board system. $135 Mac.

Sensible Grammar
Sensible Software
335 E. Big Beaver, Suite 207
Troy, MI 49083
(313)528-1950
Grammar checker or proofreader. $99.95 Mac.

Series 300
Pixsys
1727 Conestoga Street
Boulder, CO 80301
(303)447-0248
3D digitizer. $12,315 PC. Additional products offered include $1,000 motion-tracking software, and $2,950 CAD/CAM software.

Service Bureau Association
5601 Roanne Way, Suite 605
Greensboro, NC 27409
(800)962-9480 or (919)632-0200
Contact: Van Tanner
An 120-member trade organization of service bureaus listing of over 1,700 service bureaus worldwide.

SIS, Incorporated
90 Canal Street
Boston, MA 02114
(617)290-0750
Macintosh training institute specializing in desktop publishing and design.

SmallTalk/V
Digitalk, Incorporated
9841 Airport Boulevard
Los Angeles, CA 90045
(800)922-8255 or (213)645-1082
Object-oriented programming language. $199.95 Mac, PC.

Smartcom II
Hayes Microcomputer Products, Incorporated
PO Box 105203
Atlanta, GA 30348
(404)441-1617 (customer service)
Telecommunications software, links to Hayes Smartmodem. $149 V. 3.0 Mac, PC.

SmartForm Designer
Claris Corporation
5201 Patrick Henry Drive
PO Box 58168
Santa Clara, CA 95052
(408)727-8227
Forms design package. SmartForm Assistant is the data entry module. $399 V. 1.1 Mac.

SmartScrap and The Clipper II
Solutions Incorporated
PO Box 783
Williston, VT 05495
(802)865-9220
Graphics library organizer and picture manipulation utilities. $89.95 Mac.

SoftPC
Insignia Solutions, Incorporated
254 Geronimo Way
Sunnyvale, CA 94086
(800)848-7677
Macintosh PC emulation software. $399 Mac. SoftPC AT also available.

SoftType
ZSoft
450 Franklin Road, Suite 100
Marietta, GA 30067
(404)428-0008
Scalable PostScript font-generation utility. $199 Win3.

Software Bridge
Systems Compatibility Corporation
401 North Wabash Avenue, Suite 600
Chicago, IL 60611
(800)333-1395 or (312)329-0700
Mac, PC file translation filters for Apple File Exchange. $129 Mac.

Sony LDP 1200
Sony Corporation of America
655 River Oaks Parkway
San Jose, CA 95134
(800)222-0878 or (408)432-0190
CD-ROM players. CDU-531 $375; CDU-541 $630; CDU-6140 $980; CDU-6201 $505.

Sound Accelerator
Digidesign, Incorporated
1360 Willow Road, Suite 101
Menlo Park, CA 94025
(415)688-0600
Digital sound processing card.
$1,295 Mac.

Sound Blaster
Creative Labs
131 S. Maple Avenue, #6
S. San Francisco, CA 94080
(415)742-6109
Sound capture board. $239.95 V.
1.5 PC.

SpectrePrint Pro
Pre-press Technologies, Incorporated
2443 Impala Drive
Carlsbad, CA 92008
(619)931-2695
Color separation and calibration
software. $5,995 Mac, PC.
SpectraPrint II $595 (desktop
package), **SpectraPrint PM**
(for PageMaker) $295. **SpectraPrint QX** (for QuarkXPress)
$295.

StandOut
Letraset USA
40 Eisenhower Drive
Paramus, NJ 07653
(201)845-6100
Presentation graphics program.
$395 Mac.

StereoLithography Apparatus
3D Systems, Incorporated
26081 Avenue Hall
Valencia, CA 91355
(805)295-5600
3D modeling apparatus.

Storybook Live!
IBM Corporation
Product Information Center
PO Box 2150
Atlanta, GA 30301
(800)426-7699
Multimedia authoring package.
$495 PC.

StrataVision 3d
Strata Incorporated
249 E. Tabernacle St, Suite 201
St. George, UT 84770
(801)628-5218
3D modeling, scene composition,
and rendering program. $495
Mac.

Studio/1, Studio/8 , Studio/32
Electronic Arts
1820 Gateway Drive
San Mateo, CA 94404
(415)571-7171 or (800)245-4525
Paint programs. Studio /1 $149.95
Mac black and white; Studio/8
$295 (Mac-8-bit color), Studio/32 $695 Mac24-bit color.

StuffIt Deluxe
Aladdin Systems
Deer Park Center 23A-171
Aptos, CA 95003
(408)685-9175
File compression utility. $99.95 V.
2.0 Mac. StuffIt Classic is a
shareware version; StuffIt V.
1.5.1 is the previous version.

Stylewriter
Apple Computer, Inc.
20525 Mariani Ave.
Cupertino, CA 95014
(408)996-1010.
TrueType ink jet printer. $599
Mac.

SuitCase II
Fifth Generation Software
10049 N. Reiger Road
Baton Rouge, LA 70809
(800)873-4384 or (504)291-7221
Font and resource management
software. $79 V. 1.2.6 Mac.

Super Cartridge 1
IQ Engineering
685 N. Pastoria Avenue
Sunnyvale, CA 94086
(800)765-3668 or (408)733-1161
Jumbo H-P font cartridge. $399.

Super 3D
Silicon Beach Software, Incorporated
9770 Carroll Center Road, Suite J
San Diego, CA 92126
(619)695-6956
3D modeling software. $495 V. 2.0
Mac.

SuperCard
Silicon Beach Software, Incorporated
9770 Carroll Center Road, Suite J
San Diego, CA 92126
(619)695-6956
Hypermedia authoring tool. V. 2.0
$299 Mac.

SuperGlue II
Solutions Incorporated
PO Box 783
Williston, VT 05495
(802)865-9220
Excellent print-to-disk utility.
$119.95 Mac.

SuperKey
Borland International
1700 Green Hills Road
Scotts Valley, CA 95066
(408)438-8400
Keyboard remapping or macro
utility. $99.95 PC.

SuperLaserSpool
Fifth Generation Systems, Incorporated
10049 N. Reiger Road
Baton Rouge, LA 70809
(504)291-7221 or (800)873-4384
Print spooler. $129.95 Mac.

SuperMatch
SuperMac Technologies
485 Potrero Avenue
Sunnyvale, CA 94086
(408)245-2202
Display color calibration system.
$4,400 Mac. For twenty-one-
inch monitor, Spectrum 24PDQ
card $3,999 includes display
calibrator.

SuperPaint II
Silicon Beach Software, Incorporated
9770 Carroll Center Road, Suite J
San Diego, CA 92126
(619)695-6956
Combination paint and draw application. $199 Mac.

SuperPrint
Zenographics, Incorporated
4 Executive Circle, Suite 200
Irvine, CA 92715
(714)851-6352
Font rendering, print spooler, and print utility. $195–$395 V. 1.1 Win.

Switchboard
Datadesk International
9314 Eaton Avenue
Chatsworth, CA 91311
(800)826-5398 or (800)592-9602 (CA)
Configurable keyboard and related input devices for IBM PCs and Macs. $293.95 (AT keyboard with trackball). Trackball, extra function keys, LCD calculator, accountant keypad, 3270 emulation keys, and other modules available at extra cost.

Swivel 3D
ParaComp, Incorporated
123 Townsend St., Suite 310
San Francisco, CA 94107
(415)543-3848
Solid modeling software. $395 Mac.

Symantec AntiVirus for the Macintosh, see SAM

Synchrony
Finalsoft Corporation
3900 NW 79th Avenue, Suite 215
Miami, FL 33166
(800)232-8228 or in FL call (305)477-2703
Groupware system. $445 (6 users). $695 (10 users). $1,195 (unlimted users) Win.

SyncMaster
J. L. Cooper Electronics
(213)306-4131
MIDI adapter. $349 Mac.

Syquest Drives and Cartridges
SyQuest Technology
47923 Warm Springs Boulevard
Fremont, CA 94539
(415)490-7511, (415)490-3487 Fax

System 7
Apple Computer, Inc.
20525 Mariani Ave.
Cupertino, CA 95014
(408)996-1010.
Macintosh Operating system software. $99 (1 user), $399 (group/network edition).

Syzgy
Information Research Corporation
414 East Market Street
Charlottesville, VA 22901
(804)979-8191
Groupware system.

T

Talking Moose
Baseline Publishing, Incorporated
5100 Poplar, Suite 527
Memphis, TN 38137
Animated talking moose head icon. $39.95 Mac.

Tandy Computers
Tandy
1800 1 Tandy Center
Fort Worth, TX 76102
(817)390-3011.

TARGA boards, see NuVista+

TekColor
Tektronix, Incorporated
PO Box 1000
M/S 63-583
Wilsonville, OR 97070
(800)835-6100
Color matching software. $50 Mac.

TeleFinder
Spider Island Software
4790 Irvine Boulevard, Suite 105-347
Irvine, CA 92720
(714)669-9260
Iconic BBS system. $575 (50 users) Mac.

TeleMax
Shaman Software
12708 Foxton Road
Foxton, CO 80441
(303)674-9784 or (800)624-8597
Software and on-line services for corporate and consumer communications. Mac.

Tempo II Plus
Affinity Microsystems
1050 Walnut Street, Suite 425
Boulder, CO 80302
(800)367-6771 or (303)442-4820
Macro utility. $149.95 Mac.

TEX
$180 per node, 10 nodes
ArborText
Ann Arbor MI.

TeXtures
Blue Sky Research
534 SW 3rd Avenue
Portland, OR 97204
(503)222-9571 or (800)622-8398
Typesetting and page layout system. $395 Mac.

3+ Open LAN
3Com Corporation
3165 Kifer Road
Santa Clara, CA 95052
(800)NET-3COM or (408)562-6400
LAN network operating system. $1,695 (10 users) V. 1.1. $3,495 (unlimited users).

Timbuktu

Farallon Computing, Incorporated

2000 Powell Street, Suite 600

Emeryville, CA 94608

(415)596-9000

File transfer/driver software for remote Macintosh operation. $149 Mac V. 3.0.

Timbuktu/Remote Access Pack

Farallon Computing, Incorporated

2000 Powell Street, Suite 600

Emeryville, CA 94608

(415)596-9000

Remote access system. $1,295 Mac.

TimeCode Machine

Opcode Systems

3641 Haven Drive, Suite A

Menlo Park, CA 94025

(415)369-8131

SMPTE/MIDI converter. $199 Mac.

Toolbook

Asymetrix Corporation

110 110th Avenue NE, Suite 717

Bellevue, WA 98004

Hypertextural development system. $395 Win3. V.1.5.

TOPS

Sitka Corporation

950 Marina Village Parkway

Alameda, CA 94501

(415)769-9669 or (800)445-8677

File server network system. $249 per node Mac V. 2.1. TOPS Network Bundle for DOS V. 3.0, $249 per node, $995 for 10 users.

Toshiba 3100 S/X

Toshiba America Information Systems, Incorporated

Computer Systems Division

9740 Irvine, CA 92718

(800)457-7777

Portable 386 s/x laptop computer.

Tpost

Coker Electronics

1430 Lexington Avenue

San Mateo, CA 94402

(415)573-5515

BBS system. $229 (1 user); $595 (2 users); $895 (4 users).

True Color Calibrator Display System

RasterOps

2500 Wlash Avenue

Santa Clara, CA 95051

(408)562-4200

$12,695 Mac.

TrueForm

Adobe Microsystems

1585 Charleston Road

Mountain View, CA 94039-7900

(415)961-4400

Computerized form completion software. $395 Mac.

TruScan TZ-3; TZ-3C (color), $10,090, TZ-3BWC (color and black-and-white), $11,000, Camera-based scanner with a fixed bed. Truvel, T Z-3 is grayscale.

TurboMouse

Kensington Microware, Limited

251 Park Avenue South

New York, NY 10010

(212)475-5200 or (800)535-4242

Trackball. $169.95 Mac, PC (PS/2 mouse emulation).

25 Cartridges in One

Pacific Data Products

6404 Nancy Ridge Drive

San Diego, CA 92121

(619)552-0880

Jumbo font cartridge for H-P LaserJet. $399.

Type Director

Hewlett-Packard

19310 Pruneridge Avenue

Cupertino, CA 95014

(800)752-0900

Font rasterizer. $40 V. 2.0. Doesn't include typefaces.

TypeAlign

Adobe Microsystems

1585 Charleston Road

Mountain View, CA 94039-7900

(415)961-4400

Display type special effects. $99.95 V. 1.0.2 Mac. Requires the Adobe Type Manager.

TypeStyler

Brøderbund Software

17 Paul Drive

San Raphael, CA 94903

(800)521-6263 or (415)492-3500

Display type special effects. $199.95 V. 1.5 Mac.

The Typist

Caere Corporation

100 Cooper Court

Los Gatos, CA 95030

(408)395-7000 or (800)535-7226

Handheld scanner and OCR package. $695 Model 2000 Mac, $595 Model 2001 PC (with AT-bus), $595 Model 2002 PC (with MCA bus).

U

ULTIMATE Electronic Pre-Press System

Ultimate Technographics, Incorporated

4980 Buchan Street, Suite 403

Montreal, Canada, PQ H4P 1S8

(514)733-1188

Electronic prepress system. Modules available include Text Conversion, Professional Publishing System, Colormask, Impostrip and Mac Impostrip.

UltraPaint

Deneba Software

3305 NW 74th Avenue

Miami, FL 33122

(305)594-6965 or (800)622-6827

Color paint program. $199.95 V. 1.0 Mac.

Unda Prepress System and Unda Design System
Unda, Incorporated
6 West 20th Street, 9th floor
New York, NY 10011
(212)727-3310
Color electronic prepress system.

USA Today Sports Center
Four Seasons Executive Center, Building 9
Terrace Way
Greensboro, NC 27403
(919)855-3491 or (800)826-9688
On-line sports information service. Mac, PC. Software $24.95, sign-up $14.95. $4.95 to $14.95 hourly rate.

V

Varityper 5300
Varityper
11 Mount Pleasant Avenue
East Hanover, NJ 07936
(800)631-8143 or (201)887-8000
Imagesetter.

Varityper VT600P
Varityper
11 Mount Pleasant Avenue
East Hanover, NJ 07936
(800)631-8143 or (201)887-8000
A 600 dpi laser printer. $16,995 Mac.

Ventura Publisher 3.0
Xerox Corporation
101 Continental Boulevard
El Segundo, CA 90245
(213)536-7000
Page layout program. $895. GEM Windows 3, OS/2.

VersaCAD
VersaCAD Corporation
2124 Main Street
Huntington Beach, CA 92648
(714)960-7720
3D CAD package. $1,995 Mac, PC.

VersaTerm
Synergy Software (PCS Inc.)
2457 Perkiomen Avenue
Reading, PA 19606
(215)779-0522
Telecommunications software with strong terminal emulation. $149 Mac.

Video Charley
Progressive Image Technologies
120 Blue Ravine Road, #2
Folsom, CA 95630
(916)985-7501
Genlock and encoder/decoder. $550 DC5150.

Video Explorer
Intelligent Resources
1626 Colonial Parkway
Inverness, IL 60067
(708)705-9388
Video board. $10,000.

Video F/X
Digital F/X
755 Ravendale Drive
Mountain View, CA 94043
(415)961-2800
Professional film editing system (hardware/software). $9,995 Mac.

Video Quill
Data Translation, Incorporated
100 Locke Drive
Marlboro, MA 01752-1192
Character generator software. $495 Mac.

VideoLogic DVA-4000
VideoLogic, Incorporated
245 First Street
Cambridge, MA 02142
(617)494-0530
Video motion board. $2,995 Mac, $2,495 PC. PC MCA and ISA boards available.

Video Toaster
NewTek Industries
215 S. E. Eighth St.
Topeka, KS
(800)843-8934
Video board for multimedia. $1,495 Amiga.

VideoWindows
New Media Graphics Corporation
780 Boston Road
Billerica, MA 01821
(508)663-0666
ISA motion video board. $2,195 PC.

Vines
Banyan Systems, Incorporated
115 Flanders Road
Westboro, MA 01581
(508)898-1000
LAN network operating system. $5,995 (unlimited users) V. 4.0.

Virex
Microcom Software Division
55 Federal Road
Danbury, CT 06810
(617)551-1999
Virus detection and vaccine. $99.95 V. 2.7 Mac.

Virex PC
Microcom Software Division
55 Federal Road
Danbury, CT 06810
(617)551-1999
Virus detection and vaccine. $129.95 PC.

Virtual
Connectix
125 Constitution Drive
Menlo Park, CA 94025
(800)950-5880
Memory expansion software. $199 V. 2.0 Mac.

Virtus Walkthrough
Virtus Corporation
117 Edinburgh S., Suite 204
Cary, NC 27511
(919)467-9700
Visual realization software. $895
V. 1.0 Mac.

Virus Detective
Jeffrey S. Shulman
PO Box 1218
Morgantown, WV 26507-1218
(304)598-2090
Available from most on-line services and bulletin board systems. Shareware $40 V. 4.0.3a.

Vision
Opcode Systems
3641 Haven Drive, Suite A
Menlo Park, CA 94025
(415)321-8977
MIDI sequencer and SMPTE synchronization. $495 Mac.

Visual Business Systems
380 Interstate N., Suite 190
Atlanta, GA 30339
(401)956-0325
Slide imaging service.

The Voice Navigator II
Articulate Systems, Incorporated
99 Erie Street
Cambridge, MA 02139
(617)876-5236
Speech input system, hardware/software. $795 Mac. **Voice Navigator Classic** $1,295.

VoxMail
VoxLink Corporation
PO Box 23306
Nashville, TN 37202
(615)331-0275
Voice E-mail system. $4,995 for cards and software for 20 users, $8,995 for unlimited users. PC.

W

Wacom SD-420L Cordless Digitizer (12 by 12 inches)
Wacom, Incorporated
W. 115 Century Road
Paramus, NJ 07652
(800)922-6613 or (201)265-4226
Graphics tablet with pressure sensitive stylus. $795 Mac. Also **Super Digitizer** $695.

Wang Freestyle System
Wang Laboratories, Incorporated
1 Industrial Avenue
Lowell, MA 01851
(800)522-WANG or (508)459-5000
Office information management and communication system. ca. $12,000 PC. Freestyle/Light software $249. The system is configurable.

Westlaw
West Publishing Company
50 W. Kellog Boulevard, PO Box 64526
St. Paul, MN 55164
(800)328-0109
On-line legal research service.

White Knight
FreeSoft Company
150 Hickory Drive
Beaver Falls, PA 15010
(412)846-2700
Telecommunications package. Sometimes bundled with the Okyto file transfer utility. $139 V. 11.7 Mac.

Who-What-When Enterprise
Chronos Software
555 DeHaro Street
San Francisco, CA 94107
(800)777-7907.

Whole Earth Catalog
Brøderbund Software
17 Paul Drive
San Raphael, CA 94903-2101
(800)521-6263 or (415)492-3200
CD-ROM catalog. $149.95 Mac.

Wildcat
Mustang Software
PO Box 2264
Bakersfield, CA 93303
(805)395-0223
BBS software. $129 (1 user); $249 (10 users); $499 (250 users).

Windows
Microsoft Corporation
1 Microsoft Way
Redmond, WA 98073
(206)882-8080
An excellent GUI for DOS that emulates a Macintosh and ships with several useful utilities including Write, Paintbrush, Terminal, NotePad, and others. Full device driver support built-in. $99 V. 3.0 (PC).

Windows ColorLab I/P
Computer Presentations
1117 Cypress Street
Cincinnati, OH 45206
(513)281-3222
Color digital image processing program.

Wingz
Informix Software, Incorporated
4100 Bohannon Drive
Menlo Park, CA 94025
(415)926-6300
Graphics-oriented spreadsheet. $399 Mac, $499 V. 3.0 Win3, OS/2.

Wiz
Calcomp
2411 West LaPalma Avenue
Anaheim, CA 92801
(800)CALCOMP or (714)821-2000
Graphics tablet with application templates. $199 Mac, DOS, Win3 ($25 per template, $75 per pen).

Word

Microsoft Corporation
1 Microsoft Way
Redmond, WA 98073
(206)882-8080
Leading Macintosh word processor. $450 V. 5.5 PC, V. 4 Mac; **Word for Windows** V. 1.0 Win3, $495 Mac, $495 Win3.

WordPerfect

WordPerfect Corporation
1555 North Technology Way
Orem, UT 84057
(801)222-5800
Leading PC word processor. V. 2.0 $395 Mac, V. 5.1 DOS, V. 1.0 Win3, OS/2.

WordPerfect Office

WordPerfect Corporation
1555 North Technology Way
Orem, UT 84057
(801)222-5800
Groupware system. $695 (5 users), $2,400 (20 users), $10,000 (100 users), 3.0 PC. **WP Office for the Macintosh** $495 (5 users).

WordScan Plus

Calera Recognition Systems
2500 Augustine Drive
Santa Clara, CA 95054
(415)986-8006
OCR package, highly rated with good accuracy. $995 PC (with /MCA co-processor $3,995), **WordScan** $595 Win3, Mac.

WordStar

MicroPro International
33 San Pablo Avenue
San Raphael, CA 94903
(415)382-8000 or (800)323-8825
Word processor. $495 V. 6.0 PC. Other versions available.

Works

Microsoft Corporation
1 Microsoft Way
Redmond, WA 98073
(206)882-8080
Integrated applications: word processor, spreadsheet, database, and communications package. $295 V. 2.0 Mac, PC.

WriteNow 2.2

T/Maker Company
1390 Villa Street
Mountain View, CA 94041
(415)962-0195
Word processor. $195 Mac.

WTI-Moonraker

Workstation Technologies, Incorporated
18004 Sky Park Circle
Irvine, CA 92714
(714)250-8983
Video board. $2,195.

WWIV Mac BBS

T. R. Teague
530 W. Dana Street
Mountain View, CA 94041
CompuServe 76354,324 or Telex: 6502792400 MCI
$30 (shareware) Mac.

X

Xerox Presents

XPORT, see **Micrografx XPORT**

XPress, see **QuarkXPress**

XtreePro Gold 1.4

Xtree Company
4330 Santa Fe Road
San Luis Obispo, CA 93401
(805)541-0604
DOS shell. $129.

Xyvision Design System 30, Pro System 40, and System 50

Xyvision (formerly Contex)
101 Edgewater Drive
Wakefield, MA 01880
(617)245-9004
Color electronic prepress system and package design systems.

XYWrite III

XyQuest, Incorporated
PO Box 372
Bedford, MA 01730
(617)275-4439
Word processor. $395 PC.

Z

Zip (PKZip/PKUnZip)

PKWare
7545 N. Port Washington Road
Glendale, WI 53217
(414)352-3670
PC telecommunication file compression standard. $25 (shareware) V. 1.10 DOS. $47 with printed manuals.

ZTerm

Dave Alverson
5635 Cross Creek Court
Mason, OH 45040
Available from: GEnie Mac RT, Category 5, Topic 8, and from CompuServe: Mac Productivity Forum/Telecom library. Telecommunications program. $30 (shareware) V. 0.85 Mac. $40 with disk.

Index